D0161638

THE GREENWOOD COMPANION TO

Shakespeare

THE GREENWOOD COMPANION TO

Shakespeare

A COMPREHENSIVE GUIDE FOR STUDENTS

Volume II

The Comedies

EDITED BY
JOSEPH ROSENBLUM

GREENWOOD PRESS

Westport, Connecticut • London

Library of Congress Cataloging-in-Publication Data

The Greenwood companion to Shakespeare : a comprehensive guide for students / edited by Joseph
Rosenblum.
    p. cm.
   Includes bibliographical references and index.
   ISBN 0–313–32779–3 (set : alk. paper)—ISBN 0–313–32780–7 (v. 1 : alk. paper)—
ISBN 0–313–32781–5 (v. 2 : alk. paper)—ISBN 0–313–32782–3 (v. 3 : alk. paper)—
ISBN 0–313–32788–2 (v. 4 : alk. paper) 1. Shakespeare, William, 1564–1616—Criticism and
interpretation—Handbooks, manuals, etc. 2. Shakespeare, William, 1564–1616—Examinations—
Study guides. I. Rosenblum, Joseph.
  PR2976.G739   2005
  822.3′3—dc22   2004028690

British Library Cataloguing in Publication Data is available.

Library of Congress Catalog Card Number: 2004028690
ISBN: 0–313–32779–3 (set)
    0–313–32780–7 (vol. I)
    0–313–32781–5 (vol. II)
    0–313–32782–3 (vol. III)
    0–313–32788–2 (vol. IV)

First published in 2005

Greenwood Press, 88 Post Road West, Westport, CT 06881
An imprint of Greenwood Publishing Group, Inc.
www.greenwood.com

Printed in the United States of America

∞™

The paper used in this book complies with the
Permanent Paper Standard issued by the National
Information Standards Organization (Z39.48–1984).

10 9 8 7 6 5 4 3 2 1

To Ida

Thou art the nonpareil

Contents

Alphabetical List of Plays and Poems   xi
A Preface for Users   xiii
A Shakespeare Chronology   xvii

VOLUME I

OVERVIEWS AND THE HISTORY PLAYS

OVERVIEWS

William Shakespeare's Age   Harold Branam   3
William Shakespeare's Life   Joseph Rosenblum   23
William Shakespeare's Theater   Robert F. Willson Jr.   47
William Shakespeare's Texts   Roze Hentschell   65
William Shakespeare's Language   Barry B. Adams   82

THE HISTORY PLAYS

Henry VI, Parts 1, 2, and 3   John D. Cox   101
Richard III   Andrew Macdonald and Gina Macdonald   130
King John   Michael Egan   156
Richard II   Nicholas Crawford   190
Henry IV, Parts 1 and 2   Rebecca Fletcher McNeer   216
Henry V   Sheryl A. Clouse   255
Henry VIII   Yashdip S. Bains   282

VOLUME II

THE COMEDIES

The Comedy of Errors   Robert Appelbaum   309
The Taming of the Shrew   Gina Macdonald   332

The Two Gentlemen of Verona   Owen E. Brady   356

Love's Labor's Lost   Jessica Winston   380

A Midsummer Night's Dream   Jay L. Halio   398

The Merchant of Venice   Jay L. Halio   428

The Merry Wives of Windsor   Michelle Ephraim   455

Much Ado about Nothing   David W. Cole   478

As You Like It   Yashdip S. Bains   502

Twelfth Night   Gina Macdonald   531

Troilus and Cressida   Charles R. Trainor   564

All's Well That Ends Well   Regina M. Buccola   586

Measure for Measure   Nicholas Birns   609

VOLUME III

THE TRAGEDIES

Titus Andronicus   Deborah Willis   635

Romeo and Juliet   Michelle M. Sauer   658

Julius Caesar   Robert G. Blake   688

Hamlet   Jay L. Halio   721

Othello   Robert F. Willson Jr.   755

King Lear   Jay L. Halio   782

Macbeth   Matthew Woodcock   827

Antony and Cleopatra   Harold Branam   860

Coriolanus   Andrew Macdonald   888

Timon of Athens   Robert Appelbaum   911

VOLUME IV

THE ROMANCES AND POETRY

THE ROMANCE PLAYS

Pericles   Gary Waller   933

Cymbeline   Gary Waller   953

The Winter's Tale   Gary Waller   973

The Tempest   Gina Macdonald   996

The Two Noble Kinsmen   Yashdip S. Bains   1027

THE SONNETS

Overview of the Sonnets   James B. Gutsell   1053

Sonnet 3   Michelle M. Sauer   1082

Sonnet 12   Charles R. Forker   1089

Sonnet 15   Patrick Perkins   1096

Sonnet 18   Roze Hentschell   1103

Sonnet 19   Priscilla Glanville   1110

Sonnet 20   Roze Hentschell   1117

Sonnet 29   Robert G. Blake   1124

Sonnet 30   Barry B. Adams   1130

Sonnet 35   Jeremy Lopez   1136

Sonnet 55   Gayle Gaskill   1141

Sonnet 60   Robert G. Blake   1148

Sonnet 65   Barry B. Adams   1153

Sonnet 71   Robert Appelbaum   1159

Sonnets 73 and 74   Nicholas Birns   1165

Sonnet 76   Yashdip S. Bains   1174

Sonnet 87   Barry B. Adams   1180

Sonnet 91   Jeremy Lopez   1185

Sonnet 94   Robert Appelbaum   1190

Sonnets 97 and 98   Jeremy Lopez   1198

Sonnet 106   Kirk Bazler Melnikoff   1204

Sonnet 116   Annalisa Castaldo   1210

Sonnet 126   Steven Doloff   1215

Sonnet 128   Gayle Gaskill   1221

Sonnet 129   Annalisa Castaldo   1228

Sonnet 130   Gina Macdonald with Andrew Macdonald   1234

Sonnets 135 and 136   Elizabeth Moore Willingham   1241

Sonnet 138   Elizabeth Moore Willingham   1247

Sonnet 144   Andrew James Hartley   1253

Sonnet 146   Yashdip S. Bains   1259

Sonnet 147   Robert Appelbaum   1266

Sonnets 153 and 154   Yashdip S. Bains   1272

THE LONG POEMS

A Lover's Complaint   Ilona Bell   1281

Venus and Adonis   Yashdip S. Bains   1291

The Rape of Lucrece   Bruce E. Brandt   1301

The Phoenix and Turtle   Nicholas Birns   1309

The Passionate Pilgrim   Peter Kanelos   1323

Appendix: Shakespeare Resources on the Web   1331

Selected Bibliography   1335

Subject Index   1343

Key Passages Index   1363

About the Editor and Contributors   1367

Alphabetical List of Plays and Poems

The Plays

All's Well That Ends Well	586
Antony and Cleopatra	860
As You Like It	502
The Comedy of Errors	309
Coriolanus	888
Cymbeline	953
Hamlet	721
Henry IV, Parts 1 and 2	216
Henry V	255
Henry VI, Parts 1, 2, and 3	101
Henry VIII	282
Julius Caesar	688
King John	156
King Lear	782
Love's Labor's Lost	380
Macbeth	827
Measure for Measure	609
The Merchant of Venice	428
The Merry Wives of Windsor	455
A Midsummer Night's Dream	398
Much Ado about Nothing	478
Othello	755
Pericles	933
Richard II	190
Richard III	130

Romeo and Juliet 658

The Taming of the Shrew 332

The Tempest 996

Timon of Athens 911

Titus Andronicus 635

Troilus and Cressida 564

Twelfth Night 531

The Two Gentlemen of Verona 356

The Two Noble Kinsmen 1027

The Winter's Tale 973

Selected Sonnets 1082

The Long Poems

A Lover's Complaint 1281

The Passionate Pilgrim 1323

The Phoenix and Turtle 1309

The Rape of Lucrece 1301

Venus and Adonis 1291

A Preface for Users

O for a Muse of fire, that would ascend
The brightest heaven of invention!

(Henry V, Prologue, 1–2)

In the latter half of the seventeenth century, John Dryden revised William Shakespeare's *Troilus and Cressida*. Explaining why he tampered with the text of the man he had called "divine," Dryden wrote,

> It must be allowed to the present age, that the tongue in general is so much refined since Shakespeare's time, that many of his words, and more of his phrases, are scarce intelligible. And of those which are understood, some are ungrammatical, others coarse; and his whole style is so pestered with figurative expressions, that it is as affected as it is obscure.

The twenty-first-century student of Shakespeare will likely concur with Dryden's judgment. Shakespeare is hard. Even seasoned scholars differ on subjects ranging from the meaning of individual words to the implications of entire plays. No wonder, then, if high school students, undergraduates, and general readers are sometimes puzzled as they read one of Shakespeare's works or watch one of his plays. Literally thousands of studies of Shakespeare are published each year and recorded in the annual *World Shakespeare Bibliography*, which is updated annually and printed in the *Shakespeare Quarterly*, but this thicket of scholarship often renders Shakespeare more forbidding to students rather than less.

Throughout, *The Greenwood Companion to Shakespeare: A Comprehensive Guide for Students* aims to demystify Shakespeare so that students and general readers will be encouraged to appreciate the artistry of the writing and will come to a fuller appreciation of Shakespeare's genius. Students will find here what his works mean, how they came to be, how they make meaning, and how critics and directors have interpreted them over the centuries. No reference work can include all that is known or thought about Shakespeare, but the editor, contributors, and publisher have sought to make this *Companion* the best place to begin a study of this great writer. We hope that you will find the contents both useful and enjoyable.

CONTENT AND ARRANGEMENT

The four-volume *Greenwood Companion to Shakespeare* includes seventy-seven essays offering a guide to the perplexed. All of these essays have been written expressly for this work by dedicated scholars commissioned because of their scholarship and teaching skills.

The first three volumes are devoted to the plays as follows:

- Volume I is divided into two sections: first, a series of essays about Shakespeare's age, his life, the theater of the time, the texts of his work, and the English language of his era—all of which will deepen the reader's understanding of the works; second, essays that focus on the history plays.

- Volume II explores the comedies.

- Volume III presents the tragedies.

- Volume IV begins with essays on the late plays called romances; the remainder of the volume discusses William Shakespeare's poetry, beginning with an overview of the sonnets. Thirty-one essays examine selected individual or paired sonnets, including full texts of each sonnet reviewed. Compared with the rest of Shakespeare's poetry, these sonnets are the most studied and reveal the widest range of subjects and attitudes. The other essays in this volume discuss the long narrative poems: *A Lover's Complaint*—that fascinating envoi to the sonnet cycle—immediately follows the sonnets, as it did when originally published with those poems; then, in chronological order, *Venus and Adonis*, *The Rape of Lucrece*, and *The Phoenix and Turtle*; *The Passionate Pilgrim* (in which two of Shakespeare's sonnets to the mysterious Dark Lady were first printed) has been placed last because most of the poems contained therein are not by Shakespeare.

The essays are arranged chronologically within genre. To further assist readers in finding essays on particular plays or poems, an alphabetical list of the works studied in this *Companion* follows immediately after the table of contents.

Other Features

"A Shakespeare Chronology," preceding the overview essays in volume I, shows when William Shakespeare's works were written and published and provides basic facts about his life. An annotated bibliography accompanies each essay. At the end of volume IV, an appendix offers a selected, annotated list of Web sites about William Shakespeare and his work. Following that list is a selected bibliography. A subject index and an index of key passages concludes the work.

THE ESSAYS

Forty scholars contributed essays to this *Companion*. Their writings add substantially to Shakespeare scholarship. These essays range in length from some 2,500 words for articles on particular sonnets to 26,000 words on *King Lear*. The articles dealing with the plays, subdivided into eleven sections for easy access, provide the following information to readers:

1. A scene-by-scene plot summary to help students understand what is happening on the stage/page.

2. A discussion of the play's publication history and, when relevant, its historical background context.

3. Sources for the play(s), including a discussion of controversies and recent findings.

4. A brief overview of how the play is put together in terms of structure and plotting.

5. The main characters, their actions, and their purposes within the play.

6. Devices and techniques (such as imagery) that Shakespeare used in the plays.

7. Themes and meanings of the play, citing opinions of various scholars.

8. A look at past and current critical discourse on the work to help students understand the issues that have engaged scholarly attention and to show that in many areas there is no single "correct" interpretation of these complex works. Students seeking topics to explore for their own papers may find this section especially helpful.

9. Production history, surveying the play's key theatrical and cinematic representation.

10. An explication of key passages, helping readers to understand sections of the play that are considered to be the most important.

11. An annotated bibliography for further study. This selection of sources will help students choose the most accessible works from the hundreds included in the *World Shakespeare Bibliography* or the dozens listed in bibliographical guides. The books and articles noted here include classic studies but concentrate on recent writing.

The Essays on the Sonnets and Long Poems

The essays in volume IV discuss the poems. Compared with the essays on the plays they are briefer and contain fewer sections. For the sonnets, the essays provide the following key elements:

1. The sonnet itself, from *The Oxford Shakespeare*, edited by W. J. Craig and published in 1914 by Oxford University Press.

2. A prose paraphrase to explain the content of the work under discussion.

3. A discussion that situates the poem within the sonnet cycle.

4. An exploration of devices and techniques, and themes and meanings.

5. A description of the relationship of the sonnet to Shakespeare's other works, particularly the plays.

6. An annotated bibliography.

In the essays on the long poems the reader will also find discussions of publication history and sources (treated in the overview essay on the sonnets for those poems). All of the essays on the long poems conclude with annotated bibliographies.

ISSUES IN THE SHAKESPEARE CANON

One poem that readers will not find in this volume is *A Funeral Elegy*. This 578-line poem was first printed by George Eld and published by Thomas Thorpe in 1612. Eld had printed and Thorpe had published Shakespeare's sonnets three years earlier. According to the title page, *A Funeral Elegy* was the work of "W. S." The identity of this W. S. has inspired some recent controversy. In 1989 Donald W. Foster published *Elegy by W. S.* (Newark: U of Delaware P), in which he discussed the question of attribution without reaching any conclusion. However, in the October 1996 issue of *PMLA* Foster argued that the poem was by Shakespeare. Because Foster had successfully identified the author of the "anonymous" novel *Primary Colors* (1996) as Joe Klein, Foster's view was credible enough for the editors of the revised Riverside edition of Shakespeare's works (Boston: Houghton Mifflin, 1997) to include the *Elegy*; they also included, however, something of a disclaimer by J.J.M. Tobin (pp. 1893–1895). In 2002 Foster recanted, arguing that the most likely author of the *Elegy* was John Ford.

This controversy reflects the unsettled state of the Shakespeare canon, which grows and shrinks. Brian Vickers's *Shakespeare, Co-Author* (Oxford: Oxford UP, 2002) assigns joint responsibility to five of Shakespeare's plays: *Titus Andronicus* (with George Peele), *Timon of Athens* (with Thomas Middleton), *Pericles* (with George Wilkins), and *Henry VIII* and *The Two Noble Kinsmen* (both with John Fletcher). Seeking to expand the canon, Eric Sams has argued that *Edward III* is an early work by Shakespeare (see *"Edward III": An Early Play Restored to the Canon* (New Haven: Yale UP, 1996).

On one point scholars agree: the William Shakespeare who wrote the plays and poems discussed in this companion was the son of John and Mary Shakespeare, was born in Stratford-upon-Avon in 1564, and died there fifty-two years later. Since the nineteenth century, various nonscholars have proposed dozens of alternative authors, including Francis Bacon, Queen Elizabeth, and Edward de Vere, seventeenth Earl of Oxford. Those readers curious about the authorship question may consult Samuel Schoenbaum's *Shakespeare's Lives*, new edition (Oxford: Clarendon P, 1991), section VI, which is aptly titled "Deviations." Arguments about the authorship of Shakespeare's works belong to the realm of abnormal psychology rather than literary criticism.

A Shakespeare Chronology

Note: Titles in **bold** are discussed in this four-volume set. Dates for the plays (e.g., 1593 for **Richard III** and **The Comedy of Errors**) indicate probable year of first performance.

1558	Elizabeth I becomes queen of England.
1564	William Shakespeare born (ca. April 23).
1576	The Theatre (Shoreditch), built by James Burbage, opens. The Theatre is regarded as the first true London playhouse.
1582	Shakespeare marries Anne Hathaway (ca. December 1).
1583	Shakespeare's elder daughter, Susannah, born (ca. May 23).
1585	Shakespeare's fraternal twins, Judith and Hamnet/Hamlet, born (ca. January 31).
1588	Defeat of the Spanish Armada (July 31–August 8).
1589	Shakespeare probably in London, begins writing *1 Henry VI* (published in 1623).
1590–1591	**2, 3 Henry VI** written. The former first published as *The First Part of the Contention betwixt the Two Famous Houses of York and Lancaster* (1594), the latter as *The True Tragedy of Richard Duke of York* (1595).
1592	Robert Greene attacks Shakespeare in *A Groatsworth of Witte*. This is the first printed reference to Shakespeare as dramatist.
1593	**Richard III** (first published in 1597).
	Venus and Adonis published.
	The Comedy of Errors (first published in 1623).
	Shakespeare begins writing his **sonnets**.
1594	**The Rape of Lucrece** published.
	Titus Andronicus (first published in 1594).
	The Taming of the Shrew (first published in 1623).
	The Two Gentlemen of Verona (first published in 1623).

Love's Labor's Lost (first published in 1598).

Lord Chamberlain's Men established.

1595 *King John* (first published in 1623).

Richard II (first published in 1597).

Romeo and Juliet (first published in 1597).

A Midsummer Night's Dream (first published in 1600).

1596 *The Merchant of Venice* (first published in 1600).

Hamnet/Hamlet Shakespeare dies, age 11 (ca. August 9).

1597 *1 Henry IV* (first published in 1598).

The Merry Wives of Windsor (first published in 1602).

Shakespeare purchases New Place, Stratford.

1598 *2 Henry IV* (first published in 1600).

Much Ado about Nothing (first published in 1600).

Francis Meres's *Palladis Tamia* lists a dozen plays by Shakespeare and praises him highly.

1599 The Globe Theater opens.

Henry V (first published in 1600).

Julius Caesar (first published in 1623).

The Passionate Pilgrim includes two of Shakespeare's sonnets (138, 144).

1600 *As You Like It* (first published in 1623).

Hamlet (first published in 1603).

1601 *Richard II* performed at the Globe (February 7) at urging of supporters of the Earl of Essex one day before his ill-fated rebellion.

The Phoenix and Turtle appears in Robert Chester's *Love's Martyr*.

John Shakespeare dies (ca. September 6).

1602 *Twelfth Night* (first published in 1623).

Troilus and Cressida (first published in 1609).

1603 Queen Elizabeth dies. James VI of Scotland becomes James I of England. James licenses the Lord Chamberlain's Men as the King's Men.

All's Well That Ends Well (first published in 1623).

1604 *Measure for Measure* (first published in 1623).

Othello (first published in 1622).

1605 *King Lear* (first published in 1608).

1606 *Macbeth* (first published in 1623).

1607 *Antony and Cleopatra* (first published in 1623).

Susannah Shakespeare marries John Hall (June 5).

Shakespeare's brother Edmund dies (ca. December 29).

1608   Elizabeth Hall, Shakespeare's only granddaughter, born (ca. February 18).

Shakespeare's mother dies (ca. September 7).

Coriolanus (first published in 1623).

Timon of Athens (first published in 1623).

Pericles (first published in 1609).

1609   Shakespeare's **Sonnets** published, with *A Lover's Complaint*.

Cymbeline (first published in 1623).

The King's Men begin using the Blackfriars as an indoor theater.

1610   *The Winter's Tale* (first published in 1623).

1611   *The Tempest* (first published in 1623).

1612   *Henry VIII* (with John Fletcher; first published in 1623).

1613   Globe Theater burns down during production of *Henry VIII*.

Cardenio (with John Fletcher; lost).

The Two Noble Kinsmen (with John Fletcher; first published in 1634).

1614   Second Globe opens on site of first Globe.

1616   Judith Shakespeare marries Thomas Quiney (February 10).

Shakespeare makes his will (March 25) and dies on April 23.

1619   Thomas Pavier attempts a collected (pirated) edition of Shakespeare. He publishes ten plays in quarto, some with false dates to conceal the piracy, before he is forced to abandon the project.

1623   The First Folio, the first collected edition of Shakespeare's plays, is published. It contains thirty-six plays, half of them printed for the first time.

THE COMEDIES

The Comedy of Errors

Robert Appelbaum

PLOT SUMMARY

1.1. As the play opens, a merchant from Syracuse named Egeon is being led captive before the Duke of Ephesus, who explains that a recent law decrees that anyone born in Syracuse who enters Ephesus shall be put to death. Syracuse and Ephesus are at war, and both have passed similar laws against one another's citizens. There is one way out: a captured stranger can buy his life and freedom by paying a fine of 1,000 marks. But Egeon doesn't have that much money with him, and he has no friends in Ephesus to help him. Therefore condemned to die, Egeon is required to give a final account of himself before the Duke, to expand on "Why thou departedst from thy native home, / And for what cause thou cam'st to Ephesus" (1.1.29–30).

Egeon relates a tale of woe that moves everyone around him to pity. He was happily married once to a fellow Syracusan, a woman named Aemilia, and the father of identical twin boys, the elder of whom was named Antipholus. The two boys were attended by another pair of twins, the elder of whom was named Dromio, boys of the very same age whom Egeon had purchased from parents who were "exceeding poor" (1.1.56). Traveling homeward by sea, Egeon, his wife, his two sons, and the two servants were caught in a tempest. The sailors abandoned ship, leaving Egeon and his family to fend for themselves. Binding themselves to the ship's masts, they survived the storm and drifted in the direction of a pair of ships coming to help them: one a fishing boat from Corinth and the other a cargo ship from Epidaurus. Just as help approached, Egeon's ship hit a great rock and split in half. Egeon, the younger son, and the younger servant, the three of them bound together for safety, drifted off in one direction; Aemilia, the elder son, and the elder servant, likewise bound together, drifted in the other. Egeon and the younger boys were saved by the merchant ship from Epidaurus; Aemilia and the elder boys were saved by the fishermen from Corinth. The two ships were separated. Unable to make for the fishing vessel and forced to head back out to sea, the cargo ship from Epidaurus set sail for home. The Corinthian vessel drifted out of sight. And so Egeon saw the last of his wife, his eldest son, and his eldest son's servant, and had no idea what happened to them.

Egeon raised the two younger boys in Syracuse, renaming them Antipholus and Dromio, in honor of their lost older brothers (a practice that would not have seemed bizarre to Shakespeare's original audience). Egeon reports that at the age of eighteen Antipholus left home with Dromio to find out what had happened to his lost brother. Sometime later Egeon himself left Syracuse in search of his surviving son. For five years Egeon has been wandering through Asia and Greece. Finally "coasting homeward," knowing that Ephesus was off limits to a Syracusan like himself but "loath to leave" it unexplored, just in case his son was there (1.1.134–135), he came to the port city. There, being discovered, he found himself arrested and condemned to die.

The play seems ready to come to an end almost as soon as it has begun. "Here must end the story of my life," Egeon says (1.1.137). But the play will soon proceed in a happier direction. Moved to pity, the Duke gives Egeon a reprieve. He cannot change the law or abrogate Egeon's sentence, but he will give Egeon a day to find benefactors from whom he might beg or borrow and purchase his freedom. Egeon has little faith; he is convinced there is nothing for him to do for the next eight hours but delay the inevitable: "Hopeless and helpless doth Egeon wend, / But to procrastinate his liveless end" (1.1.157–158).

1.2. The first plot twist comes immediately. It turns out there is another merchant from Syracuse who has broken the law and set ashore in Ephesus: and this is none other than Antipholus, the son Egeon had raised, traveling along with his servant Dromio. Antipholus is aware of the danger and advised by a merchant who has befriended him to pretend he comes from another town, Epidamnum. But like his father, he is also determined to visit the place. Antipholus is a young man who inspires confidence in others, but he is given to sadness. He feels that there is something missing in his life, and he is going to do all he can to make up for it. Yet trying to find what he is missing only makes him feel what he is missing all the more. No less than his father, he seems to be on a helpless, hopeless quest:

> He that commends me to mine own content,
> Commends me to the thing I cannot get:
> I to the world am like a drop of water,
> That in the ocean seeks another drop,
> Who, falling there to find his fellow forth
> (Unseen, inquisitive), confounds himself.
> So I, to find a mother and a brother,
> In quest of them (unhappy), ah, lose myself. (1.2.33–40)

In spite of his melancholy, or perhaps because of it, Antipholus gives Dromio a sum of money he had earlier deposited with a merchant, tells him to stow the money at an inn, the Centaur, and there wait for him till dinnertime while he plays the tourist. Dromio takes off. Antipholus says good-bye to the merchant, who will meet up with him again later after conducting some business in the town, and barely takes a step before he encounters a breathless, nervous . . . Dromio.

This is the other Dromio: Dromio of Ephesus, his servant's long lost twin, apparently (however absurd this may seem) dressed exactly like the Dromio of Syracuse who has just wandered off to the Centaur. This local Dromio is upset. Why haven't you come home to dinner, he asks the man he mistakes for his master. Antipholus's wife, he says, is angry. His mistress has given Dromio a smack for allowing his master to be late. The food has gotten cold. Of course, Antipholus of Syracuse doesn't know what Dromio of Ephesus is talking about. But he asks this Dromio what he has done with the large sum of money he just received. Dromio of Ephesus has no idea what Antipholus of Syracuse is talking about, and the two men argue at cross-purposes. As passions rise, Antipholus of Syracuse raises his hand against Dromio of Ephesus and Dromio flees. Antipholus fears that he has been cheated. But he reflects on something he has heard, part of the legend of Ephesus, a town of some importance in Christian tradition: "They say this town is full of cozenage," that is, con-artists; it is the home of "jugglers," "sorcerers," "witches," "cheaters," "mountebanks" (1.2.97–101).

2.1. We are now at the home of Antipholus of Ephesus, where Adriana, his wife, and Luciana, Adriana's sister, worry over Antipholus's absence. Luciana tries to excuse him. He is a man, the head of the family, so he can come and go as he pleases. But Adriana will not buy the argument. She does not see why men should have more liberty than women, who certainly are not entitled to come and go as they please. When Luciana asserts that it is in the order of nature that men should dominate over women, Adriana says that that is easy for Luciana to say, since she is single. They are interrupted by Dromio of Ephesus, who rushes in to report on the odd behavior of the man he took to be Adriana's husband, refusing to come home for dinner or even to recognize that he had a wife and home here in Ephesus. Adriana commands Dromio to return and fetch his master.

2.2. Meanwhile, Antipholus of Syracuse has found out that his Dromio deposited the money at the Centaur just as he was ordered to do. Encountering Dromio of Syracuse on the street, he chides Dromio for the joke he apparently played on him. Dromio of Syracuse doesn't know what Antipholus is talking about and is puzzled by the joke Antipholus is playing on *him*. Soon the two are arguing about who did what. Indignant, Antipholus starts to beat his servant. When Antipholus calms down, the two men proceed to discuss their relationship and the proper roles of master and servant.

They seem to have made up with one another when Adriana and Luciana suddenly appear before them. Adriana takes center stage. Why are you giving me strange looks, as if you have never seen me before, Adriana asks the man she erroneously takes to be her husband. And more importantly, why don't you love me the way you used to do? Why are you estranged from me, and hence "estranged from thyself," since husband and wife are supposed to be one indivisible self? (2.2.120). She is accusing him of cheating on her with an unnamed harlot, and she demands to know how he would feel if she were found to be cheating on him.

Antipholus of Syracuse, having no idea who she is or what she is talking about, tries to be polite, and allows Adriana's strange talk to raise suspicions in his mind about Dromio again. But when Adriana softens her tone and tries to coax him to join her for dinner, Antipholus gives in. Am I dreaming or hallucinating, Antipholus wonders? "Am I in earth, in heaven, or in hell? / Sleeping or waking, mad or well-advis'd?" (2.2.212–213). He agrees to accompany Adriana and Luciana upstairs in their house at their belated mid-day dinner. At Adriana and Luciana's prompting, he commands Dromio to stand guard at the door below, with the other servants, and not let anyone interrupt them.

3.1. For the first time we meet Antipholus of Ephesus, approaching his front door in the company of Dromio of Ephesus, Angelo the goldsmith, and Balthazar the merchant. Antipholus has had the goldsmith make a necklace for Adriana, and he has also been conducting business with Balthazar. Abashed at being late for dinner, Antipholus asks Angelo to make excuses for him; angry with Dromio for telling him stories about how he just recently met him in the mart and pretended not to have a wife or wish to come home to dinner, he chides him for his nonsense. But otherwise, with a clear conscience, he invites Angelo and Balthazar in to dine with him. And so more trouble begins.

Behind the door to the house and so unseen, Dromio of Syracuse stands guard and refuses to let the men in. Challenged to identify himself, he tells them that "my name is Dromio." The other Dromio is incensed: "O villain, thou hast stol'n both mine office and my name" (3.1.44). Adriana briefly enters the scene; and though her husband calls out to her through the door, she believes him to be an imposter and a troublemaker whom it is better to ignore. She leaves Dromio of Syracuse at the door, and he continues to challenge the men outside. Finally, the men give up. Balthazar convinces Antipholus to let matters lie for the time being, lest a scandal break out. He suggests they all go to an inn for dinner, but Antipholus of Ephesus has a better idea: they will go to dine with a woman friend of his, a courtesan, "a wench of excellent discourse, / Pretty and witty" (3.1.109–110), with whom his wife has mistakenly suspected him of having an affair. To "spite" his wife (3.1.118), he asks the goldsmith to fetch the necklace and bring it to the woman's house; he'll give the gold chain to her instead.

3.2. Once more in front of the house, Luciana and Antipholus of Syracuse have an odd discussion. Luciana upbraids Antipholus for being a truant husband; but her advice is unexpected: she cautions him not to have a change of heart and love his wife better, but only to hide his true feelings and behavior from her. "[I]f you like elsewhere [that is, are in love with someone besides your wife], do it by stealth / . . . Be secret-false: what need she be acquainted?" (3.2.7, 15). As she says this, and urges Antipholus to go back inside and "comfort" her sister (3.2.26), Antipholus responds by falling in love with Luciana, and, taking his cue from Luciana's pedantic inclinations, asks her to "Teach me, dear creature, how to think and speak. / . . . Would you create me new? Transform me then, and to your pow'r I'll yield" (3.2.33, 39–40). Luciana is appalled, but Antipholus of Syracuse persists in declaring his love.

When she runs off, Dromio of Syracuse enters. He has just had an unusual romantic encounter as well. The "kitchen wench" Nell (or Luce) seems to think that Dromio is her fiancé: she lays claim to Dromio, "such claim as you would lay to your horse, and she would have me as a beast" (3.2.85–86). Antipholus and Dromio trade quips about her, including embarrassed jokes about her obesity and bawdy jokes about her body parts. But Dromio's situation convinces Antipholus not to put up with the state of affairs in Ephesus. In spite of his attraction to Luciana, he is determined to quit Ephesus by evening if he can find a ship ready to depart. He sends Dromio off to inquire. Then he runs into Angelo the goldsmith, who mistakes this Antipholus for Antipholus of Ephesus. Angelo gives Antipholus of Syracuse the necklace he has made, refusing to be paid for it until later in the day, when they are supposed to meet up again. "What I should think of this," Antipholus of Syracuse says to himself, "I cannot tell" (3.2.179).

4.1. Now the action gets further knotted up. Angelo is talking to a merchant. He owes the merchant money and needs to pay him immediately, since the merchant is about to embark for Persia. Angelo tells the merchant that he shall have his money shortly, for his friend Antipholus owes him exactly that amount of money, and is about to pay him. They therefore head for Antipholus's house, but before they get there they encounter Antipholus of Ephesus on the street. Antipholus is telling Dromio of Syracuse to buy a "rope's end" with which he is going to beat his wife and "her confederates" for locking him out of doors (4.1.16, 17). Coming up to him, Angelo requests payment for the necklace. Fine, says Antipholus of Ephesus. Go fetch the chain (which you failed to give me at lunch at my woman friend's house), take it to my wife, and have her pay you the money. But I don't have the chain, Angelo objects; you do. No I don't, says Antipholus of Ephesus, you do. The merchant, impatient with this "dalliance" between Angelo and Antipholus (4.1.59), demands that a police officer standing by arrest the goldsmith for failure to pay a debt. The goldsmith then demands that the police officer arrest Antipholus for his refusal to pay for the necklace.

As the officer takes both Angelo and Antipholus into custody, Dromio of Syracuse shows up and tells Antipholus of Ephesus that he has found a ship for them to set sail in. What are you talking about, Antipholus demands, and where is the rope I sent you for? I don't know what you are talking about, says Dromio of Syracuse. Enough, says Antipholus; go to my wife and have her bring bail money to the prison he is being led to.

4.2. Back home, Luciana is telling Adriana all about Antipholus's declaration of love to her. Adriana is angry and curses her husband bitterly, but her feelings of devotion to Antipholus (of Ephesus) haven't really changed: "I think him better than I say, / . . . My heart prays for him, though my tongue do curse" (4.2.25, 28). Dromio of Syracuse interrupts the two women with news of Antipholus of Ephesus's arrest. Adriana gets the money and gives it to Dromio of Syracuse, with orders to bring her husband home.

4.3. Antipholus of Syracuse, oblivious to all the fuss over the necklace and the arrests, thinks aloud about how well he is treated in Ephesus, everyone calling him by his name, offering him money, invitations, thanks for favors performed, "commodities to buy" (4.3.6). Yet "these are but imaginary wiles," he concludes. The place is inhabited by "sorcerers" (4.3.10–11). He is interrupted by Dromio of Syracuse, fresh from Adriana and Luciana, who gives him the bail money he (that is, the other Antipholus) sent for and asks what happened to the police officer. Antipholus of Syracuse doesn't know what he is talking about, but inquires after the ship that Dromio was supposed to find. I've already told you about the ship, Dromio replies. Antipholus of Syracuse knows that he hasn't.

The Courtesan with whom Antipholus of Ephesus had dinner enters the scene. She sees Antipholus of Syracuse wearing a gold chain around his neck and asks whether that is the necklace he promised her earlier. Antipholus of Syracuse is flabbergasted. Calling her a devil and a witch, he demands she go away and forget about the chain. The Courtesan replies, give me my ring back then, the one I gave to you earlier today. Antipholus and Dromio flee her. The woman resolves to go to Antipholus's wife and complain about Antipholus's lunacy.

4.4. Meanwhile, Antipholus of Ephesus is being led away by the Officer, when Dromio of Ephesus comes up to them, bearing not the bail money Antipholus sent for (by the other Dromio), but the rope's end Antipholus had requested before he was arrested. Exasperated, Antipholus beats him. Then Adriana, Luciana, the Courtesan, and a schoolmaster (Pinch) come upon them. The women ask the teacher to exorcize the demon possessing Antipholus and so causing him to act as if he were mad. Antipholus insists that he is sane. Antipholus and Adriana argue at cross-purposes. When Antipholus begins to rage at his wife, she has several bystanders come and bind him and bring him to her house. The Officer insists that Antipholus go to prison. The schoolmaster calls for Dromio to be bound as well. Adriana prevails by promising to pay the Officer the bail money. So Antipholus and Dromio of Ephesus are led away to the house. A moment later Antipholus and Dromio of Syracuse enter, armed. Adriana and the others run away in fright.

5.1. Angelo and the Merchant, discussing the problem between them, encounter Antipholus and Dromio of Syracuse. The argument continues about the necklace; this time Angelo complains to Antipholus of Syracuse about the behavior of Antipholus of Ephesus. Antipholus of Syracuse takes offense and the men draw swords. Adriana and the others interrupt them, and Antipholus and Dromio run off, entering a "priory," or convent, for safety.

The Abbess of the priory comes out to ask the crowd about the fuss before her door. Adriana tells a tale about the madness of her husband, but the Abbess blames this insanity on Adriana, whose excessive jealousy and shrewishness have driven her husband out of his wits. The Abbess refuses to help Adriana any further except to go back inside to see what she can do on her own about curing Antipholus (of Syracuse) of his madness.

By now evening is coming on. The Duke of Ephesus enters with his henchmen, leading Egeon, the hapless individual condemned at the beginning of the play, to his place of death. The Duke still wishes that he didn't have to go through with the execution. Adriana rushes up to petition the Duke. She tells him the story of her husband's madness, as she understands it, and asks that Antipholus be ordered out of the priory. A messenger enters to tell Adriana and the others that Antipholus and Dromio (of Ephesus in this case) have escaped from the schoolmaster and the others who were leading them home and have physically threatened the schoolmaster. That is impossible, Adriana replies, the two men are here, locked up inside the priory. But then Antipholus and Dromio of Ephesus enter, Antipholus throwing himself at the feet of the Duke, demanding justice against his wife for having "abused and dishonoured" him (5.1.199). Bound together with Dromio, he had been left in a "dark and dankish vault" at home (5.1.248), until, gnawing at the rope that bound them, he gained his freedom and hurried here to find the Duke. Antipholus, Adriana, Angelo, and the Merchant argue. The Duke accuses all of them of being mad and sends for the Abbess.

Suddenly, the captive Egeon recognizes Antipholus, or thinks he does, for the man he sees is Antipholus of Ephesus, not the son with whom he is familiar. Egeon thinks this Antipholus will save him, but neither this Antipholus nor this Dromio claims to know him. Then the Abbess comes out, along with Antipholus and Dromio of Syracuse. "I see two husbands," Adriana says, "or mine eyes deceive me" (5.1.332), and the two Dromio accuse each other of being imposters. Then, surprisingly, the Abbess recognizes Egeon. She is Aemilia, Egeon's long-lost wife. After she was saved in the shipwreck, she tells us, she was separated by the Corinthian fishermen from the two boys who were with her; she never knew what became of them, and she entered into religious orders. The mystery, as the Duke declares, is cleared up: the two parents, the two sets of Antipholuses, the two sets of Dromios, the misunderstandings. Antipholus of Ephesus reconciles with Adriana, Antipholus of Syracuse repeats his vows of love to Luciana, who can now perhaps accept his suit, and everybody can perhaps live happily ever after. The play ends with the two Dromios taking satisfaction in one another: "I see by you I am a sweet-fac'd youth," says one to the other (5.1.419). Nor will either attempt to claim precedence over the other, the elder over the younger or the guest over the host. "We came into the world like brother and brother," says Dromio of Ephesus; "And now let's go hand in hand, not one before another" (5.1.425–426).

PUBLICATION HISTORY

The Comedy of Errors was performed at least as early as 1594, and it was certainly one of Shakespeare's earliest plays, though exactly when it was written or first performed is impossible to say. First printed in 1623 in the First Folio edition of Shakespeare's plays, which was issued after Shakespeare died, in 1616, it bears thematic and linguistic similarities with Shakespeare's other early comedies, *The Taming of the Shrew*, *Two Gentlemen of Verona*, and *Love's Labor's Lost*. It is believed that the edition was set from an authorial manuscript and that the play as we have it offers no major textual problems. Not a romantic comedy in the sense that *A Midsummer Night's Dream*, *Much Ado about Nothing*, or *As You Like It* is "romantic," it is nevertheless concerned with relationships between family members and romantic partners; it ends happily when estranged individuals are reconciled, when couples reunite, when parents and children are rejoined, and when society as a whole, earlier rifted by dissension, seems to be reintegrated—its order restored, its future happiness assured. As in other early comedies, the language is often self-consciously artificial, dwelling broadly on wordplay and often adopting a style now called euphuistic, after the popular prose fiction by John Lyly, *Euphues: An Anatomy of Wit* (1578). Like other early plays, most notably *The Taming of the Shrew*, it is concerned with the rules according to which husbands and wives get along with one another, and especially with the problem of unruly or shrewish women and their resistance to male domination. The play also examines relations between masters and servants and among merchants. *The Comedy of Errors*, like other of Shakespeare's comedies, carries its audience to an exotic locale, in this case the ancient city of Ephesus on the coast of Asia Minor, to dramatize behavior that is identifiably contemporary and local. Ephesus is much like Shakespeare's London.

The Comedy of Errors differs from Shakespeare's other early comedies in two ways: first of all, its adherence to classical theatrical form; second, its emphasis on farce. Most Shakespearean plays (the most notable exception being the very late *The Tempest*) range broadly over times and places. Here, however, Shakespeare adheres to what the Renaissance took to be the Aristotelian unities: rules according to which the action of a play needed to be confined to one place and to occur within the time span of no more than a single day. As for engagement with farce in *The Comedy of Errors*, most Shakespearean comedies, even when they contain a lot of broad humor, incline in the direction of sentimentality and thematic development. The comedies are "about" something, and they are designed to make its audience feel something about what the plays are about. Here, however, Shakespeare seems to surrender to the requirements of "farce." A farce like *The Comedy of Errors*, wrote Samuel Taylor Coleridge, "is mainly distinguished from comedy by the license allowed, and even required in the fable, in order to produce strange and laughable situations" (*Literary Remains*, ed. Henry Nelson Coleridge, 4 vols. [London, 1836–1839], 2: 114–115). The absurd scenarios, the silly misunderstandings, the slapstick humor—all of this makes for a high-spirited "farce," aiming for laughs.

Because of its unique qualities, *The Comedy of Errors* has often been reckoned as an early experiment in a form that Shakespeare would soon tire of in favor of deeper, more characteristically "Shakespearean" drama. Its affinity with classical comedy has made it seem like a youthful exploration of a theatrical country that the maturing playwright would never feel the need to visit again. Classical comedy—often quite raunchy and farcical in its own right—was a part of the curriculum in schools and colleges in Shakespeare's day. For Shakespeare to write a classical comedy of his own would seem to be an expression of a taste acquired in his youth and an experimental device tied to his apprenticeship as a playwright. However, although the play is certainly an early work, and broadly appealing as a very funny comedy, it is also highly accomplished. Indeed, it is something of a tour de force, and it contains a great deal of what for any other playwright would be considered mature thought and deep emotions.

From a conventional point of view, apart from its position as an early but important experiment in theatrical form and meaning and its association with the classical comedy studied in the schools of Shakespeare's day, *The Comedy of Errors* is a play whose historical background is of little significance. You do not need to know anything about the kings and queens of Shakespeare's Europe to understand this play, or be familiar with the political and religious history of England. However, *The Comedy of Errors* is very much a part of the cultural history of England through the end of the sixteenth century, and matters of political and religious interest are not so absent from the play as they might at first appear to be.

At the time that this play about a seafaring family of merchants was written, England was experiencing a period of commercial expansion and intensifying global rivalries over seaward-looking trade. The 1590s would not prove to be a prosperous decade. In fact, at the time of the play's first known performance, England was entering an economic depression, aggravated by bad weather and some of the worst harvests in early modern history (see *A Midsummer Night's Dream*, 2.1.88–114). However, conditions of economic life were rapidly being transformed, particularly in commercial centers like London and other major ports in England. The old economy based on conventional, local relationships between landlords and tenants, aristocrats and craftsmen and other suppliers of goods, had been giving way for a long time to a cash economy—where consumer goods were produced and traded on regional, national, and international scales, irrespective of traditional loyalties. Moreover, religious, political, and economic conflicts between Catholic Spain and Protestant England had been spilling over into privateering, naval skirmishes, raids, and battles as far afield as the New World and the East Indies. Shortly before the earliest date at which *The Comedy of Errors* could have been written, 1589, England had just won the great battle against the Spanish Armada. But conflicts with Spain and other nations, and the shifting loyalties that these conflicts demanded, would continue for another decade. England, with trading partners in North Africa and Russia, a problematic colony in Ireland, and business and military interests expanding into the Atlantic, would get involved for the first time in the slave trade that Portugal had long dominated, and many Englishmen, whether unsuccessful pirates or hapless journeymen, would find themselves captured, imprisoned in a far off land, or even sold into slavery to work the galleys of Spanish or Ottoman vessels.

In such circumstances, it is not surprising to see a play whose main action is based on the separation of a merchant family at sea, its members saved by rival ships, and indeed two of its members quite openly slaves purchased from their parents. Nor is it surprising that so much of the conflict depends on understandings and misunderstandings among merchants and tradesmen, about debts and purchases and deposits of funds, or that the framing story—that is, Egeon's capture by the Ephesians—should feature the cruel wartime laws established by competing maritime powers, Ephesus and Syracuse. Finally, it is not surprising given these conditions that the play not only ends with forgiveness, reconciliation, and peace—the happiest of endings in a world of maritime conflict—but also includes many allusions to Pauline Christianity, the religion of personal redemption that Protestants of Shakespeare's day read in St. Paul, including his travels (and notable epistle) to Ephesus. Indeed, the juxtaposition of classical, farcical comedy with Christian ideas reveals yet another historically significant context of the play: the Renaissance in England was composed of such juxtaposition. Shakespeare wrote his play in an age when educated people were trained at one and the same time in classical learning and biblical lore—a time when the secular culture of economics, politics, and the arts existed side by side with a religious culture enforced by a powerful, state-sponsored Church, at whose temples it was mandatory to worship.

Besides these topical concerns one may also note how this play, like many other Shakespearean texts, is concerned with shifting gender relations and the status of women, with the nature of magic and witchcraft and madness, and the relations between masters and servants. And finally, on a biographical note, one may also observe that this play about separated parents and twins comes from the pen of a man who himself had twin children (a boy, Hamnet, and a girl, Judith) and who lived a good deal of his time, as a principal in the rapidly growing business of the commercial stage, away from his family. Shakespeare left his family behind him in the sleepy market town of Stratford while he pursued a career in the theater: perhaps traveling with a stage troupe during his first few years in the business and then taking up quasi-permanent residence in the bustling city of London. Like many other young men seeking their fortunes in the brave new world of commerce, the young Will Shakespeare, newly separated from his wife for long stretches of time, may well have known firsthand what it was like to be suffering from what Egeon calls an "unjust divorce" where "Fortune" might leave to "both of us alike / What to delight in, what to sorrow for" (1.1.105–106).

SOURCES FOR THE PLAY

The Comedy of Errors is closely based on *The Menaechmi*, a play by the Roman dramatist Plautus dating from the second century B.C. In Plautus's play, a merchant of Syracuse traveling to the town of Tarentum loses one of his twin sons to a kidnaper. The father soon dies of grief. The remaining son is renamed for his lost brother and grows up in Syracuse raised by his mother and grandfather. Meanwhile the lost son is raised in the town of Epidamnum by his kidnaper, a prosperous merchant of the town. This original Menachmus inherits the merchant's estate, marries a rich wife, and prospers. Unlike the Antipholus of Shakespeare's play, this twin really does have a lover, the aptly named Erotium, for whose pleasure he does not scruple to steal from his wife. Unlike Shakespeare's Adriana, moreover, the wife is a real shrew, as wives in Roman comedy generally were. This Menachmus of Epidamnum associates not with merchants and craftsmen but with a freeloader, or Parasite. But when Menachmus of Syracuse shows up in Epidamnum along with his slave, Messenio, to search for his twin brother, the action is much the same as in Shakespeare's play, though not nearly so complicated. It concludes when the two brothers discover one another. They agree between themselves to give the slave, Messenio, his freedom, and Menachmus of Epidamnum resolves to sell everything he has, give up his wife, and return with his brother to Syracuse.

The main difference between *The Menaechmi* and *The Comedy of Errors* is that Shakespeare, apart from changing the ending, has added the complication of a second pair of identical twins, the two Dromios. For this idea he was probably inspired by *Amphitruo*, another play by Plautus. *Amphitruo* is the story of a military hero named Amphitryon whose wife, in his absence, has been having an affair with the god Jove, who has made himself to look exactly like her husband. Jove is served in his underhanded assignations by his son Mercury, the god of thieves among other things, and Mercury has made himself up to look exactly like Amphitryon's servant, Sosia. The action includes a scene where the real Amphitryon finds himself locked out of his house while Jupiter dallies with his wife.

In taking the main plot from *The Menaechmi* and adding new characters and twists inspired by *Amphitruo*, Shakespeare both multiplies the comic possibilities of his play and makes its plot significantly more complicated, generating many new incidents and new occasions for comic misunderstanding. He seems to have thrown himself a challenge to out-Plautus Plautus. Many agree that he has succeeded. But in bringing together plot elements and comic premises from two different plays, Shakespeare has also added elements from two other sources, both of them serious rather than comic. For the story of Egeon and Aemelia that frames the tale of mistaken identities, Shakespeare drew upon the story of Apollonius of Tyre, a traditional Greek romance, which Shakespeare may have read in a version by John Gower, though the tale also circulated in many other forms. Gower was a contemporary of Chaucer, and in Shakespeare's day Gower's collection of stories, the *Confessio Amantis*, was nearly as well known and well liked as *The Canterbury Tales*. Shakespeare would return to this story of a married couple separated by a shipwreck at sea in the much later play *Pericles*. In the story of Apollonius, a husband is separated from his wife for years by ill fortune, and his wife is discovered to have lived as a priestess in a temple dedicated to the goddess Diana. In *The Comedy of Errors*, in keeping with the Christianization of the theme, the pagan temple has been changed into a priory, a kind of convent; the wife has been changed from a priestess into a prioress, or head nun.

As for much of the tone and thematic material of play, if not any specific plot elements, Shakespeare clearly drew on the New Testament, especially Acts 19 and Paul's Epistle to the Ephesians. Paul's experience with the Ephesians inspired Shakespeare to move the action from Plautus's Epidamnum to the similar but more remote port town of Ephesus. We read in Acts that Paul founded a community of

Christians at Ephesus, though only with difficulty, and that the Christian community came to rival the cult of Diana, for which a temple had been built—this temple reminding us again of the priory to which Aemilia belongs. Exorcists and witches are said to have practiced their craft in Ephesus in the name of Christ, and books of magic were burned in the town as people began moving toward Christianity.

From the Epistle to the Ephesians we get several messages that work their way through Shakespeare's text. One is the idea that Christianity involves a kind of rebirth. In the language of the Geneva Bible of 1560, one of the English-language Bibles that Shakespeare would have had at his disposal, the Christian is exhorted to "cast off . . . the old man," to "be renewed in the spirit of your mind," and "put on the new man" (Ephesians 4.22–24). Paul also writes that husbands and wives must learn to get along with one another in an asymmetrical arrangement, according to which the woman must obey her husband and her husband must cherish his wife, to the end that they may live together as one self: "Wives, submit your selves unto your husbands . . . For the husband is the wife's head. . . . Husbands, love your wives, even as Christ loved the church." Men ought "to love their wives, as their own bodies: he that loveth his wife, loveth himself" (5.22–28). Servants, writes Paul, should be "obedient unto them that are your masters," and masters should be kind to their servants, "putting away threatening" (6.5–9).

Another source of *The Comedy of Errors* may be George Gascoigne's *The Supposes* (1575), an English adaptation of a comedy by the Italian writer Ariosto. Shakespeare used *The Supposes* as the model for the subplot of *The Taming of the Shrew*, and the compounded errors (or "supposes") that pervade the Ariosto-Gascoigne play—and several specific situations—may have influenced Shakespeare as he was shaping his own comedy of compounded errors.

STRUCTURE AND PLOTTING

As mentioned above, *The Comedy of Errors* is a tour de force: literally, a "feat of strength," where an artist vaunts his ability to overcome seemingly insuperable difficulties in fashioning a work of demonstrable complexity and originality. The tour de force in this case begins with the addition of a second pair of twins and thus a second set of mistaken identities, but it also includes the way in which Shakespeare has tied the two sets of mistaken identities with a third set, the matter of Egeon and Aemilia that frames the action of the play. *The Comedy of Errors* plays seamlessly; audiences have little trouble following the action when performed on the stage and find themselves delighted by all the errors that the characters commit even while they, the audience, can see through the errors perfectly. That this wildly complex, absurd, and funny comedy nevertheless comes together in the end as a reflection on reconciliation, redemption, and forgiveness further confirms critical appreciation of the play.

The action begins and ends with the presence of the two father figures of the play, Egeon and the Duke, negotiating competing claims of paternalistic love, civil law, and the requirements of mercy. Paternal love causes Egeon to leave home in search of his son and to break the law, and thereby require an exercise of mercy at the hands of the Duke. Out of his paternalistic love for his people, the Duke tries to play the good ruler by adhering to the letter of the law, so he allows himself no latitude to exercise mercy prompted by the stirring of private sentiment. It might be expected that the play would thus end with the Duke's learning that he could be merciful in spite of the laws of his land, or that the polities of Syracuse and Ephesus might become reconciled at the conclusion, and their harsh laws against one another's citizens relaxed. Such further closure is featured in later plays by Shakespeare, such as *Cymbeline*. Here, however, impulses toward global resolution are ignored. The happiness of the ending of the play turns entirely on the resolution of the problems of mistaken identity and alienation by way of the reuniting of Egeon's family. The Duke can be merciful because he does not have to be: the sons offer to redeem their father before the Duke resolves that Egeon does not have to be redeemed. The rivalry between Syracuse and Ephesus can be ignored, not because such rivalries are wrong or because the two city-states have found a means of reconciliation, but because in one particular case family members who have long resided in Ephesus and become integral parts of the community are shown to be intimately related to family members who have long since become identified with the community of Syracuse.

The separation of the family members is not the only conflict motivating the plot of the play. Also featured is a long series of disturbances that need to be resolved—disturbances that the play generally characterizes as unfulfilled desires and nagging inclinations. Objects of attention and affection are absent, missing, or wayward, and so they motivate "errors" (see "Themes and Meanings," below). Egeon has "labored of a love to see" his missing son of Syracuse (1.1.130). Antipholus of Syracuse has lived his life, he tells us in a speech that has already been cited, lacking "content," by which he means both his happiness and the fundamental substance of his life. As he seeks to satisfy his need to find his brother and mother, he only further "confounds himself," at once confusing himself all the more and losing his sense of personal identity in the ocean of his wanderings (1.2.34–40). Meanwhile, in Ephesus, we find out that the Antipholus of that town, though well regarded in his community and well-intentioned generally, has a tendency to be negligent of his wife and is touchy about her recriminations. His marriage is not as happy as it could be. His wife is especially aggrieved, feeling unloved and expressing her frustration with nagging and jealous rages. His wife's sister has "troubles of the marriage-bed," issues apparently about her sexuality, which prevent her from finding a husband (2.1.27), or for that matter understanding what it is that men want from women. Aemilia, the mother and mother-in-law, and the only figure of maternal authority in the play, is living not only separated from her family and ignorant of their whereabouts but also as a prioress. Though her authority as the head of a convent and as a maternal figure generally in the play is important enough to serve as a device of the action's resolution, she too lives in the condition of lack: isolated in her priory. As for the two Dromios, though neither of them confesses the kinds of feelings of regret and frustration to the audience that Egeon or the Antipholuses express, they are evidently unhappy. Faithful servants, high-spirited and fun loving, they feel abused by their masters. They are quick to complain about the indignities they suffer, and though modern readers may applaud them for this attitude, they are obviously lacking in what today we call self-esteem.

Not all of these disturbances and lacks are entirely satisfied at the conclusion of the play. When the Abbess promises the Duke and the other members of the community that the family "shall make full satisfaction" for the day's events (5.1.399), she means that if everyone goes in together to the priory the family will explain all the mysteries and controversies of the "one day's error" (5.1.398). Perhaps she also implies that something greater will result from the coming coda to the day's events, but we do not in fact know how everyone is going to live after the grand reunion. We don't know for sure that Luciana is going to accept Antipholus of Syracuse as a suitor, much less marry him; she says nothing at the end. Significantly, moreover, while the trials of the slave in *The Menaechmi* end with his manumission, our two Dromios end by still being the same slaves they always have been, following the precedent not of Plautus but of Paul. Nor do they recover their own lost parents. The grand comic resolution of *The Comedy Errors*, as in many of Shakespeare's comedies, leaves some threads untied.

MAIN CHARACTERS

Antipholus of Syracuse and Antipholus of Ephesus

The main interest of the play's dramatis personae has less to do with character—the bundle of traits, dispositions, and acts that add up to what a person is—than with identity, the circumstances and roles in life that make a person who he or she is. To be one's self, the play suggests, is not only to be the self-same person from day to day, as when we may say that Antipholus of Syracuse today is Antipholus of Syracuse tomorrow. To be one's self is also to live in relation to other selves. It is because he is *out* of relation to people dear to him, as it were, that Antipholus of Syracuse claims to have "lost" himself. Similarly, because he is estranged from his wife, Adriana says to Antipholus of Ephesus (though she is actually speaking to Antipholus of Syracuse), "[You are] estranged from thyself[.] / Thyself I call it, being strange to me" (2.2.120–121). When Antipholus of Syracuse wanders through the streets of Ephesus, he encounters what is, in fact, the identity of his brother:

> There's not a man I meet but doth salute me
> As if I were their well-acquainted friend,
> And every one doth call me by my name:
> Some tender money to me, some invite me;
> Some other give me thanks for kindnesses;
> Some offer me commodities to buy.
> Even now a tailor call'd me in his shop,
> And show'd me silks that he had bought for me,
> And therewithal took measure of my body. (4.3.1–9)

A whole life is revealed to Antipholus of Syracuse as he wanders through the streets of Ephesus, a life he never had. The other Antipholus is a man well-known and well-liked, a man people greet on the street and with whom they conduct all sorts of transactions. That is not merely what he is; that is who he is. And it is because Antipholus of Syracuse knows that this is not the man he really is that he attributes his treatment in the town to witchcraft and sorcery.

One might say that Shakespeare is concerned in this play to show how identity is malleable, unstable, and contingent. One is who one is largely because of the series of accidents that make up the story of one's life, what Egeon characteristically calls "fortune" (1.1.105). One is largely who one is not because of who one feels oneself to be, but who other people recognize one to be. The instability of identity is further emphasized by the many allusions to witchcraft, sorcery, magical transformations, and hallucinations. Dromio of Syracuse, for example, seems to be in constant danger, at least metaphorically, of being transformed—like the main character in *The Golden Ass*, the ancient novel by Apuleius—into a laughable beast of burden.

However, the vagaries of identity exposed in the play do not mean that its dramatic personae lack character in the traditional sense, and *The Comedy of Errors* gives character-motivated actors plenty with which to work. Antipholus of Syracuse is among other things a melancholic figure, world weary and mistrustful. Antipholus of Ephesus, by contrast, is an easygoing man. It is indicative of what kind of man he is that, in the midst of puzzling good fortune, Antipholus of Syracuse is quick to suspect that a terrible, supernatural conspiracy is being waged against him, or that, in the face of danger, he is quick to run into a convent for safety. Antipholus of Ephesus, however, seems unafraid to demand his rights, to court danger, and, in the face of adversity, to exact revenge against his detractors.

Egeon and Aemilia

Egeon is a pitiful figure. Like Antipholus of Syracuse, he seems unwilling to take the initiative to solve his problems, even though it was originally by taking the great initiative to wander from home that he has brought his current problems upon himself. Aemilia in a sense is just the opposite. She has responded to her troubles, it is true, not by wandering in search of her loved ones but by allowing herself to be confined to a convent for a good many years. But she is quick of tongue and authoritative and stands upon her dignity. It is significant that it is to her "home," the priory, that everyone is invited in the end (and not, say, to the household of Antipholus and Adriana or to the residence of the Duke), even though a priory is not usually a place to which guests of both sexes and several walks of life are generally invited to visit. As a prioress with roots in ancient practices, apparently occupying the site of an ancient pagan temple, she is metaphorically a kind of high priestess and represents the tradition of female power that goes back to legends of the goddesses like Astarte and Lilith.

Adriana and Luciana

Adriana and Luciana may be the most interesting characters from a psychological point of view. Luciana blames Adriana for the waywardness of her sister's husband. Chaste and proper, as some critics have admiringly observed, Luciana after all is a bit of a pedant and a prude, quick to tell others how to behave and why, even though she mixes in matters, as Adriana observes, in which she has little experience. Luciana has believed what she has been told: women should passively submit to the wills of their husbands. When Antipholus of Syracuse makes vows to her, she responds by tattling on him. She seems to be the kind of person who needs always to be in the right and who, perhaps as a result, doesn't get much out of life. Yet in an interesting complication we find that she is also capable of recommending hypocrisy and deceit as a solution to one's problems.

Adriana is a woman of strong needs and a strong will. She will not simply play the submissive wife: she knows that marriage is a two-way street, that the woman has rights, too, and that the woman is justified in insisting upon them. She has considerable powers of eloquence and seduction. But she is in love with her husband, and she needs to feel loved by him. She is not above complaining when she doesn't get her way, and yet, in another interesting complication, she shows herself capable of seeing through and admitting to her own foibles. If she will berate her husband when she feels mistreated, she will not stand for hypocrisy and readily acknowledges that her open anger is a defense mechanism, a way of coping with her hurt feelings. When her husband gets into trouble, she does not hesitate a moment to do all she can to help him, although in doing so, it is true, she is also expressing the possessive side of her nature.

The Two Dromios

As for the two Dromios, they are clownish figures and were no doubt played by the clowns of Shakespeare's acting company. Quick to jest, eager to do the bidding of their masters, but also quick to complain (if not to rebel) when they are treated cruelly by their masters, they seem identical. But it is only in Dromio of Syracuse, who is used by his master to help dispel his melancholic moods, that we see the exercise of a resourceful wit and an easygoing inclination to make jokes. Dromio of Ephesus, like his master, has settled into his household's way of life; perhaps his established position has abrogated his need to be as resourceful as his twin.

DEVICES AND TECHNIQUES

The language of *The Comedy of Errors* is a mixed bag, juxtaposing high, medium, and low forms of speech, oscillating between passages in verse and passages in prose; the verse itself oscillates between the "blank," loose, spontaneous versification of oral discourse that would mark Shakespeare's later plays and several more tightly controlled and artificial-seeming forms, including exchanges of rhymed couplets and quatrains and extended speeches that seem to owe a lot to euphuism (see "Publication History," above). Some of the versification is also, in another artificial-seeming technique, made to conform to rhythmic patterns other than the standard, supple iambic pentameter of Shakespearean blank verse. These earlier, artificial verse forms are characteristic of Shakespeare's early plays, but their prevalence is not merely a sign of the playwright's immaturity, for there is a method to the mixture of styles and modes. The variety of forms provides contrasting rhythms of tone, action, and meaning that underscore the comic logic of the play and punctuate differences of character, situation, and thought.

To illustrate this point one may look at a good example of euphuistic verse in Adriana's speech to Antipholus of Syracuse in the following lines:

> The time was once, when thou unurg'd wouldst vow
> That never words were music to thine ear,
> That never object pleasing in thine eye,
> That never touch well welcome to thy hand,
> That never meat sweet-savor'd in thy taste,
> Unless I spake, or look'd, or touch'd, or carv'd to thee. (2.2.113–18)

Such language calls attention to its own structure in a highly unnatural way by using the repetition of sounds and word forms, parallelisms, analogies, and other rhetorical devices. Here the speaker uses "anaphora," repeating the same lead words and grammatical structure from line to line: "That never . . . That never." She also places her argument in the context of a tightly controlled series of analogies: as the first repetitive line here talks about the ear, the second the eye, the third the hand, the fourth the sense of taste (that is, the tongue), so the last line of the sequence covers all four topics in the same order, expressed in the same grammatical form: "Unless I spake, or look'd, . . ." The parallelism is further emphasized by the recurrent sounds: four one-syllable words beginning and ending with hard consonants and filled with long vowels, the sounds marching into one another on the same heavily accented beat: "I spake, or look'd, or touch'd, or carv'd. . . ." With such techniques, Adriana's speech is not only self-consciously ornate; it is also aggressively argumentative, as if Adriana were pressing her case in a court of law.

Right before this highly ornate speech, however, we are treated to a prose exchange between Antipholus and Dromio of Syracuse, which is marked by forced quibbles and even more forced analogies, a passage with irregular rhythms that seems to have little aim. The wordplay is very complicated and hard for a novice or for that matter even experts to follow: time is shown to be a scanty resource to draw upon since it is associated with baldness, the loss of hair that comes to men with age; hairiness by contrast is associated with beasts; yet though baldness may be associated with human rationality, it may also be associated with syphilis, although again "many a man hath more hair than wit" (2.2.82). It all adds up to what Antipholus calls a "bald conclusion" (2.2.108), a proposition without much point to it, and so we may agree. Yet the silliness of the exchange and baggy energy of the language occasion a helpful pause in the action and remind us of the bawdy world that in Shakespeare is generally found to underlie the highflown world of love and marriage and obligation that Adriana is about to expound. Adriana's speech seems all the more artificial, and therefore uncalled for (after all, she is speaking to the wrong Antipholus!), by way of its sharp contrast with the tone, quality, and sound of the silly exchange that precedes it.

Nor is this the only contrast of language in this same sequence. Before Antipholus and Dromio of Syracuse enter upon their prose exchange, they speak in a blank verse that seems natural, paced according to the psychology and dramatic requirements of the situation, as when Antipholus says to Dromio,

> Because that I familiarly sometimes
> Do use you for my fool, and chat with you,
> Your sauciness will jest upon my love,
> And make a common [that is, a public playground] of my serious hours.
>   (2.2.26–29)

In this speech there is also an argument with analogies and versification built on patterns of sound, but the analogies are unforced and the speech unfolds naturalistically; scanning irregularly, it has a rhythm approaching prose. It shows Antipholus of Syracuse in a moment when he is in control of himself and the language he uses, speaking seriously but without the high diction and cadence necessary when one speaks to one's equals or betters: rather, he is speaking the poetry befitting an address to one's slave.

Antipholus's language here may be juxtaposed, to underscore one final contrast, with the kind of language we are treated to in an exchange between Luciana and Adriana in the previous scene, where the two women debate the role of women in a man's world. Luciana remarks, for example,

> There's nothing situate under heaven's eye
> But hath his bound in earth, in sea, in sky.
> The beasts, the fishes, and the winged fowls
> Are their males' subject and at their controls. (2.1.16–19)

This speech features rhymed couplets (eye/sky, fowls/controls) developed with alternating end-stopped lines, finishing in periods. The rhythm is measured and almost plodding; it lacks the dramatic rhythm of Antipholus's speech, yet it does not seem as overdone as Adriana's. The effect is a quality known as sententiousness. Luciana's speech develops as if to pass sentence on the meaning of life (somewhat following Paul's Epistle to the Ephesians), and its "sentences" seem reasonable; they are likeably persuasive, as "sentences" were supposed to be. But Luciana's arguments are sententious in a negative sense as well: we know by the form of her language that she is repeating the thoughts of others, the commonplaces of the culture. Her language lacks naturalism: we know by the way she speaks that she is expressing not so much what she thinks and feels as what she believes people are supposed to think and feel.

The linguistic techniques of this play warrant patient study. But one must also note that the most magisterial technique of this play is its comic pacing. Following the classical model, the play moves from exposition to development to complication to crisis to resolution with a masterful rhythm. It manages to link what are in fact two plots, where the people visiting from Syracuse have one kind of experience and the people of Ephesus another, by featuring moments of crisis where the two trajectories of action confront one another to comic effect, as when the Syracuse men lock the Ephesus men out of the latter's own house and then finally link together entirely, in the concluding scene.

THEMES AND MEANINGS

An "error" is a mistake. I see someone I don't know from Syracuse but think I see someone I do know from Ephesus. I have committed an error. I have erred. But an error is also a "wrong," a moral shortcoming, as when, according to the age-old expression, I see the error of my ways. To err in this sense, to be "in error," is to go astray, to wander off course, to deviate from the right path. I was in error when I lied about what happened. I erred when I skipped practice and went to a party. The Latin word from which our word "error" derives, *errare*, in fact means to stray, to wander, and from that root we get not only "error" but also "errant," "errand," and "erratic." A "knight errant" goes off in search of adventures, with no particular itinerary. To "go on an errand" is to embark on a short journey in order to deliver or collect something that someone needs. To be "erratic" is to be engaged in an uneven or irregular pattern of action, so that one's behavior is volatile, mercurial, unpredictable. One never knows in the case of erratic behavior in which way a person is going, or likely to go.

The Comedy of Errors is a play about all these things: cognitive mistakes (especially those involving mistaken identity), moral shortcomings, wanderings and adventure seeking, errands, erratic behaviors. While it is a very funny play, written for laughs, it is also an extended meditation on the meaning of error. When all of the errors of the characters have been put aright, we are led to believe, all of their wandering will have come to an end. The characters have found themselves, and they have found themselves by finding each other. In the meantime, as the play treats us to the broad comedy of mistaken identity and its repercussions, it also exposes as rather hollow some of the devices people may use to cope with error: the hocus-pocus of the exorcist-schoolmaster, the unnecessarily harsh criminal justice system of the city-state of Ephesus, the jealousy of Adriana, the hypocritical pedantry of Luciana.

The Comedy of Errors is not a satire, but it seems clear what kinds of sympathies it wants to evoke in its audience and, by contrast, what kinds of practices and behaviors it wants the audience to share in ridiculing. The play also asks us to think about the different kinds of bonds that tie us together, or ought to tie us together: symbolic bonds like the gold chain that circulates throughout the play, or the Courtesan's ring; behavioral bonds like the dinner to which a husband is thoughtlessly late; the deeper bonds of trust that ought to unite a husband and a wife, or that enable mercantile society to function both socially and economically—in other words, the credit that makes it possible for couples, townspeople, and merchants of different locales to live and work together; and, finally, the bonds of law and mercy, according to which people may both follow the rules and bend the rules in the interest of justice, cooperation, charity, and love.

It should also be stressed that the resolution of the themes of the play does not always satisfy modern expectations: *The Comedy of Errors* embraces the order of a society where everything depends upon the will of an absolute ruler, the Duke, and where the question of freeing the two enslaved Dromios is not even raised. Blind obedience and deference are encouraged in this play no less than the exercise of mercy. The play embraces zaniness, but only so far as the disorder that the zaniness brings on may be resolved, and the kind of hierarchical order embraced in the Epistle to the Ephesians may be restored. However, the play also points out that human affairs are ruled to some extent by the capricious whims of fortune. Egeon's opening speech (see "Explication of Key Passages," below) emphasizes that fortune may rule over the best of human intentions, and the many absurd twists and turns of the plot—both those that get people into trouble and those that solve their problems—are delightful, comic examples of how the lives of people may be ruled by accidents of time that are well beyond their control.

CRITICAL CONTROVERSIES

The controversies traditionally surrounding the comedy have to do with whether Shakespeare wrote the play and, if he did, if the achievement was worthy of the mature playwright: the author of *Hamlet* and *King Lear*. During Shakespeare's lifetime the play may well have been popular, although we have a record of only two performances, in 1594 and 1604. The title became proverbial, and we know of at least one early spectator who responded to it approvingly. By the late seventeenth century, however, it came to be doubted whether Shakespeare was even capable of creating so raucous and "classical" a play. It was sometimes thought that he knew too little Latin to have been able to write a comedy based on Roman models. (The only English translation of *The Menaechmi* of the period, by William Warner, was issued a year after the play is known to have been performed successfully at Gray's Inn.) It was also thought that because later Shakespearean plays were noteworthy for their intensive character development, often articulated by great soliloquies like Hamlet's "To be or not to be" (*Hamlet*, 3.1.55ff), and because the characters in *The Comedy of Errors* seem comparatively slight, even if the play was a work of Shakespeare's apprenticeship it could not be reckoned a very good Shakespearean play. The focus on farce, moreover, seemed unworthy of the Bard.

By now, however, critics generally agree that Shakespeare was probably more than sufficiently accomplished in Latin to have read *The Menaechmi* in the original (although it is also now thought that Shakespeare could have seen the English translation in manuscript); they also agree that the play is a significant accomplishment. While one school of thought, dismissive of the play's quality, identified it as Shakespeare's earliest comedy, critics are now sufficiently admiring and careful in the use of evidence to place it toward the end of his so-called apprenticeship, dating it after *The Taming of the Shrew* and *The Two Gentlemen of Verona*, the early history plays up to *Richard III*, and perhaps even after *Love's Labor's Lost*. As for the lack of moral weight in the play, since the 1930s critics have been laboring to show that the farcical elements of the play are in fact framed and perhaps wedded to the serious thematic elements suggested from the beginning in Egeon's plight and speech, as well as in the allusions to Paul. Some scholars stress that the comedy of the play is tied not only to the romance elements borrowed from the story of Apollonius of Tyre but also to the moral and religious messages borrowed from the Bible.

Some critics emphasize the play's serious thematic material: the mysteries of personal identity, the competing roles of women in a man's world, the problem of service and slavery in the Shakespearean universe. Criticism today by and large takes the play very seriously indeed. One may sometimes wonder, though, whether critics are responding to the actual seriousness of the play as Shakespeare wrote it or to the fact that all comedy, no matter how amusing, broad, or silly, is, if one thinks about it enough, based on serious structures in the human psyche and serious tensions in the composition of human society.

What remains for critics to think about and sometimes dispute is how the play should be contextualized. There is a consensus that the play is a Roman-style farce that has been moralized, Christianized, and romanticized and that such a mixture involves a complex representation of life. What should one make of the mixture, though? If it is an expression of Shakespearean intention, what does it express? If it derives rather from the social conditions of Shakespearean theater and the world of the 1590s, what are those conditions? As for the play's comedy of identity and mis-identification, can we consider it as the development of a savvy psychological framework—one that can be explained by way of psychoanalytic or some other modern psychological theory of identity formation—or should we consider it in terms of the material circumstances of identity in Shakespeare's London? Perhaps what we see in this play is a rehearsal of the basis of identity in forms of doubling, mirroring, and desire. But perhaps the real identity crises in this play derive from crises in early modern culture, as notions of personal and biological singularity came to vie with more traditional notions of identity as bound in the conditions of one's birth, the nature of one's trade, and even in the clothes one wore.

Recent trends in Shakespearean criticism include a number of topics to which a reading of *The Comedy of Errors* readily lends itself: marginalized figures in the plays, like servants, slaves, and unmarried women; the construction of gender identity; the political, social, and economic geography of Shakespeare's plays, with an emphasis on travel, trade, and markets. *The Comedy of Errors*, however, has been relatively neglected in these areas, though the few available studies of these topics have much to commend themselves. (See, for example, Elizabeth F. Hart and Maurice Hunt in the bibliography below. Also see Lorna Hutson, *The Usurer's Daughter: Male Friendship and Fictions of Women in Sixteenth-Century England* [New York: Routledge, 1994].)

PRODUCTION HISTORY

We know of two performances of *The Comedy of Errors* during Shakespeare's lifetime, and about the first one we know quite a lot. It was held in the great hall of a major law school, Gray's Inn, London, as part of festivities that lasted several days marking the Christmas season, 1594. Some of the festivities failed to work out, with too many people crowding onto the stage area and giving rise to a "disordered tumult," as an eyewitness account published in Henry Helmes's *Gesta Grayorum* in 1666 put it. When things had settled down, "it was thought good not to offer any thing of Account, saving Dancing and Revelling with Gentlewomen; and after such Sports, a Comedy of Errors (like to *Plautus* his *Menechmus*) was played by the Players" (cited in *Gesta Grayorum* [London: printed for W. Canning, 1688], 22). About the next known performance, in 1604, we know little; but it too was given on a special occasion in a private hall. We do not know of any performances in a public theater like the Globe in Shakespeare's lifetime.

The next few generations ignored the play, and it was not revived until the eighteenth century, when it was usually adapted, sometimes to make it a more serious or sentimental play, sometimes to add music and additional comic or romantic scenes. Not until the nineteenth century was the play regularly performed in its original state, and even then it was often poorly reviewed.

In the twentieth century, *The Comedy of Errors* was often successfully revived, and it is now a regular part of the repertoire, although it has never been among the most popular works of the Shakespearean canon. With the rise in the early twentieth century of film and vaudeville and their natural inclinations toward farce (think Charlie Chaplin and Buster Keaton, or the Three Stooges), public tastes were transformed and audiences were more apt to take pleasure in the broad comedy of this play. Many modern performances of the play have emphasized its vaudevillian aspects, the absurdity of some of its situations, the slapstick humor. *The Comedy of Errors* has even been presented, with much stage business, by circus performers and stand-up comedians. In this spirit, too, the play has been adapted for the stage as the 1938 Rogers and Hart musical *The Boys from Syracuse* and several short-lived operatic and music hall productions. Directors since World War II, however, have also found ways of presenting the play without sacrificing its more serious aspects— transporting the scene to thematically interesting new locales, like a modern touristy beach town, or underscoring the mysteries of the situation, the characters' desire for wholeness, and the quandaries of the female characters and the servants. The problem of presenting twins has sometimes been solved by casting real twins, or people who when properly costumed can nearly pass for twins. In the charming 1984 British Broadcasting Company television production (directed by James Cellan Jones and available on video), the magic of videotape has allowed the director to solve the problem by casting one individual as both Antipholuses and one individual, the rock star Roger Daltry, as both Dromios. Other directors for the stage, by contrast, have experimented with the comedy by casting it against type, even including twins who look nothing like one another.

EXPLICATION OF KEY PASSAGES

1.1.31–120. "A heavier task . . . my own mishaps." In Egeon's opening speech we encounter a passage in blank verse that is ornate yet emotionally charged. Egeon often seems to take too long to say what he needs to say and to expand on points through complicated metaphors that ought to speak for themselves. But the delays in the pace of the speech capture the sense of time gone by that Egeon is discussing and Egeon's idea that the tale he has to tell is too painful to revisit. It also produces for the audience a sense of the wide world that people like Egeon inhabit, a world both united and divided by the navigable but dangerous sea; it announces the idea that despite our best intentions life is often ruled by circumstances beyond our control. At times the speech seems to descend to the level of the bathetic and is sometimes, therefore, played for laughs:

> Yet the incessant weepings of my wife,
> Weeping before for what she saw must come,
> And piteous plaining of the pretty babes,
> That mourn'd for fashion, ignorant what to fear,
> Forc'd me to seek delays for them and me. (1.1.70–74)

The plodding repetitiveness of the language, the heavy alliteration ("weeping of my wife," "piteous plainings of the pretty babes") has the inadvertent effect (from Egeon's point of view) of emphasizing the bathos. But it also captures the drama of a vivid, horrid scene. The indirectness with which Egeon explains his behavior, to the effect that he acted only under the compulsion of the cries of his wards, and the odd way of putting what it was that those cries compelled him to do ("to seek delays") underscore what was for Egeon at the time a scene of helpless desperation.

1.2.33–40. "He that commends . . . ah, lose myself." Antipholus of Syracuse here reveals his melancholy nature: he cannot find contentment. In one sense, his unhappiness derives from his loss of mother and brother, that is, his isolation. Yet he also speaks of a loss of self-identity. He compares himself to a drop of water that falls into the ocean and so vanishes. This short speech introduces a key theme in the play: how does one define (in the sense of explain and also in the sense of determining the boundaries between self and other) oneself? Is one's identity determined by birth? In that case both Antipholuses are Antipholus of Syracuse. Is it determined by where one is raised? By one's own actions? By how others act toward an individual? In this last case, both Antipholuses are Antipholus of Ephesus. Shakespeare will continue to explore this question until on a desert island a magician-duke and a shipwrecked crew will find themselves "When no man was his own" (*Tempest*, 5.1.213).

Eddie Albert and Jimmy Savo in *The Boys from Syracuse*. The musical comedy, which opened on Broadway on November 23, 1938, was based on Shakespeare's *The Comedy of Errors*. Music by Rodgers and Hart. Courtesy of Photofest.

5.1.68–86. "And thereof came it . . . from the use of wits." Like Luciana's similar speeches before these lines, Aemilia's words to Adriana toward the end of the play seem sententious: "The venom clamors of a jealous woman / Poisons more deadly than a mad dog's tooth" (69–70). Aemilia, like Luciana, instructs Adriana on how to behave toward one's husband. But Aemilia's speech is generally free of the end-stopped rhymes Luciana uses. It has a free and easy logic to it. If Antipholus is acting like a madman, she argues, it is only to be expected. "In food, in sport, and life-preserving rest," she says in a pair of lines that do, in fact, include an end-stopped rhyme, "To be disturb'd, would mad or man or beast" (5.1.83–84). Aemilia is speaking from a position of authority with an eye toward experience, not toward what in Luciana's dialogue are mere commonplaces. Her approach is inductive rather than deductive. And notably, although Luciana's arguments had no effect on Adriana, Aemilia's speech touches Adriana to the quick. "She did betray me to my own reproof," Adriana says guiltily (90). However, Aemilia is wrong: Adriana's jealousy and shrewishness had nothing to do with what has happened. Aemilia, too, at this point, no less than Adriana and everybody else, is still in error.

Annotated Bibliography

Foakes, R. A., ed. *The Comedy of Errors*. The Arden Shakespeare. London: Routledge, 1962. A fine, if dated, edition with a clear and informative introduction. A good resource for the beginning student. Includes some source material.

Freedman, Barbara. "Reading Errantly: Misrecognition and the Uncanny in *The Comedy of Errors*." In Freedman, *Staging the Gaze: Postmodernism, Psychoanalysis, and the Shakespearean Comedy*. Ithaca: Cornell UP, 1991. Reprinted in *"The Comedy of Errors": Critical Essays*. Ed. R. S. Miola. 261–293. An influential reading that draws on the psychological theories of Jacques Lacan, which focus on the role of language in the creation of personal identity.

Hart, Elizabeth F. "'Great Is Diana' of Shakespeare's Ephesus." *SEL: Studies in English Literature* 43.2 (2003): 347–374. A feminist exploration of the mythic and ideological dimensions of Aemilia and the priory.

Hunt, Maurice. "Slavery, English Servitude, and *The Comedy of Errors*." *English Literary Renaissance* 27.1 (1997): 31–56. A clear and important article that illuminates the relationship between masters and servants in the play and the meaning of servitude in Shakespeare's England. It raises some disturbing questions about power and obedience in Shakespeare but unfortunately backs away from its more provocative implications.

Lanier, Douglas. "'Stigmatical in making': The Material Character of *The Comedy of Errors*." *English Literary Renaissance* 23 (1993): 81–112. Reprinted in *"The Comedy of Errors": Critical Essays*. Ed. R. S. Miola. 299–334. An attempt to counter psychoanalytic arguments with a historical reading of identity.

Leggatt, Alexander. "Shakespeare's Comedy of Love: *The Comedy of Errors*." In Leggatt, *Shakespeare's Comedy of Love*. London: Methuen, 1974. 1–19. Reprinted in *"The Comedy of Errors": Critical Essays*. Ed. R. S. Miola. 135–152. A fine formalistic account of the play, raising thematic issues.

Miola, Robert S., ed. *"The Comedy of Errors": Critical Essays*. New York: Garland, 1997. An excellent collection. A few of the essays reprinted are singled out here for special mention, but all of them are worth reading.

O'Donnell, Brennan. "The Errors of the Verse: Metrical Reading and Performance of *The Comedy of Errors*." In *"The Comedy of Errors": Critical Essays*. Ed. R. S. Miola. 393–424. Clear and informative. Explains how verse forms and metrics affect the meaning of what the characters say.

Whitworth, Charles, ed. *The Comedy of Errors*. Oxford Shakespeare. Oxford: Oxford UP, 2002. A bit tendentious and overheated in its editorial introduction and commentary, this edition nevertheless contains important new interpretive material and reprints William Warner's translation of *The Menaechmi*.

The Taming of the Shrew

Gina Macdonald

PLOT SUMMARY

Induction, scenes 1 and 2. The Induction provides a pretext for the play to follow, making *The Taming of the Shrew* a play within a play. In the Induction, scene 1, a nobleman decides to entertain himself by playing a joke on Christopher Sly, a very drunk tinker (someone who repairs pots and pans), by having the lord's servants dress Sly in rich clothes and place him in an expensive bedroom. Scene 1 develops the details of the conspiracy and then scene 2 shows the scheme at work, so that when Sly wakes up from his drunken slumber he is surrounded by the real nobleman's attendants, who wait upon him. There is also a boy, a page, disguised as Sly's wife, who pretends to be overjoyed that Sly has recovered from a fifteen-year-long fit of insanity. The premise is that Shakespeare's play is the entertainment provided Sly by a company of itinerant players. Sly's "wife" and attendants claim that viewing the play will help prevent a return of his madness. Presumably, the instigator of this joke is watching from the sidelines, just as Sly and the audience watch Shakespeare's play. The Induction calls attention to the artificiality of the play, especially if Sly, his boy-wife, and entourage remain on stage throughout the production of Shakespeare's shrew play. After 1.1 Sly comments on the production, calling it "a very excellent piece of work" (1.1.253) but wishing it had already ended. Shakespeare thus has several levels of reality at work as characters in the play-within-the-play disguise themselves and assume roles at odds with their reality.

1.1. Lucentio speaks to his servant, Tranio, about how pleased he is to arrive in Padua, Italy, to study, financed by his wealthy merchant father, Vincentio. Tranio pleads for fun as well ("Let's be no Stoics, nor no stocks," 1.1.31), suggesting in what would have been a pun for Shakespeare's audience that stoic devotion to work makes people dull (stocks or blocks of wood). The pair overhear Baptista Minola refusing to allow his much-courted young daughter, Bianca, to marry before her older sister, Katherina (Kate), the shrew of the play within a play. Bianca's suitors, Gremio and Hortensio, complain that Kate is too rude and shrewish to get a husband, for while Bianca seems obedient, maidenly, and modest, Kate speaks her mind. Baptista seeks a tutor for his daughter, and Gremio and Hortensio conspire to find Kate a husband in order to reopen the field for Bianca, their target and hoped for prize.

Lucentio is smitten by love for Bianca at first sight ("I burn, I pine, I perish," 1.1.155) and turns to Tranio for advice about how to pursue the matter. Lucentio thinks of Bianca's beauty only in Petrarchan conceits (coral lips, perfumed breath), while Tranio reviews the facts. He suggests that Lucentio play schoolmaster to court Bianca. Tranio will pretend to be Lucentio, and Lucentio's other servant, Biondello, will pretend to be Tranio's servant. They tell the stunned Biondello that the disguise is to protect Lucentio from a murder charge, so secrecy is imperative. (Sly at this point is nodding off from boredom, 1.1.249).

1.2. Petruchio, an adventurer from Verona, has come with his man, Grumio, to see his friend Hortensio. Grumio is thickheaded and quarrelsome; he mistakes Petruchio's instructions to knock on the door to mean he should strike Petruchio; verbal and physical sparring ensue. Hortensio welcomes Petruchio in Latin, and, when he understands that Petruchio has come seeking his fortune and a wife, Hortensio perceives an opportunity to find Kate a husband, since Petruchio claims to be willing to marry an ugly shrew if she is rich enough: "I come to wive it wealthily in Padua; / If wealthily, then happily in Padua" (1.2.75–76). Petruchio agrees to woo Kate to help his friend Hortensio win Bianca and to gain himself a rich dowry.

Gremio, meanwhile, has hired a schoolmaster (Lucentio in disguise) to court Bianca for him under the guise of giving lessons, though Lucentio has his own courtship agenda in mind. Gremio and Hortensio both promote Petruchio's courtship of Kate, agreeing to pay his wooing costs (and making the disguised Tranio do so, too). Petruchio brags about his past exploits at sea, at war, and with fierce animals to prove himself prepared to face down a sharp-tongued woman. Tranio, masquerading as Lucentio, seeks Baptista's permission to court Bianca based on her high reputation. In this guise he plans to promote his master's cause.

2.1. Kate teases Bianca about her suitors, and Bianca accuses Kate of jealousy. Bianca's tears bring Baptista to her rescue, and Kate chides him for feeling more affection for Bianca than for her. Gremio, Lucentio, Hortensio, Petruchio, Tranio, and Biondello all arrive. Petruchio introduces himself, his background, and his purpose, praising Kate extravagantly and offering a disguised Hortensio as a musical tutor, Litio. Likewise, Gremio presents Lucentio as a young scholar named Cambio (meaning "change"), and Tranio introduces himself as the son of Vincentio, a mighty man of Pisa, bearing the gift of a lute and some books in Greek and Latin. As the fake Litio and Cambio go off to begin their lessons, Petruchio inquires about Kate's dowry. Baptista promises 20,000 crowns immediately and, after Baptista's death, half of his lands. Petruchio, in turn, offers Kate his lands and leases if he dies before her. He wants to draw up the marriage agreement right away, but Baptista insists he must first win Kate's love, a matter Petruchio dismisses as easy, because, he says, they are both proud and raging so their encounter will "consume" what "feeds their fury" (2.1.133). He will woo fiercely but will be careful not to destroy her spirit. He leaves with Baptista's good wishes.

Hortensio experiences Kate's temper firsthand, for she breaks the lute over his head and calls him names, actions Petruchio claims to find inviting. In a brief soliloquy he shares with the audience his madcap plan—to greet every abuse with feigned affability. Kate lives up to her reputation in their first meeting, engaging in a violent tongue-lashing. Petruchio praises her gentleness and puns on Kate as cakes to be eaten, while she denigrates him. They wittily fence verbally, as Petruchio turns Kate's insults into compliments or into clever sexual jokes. When she calls him "A join'd stool" (2.1.198), he invites her to sit on him and turns her image of him as an ass into a comment on women bearing the burden of men. Despite the world's report of her nature, Petruchio continues to praise Kate in high-flown poetic diction. When she strikes him, he warns her that he will slap her if she hits him again. He asserts that he will marry her no matter what and will tame her, making a wildcat into a house cat (punning on her name). When Baptista asks how the courtship is going, Kate complains about this "half lunatic" (2.1.287), but Petruchio claims that she complains out of "policy" (2.1.292) because of her natural modesty, and he says that they have set the wedding date for Sunday. He tells the mockers that he has chosen her for himself and that as long as he and she are pleased, their relationship is no one else's business. They have agreed, he claims, for her to continue to be contrary in public to save face, but, in fact, this is a love match and in private she is most affectionate. Baptista is stunned (as is Kate) but agrees to the wedding.

While Baptista seeks a love match for Kate, he agrees to give Bianca to whichever suitor offers (and can produce) the largest dowry. She is then bid for, with suitors expanding on what they offer her. Gremio offers his rich city house and its fine furnishings as well as his rich farm, upon his death, while Tranio offers multiple rich houses in Pisa and a fruitful country estate that produces 20,000 ducats annually. Gremio adds an argosy (a rich merchant ship) to his bid, and Tranio tops it with three argosies, two large galleys, and twelve smaller ones. Gremio says that all he has is Bianca's, but Tranio (as Lucentio) claims greater wealth than Gremio. Baptista wants Tranio's father's consent to this agreement in case Tranio dies before his father; if that consent is forthcoming, he will let Tranio/Lucentio marry Bianca the Sunday after Kate's wedding. If Tranio cannot get his father's consent, then Bianca will marry Gremio. Consequently, Tranio must find someone to impersonate Vincentio, Lucentio's father.

3.1. The disguised rivals for Bianca's hand, Lucentio as Cambio and Hortensio as Litio, compete for time to court Bianca under the guise of educating her. Lucentio's insults about Hortensio's out-of-tune instrument send the supposed musician off to correct the problem, leaving Lucentio to use a Latin translation of Ovid's *Heroides* (imaginary love letters from abandoned women) to introduce himself and his cause. Bianca repeats the Latin with her own gloss, concluding, " '*regia*,' presume not, '*celsa senis*,' despair not" (3.1.44–45). Hortensio uses the same device, a musical poem telling of his love. Bianca leaves them both to help Kate prepare for her wedding.

3.2. The day of the wedding finds Kate humiliated, fretting at Petruchio's failure to appear and weeping despite her sharp criticism of him. Biondello enters and comically describes Petruchio's approach in disreputable apparel, atop a swaybacked, broken-down nag. When Petruchio enters, Baptista urges him to dress himself more appropriately, but he replies that Kate is marrying him, not his clothes. His crafty lessons to Kate on humility and obedience begin here, as Tranio seems to perceive.

The wedding occurs offstage. Gremio describes the madcap ceremony, in which Petruchio behaves outrageously, making his responses with an oath, knocking down the priest, stamping and swearing, tossing his drink in the sexton's face, and kissing his bride with a "clamorous smack" (3.2.178). Petruchio refuses to stay for the wedding feast, despite Kate's insistence, and carries her away despite her vigorous protests. He pretends to fight off attackers as they leave. All laugh and return to the wedding banquet, presided over by Tranio/Lucentio and Bianca, a practice for their upcoming wedding, Tranio jokes.

4.1. Petruchio begins the taming of Kate, using the same strategies he earlier employed to tame a hawk or falcon to his call: depriving her of sleep and food, all under the guise of caring for her. A cold, wet, bedraggled Grumio reports the nightmare trip. Even on the way to his home Petruchio manages to make Kate's horse stumble so that she falls in the mire and the horses run away. He beats the servants for causing their mistress pain, though he guides her so she must trudge through mud to stay on his arm. Curtis and Grumio agree that Petruchio is perhaps more the shrew than Kate, and as the taming continues they feel more sympathy for her, as do we.

Once home, feigning loving consideration for her, he curses the servants for not having properly prepared for their new mistress, calls for water to clean up with, and introduces his spaniel to her. He throws out the food because it is badly prepared (a hungry Kate is quite willing to eat anything) and takes her to bed cold, wet, dirty, and hungry. The servants agree that "he kills her in her own humor" (4.1.180). Later, he keeps her awake all night, finding fault with the bed and tossing the covers around.

4.2. Back in Padua Tranio persuades Hortensio, in the light of Lucentio's behavior as Cambio, to give up his courtship of Bianca if he too swears never to marry her. The disgusted Hortensio consoles himself with a rich widow who claims to have long loved him. Then Tranio bullies an aged pedant from Mantua into impersonating his master's parent (arguing that it is death for any Mantuan to come to Padua, so the disguise will save his life). Tranio hopes this fake Vincentio will satisfy Baptista's concerns about the marriage proposal and Lucentio's courtship can thrive.

4.3. The taming of Kate continues, with Grumio aiding his master. Petruchio brings in a tailor to dress Kate appropriately for a visit to her family, but when she contests her husband's fashion sense Petruchio scornfully rejects the fine dresses he has ordered for her, bullies the tailor, and drives him away with insults, whispering to Hortensio, who has come to visit, to pay for the gown Petruchio has destroyed. Petruchio tells her that they will go to Padua just as they are and will depart now, at 7:00 A.M. Kate replies that it is already 2:00 P.M. Petruchio replies that they will not depart until "It shall be what a' clock I say it is" (4.3.195).

4.4. Tranio and the Pedant, who is dressed like Vincentio, proceed with the deception of Baptista while Lucentio elopes with Biondello's aid.

4.5. Petruchio, Kate, and Hortensio set out for Padua. Kate has clearly learned to play Petruchio's game: to anticipate the response he desires and to submit to his will. Petruchio tests her willingness to conform, asking her questions that guide her to accept his interpretation of reality, no matter how mad it sounds. When he calls the sun the moon, and then reverses his statement when she agrees with him, she finally says, "What you will have it nam'd, even that it is" (4.5.21), and Hortensio and Petruchio both know that he has won the battle. Then, when the couple meets with old Vincentio, Lucentio's father, on his way to visit his son, Petruchio makes Kate greet him as if he were a beautiful young maiden, then chides her blindness in not recognizing the old man's gender and age. Kate apologizes for her "mad mistaking" (4.5.49). Hortensio looks forward to following Petruchio's example in training his own wife.

5.1. The real Vincentio, arriving at his son's residence, is shocked to confront an imposter pretending to be himself, Biondello returning to the house, and Tranio his servant pretending to be his son. Tranio tries to keep up the pretense, but Vincentio fears for his son's life and is about to have all the pretenders arrested when the real Lucentio appears with Bianca, whom he has just married. Lucentio has outwitted his rivals and won the fair maiden. He asks for and receives his father's blessing, though Baptista is shocked that Lucentio would marry his daughter without his permission. Vincentio promises to make all right, Lucentio promises to protect Bianca from her father's wrath, and Gremio, like Baptista, feels cheated and deceived in every way.

When Petruchio asks Kate to kiss him, she is embarrassed to do so in public, but when he threatens to take her home, she yields to his request.

5.2. The play concludes with a celebration of three weddings (Kate-Petruchio, Bianca-Lucentio, the widow-Hortensio). Kate thus finally has the wedding banquet Petruchio had denied her. Hortensio's widow is catty about Kate, and Petruchio immediately bets on his wife's ability to put down the widow. Bianca responds to Petruchio's repartee by leading the women away. Amid much jesting still about Petruchio's marital choice and Kate's sharp tongue, Petruchio bets with the other newlyweds, Lucentio and Hortensio, on whose wife will prove most submissive when summoned before their husbands. Petruchio wins easily, for Bianca refuses Lucentio's requests, as does the haughty widow, but Kate not only comes at his call, but brings with her the other two resisting wives. Having won her husband's wager for him and shown up the other two women, she completes her conquest of Petruchio, the wedding guests, her beauteous sister, and the rich widow in her final speech exhorting wives to obey their husbands and take pleasure in their duties. And thus the shrew is tamed.

Shakespeare's play as we have it does not return to the Sly sequence of the Induction. In some productions Sly dozes throughout most of the play, awakening sleepily at the end and staggering off, but other productions follow the ending of the anonymous *The Taming of a Shrew* (published in 1594), which has additional dialogue. Adding this second part of the frame again calls attention to the art, artifice, and illusions of the theater. The frame emphasizes Shakespeare's power to make the artificial take on a reality of its own, to breathe life into the bare bones of a stage production and make its characters seem to live.

PUBLICATION HISTORY

The internal content, themes, and comedic games make *The Taming of the Shrew* seem very much of a piece with Shakespeare's other early plays, *The Two Gentlemen of Verona* and *The Comedy of Errors*. Consequently, it is thought to belong to that period of the early 1590s when these comedies were produced. The anonymous play entitled *The Taming of a Shrew* was published in 1594, setting the date for Shakespeare's play more firmly in the early 1590s. Curiously, the play was not mentioned by Francis Meres in his 1598 list of Shakespeare's plays.

Shakespeare's play, in which women legally have no control over whom they will marry, reflects the reality of the time. The idea of romantic love as a basis for marriage is a nineteenth- and twentieth-century phenomenon, at least for the upper classes. Elizabethans thought love was not a requirement; it might come after marriage, but family connections were far more important. Not until the late nineteenth century did aristocratic women in British and European cultures begin to have some say in their choice of spouses and some recognition of their right to own property. Thus Petruchio's attitudes reflect the consensus of opinion in his day. Romantic love certainly existed, but it was associated with foolish adolescent behavior, like that of a Romeo or a Lucentio. The theory of the Chain of Being—the idea of parallel analogies between all social levels—provided a standard for relationships, with fathers and husbands ruling their families as the king ruled his kingdom and as God ruled the universe.

The First Folio text of Shakespeare's plays contains the only surviving version of *The Taming of the Shrew*. It is the eleventh play in the Comedy section. The play is a fair text, an acting version, set up from foul papers (that is, the author's rough draft) though perhaps revised by the stage manager. The Folio lacks stage directions and confuses speech prefixes, so scholars doubt it could have been a promptbook copy. All later texts derive from the Folio edition. A quarto edition based on the Folio was printed in 1631.

Since the Folio edition contains no resolution or conclusion to the Sly frame set up in the Induction, the anonymous *The Taming of a Shrew* has helped scholars reconstruct the conclusion of the Sly framework and four short Sly inter-scenes, which are absent from the Folio text. Alexander Pope, an early eighteenth-century poet and editor of Shakespeare, inserted these scenes into his edition of the play. However, scholars differ on the relationship between *A Shrew* and *The Shrew*. Most modern editors regard the former as a "bad" quarto, that is, a memorial reconstruction, of Shakespeare's play, though others have suggested that it is a flawed version of Shakespeare's source. Questions also linger over whether Shakespeare returned to the Sly plot at the end of his play and whether at some point he or his company decided to eliminate the entire framing device and the various inter-scenes.

SOURCES FOR THE PLAY

The issue of the sources is complicated since some of the plot elements are ancient. The shrew play, for example, derives from old jokes about shrewish wives going back at least as far as Socrates' wife, Xanthippe, who is mentioned in the play (1.2.71). The shrewish wife has a long tradition in English drama, evidenced in the scolding Mrs. Noah in the medieval mystery plays (that is, plays having religious themes). Traditionally, Noah's wife berates him mercilessly for his crazy scheme and refuses to get into the Ark even though the whole world might go under water. Roman comedy also had a tradition of the loud and pushy woman, a character type easily adapted to the Elizabethan stage. Comedies of the Roman playwright Plautus include clever servants, mistaken identities and disguised characters, erroneous conclusions, and comic situations—all evident in Shakespeare's play.

When Shakespeare began work on *The Taming of the Shrew*, he probably had at his disposal an early play of a similar title, *The Taming of a Shrew*, already used in performances by the Earl of Pembroke's theater company. Some scholars speculate that the 1594 published version of *A Shrew* is a bad quarto of the lost source play on which Shakespeare built. In other words, some believe that *A Shrew* and *The Shrew* derive from a common source. The differences in psychological conception of the characters and their interaction make *A Shrew* seem quite different from Shakespeare's treatment. The plot line and structure are very much like that of Shakespeare's play, but the verbal parallels and the marked inferiority of *A Shrew* make it seem the work of another author, not an early or corrupt version of Shakespeare's play.

The main plot of this play was drawn from medieval fabliaux and Elizabethan jests about cures for nagging wives. Like Shakespeare's play, it contains a frame around the main body of the production. In the play's frame, as in Shakespeare's play, Sly, a drunken tinker, is tricked into believing he is a lord for whom the *Shrew* play is presented; he is plied with wine, snores through much of the performance, and flirts occasionally with the young male servant who pretends to be a lady. The play focuses on the realistic humor of Sly, the earthy humor of Saunders (the character whom Shakespeare made Grumio), and the lively farce between Kate and Fernando (the source equivalent of Petruchio) in an attempt to portray the affection underlying the shrew's strong will.

Shakespeare seems to have borrowed freely from *A Shrew*'s plot and language. He improves on but does not really change the leading couple or their scenes. His major changes are adding more and improved poetic imagery and increasing the psychological motivations for action. Since the subplot of *A Shrew*, with two sisters and two suitors, is dull, and since its long, high-flung speeches are reworkings of passages from Christopher Marlowe's *Tamburlaine* and *Dr. Faustus*, Shakespeare apparently turned directly to the original of the subplot, George Gascoigne's translation of Ludovico Ariosto's *I Suppositi* (1509), a play performed by and for law students at Gray's Inn in 1566. *Supposes*, as it was called in English, contains the stock ingredients of Latin comedy, particularly the clever servant who manipulates the plot, mistaken identity, and the long-lost child.

A few samples from *Supposes* make clear the degree of Shakespeare's reliance on his source. For instance, in *Supposes* Polynesta, the source equivalent of Shakespeare's Bianca, rarely appears on stage and is more the excuse for intrigue than a developed character. She is pregnant in the source (not the virgin of Shakespeare's tale), and she gives her longest speech when she sums up her young lover's scheme to court her:

> The man whome to this day you have supposed to be *Dulipo*, is (as I say) *Erostrato*, a gentleman that came from *Sicilia* to studie in this Citie, & even at his first arrivall met me in the street, fel enamored of me, & of suche vehement force were the passions he suffred, that immediately he cast aside both long gowne and bookes, & determined on me only to apply his study. And to the ende he might the more commodiously bothe see me and talke with me, he exchanged both name, habite, clothes and credite with his servant *Dulipo*. (1.1; quoted in *Narrative and Dramatic Sources of Shakespeare*, ed. Geoffrey Bullough [New York: Columbia UP, 1961], 1.114)

From *Supposes* Shakespeare directly borrows both the servant's story of danger to persuade an older man to pretend to be the father and the discovery scene, in which the real father is turned away from his son's door and fears that the servant has murdered his son. False suppositions occur with regularity, and references to "madness" and an emphasis on a "rich dowry" as vital to any marriage also find their origins in the source play. Shakespeare rejects, however, the motif of the child lost in infancy and reared as a servant (the servant Dulipo as the long-lost son of the Gremio figure). The strategies Petruchio relies on to transform his bride into an obedient wife also appear in *A Shrew*, wherein the Petruchio figure Fernando, after beating his servants for burning the food, proclaims:

> This humor must I holde me to a while,
> To bridle and hold backe my headstrong wife,
> With curbes of hunger: ease: and want of sleepe,
> Nor sleepe nor meate shall she injoie to night,
> Ile mew her up as men do mew their hawkes,
> And make her gentile come unto the lure,
> Were she as stuborne or as full of strength
> As were the *Thracian* horse *Alcides* [Hercules] tamde,
> That King *Egeus* fed with flesh of men,
> Yet would I pull her downe and make her come
> As hungry hawkes do flie unto there lure. (scene 9, ll. 42–52; cited in *Narrative and Dramatic Sources of Shakespeare*, ed. Geoffrey Bullough [New York: Columbia UP, 1961], 1.90–91)

Likewise, Kate in *A Shrew*, starved and abused, finds that even the servants mock her plight, as they do in *The Shrew*. When Kate in *A Shrew* calls on the head servant to feed her, the following dialogue ensues:

Kate: *Sander*, I prethe helpe me to some meate,
I am so faint that I can scarsely stande.

Sander: I marry mistris but you know my maister
Has given me a charge that you must eate nothing,
But that which he himselfe giveth you.

Kate: Why man thy Maister needs never know it.

Sander: You say true indeed: why looke you Mistris,
What say you to a peese of beeffe and mustard now?

Kate: Why I say tis excellent meate, canst thou helpe me to some?

Sander: I, I could helpe you to some but that
I doubt the mustard is too collerick for you,
But what say you to a sheepes head and garlick?

Kate: Why any thing, I care not what it be.

Sander: I but the garlike I doubt will make your breath
Stincke, and then my Maister will course [curse] me for letting
You eate it: But what say you to a fat Capon?

Kate: Thats meate for a King sweet *Sander* helpe
Me to some of it.

Sander: Nay, berlady then tis too deere for us, we must
Not meddle with the Kings meate.

Kate: Out villaine dost thou mocke me,
Take that for thy sawsinesse.
    She beats him. (scene 11, ll. 1–21; in Bullough, 1.92)

Even Kate's psychologically intriguing final speech on the duty wives owe to their husbands appears in *A Shrew*:

> The King of Kings, the glorious God of heaven,
>
>   *   *   *
>
> Then to his image he did make a man,
> Olde *Adam* and from his side asleepe,
> A rib was taken, of which the Lord did make,
> The woe of man so termd by *Adam* then,
> Woman for that, by her came sinne to us,
> And for her sin was *Adam* doomd to die,
> As *Sara* to her husband, so should we,
> Obey them, love them, keepe and nourish them,
> If they by any meanes doo want our helpes,
> Laying our handes under theire feete to tread,
> If that by that we, might procure there ease,
> And for a president [precedent] Ile first begin,
> And lay my hand under my husbands feete. (scene 18, ll. 28, 31–43; in Bullough,
>   1.107)

One of the newlywed husbands in *A Shrew*, after this speech and his own wife's obvious disobedience, says, "I say thou art a shrew," but she has a quick and final retort: "Thats better then a sheepe" (scene 18, ll. 59–60). In the final scene with Sly, the lord's men bear him, in drunken slumber, to the tavern where they found him and leave him there to be found by the tapster, who wakes him up and sends him home to his wife. The play's events are "the bravest dreame to night, that ever thou / Hardest in all thy life," asserts Sly (scene 19, ll. 11–12). What matters, however, is not so much Shakespeare's borrowings as his skillful re-creation of these materials.

STRUCTURE AND PLOTTING

Shakespeare carefully balances the shrew play (Kate and Petruchio) and the tale of the young lovers (Lucentio and Bianca), alternating between them. Until our attention is called to it, we may not even notice the way in which the two stories run increasingly separate courses until Shakespeare reunites them in 4.5, when Petruchio arrives in Padua with Lucentio's father. The two plots have been resolved by 5.1. The last scene defines the harmony that has been brought out of discord ("At last, though long, our jarring notes agree," 5.2.1) and allows some jovial sparring to keep the relationship realistic. Here, the wedding that typically ends Shakespearean comedies takes the form of a delayed wedding banquet for Kate and Petruchio as they celebrate the marriage of Kate's sister.

Basically, act 1 establishes the situation and characters, while act 2 shows the suitors in competition and their marital matters seemingly settled. Act 3 sees the competition for Bianca still being carried on, as the marriage of Kate and Petruchio ensues. Act 4 presents the taming of Kate, and in act 5 all plots and schemes are resolved. The true Lucentio and his father appear, Lucentio having already eloped with Bianca, and a triple wedding feast allows Shakespeare to explore his questions about marriage and love through three brides. The technique employed here is one of "foils," in which the same theme or themes (love and courtship; appearance and art versus reality) are explored through different sets of characters to provide a well-rounded exploration of the topic.

MAIN CHARACTERS

On the surface Shakespeare's characters are stock figures of comedy, ones the audience would recognize from past productions: the shrewish woman, the pedant, the cheeky or contrary servant, the confused father, the smitten lover, the competing suitors. The witty servant who helps a romantic young lover trick his father is a staple of Roman comedy. The supposed lunatic was a popular Elizabethan stage figure; audiences apparently enjoyed watching characters affect madness as a strategy to gain what they wanted. Shakespeare's use of these stereotypes, however, makes them original creations. Kate's shrewishness, which seems to be the tantrums of a rich man's spoiled young daughter, perfectly balances Petruchio's eccentricity, which he seems able to put on and off at will, just as Kate learns to control her temper at the end of the play.

Kate

Kate, whose name is subject to much wordplay on cat and catty, "cates," or cakes, is strong-willed, though ultimately all of the women in the play prove to be so. Her father has provided her with a large dowry, so she is the would-be prey of poorer suitors hoping to enlarge their fortunes and raise their social position. As she is quite aware, she is being wooed for money rather than for love. Her situation is made more unbearable by the fact that her seemingly docile, beautiful younger sister attracts her suitors with a more traditional passivity. Kate disobeys her father because it is rational to do so even though her father is convinced that he knows what is best for his daughters. Because Kate's father has set her up to be bought by any man seeking to better his position in life, Kate tests the sincerity of her suitors with her hostility. She employs a shrill tone, shrewish retorts, and a sharp wit as weapons to protect herself from fortune hunters, defenses Petruchio quickly sees through and penetrates.

At the end of the play Kate accepts the game of female submission and the expected role to her own ends. In this way, she stands in stark contrast to another strong Shakespearean female: Portia in *The Merchant of Venice*, who already has her freedom to run her household, to demonstrate grace and wisdom that put males to shame, to outwit all, to shape the destiny of men, and to save Antonio from Shylock. Kate's battle seems in the main a physical one, for food, for clothing, for rest, but it is obviously also a battle for control. Like Portia, Kate saves the day for her husband at the end of the play, but she does so by bowing to convention—or at least appearing to do so—rather than by overcoming them, as Portia does.

Petruchio

Petruchio's style of speaking (not what he says but his way of saying it) communicates his nature: loud, boisterous, a hunter who enjoys the hunt, a man of huge appetites. But we cannot be sure exactly what he is truly like because from the beginning he is playing a clever game, showing off to his fellow males and competing with Kate to wear her down, win her, and then force her to his will. At the banquet, he is still on stage, so to speak, showing off to the other males the successful results of his strategies. He certainly values making money: witness how many times in the play he receives funds—from Bianca's suitors, from Kate's father, from the final bet. Yet he has a house, servants, a respectable reputation, a known family, and local friends among the wealthy. Most of all, he is a sportsman, proud of his hunting dogs and of his skill at taming falcons and hunting with them. His antics are all contrived to embarrass and manipulate Kate, but his true nature remains hidden from Shakespeare's audience. In his introduction to *The Taming of the Shrew* in *The Complete Works of Shakespeare* (Chicago: Scott, Foresman, 1961), Hardin Craig says that Petruchio "wishes to make Kate see herself as others see her," and his madness is simply a way of showing her what her effect is on others (155). Petruchio's one soliloquy to the audience confirms his strategy and the seriousness that lies behind his humorous pose.

Lucentio and Bianca

The names suggest the personality characteristics of Lucentio and Bianca, both associated with light, brightness, and white in Italian, but with Bianca also associated with "target," that is, the white center or bull's eye, as she is indeed the target of a number of suitors, both real and pretended. Lucentio brightens her day and gives her a chance to choose a husband for herself. The play suggests, however, that her sweetness is a pose aimed at getting her man and that Lucentio's view of her as lovestruck is an illusion. Lucentio learns the reality of his catch after marriage. Bianca is as headstrong and contrary as her sister, as their violent sisterly fight at the beginning of the play should have warned the audience.

Most of the men in the play are dupes. Lucentio, Hortensio, and Gremio are each duped in some way by Bianca. Baptista is also duped by his daughter Bianca, who elopes against his wishes, and by Tranio, a servant pretending to be a master. Vincentio thinks his son is studying when he is really playing, so maybe Lucentio and Bianca, both deceivers of their parents, deserve each other. Hortensio thinks his rich widow is in love with him, but at the end of the play she too proves a haughty, catty shrew, contemptuous of his commands.

DEVICES AND TECHNIQUES

In this play Shakespeare employs a number of devices and techniques drawn from the comedic repertoire of his day. For example, the play is a punster's paradise, and much of its fun comes from the typically Elizabethan joy in language, in double entendres, puns, outright bawdy jokes, "duels" of insults, witty put-downs, intentional misunderstandings, and other forms of wordplay. Readers and viewers who suspect a pun or bawdy joke are probably right; but the pun can be confirmed by checking Eric Partridge's *Shakespeare's Bawdy* (London: Routledge & Kegan Paul, 1947). Many texts do not gloss dirty jokes, but in passages like the following the sexual intent is obvious:

Kate: If I be waspish, best beware my sting.

Petruchio: My remedy is then to pluck it out.

Kate: Ay, if the fool could find it where it lies.

Petruchio: Who knows not where a wasp does wear his sting?
In his tail.

Kate: In his tongue.

Petruchio: Whose tongue?

Kate: Yours, if you talk of tales, and so farewell.

Petruchio: What, with my tongue in your tail? (2.1.210–218)

In this play the bawdy language is inescapable and is an important part of the battle of the sexes as Kate sharpens her verbal skills to lash Petruchio, and he turns her
insults into sexual innuendoes suggesting a more intimate physical relationship.

Comic techniques used by Shakespeare in this play build on a number of strategies. For example, he uses comedy evoked by disguises, as when the page disguised
as Sly's wife creates an absurd situation. Hortensio, Lucentio, Tranio, and the Pad-
uan schoolmaster pretend to be people they are not and contribute to comic confusion. Shakespeare also creates comedy from exaggerated behavior, such as love
at first sight (Lucentio), extreme shrewishness or feigned madness (Kate and Petruchio), and Petrarchan mannerisms, as when Hortensio gives Bianca a poem claiming that he will die unless she reciprocates his love (2.1.73–78). Of course, she does
not, and neither does he. Lucentio similarly employs the exaggerated language of
Petrarchan convention when he speaks of Bianca's "coral lips" and "breath [that]
did perfume the air" (1.1.174–175). Comic repetition is a Shakespearean favorite, as
when Gremio declares of Petruchio, "Why, he's a devil, a devil, a very fiend!" and
Tranio retorts of Kate, "Why she's a devil, a devil, the devil's dam" (3.2.155–156).

Other comic wordplay includes various forms of put-downs or insults. Kate, for
example, devises clever insults. She tells Hortensio that she would "comb [his] noo-
dle with a three-legg'd stool" (1.1.64), that is, hit his head with a stool. She calls
Petruchio a "join'd stool," a "jade," a "buzzard," "a craven," and "a crab" (2.1.198,
201, 206, 227, 239). Petruchio and his servants engage in equivocation, a form of
comic misunderstanding in which the same word is used with a different meaning,
as when the word "knock" means variously to "knock on a door" for admission or
to "knock" a person down. Petruchio asks his servant to knock on the door and the
servant takes him to mean knock him down: "Knock me here soundly," Petruchio
orders. "Knock you here, sir? Why, sir, what am I, sir, that I should knock you here,
sir?" Grumio retorts. "Villain, I say, knock me at this gate, / And rap me well, or
I'll knock you at your knave's pate." (1.1.9–12). This exchange ends with a bit of
slapstick, for when Grumio continues to misunderstand his master's order to
knock, Petruchio wrings Grumio's ear.

Recurring puns include plays on ring/wring, tale/tail, deer/dear, Kate/cates
(cakes)/cat, hoar/whore, among others. In Shakespeare's comedies, names are always significant and often carry a sharp or expository implication. For example,
Bianca means both "white" and "target" and thus is a type of pun that contrasts
her appearance (seeming pure and innocent) with that of her sister and emphasizes
her function in the play (the target that all the suitors try to hit on). Another quite
common form of Shakespearean humor that recurs in many of his comedies is fake
erudition. Lucentio's Latin lesson in 3.1 provides a good illustration. Thus, he
glosses "Hic ibat Simois," which actually means, "Here flowed the River Simois" to

signify "as I told you before, . . . I am Lucentio." Bianca's translation is equally wide of the mark as she renders the phrase, "I know you not" (3.1.31–32, 42). Both cleverly use Ovid's lines to express their feelings.

A hilarious Shakespearean strategy that serves to compact the action and to make it far more amusing than it would be if actually depicted on stage is comic description, like Biondello's account of Petruchio's horse and mad attire or Gremio's description of the wedding (3.2). Shakespeare's comic figures also engage in vaudeville-like comedy routines such as the following:

> *Tranio*: Let us entreat you stay till after dinner.
>
> *Petruchio*: It may not be.
>
> *Gremio*: Let me entreat you.
>
> *Petruchio*: It cannot be.
>
> *Kate*: Let me entreat you.
>
> *Petruchio*: I am content.
>
> *Kate*: Are you content to stay?
>
> *Petruchio*: I am content you shall entreat me stay. (3.2.198–202)

Comedy sometimes comes from a reversal of meaning or expectation, as when Petruchio asks Baptista, "Pray have you not a daughter / Call'd Katherina, fair and virtuous?" (2.1.42–43). This query immediately follows a cattish and shrill battle scene between Kate and Bianca. Petruchio employs this technique throughout the play. Even before he meets Kate he announces, "Say that she rail, why then I'll tell her plain / She sings as sweetly as a nightingale" (2.1.170–171). Late in the play he indulges in the same sort of inversion in calling the sun the moon and in addressing the old Vincentio as "Fair lovely maid" (4.5.2, 33). By then, Kate is willing to play along. And, indeed, her final speech that urges wifely obedience may be another example of her adopting her husband's game of saying the opposite of the truth. Exaggeration through reference to legendary figures quite different from Kate, like patient Griselda or the chaste and virtuous Roman Lucrece (2.1.295–296), continue a humor based on a form of comic contrast and ironic image.

In other instances Shakespeare reverses convention, for example, changing the standard Renaissance image of the meek and gentle deer (dear) submitting to the male hunter into that of the deer (Kate) holding the hunter (Petruchio) at bay. Finally, there is comic deflation, the intentional lowering of high-flown diction or sentiment for comic effect, as when Petruchio tells the wedding guests: "Go to the feast, revel and domineer, / . . . Be mad and merry, or, go hang yourselves" (3.2.224–226).

In addition to the comedy in the lines there is the visual comedy, often in great part created by the situation and by the actors. Slapstick, for instance, with actors fumbling and falling, bumping into each other, engaging in food fights or visual mimicry of the movements of a fellow actor, all add their part to the humor, as watching the Burton-Taylor film production of this play makes very clear. The incongruity of the situation can just as easily create humor—Lucentio engaging in courtship under the guise of being a strict schoolmaster. In the humorous encounter between Kate and Petruchio in 2.1, Petruchio's reference to the world's reporting "that Kate doth limp" (l. 252) usually follows some stage business in which he has tripped her in one of her assaults on him and she does limp, bent over with pain, as he goes on to describe her as "straight and slender" with a "princely gait" (2.1.254, 259).

Another technique that serves Shakespeare well is his use of imagery, sometimes for comic effect, but also to help him compactly sum up his characters. For example, Lucentio breaks into Petrarchan images to describe Bianca, images just like the ones Romeo used for both Rosaline and Juliet in *Romeo and Juliet*, images Shakespeare himself mocked in his Sonnet 130: perfumed breath, coral lips, a jewel even the gods envy. Shakespeare's point is that Lucentio is a typical young man in love, seeing what he dreams of seeing and blind to the more unpleasant realities that the ending reveals about Bianca. Petruchio, too, uses exaggerated images and adjectives to praise Kate ("soft, and affable," 2.1.251) and to describe the larger-than-life quality of their encounter (himself a mountain, unmoved by her blowing wind, 2.1.140–141).

An interesting image in the final scene is a standard Elizabethan one, used by Thomas Wyatt and Edmund Spenser, among others: the man as hunter and the female as the prey, usually a deer, an animal associated in the mythology of the time with being "gentle, tame, and meek," in Wyatt's words. These were considered the ideal characteristics of a woman, the "dear" associated by pun with the "deer" of traditional imagery. Thus, Kate, the wildcat, is totally at odds with the deer image, but Shakespeare's ending suggests that perhaps many of those seemingly tame deer were quite different behind their conventional facade. And Kate herself may not be as shrewish as she has seemed. Perhaps the greatest irony in the play is that Petruchio's description of Kate as "passing gentle" (2.1.242) is accurate. When Petruchio comments, "If she be curst, it is for policy" (2.1.292), he is wittingly or unwittingly revealing Kate's true character.

THEMES AND MEANINGS

The Taming of the Shrew is among Shakespeare's wittiest comedies, due to its complicated yet well-balanced plot, its extreme but convincing characters, and its bawdy though clever puns and jokes. The themes of the shrewish woman and of the battle of the sexes obviously dominate the play. Kate is the shrew who battles all would-be suitors and repeatedly overcomes them until she meets her match in a man who could suit her, Petruchio, who turns her insults into flattery, and who knows the way to win her heart as well as her hand. However, Shakespeare goes far beyond his sources to teach a number of lessons about art, love, and marriage.

In his poems Shakespeare calls attention to the power of art to transform reality, as well as to his skill at artifice, using highly artificial language and forms to reveal complex truths. Shakespeare argues the power of his art in this play, calling attention to the artificial tricks of the stage in his "Induction" and then involving the viewers so thoroughly in his story that they forget the artifice. The induction reveals the artifice of the Shakespearean stage: boys playing the parts of women; onions used to induce fake tears; the clothes and diction of actors making the man (or the role). Shakespeare's play itself builds on artifice: a play within a play; actors watching actors; wordplay and horseplay; disguises; and exaggerated descriptions of action that cannot be performed on stage.

Nevertheless, art has great power to engage the mind and make the unreal seem real. Shakespeare's proof is that the characters in his play within the play come to seem far more real than those of his "Induction" (reality, within the terms of the play). Shakespeare can tell us that boys are playing the parts of women and that tears result from onions in handkerchiefs, but we the audience experience a willing suspension of disbelief as the play proceeds. Art entertains (as is obvious from the comedy throughout the play). However, its second goal is to teach. In this case, the play highlights the deceptive nature of appearances, provides warnings about love at first sight, and draws a model of a "good marriage." In addition, there are favorable comments about the value of art throughout the play: "Music and poesy . . . quicken you," advises Tranio (1.1.36); Bianca claims that "books and instruments" (1.1.82) will provide her company. There is also the suggestion that only dumb, dull clods like Christopher Sly fail to appreciate the value of art. In the Induction and then inside the play within the play, Shakespeare suggests that a knowledge of art, from music to poetry, indicates proper upbringing and high social class, qualities Sly cannot pretend to have. Furthermore, the visual arts offered Sly, artistic creations Sly cannot understand, are subtle imitations of life, paintings as lifelike as if they had been reality, raising the whole question of the nature and role of art in life.

This play also provides a number of lessons about love. Shakespeare suggests that love at first sight sees only the most readily apparent virtues of the beloved and is blind to the realities, a fact the experiences of Shakespeare's males confirm. Hortensio initially believes that Bianca is not only fair but also virtuous and returns his love, only to learn that she prefers a younger, more handsome rival. Lucentio sees only Bianca's beautiful exterior and her appearance of maidenly charm, innocence, and submission; he ignores her sharp tongue and her all-too-ready willingness to deceive her father and to ignore his admonitions. His is a totally physical response: "I saw her coral lips to move, / And with her breath she did perfume the air" (1.1.174–175); "I burn, I pine, I perish" (1.1.155). Shakespeare makes Lucentio look silly in contrast to Tranio, with the latter's practical analysis of the situation. A related Shakespearean lesson about love is that outward appearances may well be misleading. Bianca's seeming virtues, which won her so many suitors, prove false. Her willingness to flout convention and tradition by eloping is the first sign that she will do the same later in marriage. After the wedding, to his embarrassment Lucentio learns that Bianca is not as innocent as she pretended (notice her bawdy jokes at the wedding feast) and is not submissive (notice her refusal to obey his commands or entreaties and her reference to Lucentio as a "fool . . . for laying on my duty," 5.2.129). Their marriage will certainly have its future problems. In this play at least, love at first sight is a sign of being silly, shallow, and immature, and it can lead to life-long regrets; its negative results are often punishment for personal dishonesty and disregard for authority and convention.

One can read the play as arguing that true love grows from following the conventional social traditions: marriage to unify families or for monetary advancement, with parental consent and approval and with clear-cut male dominance. But marriage also involves an interplay of wills, a meeting of the minds by means of interaction whereby one must face both the virtues and the vices of one's love. Within the play, surprisingly, the final model of a conventional and ultimately happy marriage is that of Petruchio and Kate—a meeting of similar minds. Petruchio and Kate, even in their fiery, witty exchange, show an equal intelligence and spirit that allows them, despite their differences, to find common ground and to learn to love and respect each other. Petruchio has followed the rules in his courtship of Kate and in his final winning of love after their marriage (a reality in an age in which arranged marriages were the rule, not the exception). Ultimately, Petruchio finds himself a greater winner than his male associates because he learns that Kate, with her high spirit, her clever tongue, and her willingness to follow his lead, is a far greater prize than Bianca, the target for whom all aimed.

Kate's seeming submission in her final speech may not, in fact, be as fully subservient as it seems, for it allows her to get revenge on her sister and the catty widow, to win the admiration of all the men, and to be the center of attention and wonder, an interpretation Elizabeth Taylor brilliantly brought to her screen portrayal of Kate to Richard Burton's Petruchio. At the end of the play, Petruchio voices the consensus Renaissance opinion: a good marriage should bring peace, love, and quiet life (5.2.107–110).

One can, of course, regard the play as a confirmation of gender roles. Within an Elizabethan marriage, the husband is lord, king, governor, head, sovereign, with all the duties that such a position demands. As Kate says in her final speech, a husband must keep his wife safe, protect her, provide a home and security for her, and maintain her (5.2.137–152). In return, the wife owes tribute: fair looks, good temper, obedience, service, duty, love (5.2.153–178). If a wife compromises her wishes to meet these duties, her husband will be proud of her, respect her, love her, and pamper her. Both will benefit and prosper, as Kate's behavior wins her husband's praise and more money for their shared coffers. In contrast, a marriage not based on mutual respect between two lovers will lead to friction, as the audience sees when Bianca and the widow snap at and disobey their husbands. While Kate and Petruchio kiss and leave for bed together, Lucentio and Hortencio bemoan their unhappy married state. The final scene suggests that beauty (Bianca) and money (the rich widow) do not guarantee marital happiness, though beauty and money do sweeten the bargain, as Petruchio would testify. Shakespeare's advice seems to be the wisdom of his time: love before marriage does not always lead to happiness, but marriage, handled properly, can lead to love.

CRITICAL CONTROVERSIES

One critical controversy deals with the relationship between Shakespeare's *The Taming of the Shrew* and the anonymous *The Taming of a Shrew*—as discussed above. The other major debate about this play is the extent to which Shakespeare here accepts the patriarchal values of Elizabethan society. While in other comedies Shakespeare can be most unconventional for his time in his depiction of gender relationships, this play disturbs modern readers because of its seemingly sexist attitudes. The sense that women are property to be obtained for the wealthy dowries they bring with them is quite openly stated. Gremio and Hortensio at 1.1.140 describe Bianca as the "ring" for which they compete, a triple pun suggesting not only the prize that the swiftest or best contestant in a sporting event will win, but also a wedding ring and the virginity of the woman to be won if they hit the target. Baptista may be a doting father, worried about obtaining good marriages for his daughters, but he clearly defines a good marriage as a financially advantageous one with someone from a good family. In 2.1 he tells Bianca's suitors that he plays "a merchant's part" and ventures "madly on a desperate mart" (ll. 236–237), or market.

He talks about commodities and exchanges and then starts the bidding on his daughter, declaring that the contender with the "greatest dower / Shall have my Bianca's love" (2.1.343–344). Tranio as Lucentio outbids Gremio and thus wins Baptista's consent to wed Bianca, as long as Tranio/Lucentio's father confirms the wealth he claims to have at his disposal. The bidding for Kate has already taken place, for only one man wants her, and his price is right. Obtaining a wealthy wife is Petruchio's frankly stated motivation in first courting Kate, and once they are married, his stated claim to her sounds offensive to modern ears: "She is my goods, my chattels, she is my house, / My household stuff, my field, my barn, / My horse, my ox, my ass, my any thing" (3.2.230–232).

Related to the financial motive in gender relationships is the question of power and dominance, and in this play the male indubitably has the upper hand and uses extreme measures to assert that power. Petruchio describes himself as a fierce woman-tamer and asserts that he is born to transform Kate from "a wild Kate to a Kate / Conformable as other household Kates" (2.1.277–278), that is, from wild-cat to household cat. Furthermore, from the start, his wit centers on sexual encounters, as when he tells Kate, "Women are made to bear, and so are you" (2.1.200), with "bear" meaning not only "to carry" (the lighter, weaker sex borne by the male), but also "to bear a man during sex" as well as "to bear children." Noted playwright and contrarian George Bernard Shaw joked about the play in a way that reflected traditional male attitudes. He described it as Shakespeare's attempt at "realistic comedy," for Petruchio's accepting a fortune to take "an ugly and ill-tempered woman off her father's hands" was "an honest and masterly picture of a real man, whose like we have all met" (quoted in Arthur M. Eastman, *A Short History of Shakespearean Criticism* [New York: Random House, 1968], 169–170).

These gender attitudes in both Shakespeare and Shaw offend modern feminists, who find in most Renaissance works a predominantly chauvinistic male perspective. In *The Taming of the Shrew* the woman is, in effect, the property of her father, who can dispose of her as he pleases, and then of the husband, both of whom view her as subservient to themselves. Kate's father chides her disobedience, and her husband punishes her for her sharp tongue. The male is the tamer who makes a civilized person of the wild Kate. Feminists see *The Merchant of Venice* as much more acceptable because the woman is the teacher. Portia teaches Bassanio that he must be faithful to her just as he expects her to be faithful. There is to be an equality in their relationship. Both Kate and Portia are dependent on their father's wishes in selecting husbands. However, whereas Kate is something to be palmed off on whoever will take her, Portia is a prize. Her husband must be willing to hazard all for her, and he must love her for her inner qualities, not her gold or her external beauty alone. Furthermore, Kate is passive in the sense that she does nothing to improve her lot except rant and rave. It is Hortensio who finally tells her to agree with whatever Petruchio says. Even after she is "civilized," it is her obedience in fetching the other wives that wins her praise. Portia, in contrast, is active. She gives Bassanio the money to cover Antonio's debts; she goes to Venice and outwits Shylock; she also outwits Bassanio in the ring test. Thus, Portia earns her respect through intelligent and merciful actions. On the one hand, Kate learns the practical value of docility in order to live in peace both with her husband and with society. On the other hand, with Portia docility stems from higher values—genuine concern for her friends and appreciation for virtue itself. Thus, in Kate, Shakespeare presents a caricature of woman as seen by man, while in Portia he presents woman as a person—someone who can equal man in wit, intelligence, honor, and love.

Opponents of this interpretation of Kate, however, argue that she is a strong woman doing her best in opposition to a cultural tradition that defines her as property to be sold to the highest bidder. By behaving like a scold, she drives off the weaker, less daring suitors until she finds a man who is truly her equal, a match for her wit. At the end of the play, she has learned new methods for manipulating her husband, has considered what he values, and then provides him the public support he requires, though in fact her actions serve her own ends quite well. It is Kate's understanding of this financial motive that gives her power in the end as she helps her husband win a wager. She also serves herself by taking revenge on her haughty sister and the equally haughty widow and by winning the admiration of every man in the room. She assures, in so doing, that her husband and hence their joint coffers will be full, so she can indeed live well. The question frequently asked, however, is whether she is happy with her situation or is simply accepting it as an inescapable fact and making the most of it. The answer onstage depends very much on the actress, who can use body language and facial expression to reveal the true relationship between Kate and Petruchio, whether it is indeed a love match or an alliance, two furies calmed by each other, or a master-subject relationship, the wildcat tamed and taught to perform, the hawk hunting for its master and then returning to his firm hand for a reward.

Some scholars take a critical line that falls in the middle of this controversy, arguing that while both Kate and Petruchio maintain a distinctive style appropriate to their character (Kate, forceful and direct; Petruchio, blunt and antic), Kate's final speech (5.2.136–179) is the one major break in the decorum of the language. Therein we hear the voice of Elizabethan male authoritarianism speaking rather than that of the character Katherina. Here, Shakespeare is simply repeating the conventional wisdom of his time, which held that the male's rule over his wife and family must be as absolute as God's rule over man. Lest we tax Shakespeare too heavily for these authoritarian sentiments, such critics observe that Kate and Petruchio often behave like friendly equals and trade quips and put-downs once she has been "tamed." Also, Bianca and Hortensio's widow behave in a most undocile fashion in the last scene. Perhaps as with many sociopolitical theories, the Elizabethan idea of male supremacy was more observed in the abstract than in practice.

PRODUCTION HISTORY

According to Henslowe's diary, on June 14, 1594, the Admiral's and Chamberlain's players performed either *The Taming of a Shrew* or *The Taming of the Shrew*. The office-book of Sir Henry Herbert, Master of the Revels, notes a November 26, 1613, production acted before the king and queen at Saint James, while the 1631 Quarto edition refers to performances by His Majesty's Servants at the Blackfriars and the Globe theaters. Samuel Pepys reports seeing on April 9, 1667, John Lacy's adaptation of the play *Sauny the Scot*, set in London with the Scot corresponding to Shakespeare's Grumio. Lacy changes much, omitting the Induction and Sly, adding a bedroom scene and another in which the servant is told to undress his new mistress. The last act has nothing to do with Shakespeare and involves toothaches, a fake burial, and a dance. Pepys called this a "silly" play.

In 1715 Christopher Bullock's *Cobbler of Preston* was performed at Lincoln's Inn Fields and was followed by a Drury Lane production of Charles Johnson's play of exactly the same name, *Cobbler of Preston* (1716), both amplifications of the scenes with Sly, though Johnson interpolated references to the 1715 rebellion and railed against the Jacobites and the Pretender, James Edward Stuart. Johnson's adaptation had little success, but Bullock's was considered quite funny by audiences at the time, partly because it had some good comic actors playing the parts. Johnson's play, however, was turned into a comic opera in 1817, with a love story and sentimental songs. Another Drury Lane production borrowed from *The Taming of the Shrew* by way of *Sauny the Scot* appeared in 1735, entitled *A Cure for a Scold, a Ballad Opera*, written by James Worsdale. Katherina is named Peg in this version, and Lacy's tooth-pulling scene is retained. The work also introduces a chambermaid to help the lovers in the subplot with their intrigue. In 1735 David Garrick staged at Drury Lane a version that held the stage for 100 years, the farce *Catherine and Petruchio* [later spelled Katherine]. Beerbohm Tree produced it in 1897, as did the Lichfield Repertory Company in 1949. These versions cut Sly and Gremio and had Bianca already married to Hortensio. The old man whom Kate/Catherine must greet as a young woman (4.5) is now Kate's own father.

In 1844 Benjamin Webster reinstated Shakespeare's play uncut (lasting three and a half hours) in a Haymarket production with screens, curtains, and locality boards instead of scenery. This was the first complete performance of the play since the theaters were closed in 1642, and Webster, who himself played Petruchio, considered this revival of Shakespeare's original his greatest success. In 1888 Augustin Daly's New York production was notable, says George C. D. O'Dell (*Shakespeare: From Betterton to Irving*, 2 vols. [New York: Scribner, 1920]), for the handsome interior of Baptista's house, like an old Italian palace; the extravagant final banquet scene set, suggesting a picture by Paul Veronese, with beautiful costumes and a choir of sweet young boys; and, finally, a magnificent Kate in a fiery wig and mahogany-red brocade gown. In 1928 Barry Jackson produced the play in modern dress at Birmingham. A 1960 Stratford production developed elaborate comic business that at times obscured the dramatic lines but provided vigorous farcical incidents, slammed doors, slapped heads, tossed plates, rigid postures, and great gusto, reports John Russell Brown in *Shakespeare's Plays in Performance* (London: Edward Arnold, 1966, 194). Brown also notes that some modern productions in which the Petruchio and Kate characters interact lovingly early in the play spoil the surprise of the genuineness of their affection that should come later on through gesture and eye contact (196). In effect, what happens, says Brown, is that actors first performing in this play focus on the laughs at the expense of line and character development. However, with time, they begin to refine their performance, as did Ian Holm as Gremio and Paul Hardwick as Baptista, as they moved from the 1962 Stratford-upon-Avon productions into their second and third seasons. Holm and Hardwick began to notice the subtlety of the text that placed them together onstage with great frequency and called attention to their age and shared perspectives. Consequently, both actors began to recognize the adversity that drew their characters together and the pity they could arouse behind the laughter (205).

Of course, the 1948 production of *Kiss Me, Kate*, the musical with such songs by Cole Porter as "So in Love," "I Hate Men," "Too Darn Hot," and "Always True to You (in My Fashion)" created a wide popular following for this play. The script was by Bela and Sam Spewack. The frame is a Baltimore theater where a divorced couple, Fred Graham and Lilli Vannessi, star as leads in a musical version of Shakespeare's *The Taming of the Shrew*. Fred currently dates a colorful lighthearted woman named Lois Lane, whose boyfriend is a gambling actor, Bill Calhoun, while Lilli has engagement plans. *Kiss Me, Kate* was revived in 1999 to much fanfare. Also adding to the modern popularity of *Shrew* is the 1967 Frank Zeffirelli film of the play, starring Richard Burton as Petruchio, Elizabeth Taylor as Kate, and Michael York as Lucentio. This is a sumptuous, boisterous film with wonderful sets and costumes and compelling performances by the main characters, who make credible the love between a man and a woman who abuse each other verbally and psychologically the way Kate and Petruchio do. It is still available on video. Another delightful version was done by the British Broadcasting Company as part of its complete Shakespeare series. Produced and directed by Jonathan Miller, this 1980 video stars John Cleese (Petruchio) and Sarah Badel (Katherina). It, too, is readily available.

EXPLICATION OF KEY PASSAGES

3.2.43–71; 157–180. "Why, Petruchio is coming . . . gentleman's lackey"; "Tut, she a lamb, . . . thence for very shame." Whereas acts 1 and 2 set up the situation and the courtship of the two sisters, Kate and Bianca, act 3 focuses on Kate and Petruchio's wedding, a public alliance that changes the nature of their relationship and of Petruchio's behavior. When he was courting Kate, his overt method was the accepted language of courtship carried to the extreme: exaggerated praise of Kate, much bawdy playing with language, and seeming courtesy. He was also careful to explain away her peevish responses as maidenly modesty and a guise to hide her genuine feelings for him. As a husband, he will employ a different strategy, and the wedding scene marks the beginning of this new approach.

He is intentionally late, and Kate has already begun to cry because she is embarrassed at being publicly stood up at the altar. Moreover, she may in fact have some feelings for this strange suitor who has not been repulsed by her independence. Petruchio finally does appear, but in a fantastical guise. Before the audience sees Petruchio, Biondello reports his appearance.

For the wedding Petruchio has bought a new hat, but the rest of his clothes are old, little better than rags. His stockings hang down because two of the "points" (3.2.48) that attach to the doublet are broken. His boots are mismatched: one is buckled, the other laced. His sword is old-fashioned and rusty, with a broken hilt. It sticks out from the scabbard because the sheath lacks its metal tip, or chape. Biondello describes Petruchio's horse (which Shakespeare could not bring onstage) as an old nag suffering from every disease the animal might contract, including a swayback, a sprained shoulder, a lame hip ("hipped," 3.2.48), tumors ("fashions . . . windgalls," 3.2.52), enflamed joints, runny nose ("like to mose in the chine," 3.2.51), worms ("bots," 3.2.55), and jaundice ("ray'd with the yellows," 3.2.53). The saddle matches Petruchio's attire in age, state of decline, and broken parts. There are no stirrups, and the bridle ("head-stall," 3.2.57), made of inferior leather to start with, is held together with knots.

Petruchio's servant Grumio is just as badly attired and equipped. He wears mismatched stockings, one of linen, the other of coarse wool ("kersey," 3.2.67), one red

Richard Burton as Petruchio and Elizabeth Taylor as Katherina/Kate in Franco Zeffirelli's 1967 film *The Taming of the Shrew*. Courtesy of Photofest.

and one blue garter, and an old hat sporting an outlandish feather. He no more looks like a gentleman's servant than Petruchio looks like a gentleman.

Petruchio's response to incredulous observers is that clothes do not make the man, though in fact during the Renaissance clothes did make the man because they indicated class, rank, achievement, wealth, and fashion. As Polonius tells his son, Laertes, "For the apparel oft proclaims the man" (*Hamlet*, 1.3.72). Saying that he wishes he could mend himself as easily as he could change his clothes, Petruchio heads off for the wedding.

The marriage ceremony is too riotous to show, and actually seeing it might elicit sympathy for the priest and the sexton, who are assaulted. Moreover, marriage is a sacrament, and Shakespeare never shows an actual wedding onstage. Gremio's report allows for unalloyed mirth. According to Gremio, when the priest asks Petruchio whether he will marry Kate, Petruchio shouts, "Ay, by gogs-wouns" (Yes, by God's wounds, 3.2.160), a strong and inappropriate oath for a church service. The priest is so astonished by the response and its volume that he drops his prayer book, and when he bends over to retrieve it, Petruchio knocks him down. When the priest rights himself and resumes the service. Petruchio stamps his foot and swears again, as if he thinks the priest intends to cheat ("cozen," 3.2.68) him somehow.

After the ceremony, Petruchio calls for wine and drinks a toast like a seaman celebrating escape from a storm. He drains the cup and throws the dregs ("sops," 3.2.173) in the sexton's face because the man's beard is scraggly and seems to require nourishment. Finally, Petruchio kisses the bride so loudly that the whole church resounds, and Gremio is so embarrassed that he leaves the building. This is indeed a "mad marriage," as Gremio says (3.2.182).

4.1.188–211. "Thus have I . . . charity to shew." Petruchio speaks directly to the audience, man to man, so to speak. Gone are the bluster and the madcap antics as he shows his true self, the man who, in accord with Elizabethan proprieties, is the master, lord, and hunter, the king of his household comparable to the king on the throne. In fact, his opening lines could come straight from the history plays about the reigns of kings and princes: "Thus have I politicly begun my reign, / And 'tis my hope to end successfully" (4.1.188–189). The image of his plan to train and temper Kate comes straight from falconry, a noble, manly pursuit. Kate is his falcon, and just as a hunter keeps his falcon hungry throughout the training so it will take the lure (a baited device used to attract the bird), so Petruchio will keep Kate hungry throughout her training so she will be more pliable. He plans to teach her to "know her keeper's call" (4.1.194) and to watch her as closely as a trainer watches "these kites / That bate and beat and will not be obedient" (4.1.195–196). As he describes his plans for taming Kate (just as he had described his plans for wooing her), the audience has a preview of events to come and confirmation that, like Hamlet, Petruchio's madness is intentional—a stratagem to gain control of a potentially controlling wife before the patterns of their relationship have been too firmly established to change. He tells us that this is indeed the "way to kill a wife with kindness" and to "curb her mad and headstrong humor" (4.1.208–209). The emphasis on "humor" suggests that, in the parlance of the time, Kate's behavior is a result of an imbalance of bodily fluids, too much of the yellow bile that makes one choleric, angry, and contrary. But it also suggests that Kate's behavior has been whimsical and capricious. She can control her shrewishness if she chooses. The last lines of this speech are directed straight at the audience in a tone of shared intimacy: "He that knows better how to tame a shrew, / Now let him speak; 'tis charity to shew" (4.1.210–211). In other words, Petruchio is doing the best he can with a difficult situation and is open to suggestions if anyone in the audience can tell him another way to achieve the desired results.

5.2.136–179. Fie, fie . . . do him ease." The effect of Petruchio's strategy is clear in the next important speech: Kate's final lecture to her sister and Hortensio's widow in 5.2. She begins by chiding Bianca and the widow, giving cues as to how those parts should be played: "Fie, fie, unknit that threat'ning unkind brow, / And dart not scornful glances from those eyes, / To wound thy lord" (5.2.136–138). She then denigrates the two with the suggestion that such behavior "blots" their beauty (5.2.139) in the same way that frost shrivels up the flowers in a field and destroys their reputation as much as a whirlwind destroys fair buds. Besides, she argues, it is not proper or friendly. An actress playing this part can have fun communicating the pleasure Kate takes in denigrating the two women, who have been so critical of her and in so doing have set themselves up as her moral superiors. She says they resemble "a fountain troubled, / Muddy, ill-seeming, thick, bereft of beauty" (5.2.142–143) and emphasizes the results of their repulsive behavior: no one will want to drink from the fountain of their beauty (with kisses), no matter how thirsty they are for love.

Kate then teaches them the conventional wisdom of the time about gender roles. The husband, says she, is "thy lord, thy life, thy keeper, / Thy head, thy sovereign"

(5.2.146–147). He is charged by his position to care for his wife, to maintain and protect her, so that while she stays safely home, he faces danger on land and sea, amid storm and cold, and engages in "painful labor" to provide for her (5.2.149). Lines 152 through 154 record the male expectations for such sacrifices: "love, fair looks, and true obedience— / Too little payment for so great a debt." Lines 155 through 164 place wifely duty within the context of the Chain of Being: a wife's duty to her husband parallels a subject's duty to a prince. Thus, a wife's failure to behave dutifully is parallel to the wrangling of a "foul contending rebel" and "graceless traitor" (5.2.159–160). The battle of the sexes is then, by extension, civil war, rebellion against king and country. Thus, Kate rejects the pattern of behavior she herself had followed because she now understands that it promotes civil discord:

> I am asham'd that women are so simple
> To offer war when they should kneel for peace,
> Or seek for rule, supremacy, and sway,
> When they are bound to serve, love, and obey. (5.2.161–164)

Her next argument is from nature, the physiological fact that women's bodies are "soft, and weak, and smooth" (5.2.165), not designed for hard labor. Her conclusion is that their hearts should be so, too. Traditionally Kate employs the sweep of her arms down her body to call her stage audience's attention to womanly attractions.

Kate then goes on the attack again, calling the other two women "froward and unable worms" (5.2.169), admitting that she, too, had once been guilty of their crime, and, she gloats, she was better at rebellion than they were in bandying "word for word and frown for frown" (5.2.172). Now she sees the weakness of women ("our lances are but straws," 5.2.173) and finds in that weakness the strength to accept her social role, even though it might be that of the "least" in the hierarchy (5.2.175).

Her final lines (176–178) call on the two women she holds under physical command to lower their pride and accept their fate, as she has done, and to place their hands beneath their husbands' feet in token of their submission. The stage tradition is for Kate to force the two women down on their knees. Her final lines confirm her willingness to do the same. Thus, nature and the hierarchy accepted as God's social and natural organizing pattern confirm the role of women as submissive and subservient to their husbands (lord, master, prince). The implication is that the breaking of this God-given and socially expected role destroys the harmony of family and universe that must be connected for peace, harmony, and a good life to ensue.

In the context of the play Kate wins the approval of every male at the banquet, especially that of her husband. She has done what her father never thought possible, outclassed her sister. She has won her husband's wager for him and will reap her reward at home, but the frustrated fury of her sister and the widow is clearly most sweet revenge. Within the older tradition of Shakespeare's source, the shrew, per audience expectation, has been tamed, but she is clearly no meek, retiring wallflower, despite the sentiments her words express. She has truly proven herself a fit partner for Petruchio, for she has learned to control and direct her rhetorical displays—not simply to complain of her situation or to rage against it but to take control, even under the guise of perfect conformity to social conventions.

Annotated Bibliography

Brown, Carolyn E. "Katherine of *The Taming of the Shrew*: 'A Second Grissel.'" *Texas Studies in Literature & Language* 37 (Fall 1995): 285–314. Brown discusses shrew literature in medieval and Renaissance times, analyzes Katherine as a shrew, and relates Shakespeare's character to the Patient Griselda stories to find plot dynamics integrating two traditions.

Daniell, David. "The Good Marriage of Katherine and Petruchio." *Shakespeare Survey* 37 (1984): 23–31. Argues that Katherine is not tamed. Rather, she learns how to behave in a way that is compatible with Petruchio so that the two help each other and thus ensure a happy marriage.

Friedenreich, Kenneth. "Shakespeare, Marlowe, and Mummers." *American Notes & Queries* 20 (March/April 1982): 98–99. Friedenreich compares *The Taming of the Shrew* to Christopher Marlowe's *The Jew of Malta*, to find Shakespeare "well attuned" to the language of his most successful contemporaries.

Haring-Smith, Tori. *From Farce to Metadrama: A Stage History of "The Taming of the Shrew," 1594–1983*. Westport, CT: Greenwood P, 1985. A survey of the various adaptations and revivals of Shakespeare's play. Haring-Smith makes a strong case for treating *Taming* as a play within a play: that is, for retaining the Induction, which is sometimes cut.

Moisan, Thomas. "Interlinear Trysting and 'Household Stuff': The Latin Lesson and the Domestication of Learning in *The Taming of the Shrew*." *Shakespeare Studies* 23 (1995): 100–120. Moisan sees the Latin lesson as a masculine puberty rite suggesting linguistic inequality and, in this case, permitting seduction under the cloak of learning. He also explores Shakespeare's treatment of education, formal learning, and domesticity.

Slights, Camille Wells. "The Raw and the Cooked in *The Taming of the Shrew*." *JEGP* 88 (1989): 168–189. In the Induction the drunken Sly must learn proper social behavior. In the play that he watches, Petruchio and Kate also learn to adapt to society's rules. Sly assumes a role, that of a lord. Petruchio and Kate also take on new roles. They recognize social restraint but at the same time find ways to assert their control over it.

The Two Gentlemen of Verona

Owen E. Brady

PLOT SUMMARY

1.1. Leaving Verona for the Duke of Milan's court where he will complete his education as a gentleman, Valentine bids his lovesick friend Proteus farewell and teases him about love keeping him "dully sluggardiz'd at home" (1.1.7). When Speed enters, Proteus anxiously waits for a report on how Julia received the letter he sent Speed to deliver. Eventually Speed tells Proteus that Julia said nothing and leaves to catch his master, Valentine. Proteus worries that Julia has rejected him.

1.2. Elsewhere in Verona, Lucetta teases her anxious mistress, Julia, about her several suitors. Revealing that she finds Proteus the best, Lucetta surprises Julia. Immediately, Lucetta produces the letter that Speed was to deliver to Julia. Protesting that her modesty prohibits seeing "wanton lines" (1.2.42), Julia refuses to read it and orders Lucetta to return it to the sender. Alone, Julia berates herself for not reading it. Swallowing her pride, she calls Lucetta—and the letter—back. Picking up the letter Lucetta cleverly dropped, Julia pretends anger at Proteus's words, tears the letter, and sends Lucetta away. Julia again berates herself for tearing "such loving words" (1.2.102). She picks up the pieces with Proteus's name on them and places them next to her heart. As Lucetta returns, Julia quickly drops the pieces but orders Lucetta to collect them.

1.3. At his house in Verona, Antonio, Proteus's father, and his servant, Panthino, discuss Proteus's decision to stay home while other young men pursue advancement by going abroad. Proteus enters enthralled by a note from Julia but tells his father it is from Valentine. Happy to reunite friends, Antonio orders Proteus to leave the next day to join Valentine and exits. Realizing he might lose Julia while away, Proteus laments that love is as uncertain as the "glory of an April day, / Which now shows all the beauty of the sun, / And by and by a cloud takes all away" (1.3.85–87).

2.1. In Milan, Valentine worships a glove belonging to Silvia, the Duke's daughter, whom he describes as "a thing divine" (2.1.4). Speed mocks Valentine, telling him that, like Proteus, he is "metamorphis'd with a mistress" (2.1.30–31). Silvia, who has asked Valentine to write a letter to one whom she loves, enters. Handing her the letter he has written, Valentine confesses that not knowing who is to receive the letter made writing it difficult. Haughtily, Silvia returns the letter. When Valentine offers to write another, she tells him to do so if he wishes and to keep it if it pleases him. Valentine is confused. Speed clarifies matters: she jests and woos Valentine with his own letter. His work done, Speed urges Valentine to go to dinner.

2.2. Back in Verona, Proteus and Julia say farewell, exchanging rings and a kiss to pledge "true constancy" (2.2.8). Julia leaves without a word, and Panthino hurries Proteus along.

2.3. Proteus's servant, Launce, and his dog, Crab, enter. Distressed because he must leave Verona, Launce berates Crab for shedding no tears and having "no more pity than a dog" (2.3.10–11). Then Launce re-enacts his departure from his family, using his shoes to play his parents; his staff to represent his sister; and his hat, the maid. Panthino enters and urges Launce to catch up with his master.

2.4. In Milan, Silvia enjoys watching Valentine and his rival, Thurio, quarrel over her as the Duke enters announcing Proteus's arrival. Valentine praises his friend as "complete in feature and in mind / With all good grace to grace a gentleman" (2.4.73–74). The Duke and Thurio leave as Proteus enters. Immediately, Valentine begs Silvia to allow Proteus to serve her, too. Thurio returns to tell Silvia to speak with her father, and they exit. Valentine then reveals to Proteus that his "life is alter'd now" (2.4.128); he is in love. Confiding in Proteus, Valentine reveals his plan to elope with Silvia because the Duke prefers the wealthy Thurio. After Valentine leaves, Proteus confesses that he, too, has fallen in love with Silvia. This new love has driven out both his love for Julia and his friendship for Valentine. Concerned, he exits stating that he will either "check my erring love" (2.4.213) or, if unable, use cunning to win Silvia.

2.5. When Speed welcomes Launce to Milan, they exchange information about their masters' love lives: Julia and Proteus are matched, and Valentine has become a "hot lover" (2.5.51). They leave for an alehouse to celebrate Launce's arrival.

2.6. Proteus enters reflecting on the irony that loving Silvia will cause him to betray both Julia and Valentine. Finally, he justifies his behavior: "I to myself am dearer than a friend" (2.6.23). Cunningly, Proteus plans to thwart Valentine by telling the Duke about the plan to elope and to use "some sly trick" (2.6.41) to defeat Thurio.

2.7. Back in Verona, unable to bear separation from Proteus, Julia decides to follow him to Milan. While Lucetta urges caution, Julia protests that Proteus's "looks are my soul's food" (2.7.15), and she is starving. Afraid of "the loose encounters of lascivious men" (2.7.41), Julia decides to disguise herself as Sebastian, a page. Lucetta says that Proteus will not be happy to see Julia, and the servant questions Proteus's fidelity. Julia insists on his love as she prepares to set off.

3.1. Proteus betrays Valentine, telling the Duke about the plan to elope. Pretending to have a conflict between friendship and duty, Proteus masks his true intention—to have Silvia for himself. When the Duke announces that he has been locking Silvia in a tower nightly, Proteus reveals Valentine's plans to use a corded ladder. Seeing Valentine approach (secretly on his way to elope with Silvia), Proteus begs the Duke not to reveal his treachery so that Proteus can continue to masquerade as Valentine's friend. The Duke promises, then plays an ironic game to uncover Valentine's plot to steal Silvia. He lies, telling Valentine that Silvia has become "peevish, sullen, forward, / Proud, disobedient, stubborn, lacking duty" (3.1.68–69) by rejecting Thurio. He will disinherit her and direct his love toward a young woman he wishes to wed. When asked for advice on how to woo a young woman, Valentine supplies it: gifts, flattery, and never taking "no" for an answer. But the Duke continues: the woman is promised to a rich, youthful gentleman and kept locked in an upper chamber. Confidently, Valentine tells the Duke to go to her by night and take a corded ladder with him. He even promises to bring the Duke a ladder that one might hide under a cloak (even as Valentine is doing at that very instant). Asking to borrow Valentine's cloak, the Duke discovers the ladder and a love letter to Silvia. After the angry Duke leaves, Proteus and Launce enter with news of Valentine's banishment and Silvia's imprisonment. Advising Valentine to go into exile but to be hopeful, Proteus promises to carry Valentine's letters to Silvia. Valentine and Proteus leave hastily. Launce, alone, reveals that his master is "a kind of a knave" (3.1.264) and that he himself loves a milkmaid. When Speed enters, Launce lets Speed read a list of the milkmaid's qualities. Because she has "more wealth than faults" (3.1.367), Launce believes he has chosen well.

3.2. At his palace, the Duke asks Proteus to advise Thurio about how to woo Silvia. Proteus craftily suggests that a friend slander Valentine "with falsehood, cowardice, and poor descent" (3.2.32), and the Duke urges Proteus to do so while also praising Thurio. After Proteus encourages Thurio to write sonnets and serenade Silvia at night, they exit to pursue Proteus's plan.

4.1. When Valentine and Speed wander into a forest, outlaws accost them. Because Valentine has good qualities and speaks several languages, the outlaws decide that he should lead them. Valentine agrees.

4.2. Back in Milan, under Silvia's window, Proteus laments being spurned but continues, "spaniel-like," (4.2.14) to fawn on her. Thurio enters, jealous because Proteus has arrived ahead of him. Disguised as Sebastian, Julia appears, accompanied by the Host. Unseen, she and the Host observe the serenade. Proteus, Thurio, and musicians sing "Who is Silvia?" praising Silvia because she "excels each mortal thing" (4.2.51). The Host notes "Sebastian's" sadness as Julia observes Proteus betray her. When Thurio leaves, Proteus addresses Silvia, who berates him as a "subtile, perjur'd, false, disloyal man" (4.2.95). When she tells him to ask his former lover to forgive him, Proteus says that Julia and Valentine are dead. Though rejected, Proteus asks for Silvia's portrait, to which he will speak and weep. Silvia agrees because a false man should adore only a false shape. As Silvia and Proteus exit, the Host startles Julia/Sebastian out of her trancelike observation.

4.3. After everyone leaves, Sir Eglamore enters. Silvia pleads with him to help her escape to Mantua, where Valentine resides in banishment. They exit agreeing to meet that night at Friar Patrick's room.

4.4. Launce tells the story of taking Crab to the Duke's court. Having lost a small dog that Proteus wanted him to give to Silvia, Launce brought Crab instead. Launce relates that Crab acted uncivilized, seeking the company of the Duke's dogs under the dining table, where he urinated. When the Duke ordered the offending dog whipped, Launce took the blame. Proteus and the disguised Julia enter, and Proteus asks "Sebastian" to give Silvia the ring that Julia had given him in Verona. The disguised Julia tells Proteus that she pities his betrayed lover and him because Silvia does not requite his love. Still urging "Sebastian" to take a letter and the ring to Silvia and to bring back Silvia's portrait, Proteus leaves. Alone, Julia reveals that she cannot be untrue to Proteus or to herself. Consequently, she will "woo for him, but yet so coldly / As, heaven it knows, I would not have him speed" (4.4.106–107). When Silvia enters, Sebastian/Julia asks for the portrait and offers Silvia Proteus's letter. While Silvia provides the picture, she refuses to read the letter, rejects the ring, and expresses sympathy for Julia. As "Sebastian," Julia thanks Silvia for her sympathy and relates Julia's feelings of sorrow and despair. Both weep, and Silvia leaves. Alone, Julia expresses respect for Silvia but also jealousy. Looking at Silvia's portrait, Julia reflects on love's blindness; she sees herself as fair as Silvia.

5.1. Eglamour and Silvia flee Milan and enter the forest.

5.2. At the Duke's palace, Proteus and "Sebastian" mock Thurio. Suspicious that Silvia has fled, the Duke urges the others to join him in pursuit.

5.3. In the forest, the outlaws capture Silvia, and Eglamour runs away. Silvia sees her predicament as a sacrifice for love: "O Valentine, this I endure for thee!" (5.3.15).

5.4. Valentine wanders into the scene, where he bewails his lost love. Startled by shouts, Valentine hides to observe Proteus, Silvia, and the disguised Julia arrive. Having rescued Silvia from the outlaws, Proteus begs her for one fair look, but she berates him for betraying Julia. In hiding, Valentine watches as Proteus seizes Silvia roughly, to woo "like a soldier, at arms end, / And love you 'gainst the nature of love—force ye" (5.4.57–58). Valentine rushes in, saves Silvia from the impending rape, and confronts Proteus. Overwhelmed by "shame and guilt" (5.4.73), Proteus begs forgiveness. Astonishingly, Valentine accepts Proteus's repentance. To renew their friendship, he offers Proteus "All that was mine in Silvia" (5.4.83). Silvia is silent; Julia faints. When Proteus and Valentine aid the fallen "Sebastian," Julia reveals her identity by showing Proteus the ring he had given her upon leaving Verona. To drive home Proteus's guilt, she points out her sacrifice of maiden modesty for him by donning "immodest raiment" (5.4.106), her male disguise. While women may change their shapes, she notes, men are more treacherous because they change their minds. Transformed again, Proteus bewails human inconstancy, wondering why he thought Silvia fairer than Julia. Valentine joins Julia and Proteus's hands. Suddenly, the outlaws enter with Thurio and the Duke. Thurio reclaims Silvia, but Valentine threatens him. A practical man, Thurio gives up his claim rather than risk harm. While upbraiding Thurio for baseness, the Duke praises Valentine, declaring him worthy of Silvia. At Valentine's request, the Duke pardons the outlaws because they are "reformed, civil, full of good" (5.4.156). As all head for Milan, Valentine promises to tell the story of Julia's disguised quest for her love. Finally, Valentine promises Proteus that they will wed the same day and there will be "One feast, one house, one mutual happiness" (5.4.173).

PUBLICATION HISTORY

One thing is certain: The First Folio (1623), produced by Shakespeare's theatrical partners John Heminge and Henry Condell, provides the first printed version of *The Two Gentlemen of Verona*. According to Clifford Leech in his "Introduction" to the Arden edition of the play, the Folio text is "a good one. It rarely needs emendation of a substantive character, and it has little mislineation" (*The Two Gentlemen of Verona*, The Arden Shakespeare [New York: Routledge, 1969], xv). Narrative inconsistencies in place and character exist, however. For example, action shifts without a clear sign from Verona to Milan. The young gentlemen are sent to the "emperor," who later apparently becomes the Duke of Milan. In terms of characterization, Sir Eglamour first seems sympathetic and brave, agreeing to help Silvia escape from Milan; but, confronted by the outlaws, he turns cowardly and runs away. In the theater, audiences rarely have difficulty with these inconsistencies, which virtually disappear.

When *The Two Gentlemen* was written and first performed are matters of speculation, but scholars agree that it was written and performed early in Shakespeare's career. Certainly it was in existence by 1598 because Francis Meres praises it in his *Palladis Tamia* as one of the plays that has made Shakespeare's reputation as a comic dramatist comparable to that of Plautus, the great Roman playwright. No internal evidence in the 1623 Folio points to a specific composition date, but literary scholars use stylistic analysis to place it with *The Comedy of Errors* and *The Taming of the Shrew* as "early Shakespeare."

Weighing a number of dating theories, E. K. Chambers locates it "early in the 1594–1595 season" (*William Shakespeare: A Study of Facts and Problems*, 2 vols. [Oxford: Clarendon P, 1930], 1.331). Other scholars lean toward a composition date between 1591 and 1594, and some, for example, Howard C. Cole, believe that *The Two Gentlemen* is Shakespeare's first comedy. Cole notes the play's simple dramatic technique and its affinity with the contemporary plays of Robert Greene and John Lyly that explored the conflict between friendship and romantic love. Because *The Two Gentlemen* relies heavily on monologue and duologue (scenes with two characters) and has few scenes handling a dynamic group of characters well, it seems less artistically mature and, therefore, earlier than the more deftly written *The Comedy of Errors* and *The Taming of the Shrew*.

Kathleen Campbell supports the argument that the play was composed in phases and settles on 1593 as the date of Shakespeare's last revision ("Shakespeare's Actors as Collaborators: Will Kempe and *The Two Gentlemen of Verona*," in "*The Two Gentlemen of Verona*": *Critical Essays*, ed. June Schlueter [New York: Garland, 1996], 179–186). Campbell argues that Launce's role may have been added in 1593, when the famous comedian William Kempe joined Shakespeare's acting company, The Lord Chamberlain's Men. Campbell observes that, like Launce's role, Kempe's parts in other plays "are only loosely attached to the plot and are regularly missing from the final scenes, presumably to allow the actor time to prepare for the jig that would follow the performance" (181).

SOURCES FOR THE PLAY

Like other Elizabethan dramatists, Shakespeare borrowed stories freely from a variety of sources, both classical and contemporary. In the case of *The Two Gentlemen*, scholars agree that Jorge de Montemayor's Spanish narrative romance *Diana Enamorada* is the story from which Shakespeare derived the plot involving Julia, Proteus, and Silvia. Written in the mid-1500s, *Diana* was available to Shakespeare in French translations produced in 1578 and 1587; it also appeared in a printed 1598 English translation that circulated in manuscript in the late 1580s. Though *Diana*, a story of faithless love between Don Felix and Felismena, provides details, Shakespeare altered the plot and characterization, as he frequently did when using narrative sources. Shakespeare adds material involving a betrayal of friendship and creates Julia, a much more active and independent character than Felismena. As

Kurt Schlueter observes: "Julia shows more sense and a clearer determination than Felismena to further her own interests" (9).

The source for the plot involving the friendship between Valentine and Proteus may come from the well-known story of Titus and Gisippus that appeared as far back as Boccaccio's *Decameron* and was retold by Sir Thomas Elyot in *The Book Named the Governor* (1531). As in the case of the material from *Diana*, Shakespeare alters the seminal Titus-Gisippus story. Rather than the perfect, self-sacrificing love of Elyot's male characters, Shakespeare creates Proteus, the selfish traitor to friendship.

Shakespeare's ingenuity in using sources may be gauged by the fact that he found material for both comedy and tragedy in the same source: Richard Brooke's *Romeus and Juliet* (1562). While this narrative poem certainly provided material for the later *Romeo and Juliet*, Shakespeare also mined it for some of the details for the love story of Valentine and Silvia. For example, both Valentine and Romeo plan to scale their beloved's walls with a corded ladder, both go into exile in Mantua, and both Silvia and Juliet meet a friar who helps them plan their escape from paternal power.

While *Diana* and *The Book Named the Governor* appear to be the most likely sources for the interlocked plots in *The Two Gentlemen*, Shakespeare's involvement in London's theatrical world exposed him to a number of plays about romance and friendship that preceded *The Two Gentlemen*. For example, Leech (xxxviii) and Anne Barton in her introductory essay to *The Two Gentlemen of Verona* (in *The Riverside Shakespeare*, ed. G. Blakemore Evans et al., 2nd ed. [Boston: Houghton Mifflin, 1997], 178) see analogues and verbal echoes in Richard Edwards's play *The Excellent Comedy of Two the Most Faithfullest Friends, Damon and Pithias*, acted in 1565 at court and printed in 1571. Critics also refer to two lost plays that may have influenced Shakespeare. In 1577, Paul's Boys acted *The History of Titus and Gisippus* at the Whitehall palace. In 1585, the Queen's Men performed the lost play *Felix and Philiomena* at court.

The plays of John Lyly and Robert Greene also influenced *The Two Gentlemen*. Lyly's popular *Endymion*, performed in 1588 and printed in 1591, provided a dramatic conflict between love and friendship as well as saucy pages that may serve as the prototype for Speed and Lucetta. Moreover, Lyly's highly popular novel, *Euphues* (1578), deals with a faithless friend and employs a prose style emphasizing wordplay and rhetorically balanced sentences evident in the language of *The Two Gentlemen*. Finally, Robert Greene's *Friar Bacon and Friar Bungay*, produced before 1592 and printed in 1594, contains a conflict between love and friendship as well as a skilful use of the double plot. Howard C. Cole also sees Greene's sympathetic treatment of characters, especially the female heroine, influencing Shakespeare's perspective (220).

STRUCTURE AND PLOTTING

The Two Gentlemen of Verona conforms to Northrop Frye's theory in his *Anatomy of Criticism* (New York: Atheneum, 1957) that sees comedy as a form portraying characters' "movement from one kind of society to another" (163). In the process, characters discover their identities and place in society; consequently, society's ideals are rejuvenated. In *The Two Gentlemen*, Valentine, Proteus, and Julia initially live in the world of adolescent innocence; but they desire to enter the adult world where love and friendship are tested and refined. The process is not easy and is at times painful, though the audience may smile or laugh at the problems the characters encounter in learning to be adults. Valentine, Proteus, and Julia all leave home in quest of their new, more mature identities as ideal gentlemen and constant lovers in the highly refined society represented by the Duke of Milan's court.

In Milan, the three characters from Verona change. The honor-seeking Valentine falls in love with the sophisticated Silvia. Ironically, his bumbling attempt to fulfill his desire causes him to appear dishonorable and to be banished from the society he intended to join. Proteus falls in love with Silvia, too, and selfishly betrays his pledge of constancy to Julia and his friendship with Valentine. Proteus's dishonorable actions forfeit his claim to the identity of gentleman. Julia's love of Proteus transforms her literally and figuratively. She assumes a male identity, and she overcomes adolescent uncertainty about love as well as her conventional concerns about losing her maiden modesty.

In pursuing adult identities, all three have ironically alienated themselves from society. To find these identities, they follow the ironic pattern of comedy that Frye articulates by literally losing themselves in the forest, a "green world" (182) where almost magical transformations occur. There, they go through a period of chaos and danger that reveals their best selves. In the woods, Valentine's nobility is recognized first by the outlaws, then by Silvia, whom he rescues from rape, and finally by the Duke, who confirms the identity Valentine sought from the beginning as well as giving him his heart's desire: "Sir Valentine, / Thou art a gentleman and well deriv'd, / Take thou thy Silvia, for thou hast deserv'd her" (5.4.145–147). Confronted by his treachery and lechery, Proteus becomes again the honorable friend and lover, but his understanding of friendship and love are now tempered by the recognition of his own flaws. Julia's constancy is rewarded as she sheds her disguise and accepts Proteus, warts and all. The action of *Two Gentlemen* ends with a typical comic resolution: marriage, a traditional image of social harmony, integration, and the beginning of a new society. Later, Shakespeare will more successfully develop this comic movement through a green world in *A Midsummer Night's Dream* and *As You Like It*.

To dramatize this comic movement, Shakespeare introduces two interlocked romantic love plots and complicates them with a third, linking plot involving friendship. In *The Two Gentlemen*, as in the comedies of Plautus and Terence, young love is blocked by older authority figures. The desire of Proteus's father to educate his son abroad stands in the way of a love match with Julia. The Duke of Milan stands between his daughter, Silvia, and Valentine because he desires that she marry the wealthy Sir Thurio. The third, less well-realized plot, relates the story of the friendship between Proteus and Valentine and connects the love plots.

Central to all three plots, Proteus links them. His transformation from faithful friend and constant lover to traitor to both friendship and love complicates the love stories. Proteus's attraction to Silvia, fueled by sexual desire and perhaps even by the ideal she represents, stands as an obstacle to Julia's love for him and as an obstacle to Valentine's love for Silvia. Proteus's lusty self-interest also blocks his own desire, as Silvia rejects and berates him for his inconstancy. Consequently, the resolution of all three plot strands lies in Proteus's counter-metamorphosis in the last scene.

The climax of all the plots (5.4) comes hastily and consequently seems a flawed resolution. Odd and sometimes disturbing to modern audiences, Valentine's offer of Silvia precipitates Proteus's final transformation (see "Critical Controversies," below). While this episode is shocking to modern audiences and apparently to the disguised Julia onstage, some critics argue that Valentine's offer is consistent with the Elizabethan idea that male friendship is more precious than romantic love. For example, Madeline Doran maintains that Shakespeare's ending is conventional rather than controversial when seen in an Elizabethan perspective: "Valentine, to have his loyal and generous friendship set off against Proteus' betrayal, must *make* the offer of Sylvia to Proteus, Proteus must not, of course, take it but repent" (*Endeavors of Art: A Study of Form in Elizabethan Drama* [Madison: U of Wisconsin P, 1964], 325).

Brought together in the forest by the outlaws, all the characters participate in the abrupt happy ending that ties up all conflicts by following the comic formula Puck proposes in *A Midsummer Night's Dream*: "Jack shall have Jill; / Nought shall go ill; / The man shall have his mare again, and all shall be well" (3.2.461–463). Both sets of lovers reconcile and move toward the permanent union of marriage; Silvia's father recognizes Valentine's worthiness to marry his daughter; the outlaws receive amnesty; and Proteus will be affectionately chastised as Valentine will publicly relate the story of his friend's strange transformations by love as his "penance" (5.4.170). Shakespeare goes beyond the idea that romantic love or ideal friendship can make two individuals one: All four friends and lovers become one. As Valentine announces to Proteus and Julia in the play's concluding lines: "our day of marriage shall be yours, / One feast, one house, one mutual happiness" (5.4.173–174).

Though they are not present on stage at the end, we might also infer that Launce has his milkmaid and, of course, Crab. For comic tone and thematic resonance, Shakespeare adds Launce's scenes. Though only loosely related to the plot action, they comment ironically on the characters and themes of the main plots. Launce's absurd loyalty to Crab contrasts sharply with Proteus's fickleness. The pragmatic choice of a wealthy milkmaid (3.1) contrasts with Valentine's idealization of his lover. Finally, Launce's acceptance of the flawed milkmaid reinforces Julia's acceptance of the flawed Proteus.

MAIN CHARACTERS

Valentine and Proteus, the friends who aspire to become gentlemen, take center stage. Young and immature, they are about to move from adolescence into adulthood, with its complicated relationships and responsibilities. Though well educated, neither has seen much of the world, and only Proteus has begun to experience the power of love. Both are bound to their fathers' wills to go to the Duke of Milan's court to become "the perfect man" (1.3.20). As their names suggest, they differ significantly. Associated with the patron saint of love, Valentine is a constant friend and lover. Not until the last scene, when Proteus intends to rape Silvia, does Valentine ever doubt Proteus's friendship. Even there, he quickly forgives his friend's lechery and treachery when Proteus repents. Once smitten by Silvia, Valentine remains unwavering in his love for her. Named after a shape-shifting god, Proteus counterpoints Valentine's constancy and naïveté. He is fickle and cunning in pursuit of his object of desire.

Valentine

Despite his admirable constancy, Valentine's inexperience in the art of courtly love sometimes makes him appear dull-witted, sometimes arrogant. About to head to Milan, Valentine reveals his smug superiority in the first scene when he teases the love-transformed Proteus about "living sluggardiz'd at home" (1.1.7). Later in Milan, Valentine resorts to "braggardism" (2.4.164), telling Proteus that he should hold Silvia superior to Julia. Once he is "metamorphis'd with a mistress" (2.1.30–31), Valentine vacillates between dull-witted insecurity in wooing Silvia and hubris in his plan to elope with her. When Silvia in a "loving jest" asks him to write a love letter to "a secret, nameless friend" (2.1.105), Valentine is baffled. His servant Speed has to explain that the joke is as "inscrutable, invisible, / As the nose on a man's face, or a weathercock on a steeple!" (2.1.135–136). Later, Valentine once again proves himself smug and inept when the Duke requests advice about how to woo a younger woman. Valentine pontificates, offering conventional wooing wisdom in rhyme to demonstrate his own worldliness. In the process, he foolishly reveals his plan to elope, ladder and all, to the wily Duke (3.1).

Despite his naïveté and youthful arrogance, Valentine affirms the value of love and friendship. In the last scene, his defense of Silvia, his incredible generosity in forgiving Proteus, and his championing the return to society of the outlaws make Valentine a beacon of gentlemanly virtue (5.4).

Proteus

While falling in love with Silvia produces constancy in Valentine, Proteus's affections are mercurial. Though "over boots in love" (1.1.25) and pledging "true constancy" (2.2.8) to Julia in Verona, Proteus immediately falls in love with Silvia in Milan. Unlike Valentine, Proteus is cunning, using his wit to justify his selfish desires and to find a way to achieve them. When his desire for Silvia conflicts with his professed love for Julia and friendship with Valentine, Proteus worries about dishonorably being "forsworn" (2.6.1–3) but settles his conflict, rationalizing that "If I keep them [Julia and Valentine], I needs must lose myself" (2.6.20; see "Explication of Key Passages," below). While Valentine cannot deceive the Duke, Proteus succeeds by appearing honorable while betraying Valentine's plan to elope. As Camille Wells Slights notes, Proteus uses and "perverts the gentlemanly ideal" (67) when he tells the Duke that his duty to his host demands that he betray his friend (3.1.17–21). Later, he fabricates a terrible lie to win Silvia, telling her that both Julia and Valentine are dead. Proteus also plans to be "unjust" (4.2.2) to Sir Thurio, eliminating the last obstacle to his desire.

Obsessed with his desire for Silvia, Proteus shows determination, pursuing her despite numerous rebuffs and lectures on his vile betrayals of love and friendship. He sends her gifts and requests a picture to cherish when she refuses his advances. But his obsessive desire manifests itself viciously in the last scene when he attempts to rape Silvia.

Proteus is, however, redeemable. He responds positively to the exposure of his villainy. Confronted by his closest friend after the attempted rape, Proteus feels "shame and guilt" (5.4.73) and begs forgiveness. When Sebastian is revealed to be the faithful Julia, Proteus realizes his all-too-human failing in trading friendship and true love for selfish desire (5.4.110–113). With this recognition, Proteus moves closer to his proper role in society: gentleman.

Silvia

Shakespeare creates Julia and Silvia to complement and counterpoint the male characters. Matched with Valentine, Silvia proves a sophisticated teacher of courtly behavior and a touchstone of constancy. Like Proteus, Julia is a dynamic character. At first all adolescence, Julia vacillates between accepting Proteus's love and worrying about her image as a modest young woman. Constancy in love, however, helps her mature, and she proves capable of initiative and bravery.

Silvia's constancy is highlighted in the song "Who Is Silvia?" sung by her would-be wooers (4.2.39–53). Like her portrait, Silvia is an unchanging image of beauty and fidelity. In her witty love letter jest with Valentine, she demonstrates her sophistication and teaches him the rules of the love game. Silvia also serves as a foil to Proteus and Julia. In her reproofs of Proteus, she staunchly advocates friendship and love, repeatedly defending herself by assailing him with charges of treachery and inconstancy. While identifying Proteus's transformation as immoral, she highlights Julia's constancy.

Silvia's strangest behavior occurs in the last scene. After Valentine offers her to his penitent friend, Silvia falls silent for the rest of play. Valentine's offer and Silvia's silence have bedeviled critics for three centuries. But Silvia's function as an emblem of all that is courtly and virtuous may warrant this strange silence. It might be taken as tolerant support for Valentine's well-intentioned but inept attempt at acting the role of courtly gentleman. Or her silence could imply dismay at Valentine's willingness to sacrifice her on the altar of friendship and to treat her as if he could dispose of her heart and hand. In the end Silvia remains enigmatic.

Julia

Like Proteus, Julia is changeable. In the opening scene with Lucetta, she reveals her own uncertainties as she moves toward adulthood. She desires to read Proteus's love letter but worries about being perceived as immodest. Julia impetuously tears the letter into pieces, but quickly reproves herself: "O hateful hands, to tear such loving words!" (1.2.102). Once in love, however, Julia lets a ring and a kiss seal her constancy as she silently bids Proteus good-bye. And love makes her bold.

Julia's boldness and constancy are ironically embodied in her assumed role of Sebastian, male servant to the inconstant Proteus. Transforming herself into "Sebastian" and defying social mores, she overflows with enthusiasm and emotion as she begs Lucetta to help her follow her lover, deified as "divine perfection" (2.7.13). Unlike Proteus's fickleness that promotes violating the social ideal of the gentleman, Julia's socially unacceptable assumption of a male identity reinforces the ideal of constancy.

While Julia's constancy leads her to serve Proteus by wooing Silvia, Julia demonstrates spirited, though covert, resistance to his plans: "I woo for him, but yet so coldly / As, heaven it knows, I would not have him speed" (4.4.106–107). Later, when Proteus follows Silvia into the forest, Julia boldly tags along to "cross that love" (5.2.55). In the last scene, as Valentine offers Silvia to Proteus, Julia does something, perhaps swoons, to distract everyone. While some critics read her swoon as anxiety over potentially losing Proteus, others see it as a calculated performance "to cross" any possible match, another demonstration of her boldness (Shapiro, 79–80). In the end, Julia reveals her generous spirit, accepting the chastened Proteus. If Silvia represents the idealized lover, Julia becomes the real woman enacting the ideal through loving forgiveness.

Lucetta and Speed

Like John Lyly's saucy pages, Lucetta and Speed are somewhat impertinent servants providing satiric commentary on the aristocratic main characters. Lucetta's superior tone in her scene with Julia (1.2) heightens our perception of Julia's adolescent conflict between maiden modesty and romantic curiosity. Speed's name both belies and defines him. He is characteristically late in performing duties because he is "fast" with words, loving to dally in order to banter with others. His banter, however, provides a comic perspective. After observing Valentine and Silvia discuss the love letter she has commissioned, Speed explains the jest, thereby highlighting Valentine's dull-witted inexperience.

Launce

Launce is Shakespeare's invention, the prototype for bumbling, good-hearted commoners like Bottom in *A Midsummer Night's Dream* and Dogberry in *Much Ado about Nothing*. Though uneducated, he has common sense; though humble by birth, he has more constancy than Proteus, his gentleman master. Launce remains loyal to his dog, Crab, and pledges love to a flawed but wealthy milkmaid. While Proteus is careless of others' feelings, Launce's feelings for others move him to ridiculous actions that reveal the constancy and sensitivity Proteus lacks. In the scene reenacting his weepy departure from home (2.3), Launce's comments on Crab's unfeeling reaction reflect on Proteus's lack of feeling for others: "He is a stone, a very pibble [pebble] stone, and has no more pity in him than a dog" (2.2.10–11). Taking the beating for Crab's unmannerly behavior under the Duke's table, Launce, like Julia, displays an almost unbelievable loyalty. Like Julia in the last scene, Launce sees some redeeming qualities in a flawed human being when he chooses to love his milkmaid.

The Duke and Antonio

The remaining characters function primarily as plot devices and create a romantic atmosphere. The Duke and Antonio are stock comic old men—drawn from the Roman drama Shakespeare studied in school—who block the young characters' desires. A precursor of Sir Andrew Aguecheek in *Twelfth Night*, Thurio provides an obstacle and a foil to Valentine. Sir Eglamour is a plot agent to help Silvia escape, but he may also be another version of the gentleman who proves false. The outlaws serve primarily to bring together all the principle characters in the forest and allow the knotty plot complications to unravel; but bringing these picturesque, alienated gentlemen back into society also completes the comic theme of redemption.

DEVICES AND TECHNIQUES

Though written early in Shakespeare's career, *The Two Gentlemen of Verona* uses a number of dramatic and literary techniques and devices that appear in more developed form in later plays. Harold C. Goddard sums up critical observations in the first volume of *The Meaning of Shakespeare* (2 vols. [Chicago: U of Chicago P, 1951], 1.41) when he writes: "In no other play of Shakespeare's are there so many premonitions of later ones as in *The Two Gentlemen of Verona*." Among the most important dramatic techniques that will appear in later works are his use of multiple plots, the disguised heroine, love letters, and characters drawn from society's lower echelon who cast an ironic light on the aristocratic world. Literary techniques include satirical prose, rhyme for special effects, and wordplay.

In *The Two Gentlemen*, Shakespeare introduces the disguised heroine, Julia, who as "Sebastian" pursues Proteus to Milan. The disguise allows her to perform bold action, giving her a freedom of movement not permitted Elizabethan women. For the audience, the girl-in-boy's-clothing ironically allows Julia's "masculine side"—boldness and critical intelligence—to emerge; it also develops sympathy for the betrayed Julia, especially in scenes where she observes Proteus wooing Silvia (4.2) or where she woos her rival Silvia for Proteus (4.4). Because boys played women in Shakespeare's theater, the disguised heroine also provides a multilayer theatrical experience of virtuoso acting. In *Gender in Play on the Shakespearean Stage: Boy Heroines and Female Pages* (Ann Arbor: U of Michigan P, 1994), Michael Shapiro comments on the role's exciting theatricality because it permitted the "lively interplay between the various identities of the play-boy [actor], female character, and male disguise" (70).

Shakespeare also borrows the literary convention of love letters from his narrative source *Diana* and turns them into a repeated visual motif of miscommunication that produces a comic effect. Seeing *The Two Gentlemen* onstage, an audience might get the impression that the postal service was working overtime. As Frederick Kiefer observes in his article "Love Letters in *The Two Gentlemen of Verona*," the use of love letters represents in "eminently theatrical terms" a human paradox: "that people seek to express the most intense emotion by the most conventional of literary modes, the epistolary" (*Shakespeare Studies* 18 [1986]: 65–85, reprinted in *"The Two Gentlemen of Verona": Critical Essays*, ed. June Schlueter [New York: Garland, 1996], 133–134). The four young lovers all suffer some sort of embarrassment or worse as they try to communicate with each other in writing. Julia impetuously tears up Proteus's love letter only to regret her action the next moment. Proteus tells his father that Julia's love note is from Valentine only to have his lie confirm his father's decision to ship him to Milan. Silvia's love letter jest only confuses Valentine. Finally, Valentine's plan to elope explodes when the Duke discovers a love letter and a corded ladder.

Shakespeare uses prose to mark social class distinctions and to provide satirical comment on the play's main characters. Aristocratic characters, like the young lovers in *The Two Gentlemen*, generally speak verse; lower class characters, notably Launce, speak prose. As Milton Crane observes in *Shakespeare's Prose* (Chicago: U of Chicago P, 1951), Speed's and Launce's prose speeches that critically reflect on their masters (2.1.18–32 and 3.1.263–278, respectively) begin Shakespeare's dramatic practice of making "virtually all satirical commentators in the plays . . . speak prose, as an emblem of their separation from the action they criticize" (6).

Shakespeare's verse in *The Two Gentlemen* is of uneven quality, sometimes old-fashioned and highly rhetorical in its use of repetition and balanced phrases, sometimes energetic and metaphorical. In either case, it gives us insight into character. Julia's language provides examples of both kinds of language and how they reveal her nature. Refuting Lucetta's comment that men are deceitful, Julia replies with repetition and balanced phrases to portray her romanticized vision of Proteus:

> His words are bonds, his oaths are oracles,
> His love sincere, his thoughts immaculate,
> His tears pure messengers sent from his heart,
> His heart as far from fraud as heaven from earth. (2.7.75–78)

Shakespeare uses her schoolbook rhetoric to suggest her inexperience in love and so to highlight the play's theme of young love.

Shakespeare represents Julia's determination to pursue Proteus in the extended metaphor of a stream, drawn from nature, not books. When Lucetta warns Julia that following Proteus is like a dangerous fire that might "burn above the bounds of reason" (2.7.23), Julia's response douses Lucetta's fears. Her speech unifies natural images and the religious language of courtly love:

> The current that with gentle murmur glides,
> Thou know'st, being stopp'd, impatiently doth rage;
> But when his fair course is not hindered,
> He makes sweet music with the enamell'd stones,
> Giving a gentle kiss to every sedge
> He overtaketh in his pilgrimage;
> And so by many winding nooks he strays
> With willing sport to the wild ocean.
> Then let me go, and hinder not my course:
> I'll be as patient as a gentle stream,
> And make a pastime of each weary step,
> Till the last step have brought me to my love,
> And there I'll rest, as after much turmoil
> A blessed soul doth in Elysium. (2.7.25–38)

Here the verse suggests Julia's emotional state and gives us a glimpse into her character: her youthful enthusiasm, the strength of her desire, her gentleness, her willingness to risk turmoil because she is hopeful.

Her language contrasts with that of the two gentlemen, who use poetic imagery associated with the Italian Petrarch's sonnets that characterize the male lover as a servant or religious devotee of the beloved. For example, Valentine calls Silvia "a heavenly saint" and tells Proteus to "Call her divine" (2.4.145, 147). In using the conventional imagery of courtly love, especially the term "idol" (2.4.144), Shakespeare suggests a lack of personal experience in his young male lovers as well as egotistical self-delusion, according to Ralph Berry (44–49).

Shakespeare appeals to the Elizabethan audience's heightened appreciation of language through rhyme, wordplay, and puns to serve his dramatic purpose in *The Two Gentlemen*. While most lines in the play are blank verse, Shakespeare does employ rhyme for specific effect: to set comic tone, to mark an insight made, or to reflect a relationship between characters. Rhyme helps create a light-hearted tone when Lucetta teases Julia about her love life (1.2). To signal the idealized unity of lovers' souls, Shakespeare presents the exchange of rings and a kiss by Proteus and Julia before his departure for Milan as a mutually composed couplet:

> *Proteus*: Why then we'll make exchange: here, take you this.
>
> *Julia*: And seal the bargain with a holy kiss. (2.2.6–7)

Rhyme may also serve to mark a special insight, as if intelligence were able to give a distinctive shape to the language that expresses it. While Speed speaks prose most of the time, his insight into Silvia's jest of having Valentine write a love letter to himself is marked by a switch to rhymed verse:

> O excellent device, was there ever heard a better,
> That my master being scribe, to himself should write the letter? (2.1.139–140)

Rhyme also satirizes Valentine's foolish pride and inexperience in love. When the Duke exposes Valentine's plan to elope, he exposes the would-be gentleman's conceit as well as his ineptitude in love poetry. Puffed up with self-importance when the Duke asks him how to woo a younger woman, Valentine resorts to sententious, sometimes inept, rhymes:

> Win her with gifts, if she respect not words:
> Dumb jewels often in their silent kind
> More than quick words do move a woman's mind. . . .
> If she do chide, 'tis not to have you gone,
> For why, the fools are mad, if left alone.
> Take no repulse, what ever she doth say;
> For "get you gone," she doth not mean "away!" (3.1.89–91, 98–101)

In the same scene, Valentine's love letter to Silvia is written as an incomplete sonnet (140–151), perhaps an indication that the relationship is about to be interrupted. Shakespeare would employ a similar device in *Romeo and Juliet* (1.5).

Because puns and wordplay rely so heavily on slang and pronunciation, today's audience may often find Shakespeare's "volleys of words" (Crane, 70) more difficult to follow than did an Elizabethan audience. The dialogue between Proteus and Speed based on a pun involving the pronunciation of "ship" and "sheep" may be hard to follow (1.1.72ff). The verbal logic revolving around the relationships between shepherd and sheep on the one hand and master and servant on the other may seem precious, even tedious to us. Only footnotes liven matters up when we read that references to horns may indicate sexual infidelity and that "lac'd mutton" (1.1.97) is slang for prostitute. Crane's suggestion that we view these interchanges as a kind of "vaudeville dialogue" between two clever actors/characters may help audiences think about the tone and staging of such scenes today.

THEMES AND MEANINGS

Understanding an Elizabethan audience's ideas about a gentleman's education, male friendship, and romantic love helps us interpret the play's action. According to Kurt Schlueter in his "Introduction" to *The Two Gentlemen of Verona*, both romantic love (especially the medieval concept of courtly love) and friendship (derived from classical sources) have "educative value" (4). Both loves assume that two individuals can be united as one soul. Through both relationships, a young man may become a perfect gentleman as described in such books as Sir Thomas Elyot's *The Book Named the Governor* and Baldassare Castiglione's *The Courtier* (1527; English translation 1561). It is through an idealized love with a woman and through male friendship that, as Bradbrook notes, a man has the freedom "to ascend to and become a god or descend to a beast" (52). Though comically presented, Valentine, the constant lover, and Proteus, the lustful traitor, embody this choice to rise or fall.

While today's audiences readily respond to dramatic action involving romantic love's power to transform characters, a more detailed understanding of courtly love would enrich a viewing of the play. In the conventions governing courtly love, the male lover puts himself in the position of his lady's servant to learn ideals of humane behavior. In *The Two Gentlemen of Verona*, Silvia embodies this ideal; all young men see her as "Holy, fair, and wise" (4.2.41). To her suitor-servants, Silvia is a sort of goddess of virtue. Many of the play's dramatic techniques and interactions can be explained by recalling that courtly love was transacted "obliquely" through "games, tokens, gifts" (Bradbrook, 52), such as the play's love letters and the rings that Proteus and Julia exchange. Courtship was public and full of playful tests of a character's virtue. Consequently, we see Silvia encouraging Valentine through a game played with love letters (2.1); however, she also teaches Proteus by railing against his betrayal of love and friendship.

The Elizabethan ideal of male friendship is more difficult for a contemporary audience to understand, especially in the play's final scene (5.4) when Valentine, having just saved Silvia from Proteus's lust, offers her to him. Jean E. Howard, placing the play in the tradition of writers like Boccaccio, Elyot, and Francis Bacon, notes that "Shakespeare joined a long tradition of writers who celebrated such friendships" and that male friendship was often privileged over love of a woman ("Introduction," in *The Two Gentlemen of Verona*, The Norton Shakespeare, ed. Stephen Greenblatt et al. [New York: W. W. Norton, 1997], 78). Thus, Valentine's perplexing offer of Silvia, seen in the light of idealized male friendship, restores a relationship with Proteus that is more important than romantic love.

Yet romantic love is not to be scorned. Ovid's *Metamorphoses*, an anthology of tales about love's transforming power, was an Elizabethan favorite. In *The Two Gentlemen of Verona*, Shakespeare proves himself a man of his historical moment as he explores the ancient yet always relevant theme of love's power. He will return to it repeatedly throughout his literary career. While *The Two Gentlemen* uses love's transformations to evoke laughter, it also hints at deeper issues: the protean nature of self-identity and love's role in the process of self-discovery. It is no surprise that the play uses disguise to suggest the shifting nature of identity and paired characters who seem to be alter egos. Ruth Nero in *Comic Transformations in Shakespeare* (New York: Methuen, 1980) sees *The Two Gentlemen* as a step beyond the sort of mistaken identities found in *The Comedy of Errors*: "The issue of mistaken identities is now predominantly within, a question of psychic identity rather than optic identification, a question of the self that the self chooses, or is driven, to be" (53).

Love is a powerful tool in the educational process by which the two gentlemen learn about the ideals and weaknesses that shape human identity. Paul Lindenbaum articulates what he sees as the play's "central organizing principle" (231) by tracing the transformations of Valentine, Proteus, and Julia as they move from youthful inexperience to a more mature understanding of love and self-identity. Ironically, Proteus's father, Antonio, concerned more about social station than self-discovery, knows the truth the play explores: without time and experience in the world, no one can "be a perfect man" (1.3.20). In the tradition of the courtier books, the "perfect gentleman" rightly values himself in the context of social relations and recognizes duties dictated by them. Whether expressed as male friendship or male-female romance, love is the great creative power that makes society harmonious and perpetuates it. This is the painful and humbling lesson that Proteus must ultimately learn.

Learning to love another properly and thus overcoming the delusions caused by egotism and selfishness becomes the main transforming movement of *The Two Gentlemen*, which focuses on two kinds of love relationships: romantic love and male friendship. Both kinds of love, in ideal form, propose an almost miraculous merger of identities, whereby two individuals feel as one. But the strange arithmetic of love, whereby one plus one equals one, confuses characters, especially the males. Proteus, Valentine, and Launce all experience the difficulty in differentiating the self from the one they love. Proteus sees fulfilling his desire for Silvia and the betrayal of Valentine and Julia as necessary to becoming himself (2.6); Valentine sees separation from Silvia as a loss of self (3.1.170–187); and Launce has difficulty leaving his parents and differentiating himself from his dog, Crab (2.3.21–32; 4.4.1–39). Ultimately, through painful confrontation of his violations of ideal love and friendship, Proteus recognizes his flawed humanity and the importance of constancy in stabilizing both society and the individual.

The constancy of Silvia and Julia educates the two male protagonists. Silvia is the ideal of constancy represented in the conventional code of courtly love; Julia risks life and reputation by assuming a male disguise and violating social convention for the sake of love. Silvia repeatedly rejects Proteus and berates him with moral lessons reinforcing the importance of constancy in love. Her silence after Valentine's shocking and bizarre yet magnanimous offer to give Silvia to his repentant friend (although women of the twenty-first century find it incredible) may be interpreted as support for the ideal of the gentleman to which Valentine has aspired. Having risked her identity as a virtuous maiden and having served Proteus even in wooing Silvia, Julia has learned that self-sacrifice in love can redeem another. Julia's discovery also reinforces in Proteus's mind love's self-sacrificing nature. So, in the end, the virtuous women help the young men take on a more mature, less egotistical view of themselves. After much bungling in the learning process, Valentine in the end displays almost superhuman generosity and mercy, the marks of "the perfect man." Through his confrontation with Valentine and Julia in the final scene, Proteus recognizes his treachery, accepts his guilt, and repents. Like a true gentleman and mature human being, he accepts his weaknesses and reconfirms his love for Julia. All have learned that human ideals are vital to society but that humans are weak in their pursuit and definition of such ideals. As Paul Lindenbaum notes, the two gentlemen have gained "a proper recognition of unaccommodated man" (237). Conscious of human susceptibility to egotism, the protagonists can, perhaps, recognize its signs and be even more dedicated to their lovers.

The Two Gentlemen of Verona introduces, in tentative notes, the great theme of love's power to bring out our best selves and to renew society. The love and forgiveness evident in the conclusion to *The Two Gentlemen* suggest a redemptive power that takes a more prominent place in *The Tempest*. Perhaps the organization of the First Folio that places *The Tempest*, one of Shakespeare's last plays, first, and *The Two Gentlemen of Verona*, one of his first plays, second, is an editorial comment: The great redemptive power of love was seminal in even an early comedy.

CRITICAL CONTROVERSIES

The Two Gentlemen of Verona generates critical controversy in two broad categories: one textual, the other interpretive. Textual controversies revolve around the manuscript sources used in printing the First Folio (1623), Shakespeare's composition process, and the play's chronological position in Shakespeare's dramatic career (see "Publication History," above, for a detailed discussion). The interpretive debates typically evaluate the play's success as an experiment in comic form. More recently, feminist and gender criticism view the play as a representation of the relationship between gender and power.

To account for inconsistencies in the location of action, the time scheme, and character, scholars propose various theories about the manuscripts used to set the Folio text in print and about Shakespeare's composition process. Eighteenth-century scholars account for the play's inconsistencies and the abrupt resolution of plot difficulties by proposing that the Folio text represents a revision by Shakespeare or others of a lost original manuscript. Some twentieth-century scholars suggest that the play was set from theatrical materials, such as a promptbook or player's parts posted backstage. Most recent editors, however, conclude that the Folio text was probably set from Shakespeare's manuscript, or foul papers. Leech and Campbell propose that Shakespeare wrote the play in phases, the main love plots around 1592 and Launce's scenes in 1593 after William Kempe joined Shakespeare's troupe.

A more spirited textual controversy concerns the dating of *The Two Gentlemen* and, consequently, its role in Shakespeare's artistic development (see "Publication History," above). Some critics argue that it comes after *The Comedy of Errors* and *The Taming of the Shrew*; others see it as Shakespeare's first comedy because it is less developed in dramatic technique than either of those plays. Neither side has clearly won the debate.

The interpretive controversies move primarily between two polar positions. One view evaluates *The Two Gentlemen* as an unsuccessful attempt to meld romantic material and Roman plots or to resolve the conflict between heterosexual romantic love and idealized friendship. The other perspective sees the play as a carefully crafted, though flawed, structure that either promotes the educational value of love and friendship or satirizes the uncritical pursuit of them. In *Shakespearean Comedy*, H. B. Charlton summarizes the first perspective. He deems the play unsuccessful because Valentine as a romantic hero "appears no better than [the play's] clowns" (43). Valentine's character fails to merge two antithetical comic traditions, one found in Roman plays, where the protagonist is a satiric target, and the other in medieval romance, where the protagonist is a noble hero. Howard C. Goddard represents the second interpretive perspective, seeing the play as intentionally satirical. In *The Meaning of Shakespeare*, he notes that in light of an analysis of Valentine's and Launce's characters "we may have to revise our opinion of its juvenility and consider whether some of its apparent flaws are not consciously contrived ironical effects" (42, 43).

Most critics who see the play as satire focus on Valentine. Ralph Berry takes Charlton's analysis of Valentine and turns it around to argue that Shakespeare was satirizing the idea of the fashionable gentleman. Seeing Valentine as "self-infatuated" and comically conventional, Berry concludes that "the fundamental critical error with *Two Gentlemen* is to take Valentine at his own evaluation as an attractive, appealing male lead. He is nothing of the sort. He is (and I gladly accept Charlton's term) a 'nincompoop'; and this is the germ of the play, not an unsightly development forced on a tyro by the exigencies of the conventions" (53). Larry S. Champion concurs in *The Evolution of Shakespeare's Comedy: A Study in Dramatic Perspective* (Cambridge, MA: Harvard UP, 1970), warning that "readers and critics" who see the work as aiming at an emotional, romantic tale "have reacted sentimentally to what Shakespeare would have us laugh at" (38).

Certainly the most troubling feature of *The Two Gentlemen* is the act 5 climax, when Valentine offers Silvia to Proteus. Muriel Bradbrook notes that the scene is "universally misunderstood, universally considered to destroy the play" (47). To many, Valentine's gesture privileges male friendship over romantic love by violating Silvia's humanity. Ralph Sargent ("Sir Thomas Elyot and the Integrity of *The Two Gentlemen of Verona*," *PMLA* 65 [1950]: 1166–1180, reprinted in J. Schlueter, 33–48) argues that Valentine's seemingly insensitive gesture must be seen in the context of courtly love and the ideal courtier. Supporting Sargent, Bradbrook asserts that Valentine's offer is a "generous but not preposterous act" (48). Valentine, firmly in charge with Proteus repentant, can offer the courtly love game's role of his lady's servant to Proteus as he had on Proteus's arrival in Milan. Valentine's gesture is a direct borrowing from Renaissance courtesy books. According to Sargent, it "comes as a shock" because Shakespeare wanted to illustrate "the noble state of friendship" as his source, the Titus and Gissipus story in Elyot's *The Book of the Governor*, had (J. Schlueter, 45).

Employing the educational process as a structuring idea, Paul Lindenbaum and Camille Wells Slights use the play's intellectual background to reveal Shakespeare's satirical but humane vision. To them, conventional behaviors are satirized, but the ideals of romantic love and ideal friendship are reaffirmed as powerfully and positively transforming. Lindenbaum views the play as an educational process for Valentine, Proteus, and Julia with the play's climax as the culminating lesson in understanding the ideal of "the perfect man" as well as "the proper recognition of unaccommodated man" (237), our flawed humanity. Slights demonstrates that both Valentine and Proteus have been extreme in their pursuit of perfection. She concludes: "If the play hints darkly that both the pursuit of an extreme standard of perfection and lawless self-will are destructive of social coherence and civilized life, it also celebrates the communal happiness possible when people combine idealism with realistic understanding of human imperfection and join self-cultivation and self-assertion with respect for other people" (73).

Feminist and gender criticism have opened new territory, shifting the critical gaze from the two gentlemen to the women in the play. These critical views explore how *The Two Gentlemen* represents gender and power. Marilyn French in *Shakespeare's Division of Experience* (New York: Summit Books, 1981) observes that Shakespeare created female characters who embody "the female principle," the "magnetic power . . . to draw others to one" (90). French contends that by placing this power in female characters who do not have a socially legitimate claim to power but who accept their position, Shakespeare endorsed but "defused" the power of the feminine principle, making "it possible for him to level radical criticism at 'masculine' structures without fear of really toppling them" (90). Jeffrey Masten analyzes women as objects of exchange among men. In that role, they allow men simultaneously to express the homoerotic element in male friendship safely and to perpetuate the homosocial power structure. Within this framework, the troubling climactic scene of *The Two Gentlemen* is an appropriate theatrical representation of the way male power is perpetuated. Masten concludes that in the Renaissance: "Homoeroticism . . . is not . . . a disruptive and unconventional deconstruction of a sex/gender system. In this play . . . homoeroticism functions as part of the network of power; it constitutes and reflects the homogeneity of the gentlemanly subject" (48).

PRODUCTION HISTORY

The stage history of *The Two Gentlemen of Verona* confirms that Shakespeare is for all ages, but each age refashions his work in its own image. The infrequent eighteenth-century and nineteenth-century productions edited the text to put a noble romantic hero and decorous ladies center stage. Popular melodrama festooned the play with songs and visual spectacle, turning into a virtual operetta. The mid-twentieth century, a more ironic age, revitalized *The Two Gentlemen* and spurred more frequent productions by emphasizing satire of youthful love and society itself.

Benjamin Victor's 1762 production at Drury Lane in London is the first documented performance. His heavily revised acting version influenced the infrequent revivals of the play for almost a century. Eliminating the Folio's many inconsistencies and adding scenes for Speed and Launce, Victor also significantly altered the last scene, cutting Valentine's offer of Silvia. Thus, romantic love was allowed to triumph without concern for ideal friendship. Victor's version also removed satiric elements, so that Valentine becomes an unambiguously noble hero. With Valentine reconstituted as an admirable, sentimental hero, Proteus stands in sharper contrast as the inconstant, selfish antagonist. In London, John Philip Kemble's productions in 1784, 1790, and 1808 adopted many of Victor's changes. Like Victor, Kemble cut much of Launce's and Speed's wordplay and bawdy comments to sanitize the original text for a more "refined" eighteenth-century public.

In 1841, Macready restored Valentine's offer of Silvia to Proteus. The action of the final scene was performed rapidly, however, emphasizing Valentine's magnanimity as both lover and friend. Macready's version became a mid-century standard mounted again by Charles Kean in New York in 1846 and in London in 1848.

By the nineteenth century, contemporary social and cultural ideas of the "proper lady" influenced productions of *The Two Gentlemen*. A study of nineteenth-century promptbooks demonstrates the type of cuts that were necessary to make Shakespeare's women conform to a more passive and proper nineteenth-century model. Julia's metaphors, used to suggest her emotional and intellectual depth, as well as her asides critical of male characters, were edited out (see Patti S. Derrick, "Feminine 'Depth' on the Nineteenth-Century Stage," in J. Schlueter, 223–229). The nineteenth-century Shakespearean heroines did not engage in deep feeling, thinking, or immodest language. And they did not challenge male hegemony.

Gender and feminist criticism in the twentieth century rejected this nineteenth-century depiction of passive, subordinate women in *The Two Gentlemen of Verona*, especially in university productions. Michael Friedman deals with Silvia's silence after Valentine's offer as a theatrical sign of female subordination to patriarchal authority (" 'To Be Slow in Words Is a Woman's Only Virtue': Silence and Satire in *The Two Gentlemen of Verona*," *Selected Papers from the West Virginia Shakespeare and Renaissance Association* 17 [1994]: 1–9, reprinted in J. Schlueter, 213–221). He also describes "feminist" productions that subvert this sexist premise. Citing Dolores Ringer's 1989 University of Kansas production and Joan Robbins's University of Scranton staging, Friedman documents experiments with the climactic scene that show resistance or unwilling subordination to male power. In Ringer's production, Silvia stood shocked and alienated, remaining on stage alone after the men exited. In Robbins's version, Silvia, gagged by the outlaws, remains so throughout the attempted rape and Valentine's offer. The gag signals that her subservience is not voluntary (J. Schlueter, 220–221). In the Shakespeare Shenandoah Express's 2003 production of *The Two Gentlemen*, directed by Fred Nelson, Julia takes her turn at resistance; she pummels Proteus, rather than swooning, to vent her anger on him.

In the nineteenth century, theatrical technology evolved as melodrama and its spectacular stage effects became popular and influenced productions of *The Two Gentlemen*. In 1821 at Covent Garden, Frederick Reynolds set a production pattern that continued, though much modified, into the twentieth century. He added numerous songs and stunning staging effects that turned the play into an operatic spectacle. According to a reviewer in the *European Magazine*, Reynolds took advantage of any scene change to add songs and elaborately staged interludes, including pigmies blowing conch shells and Cleopatra entering a flooded stage in a gilded barge (Salgado Gamini, ed., *Eyewitnesses of Shakespeare: First Hand Accounts of Performances, 1590–1890* [London: Chatto and Windus for Sussex UP; New York: Barnes and Noble], 1975, 78–80, reprinted in J. Schlueter, 233).

Adding music and trendy staging continues. Joseph Papp's 1971 adaptation at the New York Shakespeare Festival, for example, became a Broadway hit and won the Tony Award for best musical of the year. Papp emphasized the youthfulness of the lovers in a contemporary setting and added pop love songs as well as politically satirical ones.

A survey of production reviews since the 1970s reveals a continuing trend to add music and spectacle to emphasize the play's focus on youth (and perhaps to develop a youthful following for Shakespeare). To emphasize the zany and absurd character of youthful love, productions have used Cole Porter, ragtime, mariachi, rock and roll, and techno-punk music. To add spectacle, the play has been transposed into twentieth-century settings. For example, in Washington, D.C., the Shakespeare Theatre's 2001 production set the action in a 1950s Verona Beach, New Jersey, "full of youthful energy, pizza parlors, and beauty salons," and a Milan that "is the sophisticated cosmopolitan city across the ocean, peopled by fashion models at cocktail parties" (www.shakespearedc.org/pastprod/twoset.html).

The Old Vic's productions in 1952 directed by Denis Carey and in 1957 directed by Michael Langham spurred renewed interest in *The Two Gentlemen*. While the 1952 production cut Valentine's offer of Silvia, it succeeded in balancing comic and romantic elements to produce a lighthearted tone, according to Kurt Schlueter (40). Reviewers noted that in this rendition Valentine's "manliness and aristocratic airs" were paramount, and the degree of Proteus's villainy was reduced greatly by presenting his fickleness "as adolescent irresponsibility and youthful excess" (quoted in J. Schlueter, 41). Michael Langham's 1957 production pushed the comic strain toward farce. The Regency costuming, with Valentine and Proteus dressed in frocked coats and frilled shirts, added an air of artificiality associated with the comedy of manners. This stylized approach allowed the audience, according to St. Claire Byrne, to "take romantic absurdity for granted" ("The Shakespeare Season at The Old Vic, 1956–57 and Stratford-upon-Avon, 1957," *Shakespeare Quarterly* 8 [1957]: 469–471, reprinted in J. Schlueter, 246). According to her, the style prepared the audience for a farcical rendition of the climax in which Proteus threatens suicide with a pistol until Valentine accepts his repentance by offering Silvia (J. Schlueter, 248).

Robin Phillips's productions at Stratford-upon-Avon in 1970 and in Stratford, Ontario, in 1975, used the comic elements to satirize the adolescent search for identity. In both productions, Valentine is a virile, athletic jock and Proteus an effeminate and envious friend, adding an element of homoeroticism to their relationship. Using stereotypical masculine identities provided a psychological explanation for Proteus's villainy. He seeks revenge on the more physically and socially favored Valentine while still admiring him. Both productions also turned Launce into a worldly wise critic of adolescent behavior. Rather than country clown, Launce became more like Shakespeare's agents of satire in later plays, Thersites in *Troilus and Cressida* or Enobarbus in *Antony and Cleopatra*.

As part of the Shakespeare Project from 1978 to 1984, the British Broadcasting Company videotaped *The Two Gentlemen of Verona*, directed by Don Taylor, in 1983. Filmed in romantic Italian gardens and with moonlit scenes, this production is conservative, subdued, and gently satirical of youthful excesses in love and friendship. Patti Derrick believes that the production prepares for the forgiveness and renewal of friendship in the conclusion. Studying Silvia's stage position and facial expressions, Derrick interprets them as a mature understanding and approval of Valentine's hesitating offer to Proteus in the name of friendship ("Two Gents: A Crucial Moment," *Shakespeare on Film Newsletter* 16.1 [December 1991]: 1–4, reprinted in J. Schlueter, 260–261).

Since the 1980s *The Two Gentlemen* has been produced often onstage, though not always by major professional companies. For example, the Royal Shakespeare Company mounted productions in 1981, 1991, and 1998. In Canada, the Stratford Festival in Ontario produced the play in 1984, 1988, 1992, and 1998. But one can see a production almost every year at regional Shakespeare Festivals, like those in Oregon and Utah; the resident Shakespeare-oriented theaters in Washington, D.C., and

(Left to right) Lloyd Bochner as Proteus, Eric House as Valentine, Ann Morrish as Julia, and Diana Maddox as Silvia in the Stratford Festival Company of Canada's 1958 production of *The Two Gentlemen of Verona*. Courtesy of Photofest.

Chicago; at outdoor summer theaters; and at universities. With its high-spirited, youthful core, it has become a vehicle for commercial success as light, almost operatic, farce; and with the development of gender and feminist criticism, it has become a vehicle for theatrical experimentation exploring gender identity and the social power of hierarchy.

EXPLICATION OF KEY PASSAGES

2.1.18–32. "Marry, by these . . . my master." In this speech, Speed echoes the theme of love's transforming power by satirizing Valentine, who has been "metamorphis'd by a mistress" (2.1.30–31). Speed delivers a set speech that characterizes Valentine in a torrent of witty comparison: he is like a malcontent, a robin redbreast, one who has the pestilence, a schoolboy, a young wench in mourning, a person afraid of robbers, and a whining beggar (2.1.20–26). These similes conjure up the stereotypical young lover who walks alone, relishes love songs, sighs, weeps, and eats poorly—a type encountered later in the lovesick Romeo in *Romeo and Juliet*. Speed notes the ironic justice in his master's transformation, since he is now like "Sir Proteus" (19), whom Valentine mocked in the opening scene. The humor is driven home when Valentine, typically slow to perceive reality, responds incredulously: "Are all these things perceiv'd in me?"(2.1.33).

2.6.1–43. "To leave my Julia . . . plot this drift." The theme of metamorphosis sounds again in Proteus's soliloquy rationalizing his treachery. True to his name, Proteus transforms himself before the audience's eyes into an inconstant man. The soliloquy has three movements. First, Proteus reflects on the consequences of betraying his lover and friend, then on an argument to support his treachery, and finally on a plot to achieve his selfish desire. In leaving Julia and wronging Valentine, Proteus will be "much foresworn" (2.6.3) and so suffer a blot on his honor and treason to love; he feels a twinge of guilt, accusing himself of "perjury" (2.6.1–5). Then he addresses Love as a capricious god who provokes the betrayal of love and prays that this sin-provoking deity now provide him with the wit "to excuse it" (2.6.7–8). The associations started in the earlier soliloquy comparing love to fire, light, and religious commitment continue here to Julia's disadvantage. While she is a "twinkling star," Silvia has become his worshipped "celestial sun" (2.6.10). The soliloquy now becomes a psychomachia, an inner struggle, as Proteus argues with himself to justify his transformation. He reasons that his vow to Julia was "unheedful" (2.6.11), made without much reflection, and that only a dim wit would not exchange "the bad [that is, Julia] for better [that is, Silvia]" (2.6.13). He immediately berates himself for speaking words that deny the "soul-confirming oaths" (2.6.16) he had made to Julia: "Fie, fie, unreverend tongue" (2.6.14). The rhythm of and the caesura in line 17 that concludes the speech's second movement bring us Proteus's decision: "I cannot leave [cease] to love, and yet I do" (2.6.17). The regular iambic rhythm of the first six syllables stops. After a breath, the line concludes with an altered rhythm stressing the vow-like words, "I do." Proteus is at the emotional nadir of the speech. He recognizes his obligation to Julia in the line's first part and his new commitment in the second part.

Once he has said, "I do" to loving Silvia, reason comes to his aid, supporting his egocentric view of the world. Using logic, Proteus tries to undo the oneness of two beings that underlies both romantic love and ideal friendship. Equating true self-identity now with love of Silvia, Proteus cannot reconcile any other partition of himself. If he keeps Julia and Valentine, his significant other selves, he concludes:

> I needs must lose myself;
> If I lose them, thus find I by their loss—
> For Valentine, myself; for Julia, Silvia. (2.6.20–22)

Having reason to thank for serving his self-seeking, Proteus reaches the peak of self-justification: "I to myself am dearer than a friend" (2.6.23). Julia is brushed away with a self-congratulatory, superficial assessment of appearances. Proteus comments that Silvia, being fair, "Shows Julia but a swarthy Ethiope" (2.6.26). From this moment on in the speech, Proteus is resolved and plans to achieve his desire. He will consider Julia dead and Valentine an enemy, thus clearing the way for his machinations to betray Valentine's plan to elope. Then he will use "some sly blunt trick" to cross Thurio (2.6.41). Proteus concludes with another prayer to the god of love, asking him to speed his plans and offering thanks for the "wit to plot this drift" (2.6.43).

3.1.263–279. "I am but a fool, . . . with clean hands." Launce, too, falls in love. This solo speech provides a silly, down-to-earth contrast to the extravagant language the two young gentlemen use to describe their goddess-like lovers. Launce sees through the romantic rhetoric of the young gentlemen. He recognizes Proteus, despite his high-flown expressions of love, as "a kind of knave" (3.1.264). Launce's language is grounded in earthy reality, and his milkmaid is a very material girl. Unlike his social betters, Launce sees his beloved clearly, flaws and all. With his characteristic ability to bend language to his purposes—perhaps paralleling Proteus in 2.6.1–43—Launce recognizes that the milkmaid is "not a maid" (virgin), though "she is her master's maid," that is, housemaid (3.1.270–271). To Launce, she has "more qualities than a water-spaniel" (3.1.272–273), a loyal dog, perhaps in contrast to the seemingly "inhumane" Crab, whom Launce also loves! While Valentine and Proteus carry around stereotypical celestial images to characterize their lovers, Launce carries around a written "cate-log," an itemized listing of his milkmaid's "condition" (3.1.274). Reading from his catalogue, Launce says that she "can fetch and carry" (3.1.275), making her superior to a horse, which can "only carry" (3.1.277). Launce ends his listing with two sexually charged puns. The milkmaid is "better than a jade" (3.1.277), a term referring to a horse in poor condition but also to a prostitute, and "she can milk" (3.1.278), a term referring both to farm work and to masturbation. Of her milking Launce notes (perhaps with raised eyebrows!): "Look you, a sweet virtue in a maid with clean hands" (3.1.278–279).

Annotated Bibliography

Berry, Ralph. *Shakespeare's Comedies: Explorations in Form*. Princeton: Princeton UP, 1972. Sees the play as a satire on following conventions in the pursuit of love and friendship.

Bradbrook, M. C. *Shakespeare in His Context: The Constellated Globe IV: The Collected Papers of Muriel C. Bradbrook*. 4 vols. Totowa, NJ: Barnes and Noble Books, 1989. Discusses the play within the traditions of courtly love and the education of a gentleman.

Charlton, H. B. *Shakespearian Comedy*. London: Methuen, 1938. Defines the play as a valuable but unsuccessful experiment in romantic comedy.

Cole, Howard C. "The Full Meaning of *The Two Gentlemen of Verona*." *Comparative Drama* 23 (Fall 1989): 201–227. Examines the comedy in light of other plays, narrative sources, and the traditions behind the sources.

Lindenbaum, Paul. "Education in *The Two Gentlemen of Verona*." *Studies in English Literature* 15 (1975): 229–244. Views the play as a series of educational processes.

Masten, Jeffrey. *Textual Intercourse: Collaboration, Authorship, and Sexualities in Renaissance Drama*. Cambridge: Cambridge UP, 1997. Uses historical and textual evidence of the homosocial power structure of Elizabethan gentlemen.

Nevo, Ruth. *Comic Transformations in Shakespeare*. New York: Methuen, 1980. Views the play as a quest for self-identity. Argues that formally it lies between farce and romantic comedy.

Schlueter, June, ed. *"The Two Gentlemen of Verona": Critical Essays*. New York: Garland, 1996. An indispensable collection of articles and theatrical reviews.

Schlueter, Kurt, ed. *The Two Gentlemen of Verona*. Cambridge: Cambridge UP, 1990. A fine edition of the play, with an excellent introduction with sections on the date of the play, themes and criticism, structure and sources, Speed and Launce, the Outlaws, and stage history. As with all the New Cambridge Shakespeare volumes, this last section is especially detailed.

Slights, Camille Wells. *Shakespeare's Comic Commonwealth*. Toronto: U of Toronto P, 1993. Presents the play as the education of gentlemen in the humanistic tradition recognizing idealism and human imperfection.

Love's Labor's Lost

Jessica Winston

PLOT SUMMARY

1.1. As the play opens, the King of Navarre explains his "late edict" (1.1.11), a recent royal proclamation. For the next three years, the court shall be an academy dedicated to philosophy. All men within a mile of it must study, fast once a week, see no women, and sleep only three hours per night. The King asks his companions, Longaville, Dumaine, and Berowne, who have already sworn to obey the decree, to affirm their oaths by signing the proclamation. The first two sign immediately, and Berowne, although initially arguing that the terms are too difficult, eventually adds his endorsement as well.

Two events immediately test the practicality of the edict. First, Berowne reminds the King that the Princess of France is about to arrive on a diplomatic mission, which will force the King to break his oath in order to accommodate her. Second, Don Adriano de Armado catches the clown Costard and the country maid Jaquenetta cuddling in the park in clear violation of the stricture against women. As punishment, the King orders Costard to fast on bran and water and remain imprisoned under the care of Armado.

1.2. This scene focuses on Armado, who is in love with Jaquenetta, despite their differences in social class. He asks the page boy Moth to console him with a song. The constable Dull brings Jaquenetta and Costard to Armado. After flirting with the country maid, Armado imprisons Costard.

2.1. Having arrived in Navarre, the Princess and her attending ladies, Maria, Katherine, and Rosaline, learn from the French Lord Boyet that the King intends to lodge the women in the fields rather than violate his recent prohibition against females at court. When the King arrives to greet the Princess, she criticizes him for his lack of hospitality and explains her complicated mission, which concerns a loan made by Navarre's father to the Princess's father. The province of Aquitaine was given to Navarre as security for the loan. Navarre still holds Aquitaine because he claims that the loan has not been repaid. The Princess maintains that it has. The meeting involves some clever wordplay between the King and Princess as well as

Berowne and Rosaline, and by the end of the act the two men are in love with the ladies, as are Longaville and Dumaine with Maria and Katherine, respectively.

3.1. The act opens with banter between Armado and his page boy, Moth. The complex wordplay reveals Armado's lovesickness and fondness for repartee as well as his page's quick wit. Later in the act, having freed Costard, Armado asks him to deliver a letter to Jaquenetta. Berowne stops the clown on the way, requesting that he deliver a letter to Rosaline. Alone onstage, Berowne wonders that he is in love and especially with Rosaline, a woman who is the least beautiful, "the worst of all" (3.1.195), among the ladies.

4.1. The Princess and her ladies hunt in the park. Costard approaches them and mistakenly delivers Armado's letter for Jaquenetta to Rosaline.

4.2. The scene introduces two new characters, the schoolmaster Holofernes and the curate Nathaniel, both of whom watch the hunt along with Dull. Holofernes and Nathaniel comment disparagingly on Dull's lack of Latin, and the schoolmaster displays his learning by spontaneously composing a poem on the deer hunt. Costard misdelivers the remaining letter, Berowne's note to Rosaline, to Jaquenetta, who asks Nathaniel to read it for her. Nathaniel quickly realizes that the correspondence violates the edict and tells Jaquenetta to take the letter to the King.

4.3. Sometimes called "the orchard scene" or "the sonnet scene," here Shakespeare constructs an elaborate eavesdropping episode in which the men unwittingly reveal that they are in love. As the scene opens, Berowne enters carrying a sonnet for Rosaline. When the King enters, Berowne hides but watches him read a sonnet composed for the Princess. The King also hides when Longaville enters and reads a sonnet composed for Maria. Longaville in turn hides when Dumaine enters with a love poem for Katherine. The characters then emerge in reverse order. Longaville steps out from hiding, chastising Dumaine for breaking the oath. The King reveals himself and chastises both. Berowne appears and self-righteously berates them all until Jaquenetta arrives bearing the letter to Rosaline. Berowne is forced to admit that he, too, is in love. The men ask Berowne to reason how they can pursue the women without being forsworn, and he responds with an elegant speech arguing that men learn more from women's eyes than books. The men thus "resolve to woo these girls of France" (4.3.368) and in particular to offer "[s]ome entertainment for them in their tents" (4.3.370).

5.1. Armado, Nathaniel, Holofernes, Costard, and Dull decide to perform a play about ancient and medieval heroes, the Pageant of the Nine Worthies, for the noblemen and women.

5.2. Two entertainments are offered. In the first, the King and courtiers dress themselves as Muscovites in order to amuse the women, but the Princess and ladies, having learned of the men's plan beforehand, disguise themselves, too. Each man thus courts the wrong woman. In the second, the non-noble characters perform the Pageant of the Nine Worthies. While the Princess politely encourages the faltering and amateur actors, the noblemen mock them relentlessly. Two events interrupt the play. First, Costard announces that Jaquenetta is pregnant with Armado's child: "She's quick, the child brags in her belly already. 'Tis yours" (5.2.676–677). Second, a French messenger, Marcade, announces that the Princess's father, the King of France, has died (5.2.719–720). The Princess and ladies prepare to depart immediately. Even so the men press their love suits. The Princess criticizes them for breaking the oaths made at the beginning of the play, observing that such actions make it difficult to trust their sudden vows of love. The Princess and her attendant women tell the men to wait a year and agree to other conditions in order to demonstrate that offers "made in the heat of blood" will last (5.2.800). The noblemen and women go their separate ways.

PUBLICATION HISTORY

As with many of Shakespeare's plays, it is unclear when *Love's Labor's Lost* was composed and initially performed, but critics now concur that it was sometime around 1594–1595. The evidence for this date is circumstantial. The earliest references to the play occur in 1598. This is the date of the earliest surviving edition, called the First Quarto. Also in this year, Robert Tofte referred to the drama in a line from a love poem: "*Love's Labour's Lost*, I once did see a play, / Yclepèd so [called so]" ("From *Alba: The Month's Minde of a Melancholy Lover*," in "*Love's Labour's Lost*": *Critical Essays*, ed. Felicia Hardison Londré [New York: Routledge, 1997], 41. Collection referred to hereafter as *Critical Essays*). In addition, Francis Meres commented in his *Palladis Tamia: Wit's Treasury* (1598) that *Love's Labor's Lost* is one of several comedies that testify to Shakespeare's greatness as a dramatist: "Shakespeare among the English is the most excellent . . . for comedy, witness his *Gentlemen of Verona*, his *Errors*, his *Love Labours Lost*. . . ." (quoted in E. K. Chambers, *William Shakespeare: A Study of Facts and Problems*, 2 vols. [Oxford: Clarendon P, 1930], 2.194). Such references do not tell us when the play was performed but indicate that it must have appeared onstage at some point before—it is difficult to say just how long before—1598.

Early critics ranked *Love's Labor's Lost* among Shakespeare's first works. Writing in 1710, Charles Gildon asserted that it was the product of an amateur playwright fairly new to his craft: "since it is one of the worst of Shakespeare's plays, nay I think I may say the very worst, I cannot but think that it is his first" ("Remarks on the Plays of Shakespeare," *Critical Essays*, 45). Since the mid-twentieth century, critics have developed a more favorable opinion of the drama, grouping it with the narrative poems, *Venus and Adonis* (1593) and *The Rape of Lucrece* (1594), and the lyrical plays of the mid-1590s, *A Midsummer Night's Dream*, *Romeo and Juliet*, and *Richard II*. This dating makes some sense given the stylistic and thematic affinities of the group. Like *Lucrece*, *Love's Labor's Lost* delights in complicated metaphors and figurative language. Like *Richard II*, the comedy depicts a king concerned more with metaphors and figures of speech than with reality. The connection with *A Midsummer Night's Dream* is particularly strong. Both bring together and mix up groups of lovers, end with noblemen mocking a play within the play, and contain similar statements about comedy. In *Love's Labor's Lost*, Berowne highlights the drama's departure from literary convention: "Our wooing doth not end like an old play: / Jack hath not Gill" (5.2.874–875). A similar statement by Puck underscores that *A Midsummer Night's Dream* keeps to tradition: "Jack shall have Jill; / Nought shall go ill" (3.2.461–462).

That the play appeared in the 1590s makes sense in light of some important historical background: the rising interest in education as a subject for literature. Over the course of the century, changing perceptions of education prompted the aristocracy—many of whom were notoriously ill-educated—to feel that they must obtain learning, especially in the form of a university education, and put their learning to good use as servants to the state: for instance, as ambassadors, judges, and administrators (J. H. Hexter, "The Education of the Aristocracy in the Renaissance," *Journal of Modern History* 22.1 [March 1950]: 1–20). As a result, in the latter part of the century, English universities gradually grew in size as increasing numbers of aristocratic men attended, as did growing numbers of young men of the merchant classes who wanted to take advantage of the opportunities that the schools could open for them. Writers of the period picked up on this trend, making education and especially the uses and abuses of education the subject of poems and plays, including Christopher Marlowe's *Dr. Faustus* (late 1580s?) as well as three anonymous plays put on at Cambridge at the turn of the century: *The Pilgrimage to Parnassus* (1598), *The First Part of the Return from Parnassus* (1599), and *The Second Part of the Return from Parnassus* (1601). In *Love's Labor's Lost*, Shakespeare also capitalized on such concerns, writing a comedy about aristocrats who use education to retreat from the world rather than to engage with it.

The earliest printings of the play may well have responded to contemporary interest in the issue of education. The First Quarto was published around the height of concern about this topic in 1598. Even so, readers' interest in the play was fairly short-lived. *Love's Labor's Lost* did not appear in print again until the publication of the First Folio in 1623 and then again in a second quarto in 1631.

The 1598 edition contains several textual oddities that cause difficulty for editors. First, the title page tells us that it is "Newly corrected and augmented," a statement that suggests an earlier edition. Such an edition has never been found. It is possible that the claim "newly corrected and augmented" was an advertising ploy used to encourage customers to purchase a seemingly already popular edition. Equally likely, two editions of the play may have appeared in fairly rapid succession and one of these is now lost. Second, despite the claim that it is "newly corrected," the First Quarto contains two passages where several lines are repeated in different versions. These occur at 4.3.292–314 and 4.3.315–362 and again at 5.2.817–822 and 5.2.837–854. Although we cannot know for certain, the repetitions may indicate that the First Quarto contains revised passages from Shakespeare's own drafts, his foul papers. G. R. Hibbard offers an accessible overview of this thesis and other textual problems in the introduction to the Oxford edition of the play (*Love's Labour's Lost* [Oxford: Clarendon P, 1990], 57–83). Most editions print and mark the repeated passages, leaving interested students with some tantalizing evidence of what might be Shakespeare's revisions.

SOURCES FOR THE PLAY

Like *A Midsummer Night's Dream*, but unlike most of Shakespeare's plays, *Love's Labor's Lost* has no known narrative or dramatic sources. Nonetheless, the play makes reference to a number of historical personages and events as well as literary texts. The names of the noblemen refer to real historical figures. King Ferdinand of Navarre refers to the Protestant King Henry of Navarre (1553–1610), who warred with the Catholic King of France in the late sixteenth century, gaining the French throne in 1589 and converting to Catholicism himself to prevent civil war in 1593. The courtiers have versions of names of those involved in the French religious wars of this period: Duc de Biron and Duc de Longueville aided Navarre. Duc de Mayenne fought against Navarre. The play does not make reference to these religious wars but may loosely represent a historical event involving the king and his wife, Marguerite de Valois, whom he married for political reasons in 1572. In 1578, Marguerite, along with a retinue of ladies, visited her then estranged husband to discuss the ownership of Aquitaine, land that was part of her dowry and referred to in the play as "a dowry for a queen" (2.1.8). This meeting had much of the atmosphere of the play, including several weeks of frivolity, dancing, and entertainments. Still, connections between the play and events involving the real King of Navarre seem little more than superficial and cursory. Shakespeare may have chosen to allude to events involving Henry of Navarre because it helped his characterization of the King in his play. After 1593, when Shakespeare probably wrote the play, Navarre was a Catholic and out of favor with Elizabeth I, the Protestant Queen of England. For educated members of the audience, Navarre's name may have signaled that he should be viewed skeptically and critically.

The play appears to refer additionally to several literary sources. Two of the non-noble characters are likely based on stock figures from classical and continental drama: Armado on the braggart soldier or miles gloriosus of Roman comedy, and Holofernes and Nathaniel on the affected schoolmaster or pedant and the flattering parasite of the Italian commedia dell'arte. The idea for the monarchic retreat may have been inspired by Pierre de la Primaudaye's *Académie française* (1577; translated and published in English, 1586) in which four young gentlemen retreat from the world to learn Latin, Greek, and moral philosophy. Inspiration for the Muscovites in act 5 may have come from an entertainment held as part of the annual Christmas festivities at one of the early English law schools, Gray's Inn, in 1594. Still, it is difficult to say how significant or likely these connections are. Armado begins as a braggart soldier but becomes more complex by the end of the play (see "Main Characters," below). The *Académie française* is interrupted by civil war, not by a diplomatic entourage of noblewomen. And the Gray's Inn entertainment may have occurred after *Love's Labor's Lost* was first performed, in which case the play may have influenced the entertainment. On the whole, throughout *Love's Labor's Lost*, Shakespeare touches on a number of historical and literary sources, none of which provides the primary narrative for the play. Yet together they highlight something characteristic of Shakespeare. As he wrote, he frequently referred to and combined historical and literary material in unexpected, creative, and sometimes even delightfully gratuitous ways.

STRUCTURE AND PLOTTING

Many of Shakespeare's comedies are structured around alternating scenes involving a main plot and subplot. *Love's Labor's Lost* likewise alternates in its first eight scenes between the noble characters of the main plot and the workaday figures of the subplot and brings them together in the ninth: the Pageant of Worthies. The alterations highlight the similarities between the nobles and others in the play. Nearly all of the characters enjoy quick verbal banter. In the main, the plot serves as a frame on which to hang a series of sparking and witty conversations.

That said, the shape of the narrative frame might be described in various ways, each of which highlights a major theme or idea in the play as a whole. For instance, one could point out that the play begins and ends with oaths. As the play opens, the men swear to study philosophy for three years and to obey the terms of the edict. As the play ends, they attempt to get and make vows of love, which the women reject. The King asks the Princess, "Now at the latest minute of the hour, / Grant us your loves" (5.2.787–788), but she refuses to pledge anything under such pressure: "A time methinks too short / To make a world-without-end bargain in" (5.2.788–789). The men then attempt to swear that they will be faithful to the women, but the women reject the oaths. As Katherine says to Dumaine: "Yet swear not, lest ye be forsworn again" (5.2.832). These framing events highlight the play's theme of oath making and oath breaking.

Alternatively, we could say that the play begins and ends with rejection. First, the men reject the women and then the women reject the men. These framing events underscore the drama's departure from the tradition of comedy, which usually begins with amorous pursuit and ends with consummation. Finally, we can say that the play is framed by two arrivals, the arrival of the women in act 2 and the messenger, Marcade, in act 5. The first disrupts the unnatural and artificial world of the all-male academy. The second disrupts the unrealistically pastoral court of Navarre. These framing events subtly draw attention to the King's problematic and naive disconnection from worldly affairs, while also highlighting the peculiar appropriateness of the Princess's demand that he live as a hermit for a year. Having frivolously abandoned diplomatic and political dealings at the beginning of the play, the King must now learn in the hardest way what real disconnection feels like.

MAIN CHARACTERS

The characters in *Love's Labor's Lost* fall into four major groups: the noblemen, consisting of the King, Berowne, Dumaine, and Longaville; the noblewomen, comprised of the Princess, Rosaline, Katherine, and Maria; the "fantastical pretenders to fashion or learning," who are Armado, Holofernes, and Nathaniel; and the "genuine country folk," Costard, Jaquenetta, and Dull (Hibbard, 14–16). Shakespeare creates his drama through the interactions of these groups. As the nineteenth-century critic Walter Pater beautifully puts it, the play has the quality of a tapestry, presenting "a series of pictorial groups, in which the same figures reappear, in different combinations, but on the same background" ("On *Love's Labour's Lost*," *Critical Essays*, 66). Certain figures from each group nonetheless become the focal point of these interactions: the King, Berowne, the Princess, Rosaline, Armado, and Costard.

The King

The first character we meet is the King, the highest ranking figure and the one who undergoes the most dramatic transformation. When the play opens, he issues his royal proclamation with much dignity and seriousness, describing the lasting renown he and the courtiers will achieve from the academy: "Let fame, that all hunt after in their lives, / Live regist'red upon our brazen tombs" (1.1.1–2). In these opening moments, he is very much in control of himself and his audience, urging his fellow courtiers to "war against [their] own affections / And the huge army of the world's desires" (9–10) and telling them with due caution to sign the decree: "If you are arm'd to do, as sworn to do, / Subscribe to your deep oaths, and keep it too" (1.1.22–23). By the Masque of the Muscovites in act 5, he has entirely forgotten his stately bearing and has lost control over his emotions as well as his body. For instance, when Boyet tells the Princess about the preparations for the masque, he says that the King and his companions, "did tumble on the ground" with such "zeal-ous laughter" that they were moved to "passion's solemn tears" (5.2.115–118). The man who urged his companions "to war against [their] own affections" now tum-bles, laughs, and cries. These changes are linked with the King's principal charac-teristic, his difficulty controlling his language, or, more accurately, connecting words and reality. The tendency is evident when he greets the Princess: "Fair Princess, welcome to the court of Navarre" (2.1.90). She quickly indicates that his words have little bearing on the situation, " 'Fair' I give you back again, and 'wel-come' I have not yet. The roof of this court is too high to be yours, and welcome to the wide fields too base to be mine" (2.1.91–94). This feature of his speech ap-pears again just after the Muscovite scene. The King greets the Princess with the conventional statement: "All hail, sweet madam, and fair time of day!" (5.2.339). Picking up on other meanings of "fair" and "hail," she replies that the statement is nonsense: " 'Fair' in 'all hail' is foul, as I conceive" (5.2.340). By the end of the play, the King regains some control over his emotions and language. One of his final lines is the entirely straightforward and courteous assertion that the men will escort the ladies out of the court: "No, madam, we will bring you on your way" (5.2.873).

Berowne

While the King has the highest social status, Berowne (pronounced "Be-roon" and sometimes spelled "Biron") is by far the dominant character, with nearly a quarter of the play's lines. He is independent-minded and quick-witted. At the be-ginning of the play, when Longaville and Dumaine immediately sign the edict, Berowne resists, maintaining that the decree is too strict, harsh, and unnatural. This argument, like most of his statements, is full of clever wordplay. Indeed, in a clas-sic essay, Thomas R. Price observes that Berowne puns and plays on words more than any other character ("Shakespeare's Word-Play and Puns," *Critical Essays*, 71–72). This habit is most evident in his compact statement in act 1 that "Light, seeking light, doth light of light beguile" (1.1.77), a line glossed as "the eye, seeking enlightenment, deprives itself of the power to see, i.e. excessive study frustrates the search for truth by making the student blind" (*The Riverside Shakespeare*, ed. G. Blakemore Evans with J.J.M. Tobin, 2nd ed. [Boston: Houghton Mifflin, 1997], 214). Like the King, Berowne also tends to lose touch with reality in his speech, concen-trating more on eloquent rhetoric than he sometimes should. Thus, just after he re-nounces ostentatiously metaphorical speech ("Taffata phrases, silken terms precise, / Three-pil'd hyperboles, spruce affection" [5.2.406–407]), he tells Rosaline, "My love to thee is sound, sans crack or flaw" (5.2.415). The use of "sans," the French word for "without," shows that he cannot entirely control his impulse to use rhetor-ical and linguistic flourish. Berowne is, however, self-deprecating and willing to rec-ognize his faults, apologizing quickly for his rhetorical flourish: "Yet I have a trick / Of the old rage [infection]. Bear with me, I am sick." Even here, though, he can-not resist playing on the idea of linguistic fever, saying, "I'll leave it by degrees" (5.2.416–418). Berowne also often speaks in proverbs, showing that he is in touch with received wisdom and common sense at least more than are his companions

(Hibbard, 37). Perhaps because of this awareness Berowne is the social leader of the four noblemen, the one whose argument against the edict threatens the academic enterprise and to whom the others look at the end of act 4 for a way to get out of their difficult position, having forsworn women but now desiring to court them.

The Princess

The intellectual equal of Berowne is the Princess. She also has a fondness for banter and quick-witted repartee. Unlike the noblemen, however, she never loses sight of reality—a fact that is plain in her initial conversation with the King, when she reminds him that lodging in the fields does not suit her station. That said, the Princess is not always serious, having a playful and mischievous spirit. She orders Boyet to read the letter delivered to Rosaline, even when she learns that it is addressed to Jaquenetta: "We will read it, I swear. / Break the neck of the wax, and every one give ear" (4.1.58–59). This spirit is evident also in 5.2, when she orders her ladies to disguise themselves so that each nobleman will court the wrong lady. As she explains, "There's no such sport as sport by sport o'erthrown" (5.2.153). Indeed, the Princess shows her love of sport when she hunts and kills a deer in act 4. Despite the impish part of her personality, she is not mean-spirited, remaining for example immensely gracious and polite during the homely Pageant of the Nine Worthies. She thanks Costard for his performance: "Great thanks, great Pompey" (5.2.558). When Nathaniel becomes flustered in the part of Alexander, the Princess observes, "The conqueror is dismay'd" and urges him to continue, "Proceed, good Alexander" (5.2.567).

Rosaline

Rosaline is a version of the Princess. The women do look different. The Princess is "the thickest and the tallest" (4.1.48) of the ladies, while Rosaline is an unconventional "beauty dark" (5.2.20), with fair skin and dark hair and eyes. Berowne disparagingly refers to her as "A whitely wanton with a velvet brow, / With two pitch-balls stuck in her face for eyes" (3.1.196–197). Nevertheless, she also has a quick wit. For instance, in the Muscovite scene, the King says that he has "measur'd many miles, / To tread a measure with her on this grass" (5.2.184–185). With the Princess's eye for realism, Rosaline replies: "[H]ow many inches / Is in one mile: if they have measured many, / The measure then of one is eas'ly told" (5.2.188–190). Even so, Rosaline's humor and personality are more extreme than that of her lady. For instance, in 5.2, when the Princess observes, "We are wise girls to mock our lovers so" (5.2.58), Rosaline details with some cruelty how she would mock hers: "That same Berowne I'll torture ere I go" (5.2.60). Likewise, at the end of the play, she demands a bizarre form of service from Berowne: to make the "speechless sick" laugh (5.2.851). Others describe Rosaline as sexually aggressive. Katherine jokes about her friend's wanton nature, her "light condition" (5.2.20), and Berowne believes that this "whitely wanton" will "do the deed," that is, have sexual intercourse, "[t]hough Argus were her eunuch and her guard" (3.1.196–199). Whether such statements are true or not, Rosaline calls our attention to the strikingly unconventional verbal and romantic freedom of the play's female characters.

Armado, Holofernes, and Nathaniel

The third set of characters consists of Armado, Holofernes, and Nathaniel, all of whom are affected and modeled on characters from traditional drama (see "Sources for the Play," above). Armado is different from Holofernes and Nathaniel, however, because he breaks out of the literary mold in which he has been cast. Armado certainly begins as a bragging soldier. The King describes him as a "child of fancy" who "shall relate, / In high-borne words, the worth of many a knight / From tawny Spain, lost in the world's debate" (1.1.170–173). As soon as he appears, though, he changes into a poet-lover. Based on the narrator of the sonnets of the Italian poet Petrarch, this melancholy and obsessive figure usually writes lyrics to his beloved, who remains unattainable and coldly rejects his advances ("Devices and Techniques," below). Armado himself announces the shift from one type to another when he says at the end of act 1 that he will turn from a soldier into a love poet:

> Adieu, valor, rust, rapier, be still, drum, for your manager is in love; yea, he loveth. Assist me, some extemporal god of rhyme, for I am sure I shall turn sonnet. Devise, wit, write, pen, for I am for whole volumes in folio. (1.2.181–185)

Armado rejects war, "valor" and "rapier," to become a sonneteer. By the end of the play, he is a peculiar combination of the two types. He reverts to the braggart when Costard accuses him of fathering Jaquenetta's child: "Dost thou infamonize [defame] me among potentates? Thou shalt die" (5.2.678–679). Later, he is a Petrarchan lover, calling himself the "votary" of Jaquenetta (who intriguingly remains single) and pledging to work three years to earn her love (5.2.883–884). While Armado shifts between these self-absorbed literary types, there is also something touchingly pathetic and unusual about his character. He breaks away from both types in the Pageant of the Nine Worthies, losing all of his narcissism when he protectively eulogizes Hector. As the noblemen interrupt, Armado responds with real feeling: "The sweet war-man is dead and rotten, sweet chucks, beat not the bones of the buried. When he breathed, he was a man" (5.2.660–662). Here, we also learn of Armado's poverty. He does not have money enough for shirts (l.710). With Armado, Shakespeare tinkers with the stock character of the braggart soldier. For this reason, Armado can be seen as an early prototype of a very different braggart soldier: the boisterous and irrepressible Falstaff in *1, 2 Henry IV*.

Costard

Costard stands out among the final group. In act 1, he helps call attention to the problems with the noblemen's pastimes. Here, he comments on the unnaturalness of the edict, telling the King that it makes little sense ("I do confess much of the hearing it, but little of the marking of it" [1.1.285–286]) and suggesting that it goes against nature: "it is the manner of a man to speak to a woman" (1.1.209–210). Like the noble characters, he has his share of verbal dexterity, punning nearly as much as Berowne (Price, 71–72). He displays this dexterity as he tries to avoid the edict, arguing that he was not with "a wench" as the edict specifies, but a "damsel," then a "virgin," then a "maid" (1.1.287–297). The failure of Costard's linguistic gymnastics points to something that the noblemen have not yet learned. As Anne Barton puts it, "facts are facts and cannot be altered by verbal description." His presence thus "constitutes a warning to the King and his courtiers, but they are not yet ready to heed it" (Introduction, *Love's Labor's Lost* in *The Riverside Shakespeare*, 209). Importantly, Costard also helps to further the plot. Like Capulet's servant in *Romeo and Juliet* (1.2.38–81), he is unable to read. Consequently, he delivers the love letters to the wrong people, a mistake that leads directly to Berowne's exposure.

DEVICES AND TECHNIQUES

The most obvious stylistic characteristic of the play is its insistent wordplay. Such banter is not due to the influence of a particular source, but grows out of the self-conscious awareness of rhetoric—the art of expressing oneself—in sixteenth-century England. Such self-consciousness is evident in the numerous manuals on the arts of speaking and writing in the period, especially Thomas Wilson's *The Art of Rhetoric* (1553), Henry Peacham's *Garden of Eloquence* (1577), and George Puttenham's *The Art of English Poetry* (1589). These manuals responded to disparaging attitudes toward the status of English at the beginning of the century, when writers viewed the language as rude, barbarous, and unpoetic. For instance, a character in John Skelton's early sixteenth-century verse *Philip Sparrow* complains:

> Our language is so rusty,
> So cankered, and so full
> Of frowards, and so dull,
> That if I would apply
> To write ornately,
> I wot [know] not where to find
> Terms to serve my mind. (ll. 777–783)

English is "rusty," "cankered," "dull," and without enough "terms" for "ornate" expression (*Renaissance Literature: An Anthology*, ed. Michael Payne and John Hunter [Oxford: Blackwell Publishing, 2003], 18). Responding to such attitudes, rhetorical and poetic manuals explored possibilities for expression, indicating that it was feasible to be eloquent in English.

The arts of rhetoric importantly became an explicit subject for literature in John Lyly's *Euphues: The Anatomy of Wit* (1578), whose main character, Euphues, grew up having practiced "those things commonly which are incident to sharp wits—fine phrases, smooth quipping, merry taunting, using jesting without mean, and abusing mirth without measure" (*John Lyly: Selected Prose and Dramatic Work*, ed. Leah Scragg [Manchester, Eng.: Fyfield Books, 1997], 3). The narrative is full of witty, carefully crafted sentences. Following the publication of *Euphues*, a form of speech called euphuism became popular, especially among courtiers who aimed to speak like Lyly's character in well-structured phrases, peppered with parallel clauses, alliteration, antitheses, repetition, assonance, and rhyme. Both *Euphues* and euphuism were popular in the 1580s and 1590s, with the character and linguistic style appearing in numerous sequels and imitations of Lyly's original work.

In *Love's Labor's Lost*, Shakespeare exemplifies the contemporary interest in rhetoric and euphuism, creating characters who speak in "Taffata phrases, silken terms precise, / Three-pil'd hyperboles, spruce affection, / Figures pedantical" (5.2.406–408).

Most notably Shakespeare fills the play with chiasmus, a rhetorical figure prominent in *Euphues*, in which a clause parallels and inverts elements of the clause preceding it. Witness: "I pretty, and my saying apt? or I apt, and my saying pretty?" (1.2.19–20) or "They have pitch'd a toil: I am toiling in a pitch" (4.3.2–3). That said, Shakespeare also satirizes the linguistic fad, especially in those many moments that divorce wordplay from reality. In act 3 Costard, whose name also means "head," trips, cuts his shin, and asks for a "salve," an ointment, to put on the wound. Moth picks up on the paradox in which a "head" is broken in the "shin," announcing to Armado: "Here's a costard broken in a shin" (3.1.69–70). Armado, however, failing to see what has happened, thinks that Moth is playing a linguistic game, "Some enigma, some riddle," and asks for the punch line, "l'envoy" (71–72). What follows is complicated banter that has nothing to do with the fact of the situation: Costard needs medical attention.

Despite the satire, Shakespeare himself obviously delights in linguistic play, word games, and puns. We see this delight in Berowne's statement, "Light, seeking light, doth light of light beguile" (1.1.77). Referring to multiple meanings of the word "light"—"brightness," "enlightenment," "truth," and "eyesight," Shakespeare here as elsewhere shows the immense associative and metaphorical richness of English and, hence, its poetic capacity.

In addition to the general concern with language arts, *Love's Labor's Lost* refers to a specific set of images and ideas from Petrarchan love poetry. Based on the sonnets of the Italian writer Petrarch, this style of poetry was quite popular in sixteenth-century England. It typically addresses an unattainable woman, characterized by her aloof indifference to her lover. The poet-lover nonetheless attempts to gain the object of his affection by devoting himself to her. Signaling its indebtedness to this poetry, the play contains several sonnets, including Longaville's poem to Maria (4.3.58–71) as well as the sonnet embedded in Berowne's rhetorically elaborate renunciation of ornate speech (5.2.402–415). A common Petrarchan image concerns the eyes of the beloved, whose all-powerful glances have the power to enliven or kill the poet. This image strongly influences the noblemen's poetry in 4.3, especially the beginning of the king's lyric: "So sweet a kiss the golden sun gives not / To those fresh morning drops upon the rose, / As thy eye-beams, when their fresh rays have smote / The night of dew that on my cheeks down flows" (25–28). The image appears also in Berowne's argument: women's eyes are "the books, the arts, the academes, / That show, contain, and nourish all the world" (4.3.349–350). All the same, Peter Erickson has shown that the lack of closure in the play stems from the men's inability to think of the women outside of Petrarchan paradigms: "[T]he psychology of male and female stereotypes expressed in the men's poetry," which give women total control, "creates a barrier which keeps the men and women apart" ("The Failure of Relationship Between Men and Women in *Love's Labour's Lost*," *Critical Essays*, 243).

THEMES AND MEANINGS

Love's Labor's Lost may seem little more than a series of witty conversations, but several themes run throughout, linking the scenes into a unified whole. The most obvious theme concerns oath making. The idea appears in the opening lines, when the King declares that his companions must "[s]ubscribe to [their] deep oaths, and keep it too" (1.1.23). The rest of the play then develops one aspect of this subject:

oaths must not be taken lightly or out of all proportion to reality. Berowne first makes this point, explaining that the edict is unnatural: "O, these are barren tasks, too hard to keep, / Not to see ladies, study, fast, not sleep" (1.1.47–48). He repeats the idea further on. When the King asserts with regard to the Princess, "We must of force dispense with this decree, / She must lie here on mere necessity" (1.1.147–148), Berowne responds that the argument sets a bad precedent: "Necessity will make us all forsworn" (1.1.149). He subtly suggests, however, that the original oath should have taken necessity into account. In act 2, the Princess articulates this position. On first meeting the King, she observes that the oath is sin against conventions of hospitality: "I hear your Grace hath sworn out house-keeping: / 'Tis deadly sin to keep that oath, my lord, / And sin to break it" (2.1.104–106). The King took the oath without regard for societal obligations. Yet the oath is also a sin against nature. In 4.3, Berowne states: "Let us once lose our oaths to find ourselves, / Or else we lose ourselves to keep our oaths" (4.3.358–359). He implies that the men have sinned against their natures by swearing to the decree. They must now reconcile themselves to nature by forswearing the oath.

Love's Labor's Lost suggests again and again that oaths must be made with due consideration of one's nature, circumstances, and societal obligations. Another theme, concerning death, suggests why the men have difficulty keeping this requirement in mind. The pattern of imagery begins with the opening description of a gravestone: "Let fame, that all hunt after in their lives, / Live regist'red upon our brazen tombs" (1.1.1–2). It appears also in the allusion to Katherine's sister, who died for love (5.2.13–15), and in the Pageant of the Nine Worthies, an entertainment about long-dead heroes. Death finally appears embodied in the figure of Marcade announcing the passing of the King of France. Such allusions underscore the court's separation from the world. Up until the end of the play, it remains distant from and unaffected by natural events, such as death. This imagery helps to account for the noblemen's behavior: they make oaths out of keeping with nature and society because their court is disconnected from both.

The theme of oath making is associated with other themes as well, including the reversal of a hierarchy that privileges men over women. Indeed, *Love's Labor's Lost* constantly reverses things that were in the period normally prioritized, such as the precedence of men over women (Patricia Parker, "Preposterous Reversals: *Love's Labour's Lost*," *Modern Language Quarterly* 54.4 [1993]: 435–482). The drama develops through a series of scenes in which the men become increasingly unruly, changing from those who "war against [their] own affections" (1.1.9) to those who "laugh," "clap," "swear," "caper," "cry," "fall," "tumble," and "laugh" (5.2.107–118). Meantime, the women continually deride the men's actions. Such criticism is pointed in 2.1, when the Princess reprimands the King for neglecting hospitality (104–106). The criticism is also evident in their censure of the men's excessive and hyperbolic language. For example, when the King greets the Princess, he says, "Fair Princess, welcome to the court of Navarre" (90). As noted above, the Princess quickly points out that the King's language is excessive and inappropriate to the reality of the situation. Similar moments occur throughout the play. The women not only correct the men but also seek to assert authority over them. In 5.2, the women repeatedly describe their actions as attempts to overthrow the men. Rosaline says of Berowne that she would "o'ersway his state" (5.2.67). The Princess suggests that the women mock the men, since "There's no such sport as sport by sport o'erthrown" (5.2.153). At the end of the scene, the Princess says to the King, "let me o'errule you now" (5.2.515). To put the conflict in terms of the play's persistent imagery of war and weaponry, *Love's Labor's Lost* is a "civil war of wits" (2.1.216) between the women and men. One could argue that the play ends in separation since the men lose this civil war by failing to control their excessive behavior or to manage their linguistic weaponry as skillfully as the women. In the end, *Love's Labor's Lost* does not suggest that women should indeed "o'errule" men; it demonstrates that a society that privileges such men over such women is comedic.

CRITICAL CONTROVERSIES

The major characteristic of *Love's Labor's Lost* is its insistent wordplay. Understandably, then, the major critical controversy concerns how to account for this feature. Even so, the criticism addresses more particularly four major topics: artistic merit; historical or topical references; festivity, including linguistic play and pastimes; and gender and relations between the sexes.

The earliest criticism focuses on relative artistic merit. As we saw earlier, Francis Meres in his *Palladis Tamia* (1598) lists *Love's Labor's Lost* as one of a series of plays that demonstrate Shakespeare's comedic greatness. Despite the promising initial reception, early critics judged the play less positively and were generally critical of its seemingly excessive wordplay. Charles Gildon asserted that it was the work of an amateur: "since it is one of the worst of Shakespeare's plays, nay I think I may say the very worst, I cannot but think that it is his first." Writing in 1765, Samuel Johnson offered conditional praise. Although some parts are "mean, childish, and vulgar," there are still "scattered, through the whole, many sparks of genius" ("Notes on Shakespeare's Plays: *Love's Labour's Lost* [Excerpts]," *Critical Essays*, 52). Into the nineteenth century readers maintained similar views. In 1817 William Hazlitt noted, "If we were to part with any of the author's comedies, it should be this." Yet he conceded, "The observations on the use and abuse of study, and on the power of beauty to quicken the understanding as well as the senses, are excellent" ("*Love's Labour's Lost* from *Characters of Shakespear's Plays*," *Critical Essays*, 61–63). Such severely qualified assessments persisted well into the twentieth century. Nonetheless, about turn of the century, critics developed a new admiration for the play, especially its wordplay. In 1898 Walter Pater published the following appreciation: "There is merriment in it also, with choice illustrations of both wit and humor" (*Critical Essays*, 65). In 1927 Harley Granville-Barker observed, "It abounds in beauties of fancy and phrase, as beautiful today as ever" (*Prefaces to Shakespeare*, first series [London: Sidgwick & Jackson, 1927], 2).

Critics turned to assess the play in an entirely different way around 1900, looking at its historical or topical references. Some writers explored links between the noblemen and the historical figures after whom they were named, showing that the play probably referred to a meeting in 1578 between Henry, King of Navarre, and his wife, Marguerite de Valois (see "Sources for the Play," above). A good deal of criticism also addressed the possibility that Holofernes and Don Armado refer to and satirize Shakespeare's literary and intellectual contemporaries, including John Florio, Thomas Nashe, Gabriel Harvey, George Chapman, and Walter Raleigh. Such arguments are too intricate to be described in detail here, and it is perhaps unnecessary since scholars today have rigorously questioned their significance and accuracy. Nonetheless, the controversy raises questions about the relative usefulness of topical approaches to literature. Students interested in this subject will find a summary of topical criticism of *Love's Labor's Lost* as well as an evenhanded discussion of the benefits and drawbacks of such approaches in Mary Ellen Lamb's "The Nature of Topicality in *Love's Labour's Lost*" (*Shakespeare Survey* 38 [1985]: 49–59).

Beginning in the mid-1950s, critics started to explore another significant aspect of the play, its festivity, both in terms of aristocratic pastimes and linguistic play. In pioneering work in this area, C. L. Barber shows that "Shakespeare made the play out of courtly pleasures" and that the play is "a set exhibition of pastimes and games" (*Shakespeare's Festive Comedy*, 87–88). Others have qualified and elaborated this view, for as much as the play depicts games it also depicts competition (John Turner, "*Love's Labour's Lost*: The Court at Play," in *Shakespeare Out of Court: Dramatizations of Court Society* [London: Macmillan, 1990], 19–48). Most recently, Edward Berry observes that the aristocratic pastime of the hunt forms an important thematic element (*Shakespeare and the Hunt: A Cultural and Social Study* [Cambridge: Cambridge UP, 2001], 59–69).

Developing alongside discussions of pastimes is criticism on language games. For instance, James Calderwood argues that Shakespeare found himself in *Love's Labor's Lost* seduced by the sensual power of language ("*Love's Labour's Lost*: A Wantoning with Words," *Studies in English Literature, 1500–1900* 5.2 [Spring 1965]: 317–332). Kier Elam links linguistic play and pastimes in his analysis of the relationship between word games and a particular kind of festivity, dramatic performance (*Shakespeare's Universe of Discourse: Language-Games in the Comedies* [Cambridge: Cambridge UP, 1984], 235–308).

For the past twenty years or so, most criticism has addressed representations of gender and especially why the play ends in separation. As noted earlier, Peter Erickson shows that the men are unable to think of the women outside of Petrarchan paradigms: "The psychology of male and female stereotypes expressed in the men's poetry," which give women total control, "creates a barrier which keeps the men and women apart." Katherine Eisaman Maus argues that the men and women have different attitudes toward language, especially oaths, and that this difference prompts their separation ("Transfer of Title in *Love's Labor's Lost*: Language, Individualism, Gender," in *Shakespeare Left and Right*, ed. Ivo Kamps [New York: Routledge, 1991], 205–223). Mark Breitenberg suggests that the play reveals and parodies a form of masculine desire, which finds the romantic chase far more fulfilling than consummation (*Anxious Masculinity in Early Modern England* [Cambridge: Cambridge UP, 1996], 128–149). Recent essays also show that explicit and implicit allusions to race, nationality, and religion illuminate topical and thematic elements of the drama (Felicia Hardison Londré, "Elizabethan Views of the 'Other': French, Spanish, and Russians in *Love's Labour's Lost*," *Critical Essays*, 325–341; and Thomas Rist, "Topical Comedy: On the Unity of *Love's Labour's Lost*," *Ben Jonson Journal* 7 (2000): 65–87).

PRODUCTION HISTORY

Love's Labor's Lost was performed several times in the late sixteenth and early seventeenth centuries, for Elizabeth I during the Christmas of 1597 or 1598, at the house of the Earl of Southampton in January 1605, and at least twice before 1631 at Blackfriars Theatre and the Globe. The play's production history mirrors its critical history. Despite such a promising early reception, it was not staged again for more than 200 years. In the eighteenth century, an age when many playwrights wrote adaptations of Shakespeare, *Love's Labor's Lost* inspired one such drama: *The Students* (1762), which seems never to have been acted. In 1836 Covent Garden Theatre mounted the first recorded revival of the play. This production was not a success, in part because the theater closed the one-shilling gallery for the opening performance, sparking demonstrations by disgruntled members of the public. After this inauspicious revival, *Love's Labor's Lost* was only rarely performed in the late nineteenth century.

A series of productions in England during the 1930s and 1940s changed the fortunes of the play. In 1936 Tyrone Guthrie successfully directed it at the Old Vic Theatre, using an elegant set with pavilions, a fountain, and wrought-iron gates. He also used eighteenth-century costumes, a choice that proved very influential. The editor and critic John Dover Wilson argued that this production changed his opinion of a play that seemed difficult to act and make funny: Guthrie "revealed it as a first-rate comedy . . . full of fun, of *permanent* wit, of brilliant and entrancing situation" ("*Love's Labour's Lost*: The Story of a Conversion," *Critical Essays*, 182). Directing in 1946 in Stratford, Peter Brook also used pastel, eighteenth-century costumes. Moreover, he innovatively staged the entrance of Marcade, who appeared dressed completely in black just as the lights began to fade. The contrast between him and the other, brightly dressed figures onstage seemed to augur the end of a golden age (Brook, "From *The Shifting Point*," *Critical Essays*, 362). This production was also a success. Since the 1950s, *Love's Labor's Lost* has been in continual performance in England, the United States, and around the world. Two productions are of particular note. In 1978 with the Royal Shakespeare Company, John Barton deliberately broke with the dominant tradition of using ornate, idealized eighteenth-century locales and dress, opting instead for a spare, naturalistic, autumnal park and homespun Elizabethan costumes. In another Royal Shakespeare Company production, in 1985, Barry Kyle cast a black actress, Josette Simon, in the role of Rosaline, thus emphasizing the character's dark beauty.

Students will most likely first see the play in one of its two film versions. In 1984 Elijah Moshinsky directed it for the British Broadcasting Company as part of their televised series of Shakespeare's complete plays. Returning to the design clichés that Barton tried to counter, Moshinsky set the film in the eighteenth century. In order to highlight the intellectual banter of the nobles, he cut many lines of other characters. The result is a bland, monotone production, described by one critic as "heavy and drained of energy" and "so serene and careful that one lost sight of Shakespeare's quicksilver comedy" (Peter Kemp, "Mellowness Is All," in *Shakespeare on Television: An Anthology of Essays and Reviews*, ed. J. C. Bulman and H. R. Coursen [Hanover, NH: U of New England P, 1988], 312–313). In 2000 Kenneth Branagh directed a feature film version titled *Love's Labour's Lost*, which remade the play in the genre of Hollywood musicals from the 1930s. He cut nearly two-thirds of the lines and replaced them with songs, such as "Cheek to Cheek," by Irving Berlin, Cole Porter, and others. Although far more radical than Moshinsky, Branagh's version is truer to the spirit of the play. The film opens with a series of 1930s newsreels, which emphasize the implications of the King's retreat. Although a world leader, he impetuously and irresponsibly turns his back on political crises that lead to world war. At the same time, the Berlin and Porter songs are now so

A scene from Kenneth Branagh's 2000 film *Love's Labour's Lost*. © Corbis Sygma.

familiar that they are for us—like Petrarchan poems of the sixteenth century—clichéd expressions of love. The songs thus give modern viewers a sense of the conventional and clichéd nature of the noblemen's poetry. The singing and dancing leave much to be desired, but overall the film still nicely captures the tone of Shakespeare's play.

EXPLICATION OF KEY PASSAGES

1.1.1–23. "Let fame, . . . keep it too." The King explains the proposal for his "little academe" (1.1.13). He aims to achieve lasting fame from the project and hopes that he and the courtiers will be "heirs of all eternity" (1.1.7). Later, he modifies this aim, wanting the academy to be a "wonder of the world" (1.1.12) in this life. He also ensures his companions' commitment to the academy, asking them to sign the edict.

The passage appears to be a careful description of objectives and plans. Its measured character is evident in the use of the rhetorical figure *ploce*, the careful reiteration of the same word with a change in sense: "And then *grace* us in the *disgrace* of death" (italics added, 1.1.3). Despite such care, the imagery signals problems with the plan. The King aims to defy nature, to act in "spite of cormorant devouring Time" (1.1.4). But he founds the academy on the impossible principle that action will bring about contemplation (1.1.14). The King uses metaphors of war to describe the project. The courtiers are "brave conquerors" who "war against [their] own affections / And the huge army of the world's desires" (1.1.8–10). They must be "arm'd to do, as sworn to do" (1.1.22). He paradoxically suggests that action, and especially heroic action, will create a "still and contemplative" philosophical academy (1.1.14). Yet as we know, at least with regard to emotions, war does not make peace. The King's closing request points to a different problem. While the men have "sworn for three years' term" to live with the King (1.1.16), they still must "[s]ubscribe to [their] deep oaths, and keep it too" (1.1.23). If oaths are binding, why affirm them in writing? The speech sets up two major issues in the play: the unnatural and illogical nature of the academy and the men's difficulty in making and keeping their oaths.

4.3.285–362. "O, 'tis more than need . . . sever love from charity?" In response to the King's request, "now prove / Our loving lawful, and our faith not torn" (4.3.280–281), Berowne offers this lengthy argument. The main points are simple: When the men swore "[t]o fast, to study, and to see no woman" they committed "[f]lat treason 'gainst the kingly state of youth" (4.3.288–289). Moreover, they denied themselves true teachers, women's eyes, which are "the books, the arts, the academes, / That show, contain, and nourish all the world" (4.3.349–350).

Berowne's strategy is to create a speech that sounds so good that we do not question its logic. He presents many ideas as commonsense truisms. While other "slow arts" (4.3.321) stay entirely within the mind, love heightens the senses: "A lover's eyes will gaze an eagle blind, / A lover's ear will hear the lowest sound" (4.3.331–332). He also appeals to ideas common in Petrarchan poetry: that the eyes of the beloved are all-powerful and that the beloved herself is the source of the male poet's inspiration. Berowne combines the two ideas, suggesting that from women's eyes men learn poetry and much else. Thus the King and courtiers learn "fiery numbers" (4.3.319) from women's eyes. Other poets are similarly inspired: "Never durst poet touch a pen to write / Until his ink were temp'red with Love's sighs" (4.3.343–344). Berowne moves to a close with a chiastic rhetorical flourish: "Let us once lose our oaths to find ourselves, / Or else we lose ourselves to keep our oaths" (4.3.358–359). At the very end, he addresses the central issue, that it is a sin to break oaths, observing that their faith is not broken. For, "It is religion to be thus forsworn" (4.3.360). Applying a general moral imperative to romantic situations, he asserts that since Christian charity requires people to love one another, then the men themselves have a duty to love the women. Over the whole of the speech, Berowne suggests that to forswear the oath is common sense as well as consistent with both nature and religion. The courtier is so eloquent that we, like his credulous friends, believe him without considering whether his argument is sound.

5.2.894–929. "When daisies pied . . . keel the pot." The play ends with the songs of spring and winter. Spring, represented by the cuckoo, describes the joys of that season. Flowers bloom and "paint the meadows with delight" (5.2.897), while shepherds make music, "pipe on oaten straws" (5.2.903). Yet along with beauty, spring brings anxiety. The song of the cuckoo is "unpleasing to a married ear" (5.2.902, 911) since it suggests cuckoldry or infidelity. Winter is a far less pleasant time, when "icicles hang by the wall" (5.2.912) and "all aloud the wind doth blow, / And coughing drowns the parson's saw" (5.2.921–922). Even so, winter brings with it a time of happy domesticity: "Tom bears logs into the hall" (5.2.914) and "greasy Joan doth keel [cool] the pot" (5.2.920, 929).

The songs provide an ambiguous but fitting ending to the play, repeating ideas that run throughout it. In focusing on spring and winter, Shakespeare united the seasons of love and death. The songs emphasize living in harmony with nature, clearly describing the cycle of the seasons, while depicting people who are "[f]it in [their] place and time" (1.1.98), whose activities change with the season. The songs also portray some of the natural ambiguity and hardship of life. While spring is pleasant, it brings fear. While winter is unpleasant, it brings content domestic life. Moreover, the tunes have a ballad-like quality that contrasts sharply with the highly stylized language of the play. They suggest what Berowne's promised rustic speech, "russet yeas" and "honest kersey noes" (5.2.413), might sound like. Most importantly, the songs show the passage of a single year, ending with a realistic and harmonious depiction of married life. In this, they suggest that after a "winter of discontent" (*Richard III*, 1.1.1), the men and women might just enjoy a glorious spring with each other after all.

Annotated Bibliography

Barber, C. L. *Shakespeare's Festive Comedy: A Study of Dramatic Form and Its Relation to Social Custom*. Princeton: Princeton UP, 1959. See especially the chapter on *Love's Labor's Lost*, 87–118. Barber shows how the play represents aristocratic pastimes.

Erickson, Peter B. "The Failure of Relationship between Men and Women in *Love's Labour's Lost*." *Women's Studies* 9.1 (1981): 65–81. Reads the play in terms of conventions of Petrarchan and sixteenth-century love poetry.

Greene, Thomas M. "*Love's Labour's Lost*: The Grace of Society." *Shakespeare Quarterly* 22.4 (Fall 1971): 315–328. According to Greene, the play reflects cultured society, and especially its concern with style and the failure of style.

Londré, Felicia Hardison, ed. *"Love's Labour's Lost": Critical Essays*. New York: Routledge, 1997. An indispensable anthology of critical responses and performance reviews from the 1590s to the mid-1990s.

A Midsummer Night's Dream

Jay L. Halio

PLOT SUMMARY

1.1. *A Midsummer Night's Dream* opens at the court of Duke Theseus in Athens. He complains to Hippolyta, his future bride whom he has captured in a victory over the Amazons, that he is impatient for their wedding day. She reassures him that the four days' wait until the new moon will soon be over. Suddenly Egeus enters with his daughter, Hermia, and her two suitors, Lysander and Demetrius. Egeus wants Hermia to marry Demetrius, but she loves Lysander. Egeus appeals to Theseus to enforce Athens' law, which compels a daughter to obey her father or die. Theseus tells Hermia that she must obey Egeus or else face death or become a nun. He then takes Egeus and Demetrius off with Hippolyta, leaving Hermia and Lysander alone.

Hermia is distraught, but Lysander comforts her and proposes that they elope. She agrees. Her friend Helena enters. Helena loves Demetrius, who has apparently jilted her for Hermia. Lysander and Hermia inform Helena of their plan to elope; then they exit. Helena decides to disclose the elopement to Demetrius, hoping thereby to get a little attention from him.

1.2. Peter Quince assembles his friends, all of them Athenian laborers, to begin planning a play they hope to perform before the duke on his wedding day. The play is "Pyramus and Thisby," and Quince distributes the parts, after overcoming difficulties that Bottom the weaver, a rather egotistical person, causes when he insists on playing more than the one role assigned to him. The would-be actors agree to meet the next night in the "palace wood" outside the town to begin rehearsing (1.2.101).

2.1. This scene is set in the forest outside Athens, but it seems a very English wood. Puck and a fairy meet and introduce themselves. Oberon, king of the fairies, and Titania, his queen, then enter with their trains. They have been quarreling over possession of a little Indian boy, whom Titania has been rearing ever since his mother, a votary of hers, died in childbirth. Oberon wants him as one of his followers, but Titania refuses to give up the child. As a result of their quarrel, nature has turned topsy-turvy. After Titania leaves with her train, Oberon plots with Puck to teach her a lesson. He sends Puck to fetch a magic flower, the juice of which spread on someone's eyes will make that person fall in love with the first living creature he or she sees.

After Puck goes for the flower, Demetrius and Helena enter. He tries to get rid of her while he pursues Hermia, but she stubbornly refuses to depart. Oberon, invisible to them, overhears their quarrel and determines to help Helena. When the young couple leave and Puck re-enters with the magic flower, Oberon tells his henchman to find the Athenian and put the magic juice on his eyes while Oberon goes and does the same to Titania.

2.2. Meanwhile, Titania is sung to sleep in her bower by her fairies. Oberon enters, puts the potion on her eyes, and leaves. Lysander and Hermia enter, and Lysander admits they are lost. Worn out, they go to sleep. Puck enters and puts the magic potion on Lysander's eyes, not realizing that this is not the Athenian Oberon meant. Puck exits, and Demetrius and Helena enter, still quarreling. Demetrius does not see Hermia sleeping and runs off. Helena finds Lysander, who awakens and immediately declares his love for her. Helena thinks he is merely mocking her and leaves, with Lysander following. Hermia awakes, frightened by a nightmare, only to find Lysander gone. She goes off to look for him.

3.1. Quince and his friends have met in the forest to rehearse their play. When Puck sees them, he decides to have some fun. Bottom goes off to await his cue, but when he returns he wears an ass's head that Puck has put on him. His friends, terribly frightened, run off, leaving Bottom alone. He consoles himself by singing a song, which wakens Titania. She at once falls in love with him and summons her fairies to take him to her bower.

3.2. Oberon wonders how his plans are working out. Puck enters and tells him that Titania has fallen in love with a monster. He also says that he has carried out Oberon's orders to anoint the Athenian man, but when Demetrius and Hermia enter, Puck confesses that is not the man he anointed. Demetrius and Hermia quarrel, and Hermia runs off, leaving Demetrius alone to lie down and sleep. Oberon commands Puck to find Helena and bring her there while he puts the magic potion on Demetrius's eyes. Puck returns with Lysander and Helena; and when Demetrius awakens, Helena finds herself now wooed by both men. She thinks it is all a trick they are playing on her; when Hermia arrives, Helena accuses her, too, of being in on the plot. Now all four lovers are at odds with each other, much to Puck's mischievous delight, though not Oberon's. The fairy king determines to make everything come out right and orders Puck to see that it does.

The quarrel between the two men over Helena and between Helena and Hermia grows more violent. Oberon therefore commands Puck to overcast the night with fog so that the lovers cannot see each other any longer. Puck does so and then leads them a merry chase, until, thoroughly worn out, they each fall asleep. Thereupon Puck places the antidote on Lysander's eyes so that he will once more be in love with Hermia, while Demetrius will continue to love Helena.

4.1. Oberon watches Titania doting on Bottom in his ass's head, while her fairies bring Bottom things to eat and play music. The fairies depart as Titania and Bottom fall asleep. Puck enters. Oberon tells him he has begun to pity his queen, who has finally surrendered the little Indian to him (offstage). Oberon places the antidote on her eyes; when she awakens, they are reconciled. Bottom sleeps on. At this point, Theseus and Hippolyta enter and see the two young couples asleep. Awakened, they cannot explain quite what has happened to them, but seeing that they are now properly matched up, Theseus overrules Egeus's insistence that Hermia marry Demetrius. He invites the young people to join him at the marriage altar, where all three couples will be wed that night.

After everyone departs, Bottom wakes up, his ass-head gone. In soliloquy he wonders at the strange experience he has had.

4.2. In Peter Quince's carpenter shop, Bottom's friends lament what has happened to him, when suddenly he appears and tells them that their play has been recommended for performance. Everyone is overjoyed to see him, and they get ready now to perform before the Duke.

5.1. Theseus and Hippolyta discuss what has happened. The young lovers enter, and Theseus calls Philostrate to plan the evening's festivities. After rejecting several proposed entertainments as unsuitable, Theseus decides on "Pyramus and Thisby," which Quince and his fellows then perform in an extremely amateurish and unintentionally hilarious fashion. Rejecting their epilogue, Theseus settles for the Bergomask dance, after which he summons all to bed. Puck enters, preparing the way for Oberon, Titania, and their trains, who come in and bless the house. When they depart, Puck recites his epilogue.

PUBLICATION HISTORY

A Midsummer Night's Dream is one of Shakespeare's "lyrical" plays, a group that includes *Romeo and Juliet*, *Richard II*, and the last act of *The Merchant of Venice*. These works are noteworthy for the prevalence of sustained flights of poetry which, while they scarcely move the action forward, are delightful in and of themselves. They include such passages as Mercutio's Queen Mab speech and Juliet's invocation to night in *Romeo and Juliet* (1.4.53–94, 3.2.1–31); John of Gaunt's apostrophe to England and Richard's last soliloquy in *Richard II* (2.1.31–68, 5.5.1–66); Lorenzo's lines on the moonlight and the music of the spheres in *The Merchant of Venice* (5.1.49–88); and Oberon's description of the flower love-in-idleness and his verses on Titania's bower (2.1.155–169, 2.1.249–256). Scholars date these plays in the mid-1590s, with *A Midsummer Night's Dream* usually 1595–1596. They are less certain whether *A Midsummer Night's Dream* preceded or followed *Romeo and Juliet*, though the farcical rendering of "Pyramus and Thisby" suggests that Shakespeare may have been spoofing his own efforts in the tragedy he had already written.

A Midsummer Night's Dream was not published until 1600, when it appeared in quarto form printed by Richard Braddock for Thomas Fisher. How Fisher came to possess a manuscript of the play for publication is not known. Since the play was entered in the Stationers' Register, its printing was most likely authorized by Shakespeare's acting company. The copy Fisher handed over to Braddock was likely Shakespeare's so-called foul papers, that is, his early draft of the play—a theory supported by signs of revision found in this quarto (Q1). For example, Theseus's lines at 5.1.2–27 are mislined in Q1, very likely because Shakespeare inserted some additional text in the margin of his copy. The compositor did his best to incorporate the additional material in the passage, but in doing so he seriously disturbed the meter. Other support for the theory of foul papers provenance includes spellings usually regarded as peculiar to Shakespeare, stage directions (or the absence of them), and a tendency to vary speech headings.

Q1 was reprinted in 1619 as one of the quartos that Thomas Pavier hoped to publish as part of a collected edition of Shakespeare's works. When that project had to be abandoned, Pavier falsely dated the quartos he had already printed, thereby hoping to sell them as the original ones. Like other reprints, Q2 *Dream* corrects some errors and introduces others, but it has no real textual authority. It is important only because a marked-up copy of this quarto, printed in William Jaggard's shop, was apparently used as copy for the text of the First Folio, 1623, which Jaggard also printed.

The reprint of the play in the Folio shows several alterations of copy that may derive from a playhouse manuscript. It adds or clarifies a good many stage directions. At the same time, it further corrupts the text beyond the errors introduced by Q2. Among the most important alterations is the substitution of Egeus for Philostrate in act 5. Furthermore, in the Folio Lysander reads the list of entertainments presented to Theseus, who comments upon them; in the Q1 version Theseus both reads and comments. Another indication of a playhouse source, probably a promptbook, is the stage direction at 5.1.126, where the entrance of Pyramus and Thisby is preceded by "*Tawyer with a Trumpet before him.*" William Tawyer was a member of the King's Men, a servant to John Heminge, who with Henry Condell collected the plays for the Folio.

Another indication of later revision and promptbook source is the stage direction at the end of act 3: "*They sleepe all the Act.*" Act divisions do not appear in Q1 or Q2 and are introduced somewhat arbitrarily in the Folio. In this new stage direction, "Act" may refer to the interval between the acts, or to the music played during the interval. Intervals were introduced in the seventeenth century, especially in the indoor private theaters, such as the Blackfriars Playhouse, which the King's Men began using in 1609. The Folio was reprinted in 1632 and again in 1663–1664 and 1685, but the changes that appear in these reprints, like those in Q2, have no authority.

Modern editions of Shakespeare's plays begin with Nicholas Rowe's of 1709. Rowe corrected some of the mislineation, and Lewis Theobald corrected still more in his 1733 edition. Eighteenth-century editors not only divided acts into numbered scenes, they also introduced scene locations—a practice not abandoned until late-twentieth-century editions. Acting versions of the play, in contrast, typically altered the text drastically to conform to neoclassical notions of decorum. The low comedy of Bottom and his fellows was usually split off into separate plays, called "drolls," and many songs were introduced into the productions, most of them by authors other than Shakespeare (see "Production History," below).

SOURCES FOR THE PLAY

Although no specific source for the action of *A Midsummer Night's Dream* has been discovered, Shakespeare drew upon a variety of works for his characters and especially for the plot of "Pyramus and Thisby." The fairies in his play were new to the stage, though fairy lore itself had a long and ancient tradition. Chaucer's Wife of Bath, for instance, mentions fairies and elves that still existed, though they could no longer be seen. Fairies were of two sorts—benign and malignant; belief in either kind was strongly opposed by the church. Malignant ones were associated with witchcraft, benign ones with helpful deeds, such as cleaning houses or leaving money in shoes. Shakespeare carefully distinguished his fairies from demons at 3.2.382–393.

Shakespeare's fairies varied in size, apparently. Oberon and Titania appear to be of human stature, whereas their trains seem to be quite small. Whether they had wings or not is uncertain; Puck can put a girdle round the earth in forty minutes (2.1.175–176), but his speed may be a function of some resource other than wings.

Oberon derives from a character in Lord Berner's translation of the French romance *Huon of Bordeaux* (1533), or possibly from a play, now lost but mentioned in Philip Henslowe's diary, that was performed in the Christmas season 1593–1594. Titania, however, comes from Ovid's *Metamorphoses*, 3.173, where she is referred to as Diana, goddess of the moon and the chase. She is clearly different from Mab, the other fairy queen, which Mercutio describes in *Romeo and Juliet* (1.4.53–95). Possibly Shakespeare got his idea for the king and queen of fairies from Chaucer's "The Merchant's Tale," where they are named Pluto and Prosperpine and quarrel about love, sex, and conjugal relations. But Shakespeare added the bit about the Indian boy that is the source for their dispute in his play.

Puck has a much richer history in fairy lore than do Oberon and Titania. He is also called Robin Goodfellow. Both names, or versions of them, appear in country lore, although Shakespeare may also have read about him in Reginald Scot's *Discoverie of Witchcraft* (1584), which deals with fairies and transformations as well as witches. While Scot denied that fairies could have emotions similar to those of human beings, Shakespeare clearly endowed his fairies with recognizable human passions.

Theseus and Hippolyta are both drawn from classical sources. For the former, Shakespeare drew upon the *Life of Theseus* in Plutarch's *Parallel Lives of Noble Greeks and Romans*, translated into English by Sir Thomas North (1579), and Chaucer's "The Knight's Tale" in the *Canterbury Tales*. Theseus was famous for his exploits in both love and war, as well as for being a great statesman. According to Plutarch, he battled the Amazons, who were at war with Athens, and captured Antiopa, also called Hippolyta, the name used by Shakespeare. Shakespeare's Theseus is a good deal more sympathetic than the notorious character in Plutarch's account. Shakespeare does not make much of Hippolyta or her Amazonian heritage in the play, although in some stage productions she is given additional attributes and actions to enhance her part.

Peter Quince and his fellows come right out of Shakespeare's own Warwickshire environs. But what are these simple workmen doing in classical Athens? Like Audrey and William in *As You Like It*, they add another level of reality to the complex whole that is this play. In other words, they help bridge the gap between imagined reality and ordinary existence.

Bottom, however, is a special case. Bottom is the only one in the play who has direct and conscious interaction with the fairies. The most obvious source for his transformation into an ass is Lucius Apuleius's *The Golden Ass*, translated into English by William Aldington (1566). Another influence may have been the story of King Midas, as told by Thomas Cooper in *Thesaurus Linguae Romanae et Britannicae* (1565). For choosing Pan over Apollo, Midas was punished by being endowed with the long ears of an ass. Another account of a man turned into an ass appears in Scot's *Discoverie of Witchcraft*. Shakespeare may have known still other stories of a man turned into an ass, such as Erasmus's *Praise of Folly*.

The story of Pyramus and Thisby is one of several Shakespeare borrowed from his favorite Latin author, Ovid. It appears in the *Metamorphoses*, Book 4, lines 67–201, as translated into English by William Golding (1567). The forbidden love of the couple appears as Shakespeare dramatizes it, only not farcically. One aspect of the story that Shakespeare omits is the way Pyramus's blood stains the mulberry tree under which he was to meet with Thisby and elope. Other variations from Ovid in Quince's representation are the introduction of Moonshine, the animation of Wall, and the change of the lioness into Lion, with some explanatory lines. Golding's fourteeners (fourteen-syllable lines), moreover, may have suggested the old-fashioned poetic style (in rhymed pentameters, not fourteeners) that Shakespeare uses for the play within the play.

STRUCTURE AND PLOTTING

A Midsummer Night's Dream has a wonderfully complex dramatic structure consisting of several planes, or levels, of reality. On one level, with which the play opens, is the court of Theseus and his nobility, which includes the young lovers and their problems. On another level is the fairy world in the moonlit forest, the world of imagination, if you will, but none the less real for that. Yet another level is the world of the mechanicals, the common workmen. Finally, we have the world of mythology or legend, the world of Pyramus and Thisby, portrayed in farcical manner by the mechanicals but nevertheless representing still another plane of reality.

Shakespeare develops the action in such a way that the various planes of reality come into contact and even intersect with each other without, however, confusing the audience. Thus, Oberon stands by and overhears the quarrel between Demetrius and Helena and determines to intervene to help the young woman. When Puck unintentionally mistakes Lysander for Demetrius and delights in the confusion that results among the four young people, Oberon insists on setting things right.

At another level, the quarrel between Oberon and Titania has dire effects on the natural world (see 2.1.81–117). Elizabethans tended to believe in an organic theory of nature, that is, everything was somehow connected and interrelated; hence, when one part of nature was disordered, other parts also became disrupted. In *Macbeth*, for example, when the rightful and hallowed King Duncan is murdered, other aspects in the world of nature go awry (see 2.4). Only when Oberon and Titania are reconciled do things resume their proper order again.

Peter Quince and his fellows add another dimension to the dramatic structure and are important components of it. Not only does Bottom play a part in Oberon's plot against his queen, but the playlet that he and the others perform has important implications. Through this device Shakespeare explores some of the aspects of performance of which both amateurs and professionals must be aware. The literal-mindedness that the mechanicals share strikes a cautionary note to all thespians concerning the nature of performance. Theseus's appeal to the imagination on the part of the audience (5.1.211–212) balances the anxiety of the mechanicals regarding such problems as bringing in moonlight or the impersonation of a lion among the ladies.

Theseus seems amused by the "very tragical mirth" of Pyramus and Thisby that Quince and his fellows propose to perform before him (5.1.57), and indeed the duke and his guests have a very good time at the laborers' expense as they bumble through their play within the play. But the tragedy of Pyramus and Thisby has significance beyond the entertainment the mechanicals provide. For the theater audience, it is a not-so-subtle reminder that not all love stories turn out as well as those of Lysander and Hermia, Demetrius and Helena, or even Theseus and Hippolyta. What determines the fate of Pyramus and Thisby is that, unlike the experience of the young Athenians, no providential character, like Oberon, and no wise ruler, like Theseus, is there to intervene in their perplexity and to make things come out right.

MAIN CHARACTERS

Theseus

As ruler over Athens, Theseus is the embodiment of right reason coupled with compassion. His reconciliation with Hippolyta, whom he has conquered in battle but now intends to wed, sets the keynote for one of the main themes of the play: bringing order out of confusion. When Egeus enters with his daughter, insisting on his prerogative as her father and invoking the laws of Athens, Theseus at first appears to have no recourse but to side with the old man and warn Hermia of the consequences if she disobeys. But later, after their adventures in the forest cause the two young couples to resolve their differences, Theseus wisely overrules Egeus and lets Hermia and Lysander get married; in fact, he invites them and the other couple to join with him and Hippolyta at the marriage altar that very evening.

As a representative of rational Athens, Theseus speaks his lines on the imagination at the beginning of act 5 and scoffs at the way some people let their fancy run away with them, specifically linking "the lunatic, the lover, and the poet" (5.1.7). He is the opposite of Hippolyta, who senses that there is something more to what the young lovers have experienced (5.1.27). Yet a little later on, he invokes the imagination as a way of enjoying drama, even the inept performance of the mechanicals, which Hippolyta regards as "the silliest stuff" that she has ever heard (5.1.210). Theseus may be little more than one of Shakespeare's stage dukes, but he is given some important lines nevertheless.

Hippolyta

As a vanquished Amazon, Hippolyta has been variously portrayed as a caged tigress, a morose victim, or a compassionate feminist where Hermia and her problem are concerned. True, she has very few lines; therefore, actors follow whatever subtext they or their directors choose. But clearly at the outset she seems reconciled or at least resigned to becoming Theseus's queen, as she attempts to assuage his impatience for their nuptial day. While she says nothing during the contretemps between Hermia and her father, she may well express through body language—perhaps even a compassionate embrace—her sympathy for the younger woman. She further complements Theseus's rationalism in 5.1 when she expresses her belief that the lovers' account of their forest adventures amounts to "something of great constancy" and not merely "fancy's images" (5.1.23–26).

Egeus

Egeus has a small role in the play but helps to trigger some of the major action by insisting that his daughter, Hermia, must marry Demetrius and not the man she loves. Although he appears to win the first round in the quarrel, when Theseus sides with him and warns Hermia what she must do, he loses out later when Theseus and his entourage find the lovers asleep in the forest the morning after their adventures. Shakespeare gives Egeus no lines to show how he reacts to Theseus's decision to let Hermia marry Lysander (4.1.179). He may disappear from the action altogether after this, but in the Folio he replaces Philostrate in bringing in the list of proposed entertainments for the wedding night festivities. Possibly he has overcome his dismay by then, although we have no certain way of telling what his demeanor is.

Hermia and Helena

These two young women have been very close friends since childhood, but when events befall them in the forest, they become temporarily opposed. Hermia is a very determined young woman, intent on marrying the man she loves, not the one her father says she must wed. She readily accepts Lysander's proposal that they elope to escape the rigors of Athenian law. She is in other ways a very proper young maiden, refusing the let Lysander lie too close to her when they decide to go to sleep in the forest (2.2.56–60). But when she thinks Helena has betrayed her by seducing Lysander, she shows how ferocious she can become.

Helena, by contrast, is rather pathetic. Having lost Demetrius's affection, she longs for him like any forlorn lover. She seizes on the opportunity to betray the confidence of Hermia and Lysander by revealing their elopement to Demetrius. She hopes that her disclosure will prompt Demetrius to throw some kind of bone her way; in fact, she calls herself his "spaniel" when she follows him into the forest (2.1.203–210). After Puck mixes everything up so that both Lysander and Demetrius pursue her as her lovers, she becomes distraught, thinking that they all, Hermia included, are playing a vile trick on her. Only at the end, when the confusion has been sorted out by Puck, do both women seem to come to their senses. Interestingly, after their few utterances in 4.1, they have no other lines for the rest of the play and sit like obedient wives with their more voluble husbands during the performance of the play within the play.

Lysander and Demetrius

Many readers find it hard to differentiate between these two young men and therefore to understand Egeus's preference for one over the other. As Lysander says, he is as well derived as Demetrius and as well possessed, that is, his fortune equals that of Demetrius (1.1.99–101). If Helena is taller than Hermia and thereby can be further differentiated from her (3.2.291), no similar distinction can be found to tell one young man from the other. Yet Hermia loves Lysander and feels nothing for Demetrius, who has apparently jilted Helena for her. But why he forsakes Helena is not clear, either. These individual preferences must simply be accepted as the givens of the play.

Oberon

Oberon is one of the more complex characters in the play. On the one hand, he is an imperious husband and ruler and perhaps not even a very faithful one (see, for example, 2.1.64ff). He demands the little Indian boy of Titania; when she refuses, he severely punishes her. Only after he finds her in a pitiable state does he relent, and only after she has acceded to his demand. On the other hand, he is very compassionate regarding the plight of the Athenian lovers and directs Puck to sort things out for them. When Puck mixes things up, Oberon becomes annoyed and makes Puck correct his errors. At the end, reconciled with Titania, he blesses the house of Theseus after all the couples have gone to bed, proving that he and his fairy band are, as he explains, not malevolent creatures but "spirits of another sort" (3.2.388).

Titania

The fairy queen is a delightful character who tries valiantly to stand up against Oberon and maintain her rights. For this self-assertion she is rightly championed by many feminists. She fails only because of Oberon's nefarious scheming. She is sexy and, like Oberon, perhaps has her affairs (2.1.74–80). When she is under the spell Oberon has cast, she makes ardent love to Bottom. After the spell is removed, she recognizes with horror what seems to her to have been a terrible "vision" (4.1.76–77).

Titania's relationship with the Indian woman who was her devoted follower shows her affectionate and compassionate nature, especially in her willingness to rear the child the woman left behind when she died. When Oberon gets his way, Titania is willing to become reconciled, calls for music, and joins with Oberon in a dance that reflects their newfound concord. She joins with him, too, in blessing Theseus's house and its occupants.

Puck

Puck, or Robin Goodfellow, is a mischievous fairy and Oberon's right-hand man. He carries out his master's orders as well and as quickly as he knows how, but he delights in the confusion he inadvertently causes by anointing Lysander's eyes instead of Demetrius's. He enjoys watching the follies of the young lovers, as they chase each other around the forest and comments, "Lord, what fools these mortals be" (3.2.115). He deliberately plays a trick on Bottom by giving him an ass's head, which frightens away all of Bottom's friends. Puck is further pleased when Titania becomes infatuated with the transformed Bottom. Under Oberon's direction, however, he has to curtail his pranks and get the lovers paired up properly, removing the potion from Lysander's eyes but leaving it on the eyes of Demetrius.

Peter Quince

Quince is the leader of the "rude mechanicals" (3.2.9), or workmen, whom he gathers together to rehearse "Pyramus and Thisby" for performance before Theseus and Hippolyta on their wedding night. Somewhat officious, he deals with his band of would-be thespians as diplomatically as he can. He seems to be the most literate of the bunch, correcting their mispronunciations and other errors. He shows his effectiveness when dealing with Bottom, who wants to have all the parts in the play.

Quince obviously suffers from some stage fright in delivering his Prologue (5.1.108–117), getting the punctuation wrong and thereby reversing his intended meaning.

Bottom

Bottom the weaver is one of the play's most important characters. While he is rather pretentious in wanting to play more than his assigned role in "Pyramus and Thisby," he is also cooperative in solving the production problems the thespians identify (see 3.1.9ff). When Puck transforms him into an ass, he refuses to be daunted by his friends' horror; he cheers himself up by singing and walking about until Titania awakens and falls in love with him. Here, Bottom is at his best. He does not let himself become overly flattered by her attentions and indeed retains his mother wit. And when Puck removes the spell, Bottom knows well enough that he has had "a most rare vision," a dream "past the wit of man to say what dream it was" (4.1.204–205); therefore, he wisely does not try to examine it too closely.

Very popular among his friends, who worry about him while he is gone, Bottom takes the lead in "Pyramus and Thisby." His overacting gets a lot of unintended laughs because of the farcical way he and the others play their roles. From time to time he interrupts the action to reassure the audience that nothing is amiss, completely unaware of the art of illusion.

DEVICES AND TECHNIQUES

Stylistic Variety

Shakespeare uses a variety of styles in *A Midsummer Night's Dream* for different effects. His basic style is the iambic pentameter blank verse with which the play begins. It is not the very elevated or "high" style of the history plays, but the formal style of the court here and elsewhere. Oberon and Titania speak in this formal style, appropriate to their characters as king and queen of the fairies, but Puck varies his verse, using trimeter and other short measures, as at 3.2.396–399. The lullaby the fairies sing in 2.2 also varies the meter, using rhyme as well. Oberon changes from blank verse to tetrameter rhymes in an incantatory style when he applies the potion to Titania's eyes at 2.2.27–34.

A more conversational style suitable for dialogue among friends characterizes the language used among the young lovers, but even then Shakespeare's style changes from time to time. For example, at 1.1.194–201 Helena and Hermia engage in rhymed stichomythia (short exchanges). Rhymed pentameters follow in the discussion between Hermia and Lysander and concluding in Helena's soliloquy, which ends the scene.

Shakespeare switches to prose for the mechanicals' scenes. It is a very simple sort of prose, again appropriate to the station and conversation of these simple working-class folk. When they perform "Pyramus and Thisby" before the duke and his guests, they employ an old-fashioned style of verse, varying rhymed dimeter and trimeter lines. A harbinger of this style appears at 1.2.31–38, when Bottom gives us a bit of "Ercles' vein" (1.2.40). In this way Shakespeare shows the naïveté of the humble thespians, but at the same time he sets off the play within the play from the action proper of the *Dream*, in a manner similar to the way he sets off "The Murder of Gonzago" in *Hamlet*.

Imagery

As in many of his romantic comedies, Shakespeare uses an abundance of imagery, particularly patterns of imagery that express the emotions of love. Interestingly, he sometimes undercuts these very expressions to suggest the complexity of attitude or emotion that the characters may or may not realize they experience. For example, at 1.1.169–178, Hermia swears to meet Lysander and elope; she begins by invoking Cupid's bow, his arrow with the golden head, Venus's doves, and so forth, but then she suddenly switches to images of betrayal, such as the fire that burned Dido after Aeneas abandoned her. Elsewhere, Oberon describes in very mellifluous language the flower-covered bank where Titania lies (2.1.249–258). He creates a most attractive picture, which tends to lull audiences and readers into complacency, until they realize that this is the setting where he will play a dirty trick upon his queen, making her "full of hateful fantasies" (2.1.258).

Images of eyes and seeing pervade *A Midsummer Night's Dream*, beginning with Hermia's complaint: "I would my father look'd but with my eyes" (1.1.56). Helena complains that Demetrius dotes on Hermia's eyes, even though she herself is just as fair. But, she says,

> Things base and vile, holding no quantity,
> Love can transpose to form and dignity.
> Love looks not with the eyes but with the mind;
> And therefore is wing'd Cupid painted blind.
> Nor hath Love's mind of any judgment taste;
> Wings, and no eyes, figure unheedy haste;
> And therefore is Love said to be a child,
> Because in choice he is so oft beguil'd. (1.1.232–239)

Until Demetrius looked on Hermia's eyes, she continues, he swore he loved her best. The senses, especially eyesight, are deceptive.

Moonlight provides the predominant imagery in this play, which after all is *A Midsummer Night's Dream*. At the very outset, Theseus is impatient for the old moon to wane so that he may wed Hippolyta under a new moon. His bride continues the imagery, describing the moon as "a silver bow / New bent in heaven" (1.1.9–10), a reflection, too, of the battles they formerly had fought. Theseus picks up the cue and promises to wed her "in another key, / With pomp, with triumph, and with revelling" (1.1.18–19).

Moon imagery suffuses 2.1. When Oberon and Titania enter, he greets his queen with "Ill met by moonlight, proud Titania" (2.1.90). A few lines later he relates how he discovered the magic flower when he saw an armed Cupid "Flying between the cold moon and the earth" (2.1.156). In the next act, as Quince and his fellows gather to rehearse, they ponder certain production problems; one of them is how to bring moonlight into their scene. In the event, they solve the problem by having one of their troupe play Moonshine, with unintended comic effect.

All of the action of the central scenes takes place at night, with a moon shining upon the lovers as they stumble across the forest as well as upon Titania and Bottom (with his ass's head) lying together in her bower. So prevalent is the imagery of moon that Caroline Spurgeon (*Shakespeare's Imagery and What It Tells Us* [Cambridge: Cambridge UP, 1971], 260) records twenty-eight uses of the word "moon" in *Dream*, three and a half times more than in any other Shakespeare play. "Moonlight" is also used more in this play than in all the other plays combined. The association of the moonlit night with midsummer madness is more implied than explicit, although Theseus's lines on the imagination at the beginning of act 5 clearly point in that direction.

Images of nature—woodlands, birds, flowers, and so forth—are not uncommon in Shakespeare's romantic comedies, but they appear here in superabundance, as Spurgeon notes (261–263). The lullaby with which Titania's fairies sing her to sleep is loaded with images of snakes, hedgehogs, and other scary creatures, curiously enough. When Puck decides to have fun with Peter Quince and his friends, he determines to lead them about in the form sometimes of a horse or a hound, "A hog, a headless bear, sometime a fire, / And neigh, and bark, and grunt, and roar, and burn, / Like horse, hound, bog, bear, fire, at every turn" (3.1.108–111). Cheering himself after his friends abandon him in the forest, Bottom sings a song about birds:

> The woosel cock so black of hue,
> > With orange-tawny bill,
> The throstle with his note so true,
> > The wren with little quill— . . .
> The finch, the sparrow, and the lark,
> > The plain-song cuckoo grey,
> Whose note full many a man doth mark,
> > And dares not answer nay— (3.1.125–128, 130–134)

Even Titania's fairies have colorful names taken from nature: Peaseblossom, Cobweb, Mustardseed, Moth.

THEMES AND MEANINGS

Love in a variety of forms is the central concern of *A Midsummer Night's Dream*. But like other Shakespeare plays, *Dream* develops many themes, often interrelated, such as the art of stage performance, reality and illusion, reason versus passion, and the creation of concord out of discord.

Romantic, Mature, and Married Love

Shakespeare knew that the varieties of love are many, if not infinite. In *A Midsummer Night's Dream* he does not treat all of them but focuses instead on a few major kinds of love: romantic young love, mature love, and married love.

The play opens with a striking contrast of romantic and mature love. Theseus and Hippolyta are experienced grownups about to be married. Yet Theseus's opening lines suggest the impatient longing of any teenager. Showing a woman's common sense (typical of Shakespeare's comic heroines), Hippolyta reassures her fiancé that the time will pass quickly enough, as assuredly it does. Recovering a measure of equanimity, Theseus sends his master of revels, Philostrate, to prepare for the wedding.

The interruption by Egeus and three of the young lovers begins part of that entertainment (and ours), though not exactly what Theseus had in mind. The love between Hermia and Lysander, and Demetrius's interference, abetted by Hermia's father, contrasts with the more settled relationship between Theseus and Hippolyta. Egeus, like Brabantio later in *Othello*, is convinced that Lysander has "bewitch'd" the bosom of his child (1.1.27). Old man that he is, he cannot understand the true beguilements of young love and believes Lysander has won his daughter's love by singing "With faining voice verses of faining love," by which he has "stol'n the impression of her fantasy" (1.1.31–32). To him, the love his daughter feels for Lysander is "fantasy," not real; it is the result of her immaturity, or "unhardened youth" (1.1.35). He insists on the prerogative of a parent to determine whom his daughter will marry, and his choice is Demetrius.

On her part, Hermia stands firm in her love for Lysander and refuses to yield to her father's demand. She has the stubbornness of youth, despite the penalties that Theseus reminds her the law retains should she disobey. Here authority as determined by law, another important theme, comes into direct conflict with love, as it will later on in the relationship between Oberon and Titania. Lysander, too, refuses to yield to Egeus's demand. But instead of insisting solely on his love, he argues in terms he thinks Egeus will better comprehend:

> I am, my lord, as well deriv'd as he,
> As well possess'd; my love is more than his;
> My fortunes every way as fairly rank'd
> (If not with vantage) as Demetrius'. (1.1.99–102)

He then brings in other arguments that he thinks will enhance his position: unlike Demetrius, he has Hermia's love, and besides, Demetrius is fickle: he has already jilted Helena.

Left alone, Hermia and Lysander commiserate with each other. Lysander reminds his love, "The course of true love never did run smooth" (1.1.134). Hermia sensibly counsels patience (1.1.152); but he immediately hits upon a different plan, one that reflects the impetuosity of youth (as it did in *Romeo and Juliet*): elopement. No sooner does Hermia swear to the plan, than Helena enters with her own love problems.

Forsaken by Demetrius, Helena bemoans the fact and envies Hermia. She asks her friend "with what art / You sway the motion of Demetrius' heart" (1.1.192–193). She knows she is as pretty as Hermia; she knows, too, that love is irrational, for in spite of everything, she still loves Demetrius. Helena comments on the transforming power of love, which subsequent events in the play demonstrate only too vividly. She is right, too, about Cupid's blindness (see 1.1.232–239, quoted above). But as subsequent events also show, love is often led by the eyes. Shakespeare says as much in the song that precedes Bassanio's choice of a casket in *The Merchant of Venice*:

> Tell me where is fancy bred,
> Or in the heart or in the head?
> How begot, how nourished?

> Reply, reply.
> It is engend'red in the eyes,
> With gazing fed, and fancy dies
> In the cradle where it lies. (3.2.63–69)

"Fancy" in this context, of course, refers to love, or perhaps imagined love, not real love. Both Lysander and Demetrius, as well as Titania, will be vigorously led astray by their eyes, once the juice of the flower, appropriately named love-in-idleness, is placed on that part of their anatomy.

After Lysander's eyes have been anointed, he awakes to see Helena before him in the forest and immediately professes his love for her. This shows how powerfully irrational love can blind the eyes and pervert the reason. Much of what he says is true, but his point of reference is distorted by the effect of the potion:

> Who will not change a raven for a dove?
> The will of man is by his reason sway'd;
> And reason says you are the worthier maid.
> Things growing are not ripe until their season,
> So I, being young, till now ripe not to reason;
> And touching now the point of human skill,
> Reason becomes the marshal to my will,
> And leads me to your eyes. (2.2.114–121)

In a well-balanced, healthy state, one is controlled by reason, but it is not reason telling Lysander that Helena is worthier than Hermia. He is, moreover, far from being "ripe," that is, mature, to the point where he is under rational control of his actions. Nor is any one of the other young lovers during the central episodes, as they chase each other about in the forest, propelled by irrational forces they barely comprehend, if at all.

All this is highly comical to the audience, though not to the lovers. It is also highly erotic. According to Jan Kott, "The *Dream* is the most erotic of Shakespeare's plays. In no other tragedy or comedy of his, except *Troilus and Cressida*, is the eroticism expressed so brutally" (*Shakespeare Our Contemporary*, 2nd ed., trans. Boleslaw Taborski [London: Methuen, 1967], 175). As evidence for the brutality, he cites, for example, the dialogue at 3.2.260–264, where Lysander yells venom at Hermia, calling her names and desperately trying to throw her off him. In many modern productions, as in the Peter Hall film, the lovers are shown scrambling about, their clothes torn and besplattered with mud (see "Production History" below). Warrant for this description lies partly in Hermia's lines after she battles with Helena and the others and wearily lies down to sleep:

> Never so weary, never so in woe,
> Bedabbled with dew, and torn with briers,
> I can no further crawl, no further go;
> My legs can keep no pace with my desires. (3.2.442–445)

The relationship between Titania and Bottom with his ass's head is further evidence that Kott gives of the brutal eroticism in the play. Although he overstates the situation, arguing that "The slender, tender and lyrical Titania longs for animal love" (183), her devotion to the "monster" whom she drags off to bed shows the depths to which irrational love can lead.

When the eyes are restored to their normal function, reason resumes control. Lysander once again loves Hermia, and Titania loathes the sight of the "monster," Bottom (4.1.76). Demetrius's eyes, however, retain the love potion. He tries as well as he can to explain to the duke what has happened to make him renounce his love for Hermia and return to Helena, but he is wise enough to admit he really does not know the reason (see 4.1.161–173).

The love potion that Oberon has directed Puck to administer thus has another function. Not only can it cause someone to fall in love, but (guided by a benevolent power) it can restore a true love that under some other, less benign influence, has been misdirected.

Love may and often does lead to marriage, as is the case for these young couples and for Theseus and Hippolyta. For the latter couple, reason and love have joined together and are no longer in opposition, despite an inauspicious beginning (1.1.16–17). But the marriage of Oberon and Titania has run into serious trouble as they quarrel over the little Indian boy. She refuses to turn him over to her husband. Their quarrel is largely though not entirely a matter of "who's boss," that is, male supremacy versus female rights. In Shakespeare's patriarchal world, there was no question about it: the husband ruled, and Oberon feels he has to teach Titania a lesson.

Although she speaks a good deal of romantic love poetry to Bottom, Titania's adoration of him is not so much romantic love as it is a function of the love-madness that characterizes the young couples' plight in the forest scenes. Titania's eyesight is distorted by the powerful influence of love-in-idleness, which has led her to view Bottom as a handsome as well as a wise man worthy of her adoration. If we can take Oberon's word for it, she is not entirely unaware of what is happening. For when he meets her in the forest gathering flowers with which to bedeck Bottom's temples, he tells Puck (4.1.47–63) that he upbraided her and fell out with her so that she began to weep and beg him to stop. Finally, once Oberon finished taunting her, she relented and straightway agreed to give him the Indian boy. In this manner Oberon resumes full control as Titania's lord and master, and in this fashion love and reason are reconciled.

Still, the magic herb may be only a pleasant fiction or device to gloss over love's fickleness. No potion compelled Demetrius to abandon Helena for Hermia, and the men's fickleness here is of a piece with similar behavior in other plays. Romeo spends the first four scenes of his play infatuated with Rosaline; then he sees Juliet. Cressida might have been faithful to Troilus had she not been sent to the Greek camp, where she promptly forgets her Trojan lover. Behind the comic confusion of *A Midsummer Night's Dream* lies the stark reality that love is a giddy thing.

The Art of Performance

For a number of critics and theater directors, the play within the play, "Pyramus and Thisby," for all its unintentional farce as performed by the rude mechanicals, lies at the heart of *A Midsummer Night's Dream*. Peter Brook, for example, at the beginning of rehearsals for his Royal Shakespeare Company production in 1970, announced that the play within the play was the "key" to everything. For Brook, it was a microcosm of the play as a whole, raising fundamental questions about the nature of reality and of acting.

At their very first meeting, Quince and his fellow thespians ponder the implications of what they are about to undertake. When Quince informs Bottom what part he is to play in their "interlude," Bottom inquires what kind of role Pyramus is— "a lover, or a tyrant" (1.2.22). Told that he is "A lover, that kills himself most gallant, for love," Bottom responds, "That will ask some tears in the true performing of it. If I do it, let the audience look to their eyes: I will move storms; I will condole in some measure" (1.2.24–28). Bottom is already aware of audience reaction and the necessity for "true" enactment of a role. Quince seconds his concern regarding the effect on an audience a few minutes later when Bottom offers to perform the role of Lion also, bragging about how well he can roar (1.2.70–84). Quince worries, "And you should do it too terribly, you would fright the Duchess and the ladies, that they would shrike [shriek]; and that were enough to hang us all" (1.2.74–77). To this Bottom responds that he "will roar you as gently as any sucking dove; I will roar you and 'twere any nightingale" (1.2.82–84).

Quince insists that Bottom play only Pyramus, to which he reluctantly agrees. But the issue Shakespeare wants to raise in all this discussion is the relationship between illusion and reality as well as the actors' and the audience's understanding of it. The issue gathers momentum in the mechanicals' next scene, when they are in the forest and beginning their rehearsals. Bottom questions the advisability of Pyramus's killing himself onstage with his sword, which, he feels, "the ladies cannot abide" (3.1.11–12). Snout agrees that it is "a parlous fear" (3.1.13); but when Starveling suggests that the killing must be omitted, Bottom comes up with a "device" to make all well: Peter Quince will write a prologue reassuring the audience that the actors will really do no harm with their swords. He goes further and says that the prologue must inform the audience that he, Pyramus, is not really Pyramus, but Bottom the weaver, and by this means put the audience out of fear (3.1.16–22).

The trepidation of the troupe is thus allayed, at least for the moment, until other questions are raised about Lion, about bringing moonlight into the chamber, and about the wall. That Quince does not end up delivering the prologue that Bottom proposes is irrelevant here. More to the point is that, during the actual performance before Theseus and his court, the various actors—and especially Bottom as Pyramus—come out of their roles at different moments to explain who they are, what they are doing, and why. For they have not fully understood, if at all, the nature of dramatic illusion, even though, as Bottom seems to know, that to get the right effect from the audience, a part must be played "truly." Their confusion, however, coupled with the stage audience's remarks, helps the theater audience make the proper connection.

Comments from the stage audience during "Pyramus and Thisby" continue throughout the performance. Among the more important ones are those imbedded in the following dialogue between Hippolyta and Theseus:

Hippolyta: This is the silliest stuff that ever I heard.

Theseus: The best in this kind are but shadows; and the worst are no worse, if imagination amend them.

Hippolyta: It must be your imagination then, and not theirs.

Theseus: If we imagine no worse of them than they of themselves, they may pass for excellent men. (5.1.210–216)

This appeal to the audience's imagination lies at the heart of any dramatic performance, for a successful stage presentation depends upon the imaginative cooperation of playwright, producers, and audience. Without what Samuel Taylor Coleridge in his *Biographia Literaria* (1816) calls "willing suspension of disbelief," we can hardly enjoy fully the performance of a play. At the same time, paradoxically, as Dr. Samuel Johnson reminds us in his famous "Preface to Shakespeare," we remain aware that we are in a theater and not in Athens, Rome, or London. This is a clear function of "multiconsciousness" that Shakespeare's *A Midsummer Night's Dream* evokes.

Reality and Illusion

If the art of performance depends on illusion—an illusion that for a while we accept as real—much else in *A Midsummer Night's Dream* also develops the basic opposition between reality and appearance. Love, as we have seen, becomes problematic when reality and illusion become confused. At night in the forest—and night, like sleep and shadows and moonshine, fosters illusion—Lysander really believes he loves Helena and rejects Hermia, but he is under an illusion induced by the magic potion derived from love-in-idleness. Demetrius believes he loves Hermia and despises Helena; no matter how real his emotions seem at the beginning of the play, however, the magic potion induces him to reconsider his position, and he eventually learns the reality of his abiding love for Helena. Similarly, Theseus's battle against the Amazons, with Hippolyta as their leader, must have seemed the result of real enough provocation. In conquest, however, his attitude toward his captive queen changes, and he recognizes a new reality—his love for Hippolyta and his wish to wed her "in another key" (1.1.18).

Like Lysander's doting upon Helena in the central scenes of the play, Titania's doting upon Bottom—monstrous as he appears with his ass's head—is also the effect of a magically induced illusion. After Oberon applies the antidote to her eyes, she sees the illusion for what it was—no matter how real her love may have seemed to her at the time of her infatuation. This, of course, is the crux of the situation: how can anyone distinguish the apparent reality—the illusion—from the reality?

Shakespeare provides a clue, ironically, in Lysander's lines when he awakens and sees Helena: "The will of man is by his reason sway'd, / And reason says you are the worthier maid" (2.2.115–116). Lysander is correct: under normal conditions, a person's will, or desire, is properly directed by the reason. When passion or emotion takes control, the will becomes misdirected. This is good Tudor reasoning, deriving from Platonic philosophy. Accordingly, Hamlet upbraids his mother in the Closet Scene (3.4), arguing that she has allowed reason to pander to her will; that is, she has permitted her reason to become subverted and hence subordinated to the dictates of lust (3.4.88). Lysander believes he is acting reasonably, unaware that he is under the influence of love-in-idleness, which has distorted his reason as well as his vision.

If one cannot depend on reason, what then? One recourse is to authority that, under the best of circumstances, is directed by right reason. Hence, Egeus appeals to authority in the person of Duke Theseus when his daughter will not listen to reason as he presents it to her. Egeus is convinced that Hermia is under the influence of illusion-producing agents, such as "rhymes," "love-tokens," and other gifts that Lysander has used to woo her (1.1.27–38). Appeals to Egeus's better reason from Lysander (99–105) as well as Hermia (50–56) fall on deaf ears. Although Shakespeare does not significantly distinguish one suitor from the other, if at all, Egeus is under the illusion that Demetrius is the better man. For the moment, authority sides with Egeus, though only on the basis of a father's right, according to law, to determine whom his child shall marry. But authority later demonstrates a superior reason, when Theseus discovers the lovers in the forest so sweetly and correctly coupled with each other. The duke, allowing superior reason to supersede law, now decides to "overbear" Egeus's "will" (4.1.179). The couples may marry whom they have chosen and are invited to join Theseus and Hippolyta at the temple for a triple wedding ceremony (4.1.177–183).

What has caused this "gentle concord in the world" (4.1.143) to come about is partly the return of right reason to the lovers. But that, of course, is not the whole story; Oberon's role has also been important. Of this the young people are imperfectly aware. Demetrius recognizes that "some power" (4.1.165) has been involved in straightening things out for them, though he does not know what power it is. We, the audience, do. But is the fairy king merely an illusion? Is there such a thing as providence directing our destiny, as the Prince of Denmark says (*Hamlet*, 5.1.10–11, 219–224)? Shakespeare lets the audience decide.

Harmony from Discord

It is axiomatic that tragedy moves from well-being to catastrophe, whereas comedy moves in the opposite direction, from difficulty to a happy resolution. Not all of Shakespeare's comedies fit neatly into the comic paradigm thus described. In *Love's Labor's Lost*, for example, Jack does not end up with his Jill but has to undergo a period of penitence and education before that possible eventuality. But in *A Midsummer Night's Dream*, finding "the concord of this discord" (5.1.60) becomes the subject not only of Theseus's question regarding the "very tragical mirth" that Quince and his fellow actors want to stage (5.1.57), but also of every aspect of the play's dramatic structure.

Although *A Midsummer Night's Dream* begins, rather than ends, with the peaceful resolution of warfare between Theseus and Hippolyta, culminating in their wedding plans, such harmony is immediately broken by Egeus's interruption. His complaint against his daughter's insubordination introduces one of the major themes of discord, followed shortly afterward by the discord between Oberon and Titania. The latter has caused discord throughout the worlds of nature and human activity, resulting in an upheaval in the seasons, the weather, and the pursuit of both work and pleasure among mortals (2.1.81–117). We have seen by what means these conflicts are resolved. Oberon's intercession leads to the proper coupling of the four young lovers, and the harsh lesson he teaches Titania brings about their subsequent reconciliation. The dialogue between Theseus and Hippolyta in 4.1 about the "music" of his Spartan hounds (4.1.110–127) is by way of commenting indirectly upon the fairy couple's newfound harmony and introducing the concord now of the young couples.

What Hippolyta describes as "So musical a discord, such sweet thunder" (4.1.118), referring to the baying of the hounds as she went hunting once with Hercules and Cadmus, epitomizes the action of *A Midsummer Night's Dream*. This is the reason, again, for including the dialogue just before Hippolyta and Theseus come upon the sleeping lovers and just after the awakening of Titania. Later, Theseus indicates to her how best to reconcile themselves to the woefully amateurish performance of the workmen as they put on "Pyramus and Thisbe" (5.1.210–216). The farcical presentation of the tragedy is Shakespeare's answer to Theseus's question on how to find "the concord of this discord," that is, the oxymoron posed by "tragical mirth" (5.1.57).

At the end, Oberon, Titania, and their train join together to bless all the newly-weds, promising them constant love and healthy progeny:

> So shall all the couples three
> Ever true in loving be;
> And the blots of Nature's hand
> Shall not in their issue stand. (5.1.407–410)

Finally, turning to the theater audience, Puck pleads for concord between them and the actors and offers a solution for any offense that the cast may have committed: the audience may simply imagine that "this weak and idle theme" (the performance) was simply a dream they experienced while they slumbered there (5.1.422–429). He promises that, if granted pardon, the actors will do better next time, and he ends by asking for conciliatory applause:

> So, good night unto you all.
> Give me your hands, if we be friends,
> And Robin shall restore amends. (5.1.436–438)

CRITICAL CONTROVERSIES

The Wedding-Play Myth

For nearly two centuries, many scholars have held to the theory that *A Midsummer Night's Dream* was written as part of the wedding celebrations of a noble family. Several weddings occurring in the 1590s have been proposed, although none with sufficiently hard evidence to prove fully convincing. Ludwig Tieck in Germany first proposed the idea in 1830 in Schlegel's translation of the play. He believed the play was written for the wedding of Shakespeare's patron, Henry Wriothesley, the Earl of Southamptom, to Elizabeth Vernon in 1598. Besides the late date, no evidence supports this proposition. E. K. Chambers many years later argued for the wedding of William Stanley and Elizabeth Vere, the daughter of the Earl of Oxford, in 1595 or, alternatively, the wedding of Elizabeth Carey, granddaughter of Henry Lord Hunsdon, the patron of Shakespeare's company, to Thomas, son of Lord Berkeley. Less likely candidates for the occasion are the wedding of Robert Earl of Essex and Frances Lady Sidney in 1590 and Henry Lord Herbert and Anne Russell at Blackfriars in 1600.

The presence of Queen Elizabeth I at one of these weddings has sometimes been adduced in support of the wedding-play myth. The theory is based upon the compliments paid to her in the dialogue of the play, such as Oberon's description of the "fair vestal throned in the west" (2.1.148–164). But, again, no conclusive evidence to show that she was, in fact, present at any of the purported occasions has been brought forward.

Such speculations have sprouted not only because of the content of *A Midsummer Night's Dream* but also because of its dramatis personae. While Shakespeare's company usually included two or three boys to perform female roles, it did not have enough for all the fairies along with the three brides, and doubling these roles was not a viable option. Hence, the children of a noble family have been suggested as participating in the action. But as several modern productions have shown, like Adrian Noble's in 1994, the roles of Titania's fairy train could have been played by the men who doubled as the mechanicals (see "Production History," below).

Stanley Wells has led the opposition to the wedding-play myth ("*A Midsummer Night's Dream* Revisited," *Critical Survey* 3 [1991], 14–29); his arguments are developed and expanded in specific detail by Gary Jay Williams in *Our Moonlight Revels* (Iowa City: U of Iowa P, 1997, 1–18). Both scholars cite the absence of any concrete evidence to support the myth. Moreover, as Williams concludes, "Plays programmed closely to court occasions would have ill suited a professional company that was primarily dependent for its livelihood on its public playhouse and moved, probably quickly, between its public and court venues" (18).

The Eroticism of *A Midsummer Night's Dream*

Ever since Jan Kott first proposed that *A Midsummer Night's Dream* "is the most erotic of Shakespeare's plays" (*Shakespeare Our Contemporary*, p. 175), critics have argued about just how erotic the play actually is. Kott believes the eroticism in the *Dream* is more brutally expressed in this play than in any of Shakespeare's other works except *Troilus and Cressida*. He even goes so far as to argue, "The slender, tender and lyrical Titania longs for animal love" (183), as shown by her devotion to the monster—Bottom with his ass's head—whom she drags off to bed. "This is the lover she wanted and dreamed of; only she never wanted to admit it, even to herself. Sleep frees her from inhibitions. The monstrous ass is being raped by the poetic Titania, while she keeps on chattering about flowers" (ibid.). Kott's view has led a number of stage directors to present Titania and Bottom engaging in sexual intercourse, although there is little in either the dialogue or the stage directions to suggest as much.

Other critics have found Kott's view excessive. Thomas MacFarland, for example, in *Shakespeare's Pastoral Comedy* (Chapel Hill: U of North Carolina P, 1972), maintains that the play's eroticism is only "a barely perceptible undercurrent, a kind of elegant hint of other things" (80). Perhaps MacFarland goes too far to the opposite extreme. Certainly the play is erotic, and certainly there is a measure of brutality in the eroticism, but one must temper one's views by taking into account, as MacFarland argues, the overall tone of the play. Undercurrents there are, and they undercut some of the loveliest passages spoken by Oberon and others (see Imagery in "Devices and Techniques," above). But one must be careful not to take under for over and turn the play upside down.

Patriarchy and Feminism

A number of critics have approached *A Midsummer Night's Dream* from the standpoint of gender criticism. Some, like Shirley Nelson Garner in her essay in *The Woman's Part* (Urbana: U of Illinois P, 1980), contend that Oberon, Theseus, and Egeus want the exclusive love of a woman and her obedience. She goes further and says they want this love to accommodate their homoerotic desires, which may or may not be recognized. More compelling is her argument concerning the relationships between the women in the play: "the breaking of the women's bonds is central in the plot involving the four young lovers" (136). The quarrel between Hermia and Helena is more demeaning than that between the men. Once Lysander and Demetrius no longer compete for the same woman, their enmity apparently vanishes. However, after the women are given over to the men whom they marry, they are permanently separated. In their new roles as wives, they remain silent and obedient, utterly submissive to the men.

In "The (In)significance of 'Lesbian' Desire in Early Modern England" (in *Erotic Politics: Desire on the Renaissance Stage*, ed. Susan Zimmerman [New York: Routledge, 1992]), Valerie Traub goes further. She compares the relationship between Hermia and Helena to that between Rosalind and Celia in *As You Like It* and notes that for these two pairs of female characters "the initial erotic investment is in one another" (157). Like Garner, Traub focuses on the divorce of female unity but contends that "the relative power of each woman is aligned according to her *denial* of homoerotic bonds" (158). The eradication of homoerotic desire, moreover, is replicated in the Titania-Oberon plot. The little Indian boy is representative not only of Titania's female order, but also of female-oriented erotic bonds. He is "the manifest link of a prior, homoerotic affection between women that doesn't so much exclude Oberon as render him temporarily superfluous" (159). Thus affronted, Oberon moves to humiliate Titania erotically by making her fall in love with a monster and then surrender the child to him.

In contrast, Christy Desmet argues that Titania is the voice of ethical commitment in the play. While the first two acts contrast the relative rights of fathers and mothers, the two plots "merge to offer a unified defense of female sexual sovereignty, the woman's rights over her own body and soul" ("Disfiguring Women with Masculine Tropes: A Rhetorical Reading of *A Midsummer Night's Dream*," in *"A Midsummer Night's Dream": Critical Essays*, ed. Dorothy Kehler [New York: Garland, 1998], 317). Like Hermia, Titania defends her retention of the Indian boy "as if in a public forum." Her speech locates the boy "within an ethically and poetically superior matriarchy that reinforces her regal and maternal rights to him" (318). Taking her stand as she does, she becomes the most ethical speaker in the play (319–320).

PRODUCTION HISTORY

We do not know where and when *A Midsummer Night's Dream* was first publicly performed. The Globe Theatre was not yet built, and the play probably was not performed at The Theatre, where Burbage was having problems with his lease for the land. It was in the repertoire of the Lord Chamberlain's Men (later, the King's Men) for many years: the title page of the 1600 quarto claims that the play was "sundry times publickely acted." Gary Williams in *Our Moonlight Revels* suggests that it might be the "play of Robin goode-fellow" performed before King James, possibly at Hampton Court, in January 1604 (36). Other allusions or references further suggest the play's popularity in the early seventeenth century, before public playing was discontinued in 1642 by the Puritans.

The original performances in the public theater took full advantage of the thrust stage, which brought the actors and audience into close proximity with each other. Unlike modern theaters, Shakespeare's stage had little, if any, scenery; hence, emphasis was on the language as spoken. With no obviously starring roles, ensemble acting and doubling of parts were almost certainly featured, though William Kempe most likely played the virtuoso role of Bottom and Richard Burbage played Oberon, perhaps doubled with Theseus. Scenery was sparse, but the First Fairy on entering at 2.1 might have hung a few boughs of greenery on the pillars (which held up the canopy over the stage) to suggest the forest, and possibly some sort of apparatus was used for Titania's bower in 2.2 or the hawthorn brake in 3.1.

Costumes often were elaborate. The finery that Theseus and Hippolyta wear as the Duke and Duchess of Athens was Elizabethan, with perhaps some classical embellishments. Oberon and Titania, as their counterparts in the forest world, dressed similarly. The young lovers were also dressed in Elizbethan fashion, though not quite so elaborately as Theseus and Hippolyta, but similarly embellished. Puck may have been dressed as a king's jester, complete with coxcomb and motley, but the more traditional costume of the English sprite—as he appears, for example, in Ben Jonson's masque *Love Restored* (1616)—fits the character much better. The fairies were not gauzy ballet dancers dressed in tutus with wings attached to them, as later represented in art and performance, and they were not female. Bottom refers to one as "Mounsieur Cobweb" and "Cavalery Cobweb," another as "Mounsieur Mustardseed" (4.1.8–23). The rude mechanicals, or "hard-handed men that work in Athens" (5.1.72), looked just like the Warwickshire craftsmen from whom they derive, all dressed as we should expect in Shakespeare's time.

After the theaters were closed in 1642, *A Midsummer Night's Dream* was not performed in its entirety for nearly the next 200 years. What were seen were various adaptations, including a "droll," or short comic piece, a Purcell opera, and other versions. One droll, called *Bottom the Weaver* (published in 1661), centers on Bottom and his friends and preserves all their episodes taken from the text of the Second Folio (1632), but it omits the young lovers; and the roles of Titania, Oberon, and Puck are severely cut. The printed list of actors indicates that a number of parts may have been doubled, especially the roles of Theseus and Oberon, possibly reflecting an earlier stage tradition. Similar adaptations had long since been known on the Continent, thanks to English strolling players, especially in Germany.

By 1660, when the theaters reopened in London, English drama was heavily influenced by the neoclassical doctrines imported from France, where the court had resided in exile during the Commonwealth period. Samuel Pepys saw a production on September 29, 1662, which he disliked intensely: "[T]hen to the King's Theatre, where we saw *Midsummers nights dreame*, which I have never seen before, nor shall ever again, for it is the most insipid ridiculous play that ever I saw in my life. I saw, I confess, some good dancing and some handsome women, which was all my pleasure." By this time, following the French lead, women had taken the female roles previously played by boys. But for the next thirty years, the play dropped out of the repertoire.

When it reemerged, it did so spectacularly but utterly transmogrified. Under continental influences, Elkanah Settle adapted Shakespeare's play as an opera called *The Fairy Queen* with music by Henry Purcell. Thomas Betterton produced it in 1692 at Dorset Gardens Theatre, where it was revived the next year with additional songs and music by Purcell. But Purcell did not score a single line of Shakespeare's text. The Shakespeare parts in this severely cut and mangled version were all spoken and acted. The lovers, the fairies, the rude mechanicals are all there, but so are a number of new characters. In addition, allegorical figures—Night, Mystery, Secrecy, Sleep—and their attendants appear, as well as Spring, Summer, Autumn, and Winter with Phoebus for a "Dance of the Four Seasons." The opera had still more for the delight of the age: Juno, a chorus of Chinese men and women, a dance of six monkeys, and "a Grand Dance of 24 *Chinese*," as recorded in Jacob Tonson's edition of 1692.

Aided by advances in theatrical machinery and movable stage sets, spectacle became increasingly important on the Restoration stage, as it was in *The Fairy Queen*. In the next century, in David Garrick and George Colman's adaptations, the text was interspersed with songs and dances as well as spectacle, which greatly appealed to audiences. The first of these adaptations was *The Fairies* (1755), an opera by David Garrick and Handel's pupil John Christopher Smith, with songs from both Shakespeare and others. The courtiers, lovers, and fairies were retained, but not the mechanicals. Though listed among the dramatis personae, Hippolyta has no lines, and speeches by other characters are sharply curtailed to make room for the songs. Unlike Purcell's opera, however, some of Shakespeare's verse is set to music. In all, twenty-one songs, besides several dances, are interspersed throughout the dialogue, but only a quarter of Shakespeare's lines remain in the text. Most of act 5 is cut, including the play within the play. Instead of Shakespeare's fairy masque at the end, Theseus summons the couples to the altar, and a chorus sings, "Hail to love, and welcome joy!"

In 1763 Garrick attempted to stage something closer to the original text of *A Midsummer Night's Dream*. As Garrick was then living abroad, his colleague, George Colman, supervised rehearsals and altered Garrick's script considerably. This version lasted only one night in performance. Three days later Colman attempted to recoup some of his losses and produced *A Fairy Tale* as an afterpiece to his *Jealous Wife*. This afterpiece, which includes the Athenian workmen and the fairies, but not the lovers and courtiers, became very popular. It was revived for the last time in 1777, but the seven performances that summer were the last of the eighteenth-century adaptations and revivals. No other adaptations took the boards until Frederick Reynolds's operatic version for John Philip Kemble in 1816, which held the stage in some form or other for many years.

Nineteenth-century productions of Shakespeare's plays are best remembered for their lavish scenic displays and corresponding attempts at historical authenticity. As theater technology advanced, so did elaborate stagings of the plays. Scene painting surpassed anything previously seen, and Mendelssohn's overture (1826) and incidental music (1843) to *A Midsummer Night's Dream* had a powerful impact on productions. Garrick's attempts to restore at least some of Shakespeare's texts gathered momentum. The most important productions of *A Midsummer Night's Dream* in that century were by Madame Vestris at Covent Garden in 1840, Samuel Phelps at Sadler's Wells in 1853, and Charles Kean at the Princess's Theatre in 1856. Although Lucia Elizabeth Vestris did much to restore some of Shakespeare's language, her production still continued the tradition of introducing spectacle and additional songs and dances to *A Midsummer Night's Dream*. Vestris set a precedent by enacting Oberon herself and kept more of Shakespeare's major passages, such as Titania's "forgeries of jealousy" speech (2.1.81–117), than had her predecessors. Although mid-Victorian decorum dictated certain cuts—for example, the reference to "big-bellied" sails and "wanton wind" (2.1.129)—Hermia still spoke of not giving up her "virgin patent" to Demetrius (1.1.80), and at the end Theseus twice summons the lovers to bed (5.1.364, 368). In later productions these would change to "maiden heart" and "Lovers, away."

The Tieck-Mendelssohn production of 1843 was the first full-scale production of *A Midsummer Night's Dream* to appear on the German stage. It used Mendelssohn's incidental music and August Wilhelm von Schlegel's 1798 translation. Shakespeare in translation was already popular in Germany, both on the page and on the stage. The costumes were a mix of Greek, old German, and sixteenth-century Spanish designs. A full orchestra played Mendelssohn's score from a pit in front of the stage. The production was a tribute to and a validation of German culture, which had by this time claimed Shakespeare as its own.

A decade later in London, Samuel Phelps produced *A Midsummer Night's Dream* emphasizing its ethereal, dreamlike quality. To achieve this effect, Phelps's scene designer, Frederick Fenton, used the newly installed gas lighting, a diorama, and a piece of greenish-blue gauze let down in front of the stage for the forest scenes. Phelps himself played Bottom and used a young but well-trained cast of actors dressed appropriately to blend in with the overall scenic effect. The production included dancing and music, but not the songs from Vestris's production. The musical score has not been found; the 1861 revival, however, used Mendelssohn's music as arranged by W. H. Montgomery.

By mid-century Mendelssohn's music—both the overture and the incidental music—was becoming a fixture in many stage productions of the play. In 1854 two New York productions, one by William Evans Burton and the other by Thomas Berry and E. A. Marshall, advertised the whole of Mendlessohn's score in their stagings. But these were not the first American productions of the work. An operatic version was staged in 1826; and in 1841, possibly inspired by Vestris's success, Charlotte Cushman played Oberon in a nonoperatic version.

To keep performances in 1856 under three hours' duration, allowing time for music, dance, and cumbersome scene shifts, Charles Kean at the Princess's Theatre cut more than 800 lines from Shakespeare's text. In addition to Mendelssohn's music, the work of other composers was used. A woman, Fanny Ternan, played Oberon, and the fairies were all played by adults. Kean outdid all others, including Vestris, in his use of spectacle, with as many as ninety fairies tripping up and down the stairs of Theseus's palace and waving bell-like lanterns in act 5.

By the end of the nineteenth century—and continuing into the twentieth—spectacle had become primary. This emphasis was especially evident in the celebrated productions of Augustin Daly and Herbert Beerbohm Tree, the most popular productions of this period. Tree even brought live birds and rabbits onto the stage. But winds of change were blowing. While some belittled Wiliam Poel's attempts at "Elizabethan" stagings of *A Midsummer Night's Dream* and other plays, the reaction against spectacle had begun to set in. Chief among those who tried new ways of producing Shakespeare's plays was Harley Granville-Barker, who staged the *Dream* in 1914. He adapted the proscenium stage that was now standard in British theaters to accommodate an apron or thrust stage, as in Elizabethan playhouses. Instead of footlights that cast long shadows of the actors, he used spotlights mounted on the front rail of the dress circle. Granville-Barker eschewed realistic settings, preferring impressionistic designs and using draped curtains to this end. Verse was spoken swiftly and naturally, with very few cuts in the text. But his greatest innovation was his use of gilded fairies, enacted by full-sized adults (men for Oberon's train, women for Titania's), instead of gauzy, bewinged children. To emphasize the fairies' supernatural quality, Granville-Barker had them walk in a stiff, dignified gait, covered as they were with gold paint and in places actual gold leaf. Cecil Sharp's English folk music replaced Mendelssohn's score.

Throughout the early twentieth century, experimental and traditional productions continued to vie with each other, both in England and on the continent of Europe, where the most important productions were those created by the German director Max Reinhardt. His productions were by no means static but evolved over time from a mixture of illusion and impressionism to a more suggestive, symbolist treatment of light and shade, with green curtains dropped before a practically bare stage to suggest the forest. A new sense of play infused the production, and the physicality of the lovers, including their sexual impulses, was apparent. His efforts culminated in his staging of *A Midsummer Night's Dream* in Hollywood in 1935 and his motion picture with William Dieterle.

After World War II, the most important production of *A Midsummer Night's Dream* is undoubtedly Peter Brook's for the Royal Shakespeare Company in 1970. Brook's aim was to see and hear the play afresh, to bring the play newly alive for audiences. In this he succeeded admirably. He began by discarding all previous production concepts, instead deciding that magic is the key, along with celebration—a celebration of the theater. Together with Sally Jacobs, his designer, he devised a set that was simply a three-sided white box, like a squash court, and he dressed the actors (except the mechanicals) in colorful, loose satin costumes like those he saw in a Chinese circus. Before rehearsals began, Brook had the cast practice juggling tricks and acrobatics, which they performed skillfully when the *Dream* opened.

To engage the audience as fully as possible, Brook had his actors, when not part of a scene, watch the action from the galleries above the walls of the squash court stage. Hence, the actors were never uninvolved. The props were distinctive. The magic flower (love-in-idleness), for example, was a silver dish spinning on a rod. The forest trees were coiled wires dropped from above, encircling and entangling the lovers. Occasionally, the fairies descended from above on swings or trapezes. Titania's bower was a large, feathery hammock, which descended and ascended as needed. Bottom's ass's head was a pair of earmuffs, a black button nose, and clogs attached to his feet. His facial expressions were thus never obscured in performance.

The music was likewise distinctive. Richard Peaslee's score involved not only a guitarist, two percussionists, and a trombone and trumpet player but also a strange instrument called a Free-Kas for the weird sounds Brook wanted. The overall effect was startling at first, like everything else in this production, but succeeded in helping to achieve Brook's ultimate goal.

If Brook occasionally played against the text, he also found ambiguities within it that could be and were exploited, uncovering new depths. His success, moreover,

(Left to right) Alan Howard as Oberon, Gemma Jones as Titania, and Robert Lloyd as Puck in a scene from the Royal Shakespeare Company's 1973 production of *A Midsummer Night's Dream*, directed by Peter Brook. Courtesy of Photofest.

may be calculated in part by the numerous imitations of the production the world over as well as by the reactions of directors at the Royal Shakespeare Company and elsewhere who, in a kind of anxiety of influence, tried to find other ways to awaken audiences newly to the play. Brook doubled several parts—Theseus and Oberon, Hippolyta and Titania, Philostrate and Puck, Egeus and Quince—but not the fairies and the mechanicals. Doubling of the major roles frequently has been a feature of other productions, though by no means all.

At the Royal Shakespeare Company, John Barton in 1977, Ron Daniels in 1981, Bill Alexander in 1986, and Adrian Noble in 1994, all tried to find interesting ways of presenting the play without imitating Brook and generally succeeded in what they set out to do. Adrian Noble was perhaps the most imaginative of the four, while paying tribute to Brook's achievement three decades earlier. His stage was, like Brook's, almost entirely bare but featured a far more colorful red box instead of Jacobs's stark white one. In place of trees, dozens of lightbulbs dropped from above, giving the appropriate illusion in the central scenes (compare Brook's wires). Titania's bower—a large, soft, pink inverted umbrella that descended from above—was another reminiscence of Brook's *Dream*, along with the swing stage right, on which Hippolyta sat at the beginning of 1.1. Otherwise, except for two smaller, green umbrellas (also inverted) on which Puck and the First Fairy rose from below, no further props were used. He followed Brook in doubling the major roles, but he went further and doubled the mechanicals and the four fairies. His overarching concept was the dream—a descent into the unconscious.

Perhaps the most astonishing *Dream* after Brook's—in some ways both a striking reaction against and a tribute to it—was Robert Lepage's at London's Royal National Theatre in 1992. Like Brook, he set out to overturn all preconceptions concerning the play and its performance. His set, designed by Michael Levine, was a large circular pool of water surrounded by a bank of mud, beyond which was a running track of somewhat firmer material. Here the lovers could race around during the forest scenes, when they were not splashing about in the water and mud. Director, designer, and cast, moreover, saw in the text of *A Midsummer Night's Dream* a good many references to floods and tempests, all of which confirmed their intuitions that water was central to the play, as mud was to the primordial experiences the play conveyed.

The performance began with a strange creature dressed in scarlet, one breast exposed, crawling crabwise across the stage to the center of the pool. This was Puck, played by Angela Laurier, walking on her hands with her feet over her shoulders. When the action of the play proper began, Theseus and Hippolyta entered perched on a brass bedstead pushed onto the pool by the four young lovers and followed on foot by Egeus and Philostrate, who later poled the bed around the pool. As Theseus and Hippolyta situated themselves at the bedhead, the lovers got aboard and lay down at the other end, their posture clearly suggesting that they were asleep. What ensued, therefore, could be understood as their collective dream. Everyone wore white, light clothing—Theseus and Hippolyta in flowing robes, the young lovers in what looked like nighties and pajamas. The fairies, who entered later, wore blue paint on their faces and dressed in black, not only to distinguish them from the mortals, but to suggest their otherworldly state. Titania and Oberon appeared as Eastern potentates, though not encumbered with heavy garments. A gamelan orchestra provided what music there was.

The production was highly physical, sometimes at the expense of the text, although Lepage cut very little. Some critics complained that Shakespeare's language got lost among all the shenanigans, as when the lovers splashed about in the pool. Bottom did not wear an ass's head exactly; in its place, Puck mounted on his back with legs upraised over his head to suggest donkey ears. With so much physical behavior to attend to, both audiences and performers had difficulty concentrating on what was said. This was a primary difference between Lepage's *Dream* and Brook's, which had emphasized clear verse speaking.

England was by no means the sole source of innovative and interesting productions of *A Midsummer Night's Dream*. By the end of the twentieth century, countless productions all over the world proved how fascinating and durable Shakespeare's play is, not only onstage but also on the large and small screens. Several noteworthy films have been made, preeminently Peter Hall's in 1968, with Ian Richardson as Oberon and Judi Dench as Titania, and Michael Hoffman's in 1999, with Kevin Kline as Bottom. Hall set his film in the English countryside, whereas Hoffman transposed the setting to Italy in the nineteenth century. The films contrast with each other in many ways, both having much to commend them, especially the verse speaking in Hall's and the lavish settings in Hoffman's.

In the summer of 2002, *A Midsummer Night's Dream* returned to the Bankside, where it may have been performed four centuries earlier. At the reconstructed Globe Theatre, the "Red Company" directed by Mike Alfreds performed their version of Shakespeare's comedy before audiences seated in the galleries or standing in the yard. This production made several concessions to modern stagings. Women played the roles of Hermia and Helena, and Geraldine Alexander doubled as Hippolyta and Titania. Since some performances were at night, artificial lighting had to be used—to illuminate the entire theater, not only the stage, to reproduce as far as possible the effect of open-air daylight performances. In addition, two intervals broke the playing time, which lasted about three hours.

The stage was essentially bare. Costumes were simple, the lovers wearing pajamas, which became more and more disheveled during their forest experience. Quince and his fellow mechanicals, in workmen's clothes, doubled as the fairies; but these fairies wore little lights over their torsos, which twinkled appropriately to suggest their otherworldliness. Bottom had "ears" that were ladies' fur-trimmed slippers stood on end, and his nose was a white cup. The costuming for "Pyramus and Thisby" was also kept simple. Lion wore a large yellow ruff; Wall was barechested and carried a sheet. Pyramus came on with a beard made of shaving-cream lather, which evoked laughter whenever it transferred to another actor through deliberate or inadvertent contact.

Musicians were placed not above, in the Lord's Room, but on the main stage in the discovery space, so that they were in view constantly. The text was only lightly cut. When Oberon and Titania were reconciled, they performed a lovely, tango-like dance. No Bergomask followed the play within the play, but Oberon sang his blessing at the end as the fairies danced and joined in as chorus. Thus *A Midsummer Night's Dream* once more graced the south bank of the Thames, bringing full circle, as it were, the performance history of this magnificent Shakespearean comedy.

EXPLICATION OF KEY PASSAGES

1.1.65–78. "I beseech your Grace . . . single blessedness." Although Egeus has mentioned only two alternatives—marriage to Demetrius or death—Theseus here gives Hermia a third choice: to become a nun. The reference is somewhat anachronistic, of course (a nun would in classical terms be a vestal virgin of some sort), but Theseus makes his point. The picture he paints of this third alternative is not very attractive. Although Theseus recognizes its religious value, becoming a nun is hardly preferable, he indicates, to the "earthlier" happiness of marriage (1.1.76), which he himself anticipates. The contrast is between the sterility of the convent—"Chaunting faint hymns to the cold fruitless moon"—and the fertility of marriage (1.1.73).

2.1.81–117. "These are the forgeries of jealousy; . . . overborne their continents." The "jealousies" Titania refers to are the accusations Oberon makes regarding her infidelities with Theseus, in response to her accusations of his infidelities (lines 64–71). She notes that Oberon has disrupted the innocent cavortings of Titania and her train at the beginning of midsummer, brawling with her about possession of the Indian boy. As a result of their discord, disorder has followed elsewhere in the world of nature. Winds have brought fogs to the land, causing rivers to flood, for example. She goes on to mention other disturbances (lines 93–114), such as the inversion of the seasons, the destruction of crops, the death of livestock, and gloom among human beings. She blames all of these evils on "our dissension; We are their parents and original" (2.1.116–117). The passage reflects the Elizabethan view of the organic relationship in all aspects of nature: human and nonhuman.

2.2.111–122. "Content with Hermia? . . . written in Love's richest book." Lysander, anointed with the juice of love-in-idleness, awakens to see Helena before him, and at once declares his love. When Helena reminds him of his love for Hermia, he gives this reply. Lysander describes good Renaissance reasoning: that is, the reason should lead the will, not vice versa. He believes he is acting rationally, unaware of the magic potion that has affected him. He says he was immature up to now and did not have the full benefit of reason; but having now grown up, he believes (erroneously) that mature reason tells him Helena is far worthier than Hermia. Of course, the audience recognizes the irony of his statements: he is hardly acting rationally.

4.1.47–70. "Her dotage now . . . the Fairy Queen." Oberon tells Puck how he has met Titania, while she was under the spell of the magic potion, gathering "sweet favors" (4.1.49) for Bottom, who is still wearing his ass's head. Oberon scolded her for her behavior toward Bottom so that the dew on the flowers she gathered seemed like tears of shame bewailing their disgrace for being so used. When Titania begged Oberon to relent, he asked her again for the Indian boy, which she immediately surrendered to him. Now that he has the boy, he says, he will remove the spell from Titania's eyes and instructs Puck to remove Bottom's ass's head so that when he awakes he can return to Athens like the others. They will all then regard their nighttime experience in the forest as nothing more than a dream, or nightmare. With Titania obedient to her husband, order is restored in both the fairy and the human realms.

4.1.112–118. "I was with Hercules . . . such sweet thunder." While Hippolyta and Theseus are hunting in the forest, she tells him of her earlier experience when hunting with Hercules and Cadmus (two legendary classical heroes). They had hunting dogs from Sparta who helped them bring a bear to bay. The sound of the dogs filled the air in "one mutual cry" (4.1.117), but the apparent discordance seemed like music, or "sweet thunder" (4.1.118). Here in brief is the theme of the play, bringing concord out of apparent discord.

4.1.200–219. "When my cue comes . . . at her death." Bottom awakens and begins calling for his friends, thinking he has just heard his cue. When he comes more fully to his senses, he realizes they have all left him asleep. Then he begins to remember the amazing things that have happened to him. In his malaprop fashion, he parodies 1 Corinthians 2:9 to describe his sense of wonderment. He is wise enough, however, not to try to relate what has happened to him as real (see Oberon's comment above, 4.1.68–69); instead, he intends to have Peter Quince write a ballad about it, which he plans to sing before the Duke at the end of the play they will perform. Of course, he does not sing the ballad, and we do not know whether or not Quince writes it, but no matter, since the whole play may be but a dream.

5.1.1–27. "'Tis strange, my Theseus . . . strange and admirable." In this dialogue, Theseus speaks as the cool rationalist. He gives a conservative, traditional account of the imagination, such as Elizabethans believed: that is, the imagination is treacherous and tricky, hardly to be trusted. Hippolyta wonders at the story the young lovers have told about what happened to them in the forest, which we the audience have witnessed, but Theseus refuses to lend their tale full credit. He groups the lunatic, the lover, and the poet together as those with vivid imaginations, supposing to be true what they only imagine. Not only does he describe imagination's transforming power, as in the lover, but also its creative power: the poet "bodies forth" (5.1.14) what does not even exist (as indeed Shakespeare has done in his play, creating fairies and monsters). Although Theseus is very persuasive, he does not entirely convince the more intuitive Hippolyta, who finds in the lovers' story an unusual and compelling consistency, something "strange and admirable," which is much more than mere "fancy's images" (5.1.27, 25). Her statement could also be taken as a comment on the play itself.

5.1.108–117. "If we offend, . . . like to know." Peter Quince speaks his prologue before Theseus and his guests on their wedding night. His stage fright and nervousness obviously cause him to mistake the punctuation; as a result, what he says comes out almost directly opposite to what he intends. For example, at the end of his first line, he should have a comma, not a period, and a period after the second line. This is not the prologue discussed in 3.2, however; that one has been scrapped or never written. But it sets the tone for the amateurish performance that ensues, making "Pyramus and Thisby" more farcical than tragic.

Annotated Bibliography

Barber, C. L. *Shakespeare's Festive Comedy: A Study of Dramatic Form and Its Relation to Social Custom.* Princeton: Princeton UP, 1959. A groundbreaking study of the nature of Shakespearean comedy, with a fine chapter on *A Midsummer Night's Dream.*

Brown, John Russell. *Shakespeare and His Comedies.* 2nd ed. London: Methuen, 1962. Contains a fine chapter on "Love's Truth and the Judgements of *A Midsummer Night's Dream* and *Much Ado About Nothing*," emphasizing the irrationality of love's choices in the former.

Carroll, D. Allen, and Gary Jay Williams, eds. *"A Midsummer Night's Dream": An Annotated Bibliography.* New York: Garland, 1986. The most extensive and useful annotated bibliography up to the date of publication.

Clayton, Tom. "'So quick bright things come to confusion'; or, What Else Is *A Midsummer Night's Dream* About?" In *Shakespeare: Text and Theater: Essays in Honor of Jay L. Halio.* Ed. Lois Potter and Arthur F. Kinney. Newark: U of Delaware P, 1999. 62–91. A wide-ranging essay that covers a number of topics, including an important account of the Indian boy and the question of "flower power."

Garber, Marjorie. *Dream in Shakespeare.* New Haven: Yale UP, 1974. An excellent analysis of Shakespeare's use of dreams and the theories that underlie many of them.

Halio, Jay L. *Shakespeare in Performance: "A Midsummer Night's Dream."* 2nd ed. Manchester, Eng.: Manchester UP, 2003. Surveys the earlier history of the play in performance and analyzes in detail a number of the most important twentieth-century stage and film productions, especially Peter Brook's.

Leggatt, Alexander. *Shakespeare's Comedy of Love.* London: Methuen, 1974. Excellent discussions of Shakespeare's romantic comedies.

Ornstein, Robert. *Shakespeare's Comedies.* Newark: U of Delaware P, 1986. Covers all the comedies in jargon-free, lucidly written language with many fine insights.

Williams, Gary Jay. *Our Moonlight Revels: "A Midsummer Night's Dream" in the Theatre.* Iowa City: U of Iowa P, 1997. The fullest account of the play's stage history up to the mid-1990s.

Young, David P. *Something of Great Constancy: The Art of "A Midsummer Night's Dream."* New Haven: Yale UP, 1966. One of the best books devoted entirely to the play. Young discusses sources, style and structure, and meanings.

The Merchant of Venice

Jay L. Halio

PLOT SUMMARY

1.1. The play opens with Antonio complaining of his depression, for which neither he nor his friends can find the cause. Bassanio enters and asks Antonio for yet another loan, this time so he can try to win the hand of the heiress, Portia, who lives in Belmont. Short of ready cash, Antonio tells Bassanio to borrow the money, using his (Antonio's) credit as the basis for the loan.

1.2. Portia laments that she is bound under the terms of her dead father's will concerning whom she may marry. Only the man who chooses the right casket among the three available may wed her. Though unhappy about this arrangement, Portia agrees with her waiting maid, Nerissa, that she must abide by her father's plan.

1.3. This scene introduces Shylock, the Jewish moneylender whom Bassanio approaches for a 3,000-ducat loan on Antonio's credit for three months. Shylock and Antonio have long been enemies, partly because of religious differences, but more because, Shylock says, Antonio gives loans out at no interest and thus forces down the rate of interest among professional moneylenders. When Antonio enters, Shylock acknowledges their enmity but nevertheless agrees to lend the money to Antonio as a gesture of friendship, charging no interest but demanding a pound of Antonio's flesh as forfeiture if he should fail to repay the loan by the date specified. Over Bassanio's objection, Antonio agrees to these terms. Antonio is confident that he will easily repay the loan as soon as one of his several ships comes in with the fortune he expects them to earn in trading abroad.

2.1. The Prince of Morocco prepares to choose among the three caskets. He asks that Portia not dislike him for his color, and she reassures him in an ambiguous statement that she thinks as well of him as of any other suitor—none of whom, however, she likes.

2.2–3. Launcelot Gobbo, who has served Shylock, prepares to leave his old master for the employ of Bassanio. Launcelot engages in some curious teasing with his nearly blind old father, telling the old man that Launcelot is dead before revealing his identity. In 2.3 Jessica, Shylock's daughter, tells Launcelot that she will miss him.

2.4. A plot is afoot for Jessica to elope with the Christian Lorenzo. Lorenzo, Gratiano, Salerio, and Solanio discuss their plans.

2.5. Launcelot summons his former master to dine with the Christians. Shylock departs, urging his daughter to lock up the house after him.

2.6. In Shylock's absence Jessica elopes with Lorenzo and takes a substantial quantity of her father's money and jewelry with her.

2.7. At Belmont, Morocco chooses the gold casket, which does not contain Portia's picture. He leaves, much to Portia's relief.

2.8. Together with his friend Gratiano, Bassanio leaves for Belmont to woo Portia. Salerio and Solanio discuss rumors of Antonio's ships being wrecked and talk of Shylock's anguish at the loss of his daughter and his money.

2.9. The Prince of Arragon tries his luck with the caskets and chooses the silver container. It, too, has no picture of Portia within, and he withdraws as Bassanio approaches.

3.1. The act opens with another dialogue between two of Antonio's friends, Solanio and Salerio, discussing Antonio's losses at sea. Shylock enters bemoaning Jessica's elopement and the ducats she has stolen. When he hears that Antonio has also suffered losses, he warns that he will make good on the terms of his loan, for he is sure that all of the Christians have been involved in his daughter's elopement with Lorenzo. Another Jew, Tubal, enters to give Shylock bad news of Jessica in Genoa and to confirm Antonio's losses. Shylock sends Tubal to arrange to have Antonio arrested for default of his loan.

3.2. Meanwhile, during Bassanio's visit to Belmont, he and Portia have fallen in love. Although Portia wants him to delay making his choice of the caskets, Bassanio is eager to know his fate. While he is deciding which casket to choose, Portia orders some music and a song to be sung. Bassanio rightly chooses the lead casket and wins Portia, and Gratiano and Nerissa announce that they too will get married. But before they have much time to celebrate, Salerio arrives from Venice along with Lorenzo and Jessica with the news of Antonio's default and imprisonment. Portia sends Bassanio back to Venice with Gratiano and with more than enough money to pay off Antonio's debt. She stipulates only that they get married first and gives him a ring. Gratiano and Nerissa follow suit.

3.3. Back in Venice, Shylock remains adamant that he will have his revenge on Antonio and demand his forfeiture.

3.4. On her part, Portia decides to depart from Belmont with Nerissa for Venice, leaving the estate in the hands of Lorenzo and Jessica. Portia will adopt the disguise of a lawyer, Balthasar, and Nerissa that of his law clerk, intent on helping Antonio deal with Shylock.

3.5. The act ends with some comic dialogue between Jessica and Launcelot about her conversion, and between Launcelot and Lorenzo.

4.1. The Duke holds court to hear Shylock's case against Antonio. He appeals to Shylock to relent, but in vain; moreover, he realizes that he cannot dismiss Shylock's claim without damaging the international reputation of Venice for law and justice, on which the city's trading empire depends. Bassanio offers thrice the amount of the loan, but still Shylock insists on his forfeiture. The Duke then reads a letter from Bellario, a famous jurist, who has sent a colleague, Balthasar (actually Portia in disguise), along with the clerk (Nerissa, also in disguise) to help adjudicate the case.

At first, Balthasar agrees that Shylock has a valid contract with Antonio, who must pay the forfeit. But just as Shylock is about to take his pound of flesh, Balthasar stops him, saying that the bond allows him only precisely one pound of flesh, not a scruple more or less, and not a single drop of blood. Foiled, Shylock tries to leave with just his money, but he is refused that as well. He has insisted on the terms of his bond, and Portia is determined that he shall have only that. Then she says that the laws of Venice decree that he, as an alien resident in Venice, is subject to death and confiscation of all his wealth for his attempt upon the life of one of Venice's citizens. The Duke allows Shylock to live, but half of his estate will go to Antonio. Shylock can keep the other half of his property on condition that he convert to Christianity and that he agree upon his death to let Lorenzo have all his remaining property. Reluctantly, Shylock agrees to these terms.

In payment for services rendered, Balthasar refuses any money but asks for the ring Bassanio wears. Since it is the ring Portia gave him, Bassanio demurs, but after Portia leaves, Antonio persuades him to let it go.

4.2. Gratiano delivers the ring, and Nerissa says she will try to get the ring she gave her husband as well.

5.1. At Belmont the two women have fun with their husbands, who no longer wear the rings they swore to keep, until Portia reveals that it was she in disguise who played the role of Balthasar and Nerissa her clerk. She also hands Antonio a letter showing that his ships have miraculously returned safely, and Nerissa hands Lorenzo Shylock's deed of gift. They then all enter Portia's house, with renewed promises of fidelity and friendship.

PUBLICATION HISTORY

Although not published until 1600, *The Merchant of Venice* was written several years earlier. It was entered in the Stationers' Register on July 22, 1598, and in his book *Palladis Tamia* (also 1598) Francis Meres mentions the play in a list of Shakespeare's comedies. Thus *The Merchant of Venice* was certainly written before 1598, though how much earlier is difficult to determine. Enough topical references, however, along with some stylistic indications suggest that the play belongs to the period 1596–1597.

Marlowe's popular play *The Jew of Malta* (ca. 1588) may have led Shakespeare to write *The Merchant of Venice*. Although written years earlier, it was still being performed in the mid-1590s. Then, too, the trial and execution in 1594 of Roderigo Lopez, Queen Elizabeth's Jewish physician who had converted to Christianity, may have excited a more than normal anti-Semitism in England and especially in London. Although Jews had been expelled from England in 1290, some converts were allowed to remain; and a few others, mainly "conversos," or refugees from the Spanish Inquisition, settled in London and elsewhere and practiced their religion secretly. Whether Shakespeare was acquainted any such Jews is not known, although a long literary tradition of Jews as villains but also as respected patriarchs still flourished in the sixteenth century.

The perennial controversies in the late sixteenth century over borrowing at interest and the rates that might be charged may have been another inducement for Shakespeare to write a play about Jewish moneylenders and Christians, though of course not all moneylenders were Jewish. Shakespeare's father had been fined for charging usurious rates for loans. Whatever the case, *The Merchant of Venice* was and remains popular on the English stage. The question of whether the play is anti-Semitic and whether Shakespeare was himself an anti-Semite will be discussed in "Critical Controversies."

On October 28, 1600, another entry concerning the play can be found in the Stationers' Register (Register C, fol. 66). It states:

> **Tho. haies** Entred for his copie vnder the handes of the Wardens & by Consent of m^r Robertes. A booke called the booke of the merchant of Venyce   vj^d [six pence] (Cited in *The Merchant of Venice*, Shakespeare Quarto Facsimiles No. 2, ed. W. W. Greg [Oxford: Clarendon P, 1957], [1].)

This second entry probably indicates that Roberts had demonstrated before the wardens that he had permission to publish the play. The curious redundancy, "A Booke called the booke," suggests that it was the promptbook that was produced before the wardens, since promptbooks were usually inscribed: "The book of. . . ." Roberts printed the play in the same year for Hayes, to whom he had transferred the rights of publication, with the following title page:

> The most excellent / Historie of the *Merchant / of Venice.* / VVith the extreame cruelitie of *Shylocke* the Iewe / towards the sayd Merchant, in cutting a just pound / of his flesh: and the obtayning of *Portia* / by the choyse of three / chests. / *As it hath beene diuers times acted by the Lord / Chamberlaine his Seruants.* / Written by William Shakespeare. / [Printer's device] / AT LONDON, / Printed by *I. R.* for Thomas Heyes, / and are to be sold in Paules Church-yard, at the / signe of the Greene Dragon. / 1600.

The copy used for printing the first quarto (Q1) was probably not the promptbook itself, which was too valuable to be put into the hands of typesetters, but a copy, possibly in Shakespeare's own hand. The presence of a number of indeterminate or descriptive stage directions points away from prompt copy, while the absence of numerous printing errors, typical of foul papers, points to fair copy provenance.

The play was printed by two of Roberts's compositors, the same ones who set the second quarto of *Titus Andronicus* and later set the second quarto of *Hamlet*. Both were competent workmen who carefully followed copy. Q1 contains ten sheets of text (A–K), including the title page. Missing capital letters, mainly at the beginning of verse lines, especially later in the text, may indicate a shortage of capital letters in the type case, or perhaps Shakespeare's tendency to omit them at the beginning of verse lines when he was composing rapidly. Variations in speech ascriptions, particularly for Shylock, may have been otherwise influenced.

Q1 was reprinted in 1619 as part of an intended collection of Shakespeare's plays printed by William Jaggard for Thomas Pavier. When the collection was aborted, Pavier put a falsely dated title page (but without Hayes's name) on the quarto, which he tried to sell as the original publication. Although this quarto (Q2) has no textual authority, it shows signs of having been carefully edited. Some obvious errors are corrected, but other alterations reveal a somewhat officious editor, revising or rewriting words and phrases. Some new stage directions also appear, while others are missing. Although on balance it seems unlikely that the editor collated his copy of Q2 against an authoritative manuscript, he may have had recourse to something other than his own judgment or guesswork. In any case, Q2 shows something about the way a Shakespeare play was read in 1619. It is possible, however, that Jaggard's compositor B, who had a major hand in the printing of the First Folio (1623), may have been at least partly responsible for Q2's variant readings.

In 1623 Shakespeare's fellow shareholders in the King's Men, John Heminge and Henry Condell, collected their late colleague's plays for publication in what is now known as the First Folio. *The Merchant of Venice* was included among the comedies and was printed from a copy of Q1, edited to some extent with reference to a play-house promptbook, as its additional stage directions imply. As in Q2, the Folio editor and/or compositor corrected some errors while introducing others. In general, the punctuation is heavier in the First Folio and the spelling is updated. Some of the corrections in the Folio previously appeared in Q2, suggesting that Q2 may have influenced the Folio, since it is likely that a copy of Q2 was still available in Jaggard's printing shop. Besides numbering scenes, the Folio also added act divisions, which most modern editions follow. Three compositors, B, C, and D, set the text, which appears between *A Midsummer Night's Dream* and *As You Like It* on pages 163 through 184.

The First Folio was reprinted in 1632, 1663–1664, and 1685, but none of these editions have any authority, deriving as they do from reprints of what is essentially a reprint of Q1. In 1637, Q was reprinted a third time (Q3), by Thomas Hayes's son, Laurence, in what is actually a more faithful reprint of Q1 than is either Q2 or the First Folio. But like the other reprints, it has no textual authority.

Modern editions begin with Nicholas Rowe's in 1709, succeeded in the eighteenth century by editions by Alexander Pope (1723–1725), Lewis Theobald (1733), Thomas Hanmer (1743–1744), Samuel Johnson (1765), Edward Capell (1767–1768), and culminating in Edmund Malone's important edition of 1790. Many of these early editors took occasion to "correct" or improve Shakespeare's plays on their own authority, a practice that editors in the nineteenth century began to modify. By the twentieth century, editors paid more careful attention to the earliest editions in attempts to uncover what Shakespeare actually wrote, and emendations of the text became far less capricious and more scientifically based. Some of the best and most reliable editions now appear from Oxford University Press, Cambridge University Press, the Folger Library, and Routledge (the Arden publications), in which editorial procedure is scrupulously outlined and followed.

SOURCES FOR THE PLAY

For his plots, Shakespeare drew upon several sources. The flesh-bond story probably derives from Giovanni Fiorentino's *Il pecorone*, in which a young man named Giannetto borrows money from his adoptive father, Ansaldo. He wants to try to win the hand of an unnamed wealthy heiress, the lady of Belmonte. After a couple of unsuccessful attempts, Giannetto finally succeeds, but in so doing he has forced Ansaldo to borrow money from a Jewish moneylender. Forgetting the due date of the loan, Giannetto allows Ansaldo to default on his bond with the moneylender, causing him to forfeit a pound of his flesh. When Giannetto belatedly tries to repay the loan, the moneylender refuses anything but the forfeit. Meanwhile, the lady appears in disguise as a lawyer and foils the moneylender's designs upon Ansaldo's life. While in disguise, she also manages to get Giannettos's ring, the very one she gave him. At the end of the story, they all return to Belmonte (except, of course, the moneylender), and the lady reveals her clever deception to Giannetto. Ansaldo marries the waiting maid who had helped Giannetto learn the secret to winning the lady's hand.

In Fiorentino's tale, there are no caskets to choose from. That part of the story derives instead from Richard Robinson's translation of the *Gesta romanorum* in 1595. Nor does the moneylender have to convert to Christianity at the end. Other differences, such as the doubling of the marriages and ring plots, suggest that Shakespeare transformed the plot for his own purposes. Shakespeare borrowed the Jessica-Lorenzo plot from Masuccio Salernitano's *Il novellino*, which depicts a young woman locked up by her father until a clever young man finds a means of elopement for the two of them. Marlowe's *The Jew of Malta*, in which the Jew Barabas has a daughter, Abigail, who loves a Christian, also may have influenced Shakespeare. Other sources may have suggested some details to Shakespeare, who might have known a now-lost play called *The Jew* that possibly told a similar story of a vicious moneylender and his daughter.

STRUCTURE AND PLOTTING

Like many of Shakespeare's comedies, *The Merchant of Venice* contains several plot lines, although these must not be confused with its dramatic structure. The several plots that make up *The Merchant of Venice* are: the Portia-Bassanio love story, or the casket-choice plot; the Antonio-Shylock, or the flesh-bond, plot; the Jessica-Lorenzo elopement; and the ring plot. The dramatic structure of the play emerges from the intersection of these plots with one another, including events involving the minor character, Launcelot Gobbo. Or, to put it another way, the dramatic structure of the play consists of its overall design and the way each scene, or elements of a scene, may relate to the scenes or passages that precede and follow it. For, as always, the scene is the basic dramatic unit in Elizabethan drama.

Parallels and contrasts are important in the dramatic structure of any Shakespearean play. For example, the first two scenes of *The Merchant of Venice* display important parallels. In 1.1, Antonio complains of depression, and in 1.2 Portia similarly, but for understandable reasons, also feels unhappy. We never learn the reason for Antonio's depression, nor does he, but Portia's despondency is alleviated when in act 3 Bassanio, whom she loves, makes the correct choice of the caskets laid out before him.

Bonds of various kinds also help to define the dramatic as well as the thematic structure of the play. In 1.1 Antonio is clearly bound to his friend Bassanio, as Bassanio is to him. In 1.2 Portia is bound to her father's will, and in 1.3 Antonio becomes bound to Shylock by his agreement to the terms of the loan Shylock proposes. In 2.1 the Prince of Morocco is bound to the terms imposed on anyone who wishes to choose among the three caskets, as are, in later scenes, the Prince of Arragon and Bassanio. In 2.2 Launcelot is bound to Shylock as his servant and debates with himself whether or not to break that bond with his master. In the scene immediately following, Jessica also feels bound to Shylock but is ready to sever that bond and marry Lorenzo. Thus all of the various plots are connected thematically and dramatically, by parallels and contrasts, by various types of bonds.

Acts 3 through 5 display the consequences of these bonds and introduce, in the ring plot, new kinds of bonds. Jessica's elopement precipitates in Shylock his strong feeling for revenge against Antonio, who has long been his antagonist. But Jessica's betrayal, with the assistance of the Christian community (at least as Shylock sees this event), is the last straw. Shylock now sees his chance to take advantage of the bond he has made with Antonio, and nothing anyone says can dissuade him from his course of vengeful action.

Once Bassanio has chosen the right casket, he becomes bound in matrimony to Portia, as the ring she gives him symbolizes. But, as Portia realizes, that bond does not nullify his bond of friendship to Antonio, and she acts to assist him in saving his friend. In act 4, appearing in disguise, she saves Antonio's life by illuminating aspects of the flesh bond that Shylock failed to consider. She goes further and reveals laws that bind Shylock as an alien to a severe sentence: death and confiscation of all his worldly goods. The Duke and Antonio, however, choose to be merciful and let Shylock live and retain at least a portion of his wealth. In return Shylock must abandon his former religion and bind himself to Christianity.

In 4.2 Portia and Nerissa manage to get Bassanio and Gratiano to relinquish the rings they gave their husbands in 3.2. This episode provides the structure for act 5 and its relation to the foregoing acts; otherwise, act 5 might seem as a mere appendage to the rest of the play. When everyone returns to Belmont, the women "discover" that their husbands no longer have the rings they gave them, symbols of their bond of fidelity. The conflict is resolved in comic fashion when the women reveal how they obtained the rings and once again bestow them on their husbands, having now taught them an important lesson in loyalty and the priority of obligations. For no matter how dear Antonio is to Bassanio, Portia must now and forever remain her husband's first and most important love.

MAIN CHARACTERS

Shylock

Although Shylock appears in only five scenes, in many ways he seems to dominate the action of *The Merchant of Venice*. He is certainly a very powerful figure as well as a very complex one. When first seen, he is extremely resentful of Antonio and the way Antonio has treated him; hence, he senses an opportunity for revenge when Bassanio comes to borrow money from him in Antonio's name. When Antonio enters the scene, however, Shylock also sees an opportunity to resolve their old enmity. As a moneylender he therefore makes an extraordinary gesture in offering Antonio the loan at no interest. As security for the loan, Shylock laughingly offers to take a "merry bond" of a pound of flesh (1.3.173), which he says would be useless if Antonio should default (1.3.163–167).

Antonio agrees. But when Jessica elopes with Antonio's friend Lorenzo, Shylock becomes enraged. At the same time, he hears of Antonio's losses at sea and perceives his advantage (3.1.44–50). He makes an oath to take his forfeiture of the bond of flesh if Antonio should default. Accordingly, when Antonio cannot repay the loan on the due date, Shylock demands his pound of flesh. Portia, disguised as the lawyer Balthasar, tries to persuade Shylock to show mercy, but instead he demands "justice." As he is about thrust his knife into Antonio's body, Portia stops him. Since the bond stipulates only flesh and no blood, Shylock is foiled. He tries to leave with only his principal, but since he has insisted on the strict terms of the bond, Portia holds him to them.

When Portia then levels the charge against him for plotting against the life of a Venetian citizen, Shylock is in danger of losing his life as well as his worldly goods. Showing mercy on his part, the Duke spares Shylock's life, and Antonio agrees to let him keep half his possessions provided that he convert to Christianity and at his death bequeath everything he has to Lorenzo and Jessica. Crushed, Shylock agrees. Here as earlier, when he refused to show mercy and determined to murder Antonio, Shylock reveals that, his protestations notwithstanding, he is not only a bad person, but a bad Jew; for he has violated some of the most serious tenets of his religion, and he is even willing to become an apostate.

Shylock's famous speech that begins "Hath not a Jew eyes" (3.1.59ff) is often taken as demonstrating his humanity, although in context it is used to justify his revenge. Showing many of the faults other human beings are prone to have, Shylock is thoroughly human and not the Elizabethan stereotype of a Jew. His relationship with Jessica is, at the very least, problematic. She hates living with him, not because he mistreats her—there is no warrant in the text for that interpretation—but because, as she says, "Our house is hell" (2.3.2). That description probably refers to Shylock's austere way of life. He dislikes music and any display of merriment, such as masques (see 2.5.28–36). When she leaves, taking with her his ducats and jewels, Shylock is nearly heartbroken. He is also furious with her. But when he learns that she has exchanged for a monkey the ring that his dead wife, Leah, had given him, he shows a tender side of his character, too (3.1.118–123), declaring, "I would not have given it for a wilderness of monkeys" (3.1.122–123).

Antonio

Antonio is the "merchant" of the play's title. He is a magnifico, that is, a wealthy man well regarded in Venetian society. His wealth derives from his import/export trade. He is devoted to his young friend, Bassanio, to whom he has lent money several times in the past; though lacking ready cash, he is willing to borrow for Bassanio's benefit. Here he may be generous to a fault.

Antonio's relationship with Bassanio in the view of some stage directors as well as critics may be homoerotic, at least latently. That may help to explain Antonio's depressed feelings at the beginning of the play, if he suspects that Bassanio is coming to say that he wants to woo someone for his wife. Salerio eloquently describes Antonio's devotion to his young friend at 2.8.35–49, and Solanio agrees that "he only loves the world for him" (2.8.50). When Antonio defaults on his bond with Shylock, he stoically faces his death. He is an avowed anti-Semite (see 1.3.130–137) and realizes that nothing he can say will deter Shylock from his revenge (4.1.70–83). When it is his turn to show mercy to Shylock, he insists on two conditions: that Shylock convert to Christianity and that Shylock bequeath everything to Lorenzo at his death. For many modern critics this is hardly mercy, though in Shakespeare's time it might have been perceived as such.

When Portia in disguise as Balthasar saves Antonio's life, she asks only for the ring on Bassanio's finger as reward. Bassanio naturally demurs, but Antonio insists that he give the ring; so he does. At the end of the play, when Portia reveals her disguise and shows Bassanio the ring, she gives it to Antonio to give back to Bassanio, thus underlining for her husband that henceforth she, not Antonio, is the primary person in his life.

Bassanio

Bassanio at first appears as a rather cavalier young man, something of a ne'er-do-well and certainly a spendthrift, though handsome and accomplished. A young lord, he is typical of the people of his social standing in Shakespeare's time. But he has other qualities, too, that make Portia as well as Antonio love him. For example, he does not want Antonio to take Shylock's money under the terms of the bond offered (1.3.154–155). He shows good insight when he chooses the right casket, proclaiming "So may the outward shows be least themselves" (3.2.73). When he gets the news of Antonio's default, he is distraught, and only when Portia sends him back to Venice with more than enough money to redeem his friend does he recover a little.

In the court scene, Bassanio does his best to fend off Shylock, offering him not only more than the original amount of the loan, but his own body as well (4.1.209–214). He offers even to sacrifice his beloved wife to save Antonio (4.1.282–287), not realizing that Portia is right there in disguise as Balthasar. Reluctant though he is to surrender the ring that Portia gave him, he nevertheless lets Antonio persuade him to do so, erring yet again. He thus stands in need of instruction, which his wife provides at the end of the play. He accepts that instruction with a good grace and a little humor, showing his true mettle once again.

Portia

Portia is the heroine of the play. A very clever woman, she also shows very human qualities, as when she laments being compelled to obey the dictates of her father's will, and even more when she confesses how much she loves Bassanio and does not want him to rush into making his choice of the caskets (3.2.1–24). She can also be somewhat arrogant, as evidenced by her attitude toward her other suitors in 1.2 and later toward Morocco and Arragon. She may also be a bit of a racist (2.7.78–79), though she does not exhibit any overt anti-Semitism.

Portia's big moment comes in the trial scene, where she appears in disguise as Bellario's colleague, Balthasar. Her appeal to Shylock to show mercy is an extremely eloquent statement on the nature of this virtue (4.1.184–205), possibly intended not only for Shylock but also for the others present, as subsequent events reveal. That her speech fails to move Shylock says more about him and his determination to commit murder than it does about her ability to persuade. When she springs the trap that Shylock falls into because of his diabolical determination, she shows that she, too, can be adamant in insisting that he get no more than the justice he has been demanding, that is, the specific terms of the bond.

Portia's appeal to mercy has its consequent effect on the Duke and on Antonio, as they spare Shylock's life and half his fortune. Throughout the court scene, Portia shows her poise and ability to deal with men of different types. She also shows her sense of humor when she comments on Bassanio's lines about sacrificing his wife (4.1.288–289) and later back in Belmont when she teases Bassanio about giving up the ring he swore to keep. She teaches him a good lesson, and while she is about it, bestows gifts upon both Lorenzo and Antonio, bringing the play to a happy conclusion, at least as far as the Christians are concerned.

Nerissa

Nerissa is Portia's lady-in-waiting and confidante. Like her mistress, she has a keen wit and ability to handle difficult situations. When Portia complains about feeling low, Nerissa reminds her lady how well off she really is. Nerissa later explains the wisdom that Portia's father showed in providing the way to find a husband who truly loved her (1.2.27–33). In the same scene she teases her mistress about her undesirable suitors and only afterward tells her that they have all decided to leave without choosing any of the caskets.

Nerissa does not have a major role, but she doubles the audience's pleasure when she and Gratiano announce they have decided to get married, too, and again later when she gets her husband's ring off his finger. She is a sprightly woman, as she shows in her argument with Gratiano in 5.1, which leads directly to the unraveling of the ring plot that Portia has devised to teach these husbands a necessary lesson.

Gratiano

Bassanio's friend Gratiano is a rather wild individual, as Bassanio notes when cautioning him to behave if he goes to Belmont (2.2.180–189). He is also the play's most outspoken and virulent anti-Semite, as his speeches against Shylock in 4.1 indicate (see, for example, 128–138). He provides a good deal of humor, nevertheless, in his relationship with Nerissa, and Shakespeare gives him the last lines in the play, with an appropriate sexual pun on "ring."

Jessica

Shylock's daughter at first appears as a troubled young woman determined to escape from an existence she finds too restrictive. To accomplish her goal, she is even willing to abandon not only her home but even her religion to marry a Christian. Some stage directors think that by the play's end she may have second thoughts about her behavior and show some regret, especially if her husband Lorenzo is played as a scamp or, worse, a gold digger.

Launcelot Gobbo

Launcelot is the clown, providing some funny wordplay as well as low comedy in *The Merchant of Venice*. He and Jessica have a friendly relationship (see 2.3.1–4), though he teases her rather harshly about her conversion to Christianity in 3.5. His role is often cut down in productions, despite his famous line ("it is a wise father that knows his own child," 2.2.76–77) in a scene with his father, Old Gobbo, that helps to develop the theme of bonds between parents and children.

DEVICES AND TECHNIQUES

Stylistic Variety

Shakespeare uses a variety of styles in *The Merchant of Venice* for different effects. His basic style is the iambic pentameter blank verse with which the play begins. It is not the "high" style of the history plays, or the formal style of the Duke's speeches in 4.1, but a more conversational one suitable for dialogue among friends. In the next scene Portia and Nerissa speak in prose, dropping the informal tone still further, as the two women discuss Portia's father's will and the various suitors who have come to visit her. Prose continues in the beginning of scene 3, as Shylock and Bassanio discuss a business deal, but Shakespeare switches again to blank verse when Antonio enters for the more formal discourse between the two major antagonists and the heightening tension in the scene.

Still greater formality characterizes the casket-choosing scenes, particularly those involving the princes of Morocco and Arragon, but again Shakespeare reverts to prose for Launcelot's comic monologue in 2.2 and his dialogue with Old Gobbo. Later in the scene Bassanio speaks mainly in blank verse, as appropriate to his rank and station, while the Gobbos continue speaking to him in prose, as appropriate to theirs. Launcelot and Jessica have a brief scene (2.3) in which she speaks in verse and he in prose, but their comic scene in 3.5 is in prose, which switches to blank verse after Lorenzo enters and Launcelot leaves. Thus Shakespeare maintains a kind of decorum, using different stylistic forms to signal shifts in character or situation.

Other verse forms than blank verse appear, as needed. For example, the scrolls within the gold and silver caskets are in tetrameter couplets that have a kind of jingling ring, appropriate to the comic action. The verse form for the song in 3.2, performed as Bassanio contemplates his choice of casket, while also tetrameter, does not jingle; rather, it is typical of the lyrics of that period put to musical accompaniment. Finally, the scroll Bassanio finds in the lead casket along with Portia's portrait does not jingle either; while still in tetrameter couplets, it conveys a more serious message, consistent with the theme of deceptive appearance that the other scrolls convey in a more satirical vein. In Shakespeare's hands, a verse form becomes a highly versatile medium of expression.

Imagery

The Merchant of Venice is a play rich in imagery. Not surprisingly, some of the most notable image patterns involve not only romantic expressions of love but also metaphors relating to the world of commerce. Salerio attributes Antonio's depression, or sadness, to his worry over his ships: his mind is "tossing on the ocean," he says, adding: "There where your argosies with portly sail / Like signiors and rich burghers on the flood, / . . . / Do overpeer the petty traffickers" (1.1.8–12). Salerio continues in this vein for several more lines, until Antonio's demurrer, whereupon Solanio suggests that Antonio is in love. Antonio at once rejects that thought, and love imagery is reserved for Portia's and Jessica's suitors and for the women.

Jessica uses a standard reference to Cupid when she greets her lover, Lorenzo, as they are about to elope. Commenting on her disguise as a boy, she says: "But love

is blind, and lovers cannot see / The pretty follies that themselves commit"
(2.6.36–37). Portia is more voluble and much more deeply in love, as her speeches
indicate in 3.2. She can scarcely maintain her maiden reserve, as she tries to get Bassanio to delay longer before his choice of a casket; her convoluted utterance conveys something of her confusion about being in love:

> Beshrew your eyes,
> They have o'erlook'd me and divided me:
> One half of me is yours, the other half yours—
> Mine own, I would say, but if mine, then yours,
> And so all yours. (3.2.14–18)

The metaphor of division suggests a business transaction, which her next words
confess:

> O these naughty times
> Puts bars between the owners and their rights!
> And so though yours, not yours. Prove it so.... (3.2.18–20)

The use of commercial metaphor in a love situation may strike the reader as odd,
except that the play is much about transactions of this sort, not only the literal business transaction undertaken between Shylock and Antonio. Portia is very mindful
of the kind of transaction that marriage to Bassanio will entail, as she says after he
chooses the right casket:

> You see me, Lord Bassanio, where I stand,
> Such as I am. Though for myself alone
> I would not be ambitious in my wish
> To wish myself much better, yet for you,
> I would be trebled twenty times myself,
> A thousand times more fair, ten thousand times more rich,
> That only to stand high in your account,
> I might in virtues, beauties, livings, friends,
> Exceed account. (3.2.149–157)

By contrast, Bassanio is the more typical romantic lover, as his words and images express his feelings after he has made his choice and found Portia's portrait in
the lead casket:

> Fair Portia's counterfeit! What demigod
> Hath come so near creation? Move these eyes?
> Or whether, riding on the balls of mine,
> Seem they in motion? Here are sever'd lips,
> Parted with sugar breath; so sweet a bar
> Should sunder such sweet friends. Here in her hairs
> The painter plays the spider, and hath woven
> A golden mesh t' entrap the hearts of men
> Faster than gnats in cobwebs. (3.2.115–123)

The "sugar breath," the "golden mesh" of hair—to "entrap the hearts of men"—are approximate clichés of the Elizabethan sonneteer describing his mistress, although here they describe merely her picture.

Caroline Spurgeon remarks in *Shakespeare's Imagery* (Cambridge: Cambridge UP, 1935), that music suffuses important moments in the play (269–271). In 3.2, for example, when Portia orders the song to be sung as Bassanio contemplates the caskets, she says:

> Let music sound while he doth make his choice;
> Then if he lose he makes a swan-like end,
> Fading in music. (3.2.43–45)

But if he wins,

>   Then music is
> Even as the flourish when true subjects bow
> To a new-crowned monarch; such it is
> As are those dulcet sounds in break of day
> That creep into the dreaming bridegroom's ear,
> And summon him to marriage. (3.2.48–53)

In another scene at the end of the play, music also plays an important role, both in actual sound as well as imagery, when Lorenzo summons the musicians to play for Jessica and himself:

> How sweet the moonlight sleeps upon this bank!
> Here will we sit, and let the sounds of music
> Creep in our ears. Soft stillness and the night
> Become the touches of sweet harmony. (5.1.54–57)

When Jessica complains that she is "never merry" when she hears sweet music, Lorenzo launches into a long speech explaining that her spirits are too "attentive" (5.1.70); he contrasts her experience with that of wild animals struck spellbound by music, and with Orpheus's effect on even inanimate objects, such as stones and trees.

Other images abound, such as the ones Portia uses to describe the quality of mercy (4.1.184–202). There she compares unforced mercy to the gentle rain that drops from heaven above, and to the power of a monarch, which mercy exceeds. The image she builds is of Mercy as an enthroned deity. The beauty of this imagery contrasts with the sordid imagery Shylock uses to explain his feelings against Antonio, who, he says, has spit upon his "Jewish gabardine" (1.3.112) and called him "cut-throat dog" (1.3.111). He dwells on this image of the "stranger cur" (1.3.118) in this first scene between them and again later after the bond is forfeit, when Shylock says, "Thou call'dst me dog before thou hadst a cause, / But since I am a dog, beware my fangs" (3.3.6–7). Gratiano picks up the image in the court scene, calling Shylock an "inexecrable dog" and referring to his "currish spirit" (4.1.128, 133). Indeed, for Gratiano, and by extension others present there, Shylock's desires "Are wolvish, bloody, starv'd, and ravenous" (4.1.138).

Classical, Biblical, and Other Allusions

Shakespeare and his audience were very well versed in the classics, and since English Bibles were available in post-Reformation England and church attendance on Sundays was compulsory, they had good knowledge of the scriptures. *The Merchant of Venice* is studded with references to both the classics and the Bible, not to show off Shakespeare's learning but functionally to develop certain aspects of the play, its characters, and its events. For example, to show how wonderful and virtuous Portia is, when Bassanio mentions her name to Antonio, he says she is "nothing undervalu'd / To Cato's daughter, Brutus' Portia" (1.1.165–166). He thus compares her to the famous daughter of the Stoic Cato the Younger, she who married Brutus, one of the conspirators who killed Julius Caesar. Later, after Bassanio has chosen the correct casket and won Portia for his wife, Gratiano boasts to Lorenzo and Salerio that Bassanio and he are "the Jasons, we have won the fleece" (3.2.241). Jason and his Argonauts were well-known for sailing to Colchis to retrieve a valued fleece of a ram. Classical allusions may be used for comic purposes, too. For instance, the Prince of Morocco, trying to show off his learning, gets his mythology mixed up when he alludes to Hercules (Alcides) and Lichas playing at dice (2.1.32–35; Hercules wins, not Lichas, in the actual story).

In a play that has important moral themes, many biblical allusions naturally arise. Shylock tells Antonio how Jacob cleverly won a large part of Laban's flock by setting up certain wands to cause the ewes to deliver parti-colored sheep and uses this example to justify his lending money at interest (1.3.77–96; alluding to Genesis 30:25–43). Antonio warns Bassanio that "the devil can cite Scripture for his purpose" (1.3.98), an allusion to Matthew 4:6 and Luke 4:10. In her set speech on the quality of mercy (4.1.184–202), Portia alludes to Ecclesiasticus of the Apocrypha 35:19 and Deuteronomy 32:2, as well as to the classical debate on conflicting claims of justice and mercy in Seneca's *De clementia*.

Shakespeare uses biblical allusion in another way, too, in the court scene. When Shylock prepares to cut his pound of flesh from Antonio and Portia stops him just in time, they reenact a very significant episode in Genesis, the Binding of Isaac. Just as the angel stopped Abraham from sacrificing his son, Portia stops Shylock from killing Antonio, who has already described himself as a kind of sacrifice (4.1.114–115, 265–266). In so doing, she prevents Shylock from committing a terrible crime, both against Antonio and himself, insofar as Shylock was not only about to violate the commandment against murder but also about to forsake his humanity in the process.

THEMES AND MEANINGS

Bonds

Much has already been said about the importance of bonds in *The Merchant of Venice*: between parent and child, master and servant, creditor and borrower. Perhaps a little more needs to be said about the bonds between human beings in general. Antonio's antipathy toward Shylock, which he confesses in 1.3, suggests that he hardly considers the Jew to be human. In his treatment of Shylock, he violates the common bond of decency that should obtain between all human beings. The anti-Semitism that he represents along with Gratiano and others is everywhere ap-

parent in the play and everywhere deplorable. Shylock's revenge against his persecutors is thus understandable, though hardly excusable. When he seeks to exact his
pound of flesh nearest Antonio's heart, he not only violates the commandment
against murder, he violates the bond between human beings, all of whom should
hold life precious. In preventing Shylock from carrying out his crime, Portia saves
both Antonio and Shylock—the latter from committing a terrible act against another human being.

Friendship

The bond of friendship is another important theme in *The Merchant of Venice.*
Most obvious is the bond between Antonio and Bassanio; it also appears in the
friendship between Bassanio and Gratiano, whom Bassanio, against his better
judgment, is willing to take with him to Belmont. Lorenzo also figures into the
friendship of these men, who assist in his elopement with Jessica. Because of Bassanio's friendship with Lorenzo, Portia is willing to entrust the care of her estate to
him when she leaves for Venice with Nerissa.

However strong the bonds of friendship are, and they are very strong indeed—
Antonio is willing to risk his life for his friend, after all—the play shows that these
bonds must give way to another, still stronger one: that between husband and wife.
This is the point of the ring plot that Portia and Nerissa contrive against their husbands after 4.1. They are determined to show the men how important their vows
are; the rings become symbolic of those vows. Perhaps they get the hint for this
plot when in the court scene each husband declares how willing he is to sacrifice
his wife if that would help save Antonio's life (4.1.282–287, 290–292). At the end of
the play, Portia cleverly gives the ring to Antonio to give back to Bassanio, by this
means showing the ascendancy of married love over the friendship that hitherto
held sway.

Deceptive Appearance and Disguise

Deceptive appearance and disguise are also important themes. The first two suitors are deceived by the outward surface appearance of the caskets, as Morocco discovers when he reads, "All that glisters is not gold" (2.7.65). Similarly, Arragon
discovers that "Some there be that shadows kiss, / Such have but a shadow's bliss"
(2.9.66–67). Bassanio is wiser. He begins his contemplation of the caskets with "So
may the outward shows be least themselves— / The world is still deceiv'd with or-
nament" (3.2.73–74). He thus chooses the lead casket, though it is outwardly the
least attractive of the three.

Elizabethans accepted the theatrical convention of "impenetrable disguise,"
which Portia and Nerissa adopt to help save Antonio; their disguise deceives everyone present in the court, including their own husbands. The disguise works further
to deceive Shylock, who in demanding justice fails to see beyond the letter of the
contract he has with Antonio and all its implications. He calls Portia, in disguise as
Dr. Balthazar, "A Daniel come to judgment! yea, a Daniel! / O wise young judge"
(4.1.223–224). Blinded by his diabolical lust for vengeance, he fails to perceive the
wisdom of Portia's appeal for mercy, which is clear and persuasive to everyone but

him. His self-deception leads directly into Portia's deceptive agreement that he has a right to his pound of flesh—until she springs her trap.

Mercy and Vengeance

In many of his plays, comedies as well as tragedies, Shakespeare examines revenge, a compelling theme in much Elizabethan literature. Both church and state vehemently opposed personal vengeance, which Francis Bacon called a kind of wild justice, not sanctioned by law or scripture ("Vengeance is mine; I will repay, sayeth the Lord," Romans 12:19). In his most eloquent speech, Shylock defends himself and his people as human beings who should be treated as such ("Hath not a Jew eyes?" 3.1.59–73). But in context, he uses his claim of common humanity to justify his action against Antonio. Listing many human attributes that Jews share with Christians, he concludes: "And if you wrong us, shall we not revenge? If we are like you in the rest, we will resemble you in that." He thus perverts his eloquent apologia to condone, he believes, his intention to take personal vengeance against his erstwhile enemy.

The counter argument appears in Portia's beautiful lines on the quality of mercy. Her plea is mercy, not revenge. She elevates the attribute of mercy even higher than the "sceptred sway" of kings (4.1.193). Mercy, she says, is an attribute of God himself, and she argues that this virtue should "season" justice (4.1.197). Note that she does not deny the importance of justice: justice comes first, then mercy follows. Shakespeare is no sentimentalist, nor does he allow Portia to be one. She recognizes, or says she does, the justice of Shylock's claim against Antonio; the contract they have made is valid, at least as far as it goes. But mercy should supervene.

This is the lesson that the Duke and Antonio, if not Shylock, learn when they spare Shylock's life. The quality of Antonio's further mercy, however, is debatable, especially in the terms he lays down (see next section). The Duke without hesitation reprieves Shylock, but Antonio insists on some provisos. Is this Antonio's revenge, masked as mercy?

CRITICAL CONTROVERSIES

Is *The Merchant of Venice* Anti-Semitic?

Much ink has been spilled over the question of whether *The Merchant of Venice* is anti-Semitic. While most critics concede that anti-Semitism exists in the play, as in Antonio's and Gratiano's attitude toward Shylock, that does not necessarily mean that the play is anti-Semitic. Other critics maintain that from the way Shylock is addressed throughout *The Merchant of Venice*, usually not by name but as "Jew," to the way Shakespeare characterizes him, making his own daughter abhor him and his household, the play is thoroughly anti-Semitic. They go further and claim that Shakespeare in writing the play displays his own anti-Semitism.

Clearly, Shylock is the villain of the piece, and his Jewishness is very much at issue. But Shakespeare makes it clear that he is not only a bad man, he is also a bad Jew. He violates some of his religion's most fundamental precepts, including his action at the end when, rather than risk death by adhering to his faith, he chooses to convert, to become an apostate. In all of his actions, then, Shylock appears by no means as a typical Jew—which would make the play anti-Semitic—but as a renegade Jew. Only the distortions of his representation, such as the Nazis under Hitler delighted in, could make him—and the play—representative of Jewish villainy.

Antonio's Mercy

How merciful is Antonio to Shylock at 4.1.380–390? True, he agrees to let Shylock have his life and half his fortune, but he stipulates two conditions. The first is that Shylock must become a Christian; the second, that he must bequeath all of his possessions to Lorenzo and his daughter. Antonio further states that he will use and render his half of Shylock's fortune, retained as part of the fine, "Upon his death unto the gentleman / That lately stole his daughter" (4.1.384–385). This is surely rubbing salt into Shylock's wounds, but much more significant is the requirement that Shylock must convert.

Perhaps many in Shakespeare's original audiences would see the requirement for conversion as Antonio's way of doing Shylock a favor. For Christian believers, the only means to salvation was acceptance of Jesus Christ as the savior. Otherwise, one was condemned to eternal damnation. But such forced conversions could not be regarded as authentic and indeed were not sanctioned by the Church. Moreover, Antonio seems to take full advantage of the power he has over Shylock at this moment. If Shylock's revenge was diabolical, how much better is Antonio's? He wounds Shylock deeply, as becomes evident when Shylock begs at last to be allowed to leave and complains that he is not well (4.1.395–396). He does not appear again in the play, and some speculate that he may even die soon afterward, as Laurence Olivier seemed to indicate in his celebrated representation of Shylock at the National Theatre in London, when he uttered a terrifying offstage scream after exiting the scene.

Jewish Justice versus Christian Mercy

Barbara Lewalski ("Biblical Allusion and Allegory in *The Merchant of Venice*," *Shakespeare Quarterly* 13 [1962]: 327–343) and some other scholars have treated *The Merchant of Venice* as allegorically opposing Jewish justice (in the Old Testament) against Christian mercy (in the New Testament). As a Jew, Shylock demands justice and rejects mercy in 4.1. As a Christian, Portia counters with the claims of mercy, which should season justice. In this way, it appears, the New Testament stands opposed to the Old. But this is to approach the play as well as scripture simplistically. Mercy is very much a highly regarded virtue in the Old Testament as well as in the New (see, for example, Psalm 106). "Love thy neighbor as thyself" is not solely a New Testament teaching. It has plenty of precedent in the Old Testament: "You shall not hate your brother in your heart, but you shall reason with your neighbor, lest you bear sin because of him. You shall not take vengeance or bear any grudge against the sons of your own people, but you shall love your neighbor as yourself" (Leviticus 19:17–18; see also 33–34). Similarly, the Golden Rule, though couched in negative terms, derives from Old Testament precepts, as propounded by the Jewish sage Hillel, who declared, "That which is hateful to you, do not do unto others. That is the fundamental lesson of the Torah. The rest is commentary."

PRODUCTION HISTORY

The Merchant of Venice is one of the most frequently performed of Shakespeare's plays. The reason for its popularity in the theater is not hard to discern. A play of rich complexity, it raises perennially significant issues of justice and mercy, friendship and (or, perhaps, *versus*) matrimony, appearance and reality. In addition, the play's many passages of engaging poetry, comic interludes, opportunities for splendid stage settings, and above all its vehicle for starring roles in Portia and Shylock make it attractive for producers.

The stage history of *The Merchant of Venice* is one of the most fascinating studies of all Shakespeare plays. First produced in 1596, it is known to have been played before King James and his court several times in February 1605. Although no hard evidence exists to describe the way Shylock was performed, or who first essayed the role, very likely he was originally played as a comic villain, complete with red wig and beard in the manner of Marlowe's Barabas in *The Jew of Malta*. In the 1950s at the Oregon Shakespeare Festival in Ashland, Oregon, Angus Bowmer followed that model when he played Shylock. To the surprise of many who had been brought up to view Shylock as a tragic hero, Bowmer's enactment worked very well. Shylock as a comic villain was clearly the way he was performed at the end of the seventeenth century and the beginning of the eighteenth, if we may judge from how Thomas Doggett enacted the role in George Granville's adaptation called *The Jew of Venice*, first produced in 1701.

Granville's Shylock held sway for forty years, although given the number of recorded performances of *The Merchant of Venice* on the professional stage, the play itself was not highly popular. Not until Charles Macklin restored Shakespeare's version in the later eighteenth century did the play's popularity really improve. In Macklin's interpretation, Shylock became a fierce villain, much in the way that Maria Edgeworth reconstructs his performance in her novel *Harrington* (1817). Macklin may have taken his cue from a remark by Rowe in the biographical essay prefaced to his 1709 edition, in which he recognizes that although the play has usually been regarded as a comedy and performed accordingly, he "cannot but think that it was design'd Tragically by the Author." He justifies his contention by arguing that "There appears in it such a deadly Spirit of Revenge, such a savage Fierceness and Fellness, and such a bloody designation of Cruelty and Mischief, as cannot agree either with the Stile or Characters of Comedy" (*The Works of Mr. William Shakespear*, ed. Nicholas Rowe [London: Printed for Jacob Tonson, 1709], 1.xix–xx). This view of the play as tragedy differs greatly from that of performers in the nineteenth century who portrayed its tragic nature but reinterpreted Shylock's position.

In 1814 Edmund Kean played Shylock with yet another original conception of Shylock: this time as a man "[m]ore sinned against than sinning" (*King Lear*, 3.2.60), which epitomized Kean's new interpretation of the play's tragic aspect. Kean violated stage tradition by appearing in a black wig, loose gaberdine, and Venetian slippers. The boxes in the theater were empty and only about fifty people were in the audience, but theater history was made on January 26, 1814, the night of Kean's initial performance as Shylock.

Kean intellectualized the role, bringing a freshness of approach and energy. Kean's performance caused the critic William Hazlitt to alter completely his view of Shylock, which had been formed not by Shakespeare's text but by earlier portrayals on the stage. Hazlitt found Shylock in Kean's representation much more human than he had realized. In Frederick William Hawkins's *Life of Edmund Kean* (London: Tinsley Brothers, 1869), Hazlitt is recorded as saying that "Shakespeare could not easily divest his characters of their entire humanity; his Jew is more than half a Christian; and Mr. Kean's manner is much nearer the mark [than earlier representations]" (1.137). Only Edwin Forrest's Shylock in America rivaled Kean's. By contrast, William Charles Macready enacted Shylock not as a persecuted martyr, à la Kean, but as a dignified and stately man consumed with malice. In many nineteenth-century productions, which highlighted the pound-of-flesh plot, the play ended with act 4; Shakespeare's fifth act was regarded as a superfluous and unfortunate distraction.

By the nineteenth century, elaborate stage settings had replaced Shakespeare's bare stage and the rudimentary stage settings of the late seventeenth and eighteenth centuries. Charles Kean (Edmund's son) is perhaps the most noteworthy for his extravagant sets, though not especially for his acting. Using multiple levels and movable pieces, Charles Kean transformed the stage of the Princess's Theatre in London into a Venetian carnival for his 1858 production. Kean and his wife, Ellen Tree, played Shylock and Portia. Music and dance concluded the elopement scene, which ended act 2, while gondolas passed to and fro upon "real" canals. To allow for all the scene shifts required for his production, Kean had to cut a good deal of the text, even while restoring the roles of Morocco and Arragon, who had disappeared in some other versions. What he presented was Shakespeare, but what he omitted was a good deal of Shakespeare, too. The omissions may not have been sorely missed by ordinary playgoers, for they were compensated by the spectacles Kean provided. Whereas his father's performance had been a compelling drama, the younger Kean's production was "a magnificent show," according to Toby Lelyveld (*Shylock on the Stage* [Cleveland: The P of Western Reserve U, 1960], 59).

Perhaps the most outstanding and certainly the most influential production of *The Merchant of Venice* in the nineteenth century was that of Henry Irving, which opened in 1879 and continued for 250 performances. Like Charles Kean, Irving provided a spectacular stage set, but his performance and Ellen Terry's as Portia shone through nonetheless. Again, much was cut, partly to accommodate the spectacle but partly to highlight Irving's role. Irving introduced a new scene, one that many later productions incorporated: Shylock returning home in act 2 after dining at Bassanio's house. He knocks on the door of his home, which of course now is empty, Jessica having departed with much of his treasure. In Irving's representation of this scene, Shylock knocks just once—enough to arouse the desired pathos of the situation—although subsequent performers have sometimes overdone the scene, allowing it to degenerate into a frenzy of despair.

Irving, who dressed Shylock as an oriental Jew, remarked that the character was "the type of a persecuted race; almost the only gentleman in the play, and most illused" (as recorded in Joseph Hatton's *Henry Irving's Impressions of America* [London: S. Low, Marston, Searle, & Rivington, 1884], 2:265). Irving emphasized Shylock's "moments of sheer humanity" and his suffering so that despite his evident greed and vengefulness, one could almost forgive him. Ellen Terry's Portia was a good match for Irving's Shylock, bringing to the role an emphasis on the heroine's womanliness. Their teaming up lasted for more than two decades, as the production continued to draw crowds.

Portia's role is fraught with pitfalls. She can be too spirited and flighty, as enacted by Kitty Clive in Macklin's production, or too snobbish and sophisticated, as Joan Plowright was in Jonathan Miller's National Theatre production in 1970. She must be at once, or alternately, romantic, sensitive, witty, and intelligent—forceful but not overbearing, loving and in love but not sentimental. Among the most successful Portias have been Peg Woffington and Sarah Siddons in the eighteenth century, and Helen Faucit, Helena Modjeska, and Julia Marlowe in the nineteenth. In the twentieth century many actresses succeeded in conveying the complexity of the role, most particularly Sinead Cusack.

By the advent of the twentieth century, reaction against spectacular productions had already begun. William Poel, for example, had advocated a return to the simplicity and swiftness that were true of performances at Shakespeare's Globe Theatre. Where *The Merchant of Venice* was concerned, he argued against the prevailing conception of Shylock as a tragic figure, a misconception Poel attributed in part to a change in Britain's religion or politics. He maintained that Shylock is a villain, despised not so much because he is a Jew, but because he is a curmudgeon who, in a romantic comedy, must be defeated—as Shylock, in fact, is. For Poel, Shylock's Jewishness is almost incidental; the play has more to do with his profession as a usurer and his rigid adherence to legalism than with religious convictions.

By the 1930s, the Victorian tradition, which had climaxed in Irving's productions and was continued by Herbert Beerbohm Tree, Arthur Bourchier, Richard Mansfield, and others, had come to an end. Its last gasp was Frank Benson's final performance at the Shakespeare Memorial Theatre in Stratford-upon-Avon in 1932. When William Bridges-Adams took over as manager of the Stratford festival, he set out to breathe new life into Shakespearean productions. He invited Russian-born Theodore Komisarjevsky to direct *The Merchant of Venice*, which opened on July 25, 1932. As James Bulman notes in *Shakespeare in Performance: "The Merchant of Venice"* (54), Komisarjevsky opposed the pictorial realism, historical detail, naturalistic acting, and moral sententiousness that had previously dominated productions. While he retained all but fourteen lines of Shakespeare's text, he added some mimed scenes, such as some commedia dell'arte masquers at the beginning and a yawning Launcelot Gobbo at the end. Morocco, Arragon, and the Duke were burlesqued, and for the trial scene Antonio wore a huge ruff that made his face look like the head of John the Baptist on a charger. For Komisarjevsky the play was a fantastic comedy, to be staged as such, as his set designs clearly indicated. Buildings veered off at odd angles, and a Bridge of Sighs was split in two. Into this extravaganza, Randle Ayrton's traditional Shylock was out of place, resisting Komisarjevsky's attempt to reduce the role to comic villainy, as J. C. Trewin pointed out in *Shakespeare on the English Stage, 1900–1964* (London: Barne & Rockliff, 1964, 137).

Following World War II, directors found it impossible to ignore the Holocaust in their productions, although their efforts to deal with this experience varied. Jonathan Miller in his 1970 National Theatre production staged the play in the Victorian age. His Venice closely resembled the London of Benjamin Disraeli and Baron Rothschild, who because he was Jewish had to wait for eleven years, or until the Oath of Uniformity was modified, before taking his seat in parliament, though he had been duly elected. Miller thus used the play to advance a social program, to show the roots of modern anti-Semitism in economics and the competition for

Laurence Olivier as Shylock and Joan Plowright as Portia in the National Theatre's production of *The Merchant of Venice*, directed by Jonathan Miller. This production opened in the United Kingdom in 1970 and appeared on television in the United States in 1974. Courtesy of Photofest.

power. To make Shylock, played by Laurence Olivier, a more sympathetic character, Miller drastically cut the text. For example, he excised Shylock's long aside in 1.3, in which he expresses his hatred for Antonio as a Christian and an opponent to usury. Launcelot Gobbo's low comedy, often at the expense of Shylock and Jewishness, was also severely cut. To emphasize the tragic aspect of the action, Miller ended his production with a startling coup de theatre. As Portia and the others enter her house, Jessica drifts away in the opposite direction, holding the deed of gift that Shylock has signed, while offstage (or voice-over in the televised version) a cantor loudly intones the mourner's kaddish.

Ten years later, Miller again became involved in a production of *The Merchant of Venice*, this time as producer for the BBC-TV series *The Shakespeare Plays*. Constrained by series policy, this production was necessarily more traditional, set in the Renaissance with appropriate costumes and sets. Jack Gold directed, and Warren Mitchell, himself a Jew, was Shylock. Whereas Olivier was dressed like an English gentleman and affected an upper-class accent, Mitchell spoke with the accent of a middle-European Jew and donned what looked something like a "Jewish gabardine" (1.3.112). In the decade between productions, Miller had come to see both sides—Christian and Jewish—as equally in the wrong, as in the trial scene, which balances Shylock's cruelty against the brutality of the conversion dictated by Antonio.

Meanwhile, another British director, John Barton, staged two productions of the play: an experimental one at the Royal Shakespeare Company's studio theater, The Other Place, in 1978, and a full-scale production in the main house in 1981. Both were set in the late nineteenth century. Two quite different actors played Shylock in two quite different conceptions of the role: Patrick Stewart at The Other Place, and David Suchet at the Royal Shakespeare Theatre. Stewart's Shylock was a mean-spirited man, primarily concerned with money: a bad man and a bad Jew. Hence, he readily accedes to Antonio's demand that he convert, since his religion is of little consequence to him. This was consistent with Barton's idea that "the play is about true and false value and not about race" (quoted from the program notes in Bill Overton, *Text and Performance: "The Merchant of Venice"* [Atlantic Highlands, NJ: Humanities P International, 1987], 49). For David Suchet, who, like Mitchell, is Jewish, matters became more complicated. For him, Shylock's Jewishness is of central importance in the play; he is "not an outsider who *happens* to be a Jew but *because* [he is] a Jew" (quoted in John Barton, *Playing Shakespeare* [London: Methuen in Association with Channel Four Television, 1984], 171). Suchet therefore adopted a slight accent, distinguishing his interpretation of the role and Shylock's pride of race from Stewart's.

Other differences between the two productions emerged, although Barton maintained that his instructions to both actors were exactly the same. Stewart showed little concern for his daughter, Jessica; in fact, at one moment in act 2 when they are together he gives her a resounding slap across the face, explaining later to some who commented on this extra-textual gesture that Shylock seems at that point to notice a look of insubordination in her eyes. Suchet was much more tenderhearted toward Jessica, although he admitted that he could not reconcile those feelings with any justification of her betrayal and his subsequent anger at her elopement with a Christian. For both actors, however, Shylock's decisive moment is in 3.1 when he laments the loss of Leah's ring and then determines on his revenge.

Two other British productions deserve consideration here. After John Caird's disastrous, over-designed production in 1984, the Royal Shakespeare Company again staged the play in 1987, with Antony Sher (a South African Jew) as Shylock. Bill Alexander directed. Unlike Olivier, Sher reverted to an unassimilated, Middle Eastern Shylock, with corresponding accent and a costume not unlike Henry Irving's. Shylock sat on huge cushions in his "office," very like an oriental potentate in the 1630s, the period of the stage settings. Deborah Goodman's Jessica was similarly attired. The production nevertheless included contemporary allusions, such as swastikas and similar graffiti scrawled on walls near Shylock's home, which seemed to intensify the problematic nature of the text deliberately to force the audience to examine the nature of their own possible prejudices. The production became highly controversial, not least because in stripping bare Shylock's own bloodthirsty motives, Sher made the character highly offensive.

Alexander tried to make his production not about anti-Semitism, but about racism in general. In the trial scene, for example, while commenting on Venetian slaveholding, Shylock held a black attendant before him, connecting discrimination against Jews and blacks and making it visually unmistakable (see Bulman, pp. 124–125). Alexander felt that setting the play in the Jacobean period was the only way to make Shylock's intention to carve out his pound of flesh credible. Moreover, he believed that the social context requires the historical setting to allow audiences to understand the position of Jews in Venice and Christian hypocrisy in dealing with them (Ralph Berry, *On Directing Shakespeare* [London: H. Hamilton, 1989], 181–182). Other aspects of Alexander's directions were also calculated to disturb the audience's presumed complacency and to arouse controversy, such as Antonio's blatant homosexuality, made unmistakable at one point when he gave Bassanio a smacking great kiss on the lips.

The Merchant of Venice also has an important stage history outside of Britain. It was the first of Shakespeare's plays to be performed by professional actors in America, when Lewis Hallam and a company from London staged it in Williamsburg, Virginia, in 1752. Edwin Booth was the greatest American actor to play Shylock, succeeding his father, Junius Brutus Booth, in the role. He surpassed even Edwin Forrest, another eminent American actor. Whereas Forrest's representation rivaled Edmund Kean's, the younger Booth's more closely resembled Macklin's or, in the late twentieth century, Stewart's. Like them, he saw Shylock driven mainly by economic concerns, moved more by the financial worth of Leah's ring than by sentiment. For his revivals of the play in New York beginning in 1867, which none surpassed until Henry Irving's, he cut or otherwise altered the text, making Shylock's threats more ominous and bringing the role into great prominence. Thus he ended the play with Shylock's exit in 4.1, completely omitting the ring plot and all of act 5.

In the nineteenth century another, less well-known American actor played Shylock with great success. Since he was black, his appearances occurred mostly in Europe, where he received great acclaim, especially in Russia—not as an oddity but for his stirring portrayal of many Shakespearean characters, King Lear as well as Shylock. This was Ira Aldridge, who was born in New York in 1807 and died in Poland sixty years later. More recently, in 1957 in Stratford, Connecticut, Morris Carnovsky played Shylock and was warmly received for the vigor and humor he brought to the role. A Jew himself, Carnovsky refused to speak with an accent, honoring Shakespeare's language for the greatness of its diction. At about the same time, Angus Bowmer enacted Shylock, as he had done several times before when he helped found the Oregon Shakespeare Festival. He elected to play Shylock in what he considered an authentic Elizabethan representation, complete with red wig and beard, putty nose, and middle European accent. A quite different, modern-dress production was performed on the same stage in 1991 that did, unfortunately, arouse spirited accusation of anti-Semitism.

The Merchant of Venice has been performed all over the world, but perhaps the most interesting performances in the non-English speaking world have been in Israel. Although understandably not the most popular Shakespeare play in that country, its several productions, beginning with the first in 1936 (before Israel became a nation), have some special appeal. In 1936 at the Habimah Theater Shylock was performed alternately by Aharon Meskin and Shim'on Finkel. As directed by Leopold Jessner, a Jewish refugee, famous for his work at Berlin's Schiller Theater, Shylock represented the Jewish people battling against the oppressions of Christian society. Meskin emphasized Shylock's heroic stature, Finkel his bitter spite, and every trace of comic villainy was removed. Nevertheless, because the Christians appeared too decent, the production evoked controversy.

Many years later, in 1959 Tyrone Guthrie directed the play after the State of Israel was established. Meskin again played Shylock in this modern-dress production, where he affected a Rothschildian appearance, anticipating Olivier's representation, to underscore Shylock's position as a financier. Guthrie attempted to keep the play within the contours of romantic comedy but was only partly successful. Portia was miscast, and Meskin's marked pathos fit awkwardly into the romantic conception. Not until 1972 was the play again staged in Israel, this time at the Cameri Theater in Tel Aviv. By this time, after Israel's stunning victory in the Six-Day War in 1967, Israeli pride and confidence were such that an unsympathetic Shylock could be risked in a version much removed from realism. A mimed Good Friday procession opened the play; in the trial scene, Antonio appeared as a Christ figure, with a large black cross fitted on his back; and throughout the play a puppet theater in the background mimicked the action of the main stage or otherwise commented on it. A noted Israeli comedian, Avner Hyskiah, grotesquely impersonated Shylock as a shrewd old Jew capable of making clever deals. Not surprisingly, the production was both an artistic and a financial flop.

In 1980 the Cameri Theater revived the play, importing Barry Kyle from the Royal Shakespeare Company to direct. The production is perhaps most notable for the elimination of Shylock's conversion at the end of 4.1. A later production at the Cameri Theater, in 1993, staged after Baruch Goldstein's massacre of Palestinians at the Tomb of the Patriarchs in Hebron, featured Shylock as a version of a modern-day terrorist.

The Merchant of Venice continues to fascinate contemporary audiences and is often staged in modern dress. In 1991 in Sofia, Bulgaria, for example, Portia's Belmont was like a luxury spa, complete with swimming pool; Portia and Nerissa entered in 1.2 riding bicycles. A better example was the Royal Shakespeare Company's production in 1993 with David Calder as Shylock. The setting for Shylock's office was a modern brokerage, complete with a host of computer screens. Launcelot's first appearance brought the house down when, before he even uttered a word, he did something on a computer keyboard that made all the screens suddenly go blank. The production showed how a modern-dress version can take the sting out of Shylock's forced conversion by de-emphasizing the religious aspect of the play. David Calder's Shylock, a businessman more than a religious Jew, accepted conversion as a relatively trivial concession.

Michael Kahn's 1999 production at the Shakespeare Theatre in Washington, D.C., went in the opposite direction. Hal Holbrook played Shylock as a devout Jew, dressed accordingly. In the trial scene, instead of entering alone, he was accompanied by a good many co-religionists, all wearing prayer shawls and moaning audibly when the tide goes against their friend. The scene ended in a near riot at the point where Shylock has to convert.

Also in 1999 the Royal National Theatre in London staged the play with Henry Goodman as Shylock. Again, it was set in modern dress. Antonio entered in 1.1 strikingly as a man thoroughly dissipated, playing noisily on an upright piano in a tavern or bar, as his friends looked on and then tried to comfort him in his misery. Goodman's Shylock was filled with inconsistencies, some of them called for in the text. He was both loving and cruel to Jessica, for example, at one time singing Yiddish folk songs with her, at another time even striking her for suspected disobedience. Originally performed at the Cottesloe Theatre (the small studio in the National Theatre complex), it was so successful that it moved to one of the larger theaters and was later adapted for television and shown in both the United States and England. Directed by Trevor Nunn, this version aired in 2001. It is distributed by Image Entertainment and the Public Broadcasting Service.

EXPLICATION OF KEY PASSAGES

1.3.41–52. "How like a fawning publican . . . If I forgive him!" Shylock's speech, usually indicated as an aside, is spoken just after Antonio enters when Shylock and Bassanio have been discussing the loan of 3,000 ducats on Antonio's credit. Important to note is not only the antipathy between Shylock the Jew and Antonio the Christian, which is of long standing, but also—and even more important to Shylock—the economic conflict. Shylock hates Antonio because he is a Christian, but *more*, he says, because the man has driven down the price of loans and thereby affected Shylock's profits as well as those of other moneylenders. Antonio lends out money at no interest, in keeping with his Christian belief that money should not breed money. Shylock promises himself that, given the opportunity, he will take revenge on Antonio for his actions and his anti-Semitism; a few moments later, however, when he speaks directly with Antonio, he seems to be trying to make friends with his enemy and to let bygones be bygones. He offers him the loan at no interest at all, requiring only a guarantee (the bond), of which he makes a kind of joke. It is an open question whether Shylock at this point is sincere or laying a cunning plot against Antonio's life.

2.8.35–49. "A kinder gentleman . . . and so they parted." Shakespeare does not show Bassanio's leavetaking for Belmont but instead provides this account by Salerio, in which Antonio appears as a noble and generous friend. He wants Bassanio to take his time and do his best as Portia's suitor. He tells Bassanio not to think about the bond with Shylock, but to enjoy himself in Belmont, courting his lady love. At the end of the speech, however, it is clear that Antonio loves Bassanio very much, so much so that some critics interpret this as Shakespeare's indication of a homoerotic relationship, at least a latent one, where Antonio is concerned. Or, as Solanio replies in the next line, "I think he [Antonio] only loves the world for him."

3.1.59–73. "Hath not a Jew eyes? . . . better the instruction." Shylock's speech must be understood in context. Although it reads for the most part like a very eloquent defense of Jews against attacks of anti-Semitism, as of course it is, Shylock uses it as a justification for taking revenge against Antonio. In the process, he indicts Christians for their supposed "humility," which in actuality, he argues, is mere hypocrisy. When wronged, Christians do not exercise forbearance, or "sufferance"; they take revenge. Hence, by their example Shylock feels justified, since he is as human as they are, in taking revenge when he is wronged, too. It is "Christian example," he claims, that instructs him. The speech may therefore also be seen as a cue for depicting the Christians in the play as in many ways as culpable as Shylock.

3.2.149–74. "You see me . . . to exclaim on you." Bassanio has just chosen the right casket, found Portia's portrait in it, and won her hand in marriage. Rather ingenuously, Portia describes herself as a simple, unsophisticated maiden, though the audience has already seen that she is anything but that, and subsequent events will further illustrate her intelligence. But for the moment, deeply in love with Bassanio, she assumes the role of a modest woman, gladly bestowing everything she is and has upon "her lord, her governor, her king" (3.2.165) as indeed in English law at the time, as her husband, Bassanio will become. He will control all of Portia's estate henceforward; she will be subject to him completely as his wife. She is glad to accept him as such, though as events later demonstrate, and as the ring she gives him will symbolize, she will continue to prove quite capable of exercising a good deal of control in the marriage. The ring here given by her to Bassanio becomes the basis, symbolically and literally, of the ring plot that is the focus of act 5.

4.1.184–205. "The quality of mercy . . . 'gainst the merchant there." In this set speech, Portia, disguised as Dr. Balthasar, Dr. Bellario's surrogate in the Duke's court, tries to get Shylock to drop his plea for justice—the execution of the forfeit of his bond with Antonio—and instead show mercy. She uses the example of both divine and temporal mercy, which she says "seasons" justice (4.1.197). Note that she does not argue that mercy should supersede justice. Mercy is truly meaningful in the context of justice: Shakespeare here, as elsewhere in his plays, does not sentimentalize his theme. Portia's first metaphor, "the gentle rain" (4.1.185) derives from scripture (see Deuteronomy 32:2 and Ecclesiasticus 35:19) and emphasizes the unforced nature of true mercy. She then appeals to every human being's need for mercy, which should teach us to render mercy to others. She ends, however, by giving Shylock the opportunity to maintain his insistence on justice and tempts him to do so by saying that if he continues in that course, the "strict court of Venice" (4.1.204) will have no option but to allow him to carry out the forfeiture against Antonio.

4.1.376–386. "So please my lord . . . his son Lorenzo and his daughter." Asked by Portia to show mercy to Shylock, who stands convicted of the capital crime of intending to murder a Venetian citizen, Antonio agrees, but with several provisos. The first is that Shylock must give Antonio half of his fortune to use as he sees fit. Upon Shylock's death, that part will go to Lorenzo. The other provisos are that Shylock must convert to Christianity and must agree to bequeath, by deed of gift, everything he dies possessed of to Lorenzo and Jessica. The quality of this "mercy" has been lately much debated, especially as concerns the forced conversion. But there is an additional jab insofar as Shylock is compelled to bequeath everything he owns to his despised son-in-law and unfaithful daughter. He reluctantly agrees to these terms, giving satisfaction to Antonio and, from a certain point of view, a measure of revenge for what he has been put through.

Annotated Bibliography

Bloom, Harold. *Shakespeare: The Invention of the Human.* New York: Riverside Books, 1998. 171–191. Bloom maintains that Shylock is a comic villain and the play is anti-Semitic. Nevertheless, he doubts that Shakespeare himself was an anti-Semite.

Bulman, James C. *Shakespeare in Performance: "The Merchant of Venice."* Manchester, Eng.: Manchester UP, 1991. The best recent, detailed study of the play on the stage and on video. A second edition with new chapters is forthcoming.

Coyle, Martin, ed. *The Merchant of Venice.* New York: St. Martin's P, 1998. In the New Casebooks series, this volume contains ten useful essays by various critics, including Kiernan Ryan, Kim Hall, Karen Newman, and Avraham Oz.

Danson, Lawrence. *The Harmonies of "The Merchant of Venice."* New Haven: Yale UP, 1978. As the dust jacket of this important book says, "Danson treads a convincing middle way between the romantic sentimentalizers of the play and the hard-headed but reductive historical school."

Gross, John. *Shylock: Four Hundred Years in the Life of a Legend.* London: Chatto and Windus, 1992. A thorough survey of the play's role, and specifically Shylock's, in the history of anti-Semitism in the Western world.

Halio, Jay L. *Understanding "The Merchant of Venice."* Westport, CT: Greenwood P, 2000. A student casebook on issues, sources, and historical documents relevant to the play. Especially designed for high school students and teachers.

Lyon, John. *The Merchant of Venice*. Twayne's New Critical Introductions to Shakespeare. Boston: Twayne, 1988. A detailed analysis of the play.

Shapiro, James. *Shakespeare and the Jews*. New York: Columbia UP, 1996. A far more extensive study of Jews in England than the title indicates. It treats of Jews in England from before the Expulsion in 1290 to the eighteenth century. A standard reference on the subject.

Yaffe, Martin D. *Shylock and the Jewish Question*. Baltimore: The Johns Hopkins UP, 1997. Yaffe challenges the view that Shakespeare is unfriendly to Jews. He attempts to show that *The Merchant of Venice* actually provides what he calls "a helpful guide for the self-understanding of the modern Jew" (1).

The Merry Wives of Windsor

Michelle Ephraim

PLOT SUMMARY

1.1. On a street in Windsor, Justice Robert Shallow, accompanied by his nephew, Abraham Slender, and the Welsh parson Sir Hugh Evans, complains about the roguish knight Sir John Falstaff. Shallow's melodramatic threat to take Falstaff to the English high court is rendered completely absurd by the men's misuse of legal terminology. Evans temporarily distracts Shallow from his obsession with Falstaff by proposing a marriage between Slender and the beautiful and prosperous Anne Page. At Shallow's suggestion, they visit the Pages' house, where Falstaff mocks Shallow's emotional state and playfully evades Shallow's accusation that he has stolen deer from his property. Slender issues his own grievance against Falstaff and his friends Bardolph, Nym, and Pistol, whom Slender calls "cony-catching rascals" (1.1.124–125), for stealing his money after plying him with liquor. Hurling insults at Slender, they each deny the charge. As everyone retires to dinner, Slender proves completely inept at courting Anne.

1.2. The Welsh parson Sir Hugh Evans gives Slender's servant Simple a letter from Slender to deliver to Mistress Quickly asking her help in the wooing of Anne Page.

1.3. At the Garter Inn Falstaff boasts to his followers and the Inn's Host that he will seduce and subsequently elicit money from both Mistress Alice Ford (wife of Francis Ford) who has offered him "the leer of invitation" (1.3.45–46) and Mistress Margaret Page (married to George Page) who also gave him "good eyes" (60). Falstaff dismisses Pistol and Nym when they refuse to deliver the identical love letters he has written to the wives, and the two men agree to revenge themselves on Falstaff by disclosing his plan to the women's husbands.

1.4. Meanwhile, the French Doctor Caius challenges Evans to a duel when he discovers that Evans has sent Simple to solicit his housekeeper, Mistress Quickly, to help in securing a marriage with Anne, whom Caius hopes to wed. With frenetic duplicity, Mistress Quickly assures the jealous Caius of Anne's affections for him while also encouraging Slender as well as Anne's third suitor, the upper-class but insolvent Master Fenton, in their romantic pursuits. Though Mistress Quickly eagerly accepts Fenton's money in exchange for commending him to Anne, she does not believe that Anne loves him.

2.1. Mistress Page is shocked to receive Falstaff's love letter in the "holiday-time of [her] beauty" (2.1.2). After Mistress Ford arrives at the Pages' house with her identical letter, the wives decide to take revenge on the lecherous knight. Although George Page is unmoved by Pistol and Nym's report of Falstaff's seductions, Francis Ford becomes deeply suspicious and cautions Page that "a man may be too confident" (2.1.186–187) with regard to his wife. The Host, after thwarting Caius and Evans's duel by sending them to separate locations, accepts Ford's bribe of liquor in exchange for arranging a meeting with Falstaff in which Ford will assume the pseudonym of "Brooke."

2.2. At the Garter Inn, Mistress Quickly, dispatched by the wives, arranges a tryst between Falstaff and Mistress Ford and convinces him to send his servant, Robin, to Mistress Page as a show of affection. In an elaborate and paranoid scheme to confirm his wife's adulterous relationship with Falstaff, Ford enters the Inn disguised as the prospective lover "Brooke" and offers money to Falstaff in exchange for seducing Mistress Ford. When Falstaff inquires about his motive, "Brooke" explains that evidence of Mistress Ford's infidelity would allow him to challenge her claim of chastity, which she uses to rebuff him. Calling Ford a "poor cuckoldly knave" (2.2.270), Falstaff enthusiastically accepts the money and unwittingly informs Ford of his future assignation with his wife. In a soliloquy, Ford rages about the public shame of cuckoldry and subsequently vows to apprehend Falstaff during the forthcoming assignation.

2.3. As Caius waits for Evans in Windsor Park, the Host arrives and lures him to Frogmore with the promise that Anne will be there.

3.1. In a field near Frogmore, Evans, joined by Simple, Shallow, Slender, and Page, nervously anticipates the swordfight with Doctor Caius. The Host arrives with Caius and subsequently disarms the men; in response to this public humiliation, Caius and Evans unite to plan their revenge.

3.2. Ford, intent on exposing his friend's naivete, invites Page, Caius, and Evans to see "a monster" (3.2.81) at his house.

3.3. Meanwhile, at Ford's house, the wives prepare for Falstaff's arrival. From her hiding place, Mistress Page secretly observes the knight's attempt to flatter Mistress Ford with intimations that she is better suited for an aristocratic lifestyle. On cue, Mistress Page "arrives" to warn of Ford's approach, unaware that her fabricated story is actually the truth. According to plan, the wives promptly hide Falstaff in a laundry basket covered with filthy clothing, which the servants, after passing Ford, Page, Caius, and Evans at the door, proceed to empty in a muddy ditch in Dachet-mead, a nearby meadow. Ford's futile manhunt inside his home provokes the men to condemn his unfounded jealousy.

3.4. Outside Page's house, Fenton explains to Anne that, even though his initial motivations for marriage were financial, he has genuinely fallen in love with her. Anne encourages Fenton to pursue her father's approbation despite his endorsement of Slender. Urged on by Shallow and Mistress Quickly, Slender interrupts the lovers but fails to assert himself, explaining to Anne that he only follows the will of his uncle and her father. When Anne's parents arrive, Page shuns Fenton, but Mistress Page, who prefers Caius for her daughter, concedes that she will consider Fenton's proposal. Mistress Quickly hastily takes credit for fulfilling her agreement to promote Fenton to Anne's family.

3.5. At the Garter Inn, Mistress Quickly convinces Falstaff to attempt another tryst with Mistress Ford. "Brooke" arrives at the Inn, and Falstaff relates details of his hasty departure in the laundry basket as well as the plan for the second rendezvous. In a fanatical soliloquy, Ford vows to "search impossible places" (3.5.148) at his home until he catches Falstaff.

4.1. Before departing for the Ford's home, Mistress Page solicits a Latin lesson for her son from Evans. In a humorous showcase of her bawdy sensibilities, Mistress Quickly continuously interrupts the lesson with lewd misinterpretations of the Latin words.

4.2. Mistress Page finally arrives at the Ford's house and, once again, issues a "fake" warning of Ford's impending arrival that turns out to be entirely accurate. At Mistress Ford's suggestion, the wives disguise Falstaff as her maid's aunt, "the fat woman of Brainford" (4.2.75–76), whom her husband loathes and believes to be a witch. Accompanied by Page, Caius, Evans, and Shallow, Ford immediately empties the suspicious laundry basket upon his arrival as his companions proclaim him a lunatic. As the wives and the men look on, Ford beats the person he believes to be the maid's aunt and expels "her" from the house before departing with the men in tow. The wives decide to disclose all to their husbands.

4.3. In this brief scene, Bardolph tells the Host of the Garter Inn that three Germans want to hire horses. The Host replies that he will overcharge his foreign guests.

4.4. At Ford's house, Ford, Page, and Evans praise the two women for successfully duping Falstaff, and Mistress Page suggests a final public shaming in which Falstaff will appear as the folk-tale legend "Herne the Hunter" as the children of the town, in disguise as fairies, goblins, and elves, physically harass him. Page secretly plans for Slender and Anne's elopement during the fairy "performance," while Mistress Page does the same for Caius and Anne.

4.5. Back at the Garter Inn, Simple, by Slender's request, seeks out the "wise woman of Brainford" (4.5.26–27) so that she may confirm Nym's theft of Slender's chain. Claiming to have consulted this woman about these matters, Falstaff gives an equivocal response to Simple's inquiries about both the theft and the outcome of Slender's proposal to Anne. In an act of vengeance, Caius and Evans convince the Host that a group of Germans have departed without paying for their rooms as well as stolen his horses. Mistress Quickly persuades Falstaff to meet the wives in disguise in Windsor forest.

4.6. Fenton relates to the Host Anne's intention to resist both her parents' schemes to marry her off during the "Herne the Hunter" ruse. Fenton divulges their own plan to elope and persuades the Host to arrange for a priest.

5.1. In his final meeting with "Brooke," Falstaff, after describing his latest escape, vows to take revenge on Ford for beating him.

5.2–3. Unaware of Anne's secret rebellion, the Pages continue to deceive one another by privately arranging the details of Anne's elopement with the two hopeful suitors.

5.4–5. That night, at Windsor Park, Evans appears as a satyr. He is accompanied by his students disguised as fairies. Falstaff, as "Herne the Hunter," encounters the wives and excitedly declares that they may "[d]ivide [him] like a brib'd-buck [stolen deer], each a haunch" (5.5.24). At the sound of the approaching spirits, the women flee on cue, leaving Falstaff at the mercy of the child "fairies," who, led by Evans as a satyr and by Mistress Quickly as the Queen of the Fairies, pinch and burn him with candles while denouncing his lust. As Fenton and Anne successfully elope during the confusion, Caius and Slender each retrieve a young boy in the guise of a fairy, whom they believe to be Anne. When the fairies depart, the Pages and the Fords reveal themselves to reprimand the shamed knight, who subsequently concedes that he is "made an ass" (5.5.119). After the perplexed Slender and Caius appear with their boys in tow, Fenton and Anne arrive and clarify the situation. Fenton urges Anne's parents to accept Anne's choice of a husband and, with Ford's encouragement, the Pages agree to do so.

PUBLICATION HISTORY

Modern editors must necessarily engage with a wide range of possibilities when assigning a date of composition to *The Merry Wives of Windsor*, which may have been performed for Queen Elizabeth I at Westminster during the Order of the Garter Feast on St. George's Day, April 23, 1597, but did not appear in print until the First Quarto edition of 1602. As Barbara Freedman points out, editors have assigned various composition dates to the play within a broad five-year spectrum, 1597–1601 ("Shakespearean Chronology, Ideological Complicity, and Floating Texts: Something is Rotten in Windsor," *Shakespeare Quarterly* 45 [1994]: 191). Leslie Hotson's highly influential *Shakespeare Versus Shallow* (Boston: Little, Brown, and Company, 1931)—which focuses on the play's possible allusions to Shakespeare's acquaintances as well as references to Queen Elizabeth and the Garter ceremony in 5.5 of the 1623 First Folio (the earliest "Collected Works" of Shakespeare) edition of *Merry Wives*—establishes that Shakespeare wrote the play between 1596 and 1597 for the 1597 celebration, a yearly induction of new knights into the Queen's Order. Although Edmond Malone, who in 1790 made the first connection between the play and the Garter tradition, argues that *Merry Wives* debuted during the 1603 Garter celebration (*The Plays and Poems of William Shakespeare*, 10 vols. [London: H. Baldwin, 1790, 1.1.329]), it is Hotson's theory that is cited as authoritative by many scholars today.

Expanding on Hotson's study, which is concerned mainly with establishing the character of Justice Shallow as a satiric portrait of William Gardiner, the Surrey Justice of the Peace, William Green in 1962 provides further support of the 1597 date in his own book-length examination of the relationship between the Garter ceremony and *Merry Wives*. The passages in the 5.5 "fairy" performance, in which one child dressed as a hobgoblin exclaims "Our radiant Queen hates sluts and sluttery" (5.5.46) and Mistress Quickly describes emblems of the Order of the Garter (55–76), Green argues, reinforce the play's external references to the specific knights who would be honored at the 1597 ceremony: the Knight-elect George Carey (Lord Hunsdon), Shakespeare's patron, and in the brief satiric allusion to the "duke de Jamany" (4.5.87), Frederick, the Duke of Wurtemberg, whom the Queen ostensibly approved for knighthood only as a result of his excessive badgering. Although the Duke, formerly "Count Mompelgard" during his initial visit to England in 1592, was absent from the ceremony itself, the term "garmombles" (used in the 1602 First Quarto edition but replaced with "cozen-germans" [4.5.77] in the 1623 Folio) "represents a verbal scrambling of Garter and Mompelgard" (*Shakespeare's The Merry Wives of Windsor*, 151–176). Hotson and Green have significantly influenced scholarly opinion about the date and historical circumstances of the play's composition, but a number of critics have recently questioned this "occasionalist" tradition, noting in particular the purely speculative basis of their claims (see "Critical Controversies," below).

Just as important as the 1597 Garter ceremony to the process of dating the play is Shakespeare's creation of Falstaff, his most famous comic character, who appears prominently in *1, 2 Henry IV* as well as in *Merry Wives*. Based on the appearance in Shakespeare's comedy of a number of other characters from *1, 2 Henry IV* and *Henry V*—Nym, Pistol, Bardolph, Mistress Quickly, and Justice Shallow—critics agree that Shakespeare wrote *Merry Wives* at some point during or immediately after his conception of the history trilogy. A 1597 date would establish that Shakespeare composed *Merry Wives* between *1 Henry IV* (1596/1597) and *2 Henry IV* (1598). The tenability of this "occasionalist" theory is undermined, however, by the striking character discrepancies between the politically subversive and wittily profound Falstaff in *1, 2 Henry IV* and the foolish, ridiculed knight who appears in Shakespeare's comedy.

Further incongruities between the Henry plays and *Merry Wives* with regard to plot and characterization raise questions about the chronology of Shakespeare's artistic process that remain unanswered. *Merry Wives* contains, for example, only one allusion to events depicted in the histories, and this reference does not cohere with Shakespeare's plot: Master Page dismisses Fenton as a prodigal because he "kept company with the wild Prince and Poins" (3.2.72–73), when in fact it is Falstaff who is the young Prince's companion in *1, 2 Henry IV*. Although Falstaff associates with Bardolph, Nym, and Pistol in *Merry Wives*, he does not seem to have a prior relationship with Mistress Quickly, his close companion in the Henry plays.

The first mention of *Merry Wives* occurs in the Stationers' Register for January 18, 1602: "A booke called An excellent and pleasant conceited commedie of Sir John Faulstof and the merry wyves of Windesor" (E. K. Chambers, *The Elizabethan Stage*, 4 vols. [Oxford: Clarendon P, 1961], 3.486). The title page of this First Quarto edition reads:

> A Most pleasaunt and excellent conceited Comedie, of Syr *Iohn Falstaffe*, and the merrie Wives of *Windsor*. Entermixed with sundrie variable and pleasing humors, of Syr *Hugh* the Welch Knight, Iustice *Shallow*, and his wise Cousin M. *Slender*. With the swaggering vaine of Auncient *Pistoll*, and Corporall *Nym*. By William Shakespeare. As it hath bene divers times Acted by the right Honorable my Lord Chamberlaines servants. Both before her Maiestie, and else-where.

Although for some critics the reference to Elizabeth provides more evidence of the 1597 debut, the precise occasions of the "divers times" remains purely speculative (see "Production History," below).

The play exists in the 1602 First Quarto (Q1) edition, a 1619 Quarto (Q2), the 1623 First Folio edition, and a 1630 Quarto based on the Folio. The Folio is believed to be a transcription by the professional scribe Ralph Crane based on the original manuscripts. At approximately half the length of the Folio text, Q1 is the shortest of Shakespeare's quartos and lacks five entire scenes (among other sections) included in the Folio: 4.1, 5.1, 5.2, 5.3, and 5.4. Only the Folio refers to Queen Eliza-beth and to the Knights of the Garter in 5.5 and, in general, contains more provin-cial references: rather than having specific allusions to Windsor, the Quarto describes a general setting that is possibly contemporary London. Finally, the Folio is written almost entirely in prose while Q1 includes a significant amount of verse. The Second Quarto (1619) reprints Q1, but the Third (1630)—the first that was based on the Folio version—is the prototype for modern editions of the play. Although this standard edition is largely a copy of the 1623 text, it also includes some ele-ments of Q1, such as stage directions, which appear only at the beginning of each scene, and Ford's pseudonym "Brooke," which appears as "Broome" in the Folio. The latter certainly does not cohere as well as "Brooke," which allows for Falstaff's punning quip when he hears that "Master Brooke" has sent "a draught of sack" (2.2.147): "Such Brooks are welcome to me, that o'erflows such liquor" (2.2.150–151).

Whether or not allusions to the Order of the Garter refer to a specific ceremony, the play's "familiar" terrain—its allusions to recognizable landmarks, such as Wind-sor Castle, Datchet-mead, Frogmore, and the Garter Inn—makes *Merry Wives* Shakespeare's "sole play set in its entirety in Elizabethan milieu" (Green, p. 3). Roy Strong argues that the Garter ceremony, established initially by King Edward III during the fourteenth century to involve knights and nobles in England's military ventures, held particular significance for Queen Elizabeth. Her brother, the late King Edward VI, began reforms of the Order that were halted from 1553 to 1558 by their Catholic sister, Mary, who maintained its traditional Mass ceremony. Eliza-beth, who ruled from 1558 to 1603, removed such Catholic conventions and em-braced the medieval chivalric tradition as a means through which to promote allegiance to her Reformist court (*The Cult of Elizabeth: Elizabethan Portraiture and Pageantry* [London: Thames and Hudson, 1977], 165–185). Thus, in addition to hon-oring the outstanding knights of the region, the Order of the Garter celebrated Eliz-abeth's own unprecedented role as a female head of church and state during the Reformation.

The play's "local" character has also lent support to a popular, if dubious, story that Shakespeare wrote the play to honor the queen herself. In 1702, the playwright John Dennis in the dedicatory letter to George Granville that accompanies his un-successful adaptation *The Comical Gallant: Or The Amours of Sir John Falstaffe* claimed that the play was Shakespeare's answer to Elizabeth's request for a roman-tic play about Falstaff. According to Dennis, the queen demanded the play to be completed within two weeks—evidence cited by some critics that she would have had the deadline of the Garter ceremony in mind: "This Comedy was written at her Command, and by her direction, and she was so eager to see it Acted, that she com-manded it to be finished in fourteen days; and was afterwards, as Tradition tells us, very well pleas'd at the Representation."

In 1709, Nicholas Rowe, in a biographical note on Shakespeare that accompa-nied his edited collection of the plays, reiterates Dennis's unlikely account: Eliza-beth "was so well pleas'd with that admirable Character of *Falstaff*, in the two parts of *Henry* the Fourth, that she commanded [Shakespeare] to continue it for one Play more, and to shew him in Love" (H. J. Oliver, *The Merry Wives of Windsor*, xliv–xlv). The theory that the queen herself exerted pressure on Shakespeare, al-though questionable (not to mention somewhat unheeded, as Falstaff's attempt to get money from Mistresses Ford and Page hardly constitutes being "in love"), does provide an appealing explanation of Falstaff's character here, whom many critics have understood as an inadequate postscript to the more ambitiously drawn figure of this character in the history plays. Expressing what has been critical consensus about Falstaff's inferior characterization in the comedy, Harry Levin concludes that "*The Merry Wives of Windsor* sags with signs of having been written to order" ("Falstaff's Encore," *Shakespeare Quarterly* 32 [1981]: 9).

SOURCES FOR THE PLAY

There is no obvious source material for *Merry Wives*, and critics have generally dismissed theories about the influence of *A Jealous Comedy*, a lost text reported to be performed in 1593, as entirely inconclusive (Geoffrey Bullough, *Narrative and Dramatic Sources of Shakespeare*, 4 vols. [London: Routledge and Kegan Paul, 1958], 2.4). Despite the absence of a clear source, however, it is evident that the play takes inspiration from a wide range of literary genres and traditions. Freedman describes the play in this sense as a provocative composite: it is "[p]art royal compliment and part bedroom farce, best known as a Falstaff play and widely recognized as Shakespeare's only topical satire, part citizen comedy, part city comedy, part humors comedy, and part court comedy" (191). As Levin notes, Falstaff in particular is a dynamic amalgamation of many classical and medieval archetypes: "a Braggart, a Parasite, a Trickster, a Scapegoat, a Fool, a Vice" (7).

Like the "Vice" character of medieval morality plays, Falstaff offers corrupt temptations that are also infused with comic elements; because of Falstaff, the play's "moral" condemnation of sexual transgression is ultimately rendered with tongue-in-cheek humor. The play in general and Falstaff in particular also recall the stock characters and farcical plots of classical Greek and Roman comedy. Bullough argues that Shakespeare draws upon Plautus's Roman comedy *Casina* (in which a husband and wife separately promote suitors for their daughter, who ultimately chooses a third lover) for the Anne Page plot (9). A. L. Bennett, expanding on Bullough's links between *Merry Wives* and Roman sources, argues that the prototype for Falstaff may be found in the English playwright Nicholas Udall's particular variation of the "braggart solider" stock character in *Ralph Roister Doister* (1552). Like Falstaff, Roister Doister attempts to seduce a "citizen's wife" for financial gain; in both plays, these wives seek revenge after receiving a seemingly presumptuous letter ("The Sources of Shakespeare's *Merry Wives*," *Renaissance Quarterly* 23 [1970]: 429–433). With its focus on the middle class, *Merry Wives* anticipates the genre of "city comedy" popular at the beginning of the seventeenth century. Nym's obsessive and arbitrary use of the term "humor" also suggests the "comedy of humors" popularized by Ben Jonson on the seventeenth-century stage. Contemporary medical authorities believed that the body was composed of four "humors"—bile, blood, choler, and phlegm—that, thrown into imbalance, would result in an extreme emotional state, such as Hamlet's melancholia (associated with bile) and Ford's fury (choler).

Shakespeare's focus on the theme of cuckoldry derives from the medieval farce or fabliau tradition employed famously during the fourteenth century by Geoffrey Chaucer in "The Miller's Tale" from *The Canterbury Tales*. Within this genre, Bullough notes in particular the story of the duped husband in the Italian writer Ser Giovanni Fiorentino's prose collection *Il Pecorone*, published in 1558. Like Falstaff, the protagonist unknowingly informs his paramour's husband about their trysts, evades the husband's subsequent attempts to catch him, and in one instance hides in a linen basket (5). Shakespeare's familiarity with the collection is evident in his play *The Merchant of Venice*, which borrows from Fiorentino's story of a Jewish moneylender and a wagered pound of flesh.

Shakespeare also makes a strong association between Falstaff as "Herne the Hunter" and the figure of Actaeon from Ovid's *Metamorphoses* (2.138–252)—the hunter transformed into a stag as punishment for glimpsing the bathing Diana and her nymphs. Just as the stag Actaeon is killed by his own dogs, Falstaff's adulterous devices are symbolically turned upon him as he is tortured and shamed by the fairies while he is dressed in horns, an adornment that the audience would have understood as a symbol of cuckoldry (see "Themes and Meanings," below). The two allusions to Actaeon in *Merry Wives*—Pistol's warning to Ford to "Prevent [Falstaff]; or go thou / Like Sir Actaeon" (2.1.117–118) and Ford's subsequent condemnation of Page as "a secure and willful Actaeon" (3.2.43)—suggest that all of the male protagonists are vulnerable to being "transformed" into this dreaded archetype. In the Folio, Falstaff is disguised as "Herne the Hunter," but in the Quarto the name of Shakespeare's fictitious character is actually "*Horne* the Hunter."

In addition to John Lyly's late sixteenth-century play *Endymion*, in which fairies harass a lover in his romantic pursuits, the "fairy" performance during the play's final scene recalls the aggressive spirits who manipulate the mortal lovers in *A Midsummer Night's Dream*. The "fake" fairies of *Merry Wives*, a product of Mistress Page's own imagination, also suggest early modern writer Reginald Scot's theory that women should be blamed for cultural anxiety about the supernatural: "Our mothers' maids have so terrified us with spirits, witches, urchins, elves, hags, fairies, satyrs . . . that we are afraid of our own shadows" (*The Discovery of Witchcraft* [London, 1584], 86, cited in "*A Midsummer Night's Dream*": *Texts and Contexts*, ed. Gail Kern Paster and Skiles Howard [Boston: Bedford/St. Martin's, 1999], 308). Leslie S. Katz notes that the concluding scene, with its elaborate staging, costumes, "amateur" actors, and intimate audience, also evokes the popular court masque (89).

STRUCTURE AND PLOTTING

Some critics have explained the plot structure of *Merry Wives* as evidence that Shakespeare did, in fact, hastily compose the play in two weeks. Undeniably, the narrative appears at times to be sporadic and incomplete. For example, the nature of Shallow's raging "complaint" against Falstaff that begins the play is not identified until later in the scene and, after a brief mention, is dropped without further clarification. More strikingly, the details of Caius and Evans's plot to convince the Host that Germans have cheated him of lodging fees and stolen his horses are never established. Does the Host ever encounter actual Germans at the Inn? Do Cauis and Evans disguise themselves as the "Germans" who apparently lead Bardolph on a horse chase? Is Bardolph himself in on the scheme? Bullough calls the scene "surely the worst handled episode in all Shakespeare's plays" (2.11).

These unresolved narrative threads stand out in particular against the tightly orchestrated main narrative of the wives' duping of Falstaff and the similarly stylized subplot of Anne's elopement with Fenton that also centers on the theme of sexual duplicity. Jeanne Addison Roberts notes that the play was well-received during the neoclassical period (1660–1785) and that writers appreciated the play's patterned interplay of plot and subplot as well as the repetition of key events, such as the wives' three tricks on Falstaff and Master Ford's three meetings in the guise of "Brooke" (66–68).

Almost all of the central characters in the play participate in acts of deception, and many of those who initially deceive are themselves duped by their intended "victims." Falstaff is victimized by the wives he intends to exploit and by his would-be cuckold Master Ford, who physically assaults him and later watches as Falstaff himself is crowned with "horns." Similarly, both Pages are fooled by their daughter, whose marital choices they intend to manipulate. Many of the play's deceitful interrelations—between the wives and Falstaff, the Host and Evans and Caius, Falstaff and Ford, and the Pages—are facilitated by messengers in the form of the numerous servants who populate the play and by Mistress Quickly, who "quickly" complies with her often treacherous assignments. Mistress Quickly intercedes in both plots of sexual intrigue, conveying the wives' invitations to Falstaff and encouraging each of Anne's suitors to pursue her.

The escalating deceptions within the Windsor community are resolved in the play's final play within a play, which shifts *Merry Wives* from a provincial comedy to one situated in a "Green World"—a critical term used to describe a place of escape and transformation. As Northrup Frye argues, Falstaff, burned by the fairies, facilitates the resolution of the community's internal disharmony by undergoing a symbolic "death" and rebirth that is imitative of folk rituals intended to purge the winter season (*Anatomy of Criticism: Four Essays* [Princeton: Princeton UP, 1957], 183). Through Falstaff, sexual transgressions and other sins are first indulged, and then purged. Though restricting his discussion of Falstaff to the *Henry IV* plays, C. L. Barber argues that Falstaff suggests the "Lord of Misrule" from country holiday celebrations, a symbol of the rowdy festivity that Prince Hal expels from his life: Falstaff's faked death and subsequent revivification during the battle of Shrewsbury as well as Prince Hal's later rejection of him establish Falstaff as a ritual scapegoat whose death (reported in *Henry V*) allows for the "purification [of Prince Hal and England] by sacrifice" (*Shakespeare's Festive Comedy: A Study of Dramatic Form and Its Relation to Social Custom* [Princeton: Princeton UP, 1972], 206). Roberts adds to the arguments of Frye and Barber that the symbolic sacrifice of Falstaff, given the play's major themes of love and marriage, specifically invokes fertility rituals: though also the victim of the community's rage, Falstaff is an "old Fertility god" sacrificed so that "order is restored to marriage" (81; see "Devices and Techniques," below).

MAIN CHARACTERS

Falstaff

For readers familiar with the Henry plays, it is difficult to understand the relationship between Falstaff—the witty and rebellious father figure who threatens the English monarchy by way of his influence on the prodigal Prince Hal—and the foolish barfly humiliated by two provincial housewives in *Merry Wives*. Rather than a voice of political subversion, the Windsor Falstaff proves to a large extent an impotent figure within a local community—a dramatic shift in characterization that has occasioned artistic condemnation from literary critics. Levin describes Falstaff as "less of a wit than a butt, more laughed at than laughed with, repeatedly dis-comfited not by other men but by women, whose practical jokes fend off his clumsy advances" ("Falstaff's Encore," 9). Making a similar point, Anne Barton compares the dramatic resonance of Prince Hal's rejection of Falstaff in *2 Henry IV* with Shakespeare's own treatment of Falstaff, "humiliated at the hands of an unremark-able, small-town society" ("Falstaff and the Comic Community," in *Essays, Mainly Shakespearean* [Cambridge: Cambridge UP, 1994], 70). Still, Falstaff proves the epi-center of *Merry Wives*. A force of comic misrule and social subversion, Falstaff un-settles the institutions represented by Justice Shallow as well as the sexual propriety ostensibly emblematized by the chaste wives.

The most verbally inventive character in the play, the corpulent Falstaff tempers his commanding physical presence by wittily rendering his body as an absurd en-tity. Describing his ordeal in the Thames River as a near-drowning, he explains that his body has a "kind of alacrity in sinking" (3.5.12–13); swollen with water, it might have become a "mountain of mummy" (3.5.18). Rather than a menacing thief or sexual predator, Falstaff appears a benign, aging hedonist more prone to pratfalls than assaults. He is "well-nigh worn to pieces with age" (2.1.21–22), a fact that he uses to woo the wives as he describes himself in his love letter as a sympathetic and jovial old drunk.

Mistress Quickly

Unlike the thieves Nym and Pistol, who with humorous claims of moral righ-teousness refuse to deliver Falstaff's love letters, the unscrupulous Mistress Quickly unhesitatingly offers herself as a panderer to numerous parties. The ambiguous na-ture of Mistress Quickly's private employment—quite different from her position as hostess of the Boar's Head Tavern in the *Henry IV* plays—is striking. Described by Evans as Caius's "nurse—or his dry-nurse—or his cook—or his laundry—his washer and his wringer" (1.2.3–5), Mistress Quickly proves her manifold uses also in a bawdy sense by reassuring each of Anne's three suitors of their sexual viabil-ity. In her role as messenger, through which she effectively offers Anne's virginity to the most persuasive (or financially generous) bidder, Mistress Quickly herself be-comes symbolic of sexual looseness. As Pistol comments of her, "this punk [pros-titute] is one of Cupid's carriers" (2.2.135). But like Falstaff, Mistress Quickly never poses a serious moral threat to the community: although she claims to control Anne Page's will (1.4.127–130), at no point does the play suggest either her influence over Anne or her familiarity with Anne's actual affection for Fenton.

Shallow

Like Mistress Quickly, the elderly Shallow also erroneously believes in his con-trol over the residents of Windsor. Shallow's penchant for referring to himself in the third person (regarding Falstaff, "Believe me, Robert Shallow, Esquire, saith he is wronged" [1.1.106–107]), his malapropisms, and his nostalgic allusions to his days as a violent youth establish him as a farcical authority figure. A court-associated "outsider," Shallow attempts to take Falstaff to the high court and to secure Slen-der's marriage to Anne, but he is unsuccessful. Rosemary Kegl suggests that Shal-low represents *Merry Wives*' ambivalence about state control—a possible antimonarchical sentiment that conflicts with the play's references to the Order of the Garter festivities (*The Rhetoric of Concealment: Figuring Gender and Class in Renaissance Literature* [Ithaca: Cornell UP, 1994], 87–96).

Slender, Caius, and Evans

Like his uncle, the dimwitted Slender (whose very name suggests a lack of substance) proves inept at mastering the social terrain of Windsor. His request for a collection of outdated verses with which to court Anne Page suggests his inability to conceive his own thoughts, and his accusations of thievery only expose him as a malleable drunk. Caius and Evans, also "outsiders" in this provincial English town, represent a "foreign" threat played out in their tale of the "duke de Jamany" and in the play's many racial epithets. With their mutilation of the English language and their absurdly violent outbursts (such as Caius's threat to castrate Evans for encouraging Slender's marriage to Anne), these men come across as buffoons. Yet Shakespeare also makes clear that these "others" represent genuine xenophobia within the community (see "Devices and Techniques," below).

Ford and Page

Both Ford and Page consider that the "outsider" figures—specifically, the higher-class Falstaff and Fenton—potentially undermine their patriarchal authority. Although he embraces Slender as a future husband for his daughter, Page condemns Fenton as of "too high a region" (3.2.73), a prodigal who seeks to take financial advantage of Anne. Fenton proves legitimately in love with Anne, yet his admission of an initial financial motivation affirms her father's cautious view of men outside of their middle-class community. Nonetheless, Page functions as the benevolent counterpart to the hostile, paranoid Master Ford, who rages against both the male "outsider" figure and his own wife. In a psychoanalytic examination of Ford's character, Nancy Cotton associates Ford's lack of children with his feelings of sexual "impotence." Unlike Ford, Page (the father of two) confidently presumes his wife's sexual fidelity ("Castrating (W)itches: Impotence and Magic in *The Merry Wives of Windsor*," *Shakespeare Quarterly* 38.3 [1987]: 322). Suspicious of his wife even before his first meeting with Falstaff, Ford imagines all men as potential cuckolds. He is determined to educate Page, whom he deems "a secure fool" who "stands so firmly on his wive's [sic] frailty" (2.1.233, 234).

Mistress Page and Mistress Ford

Ford certainly underestimates his wife. Yet the play slyly hints that the middle-aged Mistress Ford and Mistress Page might be enticed by Falstaff's advances. Mistress Page raises the possibility that Falstaff may recognize some dishonest "strain" in her of which she is unaware (2.1.87–88); even more ambiguously, Mistress Ford, before the (potentially disappointing) discovery that Falstaff has sent her friend an identical missive, playfully alludes to an opportunity for an extramarital affair: "If I would but go to hell for an eternal moment or so, I could be knighted" (2.1.49–50). Although innocent of adultery, the wives do prove threatening to male authority: their ability to act as the "ministers" (4.2.219) of Falstaff's fate, to "forge" and "shape" (4.2.223) his public shame, suggests their potential to humiliate their husbands as well. As Kegl argues, ostensible authority figures, such as Shallow (representing the state) and Evans (representing the church), are overshadowed by the wives' skilled enforcement of social and moral codes within the community (102). Yet the wives also embrace the status quo: to Ford's provocative suggestion that the women "would marry" (that is, each other) should their husbands die—an intimation of both homoerotic and feminist desires—Mistress Page responds quickly, "Be sure of that—two other husbands" (3.2.15–17)—thus assuring Ford of their sexual preference for men that is also an affirmation of the traditional patriarchal order of Windsor.

Anne Page

The "seemingly obedient" (4.6.33) Anne Page is a benign version of the subversive older women. Kegl suggests that Anne's duping of both parents safely displaces anxiety about the wives' authority onto a daughter's rebellion (124–125). Like Anne, the wives ultimately suggest ideal, chaste female partners in a "companionate marriage," a term used by early modern historians to describe the sanctity of marital relations and the elevated status of wifehood (as opposed to the concept of "holy virginity" upheld by the Catholic church) during the Protestant Reformation.

DEVICES AND TECHNIQUES

Merry Wives presents 86.6 percent of its lines in prose, the highest volume of prose in any play in Shakespeare's canon, followed by *Much Ado about Nothing* at 71.7 percent (*The Complete Pelican Guide to Shakespeare*, ed. Alfred Harbage [Baltimore: Penguin, 1969], 31). Critics have long questioned the once popular generalization that Shakespeare associates prose with his nonaristocratic characters, yet Shakespeare does in fact distinguish the upper-class Fenton by his use of blank verse. Language certainly conveys Windsor's provincial flavor, and the play is filled with clichés, quaint proverbs, and references to popular culture. Mistress Ford's comment that Falstaff's professions of love are as disjointed as the "hundred Psalms to the tune of Green-sleeves" (2.1.61–63), for example, makes an analogy between Falstaff's scandalous behavior and the subjects of the broadside ballad, a printed sheet on which sensational news stories on such topics as cross-dressing, foolish foreigners, lascivious wives, and cuckolded husbands were set to popular tunes. Barry Reay notes that approximately 15,000 different ballads were published during the sixteenth and seventeenth centuries; their circulation could have numbered in the millions (*Popular Cultures in England 1550–1750* [London: Longman, 1998], 36–70). The rogue Autolycus in Shakespeare's romance *The Winter's Tale* peddles these scandalous sheets, including one set "to a very doleful tune" about a moneylender's wife who gave birth to twenty moneybags (4.4.262–264).

It may first appear that language establishes a clear line between "insider" and "outsider" in Windsor. Evans's and Caius's humorous distortions of the English language provoke the natives' constant ridicule: in his first appearance, the Welsh Evans turns references to Shallow's ancestors' "luces" (fish) on a coat of arms to "louses" (lice) (1.1.16, 19). As Falstaff remarks about the Welshman at the end of the play, "Have I liv'd to stand at the taunt of one that makes fritters of English?" (5.5.142–143).

The numerous racial epithets peppered throughout the play conceive "foreign" as tantamount to "immoral behavior." For example, Pistol condemns Falstaff as a "Base Phrygian Turk" (1.3.88) for his adulterous solicitations, and Mistress Page, upon reading Falstaff's love letter, refers to him as a "Flemish drunkard" (2.1.23).

Yet Nym's own misuse of language (through which he "frights English out of his wits" [2.1.139], according to Page) in fact collapses distinctions between provincial middle-class England and its elite and foreign visitors. Characters from every class of English society employ malapropisms, verbal distortions of the native tongue that symbolize possible fissures underneath the moral facade of Windsor. Slender refers to his uncle as "Justice of the Peace and Coram" (1.1.5–6), a term meaning "discipline," rather than "quorum" (a legitimate number of judges for a trial); thus Slender emphasizes his uncle's affinity for punitive rather than moral action. With another linguistic slip, Slender unwittingly conveys the discordant reality of matrimony: instead of being "resolved . . . resolutely" to marry Anne, he announces to Shallow that "if you say, 'Marry her,' I will marry her; that I am freely dissolv'd, and dissolutely" (1.1.250–252). Mistress Quickly creates the most outrageous and bawdy malapropisms. Instead of "virtuous," she deems Mistress Ford a "fartuous . . . civil modest wife" (2.2.97–98). Later, defending the laundry basket incident as the servants' misunderstanding of Mistress Ford's "direction," Mistress Quickly tells Falstaff that "they mistook their erection" (3.5.39–40). From Evans's Welsh rendition of the Latinate term "vocative" as "focative" (4.1.51) and the Latin declension "*horum, harum, horum*" (l. 61) in William Page's Latin lesson, she construes the "genitive" case as the whore "Jinny's case" (l. 62), involving venereal disease.

In Falstaff, the comic devices of wit and physical farce diffuse such implications of sexual aggression, adultery, and prostitution. Dressed as the woman from Brainford, Falstaff makes slapstick of Ford's disturbing act of misogyny; his verbal retorts work similarly to generate a comic effect after the fairies' menacing chants ("Lust is but a bloody fire, / Kindled with unchaste desire" [5.5.95–96]) and subsequent physical assaults. Falstaff also inspires the play's most striking imagery: the man/stag whose horns appear throughout the play as a symbol of the cuckold, and the aquatic whale/leviathan captured and exploited by the community. As Barton points out, the large and out-of-place Falstaff is in some sense "beached" in Windsor (80). After hearing of Mistress Page's identical love letter, Mistress Ford evokes the image of the whale with which Falstaff is associated metaphorically throughout the play:

> What tempest, I trow, threw this whale, (with so many tuns of oil in his belly) ashore at Windsor? How shall I be reveng'd on him? I think the best way were to entertain him with hope, till the wicked fire of lust have melted him in his own grease. (2.1.64–68)

In her analogy, Falstaff's oily composition—a reference to his fat and to his sleazy scheme—is emblematic of the "wicked fire of lust."

The "wicked fire" anticipates Mistress Quickly's "trial fire" as Queen of the Fairies: "touch me his finger-end. / If he be chaste, the flame will back descend / And turn him to no pain; but if he start, / It is the flesh of a corrupted heart" (5.5.84–87). Punished by the "wicked fire" he has generated, Falstaff becomes a type of burnt sacrifice that affirms the moral well-being of the community. Imagining the public's discovery of his treacherous adventures, Falstaff describes himself similarly as both the victim of the community's aggression and its source of sustenance: "If it should come to the ear of the court, how I have been transform'd, and how my transformation hath been wash'd and cudgell'd, they would melt me out of my fat drop by drop, and liquor fishermen's boots with me" (4.5.94–99).

THEMES AND MEANINGS

Mary Beth Rose notes that *Merry Wives* is unusual in Shakespeare's canon for its benevolent representation of a mother figure, Mistress Page. Although Mistress Ford has no children of her own, she signifies, along with Mistress Page, the emerging authority of the married woman in early modern England. Rose observes that women did have some legal agency over such matters as the buying and selling of homes and their children's marriages and education ("Where are the Mothers in Shakespeare? Options for Gender Representation in the English Renaissance," *Shakespeare Quarterly* 42 [1991]: 291–314).

Together, the wives in the play exercise a broad realm of "local" authority over their husbands, servants, and Falstaff that suggests also the autonomy of Queen Elizabeth, who would have been on the throne for approximately four decades when Shakespeare composed this comedy. Regardless of whether or not the queen commanded Shakespeare to portray Falstaff in love as the tradition of John Dennis maintains, *Merry Wives* acknowledges female authority in a way that inevitably implicates the female monarch. Interestingly, while Falstaff signifies the vulnerability of King Henry IV in the histories, he is firmly kept under control by the mother/wife/queen figures Mistresses Ford and Page.

Yet *Merry Wives*, like some public proclamations made against Elizabeth herself, also expresses ambivalence about this level of female authority. The wives do not exploit their husbands sexually or financially, but it is clear that Falstaff's invitation places them in a position in which they may choose to do so. Peter Erikson compares the wives' mock-flirtations with Elizabeth's own strategic use of her sexuality in political self-representations: "Like Elizabeth, the wives use love as a political device to shape, contain, and deny male desire" ("The Order of the Garter, the Cult of Elizabeth, and Class-Gender Tension in *The Merry Wives of Windsor*," in *Shakespeare Reproduced: The Text in History and Ideology*, ed. Jean E. Howard and Marion F. O'Connor [New York: Methuen, 1987], 130). In addition to describing herself in her political speeches as both a wife and mother to England, the unmarried Elizabeth also cultivated her persona as the "Virgin Queen," a model of chastity and strength. In *Merry Wives*, Mistresses Page and Ford insist on their marital chastity, yet chaste women also spark suspicion in the play, as Ford demonstrates most strikingly in his "story" about his wife that he relates to Falstaff while in the guise of her lover: her "chastity," he claims, is only a ruse that allows her to conceal her illicit behavior. Ironically, the label of "chaste" also suggests a woman's potential for deception (see "Explication of Key Passages," below).

D. E. Underdown contends that Shakespearean England demonstrated a "fascination with rebellious women," such as shrews, adulteresses, and witches. Local court cases during this time record a striking number of women accused of local disputes, beating their husbands, and witchcraft ("The Taming of the Scold: the Enforcement of Patriarchal Authority in Early Modern England," in *Order and Disorder in Early Modern England*, ed. Anthony Fletcher and John Stevenson [Cambridge:

Cambridge UP, 1985], 118–119). The play's suggestion that an ostensibly chaste woman may have an affinity for adultery establishes the central theme of cuckoldry that is expressed most powerfully in Ford's paranoid fantasies about his wife. Coppélia Kahn notes the pervasive cultural threat signified by the term "cuckold," which dates from the mid-thirteenth century: "Man's vulnerability to woman in marriage is symbolized by the cuckold, who skulks through Shakespeare's works from early to late, his horns publishing his shame" (" 'The Savage Yoke': Cuckoldry and Marriage," p. 119). Consumed by such anxieties, Ford invites Page, Caius, and Evans to see the "monster" at his house—a term that suggests either Falstaff or Ford's unfaithful wife, inhuman because of her predisposition to adultery.

The image of the cuckold figures prominently in the "shaming rituals" of "charivari" or "skimmington," which would have been familiar to Shakespeare's audience as a local form of justice used against men who beat their wives as well as those "guilty" of harboring an unfaithful wife. Like Falstaff's own punishment in *Merry Wives*, the custom might involve female clothing or the particularly humiliating adornment of horns, thus mimicking the particular sexual transgression (Reay, pp. 155–161). Cultural anxiety about female authority over men is expressed also in the play's allusions to witchcraft, a central topic in *Demonology* (1597), authored by Elizabeth's successor, King James I. His denunciation of suspected "witches," women accused of inciting rebellion and anarchy within the kingdom, resembles Ford's condemnation of the woman of Brainford to whom he refers as a "witch, a quean [hussy], an old, cozening quean!" (4.2.172): "We are simple men, we do not know what's brought to pass under the profession of fortune-telling. She works by charms, by spells, by th' figure [astrological chart], and such daub'ry as this is, beyond our element; we know nothing" (4.2.174–178). "What's brought to pass" in this sense represents not only a potential sexual threat but also a wider scope of subversive behavior of which he knows "nothing."

For Ford, this "Mother *Prat*" (4.2.182; "prat" is defined by the *Oxford English Dictionary* as slang for "buttock"; it can also mean "trick"), a figure of the wives themselves, represents the limits of male knowledge and, subsequently, a woman's formidable potential to control the men in her community either through sex or chicanery. Cotton emphasizes that the violent scene of Ford's attack on the disguised Falstaff—a "symbolic wife-beating"—is remarkable also for the men's passive responses to someone whom they have already determined to be mentally unstable: "their lack of action rests on the unspoken premise that it is acceptable to beat, not just a witch, but a woman" (321). Mistress Quickly's later story that the husbands have beaten the wives for their dalliances with Falstaff similarly places a thin gloss over the disturbing image of domestic abuse: "Mistress Ford, good heart, is beaten black and blue, that you cannot see a white spot about her" (4.5.111–113).

Although the fairy play within a play provides the meta-theatrical climax of *Merry Wives*, such "performances" function throughout *Merry Wives* both to reveal and to suppress intimations of tragedy. In the wives' "act" of infidelity and Master Ford's role as "Brooke," for example, the characters stage their own illicit desires and fears. A central theme in *Merry Wives* is the blurring of fiction and reality to achieve these ends; Shakespeare underscores the short distance (if any) between the characters' contrived performances and their actual concerns. The story that Mistress Quickly tells Falstaff about Mistress Ford's unhappiness with her husband (2.2.88–91), for example, is actually suggested in the play's "real" exchanges between

Mistress Page and Mistress Ford (to Mistress Page's comment that her husband is "as far from jealousy as I am from giving him cause," she responds, "You are the happier woman" 2.1.103–104, 106) and by Master Ford's swift and unsubstantiated denunciation of his wife. Similarly, in the wives' plot to scare Falstaff, Mistress Page's contrived news of an enraged Master Ford proves factual.

These performances also call attention to the function of the theater itself, and in this sense point to the play's larger meta-theatrical theme. The disguised boy actors whom Caius and Slender each believe to be Anne Page represent the conditions of the early modern English theater in which male actors cross-dressed to play women's roles. Falstaff's disguise and performance as "Mother Prat"—like Evans's intimation that the fearful and unstable Page might be best suited with his wife's clothes (4.2.141–142)—creates an association between the experience of the theater and the spectacle of emasculation. Katz argues that Falstaff's role is to play out Master Ford's own masochistic fantasies of his cuckoldry as well as to articulate the audience's similar desires to see their anxieties represented—and subsequently purged—through the safe artifice of the theater. In his role as a "woman" and later as the horned "Herne the Hunter," Katz argues, Falstaff functions as a person on whom male viewers (within the play and in Shakespeare's actual audience) may project their own anxieties. Appropriately, Falstaff concedes after being denounced for his drinking, his lust, his altercations, and his general social misconduct, "I am your theme. . . . use me as you will" (5.5.161, 163–164).

But Katz also takes further the significance of the cuckold-spectacle to suggest a long-sought link between the two disparate Falstaffs in Shakespeare's dramatic work: "A set of poetic associations travels via Falstaff between the world of Windsor and Shakespeare's history plays. Taken together, these associations imagine a fantastical relationship among kingship, theatricality, and lecherous desire" (84). The "horned" Falstaff in *Merry Wives* recalls Falstaff's condition at the conclusion of *1 Henry IV* when Prince Hal remarks of the supposedly "dead" Falstaff: "Death hath not strook so fat a deer to-day, / Though many dearer, in this bloody fray" (5.4.107–108). A type of wounded animal in both scenes, Falstaff represents Prince Hal's political shame, the dishonorable past that he desires to leave behind, as well as the shame signified by the Garter motto *Honi soit qui mal y pense* (evil be to him who evil thinks) to which Mistress Quickly alludes (5.5.69). Ostensibly inspired by King Edward III's declaration to onlookers while holding a woman's garter, the inscription on the Garter emblem reminds spectators to dispense with their lustful thoughts. Shame in the form of King Henry IV's usurpation of Richard II's crown, Prince Hal's seeming rebellion against his father, and Ford's own fantasies of deception are displaced onto Falstaff, who effectively links "national shame" with "the Garter Day/Windsor imagery of sexual appetite and violation" (88).

CRITICAL CONTROVERSIES

The performance history of *Merry Wives* remains very much under debate. The "occasionalist" theory that the play was written for the April 23, 1597, Order of the Garter ceremony and perhaps in answer to Elizabeth's own command to see a play about Falstaff in love, while a crucial part of the play's critical history acknowledged in every modern edition of *Merry Wives*, has never been definitely established. Editors continue to offer their own theories about when Shakespeare composed the play. G. R. Hibbard, for example, in the New Penguin (Baltimore, 1973) edition of *Merry Wives* suggests that Evans's sharply defined Welsh accent dates the play later than the Henry plays, in which the language of the Welsh characters Glendower and Fluellen is not characterized with the same authentic detail (48–49).

Rather than debating the merits of one date over another, recent critics have turned to focus on the significance of these "myths" of origin that so famously surround the play. Freedman notes that *Merry Wives* "boasts the stunning fact of being the only play in the corpus still generally believed to have been composed for a specific court occasion and, even more specifically, as a compliment to Elizabeth" (190). Disputing many of Hotson's and Green's claims about topical references in the play, she points out that in 1597, a year in which English-German relations were particularly tense because of the German ban on English merchants by Emperor Rudolph II, Shakespeare would not have written a play that satirized the German duke (199–203). Katz contends that the legend of Elizabeth's demand for an amorous Falstaff expresses a fantasy of the queen's own sensual desires (78). Committed to a life as the "Virgin Queen," Elizabeth continually frustrated national hopes for her marriage—as much a political strategy for a Protestant heir as a cultural desire to place her in the traditional roles of wife and mother.

The Folio text's Garter allusions also raise questions about textual editing, which figure prominently in critical debates about *Merry Wives*. One of the most perplexing discrepancies between the Quarto and Folio is Ford's pseudonym: in the former, he is represented as "Brooke," and in the latter, "Broome." Critics such as Green have cited the shift as evidence that the Folio is closest to Shakespeare's original manuscript prepared for the 1597 Garter event. Green explains that Shakespeare's initial choice was "Brooke," the same name as Lord Cobham of the aristocratic Oldcastle family, who had protested also against Shakespeare's invocation of another family member, "Sir John Oldcastle," Falstaff's original name that appears in parts of the First Quarto of *1 Henry IV*. Some observer of the play in rehearsal during the weeks before the 1597 Garter ceremony, Green conjectures, perhaps Shakespeare's patron Lord Hunsdon, might have alerted the playwright to the fact of Lord Cobham's recent death and his family's subsequent sensitivity about the use of his name. The textual discrepancy between "Broome" and "Brooke" continues to bewilder literary critics, however, and reflects the major—and ongoing—debate about the construction of the text of *Merry Wives* and the relationship between the initial performance of the play, the 1602 Quarto, and the Folio (Green, pp. 107–120).

In 1881 P. A. Daniel challenged Alexander Pope's 1725 theory that the Quarto is an earlier draft of the Folio, contending instead that the former is a poor reproduction of the original constructed from memory by someone involved with the theater (Green, p. 77; Oliver, p. xiv). Daniel's argument, based on scene-by-scene comparisons between the two texts, has significantly influenced twentieth-century interpretations of the relationship between the extant versions of *Merry Wives*. Critics have also applied this theory of an actor/reporter's "memorial reconstruction" to other Shakespearean quartos, such as *Hamlet* and *Henry V*. Building on A. W. Pollard's theory that the Quarto is the result of textual piracy, W. W. Greg in 1910 argued that the actor who played the Host (whose lines in Q1 appear most like those in the Folio) most likely reconstructed this incomplete and inferior "Bad" Quarto from memory in order to revive the play in provincial performances. Though he considers the possibility that the 1602 Quarto may have been intentionally shortened to suit these traveling shows and perhaps a smaller acting cast, Greg ultimately rejects this theory (i–lvi). In 1971 H. J. Oliver added to Greg's argument the possibility that the actor playing Falstaff (based on the "memorized" clarity of his lines in Q1) might also be the "pirate actor" (xxvii). Recently, however, Gerald J. Johnson's "stringent analysis of the casting pattern in the Quarto" effectively disputes Pollard's and Greg's "memorial reconstruction" theory as well as W. J. Lawrence's argument in 1935 that the Quarto is adjusted for a stage production of fewer actors in which parts are subsequently doubled. Noting its distinctly "urban" setting, Johnson suggests that the Quarto might have been prepared for the London stage and the Folio for the Garter ceremony ("*The Merry Wives of Windsor*, Q1: Provincial Touring and Adapted Texts," *Shakespeare Quarterly* 38 [1987]: 164).

At stake in the long-standing debates about the origins of and relationships between the various versions of *Merry Wives* is Shakespeare's own authorial "authority." To what extent does either the Quarto or the Folio reflect Shakespeare's personal drafts? The practical aspects of printing in Shakespearean England make the relationship between authorial intent and textual reality a slippery one. Shakespeare's manuscripts, initially separated into individual parts during the process of preparing the text for the actors to use during rehearsal, would have been altered by professional scribes as well as by the actors themselves. Although Pollard along with John Dover Wilson in 1919 concluded that the "bad" Quarto of *Merry Wives* may have derived from a combination of Shakespeare's own revisions as well as those done by other agents, many modern critics still insist upon Shakespeare's connection to only the "superior," more cohesive texts (Werstine, p. 66). Greg himself would question his earlier conviction that the "bad" Quartos were the work of a non-Shakespearean, inauthentic agent and the "good" a reflection of Shakespeare's own work, yet his earlier perceptions of "good" and "bad" texts (the terms with which Pollard first classified Shakespearean quartos) have greatly shaped popular belief in the Folio's artistic and authorial superiority (Greg, "Notes and Observations," *Review of English Studies* 4 [1928]: 202).

Over the past two decades, however, critics have issued a substantial challenge to Greg's 1910 perception of the Quarto. As Leah Marcus shows, this reconsideration of the *Merry Wives* Quarto reflects a broader trend in literary criticism: the quarto editions of such plays as *King Lear* and *Richard III* have also been the subjects of such inquiries (*Puzzling Shakespeare: Local Reading and Its Discontents* [Berkeley: U of California P, 1988]). Werstine argues that modern critics have hastily continued Greg's use of "good" and "bad," sustaining the erroneous idea that Shakespeare should be associated only with the former. Steven Urkowitz also argues against Greg's early arguments about the texts and suggests that the Quarto, rather than "bad," could be a "tentative and exploratory" text composed by Shakespeare himself ("Good News about 'Bad' Quartos," in *"Bad" Shakespeare: Revaluations of the Shakespeare Canon*, ed. Maurice Charney [Madison, NJ: Farleigh Dickinson UP, 1988], 195).

PRODUCTION HISTORY

The cover of the 1602 Quarto states that *Merry Wives* was "divers times Acted . . . before her Maiestie, and else-where," but this interesting piece of information does not establish the precise dates and circumstances for these royal performances. There are, however, clear records of when the play was performed for Elizabeth's successor, King James I. According to the Revels Accounts of 1604, *Merry Wives* was performed for the king on Sunday, November 4, in the Banqueting Hall at Whitehall by the King's Men (Chambers, 4.171). Oliver suggests that a record of a play entitled *Sir John ffalstaffe* for which the King's Men were paid on May 20, 1613 may refer to *Merry Wives*, but the next indisputable account of a stage production is the King's Men performance at court on November 15, 1638 (Oliver, p. x; *The Jacobean and Caroline Stage*, ed. G. E. Bentley, 5 vols. [Oxford: Clarendon P, 1941–1968], 1.99). The famous Elizabethan comic actor William Kempe was likely the first Falstaff, and some critics believe that it was his act of textual piracy that prompted his expulsion from Shakespeare's company, the Chamberlain's Men, in 1599 (Andrew Gurr, *The Shakespearean Stage, 1574–1642* [Cambridge: Cambridge UP, 1970], 66).

Merry Wives was one of the first plays performed when the Puritans' eighteen-year ban on the theaters was removed in 1660. Even though major theaters produced *Merry Wives* more than thirty times during the eighteenth and nineteenth centuries, the play was not initially well-received by the Restoration audience. The writer and critic Samuel Pepys, for example, responded unfavorably to the performances he attended on December 5, 1660; September 25, 1661; and August 15, 1667 (Oliver, p. xi; *The Merry Wives of Windsor*, ed. David Crane [Cambridge: Cambridge UP, 1997], 19–24). Oliver explains Pepys's distaste for the play as indicative of the late seventeenth-century theatergoing public's lack of interest in a play that celebrates the English middle class, though Pepys's strictures on the first two performances suggest that the acting was to blame for his dissatisfaction. John Dennis, reacting against Shakespeare's excessive use of plot, attempted to condense the original narrative in his unpopular 1702 adaptation, *The Comical Gallant: Or The Amours of Sir John Falstaffe*. The play centers on Fenton, expands Anne Page's role, and substitutes Ford for Falstaff in the final scenes (Oliver, pp. x–xii; Roberts, p. 73).

Despite its inauspicious beginnings after the Restoration, *Merry Wives* achieved great popularity during the early eighteenth century and was produced more than any other Shakespearean play (Roberts, p. 62). The play made its debut on the American stage in Philadelphia in 1770 (Oliver, p. xii). Falstaff in particular has inspired operatic adaptations of Shakespeare's text, such as Otto Nicolai's *The Merry Wives of Windsor* (1849); Ralph Vaughan Williams's *Sir John in Love* (1929); and, most famously, Giuseppe Verdi's *Falstaff* (1893), which also includes scenes from the *Henry IV* plays. Embraced by actors for its variety of humorous parts, *Merry Wives* has appeared with some regularity on the twentieth-century stage. The Royal Shakespeare Company, for example, offered performances in 1968, 1975, and 1992 (Crane, p. 27).

Modern productions of *Merry Wives*, however, have also encountered particular obstacles because of the play's topicality; unlike Shakespeare's tragedies, for example, which offer archetypal, universal characters and plots, the Windsor comedy is somewhat restricted by its careful detailing of citizens' lives during a specific historical moment in Elizabethan England. The controversial director Oscar Asche (who also often played the role of Falstaff), for example, caused a critical uproar when he gave the play a winter setting in a 1911 production in London's West End. A production in 1955 provoked the same response in an audience similarly insistent on the play's festive, spring setting. Critical reactions to Asche's modernized

Charles Coburn (as Falstaff) and Jessie Royce Landis (as Mistress Ford) in *The Merry Wives of Windsor*. The Theatre Guild Shakespeare Company, presented by the Theatre Guild, 1949. Courtesy of Photofest.

Merry Wives in 1929 also convey how audiences familiar with the play expect a certain loyalty to Shakespeare's slapstick, middle-class, Elizabethan text. One review of the 1929 production in the London *Times* explains that Asche errs in modernizing the play because *Merry Wives* "stands for Old England in its healthiest, sanest, and most full-bloodied spirit" ("Oscar Asche: an Edwardian in Transition," *New Theatre Quarterly* 47 [1996]: 226). While viewers can be skeptical about the modernization of any Shakespearean play, the provincial, nostalgic "Old England" flavor of *Merry Wives* perhaps inspires more resistance to its interpretive possibilities.

EXPLICATION OF KEY PASSAGES

1.3.41–74. "No quips now, . . . we will thrive." After announcing to his companions at the Garter Inn that he plans to seduce Mistresses Page and Ford, Falstaff anticipates his success in this financial venture: "We will thrive, lads, we will thrive" (l. 74). Making an analogy between England's foreign expeditions during the sixteenth century and his own attempt at conquest, Falstaff describes Mistress Page metaphorically as an exotic and enticing land: she is like a "region in Guiana, all gold and bounty" (l. 69). In his role of adventurer, Falstaff also imagines himself a type of cheater/escheator, a robber as well as a revenue collector enabled by the office of the "exchequer" (the office that collected estates and lands forfeited to the monarch): "I will be cheaters to them both, and they shall be exchequers to me. They shall be my East and West Indies, and I will trade to them both" (ll. 69–72). With these analogies, Falstaff recasts his devious plan to procure money from Ford and Page as an action sanctioned by the English government itself. His seduction will yield material goods that are of both personal and national value. Falstaff suggests that the wives' own provocations make clear their need for this type of patriarchal control. He "[spies] entertainment" (l. 44) in Mistress Ford and "the leer of invitation" (ll. 45–46); Mistress Page has similarly "examined [his] parts with most judicious iliads [flirtatious looks]" (ll. 60–61) and admired his "portly belly" (l. 62). When "English'd rightly" (interpreted correctly; l. 48), the wives, like the foreigners to whom he alludes, will be tamed and controlled by the English patriarchy. Ironically, Falstaff's fantasy of men in power reads also as a re-action to the actual English monarchy itself, which was headed by the domineer-ing Queen Elizabeth.

Yet Falstaff also relates how Mistress Page did "course o'er [his] exteriors, with such a greedy intention, that the appetite of her eye did seem to scorch [him] up like a burning-glass!" (ll. 65–67), which suggests that he does not conquer the wives but is rather consumed by them. Mistress Page has an "appetite" for him; this in-timation of lascivious female desire evokes also Othello's intimations of his wife Desdemona as such a "consuming" woman guilty of an excessive (and adulterous) sexual appetite. The "burning glass" suggests an instrument with which to start a fire, and the image anticipates other descriptions of Falstaff as a cooked substance for the wives to consume and digest. After the laundry basket incident, Falstaff won-ders, "Have I liv'd to be carried in a basket like a barrow of butcher's offal?" (3.5.4–5) and claims that if he were to make himself vulnerable to another such trick, he would have his "brains ta'en out and butter'd" (ll. 7–8). Describing his ordeal to "Brooke," Falstaff explains that, as he is "as subject to heat as butter; a man of con-tinual dissolution and thaw," he became "half-stew'd in grease, like a Dutch dish" in the basket of dirty laundry (3.5.115–116, 119). In addition to establishing Falstaff as a type of sacrificial offering, the "burning" metaphors emphasize how the wives' domestic realm poses a legitimate threat to his well-being.

This passage, inspired by Falstaff's ambitious plans to exploit these women, ul-timately foreshadows the wives' exploitation of Falstaff. He relates that Mistress Page's eyes "sometimes gilded [his] foot" (l. 61), an illusion to how her affections will "gild" him with riches but an implication too that her lustful gaze will turn Falstaff himself into gold. She will objectify him for her own personal gain.

2.2.287–314. "What a damn'd . . . cuckold!" At the Garter Inn, in the soliloquy that concludes his first of three meetings with Falstaff under the pseudonym of "Brooke," Ford rages at what he believes is indisputable proof of his wife's adulter-ous liaison: "Who says this is improvident jealousy?" (ll. 288–289). Ford, always sus-pecting female infidelity, is here perversely vindicated by what seem to be the ostensible facts of his wife's impending assignation with Falstaff: "My heart is ready to crack with impatience! . . . My wife hath sent to him, the hour is fix'd, the match is made. . . . God be prais'd for my jealousy!" (ll. 288, 289–290, 309). In a paranoid frenzy, he imagines the repercussions of the incident: "My bed shall be abus'd, my coffers ransack'd, my reputation gnawn at, and I shall not only receive this villain-ous wrong, but stand under the adoption of abominable terms, and by him that does me this wrong" (ll. 292–296).

The terms "wittol" and "cuckold," he argues, far surpass the names of the devil himself. As Kahn points out, "wittol," defined in the *Oxford English Dictionary* as a cuckold who passively accepts his wife's adultery, suggests an exceedingly "unmanly" condition (129). After confirming his own public humiliation, Ford deems Page "a secure ass" (ll. 300–301) for trusting his wife and claims that he would rather trust a foreigner than a woman, a comparison that is significant in a play in which foreigners represent a threat to English sensibility: "I will rather trust a Fleming with my butter, Parson Hugh the Welshman with my cheese, an Irishman with my aqua-vitae bottle, or a thief to walk my ambling gelding, than my wife with herself" (ll. 302–305). With knowledge of the details of Falstaff's meeting with his wife, Ford plans to prove to all that doubted his suspicions that he is correct. The pervasive cultural image of the "cuckold" unsettles him most profoundly, and he ends his rant with a frantic repetition of the term: "Fie, fie, fie! cuckold, cuckold, cuckold!" (ll. 312–314).

4.2.102–107. "Hang him . . . all the draff." These lines, spoken by Mistress Page, occur during the second of her three meetings with Falstaff. After contriving the story of the approaching Master Ford, Mistresses Page and Ford send Falstaff upstairs to disguise himself in the maid's aunt's gown. As Mistress Ford imagines what her husband's reaction to Falstaff might be, given that he "cannot abide the old woman of Brainford" (4.2.85–86), her friend discloses that the story of her husband is no trick. Excited by these developments, Mistress Ford goes upstairs to expedite Falstaff's cross-dressing. Unlike the first meeting, here the wives plot a confrontation between Falstaff and Ford that anticipates the "shaming ritual" with which the play ultimately concludes. Declaring "we cannot misuse [Falstaff] enough!" (ll. 102–103), Mistress Page offers this explanation of their behavior:

> We'll leave a proof, by that which we will do,
> Wives may be merry, and yet honest too:
> We do not act that often jest and laugh;
> 'Tis old, but true: still swine eats all the draff. (ll. 104–107)

The outcome of the tricks, she suggests, will offer "proof" that their merriment is indicative of marital chastity and moral justice. She equates "merry" with "honest": the quaint adage in the final line above intimates that silent women should cause more concern than women who display their emotions publicly. There are important contradictions in Mistress Page's argument, however, that signify the play's ambivalent representation of female authority. She claims that, as women who "often jest and laugh," they do not "act"—yet "acting" is precisely what the wives do throughout the play in their mock-trysts with Falstaff and in their disingenuous interactions with their husbands. As Mistress Page tells Mistress Ford as they anticipate Falstaff's arrival for the first of their meetings, "[I]f I do not act it, hiss me" (3.3.38–39). Also, Ford suggests that chastity itself is a type of performance. In a meeting with Falstaff, Ford explains that his desire to prove Mistress Ford unchaste is motivated by rumors that she "enlargeth her mirth" away from home "so far that there is shrewd construction made of her" (2.2.222–223), thus making a connection between merriment and sexual promiscuity. As "merry" wives they are satisfied and jovial under the wings of their husbands in this provincial town; at the same time, the comic spirit of "merriment" also suggests Falstaff's own disruptions that aggravate the conservative social structures of Windsor. By asserting her chastity, Mistress Page emphasizes her difference from Falstaff; yet like the knight, the wives also evoke the "Falstaffian," or unruly, elements of society even as they strive to repress those anarchic aspects.

Annotated Bibliography

Green, William. *Shakespeare's "The Merry Wives of Windsor."* Princeton: Princeton UP, 1962. The most influential and extensive explanation of the play's possible connection to the 1597 Order of the Garter ceremony.

Greg, W. W., ed. *Shakespeare's "Merry Wives of Windsor" 1602.* Oxford: Clarendon P, 1910. The Quarto text and Greg's controversial introduction. Greg's theory of this text as a "memorial reconstruction" of the original Folio has shaped modern ideas about play's textual history.

Kahn, Coppélia. "'The Savage Yoke': Cuckoldry and Marriage." In *Man's Estate: Masculine Identity in Shakespeare.* Berkeley: U of California P, 1981. 119–150. An examination of the literary history of the "cuckold" and Shakespeare's use of this provocative term in *Merry Wives.*

Katz, Leslie S. "*The Merry Wives of Windsor*: Sharing the Queen's Holiday." *Representations* 51 (1995): 77–93. Katz traces the development of Falstaff's character through Shakespeare's histories and *Merry Wives.*

Oliver, H. J., ed. *The Merry Wives of Windsor.* London: Methuen, 1971. Oliver's introduction, an excellent overview of the play, provides the most comprehensive summary of critical debates about the Quarto and Folio.

Roberts, Jeanne Addison. *Shakespeare's English Comedy: "The Merry Wives of Windsor" in Context.* Lincoln: U of Nebraska P, 1979. One of the few books devoted entirely to *Merry Wives,* Roberts's study treats every dimension of the text and its critical history.

Werstine, Paul. "Narratives about Printed Shakespeare Texts: 'Foul Papers' and 'Bad' Quartos." *Shakespeare Quarterly* 41 (1990): 65–86. This essay, which refutes traditional ideas about Shakespeare's own role in the writing of "good" and "bad" versions of the play, represents the most recent trend in textual criticism about *Merry Wives.*

Much Ado about Nothing

David W. Cole

PLOT SUMMARY

1.1. Don Pedro, Prince of Arragon, has just quelled a revolt by his illegitimate half-brother, Don John. Returning triumphantly to Messina, Don Pedro and his followers, the Counts Claudio and Benedick, are invited by Leonato, the Governor, to stay at his estate. Don Pedro threatens that they will stay for a month, and Leonato assures him that they will be welcome even longer.

Three interlocked plots follow: two of them love stories and the last a story of thwarted vengeance. Earlier the young Count Claudio had taken no special notice of Leonato's daughter, Hero. Now, however, struck by her beauty and her modesty, he asks what his friend Benedick thinks of her. Benedick, an outspoken bachelor, tries to laugh the request off, but Claudio calls her the sweetest lady he has ever seen. Subsequently Don Pedro makes the lady even sweeter to Claudio by revealing that she is her father's only heir. Don Pedro promises to arrange her marriage to Claudio.

1.2. A servant overhears Don Pedro and Claudio and mistakenly reports that the Prince will woo Hero for himself. Leonato responds cautiously, "We will hold this as a dream till it appear itself" (1.2.20–21).

1.3. Claudio and Don Pedro are also overheard by Borachio, one of Don John's followers. Claudio has won glory in the war, and Don John, full of venom, would like in return to embarrass Claudio. He plans to thwart the contemplated engagement by convincing Claudio that Don Pedro has played him false.

2.1. At a masquerade in the evening, Don Pedro goes aside with Hero, while Don John suggests to Claudio that Don Pedro is courting her for himself. Easily persuaded, Claudio is petulantly disappointed. Meanwhile, instead of pursuing romance Benedick tries to escape the sharp tongue of Hero's cousin, Beatrice, who pretends not to recognize him in his disguise so that she can accuse him of many shortcomings. Soon, Claudio learns that the Prince has been a faithful proxy after all, gaining for him the hand of the modest Hero and the consent of her aristocratic father. At a loss for words, Claudio can declare only, "Silence is the perfectest heralt of joy" (2.1.306).

Claudio wants his marriage ceremony to be held the next day, but Leonato demurs—a week will hardly be time enough to make the necessary preparations. To pass the time, Don Pedro proposes that he, Leonato, Claudio, and Hero make a match between Benedick and Beatrice. Beatrice, as outspoken as Hero has been quiet, has declared her devotion to maidenhood and her aversion to men, and most especially to Benedick, whom she mocks mercilessly. Benedick has been equally outspoken in his devotion to bachelorhood, and almost as quick witted in his repartee as Beatrice. Apparently Beatrice and Benedick had been attracted to one another earlier, but, she says, he played her false.

2.2. Frustrated in his first attempt to cross Claudio, Don John welcomes Borachio's suggestion that they convince Claudio that Hero is unchaste. Borachio offers to have one of Hero's serving women, Margaret, dress herself in Hero's clothes and meet him in the night at Hero's window. If Don John gets Don Pedro and Claudio to witness the meeting, the proposed marriage can still be thwarted. Don John promises Borachio a thousand ducats for this effort.

2.3. Later, Benedick conceals himself in Leonato's orchard rather than join Leonato, Claudio, and Don Pedro to talk of love and marriage. They pretend not to see him and by prearrangement discuss Beatrice's supposedly desperate passion for Benedick, which, they say, she will never expose to Benedick's scorn. Benedick believes they are sincere and, guilt-stricken, vows to reform. "I will be horribly in love with her. I may chance have some odd quirks and remnants of wit broken on me, because I have rail'd so long against marriage; but doth not the appetite alter?" (2.3.235–238). Beatrice, as yet untouched by the conspiracy, is sent to call Benedick to dinner. He imagines a hidden meaning in her open antagonism, and after she has left he says that he will get her picture.

3.1. Hero and two of her serving women, Margaret and Ursula, plot to trick Beatrice very much as Don Pedro, Claudio, and Leonato have tricked Benedick. Margaret tells Beatrice that Hero and Ursula are walking in the orchard talking about her. Beatrice, hiding to eavesdrop, hears that Benedick is hopelessly in love with her. Beatrice is convinced; in ten lines of poetry she declares that she will requite him.

3.2. In the meantime, Don John accuses Hero of infidelity. Claudio is almost as ready to believe this lie as he was to believe that Don Pedro betrayed him, and the Prince offers to accompany Claudio to see whether Hero meets the alleged clandestine lover. Claudio promises that if Hero is proved false, he will repudiate her at the altar.

3.3. As night falls, Dogberry, the master constable, and his assistant, Verges, muster the watch. Supremely self-assured, Dogberry is unconscious of his abuse of logic and the language; his instructions almost guarantee that the watch will be ineffectual. "This is your charge: you shall comprehend all vagrom [that is, vagrant] men; you are to bid any man stand, in the Prince's name" says Dogberry. But if a man will not stand, "Why then, take no note of him, but let him go, and presently call the rest of the watch together, and thank God you are rid of the knave" (3.3.24–30). Despite their leader's instructions and their own ineptitude, members of the watch overhear Borachio drunkenly tell his companion, Conrade, about Don John's success in persuading Don Pedro and Claudio of Hero's infidelity. Although the watchmen do not quite understand what they have heard, they recognize villainy and apprehend Borachio and Conrade.

3.4. In the morning Hero, Ursula, Margaret, and Beatrice prepare for the wedding. Just as the Prince, Claudio, and Leonato had earlier made fun of Benedick's signs of love, Hero and her serving women tease Beatrice about Benedick.

3.5. Meanwhile, master constable Dogberry and Verges report to the governor, Leonato. Dogberry cannot make himself understood, however, and Leonato, impatient and distracted because of the impending marriage ceremony, tells Dogberry and Verges to conduct the examination of the prisoners themselves and bring him the results.

4.1. The Prince, Don John, Leonato, Claudio, Benedick, Hero, Beatrice, a Friar, and others assemble for the marriage ceremony. The Friar asks Claudio, "You come hither, my lord, to marry this lady?" (4.1.4–5). Claudio answers, "No." Bitterly he makes himself clear, accusing Hero of being unchaste. Hero denies his charges, but the Prince and Don John bear witness to Claudio's accusation. As the Prince, Don John, and Claudio leave, Hero faints. Benedick remains behind. Leonato is frantic with shame:

> O, she is fall'n
> Into a pit of ink, that the wide sea
> Hath drops too few to wash her clean again. (4.1.139–141)

But Beatrice declares, "O, on my soul, my cousin is belied!" (4.1.146). Still, she must admit that she was not with Hero the night before, although she and Hero had shared a bed on every other night for the past year. Leonato takes this admission as confirmation of Claudio's charge, but the Friar observes that Hero does not look guilty. Surely, he says, there is some mistake. Then the Friar proposes that they report the death of Hero, who had been prostrate in a swoon. In time, he predicts, her accuser will remember her loveliness and grow to regret his accusation, while her friends will have time to find the truth. Benedick and Leonato agree, and the Friar and Leonato leave with Hero.

Left alone, Beatrice and Benedick discuss what has transpired. Benedick declares that Hero has been wronged. Beatrice says that a man—but not Benedick—could right that wrong. Benedick confesses that he loves Beatrice, and she finally admits that she loves him, too. "Come, bid me do anything for thee," he says, and she responds simply, "Kill Claudio!" (4.1.288–289). Faced with a conflict between love and friendship, Benedick demurs. Beatrice, furious, exclaims, "O God, that I were a man! I would eat his heart out in the market-place" (4.1.306–307). Moved by her conviction and her depth of feeling, Benedick finally agrees to challenge Claudio.

4.2. Meanwhile, Dogberry and Verges conduct their examination of Borachio and Conrade, while the sexton, who alone is literate, records the proceeding. The constables have no idea of what they are about, but the sexton, understanding the deception that has been practiced, leaves to show Leonato the record. Conrade, offended by Dogberry's pompous ineptitude, calls Dogberry an ass, and Dogberry laments that this insult has not been recorded: "O that I had been writ down an ass!" (4.2.86–87).

5.1. Leonato's brother, Antonio, attempts unsuccessfully to console him for his humiliation. When Claudio and the Prince appear, first Leonato and then Antonio confront Claudio, who will not accept the challenges of these old men. The Prince again asserts the truth of Claudio's charge and refuses to hear any protest. As

Leonato and Antonio leave, Benedick appears, and the Prince and Claudio try to joke about the confrontation. Benedick does not join in, but instead challenges Claudio himself and dissociates himself from the Prince. He adds that Don John has fled. Dogberry, Verges, and the watch now appear with their prisoners. Once again Dogberry is comically unable to give a clear account of their offenses, but Borachio confesses. Now Claudio can think only of the modesty and beauty he first saw in Hero. Leonato, Antonio, and the sexton enter, and Claudio asks Leonato to impose any penance on him. Leonato's revenge is to require Claudio to publish Hero's innocence, to sing an epitaph at her tomb, and then to marry his brother's hitherto unseen daughter who, he says, is now the sole heir of both of them, and is moreover almost the copy of the dead Hero. Claudio gratefully accepts this penance.

5.2. Benedick complains of the ominous rhymes and allusions that occur to him as he tries to write love poetry. He sends for Beatrice, and when she appears, he tells her that he has challenged Claudio.

5.3. That night Claudio and Don Pedro conduct their promised rites of mourning at Hero's tomb.

5.4. In the morning Leonato directs the women, including Hero and Beatrice, to withdraw and mask themselves before the marriage ceremony. Benedick takes advantage of their absence to gain Leonato's consent for his marriage to Beatrice. Claudio arrives with Don Pedro and makes a binding pledge of marriage before he sees his bride's face. Only then does Hero reveal herself. Beatrice and Benedick discover the tricks that have been played on them but agree to marry anyway. Benedick and Claudio are reconciled. Word comes that Don John has been apprehended. Benedick promises to devise "brave punishments" the next day (5.4.128), and the play ends with a festive dance.

PUBLICATION HISTORY

The received text of *Much Ado about Nothing* is relatively reliable. The only quarto of the play was published in 1600. The First Folio and modern editions follow the 1600 text with infrequent minor changes.

The typesetter of the Quarto apparently worked from Shakespeare's foul papers. Evidence that the source was not a final draft includes the naming of Leonato's wife ("Innogen" or "Imogen") in stage directions, although she never speaks, and confusions and omissions in the naming of other characters in the stage directions. Dogberry and Verges are indicated in 4.2 by the actors' names, "Kemp[e]" and "Cowley." Some entrances are not indicated at all in the sketchy stage directions. In 1923 Sir Arthur Quiller-Couch and John Dover Wilson hypothesized that rather than being printed from foul papers, the text of the play as we have it shows evidence of revision, but this suggestion has been convincingly refuted by the subsequent bibliographic research of W. C. Ferguson and Charlton Hinman, among others. The typesetter of the Quarto apparently followed his copy-text fairly faithfully. Modern editors have restored occasional corruptions in the text, but none have come up with a completely convincing emendation for the Quarto's "and sorrow, wagge" (5.1.16).

In September 1598, in *Palladis Tamia*, Francis Meres provides a presumably complete list of Shakespeare's comedies to that date, including "his *Gentlemen of Verona*, his *Errors*, his *Love labors lost*, his *Love labors wonne*, his *Midsummers night dreame*, and his *Merchant of Venice*"—but not *Much Ado about Nothing*. It has been suggested that *Much Ado* is the otherwise unknown *Love's Labor's Won*, but there is no recognizable contemporary reference to *Much Ado* by the other title; when *Much Ado* is not called by its title in the 1600 Quarto, it is named after Beatrice and Benedick. Moreover the August 1603 inventory of bookseller Christopher Hunt lists *Love's Labor's Won* along with other titles by Shakespeare; it seems improbable that he would list the play by any title other than that on the title page of the 1600 Quarto. A. R. Humphreys concludes, then, that *Much Ado about Nothing* is not the mysterious *Love's Labor's Won*, and that *Much Ado* had not yet been performed when Meres made his list in the summer of 1598. However, since William Kempe's name appears in some of the speech headings for Dogberry, the play must have been written before early 1599, when Kempe left Shakespeare's company, the Lord Chamberlain's Men. Stylistic analysts place *Much Ado* with *As You Like It* between the *Henry IV* plays and *The Merry Wives of Windsor* (1596–1597), on the one hand, and *Julius Caesar* and *Henry V* (1599), on the other, making a date of late 1598 plausible (*Much Ado about Nothing*, New Arden Edition, ed. A. R. Humphreys [London: Thomson, 2002], 2–4).

SOURCES FOR THE PLAY

Stories involving a lover or husband deceived into believing that his beloved is unfaithful are very old. They were especially popular in the Renaissance, and Shakespeare, who may have known several of them, appears to have used two in writing *Much Ado about Nothing*. The most important is Bandello's *La Prima Parte de la Novelle*, of 1554, which tells the story of Don Timbreo, who, having distinguished himself in the army of King Piero of Arragon, is attracted to Fenicia, the beautiful daughter of Lionato, a poor nobleman of Messina. Timbreo tries to make Fenicia his mistress—she is too poor, he thinks, to be his wife—but she is as modest as she is beautiful; so, to win her, Timbreo asks a noble friend to arrange a marriage. However, Timbreo's friend Girondo, secretly in love with Fenicia, employs an agent to accuse her of receiving a lover at her bedroom window at night and invites Timbreo to see the proof. From Lionato's garden that night, Timbreo sees a ladder placed under Fenicia's window and Girondo's servant entering the room. Jealous and angry, Timbreo sends his intermediary back to Lionato to charge Fenicia with infidelity and to call off the match.

Fenicia denies any unchasteness and falls into a deathlike swoon. When she is being prepared for burial, she revives, and her father sends her secretly to his brother's country house. Burial rites are performed, an epitaph is placed on her tomb declaring her innocence, and the whole city mourns her. Timbreo begins to feel he has been too hasty, and Girondo is overcome with guilt. Meeting Timbreo at Fenicia's tomb, Girondo confesses, asking Timbreo to kill him. Their friendship is so strong, however, that Timbreo forgives him, and even declares that had he known of Girondo's passion, he would have resigned Fenicia to him. Together Timbreo and Girondo confess to Lionato; Timbreo pledges to atone in any way that Lionato wishes. Lionato asks that when Timbreo marries, he take as his wife whomever Lionato chooses, and Timbreo agrees. Meanwhile, Fenicia, having taken the name of Lucilla, grows ever more beautiful. After a year, Timbreo goes with Lionato, Girondo, and others to take her as his bride. Timbreo does not recognize her, but at the wedding feast, her identity is revealed. After the happy reconciliation of Timbreo and Fenecia, Girondo is given the hand of Belfiore, Fenecia's sister. In Messina, the two couples and Lionato are received by the king with gifts and celebration.

From this story Shakespeare has taken the setting, the names of Leonato and Don Pedro, the false accusation confirmed by misleading appearances, the ladder at the bedroom window, the apparent death of the slandered woman, a conflict between friendship and heterosexual love, the atonement by marriage to Lionato's choice of bride, and the happy reunion of the lovers. From a second, somewhat similar story, in Ariosto's *Orlando Furioso*, Shakespeare takes the characters of a thoroughly villainous slanderer and a servant who unknowingly cooperates in the deception.

The Beatrice and Benedick plot has no such close analog, although Beatrice and Benedick themselves resemble characters in literary tradition and in Shakespeare's own earlier works. Beatrice resembles Chaucer's Wife of Bath in her independence, and in her aversion to heterosexual love she is also like a woman described in Baldassare Castiglione's *The Courtier* (1528; English translation, 1561) who rejected a man until she heard that he and she were reputed to be lovers. Forerunners of Beatrice in Shakespeare's plays include Kate in *The Taming of the Shrew*, Portia in *The Merchant of Venice*, and the ladies of *Love's Labor's Lost*. Benedick, the outspoken bachelor, resembles Berowne and the other scorners of love in *Love's Labor's Lost* and Valentine in *The Two Gentlemen of Verona*. Dogberry, too, recalls characters in earlier Shakespearean plays, most notably Bottom the Weaver in *A Midsummer Night's Dream*—also played by William Kempe, whose talents must have helped to shape both roles. Two generations after *Much Ado* was written, John Aubrey reported that "the Constable in a *Midsomernight's Dreame*" was based on a constable in Grendon Underwood in Buckinghamshire. No constable, however, appears in *A Midsummer Night's Dream*; perhaps Aubrey refers to a local tradition about the origins of Dogberry. *Much Ado*'s close and intricate interconnecting of the stories of the slandered woman, the reluctant lovers, and the incompetent and egotistical constable is Shakespeare's original creation.

STRUCTURE AND PLOTTING

In *Much Ado about Nothing* Shakespeare makes Bandello's story more dramatically effective, simplifying and sharpening its focus by redefining the characters and their relationships. Shakespeare gives Hero not only beauty and modesty, like Bandello's heroine, but rank and wealth. Claudio is younger than Bandello's hero, shy enough that he really needs Don Pedro to woo for him by proxy, and so innocent that his denial of sexual relations with Hero during their betrothal resonates with his real shock at such an idea. Shakespeare makes Claudio consistently gullible, unlike Bandello's hero, and presents him almost always in the company of a dominant male companion. These changes in the character of the story's protagonist necessitate an expansion in the role of Don Pedro in Shakespeare's revision. Shakespeare also radically transforms Bandello's plot by eliminating any suggestion of rivalry between the protagonist and his friend. Shakespeare must then find a new motive for deception, which he does by creating a new character. Don John is moved not by romantic jealousy but by military jealousy and resentment, and by the inherent malignity of his bastardy. Shakespeare alters his heroine's family as well, giving her only a father who at least initially doubts her, instead of two unwaveringly supportive parents.

Shakespeare brings all of these characters together in the theatrically very effective scene in which Claudio accuses and repudiates Hero at the altar (4.1). The explosive emotional power of this dramatic rejection is such that Shakespeare must create more visible assurances that all will work out for the best. Hence he adds the watch, who discover the falseness of the accusation even before it is made. The changes that Shakespeare has made in the main plot lead him to add the two subplots of the play. Elizabethan aesthetics, leaning always to copy, make it natural to give the protagonist's friend a romantic interest also, and the involvement of the watch invited the creation of a role for William Kempe that grew into a subplot itself.

Some critics of *Much Ado* have found the resulting tripartite plot structure flawed. The story of Claudio and Hero seems underwritten. Hero, whose character and motivations are only sketchily developed, seems equally ready to accept Don Pedro or Claudio as a suitor, and her forgiveness of Claudio at the end seems unmotivated. Claudio's acceptance of his penance also seems arbitrary, leaving him an undefined and unsympathetic character. The nature of Margaret's involvement in Don John's deception and the reasons for her prompt exoneration are also unexplained at the play's end. The underdevelopment of the play's main plot creates a potentially troubling imbalance with the fully developed story of Beatrice and Benedick and their fully realized characterization.

The various story lines of *Much Ado about Nothing*, however, can also be seen to work well together. Beatrice and Benedick are foils to Claudio and Hero. As Claudio and Hero are eager lovers, Beatrice and Benedick are reluctant. As Claudio and Hero are quiet, Beatrice and Benedick unloose a flood of words. Each couple encounters a problem of fidelity—deceitfully imposed on Claudio and Hero, obsessively imagined by Benedick, but—if Beatrice is to be believed—perhaps at one time real in Benedick's own behavior. Harold Goddard observes that despite all of these antitheses between the two couples, the sentimental and romantic egotism of Claudio and Hero is really not significantly different than the antiromantic and intellectual egotism of Benedick and Beatrice. Goddard sees Beatrice and Benedick as satirizing Claudio and Hero, and Dogberry as satirizing Beatrice and Benedick in turn by his egotistical use of words (vol. 1, 277). The relationship of Dogberry and Verges also satirizes the relationship of Don Pedro and Claudio. Finally, the grace of comedy corrects and forgives the excesses of almost all of these characters whom Shakespeare has brought together. Don John alone faces "brave [severe] punishments" in the end (5.4.128).

MAIN CHARACTERS

Much Ado about Nothing contrasts Benedick and Beatrice with everyone else in Messina. In the beginning of the play, Don Pedro, Claudio, Benedick, Leonato, and his brother (Antonio) inhabit the comfortable, cultivated world of aristocratic male fellowship. Accompanied by trusted friends, their social dominance assured, their values conventional and unquestioned, they have lives apparently secure in every way. Even the recent war has been for them more an occasion of self-advancement or self-advertisement than an experience of discomfort or danger. The privileged world of aristocratic male fellowship has limits, clearly, yet those who enjoy it can quite legitimately appreciate the stability and security it offers.

Don Pedro

Don Pedro is the focal character in this privileged world: the source of order, the embodiment of decorum, and Claudio's mentor. Although he seems sophisticated, he, like Claudio, is taken in by Don John's deception, and his sober confirmation of Hero's wantonness greatly strengthens Claudio's wild charges. That Don Pedro shares Claudio's guilt may make Claudio's error more forgivable in the eyes of some interpreters. Significantly, however, the Prince is not challenged when Claudio is (5.1.45–193), although he participates with Claudio in the mourning rites before Hero's tomb and even presides over the ritual.

Claudio

From beginning to end, Claudio inhabits the world of masculine friendship, at first asking Benedick to confirm his choice in love and then asking Don Pedro to woo in his stead. Later with Don Pedro and Don John as friends, he accuses Hero. Finally, he accepts Leonato's choice of a bride. He seems never to speak for himself, only repeating or amplifying what a comrade (usually Don Pedro) has said. His accusations of Hero are no more than what Don Pedro and Don John expect. Even in his engagingly humble lines "I am your husband if you like of me" (5.4.59), he speaks as Leonato has determined.

Leonato

Leonato is comfortable and quite conventional in the aristocratic brotherhood until he is faced with a conflict between male fellowship and paternal trust. In the crisis he first joins his daughter's accusers, then doubts them, then confesses his confusion. Through act 4 and the early part of act 5 he is constant only in his overwhelming self-pity. Not until Don John's plot is discovered is the conflict between his masculine values and his paternal duty resolved, so that he can again play a graceful and generous role as Claudio's benefactor.

Antonio

Antonio's status is not quite that of his brother the Governor, but he is a wealthy landowner and a gentleman. Although he is Leonato's brother, Leonato's niece, Beatrice, is not his daughter, and despite the "daughter" referred to in the last act, he seems to have no family of his own. Antonio is old, with a waggling head, and he is more excitable than Leonato. He is stirred in act 1, scene 2 by the report that the Prince will court Hero, and after counseling patience to his distraught brother at the beginning of the last act, Antonio injects himself into the quarrel between Leonato and Claudio, demanding, "Come follow me, boy; come, sir boy, come follow me, / Sir boy, I'll whip you from your foining fence [thrusting fencing] (5.1.83–84).

Friar Francis

Friar Francis appears only twice in the play, but he has an important role. He believes the best of everyone. He perceives Hero's innocence, and he believes that, given time, Claudio's better nature will allow him to discover his strange error. Although events move too fast for the Friar's prediction to prove itself, his wisdom, ingenuity, and initiative provide an opportunity for the resolution of the conflict. Given the religious controversy of Shakespeare's day, one may note with interest this very sympathetic characterization of a Roman Catholic ecclesiastic. He recalls the similarly well-meaning if less effectual Friar Lawrence of *Romeo and Juliet.*

Don John

Don John has none of the depth that Edmund, Iago, or even Malvolio has; an actor must flesh out the role. Don John maintains with Borachio, the drunken womanizer, and Conrade, the spoiled gentleman, a kind of anti-court opposed to Don Pedro, Claudio, and Benedick. Coming from the cultivated and secure world of privilege but not really of it, Don John resents that world and attacks it in the person of Claudio, the prodigy who has won favor at Don John's expense. Perhaps as a bastard Don John also resents the legitimacy of the impending marriage. As a dependent with a somewhat ambiguous status, Don John is an interesting foil to Beatrice: he is as saturnine as she is merry, and he rejects community while Beatrice creates a place for herself in the world of the play. In the denouement there is celebration for her, but for Don John there will be unspecified but fully deserved retribution.

Conrade and Borachio

Conrade and Borachio, Don John's followers, play roles quite different from one another, although they are arrested together. Borachio prompts Don John to tell Claudio that Don Pedro was wooing Hero for himself and then devises the plot to use Margaret to make Claudio think that Hero is unfaithful. Borachio devises these plots apparently not to injure Claudio but to win Don John's approval, which, when it comes, appears in the quite substantial form of a thousand ducats. Borachio spends some of this on drink and drunkenly reveals his story to Conrade, whose guilt is only by association. Conrade has actually counseled Don John to reconcile with his brother. As a gentleman, he is offended by his arrest and by Dogberry's overweening officiousness. Conrade gives Dogberry the title of "ass," which the constable is so eager to have recorded for posterity.

Hero

Hero is lively and playful only with the other women. Submissive in a male-dominated world, she acquiesces to the Prince's anticipated suit and then quickly accepts Claudio instead. Claudio finds her submissiveness attractive. Hero's responses when the masculine order betrays her in the church are stunned silence, then passionate denial of Claudio's slander, then a swoon—what more could she do? In the end she is forgiving, either from her dutiful acceptance of her father's wishes or from the grace and generosity of her simple and pure nature.

Margaret and Ursula

Margaret and Ursula, Hero's serving women, enjoy with her and Beatrice a feminine fellowship very similar to the masculine fellowship of Don Pedro, Claudio, Benedick, Leonato, and Antonio. All of these women are lively among themselves— and, interestingly, at the masquerade. Margaret and Ursula cooperate readily with Hero in the gulling of Beatrice. Ursula is the more sensitive of the serving women— note the delicate imagery of

> The pleasant'st angling is to see the fish
> Cut with her golden oars the silver stream,
> And greedily devour the treacherous bait. (3.1.26–28)

Margaret is more forward and more bawdy, both when Hero is preparing to be married in 3.4 and in her exchange with Benedick in 5.2. She has been involved in a year-long love affair with Borachio. She is said not to be guilty of conspiring against her mistress, but Margaret does not come forward to defend her, either. Perhaps she has no opportunity to do so.

Dogberry

Master Constable Dogberry comes from a different milieu than the other characters, both because he is so distinctively English and because he is from the working class. He is aggressively aware of social status, but everything he says and does to assert his material and intellectual advantages advertises instead his limits to his betters if not to his peers. His instructions to the watch run exactly counter to his obviously sincere desire to maintain the good order of the Prince's people, but his misstatements don't matter—the watch will serve as it always serves. Dogberry may be "writ down an ass" (4.1.87) not in the record of the malefactors' examination, but in the play itself; yet by the grace of comedy he also successfully maintains his human dignity. Verges, Dogberry's "compartner" (Stage Direction at head of 3.3), who can turn a malapropism as well as the Master Constable, is usually content simply to agree with whatever Dogberry says, following Dogberry's lead much as Claudio follows the lead of Don Pedro.

Beatrice and Benedick

Beatrice and Benedick are far more thoroughly developed as characters than are any others in the play. If Claudio seems almost devoid of self-consciousness, Benedick is the opposite. In railing against marriage he is playing a role in the world of male fellowship, and in all of his role playing, Benedick is his own first audience. Ironically, he has been attracted to marriage as long as he has resisted it, and has been attracted to Beatrice even longer than he has complained about her. When he is fooled by Don Pedro, Claudio, and Leonato into admitting his love for Beatrice, Benedick at first expects that he will merely change his role a little in the masculine world. Only after Beatrice demands that he kill Claudio does he realize the fundamental revolution that has occurred in his values and consequently in all his relationships. He sacrifices the superficiality and the security of masculine society for a more engaging, more intense, more dangerous, and more rewarding commitment to Beatrice.

Beatrice, Hero's foil, is anything but acquiescent. An orphan in her uncle's household, she is resolutely independent. Having felt betrayed by Benedick, she fights back with her wit and, she says, has sent "four of his five wits . . . halting off" (1.1.65–66). She is, she says—perhaps not quite so credibly—determined to live and die a maid. Tricked into accepting Benedick's courtship, she admits her own love reluctantly. In the end, though, she allows Benedick to stop her mouth with a kiss (5.4.97) as she had earlier urged Hero to stop Claudio's mouth (2.1.310–311), and thus she does give up the last word. Beatrice is the most self-aware, self-contained, and self-sufficient character in *Much Ado about Nothing*, and one of the most articulate and appealing characters in all of Shakespeare's plays.

DEVICES AND TECHNIQUES

In the title *Much Ado about Nothing*, Harold Goddard finds an elaborate conceit. Shakespeare would have pronounced "nothing" as "noting," which Goddard suggests could be synonymous with the observing and overhearing so central to the plots of the play. Claudio and Don Pedro observe a malicious deception that, although nothing in itself, is an attempt to destroy something good that does exist. Benedick and Beatrice overhear creative deceptions that are attempts to bring into being something good out of nothing (271–277).

James C. Wey suggests that the title involves a pun on "noting" in the sense of slander (the first deception above) and musical noting (" 'To Grace Harmony': Musical Design in *Much Ado about Nothing*," in *Twentieth Century Interpretations of "Much Ado about Nothing,"* ed. W. R. Davis, 80–87). Wey observes that when the play's characters are in accord—when Leonato and Antonio talk about the possibility that Don Pedro will court Hero (1.2), when the courtship in the masque follows (2.1.85ff), and when Benedick is tricked into loving Beatrice (2.3.37ff), harmony is accompanied by music. Remarkably, no music at all is indicated in the wedding scene (4.1), even before Claudio interrupts the ceremony. Only as Benedick attempts to learn the decorum of courtship (5.2.25–28) and as Claudio later performs his penance (5.3.12–21) does music return to the play, and the final harmony of the play's resolution is emphatically expressed in the music of a dance (5.4.128–129). Moreover, Wey notes a motif associating music with love; for example, Don John, the enemy of love, refuses "to sing in [his] cage" (1.3.34). Don Pedro promises to "teach them [baby birds] to sing" (2.1.232), by which he means that he will teach Hero to love before giving her to Claudio; and Beatrice compares love to music and summarizes the course of love as "a Scotch jig, a measure, and a cinquepace" (2.1.74).

The language of the play owes much to the tradition of courtly literature beginning with Castiglione's *Book of the Courtier*. The men and women of the *Courtier*, who debate one another in a style that is cultivated but not excessively artificial, served as a model for the English elite in the decades that followed the book's English publication in 1561. The elegant epigrams and antitheses of John Lyly's dramatic characters recall the *Courtier* and anticipate the language of Beatrice and Benedick and everyone else in the Messina of *Much Ado*.

The play's prose is remarkable for its suppleness, its aptness, and its brilliance.

William G. McCollum observes that style can be used to establish a work's tone as well as to characterize particular speakers: "In Renaissance terms, the decorum of the genre will sometimes take precedence over the decorum of the speaker" ("The Role of Wit in *Much Ado About Nothing*," in *Twentieth Century Interpretations*, ed. Davis, 70). The measured rhythms and the balance and antithesis of Borachio's confession belong to the decorum of the genre; Borachio speaks in the voice of the play rather than with an individual voice:

> [D]o you hear me, and let this count kill me. I have deceiv'd even your very eyes. What your wisdoms could not discover, these shallow fools have brought to light, who in the night overheard me confessing to this man how Don John your brother incens'd me to slander the Lady Hero, how you were brought into the orchard, and saw me court Margaret in Hero's garments, how you disgrac'd her when you should marry her. (5.1.231–239)

This is much the same cultivated style as Leonato's to Don Pedro in the first act: "Never came trouble to my house in the likeness of your Grace, for trouble being gone, comfort should remain; but when you depart from me, sorrow abides and happiness takes his leave" (1.1.99–102).

Many of the play's characters do have their own voices, of course—for instance, Don John's flood of bitter antitheses, his insistent rhythms, and his violent images, each strikingly different from the others. Similar only in its energy, its overflowing emotion, and its rapid succession of unexpected images is the apparently spontaneous yet artfully turned expression of Benedick: "Shall I never see a bachelor of threescore again? Go to, i' faith, and thou wilt needs thrust thy neck into a yoke, wear the print of it, and sigh away Sundays," he tells the newly enamored Claudio (1.1.199–202). Benedick's speeches throughout the play reveal a growing sense of ironic self-knowledge expressed with consistently lighthearted hyperbole. Soon after his complaint about Claudio, he bemoans his own treatment by Beatrice, and compares her to Omphale (who enslaved Hercules), to Ate (goddess of discord), and to a spirit from hell (2.1.239–261). He is just as energetic and just as rhetorically inventive in his self-justification when he surrenders himself to love after being gulled by Don Pedro, Leonato, and Claudio (2.3.220–246).

Benedick's foil, Claudio, has no such distinctive voice. Perhaps his most memorable line, "Silence is the perfectest herald of joy" (2.1.306), is an aphorism that might have come as well from the lips of Leonato as from his own. Claudio appears often in the company of Don Pedro and tends to echo the Prince's sentiments in language very much like the Prince's.

The most distinctive voice in the play belongs to Beatrice. She is resolutely independent—witness the crisp antithesis of "it is my cousin's duty to make cur'sy and say, 'Father, as it please you.' But yet for all that, cousin, let him be a handsome fellow, or else make another cur'sy and say, 'Father, as it please me'" (2.1.52–56). Note, too, the witty allusion and double entendre as she asks, "Would it not grieve a woman to be overmaster'd with a piece of valiant dust? to make an account of her life to a clod of wayward marl [clay]?" (2.1.60–63).

Having been jilted by Benedick, Beatrice is bitter; she says of Benedick that he won her heart "with false dice" (2.1.280–281), and she does indeed, as he says, speak "poniards" to him and about him (2.1.247). Yet, the church scene excepted, there is also a lightness in almost all that she says to him and about him, or for that matter, about herself. As she states, when she was born, "my mother cried, but there was a star danc'd, and under that was I born (2.1.334–335). The evenly divided conflict of her psyche is reflected in this neatly antithetical imagery. Her mixed feelings as she admits her love are also reflected in her sudden inarticulateness, with its interrupted rhythms: "believe me not; and yet I lie not: I confess nothing, nor I deny nothing" (4.1.271–272).

A. R. Humphreys says of the verse in *Much Ado* that it, like the prose, "offers courteous decorum on the one hand and impulsive energies on the other." Humphreys praises the "gentle colorings" of lines like Hero's "For look where Beatrice like a lapwing runs / Close by the ground, to hear our conference" (3.1.24–25) and Don Pedro's

> Good morrow, masters, put your torches out.
> The wolves have preyed, and look, the gentle day,
> Before the wheels of Phoebus, round about
> Dapples the drowsy east with spots of grey. (5.3.24–27)

Humphreys calls this last passage "a delicate aubade [love song at dawn], dispelling the gloom and grief of Act IV" (*Much Ado about Nothing*, ed. A. R. Humphreys, 31). One might further note the counterpoint in the surprising aptness of the mention of wolves in these lines.

In verse Leonato finds his true voice: Listen to the tolling of "mine" in these lines so much more deeply felt than the courtly wit of Leonato's earlier, merely impersonal badinage with Don Pedro and Benedick:

> I might have said, "No part of it is mine;
> This shame derives itself from unknown loins[.]"
> But mine, and mine I lov'd, and mine I prais'd.
> And mine that I was proud on, mine so much
> That I myself was to myself not mine,
> Valuing of her—why, she, O she is fall'n
> Into a pit of ink, that the wide sea
> Hath drops too few to wash her clean again. (4.1.134–141)

Leonato's outburst in the church, effectively expressed in verse, is not the voice of grief but of sincere self-pity—which is evident too in his long complaint to his brother (5.1.3–32).

Perhaps the most telling use of verse in the play is in Beatrice's response to her gulling by Margaret, Ursula, and Hero:

> What fire is in mine ears? Can this be true?
> Stand I condemn'd for pride and scorn so much?
> Contempt, farewell, and maiden pride, adieu!
> No glory lies behind the back of such.
> And, Benedick, love on, I will requite thee,
> Taming my wild heart to thy loving hand.
> If thou dost love, my kindness shall incite thee

To bind our loves up in a holy band;
For others say thou dost deserve, and I
Believe it better than reportingly. (3.1.107–116)

The rhythms of these lines, with their frequent caesuras, suggest the difficulty of her self-assessment. The metaphors of fire in line 107 and of the falconer and the haggard in line 112 convey effectively her emotional intensity. Almost—but not quite—a sonnet, Beatrice's response is far more profound in its self-knowledge and commitment than Benedick's reaction to his own earlier deception, and it reflects Beatrice's sharper intellect and her greater depth of character.

THEMES AND MEANINGS

Much Ado about Nothing obviously develops the theme of love. The play repeatedly catalogues the qualities a lover might be expected to seek in a spouse. Hero attracts Claudio because of her beauty, her modesty, and her inheritance. Later, Benedick lists all the qualities he requires in a wife (although he expects never to marry): she must be rich, wise, virtuous, mild, noble, of good discourse, an excellent musician—and her hair may be "of what color it please God" (2.3.35). In the gulling scene that follows, Beatrice is recommended as "an excellent sweet lady," wise and virtuous (2.3.159–160). This last quality is particularly important, given Benedick's obsession about being cuckolded. In the same scene, Benedick's qualifications are also listed: he is proper, handsome, wise, witty, and valiant—although prudent—in the management of quarrels. In the next scene, Ursula again praises Benedick "For shape, for bearing, argument, and valor" (3.1.96). With the exception of excellence in argument, the noble Claudio is similarly qualified.

The two pairs of lovers are contrasted, however, in the course of their loves. Claudio engages himself to a woman he hardly knows, and in his ignorance of her is deceived into believing she has betrayed him. Beatrice and Benedick, in contrast, are quite preoccupied with one another and know each other well before they are brought to recognize their love. Claudio's inarticulate courtship is prompted in part by the wealth that Hero brings; but Beatrice's prospects are nowhere specified: Benedick is attracted to her as an individual, who insists, despite convention, that she is fully Benedick's equal. At the end of act 5 he stops her mouth with a kiss, but only because she lets him. From Shakespeare's day until the present, Beatrice and Benedick have been recognized as preeminent in the play and as the norm for lovers.

Much Ado about Nothing further prompts the reader to consider the power of language, which is not only the vehicle for deception, benign or malignant, and for misunderstanding, but also, in the vows that Benedick and Claudio make, the vehicle for understandings. Claudio's vow before witnesses in the last act, "I am your husband if you like of me" (5.4.59), is legally binding, whereas his statement that "Silence is the perfectest herald of joy" (2.1.306) is not. Above all, language in this play is power. By words Dogberry tries and fails to assert his standing among his social betters; but words are the tools, however ludicrously misused, by which he ensures his standing among his peers. More formidably, language is also the weapon that Beatrice wields against Benedick in their war of wits, and by which she, a woman and an orphan, creates for herself a secure place.

Finally, *Much Ado about Nothing* explores the relationships between illusion and reality, between knowledge and faith, and between belief and action. At the prompting of Don John, both the foolish Claudio and the wiser Don Pedro mistakenly believe their eyes. To them Don John appears honorable and Hero dishonorable, and they act cruelly and unjustly in consequence. To Claudio, Hero's beauty and apparent innocence are false, and she is the more to be condemned for her apparent innocence:

> You seem to me as Dian in her orb,
> As chaste as is the bud ere it be blown;
> But you are the more intemperate in your blood
> Than Venus, or those pamp'red animals
> That rage in savage sensuality. (4.1.57–61)

However, the Friar, viewing Hero at the same time, has a different impression of her:

> A thousand blushing apparitions
> To start into her face, a thousand innocent shames
> In angel whiteness beat away those blushes,
> And in her eye there hath appear'd a fire
> To burn the errors that these princes hold
> Against her maiden truth. (4.1.159–164)

As David Horowitz observes, "the play . . . is as relentlessly 'for' the view that appearances are the whole of reality (or at least accurately reflect reality) as it is 'for' the contrary position, that appearances are deceptions, at best, not to be trusted." ("Imagining the Real," from *Shakespeare: An Existential View* [New York: Hill and Wang, 1965], 19–36, reprinted in *Twentieth Century Interpretations*, ed. W. R. Davis, 39–53). Horowitz goes on to note that mistaking appearances for reality can have good consequences as well as ill. When Dogberry and the watch apprehend Borachio and Conrade, they charge the malefactors not with slandering Hero but with slandering Don John; but out of their mistake true conclusions are drawn and justice is done.

Is it possible, finally, to state what the characters of the play should believe? If appearances are neither reliably true nor reliably false, how is a person to know the truth? Leonato is wrong to trust his superficial acquaintance of Claudio and Don Pedro, the two honorable men. Beatrice knows, from her long acquaintance with Hero, that her cousin "is belied" (4.1.146). After having seen and heard Claudio's charge and Don Pedro's confirmation, the Friar's observation, Beatrice's defense, and Leonato's doubt, Benedick is forced to interpret the situation and to locate the truth. "Think you in your soul the Count Claudio hath wronged Hero?" he asks. Beatrice answers, "Yea, as sure as I have a thought or a soul" (4.1.328–330), and believing becomes seeing. Beatrice's knowledge of the heart proves more trustworthy than mere appearance or convention.

Shakespeare would return to this theme repeatedly. Invariably in his plays, truth lies on the side of love, yet with equal consistency the men—significantly, not the women—trust the forces of hate. Othello believes Iago rather than Desdemona; Leontes in *The Winter's Tale* trusts his own jealousy even after the Delphic oracle declares Leontes's wife chaste. Posthumus accepts Jachimo's baseless accusation that

Imogen, Posthumus's wife, is unfaithful (*Cymbeline*). In the comedies and romances the men learn to love, and so they and the plays end happily. The tragedies show what happens when men fail to believe in love until too much damage has been done. In *Much Ado* and elsewhere Shakespeare warns that the world is ambiguous ("I have deceived even your very eyes," Borachio declares [5.1.232]). The only certain guides prove to be faith, hope, and love.

At the beginning of the play Benedick fears marriage because a married man cannot be sure he will not be cuckolded and cannot be sure that his wife's child is his own. Even with the knowledge of himself and Beatrice that he gains through the events of the play—revealing deception and true experience alike—Benedick is still not sure that he will not be cuckolded. Yet he commits himself both to challenge his best friend and to marry Beatrice. He may be wrong to act—"man is a giddy thing," he concludes (5.4.108)—but, amid general rejoicing, he commits himself. The need for commitment and action, despite the uncertainty of knowledge, lies at the very heart of the meaning of *Much Ado about Nothing*.

CRITICAL CONTROVERSIES

Critical controversies concerning the dating of the play, the relationship of the play to *Love's Labor's Won* or some possible earlier version, and the harmony of the various subplots within the play have all been touched on above (see "Publication History" and "Sources for the Play"). Much of the current critical controversy concerning *Much Ado about Nothing* centers on the interpretation of Claudio. He is attracted to Hero in part because of her physical beauty; that love should come through the eyes would be recognized by a sixteenth-century audience as good Neoplatonic doctrine, although they would also be aware, as Claudio himself later is, that beauty may prove false. Claudio is also moved by the fortune Hero brings with her as Leonato's only heir: the marriage is, as C. J. Prouty observes, a business proposition (*The Source of "Much Ado about Nothing": A Critical Study* [Freeport, NY: Books for Libraries, 1950]). Claudio gains a presumably generous dowry and, eventually, a far greater inheritance; in return, Leonato gains a family alliance to nobility. This business proposition remains the one constant factor after Hero's supposed death and the substitution of Leonato's veiled "niece." Critics who judge by what they understand of sixteenth-century values find Claudio's motive normal for the times; critics (not only feminists) who judge according to the values of our own times are more censorious.

Claudio's condemnation of Hero is also the subject of controversy. Some interpreters who see him finally as a more or less conventional romantic protagonist defend him and blame Don John's villainy for Claudio's conduct in the church. Further, they observe that Claudio is not the only gullible one; Don Pedro, too, is fooled. Sir Arthur Quiller-Couch and John Dover Wilson even hypothesized that Shakespeare must originally have written a balcony scene to show Claudio being fooled, and some productions do present such a scene to make Claudio's mistake more understandable and forgivable. But another critical school finds no textual authority for such an interpolation and finds Claudio's decision to repudiate Hero in the church gratuitously cruel (Friedman, pp. 93–96). Shakespeare after all makes Claudio's repudiation more public and more dramatic than that of Bandello's hero, who calls off the marriage privately.

Interpreters sympathetic to Claudio read or perform the final scene of the play to underscore his repentance and his forgiveness. Although the Quarto and the First Folio both assign Hero's epitaph and the song of mourning in 5.3 to an attendant lord, Quiller-Couch and Wilson speculated that the compositor of the Quarto might have misread a "cla" in the margin for "lo" and thus provided the wrong stage direction. In the New Arden edition of the play, Humphreys adopts their speech assignment, if not their rationale, observing that it "seems natural" for Claudio to read the epitaph (210 n). But F. H. Mares, in the New Cambridge Edition, observes that Claudio might naturally do his grieving as he had done his wooing, by proxy (*Much Ado about Nothing* [Cambridge: Cambridge UP, 2003], 131 n). If the epitaph and the song in this scene are not assigned to Claudio, his only expression of repentance is his statement to Leonato,

> I know not how to pray your patience,
> Yet I must speak. Choose your revenge yourself,
> Impose me to what penance your invention
> Can lay upon my sin; yet sinn'd I not
> But in mistaking. (5.1.271–275)

To Claudio's detractors these last words are a weak excuse and a shabby defense.

Harold Bloom views critical controversies such as these about Claudio with a jaundiced eye: "What does not work, pragmatically, is any critical or theatrical attempt to assimilate Shakespeare to contexts, whether historical or here-and-now." Shakespeare, he says, transcends generation, gender, and ideology, and in doing so creates nothing less than modern human consciousness (10–11).

PRODUCTION HISTORY

Much Ado about Nothing was almost certainly first performed late in 1598 or perhaps very early in 1599. The title page of the 1600 Quarto states that the play "*hath been sundrie times publikely* acted by the right honourable, the Lord Chamberlaine his seruants." Frequent mentions of *Much Ado*, identified either by its published title or by the names of Beatrice and Benedick, show that the play was popular in performance until the closing of the theaters in 1642. When the theaters reopened in 1660, William Davenant was assigned rights to *Much Ado*. The Restoration theater found Shakespeare's works in need of modernization; Davenant accomplished this revision for *Much Ado* by fusing it with *Measure for Measure* in a work called *The Law Against Lovers*, described by A. R. Humphreys in his New Arden edition of *Much Ado*. Little of *Much Ado about Nothing* survives in this Restoration play; Don John, Don Pedro, and Hero are gone entirely. So is Hero's lover Claudio; the Claudio of Davenant's play is based on the Claudio in *Measure for Measure*, quite a different character. However, the Beatrice and Benedick in *The Law Against Lovers* are based on the lovers in *Much Ado*. Much of their wit combat in the first acts reflects or reproduces Shakespeare's play, but their lines and actions in the second half of the play are shaped by Davenant's plot, which is loosely based on *Measure for Measure* (*Much Ado about Nothing*, ed. A. R. Humphreys, 229).

In the early eighteenth century *Much Ado* contributed to two other bastardized adaptations, but *Much Ado about Nothing* itself also re-emerged. The comic Benedick/Beatrice action dominated the play, and stars dominated the stage; Garrick played Benedick in mid-century, as Charles Kemble did well into the next century. In the first years of the nineteenth century, Beatrice's liveliness had descended into shrewishness in many productions. However, in 1836 Helen Faucit, playing opposite Kemble, brought warmth, femininity, and earnestness to the role, which she played successfully for forty years.

The nineteenth-century theater devoted much effort to realistic stage sets—the more elaborate, the better. Critics praised Charles Kean's production of *Much Ado* in 1858 for its beautiful scene painting. The 1882 production by Henry Irving and Ellen Terry in the Lyceum Theater was even more elaborate. Many sets in this production depended on painted drops that gave the illusion of three dimensionality through the lighting. Irving had considered using electric lighting but acquiesced to Ellen Terry's urging that he use gas. Most notable was the very elaborate set for the church scene (4.1), which is depicted in the painting by Johnston Forbes-Robertson reproduced in Robert Speaight's *Shakespeare on the Stage* ([Boston: Little, Brown, 1973], 54–55).

Henry Irving's characterization of Benedick was chivalric and patrician—according to one reviewer quoted by Humphreys, his Benedick was "a soldier first, a lover next, and always a gentleman," although Irving's co-star Ellen Terry found him "too deliberate, though polished and thoughtful" in the role. Johnston Forbes-Robertson, the painter of the church scene referred to above, played Claudio, making him a more sympathetic figure than he had usually been. Like Helen Faucit, Ellen Terry brought warmth and femininity to the role of Beatrice. Terry felt that she was "never swift enough" playing opposite Irving's deliberate Benedick, but a critic at the time found her "buoyant, winsome, merry [and] enchanting" until the overwhelming passion and pathos of her "futile helpless anger" against Claudio took over (quoted in *Much Ado about Nothing*, ed. A. R. Humphreys, pp. 37–38). Terry and Irving were partners as well as co-stars. If Terry carried her point with Irving concerning the lighting, she lost an argument about an interpolation Irving made at the end of the church scene. Irving was not content with the closing line Shakespeare provided: "Go comfort your cousin. I must say she is dead; and so farewell" (4.1.334–336). He added two dramatically redundant lines to draw even more applause than the scene had ordinarily evoked (Speaight, p. 58):

Beatrice: Benedick, kill him—kill him if you can.

Benedick: As sure as I'm alive, I will!

Ellen Terry played Beatrice again in 1903 in a production designed and directed by her son Gordon Craig. The production was ahead of its time with its nonrepresentational set. In contrast to the sumptuous church set of the Irving/Terry production in 1882, Craig provided merely a large cross; other scenes were suggested by pillars painted on the folds of curtains. Leonato's garden was represented by a large wickerwork structure that, according to the *Athenaeum*'s reviewer, "fail[ed] to convey . . . any intelligible idea" (quoted in Humphreys, p. 40). In the early 1920s Robert Atkins produced *Much Ado about Nothing* without ponderous scenery that would impede the energetic flow of the action, and in the mid-1930s Atkins took *Much Ado* to the Ring at Blackfriars—normally a boxing arena—where it was produced under the bright lights of the boxing ring with the audience on three sides and an inner stage and balcony on the fourth.

In 1949 John Gielgud directed *Much Ado about Nothing* at Stratford-upon-Avon. Diana Wynyard played Beatrice, and Anthony Quayle was Benedick. The set and costuming represented the Renaissance; the ingenious set allowed quick changes of scene. The production was revived the next year at Stratford-upon-Avon with Peggy Ashcroft and Gielgud as Beatrice and Benedick; Harold Bloom regards their performance as definitive (192). The production was revived again in London in 1952 with Wynyard playing to Gielgud and toured the continent before reappearing in London in 1955.

In 1957 John Houseman and Jack Landau co-directed a largely successful production of *Much Ado* at Stratford, Connecticut. Katharine Hepburn and Alfred Drake played Beatrice and Benedick; Virgil Thompson provided an original score for the music of the play. This production, like several others in the second half of the twentieth century, changed the setting from sixteenth-century Sicily, which had been ruled by Spain. Houseman and Landau still saw the ethos of the play as colonial Spanish, and to make this ethos more easily accessible to a contemporary audience they chose to set the play in mid-nineteenth-century northern Mexico, where most of the characters can be plausibly placed. But Brooks Atkinson, at least, found Dogberry, Verges, and the watch too English and too Elizabethan to fit in that context ("The Theatre: 'Much Ado,'" *The New York Times*, August 8, 1957, 15, col. 2). Other twentieth-century performances with innovative treatments include a 1958 production at Stratford-upon-Avon in a setting variously described as Regency or Risorgimento, Zeffirelli's 1965 production set in Sicily around 1900, and John Barton's 1976 production set in British colonial India. From 1999 to 2001 Peter Meinck set the play fantastically, recalling popular action films and television series in a kind of meta-drama.

In 1972 Joseph Papp's New York Shakespeare Festival produced *Much Ado about Nothing* first in Central Park, then on Broadway, and finally, on February 2, 1973, on CBS Television. In this production, directed by A. J. Antoon, the play unfolds in the American South on a scrupulously recreated turn-of-the-century estate. The counts become captains, and Dogberry's watch deals with the governor's citizens rather than the Prince's subjects, but the language of the play is otherwise Elizabethan and produces a potentially jarring contrast with the turn-of-the-century costumes and the detailed realism of the set. Sam Waterston defines the role of Benedick in his performance, which is the high point of the production, and Kathleen Widdoes is convincing as Beatrice. Glenn Walken is fresh-faced and somewhat spoiled as Claudio; April Shawhan is almost childlike in her innocence as Hero; and Bernard Hughes is a remarkably dignified Keystone Cop as Dogberry. Douglas Watson is a fatherly Don Pedro; Jerry Mayer is melodramatically villainous as Don John. This production, although extravagant at times, contains many very effective sequences. A videotape of the CBS performance is available through the Broadway Theatre Archive.

In 1988 there were both Di Trevis's very feminist and very heavily criticized Royal Shakespeare Company production of *Much Ado*, which threw the Claudio-Hero relationship into a clear and unattractive light, and Judi Dench's much simpler, psychologically persuasive and theatrically effective production. Kenneth Branagh's 1993 notable production of *Much Ado about Nothing* is, like Papp's production,

(Left to right) Denzel Washington as Don Pedro, Kenneth Branagh as Benedick, Emma Thompson as Beatrice, Richard Briers as Leonato, Brian Blessed as Antonio, Kate Beckinsale as Hero, and Robert Sean Leonard as Claudio celebrate their wedding in Kenneth Branagh's 1993 film *Much Ado about Nothing*. Courtesy of Photofest.

available on videotape. The film makes the most of its beautiful Tuscan setting. Robert Sean Leonard is a sympathetic Claudio, and Kate Beckinsale is winsome and vulnerable in Hero's role. Denzel Washington presents Don Pedro with gravitas; Keanu Reeves is Don John; and Michael Keaton plays a broadly farcical Dogberry. Branagh directs and plays Benedick to Emma Thompson's high-spirited and sensitive Beatrice. Her performance is as definitive as Sam Waterston's was in the 1973 production. Michael D. Friedman analyzes compromises that Branagh makes as he tries to integrate his wish to exonerate Claudio and his essentially feminist sympathies with Beatrice and Hero (102–107). Branagh's production succeeded commercially but not always critically, prompting Peter Holland, for example, to deplore its "banal populism" ("Shakespeare Performances in England," *Shakespeare Survey* 47 [1994]: 192).

Shakespeare's Globe Theater-Restored is a half-hour videotape produced by associates of the New Globe Theatre in Southwark and the Shakespeare program in the English Department of the University of California-Berkeley. The tape includes not only scenes from *Much Ado about Nothing* played in 1996 by students from Berkeley's Shakespeare program in the yard of The George in Southwark and on the stage at the restored Globe Theatre but also illuminating discussion of how the physical environment of the Shakespearean stage influences performances.

Much Ado continues to be popular. Among notable more recent productions has been Michael Boyd's interesting, ambitious, and eccentric production at Stratford in 1997. Writing in the *Shakespeare Survey*, Michael Smallwood admired the actors' performances in this production, but he felt that the stage set was confusing and incompatible with the seventeenth-century costuming; and he found the whole production too complicated and too fussy in its enigmatic and obtrusive attempts at symbolism ("Shakespeare Performances in England," *Shakespeare Survey* 51 [1998]: 230–235).

EXPLICATION OF KEY PASSAGES

1.1.96–112. "Good Signior Leonato . . . an honorable father." "The fashion of the world is to avoid cost, and you encounter it," Don Pedro tells Leonato (1.1.97–98). The costs of hospitality will indeed be substantial, as Elizabethans familiar with their monarch's Progresses would well have known. Leonato's response, "Never came trouble to my house in the likeness of your Grace, for trouble being gone, comfort should remain; but when you depart from me, sorrow abides and happiness takes his leave" (1.1.99–102), is a rhetorically polished expression of a quite conventional sentiment, and it strikes a note of superficial insincerity and conventionality that bears its fruit later in Leonato's ready belief of Claudio's accusations against Hero. The passage employs dramatic irony to foreshadow events that follow. Don Pedro and his entourage will in fact cause much trouble, banishing happiness and bringing sorrow to Leonato and his family.

Don Pedro's statement, "I think this is your daughter" (1.1.104), when Leonato presents Hero, first gives rise to what will become a central issue of the play. Leonato's response that Hero's mother told him that he was Hero's father is mere courtly wit. Benedick's question "Were you in doubt, sir, that you ask'd her?" (1.1.106) reflects his own very real doubts and insecurities, with which he must come to terms before he can fulfill a mature man's role by marrying and making his own contribution to the peopling of the world.

Benedick is not alone in his concern about womanly chastity: Claudio is first attracted to Hero for her modesty, and his subsequent doubt of her fidelity is the driving force of the main plot of the play. Leonato retorts, "Signior Benedick, no, for then were you a child" (1.1.107–108); this may be more cleverness, mere masculine foolery, but it also suggests that Benedick is recognized for his sexual aggressiveness and thus tends to corroborate Beatrice's bitter complaint in 2.1.280–281 that Benedick earlier played her false.

1.3.1–40. "What the good-year . . . Who comes here?" "Why are you thus out of measure sad?" Conrade asks Don John, who replies, "There is no measure in the occasion that breeds, therefore the sadness is without limit" (1.3.1–4). Conrade urges him to take advantage of his brother's grace, but Don John declares, "I had rather be a canker in a hedge than a rose in his grace" (1.3.27–28). He says he would bite if he had his mouth; he recognizes himself as a villain and will use only his discontent. What breeds Don John's discontent? Is it simply the Prince's distrust? The defeat of his rebellion? His bastardy? His hostility seems excessive to any cause. Almost a caricature of villainy, Don John cannot reconcile himself to order or harmony of any kind and will, when opportunity offers, spoil any harmony he encounters. Here Shakespeare introduces the prototype of the much more cunning Iago of *Othello*, who, like Don John, delights in evil for its own sake.

2.1.331–346. "Your silence . . . herself with laughing." "[O]ut a' question, you were born in a merry hour," the Prince says to Beatrice, who replies, "No, sure, my lord, my mother cried, but then there was a star danc'd, and under that was I born" (2.1.332–335). A moment later, her uncle reports that she has "often dreamt of unhappiness, and wak'd herself with laughing" (2.1.345–346).

In his essay "Laughter," the French philosopher Henri Bergson cites as one of the prerequisites of laughter "something like a momentary anesthesia of the heart" (in *Comedy*, ed. Wylie Sypher [Garden City, NY: Doubleday, 1956], 64). The star that dances suggests detachment from terrestrial woe, yet Beatrice gives clear and emphatic evidence of feeling pain. Shakespeare's comedy is often allied to deeply felt suffering, and Beatrice's stinging wit often takes its impulse from her own griefs as well as from her perception of others' embarrassments. Bergson also believes that laughter demands to be shared socially, yet Beatrice laughs even when she is alone in her dreams. In her, the saturnalian rhythm is inverted, and laughter is her every-day wear (Barber, p. 6).

3.2.1–20. "I do but stay . . . he wants money." These lines reveal the very different priorities of Claudio and Benedick as their love affairs conflict with masculine fellowship. Claudio clearly shows that he values his loyalty to Don Pedro—his lord, his mentor, and his friend—above his duty and his love for Hero, his wife-to-be. Leonato takes no exception to Claudio's offer to accompany the Prince to Arragon, perhaps because the Prince refuses the offer immediately and mildly reproaches Claudio for not valuing his newlywed status more highly. Don Pedro, Claudio, and Leonato all tease Benedick, whose clean-shaven face and melancholy expression are signs of love, and Benedick admits that his priorities as well as his appearance have changed; he is not nearly as willing as Claudio to leave Messina and his newly recognized love. However, he is not yet willing to admit the cause of this transformation and attributes his new seriousness to "the toothache" (3.2.21). He knows that a confession will make him the butt of ridicule. Despite his earlier claim that he would not mind "quips and sentences and these paper bullets of the brain" (2.3.240–241), he is in fact still wary of them. The Prince's words to Claudio about the new gloss of matrimony raise a question about his attitude toward the possibility of his own marriage, an attitude which seems enigmatic here, as it does in his exchange with Beatrice in 2.1.318–330 and again at the end of the play.

4.1.289–336. "Kill Claudio . . . and so farewell." Beatrice's demand "Kill Claudio" is the emotional fulcrum not only of this scene but also of the play as a whole. Beatrice is poised between frustration and hope. To uphold her cousin's honor is a man's office, but Hero's husband-to-be is guilty himself of slandering her. Her father, who should be her protector, is unsure of her honesty. Beatrice, as a woman, lacks both the status and the ability to defend her. "O God, that I were a man!" she exclaims (4.1.306). Benedick, who has professed both his belief in Hero's innocence and his love for Beatrice, might do what she cannot. However, many Elizabethans believed that men possessed intellects and souls superior to women's and therefore valued male friendship highly. Beatrice, knowing that what she asks is extreme, has already told Benedick that what she wants "is a man's office, but not yours" (4.1.266), and Benedick's immediate refusal of her demand, when she does make it, bears out the difficulty of violating masculine friendship.

If "Kill Claudio" is the emotional fulcrum of the play, Benedick's question at the end of the scene, "Think you in your soul that the Count Claudio hath wrong'd Hero?" (4.1.328–329), is the epistemological fulcrum. Beatrice answers as Benedick asks, not with the fallible knowledge of eyes but with knowledge of the heart—true knowledge of her cousin's character. Benedick believes her and commits himself. This act of faith by a hitherto confirmed skeptic is the turning point not only in the courtship of Beatrice and Benedick but also in Benedick's personal growth. Benedick here shifts his allegiance from the masculine world he has hitherto endorsed to the feminine world of Beatrice and Hero. Yet Shakespeare problematizes the conversion by making it hinge on Benedick's agreeing to fight a duel, a decidedly male activity. As Shakespeare so often does in his plays and poems, he here elides masculine and feminine, a fusion compounded by the fact that Beatrice, to whom Benedick now gives his allegiance, is, in fact, played by a boy.

5.2.26–41. "The god of love . . . festival terms." W. H. Auden's observation that men do not take their identities or make their choices independently of those around them applies clearly to Benedick (*Lectures on Shakespeare*, reconstructed and edited by Arthur Kirsch [Princeton: Princeton UP, 2000], xiv–xv). Benedick has been a conventional antiromantic—albeit an amusing one—and his conversion has not been easy. Attempting now to adopt the conventions of a lover, he has resolved to get Beatrice's picture and has even shaved his martial beard, but, he says, he cannot woo conventionally, "in festival terms" (5.2.41). Conventional lovers court their ladies in serenades, but he is a pitiful singer. Conventional lovers display their loves in sonnets, but he "was not born under a rhyming planet" (5.2.40).

His awkwardness in his new role stems from deeper and less easily expressed feelings than those of the thoroughly conventional lover Claudio. Benedick's ineptitude in music and in verse is emblematic of the difficulties he fears in love itself. As a onetime skeptic, he is perceptive enough to see that love may not bring pure harmony and eternally happy endings. His allusions to legendary lovers in this speech are particularly significant. That he should think of Leander is fitting, revealing, and ominous. Marlowe's "Hero and Leander," familiar to Shakespeare and many in his audience, presents Leander as initially free of love and then passionately attracted to Hero, who withholds herself at the same time that she reciprocates his passion. Marlowe dwells on Leander's physical beauty—perhaps another point of similarity in the mind of the self-centered Benedick—but the inescapable focus of the legend of Leander is his death for love. Benedick also compares himself to Troilus, an even more revealing allusion. Troilus, a noble and valiant knight, gives himself utterly in love, is briefly rewarded with Cressida's affection, but must then helplessly witness his betrayal by his beloved. Benedick has repeatedly argued that marriage leads to cuckoldry; his fear has amounted to an obsession, and this allusion shows that the fear has not left him. When he tries to write poetry, the only word he can think of to rhyme with "scorn" is "horn" (5.2.38). Thus he again reveals his fear of cuckoldry that first shows itself in 1.1.106. Words like "born," "corn," "torn," and "worn" are crowded out of his brain by this apprehension. Yet he perseveres in his courtship. Whatever the outcome, he is committed.

Annotated Bibliography

Adams, Barry B. *Coming-to-Know: Recognition and the Complex Plot in Shakespeare*. New York: Peter Lang, 2000. An Aristotelian study of discovery and recognition in Shakespeare's comedies.

Barber, C. L. *Shakespeare's Festive Comedy: A Study of Dramatic Form and Its Relation to Social Custom*. Princeton: Princeton UP, 1959. An analysis of Shakespearean comedies with reference to saturnalian social patterns using inversion, statement, and counterstatement to move "through release to clarification" (6).

Bloom, Harold. *Shakespeare: The Invention of the Human*. New York: Riverhead, 1998. An often brilliant, always provocative study of the plays, in which Bloom believes Shakespeare created, through his nihilistic and simultaneously affirmative vision, the modern idea of essential humanity. *Much Ado* is discussed on pages 192–201.

Davis, Walter R., ed., *Twentieth Century Interpretations of "Much Ado about Nothing": A Collection of Critical Essays*. Englewood Cliffs, NJ: Prentice Hall, 1969. Critical essays and short excerpts from longer works treating a variety of topics and employing a variety of approaches.

Friedman, Michael D. *The World Must Be Peopled: Shakespeare's Comedies of Forgiveness*. Madison, NJ: Fairleigh Dickinson UP, 2002. A "theatrically conscious reading" (15) of the comedies from a feminist perspective—incisive, thorough, and thoughtful.

Goddard, Harold C. *The Meaning of Shakespeare*. 2 vols. Chicago: U of Chicago P, 1951. A classic of Shakespeare criticism—personal, sensible, and humane.

Levin, Richard A. *Love and Society in Shakespearean Comedy: A Study of Dramatic Form and Content*. Newark: U of Delaware P, 1985. An alternative to C. L. Barber's approach to Shakespearean comedy; a study examining losers as well as winners in "the struggle for inclusion into society" (21).

As You Like It

Yashdip S. Bains

PLOT SUMMARY

1.1. In the garden of Oliver's manor house, Orlando complains to his old servant, Adam, that Oliver, his elder brother, has abused him by not educating him and by not honoring their late father's wishes. When Oliver enters, Orlando insists that his brother give him his patrimony. Rudely dismissing Orlando, Oliver speaks to Charles, a wrestler. Charles shares with him the old news that Duke Frederick has forced Duke Senior to go into exile in the forest of Arden but has kept Duke Senior's daughter, Rosalind, at court for the sake of her companionship with his own daughter, Celia. Oliver speaks ill of Orlando and asks Charles to kill him in the wrestling match the next day. As Charles leaves, Oliver enviously broods over his brother's popularity and noble qualities.

1.2. On the lawn before the Duke's palace, Celia tries to cheer up Rosalind. They exchange pleasantries with Touchstone, a jester. Then the courtier Le Beau informs them of the wrestling match. Duke Frederick and his courtiers enter to watch the match, while Celia and Rosalind urge Orlando to withdraw from the fight. Applauded by Rosalind and Celia, Orlando defeats Charles. Upon learning the identity of Orlando's father, who supported the previous duke, Frederick grows annoyed and leaves the scene without giving him a reward. Celia and Rosalind congratulate Orlando, and Rosalind offers her necklace to him as his prize. Orlando is too shy to respond to her gesture. Le Beau advises Orlando to leave the court to save himself from Frederick's wrath.

1.3. Rosalind shares with Celia the secret of her love for Orlando. Duke Frederick orders Rosalind into exile. Celia suggests that they escape to the forest of Arden together in disguise. The taller Rosalind dresses as a man and gives herself the name of Ganymede. Celia changes her name to Aliena. They beseech Touchstone to join them on their journey.

2.1. In the forest of Arden, Duke Senior talks to his lords, dressed like foresters, about the moral principles which have helped him to accept the discomforts of their pastoral surroundings. They go in search of Jaques, who had been weeping and commenting on the fate of a wounded deer.

2.2. Duke Frederick questions his courtiers about the missing Celia and seeks Oliver's assistance in finding her.

2.3. Adam advises Orlando to slip away from his brutal brother and volunteers to go with him as his servant.

2.4. In the forest of Arden, Rosalind, Celia, and Touchstone happen upon young Silvius, who is telling old Corin about his (Silvius's) love for Phebe. Rosalind learns from Corin that his master's property is for sale. The two cousins decide to buy it.

2.5. Amiens sings, "Under the greenwood tree" to Jaques and others (2.5.1–8). Jaques replies with satirical verses of his own.

2.6. Adam is hungry. Orlando leaves him in a shelter and goes in search of food for him.

2.7. Dressed like outlaws, Duke Senior and his lords have a table set for dinner. Jaques comes in and reports on his meeting with Touchstone. Orlando barges in, his sword drawn, and demands food. Duke Senior courteously invites Orlando to join in the meal. Orlando thanks Duke Senior but leaves so that he can fetch Adam. After Orlando leaves, Duke Senior observes that he and his men are not the only unfortunates in the world.

This comment provides the occasion for Jaques to deliver his "All the world's a stage" speech (2.7.139–166). Orlando and Adam return and eat. Amiens entertains the group by singing, "Blow, blow, thou winter wind" (2.7.174ff). Duke Senior explains that he loved Orlando's late father and welcomes Orlando to the forest.

3.1. Frederick forces Oliver to go in search of Orlando and has seized Oliver's property until Orlando is found.

3.2. Orlando hangs a poem on a tree in witness of his love for Rosalind and plans to hang many more verses throughout the forest. Corin and Touchstone argue about the merits of country versus court life. Rosalind as Ganymede enters, reading verses in her own praise, and Touchstone ridicules her with a parody of his own. Alone with Rosalind, Celia reveals that Orlando the versifier is in the forest. Rosalind and Celia observe Orlando and Jaques as the latter mocks the earnest lover. The disguised Rosalind queries Orlando about his poems and offers to cure him of his malady of love by pretending to be a temperamental Rosalind.

3.3. Jaques convinces Touchstone to delay his marriage with Audrey, an ignorant goatherd, on the ground that he should have a more reliable priest than Sir Oliver Martext.

3.4. Rosalind is furious that Orlando is late for his meeting with her. Celia teases her that she should not trust Orlando. Corin leads Celia and Rosalind to watch Silvius trying to woo a scornful Phebe.

3.5. Phebe spurns Silvius. Agitated over Phebe's disdain for the man who loves her, Rosalind comes forward and reminds Phebe how ungrateful she is. Phebe immediately falls in love with "Ganymede" and asks Silvius to deliver a letter to the youth. She says that the letter will taunt Ganymede, but in fact she sends a love poem.

4.1. Rosalind gently mocks Jaques' melancholy. Jaques leaves upon Orlando's entry. Rosalind takes Orlando to task for his late arrival. She dismisses his worn-out, conventional language of love and makes him aware of the awful reality of husband-wife relationships. Celia consents to act as a priest for Rosalind's mock marriage. Rosalind gets Orlando to agree to meet her on time the next day. Then she confides in Celia the sincerity of her love for Orlando.

4.2. Jaques and some of the Duke's lords dressed as foresters sing, "What shall he have that killed the deer?" (4.2.10–18).

4.3. Orlando is late again for his appointment with Ganymede. Rosalind and Celia get Phebe's letter from Silvius. Rosalind reads it aloud and then sends the youth back to Phebe with the message, "[I]f she love me, I charge her to love thee; if she will not, I will never have her unless thou entreat for her" (4.3.71–73).

Oliver enters with a bloody cloth in his hands and recognizes Ganymede from Orlando's description. He tells the two cousins that Orlando found him asleep in the forest and a lioness crouched to attack him. Orlando disregarded his hatred for his brother and killed the beast. The lion wounded Orlando's arm in the struggle. When Oliver awoke, he underwent an instant conversion from his hateful ways and became friends with Orlando. Orlando had lost blood during the encounter and fainted, but he has joined Duke Senior and sent Oliver with a bloody cloth to Ganymede to account for his absence. When she sees blood, Rosalind faints and so almost ruins her disguise. However, she quickly recovers and claims that her swoon was "Counterfeit, I assure you" (4.3.172).

5.1. Touchstone assures Audrey that they will marry. William, in love with Audrey, enters, but Touchstone warns him to "abandon the society of this female, or, clown, thou perishest" (5.1.50–51). William departs, and Corin enters to summon Touchstone and Audrey to join Rosalind and Celia.

5.2. Oliver has fallen in love with Celia/Aliena after their brief acquaintance, and he wants to marry her right away. He assures Orlando that he will bestow his estate upon his younger brother, since Oliver is resolved to live and die a shepherd in the forest. Orlando agrees with Oliver's plans and suggests that the marriage take place in the presence of Duke Senior and his lords. Entering after Oliver has departed, Rosalind informs Orlando that he can marry his Rosalind at the same hour that his brother weds Celia. She will use her magic to produce Rosalind for the ceremony. When she meets Phebe and Silvius, Rosalind announces that if she decides to marry a woman, she will choose Phebe. She promises Silvius that he will also get married. Rosalind advises Orlando, Silvius, and Phebe to come to her the next day properly dressed for their weddings.

5.3. Touchstone and Audrey enter discussing their impending marriage, apparently also arranged by Rosalind. Two pages come in and sing for them "It was a lover and his lass" (5.3.16–33).

5.4. In the presence of Duke Senior, Amiens, Jaques, Orlando, and Oliver, Rosalind as Ganymede has everybody agree to her plan. Duke Senior will give Rosalind to Orlando if she be found and brought in, and Orlando will marry her. Phebe will marry Ganymede, but if Phebe refuses "him," she'll marry Silvius, who promises to wed Phebe "Though to have her and death were both one thing" (5.4.17). Rosalind and Celia then depart. Touchstone and Audrey enter, and Jaques rouses Touchstone to entertain the group with his account of "a lie seven times remov'd" (5.4.68). This conversation provides some entertaining wit and allows Rosalind time to change back from Ganymede to herself.

Guided by Hymen, the god of marriage, Rosalind and Celia now appear in their own persons. Rosalind is united with her father and weds Orlando. Phebe abandons her claim to "Ganymede." Hymen gives his blessing to the four couples and sings "Wedding is great Juno's crown" (5.4.141–146). Jaques de Bois, Sir Rowland's second son and hence brother to Orlando and Oliver, brings news that Duke Frederick had gathered an army to arrest and kill Duke Senior, but in the vicinity of the forest the usurper met an old hermit, who converted him. Jaques delivers a benediction for the couples but will not attend the celebration. Instead, he will join the company of Duke Frederick and the other religious converts. Duke Senior invites everyone else to join in a dance.

Epilogue. Rosalind cleverly begs for the spectators' approval.

PUBLICATION HISTORY

As You Like It was entered on a preliminary leaf of Book C of the Stationers' Register on August 4, 1600, but it was not printed until 1623 in the First Folio. A fairly reliable text, it was based probably on a playhouse promptbook or a literary transcript of the playwright's foul papers. Since Francis Meres did not include this play in his 1598 list of Shakespeare's works, it may be assumed that Shakespeare had not yet written it. Shakespeare's use of Thomas Morley's song, "It was a lover and his lass," printed in Morley's *First Book of Airs* in 1600 but prepared in 1599, may also justify 1599–1600 as a likely date for composition. Pastoral plays, stories, and poems had become extremely popular by the late 1590s, and Shakespeare may have composed *As You Like It* for the Chamberlain's Men to compete with other professional companies for a share of the audience. Most modern critics and editors place *As You Like It* chronologically between *Much Ado about Nothing* and *Twelfth Night*.

SOURCES FOR THE PLAY

The primary source for the play is Thomas Lodge's *Rosalynde* (1590), written in prose mixed with poems. A popular pastoral, its fourth edition appeared in 1598. However, Shakespeare introduced many changes. He turned Lodge's rivals into brothers. The usurper Duke Frederick repented and thus made possible the restoration of the exiled court without the battle that Lodge introduces. Shakespeare altered the names of all the characters except Phebe and Rosalind, and he added a number of characters: Touchstone, Le Beau, Amiens, Jaques, William, Sir Oliver Martex, and the old shepherd, Corin. Lodge based his work to some extent on the medieval narrative poem *The Tale of Gamelyn*; hence it is possible that this work also may have influenced Shakespeare's play. Whenever Shakespeare relied on sources, and he usually did, he invariably selected, omitted, and added material to create the distinctive features of his new work. In *As You Like It* he alters the source material substantially to suit his intentions.

STRUCTURE AND PLOTTING

One of the prominent features of plotting in the play is the variety of elements Shakespeare has combined, from a wrestling bout to Hymen's celebration of marriage in a masque. Anthony R. Dawson has stressed these structural elements:

> The full flavour of *As You Like It* is thus one that includes a blend of different tastes: elements of variety show, love, and fairy tale are mixed together with close psychological observation and acute social awareness. During the central part of the play, an artificial convention, this time the "pastoral," is offset by a sharply realistic set of at-

titudes towards love—the central subject of *As You Like It* as it is of much pastoral literature. The play continually brings together the differing effects wrought by conventional forms and realistic presentation. In doing so, it uses widely various theatrical means, such as athletic displays, elaborate set-pieces, disguises, mock debates, songs, recitations, parodies and a masque. (Tomarken, p. 583)

Shakespeare provides something for everybody to jolt the spectators out of the smugness of their dream of a golden world and to return them to the complexity of their own lives.

Shakespeare builds the play around the contrasting worlds of the court and the forest, which also reflect on one another and create the impression that neither is an ideal place. Power struggles at the court have led to Duke Frederick's usurpation of authority and the expulsion of Duke Senior. Duke Senior withdraws into the green world of the forest, where he does not find any ingratitude and jealousy—but it is not an ideal location, either, as Touchstone points out (3.2.13–22). Duke Senior asks his courtiers, "Are not these woods / More free from peril than the envious court?" (2.1.3–4). But Corin reveals the inequities in the forest when he tells Rosalind and Celia that he is "shepherd to another man" and does not "shear the fleeces" that he grazes; moreover, his "master is of churlish disposition" (2.4.78–80).

Shakespeare creates a set of oppositions between the natural and the artificial. The antithesis between the two allows the playwright to question the view that the natural is free and wholesome while the artificial and manmade is restricted and somehow unnatural. The tyrannical practices of the usurping Duke stand in opposition to the freedom and simplicity of the forest, but Shakespeare is not implying that every court is inherently corrupt and or that everyone in a forest is happy. One brother may turn against the other in fratricidal feuds, but peace and harmony in the family are always preferable to living in exile. Hence, instead of making absolutes out of the court and the country, Shakespeare's setting emphasizes the return to harmony. Old hermits can convert even bloodthirsty tyrants to change their ways and to return their usurped dukedoms to the rightful heir.

Shakespeare shows ambivalence and skepticism about the oaths of loyalty and stresses the need for the right orientation in matters of love. Jaques has had a reckless past and is not interested in love or marriage. Touchstone harbors no romantic illusions about either, for "man hath his desires; and as pigeons bill, so wedlock would be nibbling" (3.3.80–82). Phebe treats Silvius disdainfully, but Rosalind challenges her arrogance: "Must you be therefore proud and pitiless?" (3.5.40). Rosalind must cure Orlando of the madness of love. Rosalind/Ganymede exposes the folly of hanging Petrarchan sonnets on trees and brings all the couples back to the state of marriage. Innocence and experience finally emerge not as two separate states of being but rather as twin aspects of the same life at court and in the country.

This play contains a large number of set-pieces to be performed for onstage audiences. Duke Frederick and others watch a wrestling match that provides the occasion for Rosalind's falling in love with Orlando. Jaques' reported elegy on the wounded and sobbing deer, which is an indictment of Duke Senior and his tyranny in the forest, is heard in 2.1. In 2.7 Jaques explains the process of decline through the seven ages of man. In 3.6, Rosalind and Celia watch the spectacle of Silvius and Phebe and become aware of the difficulties of courtship in love. In 4.1 Celia is a spectator during the scene between Orlando and Rosalind and so observes another example of love's complexity. In 4.3 Oliver narrates the story of his rescue from a lioness and a snake by Orlando and introduces the idea of sudden conversion. In 5.3, two Pages sing a song for Touchstone and Audrey about spring and love and the passing of time. In the last scene, 5.4, Touchstone gives his speech about the lie, Hymen performs a ceremony of marriages, Jaques de Boys tells the group about Duke Frederick's meeting with an old religious man and his conversion from the world. Shakespeare is using such plays within the play to extend the connections between life on and off stage and to enrich the levels of meaning.

As You Like It gives the impression that it has more talk than action. It is true that Jaques and others talk and Rosalind and Orlando enjoy long conversations, but the play is not devoid of movement and action in and outside the forest of Arden. There are major political and family conflicts, and people leave the court to escape into a pastoral setting. The wrestling match is a major site for action and conflict over loyalty and love. Duke Senior's companions amuse themselves when they walk around dressed as foresters sometimes and as outlaws other times. Conversations in the forest console the exiles. People sit around and sing songs.

Although time is supposed to stand still in a pastoral setting, it does not do so in the forest. As Touchstone broods, the clock is constantly ticking: "It is ten a' clock. / . . . / 'Tis but an hour ago since it was nine, / And after one hour more 'twill be eleven" (2.7.22–25). Jaques strikes the gloomy note of the passage of time in his monologue on the seven ages of man in the midst of the forest's supposed time-lessness. Orlando cannot be late, Rosalind insists. The play keeps time in the fore-front from scene to scene. The clock exposes the fallacy of timeless tranquility in the forest. Seasons change; property changes hands. "These times" are on Orlando's mind when he compliments old Adam for his "constant service of the antique world":

> Thou art not for the fashion of these times,
> Where none will sweat but for promotion,
> And having that do choke their service up
> Even with the having. (2.3.57, 59–62)

These times are very different from what they had been; they change again when the restored Duke Senior invites everyone to "share the good of our returned fortune" (5.4.174).

Shakespeare has placed more songs in *As You Like It* than in any other play. The songs enable Duke Senior and others to while away the time in the forest, but they also reflect on their fortune. Richmond Noble gives a one-sided view when he asserts: "To such a comedy the service of song is indispensable, for without the aid of music we should be unable to realize its ideality or its entire removal from any kind of life with which we are acquainted" (*Shakespeare's Use of Song with the Text of the Principal Songs* [Oxford: Oxford UP, 1923], 71). Some of the songs are about the life people are acquainted with; some of them capture the mood of the festive and the elegiac. Amiens's song "Under the greenwood tree" (2.5.1–8) rejoices in love in the forest with no enemy but winter and rough weather, but it also contains a note of sadness. The melancholic Jaques cannot help but call his fellow lords "gross fools" (2.5.56) who are deluded. The songs augment their scenes in complex ways instead of just reaffirming the ideal setting of the pastoral.

MAIN CHARACTERS

Rosalind

The one figure that has caught the fancy of the spectators over the past 400 years is Rosalind. In a play of 2,636 lines, she speaks 668; her part is larger than that of any other woman in Shakespeare's plays. The daughter of the exiled Duke Senior, she is fair-skinned (3.2.95; 4.3.85), "slender" (3.2.106), "more than common tall" (1.3.115), and able to pass herself off as a man with "a swashing and a martial outside" (1.3.120). Yet her disguise hardly conceals her femininity (3.5.115–23; 4.3.85–88). She is grief-stricken and unhappy, but she wants to leave her sadness aside and be happy. When Celia earnestly urges her to be so, Rosalind declares exuberantly: "From henceforth I will, coz, and devise sports. Let me see—what think you of falling in love?" (1.2.24–25).

Le Beau informs Orlando that "the people praise [Rosalind] for her virtues, / And pity her for her good father's sake" (1.2.280–281). In a state of anxiety, she watches Orlando defeat Charles in wrestling and then gives Orlando her chain. She congratulates him, for he has "wrastled well, and overthrown / More than your enemies" (1.2.254–255). When Duke Frederick accuses her of disloyalty because she is her father's daughter, she defends herself vigorously in a firm and forthright manner: "Treason is not inherited, my lord" (1.3.61–63). She exhibits her independence of mind and sense of reality in her exchanges in the court of Duke Frederick.

One of Shakespeare's favorite techniques is disguises, and Rosalind is the main beneficiary of this device. By putting on her male dress, Rosalind begins to savor the opportunity to act like a man. "A gallant curtle-axe upon my thigh, / A boar-spear in my hand"(1.3.117–118), Rosalind can pretend to be brave, just as many men "do outface it with their semblances" (1.3.122). She adopts the name of Ganymede, a beautiful young man who was the cupbearer of Jove, the king of the gods. Her great challenge will be to speak the language of men and to avoid the sentimentalities and tears of women.

Once in the forest of Arden, Rosalind concentrates entirely on love and does not disclose her identity even to her father. Her first encounter in the forest is with Silvius, who explains his woes in unrequited love (2.4). Silvius's complaint opens up Rosalind's own wound: "Alas, poor shepherd, searching thy wound, / I have by hard adventure found mine own" (2.4.44–45).

Yet Rosalind can cherish her ideals in love and at the same time be realistic enough to say to Phebe, "Sell when you can, you are not for all markets" (3.5.60). She also understands that "men have died from time to time, and worms have eaten them, but not for love" (4.1.106–108). Shakespeare injected great humor into the play by showing a woman instead of a man pursuing her lover with skill and ease. Bernard Shaw considered it admirable that Rosalind "makes love to the man instead of waiting for the man to make love to her—a piece of natural history which has kept Shakespeare's heroines alive, whilst generations of properly governessed young ladies, taught to say 'No' three times at least, have miserably perished" (*Saturday Review*, 5 December 1896, in Tomarken, 533–534).

In the guise of Ganymede, Rosalind commands the linguistic power she might not have displayed as a woman. Between falling in love at first sight in act 1 and marrying Orlando at the end of act 5, she has a great deal of time to ascertain Orlando's worth. She and Celia have bought property, and she acts as the head of a household. Celia accuses Rosalind of maligning women when she seeks to educate Orlando in female temperament: "I will be more jealous of thee than a Barbary cock-pigeon over his hen, more clamorous than a parrot against rain, more new-fangled than an ape, more giddy in my desires than a monkey" (4.1.149–153). She claims to possess the powers of a magician: "I have, since I was three years old, convers'd with a magician, most profound in his art, and yet not damnable" (5.2.59–61). Her disguise has given her the ability to direct and manage her love and marriage. Still, she also never forgets that she is a woman and declares, "When I think, I must speak" (3.2.249–250). She weeps when she has cause.

Michael D. Bristol examines Rosalind's role in terms of the conflict between feudal patriarchy and free-market individualism: "Rosalind, whoever or whatever she is, represents the new social reality of the market, where desire is a polymorphous commodity requiring only mutual consent between parties to the exchange of sexual goods." The play "experiments with a social world where the idea of mutual consent is really taken seriously," and Rosalind "asserts the values of autonomy and self-determination over and against the tradition of patriarchal authority" (303). According to Bristol, Rosalind emerges as one of the strong Shakespearean women who want to be taken at their word and who value the right to give consent in their own right.

Jaques

Shakespeare invented Jaques the melancholic to reflect on the unhappy aspects of both the court and the country. A discordant figure in Duke Senior's court, Jaques labels Duke Senior and his lords as "mere usurpers, tyrants" who kill the animals "[i]n their assign'd and native dwelling-place" (2.1.61, 63). When Amiens sings in praise of the ideal forest of Arden, Jaques labels the inhabitants as asses who have given up their "wealth and ease" and become "[g]ross fools" (2.5.52, 56). Since Jaques believes that the world is full of fools, he would like to change it. Yet after spending an hour with a fool, Touchstone, Jaques wants to be a fool who knows that "we ripe and ripe" and then "we rot and rot" (2.7.26–27). Only fools possess this wisdom about mortality. If granted the freedom to speak his mind, he "will through and through / Cleanse the foul body of th' infected world" (2.7.59–60). But Duke Senior reminds him that he "has been a libertine" and would unload his "embossed sores, and headed evils" on the world (2.7.65, 67).

Jaques' famous dissertation on the seven ages of man presents a dark view of human life. One of his favorite pastimes is to sit down and "rail against our mistress the world, and all our misery" (3.2.278–279). One of his good deeds is to advise Touchstone to "have a good priest that can tell you what marriage is" instead of letting Sir Oliver Martext perform the ceremony (3.3.85–86).

Some readers have idealized him for his contemplative tendencies; others have found him diseased and sickly. William Hazlitt and Sander Gilman can be cited here as proponents of two extreme views. For William Hazlitt, he "is the only purely contemplative character in Shakespeare. He thinks, and does nothing. His whole occupation is to amuse his mind, and he is totally regardless of his body and his fortunes" (Knowles, p. 583). For Sander Gilman, however, Jaques is syphilitic and unsound: his disease "is a sign of his role as the infected and the source of infection within the sexual economy of the comedy. It is also the source of his world-view, his melancholy, and his illness is in turn shaped by his manner of seeing the world." Diagnosing his life as a case of the progress of a disease from youth to old age, Gilman believes that "Jaques's soliloquy signals the most pessimistic course of life and decay" ("Love and Marriage = Death," in *Sex Positives? The Cultural Politics of Dissident Sexualities*, ed. Thomas Foster, Carol Siegel, and Ellen R. Berry [New York: New York UP, 1997], 210).

Rosalind finds Jaques' melancholy repulsive and abominable. He takes pride in claiming that his "is a melancholy of mine own, compounded of many simples, extracted from many objects, and indeed the sundry contemplation of my travels, in which my often ruination wraps me in a most humorous sadness" (4.1.15–20). Rosalind acutely tells him that his experience has deformed his identity: "[L]ook you lisp and wear strange suits; disable all the benefits of your own country; be out of love with your own nativity, and almost chide God for making you that countenance you are" (4.1.33–37). Jaques does not belong in the final scene of marriage and joy; he is "for other than for dancing measures" (5.4.193). Though he momentarily stays behind in Duke Senior's "abandon'd cave," he looks forward to conversing with an old religious man and Duke Frederick (5.4.196).

Jaques seems to derive from Ben Jonson's humor characters popularized in *Every Man in His Humor* (1598), in which Shakespeare performed, and *Every Man out of His Humor* (1599), staged by the Lord Chamberlain's Men. He also resembles the various satiric characters appearing on the stage at this time in the plays produced by the boys' acting companies. In the culture outside of the theater, satire was also enjoying a vogue on which Shakespeare may have been trying to capitalize.

Touchstone

Shakespeare created Touchstone as the wise fool in contrast to Jaques-the-melancholic. As a jester Touchstone is a privileged person who holds no delusions about the idyllic forest or the ideals of love. Celia acknowledges "the great heap of [his] knowledge," and Rosalind invites him jokingly to "unmuzzle [his] wisdom" (1.2.68–70). He regrets that "fools may not speak wisely what wise men do foolishly" (1.2.86–87). While Jaques has renounced the world and its pleasures, Touchstone observes human follies and enjoys all the pleasures offered by the world. Unlike Duke Senior and his lords, he carries no illusions: "Ay, now am I in Arden, the more fool I. When I was at home, I was in a better place, but travellers must be content" (2.4.16–18). But he is not pessimistic or cynical. He keeps an objective eye on mortal beings who show their humanity by falling in love: "We that are true lovers run into strange capers; but as all is mortal in nature, so is all nature in love mortal in folly" (2.4.54–56). Touchstone supplies the most persuasive case for marriage: "As the ox hath his bow, sir, the horse his curb, and the falcon her bells, so man hath his desires; and as pigeons bill, so wedlock would be nibbling" (3.3.79–82). Having decided, at Jaques' urging, to postpone marriage with Audrey, Touchstone says to her: "We must be married, or we must live in bawdry" (3.3.97). Like Rosalind, he takes a realistic view of love and male-female relationships. But he is no cynic. When Ganymede and Aliena have left and Duke Senior and others are waiting for the appearance of Rosalind and Celia, Jaques incites Touchstone, "the motley-minded gentleman," to display his wit. Touchstone speaks earnestly and modestly about Audrey and goes against his usual manner to affirm honesty and honor in marriage: "A poor virgin, sir, an ill-favor'd thing, sir, but mine own; a poor humor of mine, sir, to take that that no man else will. Rich honesty dwells like a miser, sir, in a poor house, as your pearl in your foul oyster" (5.4.57–61).

The Touchstone Jaques encounters in the forest broods over the process of aging and decay and is concerned with "how the world wags" (2.7.23). He derives his wisdom from his grasp of the ways of the world. He can exchange wit with Corin and Rosalind with equal ease and facility. He can prove to Corin that the old shepherd is damned, and he can parody Orlando's verses for Rosalind and ask her: "Why do you infect yourself with them?" (3.2.113–114). As C. L. Barber observes, Touchstone "is only making manifest the folly which others, including the audience, hide from themselves" (233). Duke Senior reminds everyone that "He uses his folly like a stalking-horse, and under the presentation of that he shoots his wit" (5.4.106–107).

Orlando

Orlando is a natural gentleman who develops his nobility and strength in spite of being kept "rustically at home, or . . . at home unkept" (1.1.7–9). Even his villainous brother, Oliver, feels envious of his inborn qualities: "Yet he's gentle, never school'd and yet learned, full of noble device, of all sorts enchantingly belov'd, and indeed so much in the heart of the world, and especially of my own people, who best know him, that I am altogether mispris'd" (1.1.166–171). Oliver tries to get him killed by Charles, the wrestler, but even here Orlando surprises everybody by defeating Charles. Duke Frederick calls him "a gallant youth," and so he proves to be (1.2.229).

Adam, the loyal old servant who has known Orlando all his life, sees in him the "memory / Of old Sir Rowland" and praises him as "gentle, strong, and valiant" (2.3.2–3, 6). Alerted to danger by Adam about Oliver's plans to kill him, Orlando finds himself in the forest of Arden, dreaming of Rosalind and composing verses in witness of his love. Having read treatises on love, he acts accordingly. Like a typical pastoral lover, Orlando looks upon trees as his books and says, "And in their barks my thoughts I'll character" (3.2.6). Since Orlando hardly knows Rosalind, he describes her in abstract and idealized diction that reflects his enthusiasm and madness in love: "Run, run, Orlando, carve on every tree / The fair, the chaste, and unexpressive she" (3.2.9–10). Through his naive verses Orlando reveals not only his sincerity, devotion, and faith in Rosalind, but also his folly in love.

In the forest of Arden, Celia spots Orlando wearing a "chain, that you once wore, about his neck," and lying "stretch'd along, like a wounded knight" (3.2.181–182, 240–241). As soon as Rosalind/Ganymede meets Orlando and questions him about time, she identifies him promptly as a "fancy-monger" who "seems to have the quotidian of love upon him" (3.2.364, 365–366). She assumes the task of curing him of his madness. He must meet Ganymede but imagine that he is with Rosalind; Ganymede will show him what women are really like. She gives him a misogynist's list of women's traits: temperamental, changeable, whimsical, proud, inconstant, and unreliable. Rosalind's therapy will drive her "suitor from his mad humor of love to a living humor of madness" (3.2.418–419). Ganymede must be glad to hear that Orlando "would not be cur'd" (3.2.425).

Still, thanks to Rosalind's play-acting, Orlando develops the assurance to display his sincere emotions. On the day of Oliver's marriage he will be "at the height of heart-heaviness" (5.2.46) because he "can no longer live by thinking" (5.2.50). Ros-alind realizes that her cure has worked and reassures him that he "is a gentleman of good conceit" (5.2.53–54). By this time Orlando has also overcome his hatred for Oliver and has saved his brother from the lioness that was waiting to devour him.

The Magician-Uncle

One of the most intriguing figures in *As You Like It* is Rosalind's magician-uncle, who never appears in any scene. When Orlando comments that her "accent is some-thing finer than you could purchase in so remov'd a dwelling," she responds that "an old religious uncle of mine taught me to speak, who was in his youth an in-land man" (3.2.344–345). This uncle taught her "how to know a man in love" (3.2.370). He also taught her to "do strange things. I have, since I was three year old, convers'd with a magician, most profound in his art, and yet not damnable" (5.2.59–61). Rosalind may have invented this figure to account for certain aspects of herself in the forest, but he is most helpful in driving the plot ahead.

DEVICES AND TECHNIQUES

As You Like It, written at a mature period in Shakespeare's career, around 1599, reflects Shakespeare's command of the artistic resources of the English language to the development of which he contributed through his diction, imagery, and verbal play, and through the projection of character through the varieties of linguistic use. A distinctive feature of language in the play is the quality of prose. More than half of the play is in prose, over 35 percent in blank verse, and only about 10 percent in rhymed verse. Duke Frederick speaks in verse when he banishes Rosalind and Or-lando, and so does Duke Senior when he is trying to keep his spirits up in the forest.

Shakespeare's prose is controlled, but it sounds informal and unadorned. Audi-ences respond to Rosalind, Orlando, Celia, Phebe, and the other characters on the basis of their rhetorical flexibility. Phebe stands apart in the way she accentuates her rhetorical pretensions in her syntax and choice of words. For example, Phebe takes twenty lines to mock Silvius's idea that eyes can kill. Her diction, syntax, rhythm, and verse reveal her ignorance and arrogance:

> Thou tell'st me there is murder in mine eye:
> 'Tis pretty, sure, and very probable,
> That eyes, that are the frail'st and softest things,
> Who shut their coward gates on atomies,
> Should be called tyrants, butchers, murtherers! (3.5.10–14)

Shakespeare is mocking a tradition that so many of the lovers accept. Phebe em-phasizes the folly of Petrarchan conceits, but at the same time she is revealing her naïveté, perhaps even her ignorance, in taking literally what should be understood as metaphor. Shakespeare had mocked this same literal-mindedness in the rude me-chanicals of *A Midsummer Night's Dream*, who think that the ducal audience will regard their playacting as reality.

Rosalind shines with her natural and unassuming phrases and the forthrightness of her syntax. She also excels in wit. She exhibits her impatience, learning, humor, and intensity when Celia tells of seeing the author of the verses praising Rosalind. Rosalind insists on knowing at once who it is:

> One inch of delay more is a South-sea of discovery. I prithee tell me who is it quickly, and speak apace. I would thou couldst stammer, that thou mightst pour this conceal'd man out of thy mouth, as wine comes out of a narrow-mouth'd bottle, either too much at once, or none at all. I prithee take the cork out of thy mouth that I may drink thy tidings. (3.2.196–203)

Comparing Celia's delay with the time it would take to explore the South Seas and her mouth with a bottle of wine, Rosalind is displaying her witty personality.

Hidden behind her male disguise, Rosalind in public has to be manly in her language. She also has a sharp eye for others' poses and pretensions. She delivers her most intense emotions and feelings in prose. She can vary her medium in relation to the person she is talking to. For example, she is stern with Phebe, who is rejecting Silvius with disdain. Rosalind reveals a great part for herself when she sets out to cure Orlando of his madness by presenting a catalogue of women's faults. If he knows enough about women, he will overcome his love, but Rosalind herself is a woman in love with Orlando. Her point is not to malign her sex but to remove Orlando's abstract fantasies about love and her beauty. Women are not what a lover may imagine they are. "Rosalind is able," says Barber, "in the midst of her golden moment, to look beyond it and mock its illusions, including the master illusion that love is an ultimate and final experience, a matter of life and death" (235).

Orlando displays his immaturity, bookish learning, and superficiality when he imagines his love's creation by a "heavenly synod" (3.2.150). He shows signs of madness when he believes that his beloved represents Helen's beauty without her fickleness, "Cleopatra's majesty" and nobility, Atalanta's fleetness of foot, and Lucretia's scrupulous chastity (3.2.147–150). His trust in the bookish language of love, his faith in classical figures, and his uncertainty about his emotions betray his inexperience. Rosalind quickly tears his classical language apart when she says that she cannot find any of her uncle's marks of love upon him. Rosalind is using her cure to make sure that he acts maturely in his understanding of women.

Shakespeare often uses antithetical phrases and words and puts one against the other. When Celia and Rosalind go into the forest, they are choosing liberty over banishment. Duke Frederick tells Orlando that "the world esteem'd thy father honorable, / But I did find him still mine enemy" (1.2.225–226). *As You Like It* is replete with conflicts of brother against brother, court against country, appearance against reality. But since the play is a comedy, these prove "but burs . . . thrown . . . in holiday foolery" (1.3.13–14); the conflicts can be resolved by mysterious conversions or good fortune. If Duke Frederick had not accidentally met a holy man during his attack against Duke Senior in the forest of Arden, Duke Senior would not have regained his dukedom. But unexpected and strange things happen and change the course of events. As Harold Jenkins has put it, "What is wisdom and what is folly is of course never decided—you may have it 'as you like it'" (Dean, p. 132).

THEMES AND MEANINGS

The title of the play refers to Shakespeare's attempt to move away from one-sided views and to recognize that reason and irrationality, love and withdrawal, the court and the forest, wisdom and folly are not absolute opposites. People try to console themselves with what they have, as Duke Senior and his lords do. All kinds of people live in the forest. Duke Senior and his company live there "like the old Robin Hood of England," and "many young gentlemen flock to him every day, and fleet the time carelessly, as they did in the golden world" (1.1.116, 117–119), but the play undermines these idealized scenes. Who are Duke Senior and his lords robbing to give to whom? Why are young men withdrawing into the harsh environment of the forest? Duke Senior supplies his own dubious picture of freedom from Adam's penalty, but Jaques and Touchstone point out that the pastoral landscape is not what it is rumored to be.

The play tries to juxtapose the seemingly opposite elements like nature and convention and justifies both. For example, Joseph Alulis looks at "the relation between nature and convention, the former understood as both standard and native impulse, the latter understood as a society's accepted ideas of right and wrong and the mechanisms by which such ideas are made to govern our lives." He elaborates Shakespeare's handling of the two:

> What makes this play the delightful affair it is, is that while it affirms an essential goodness of nature, hence the deficiencies of convention that depart from nature's standard, it also shows the necessary role of convention in relation to natural impulses, both in curbing those that are harmful and in protecting and fostering those that are beneficial. It rejects the melancholy view, occasioned by the spectacle of human injustice, that both nature and convention are meaningless, respectively teaching and serving only the pursuit of selfish ends by the most powerful; Shakespeare invites us to see our condition in nature and the world rather as an occasion of mirth. ("Fathers and Children: Matter, Mirth, and Melancholy in *As You Like It*," in *Shakespeare's Political Pageant: Essays in Politics and Literature*, ed. Joseph Alulis and Vickie Sullivan [London: Rowman and Littlefield, 1996], 38–39.)

The contradictory reality of human condition is the basis of Shakespeare's comedy and humor.

For Keir Elam, the play qualifies as "a pastoral romance that presents no longer a yearning for the inaccessible but an affirmation of the achievable, namely of the capacity of dramatic theatre itself to create a world at once remote and present, oneiric [dreamlike] and pragmatic, magical and ironical" ("As They Did It in the Golden World: Romantic Rapture and Semantic Rupture in *As You Like It*," in *Reading the Renaissance: Culture, Poetics, and Drama*, ed. Jonathan Hart [London and New York: Garland, 1996], 175). According to Elam, "Shakespeare's way with nostalgia in the play is more of a doing away with nostalgia, in favour of a forward-looking assertion of the erotic, the ludic [playful], and the magical potentials of the drama in a freshly re-invented pastoral romance mode" (175–176). Shakespeare adopts the pastoral, which was so popular in the 1590s, to draw audiences and to reveal its irrelevance.

Shakespeare presents the pastoral world as a mislabeled arcadia, with little sunshine and peace. David Young explains Shakespeare's use of antithesis:

> To be a credit to art, however, pastoral had to avoid the limited accomplishments of escape and wish-fulfillment, and had to face the issues it raised. In its function as an alternative it was to be dialectical, a kind of discourse between reality and the imagi-

nation. This process quite naturally called for continual recourse to antithesis, a favorite stylistic device, and it should be obvious, even to the most casual reader of pastoral, that it is founded on a series of tensions and oppositions. (Tomarken, p. 50)

These tensions and oppositions enable Shakespeare to mock illusions about the
world, restore Duke Senior to power, and reposition the audience in a realistically
drawn society.

The vagaries of Fortune, according to Shakespeare, affect everyone in *As You Like
It*. The dark clouds have cast such a shadow that Celia proposes to Rosalind that
they "sit and mock the good huswife Fortune from her wheel, that her gifts may
henceforth be bestow'd equally" (1.2.31–33). Rosalind agrees that Fortune's "benefits are mightily misplac'd, and the bountiful blind woman doth most mistake in
her gifts to women" (1.2.34–36). Rosalind distinguishes the gifts of Fortune (wealth,
power, and success) from those of Nature (beauty and intelligence) when she assures her cousin: "Fortune reigns in the gifts of the world, not in the lineaments of
Nature" (1.2.41–42).

Shakespeare does not believe that the court is under the domain of Fortune and
the forest of Arden under Nature. What he is suggesting is that Fortune and Nature play a role in everybody's life, regardless of one's location. Orlando's act of
kindness under the influence of his nature in saving his brother's life changes
Oliver's fortune; Duke Frederick's chance encounter with an old hermit changes
his.

Shakespeare similarly reconciles the contradictory ideas of reason and irrationality in the play to suggest that both have a place in people's lives. Touchstone-
the-fool makes most sense when he expresses his opinions in an irrational manner.
His irrational witticisms reveal the limits of reason. Orlando is a mad man in love
who writes poetry, but his madness is not a disease. There is room for melancholy
in Shakespeare's scheme of things, but Jaques' melancholy is too pessimistic to be
tolerated. Ruth Morse brings out the beneficial and harmful sides of reason and irrationality:

The madness of the lover, appropriate to youth, is constitutive of social bonds and
the future of the age; the irrationality of the natural or fool offers a running commentary on the limits of reason, and has method in it; while the excessive and un-
balanced logic of the Melancholy challenges reason by reason of its own excess.
(Debax, p. 74)

The playwright's concern is not with reason as such; it is rather with every man or
woman in his or her humor.

Shakespeare has infused the play with different humors of love in men and
women. Orlando, Oliver, Touchstone, and Silvius amuse and instruct the audience
with their situations, as do the four women. Oliver was the luckiest one to snatch
Celia in a short time. Touchstone is the wise fool who drives away his rival, William,
and chooses Audrey without any illusions. Silvius is the unfortunate one caught in
a web of words: "If you do sorrow at my grief in love, / By giving love, your sorrow and my grief / Were both extermin'd" (3.5.87–89). Phebe is a suitable match
for him because she is caught up in her own delusions. Orlando, the wrestler turned
poet, is reluctantly cured of his madness in love by his beloved disguised as a man
who pretends to be his beloved. In this pageant of love's humors, all pursue their

fortunes in love as they like it. When Phebe asks Silvius to clarify to Rosalind/Ganymede "what 'tis to love," Silvius answers,

> It is to be all made of sighs and tears, . . .
> It is to be all made of fantasy,
> All made of passion, and all made of wishes,
> All adoration, duty, and observance,
> All humbleness, all patience, and impatience,
> All purity, all trial, all observance. (5.2.84–98)

"If this be so" (52.2.103ff) one should not blame any of them for falling in love with another. Even though Rosalind proclaims that "men have died from time to time, and worms have eaten them, but not for love" (4.1.106–108), she concurs with Silvius at the end when she has removed, like a magician, all the impediments to marriage.

Shakespeare deals with change in a variety of ways, from the external transformation of Rosalind and Celia into Ganymede and Aliena to the inner reformation of Oliver and Duke Frederick. Duke Senior used the word when inquiring about Jaques in the forest: "I think he be transform'd into a beast, / For I can no where find him like a man (2.7.1–2). Orlando compares himself to "a doe [going] to find my fawn" when he leaves Duke Senior to retrieve Adam (2.7.128). Rosalind brings up the Pythagorean doctrine of the transmigration of souls after finding verses on a palm tree: "I was never so berhym'd since Pythagoras' time, that I was an Irish rat, which I can hardly remember" (3.2.176–178). Even though Audrey is too ignorant to appreciate the learned allusion to Shakespeare's favorite poet, author of the *Metamorphoses*, Touchstone tells her that he is "here with thee and thy goats as the most capricious poet, honest Ovid, was among the Goths" (3.3.7–9). Playing on "Goths" and "goats", he is indulging in linguistic transformation with a pun.

Almost everyone undergoes change when he or she goes into the forest, though some of the natives like Corin remain what they are. These changes occur because of interaction among Rosalind and Orlando and Duke Senior and others, aided by Rosalind's magic presentation of herself and Celia with Hymen the god of marriage. Hymen transforms single men and women into husbands and wives. Threatened by a lioness and a snake, Oliver repents his past and makes himself anew. When Duke Frederick is marching into the forest at the head of an army to capture his brother, his chance encounter with an old religious man transforms him. This metamorphosis leads to the final transformation—Duke Senior's return as ruler of his court. Shakespeare does not account for all the changes, but he upholds the inevitability of renewal or reform. Even Jaques has not been a melancholic all the time; in the past he was a libertine (2.7.65–66). Time, chance, and mutability rule. In tragedies the consequences are death and loss, but in comedies like *As You Like It* the results are love, marriage, and restoration.

CRITICAL CONTROVERSIES

Critical controversies about *As You Like It* have focused on different topics, depending on the literary and cultural climate of an age. Eighteenth-century critics debated the play's lax moral outlook but praised it in general. With the Romantics began an appreciation of the idyllic atmosphere of the forest of Arden. In the second half of the nineteenth century, a number of women drew attention to the glorious charms of Rosalind. Since the 1950s, critics have focused on the nature of Shakespearean comedy and *As You Like It*. Others have sought to read the play in the context of political and social changes in Shakespeare's time and in the modern world. Feminists have taken up the questions of Shakespeare in relation to women's oppression and patriarchy.

Samuel Johnson in 1765 remarked that the play's "fable is wild and pleasing," but he wondered how "the ladies will approve the facility with which both Rosalind and Celia give away their hearts." Similarly, he did not approve of the ending: "By hastening to the end of his work Shakespeare suppressed the dialogue between the usurper and the hermit, and lost an opportunity of exhibiting a moral lesson in which he might have found matter worthy of his highest powers" (in Knowles, p. 504). Five years later, Francis Gentleman faulted Shakespeare for not observing the Aristotelian unities of time, place, and action and for letting Oliver escape punishment altogether; he had "a strong objection to crowning such a monster with fortune and love" (ibid.).

The Romantics shifted the focus from moral and structural issues to the ideal setting of the forest of Arden. William Hazlitt praised *As You Like It* as "the most ideal of any" of Shakespeare's plays:

> It is a pastoral drama in which the interest arises more out of the sentiments and characters than out of the actions and situations. It is not what is done, but what is said, that claims our attention. Nursed in solitude, "Under the shade of melancholy boughs," the imagination grows soft and delicate, and the wit runs riot in idleness, like a spoiled child that is never sent to school. (Ibid., 505)

Hazlitt adores the forest: "The very air of the place seems to breathe a spirit of philosophical poetry; to stir the thoughts, to touch the heart with pity, as the drowsy forest rustles to the sighing gale" (ibid., 554).

Like Hazlitt, many other critics saw more in the forest than perhaps even the playwright had allowed. Shakespeare's imagination inspired Hartley Coleridge, in 1851, to wax lyrical over various sights and sounds: "The leaves rustle and glisten, the brooks murmur unseen in the copses, the flowers enamel the savannahs, the sheep wander on the distant hills, the deer glance by and hide themselves in the thickets, and the sheepcotes sprinkle the far landscape all spontaneously, without being shown off, or talked about" (ibid., pp. 555–556). Hartley Coleridge and other writers were fascinated by what Shakespeare barely hinted. It does not matter that Shakespeare did not name specific birds or insects or flowers, and mentioned only the deer, a lioness, and a "green and gilded snake" (4.3.108).

Later critics have turned from this "never land" of the forest of Arden and stressed the political and social contexts in which they can situate the author. The main strength of political criticism lies in its understanding of actions and plot in terms of the power relations and social structure of a society. Duke Senior, Duke Frederick, and the absent uncle reflect the issues of losing or retaining authority and social stratification of England and other countries. These characters live in a society that was engaged in problems of social transformation and the dynamics of patriarchy. People in the forest do not "fleet the time carelessly" (1.1.118). They have their social hierarchy; they are concerned about property; and they cannot live without money. When Celia and Rosalind prepare for their departure for the forest of Arden, they make sure that they take their jewels and their wealth (1.3.134). In the forest they inquire "if that love or gold / Can in this desert place buy entertainment" (2.4.71–72). They immediately purchase "the cottage, pasture, and the flock" (2.4.92).

Hugh Grady (1996) examines another political subject in *As You Like It*—the building of alternatives to the oppressive court headed by Duke Frederick. Shakespeare highlights the independence and the personal integrity of Duke Senior and other inhabitants of the forest of Arden. Rejecting the Romantic fascination with the forest of Arden, Grady argues that in *As You Like It*, instead of naively exercising a nostalgia for the pastoral, Shakespeare is dramatizing the possibility of "utopian alternatives to new reifications of market and state power" (182). Grady explains:

> From the molecular "private" of Adam and Orlando (and of Rosalind and Celia), we move to a larger, more inclusive community of refugees in the process of founding new social relations out of the material of their older ones—relations radically transformed, however, by the new rough egalitarianism and communal solidarity of the cleared space of Arden. (190)

This view establishes a link between Shakespeare's search for alternatives to feudalism and modern searches for alternatives to a market economy.

In the ideal setting, described by Hazlitt and others, Anna B. Jameson and other women writers have perceived in Rosalind the many colors and shades of their own fancy. In 1833 Jameson considered Rosalind "like a compound of essences, so volatile in their nature, and so exquisitely blended, that on any attempt to analyze them, they seem to escape us" (in Knowles, p. 572). Jameson compared Rosalind to "silvery summer clouds," "the May-morning, flush with opening blossoms and roseate dews," and "a mountain streamlet." Thirty years later, Mary Cowden Clarke remarked that Rosalind "is like the sunshine, cheerful, beaming full of life, and glow, and warmth, and animation" (ibid., 574).

In 1892 Grace Latham remarked that "the underlying thought in the play is this struggle between good and evil; going on in different form, according to the nature of the dramatis personae, Rosalind being its central figure; Jaques is the hero of evil; Orlando, that of goodness" (ibid., 507). Latham explains how Rosalind joins this struggle: "Keen-witted and keen-sighted, she sees through the people with whom she comes in contact at a glance; has a rooted hatred of all that is mean or false, and a love of truth and uprightness which is one of her best features, but the very clearness of her vision makes her less trustful, more prone to suspect evil than her friend" (ibid., 576).

Unlike Jameson and other women who regard Rosalind as one of Shakespeare's most endearing and charming creations, feminist critics evaluate the play in terms of its support for patriarchy and oppression of women. Every patriarchal relationship deprives women of their identity and independence; it has hindered the growth of a healthy environment for the welfare of Rosalind, Celia, Audrey, and Phebe. According to this view, the marriages at the end of *As You Like It* affirm and restore the oppressive values of an authoritarian society. Penny Gay describes the cycle of

Shakespeare's conflict over the problem of patriarchy (*As She Likes It: Shakespeare's Unruly Women* [London and New York: Routledge, 1994]). Shakespeare first rejects, then restores patriarchal order:

> *As You Like It* effects, through Rosalind's behaviour, the most thorough deconstruction of patriarchy and its gender roles in the Shakespearean canon; yet it is a carnival license allowed only in the magic space of the greenwood. At the end, all must return to the real world and its social constraints. (49)

According to feminist critics like Gay, Shakespeare, by not finally abolishing patriarchy, contributed little to the process of social change and the amelioration of women's lives.

However, many of the feminist readings of the play are more positive about Shakespeare's depiction of Rosalind and other rebellious women. Katy Emck argues that Shakespeare's stress on rebellious women "embodies the desire for expanded self-sovereignty in a world where the power of domestic patriarchs and of monarchs was being absolutised" ("Female Transvestism and Male Self-Fashioning in *As You Like It* and *La vida es sueno*," in *Reading the Renaissance: Culture, Poetics, and Drama*, ed. Jonathan Hart [New York: Garland, 1996], 77). She acknowledges the difficulty of limiting discussions of the play to polarizations of male and female:

> Rosalind's erotic play on her identity with the audience suggests the pleasurable incommensurability and reality which cannot be contained in gender binarisms or class binarism of low to high, or controlled by figures of the sovereign masculine subject, here parades its disturbing, and intensely pleasurable, irrepressibility. (Ibid., 88)

One area in which Shakespeare's delineation of Rosalind has disappointed many critics is the denial of "the female homosocial or homoerotic alliance"; as Jessica Tvordi points out: "Female transvestite figures in Shakespeare's plays are primarily interested in heterosexual relationships, and their engagement in activities that are limiting both for themselves and for other women often works to dissolve the female homosocial or homoerotic alliance" (115). Tvordi and others wish that Rosalind and Celia had continued to set up house together upon their return from the forest of Arden instead of marrying the two brothers.

Like the shifts from vague praise for the forest of Arden and Rosalind to the exploration of social and political realities of Elizabethan and Jacobean England, criticism has moved from applauding Shakespeare's verse and prose to recognizing its instability and uncertainty of meaning. Hazlitt remarked about *As You Like It* that "hardly any of Shakespeare's plays contain more quoted passages, or [more] that have become proverbial" (*Characters of Shakespeare's Plays* [London: Macmillan, 1925], 189). In 1894 J. C. Smith, commented: "The lines are surcharged with feeling, or eloquence, or imagination. They are intrusted with the sentiment, the reflection, and not a little of the action of the piece" (in Knowles, p. 560). Caroline Spurgeon, among others, assessed the effectiveness of the play's figurative language (*Shakespeare's Imagery and What It Tells Us* (Cambridge: Cambridge UP, 1935). Numerous scholars have paid attention to the ambiguities of syntax and diction and the difficulties of interpreting some of the passages. This approach finds its climax in critical theory that dwells on the instability of language and refers to the uncertainties of sense. It argues that there is no stable center of significance in the play.

Malcolm Evans (*Signifying Nothing: Truth's True Contents in Shakespeare's Text*, 2nd ed. [Athens: U of Georgia P, 1989], 161) suggests that Hymen's line "If truth holds true contents" (5.4.130) can be read in at least 168 ways. While such criticism opens up Shakespeare's text to numerous interpretations, it renders problematic any specific meanings of any text.

PRODUCTION HISTORY

Historians have discovered no evidence that *As You Like It* was performed between 1603 and 1740, although it is fairly certain that it was staged at the Globe and other venues during Shakespeare's lifetime. In 1669, it was one of the twenty-one Shakespeare plays assigned to Thomas Killigrew, Master of the Theatre Royal in Bridges Street, but this is not a proof of performance. Historians have found no records of any production in the years after the Restoration of 1660 and before 1740. Since the play deals with political usurpation of power, professional companies, after the return of Charles II to England, may have stayed away from the sensitive issue of the stability of monarchy.

In 1723 Charles Johnson created an altered version entitled *Love in a Forest*, which minimized the usurpation theme and focused on marriage. While keeping the main plot, he dropped Touchstone, Silvius, Phebe, Audrey, William, and Sir Oliver Martext. He renamed Duke Senior as Alberto. Johnson inserted the subplot of Pyramus and Thisbe from *A Midsummer Night's Dream* in place of Touchstone's comments on the degrees of the lie. He showed Jaques "as joining others at the end in marriage in order to demonstrate that his satire is not directed at establishment institutions" (Tomarken, p. 6). He made the play "a comedy about the process of creating a family, the courtship rites that lead to marriage, which is the basis and result of stable government" (ibid.). In 1739 James Carrington prepared another adaptation, *The Modern Receipt or a Cure for Love*. One of his innovations was to enlarge the role of Jaques, "who is taught, after some initial reluctance, how to court a woman and finally marry her" (ibid.). Carrington's piece was never staged.

Michael Jamieson has identified the first production of *As You Like It* since Shakespeare's time. It opened on December 20, 1740, at Drury Lane as "Not Acted these forty Years." Women in breeches parts, or men's roles, had become extremely popular on the stage in the 1730s. Hannah Pritchard played Rosalind, and the spirited Kitty Clive was Celia:

> There was a strong cast and three of Shakespeare's songs were given new settings by Thomas Arne. The Rosalind was Hannah Pritchard, then twenty-nine, who got off to a bad start. In those more boisterous days, when the auditorium remained illuminated, a performer's "points" were applauded. It was only when Pritchard, given an unbecoming gown by the management, reached the line "Take the cork out of thy mouth that I may drink thy tidings" that she was applauded loudly for her spirited delivery. (Ibid., 626)

Thomas Arne composed music for the songs and included the Cuckoo Song from *Love's Labor's Lost*. Professionals continued to use the Cuckoo song for almost 200 years. This performance solidified Mrs. Pritchard's reputation as an actress and established the popularity of Shakespeare's comedies in the eighteenth century and beyond. In October 1741, Drury Lane and Covent Garden featured *As You Like It* at the same time, with Margaret Woffington as Rosalind at the first and Mrs. Pritchard at the second. It was in the role of Rosalind that Mrs. Woffington suffered a stroke on May 3, 1757, in the midst of delivering the Epilogue.

What interested eighteenth-century spectators most were the characters of Rosalind and Jaques and the interludes of music and dance. They wanted their Rosalinds to be beautiful, vivacious, and elegant. Mrs. Sarah Siddons failed twice as Rosalind in 1785 and 1786 because she did not feel comfortable in the male dress. The reviewer of the London *Times* (7 February 1786; Tomarken, p. 515) reflected the audience's expectations when he explained why Mrs. Wells failed as Rosalind at Covent Garden. She disappointed because "the beauty of her face is not expressive of the vivacity which is the characteristic of Rosalind; nor has her person, though finely formed, the elegance and ease of a woman bred in the high fashion of court."

Similar standards prevailed through the middle of the nineteenth century. When Louisa Nisbett played Rosalind in 1842 in a William Charles Macready production at Drury Lane, she "did not certainly fulfill every requisite of the character," stated the London *Times* (3 October 1842; Tomarken, p. 525):

> Joyous indeed she was and merry, it was not the joy and merriment of the banished Duke's daughter; it betrayed an inward heaviness of heart, it was thoughtless when it should have been thoughtful. In short, there was an absence of that graceful sensibility which is the very soul of the character, and without which it loses all its poetry.

For the *Spectator*, Louisa Nesbitt was "utterly devoid of sentiment, and deficient in depth and earnestness"; she was pleasant but showed "no under-current of tender and impassioned feeling." Macready's "delivery of the celebrated passage 'All the world's a stage' was particularly forceful and free from that overstriving at light and shade which is the prevailing blemish of his acting," wrote the *Times* critic (ibid.).

By this time, producers like Macready had decided to lavish money on elaborate sets and costumes in a move toward realism. The *Times* reviewer found that "[e]very scene was a complete picturesque study, and above all the wrestling scene deserves mention, in which the new effect was introduced of including the space where the wrestlers encounter with ropes and staves round which the courtiers and spectators stand pressing eagerly forward, watching every movement of the combatants" (Tomarken, p. 526). Bernard Shaw mocked this stress on scenery in his review of a revival at St. James Theatre (*The Saturday Review*, 5 December 1896; Tomarken, p. 535): "The children will find the virtue of Adam and the philosophy of Jaques just the thing for them; whilst their elders will be delighted by the pageantry and the wrestling."

Helen Faucit exhibited "tenderness and impassioned feeling" in her Rosalind and became the most famous in that role from 1839 to 1879. In "Some of Shakespeare's Female Characters" (1884), which she addressed to Robert Browning, she revealed that the secret of her success as Rosalind was her early realization that it was wrong to assign it "to actresses whose strength lay only in comedy." Faucit explained that the play "deals with happy love" and is "full of imagination, of the glad rapture of the tender passion, of its impulsiveness, its generosity, its pathos" (Tomarken, p. 351). Ellen Terry recalled in 1908 in *The Story of My Life* how Faucit, in the mock-marriage scene (4.1.127ff), "flushed up and said the line ["I do take thee, Orlando, for my husband," 4.1.139] with deep and true emotion, suggesting that she was, indeed, giving herself to Orlando. There was a world of poetry in the way she drooped over his hand" (Tomarken, p. 547).

As You Like It had been popular on the American stage since the late eighteenth century. The most outstanding of the actresses in America was Charlotte Cushman, who performed on both sides of the Atlantic. She won applause with her "masculinity." The London *Observer* (2 March 1845) pointed out that Cushman "looks in every inch a man; and a man she is in voice and manner also, and gesture, so long as she retains these outwards and visible symbols of the stronger sex." Cushman "spoke her speeches trippingly, and seeming to see nothing equivocal in the meaning of the words she uttered, and nothing obnoxious to good taste in the dialogue as set down by the author."

Born in Ireland, Rose Coghlan moved to the United States, and "her Rosalind became a genuine American favorite," says Charles H. Shattuck, who cites a Boston critic in 1886: "Hers is no rose-petal Rosalind, all nerves and no blood. She is brimming with animal spirits, fantastic in a wholesome way" (*Shakespeare on the American Stage*, 2 vols. [Washington, DC: Folger Books, 1987], 2.96–97).

By the 1880s Mary Anderson had emerged as an "ideal actress of the classic kind" who "was tall, strong, statuesque" (Shattuck, 2.103). She was a strong Rosalind and received acclamations in the role in London. William Archer considered her beauty as "good, honest, healthy comeliness, a precious gift, but not a talisman to conjure with" and commended her nobility and loveliness in Rosalind during her two seasons in London:

> It is a work of a most intelligent artist, who happens to possess some peculiar quali-
> fications for this very character . . . a very rare combination of beauty, grace, and what
> may be called physical as well mental talent. . . . Youth, health, and high spirits form
> the charm of her performances. Had it been a little less graceful we should have had
> to call it bouncing, but the actress's consummate charm of pose and movement saves
> it from this reproach. (Shattuck, 2.107)

The stress in this production was on scenery. Lewis Wingfield, the designer, had set the action in the time of Charles VII of France. The *Atheneum* (31 January 1885) praised Wingfield's realism. The American audiences, however, did not warm up to Anderson.

In the twentieth century, *As You Like It* became a popular item in the repertory of professional companies. The directors shifted their attention from extravagant scenery to more credibly realistic settings of some kind. When the Royal Shakespeare Company performed the play in 1919, the London *Times* wrote that it based its setting on "obviously some illuminated manuscript of the early 15th century." Thus, "The forest, for instance, is ruthlessly simplified, while the costumes are all 15th century, and very brilliant and exciting they are, even in the dim lighting affected by the modern stage artist" (London *Times*, 23 April 1919; Tomarken, p. 550). Athene Seyler's Rosalind was "tingling with life and humour and femininity from start to finish," and the entire production was "full of life and direction," remarked the same reviewer.

One of the most memorable productions of *As You Like It* by the Royal Shakespeare Company at Stratford-upon-Avon came in 1961 with Vanessa Redgrave as Rosalind. Reviewing for *The Spectator* (14 July 1961), Bamber Gascoigne found its

Ian Bannen as Orlando and Vanessa Redgrave as Rosalind in a scene in the Forest of Arden from *As You Like It* at the Aldwych Theatre, 1962. © Hulton-Deutsch Collection/Corbis.

set delightful: "[Richard] Negri's set is a steep green breast of a hill; from its top a mighty tree soars up and out of sight; branches jet from it like elephant tusks, supporting flat palletes of leaves" (207: 59–60). Gascoigne reserved enthusiasm for Vanessa Redgrave as "a triumph":

> For the first few scenes it looked as she was going to seem gawky in the part, but I suspect she intended it. Her Rosalind, very properly, is mewed up in court clothes. As soon as she gets into the forest she expands, throws her arms wide to the air, and frolics up and down Negri's hill like one of shepherd Corin's long-legged lambs. Between leaps she pants out Rosalind's euphuistic conceits with all the excitement of someone

who has just found that she too can play the game of fashionable wit. In every way
the forest of Arden is a place of discovery for her. (Ibid., 60)

Redgrave, according to Gascoigne, "has done the most alarming admirable thing—
she has thrown herself so fully into her role that, if it goes wrong, she will merely
look foolish." Michael Jamieson tried to capture the magic of her appeal thus:
"More than common tall, she played Ganymede barefoot, with a working-man's
cap pulled down over her eyes. When she finally came running round the great in
her wedding dress, the audience gasped" (Tomarken, p. 638). The final scene, according to Robert Speaight, "celebrated the sanctification of nature by sacrament,
the coming together of all kinds and classes of men beneath the shelter of a common benediction" (*Shakespeare on the Stage* [Boston: Little, Brown, 1973], 282).
Speaight recommends the production as the finest work by the Royal Shakespeare
Company: "The lighting was beautiful without being fussy; the sunlight fell though
dappled leaves; and the birds sang. Earth has not anything to show more fair than
a production of this quality at Stratford" (283).

In 1971 the Royal National Theatre attempted an all-male production that fascinated the public because it recalled the tradition of men playing women's role during Shakespeare's time. People had a curiosity about watching Ronald Pickup's
Rosalind. He played it "with mental tact in a trouser-suit, chiffon scarf and jaunty
cap. Charles Kay was a watchful, waspish Celia in granny glasses and mini-skirted
frock. Richard Kay as Phebe played more in the sixth-form, serious schoolboy
mode, while Antony Hopkins as Audrey was a bit like a Welsh rugby player in drag"
(Michael Jamieson; Tomarken, p. 640). *The Sunday Telegraph* provided more details:

> Ronald Pickup's Rosalind, willowy and breastless, is the one most clinically drained
> of sensuality. This duke's daughter radiates the lanky, coltish, androgynous sweetness
> of a young Garbo, sex without gender, a platonic readiness to accept love as an emo-
> tion not yet awoken into physical passion. Curiously enough, with darkly widened
> eyes and generously pinked mouth setting off a cheeky beak of a nose, Mr. Pickup
> looks more feminine in the white simulated-leather of his Ganymede disguise than in
> his floor-length knitted dress at court.

Robert Smallwood quotes the director's program note as saying that he sought to
evoke "an atmosphere of spiritual purity which transcends sensuality in the search
for poetic sexuality" (7).

In 1973 Buzz Goodbody got an opportunity to direct *As You Like It* at the Royal
Shakespeare Company in Stratford-upon-Avon. "A feminist and a Communist, she
strove to reclaim the text for women," says Michael Jamieson (Tomarken, p. 640):

> The setting by Christopher Morley consisted of metal tubes hanging round a circular
> playing space—an allusion to Koltai. The court was Edwardian, with Touchstone as
> a cheeky chappie from the Music Hall. In Arden the banished Duke and his follow-
> ers seemed like gentry weekending in the country, with Richard Pasco's detached
> Jaques acknowledging kinship with Chekhov's doctors.

It "had a rock-and-roll score by Guy Woolfenden" and "1970s denim jeans for Rosalind and Orlando in the forest scenes" (Smallwood, p. 14). Eileen Atkins stressed

Rosalind's "sceptical intelligence" and portrayed her as a "mordant satirist of romantic attitudes" (Smallwood, p. 116). Richard David considered her "self-doubting, ironic, inward, almost," a young woman with "a highly alert intelligence combined with a quick and passionate sympathy and a sense of the comic all the more bubbling for the fact that, for much of the play, the lid must be kept firmly clamped upon it" (ibid.).

In 1991 Cheek by Jowl Company's all-male production received immense praise, directed by Declan Donnellan and designed by Nick Ormerod. For Peter Holland, "this was like watching a much-loved picture restored, the colours bright and shining, unnoticed details newly apparent, the brilliance of the whole pristine and exhilarating" (*English Shakespeares* [Cambridge: Cambridge UP, 1997], 91). Its "adaptable basic set was of white canvas," writes Jamieson:

> Fourteen actors trooped in wearing black pants, white collarless shirts, and braces. Jaques, played by a black actor Joe Dixon, spoke the first lines of "All the world's a stage." At "And all the men and women merely players" two men (soon to be Rosalind and Celia) stepped aside. Seconds later the play began. There was no attempt at illusion. Lighting was brilliant and bright. (Tomarken, p. 645)

Adrian Lester took up the role of Rosalind:

> Rosalind was dazzlingly played by Adrian Lester, a young black Londoner of six-foot two, clearly never a French princess but always a male actor. Rosalind's character by some alchemy became more feminine once Lester was doubly disguised as Ganymede, with a straw hat pulled over a headscarf. (Michael Jamieson; Tomarken, p. 645)

"The play-acting of Rosalind-Ganymede," says Peter Holland, "was both more intriguing and simpler than it is when a woman plays Rosalind but the tremendous erotic charge between Rosalind and Orlando had nothing glibly homoerotic about it" (91). This performance "built up to a final scene of dizzying ambiguities, and the conclusion was extraordinarily joyous and celebratory" (Jamieson; Tomarken, p. 645).

In the summer of 1998, Shakespeare's Globe Company mounted an *As You Like It*, and one of their innovations is worth mentioning here. In order to facilitate passing from stage to yard, which was used extensively as an acting space, especially for the wrestling, they built steps in front of the stage. The actors and musicians walked among the groundlings. Duke Frederick, Rosalind, Celia, and others became part of the audience.

Three revivals (in Sheffield, in Manchester, and in Stratford) made 2000 "the year of *As You Like It*" (Michael Dobson, "Shakespeare Performances in England, 2000," *Shakespeare Survey* 54 (2001): 267). Dobson enumerates reasons for this:

> With sheep farming in deep crisis, the relations between the country and the city making regular front-page news, and even the ethics of deer-hunting a topic of national debate, the play suddenly looked more topical than at almost any time since the 1590s. (267)

These productions established Shakespeare's ability to continue to illuminate and entertain the public about their issues and anxieties in the twenty-first century.

As You Like It has been shown on screen only five times. The earliest is a thirty-minute Vitagraph, made in 1912, directed by Charles Kent and featuring Rose Coghlan as Rosalind. Next came Paul Czinner's ninety-seven-minute version by Twentieth-Century Fox in 1936 with Laurence Olivier. Reviewers did not find this to be one of Olivier's happier roles. According to Kenneth Rothwell, Olivier "looks all the more gloomy and morose, better suited as Oliver than as Orlando, for being paired opposite the effervescent Polish-born actress, Elisabeth Bergner, wife of director Paul Czinner, whose sprightly Rosalind saves the picture from utter ruin" (Kenneth S. Rothwell, *A History of Shakespeare on Screen: A Century of Film and Television* [Cambridge: Cambridge UP, 1999], 49). As Rosalind, Bergner "with her charmingly accented English, whirls, turns, sparkles, dazzles, giggles, crosses her arms and offers unconditional love to her best friend, Celia, now cross-dressed as Aliena" (50).

In 1992 Christine Edzard attempted to represent the play by taking "exactly the opposite approach from the 1936 film":

> The Forest of Arden has been transmogrified into a vacant lot on the East London waterfront, and Duke Senior and his merry crew are making sweet the uses of adversity by living out of packing cases. (Ibid., 216–217)

Instead of the pastoral contrast between the city and the country, "it is the wretched of the earth within the city itself that implicitly condemn the callous Thatcherites" (ibid., 217):

> Appropriately for this reading, the court of the bad Duke Frederick seems to have been constructed out of an abandoned bank lobby, and he and his friends cavort in splendid clothing vastly superior to the rags of his good brother's cohorts. (Ibid.)

Emma Croft as Rosalind "brings energy, youth, bounce to the demanding role but there is so much bounce as she leaps and swirls and cavorts that it distracts from the bouncy language" (ibid.). This film was a little better than Olivier's, "but the first truly successful film of this challenging play has yet to be seen," concludes Rothwell (ibid., 218).

The British Broadcasting Company has made *As You Like It* twice for the small screen. In 1937 it broadcast an eleven-minute segment. It was directed by Robert Atkins and featured Margaretta Scott as Rosalind and Ion Swinley as Orlando (Rothwell, p. 95). Between 1978 and 1979 the BBC produced the entire text in 150 minutes. According to Rothwell, it was "an outdoorsy *As You Like It*, filmed on location in May and June at Glamis Castle, Scotland," with Helen Mirren "as a somewhat sullen Rosalind" and Richard Pasco as Jaques (112).

Since film and television are visually oriented forms they presented a problem to Basil Coleman, director of the BBC production. According to James Bulman, Coleman modified the play to accommodate the images of television in this way:

> Taking his cue from satirical qualifications of pastoral inherent in the play, he apparently decided that no television audience could swallow pastoral artifices straight, especially when they are played out in a "location" that by tradition demands realism. Thus he chose to alienate us from the fiction, to make the retreat to Arden seem a game that the players play only to keep from acknowledging the darker lessons of

human nature that Jaques insists on. This is a peculiarly contemporary bias. As a response to Shakespeare's comedy, we may find it inadequate or discomforting. But to find it so, we ought not to dismiss it before considering how it reflects, or speaks to our age. (Tomarken, p. 602)

The production was lop-sided because, on account of its location, it "very nearly became a production more about Mother Nature than about Rosalind, Orlando, or the dukes," comments Susan Willis. "The acting had trouble getting momentum; though Rosalind and Touchstone had moments and Richard Pasco's Jaques was eloquently morose, the overall production never quite sparked into sustained life in its woodland setting" (Tomarken, pp. 619, 622).

EXPLICATION OF KEY PASSAGES

2.1.1–17. "Now, my co-mates . . . in every thing." Audiences already have heard that Duke Senior and a group of merry men are living in exile in the forest of Arden, according to Charles the wrestler, "like the old Robin Hood of England [and] many young gentlemen flock to him . . . and fleet the time carelessly, as they did in the golden world" (1.1.116–119). When Duke Senior asks his companions if "old custom" (2.1.2), that is, long-continued habit (the result of having lived in the forest for a long time) has not made their lives more comfortable than living under the hollow pomp and ceremonies of the court from which he has been expelled by his brother, Duke Frederick, he is ambiguous about the beneficial effects. Are they not feeling freer and safer from peril here than they would have in the malicious and spiteful court torn apart by envy and jealousy? The forests were full of perils, however, like lions and snakes; hence it is a matter of the Duke's honesty that he should be evasive and equivocal in his remarks. His assertion that they do not feel the penalty or consequences of Adam's fall, which brought cold, suffering, disease, and death to the world, is, however, not true. They have no perpetual spring in the forest as there was in Eden. Duke Senior and others experience the differences of the seasons. Duke Senior acknowledges this fact when he says that the icy fangs and rough wind of the winter bite and blow on his body. But while he is freezing with cold, he smiles and says, "This is no flattery: these are counsellors / That feelingly persuade me what I am" (2.1.10–11): that is, a mortal. Again, Duke Senior is conceding that he is living in a post-lapsarian forest, not in Eden, where death did not enter until Adam's fall.

Citing proverbial phrases about the sweetness of adversity, he compares it to an "ugly and venomous" toad that carries in its head a precious stone or pearl that has many virtues, such as the power to cure diseases and to act as an antidote to poison (2.1.13). Living in nature rather than the court, Duke Senior and his lords converse with trees; they find their "books in the running brooks, / Sermons in stones, and good in every thing" (2.1.16–17). This picture of life in the forest rebuts the ideal of pastoral life invoked by Charles. Duke Senior is trying to cheer everybody up and persuade them to accept their hardship, which teaches them fortitude. Without a hint of irony, Amiens calls him "happy" because he "can translate the stubbornness of fortune / Into so quiet and so sweet a style" (2.1.18–20).

2.7.139–166. "All the world's . . . sans every thing." Duke Senior's remark that "This wide and universal theatre / Presents more woeful pageants than the scene"

(2.7.137–138) that they are in gives Jaques the opening to present the most famous speech of this play. The first line may refer to the Latin motto on the sign of the Globe Theatre, in which the play was being performed: "*Totus mundus agit histrionem*" (The whole world plays the actor). The idea of dividing human life into seven ages or stages was a commonplace and regularly taught in schools. Jaques says that all human beings are but actors, for whom a script has already been written. They have their births and deaths, and one person during his or her lifetime plays seven roles or parts. Jaques' is a pessimistic view of human development. First he describes the infant as crying and "puking" (2.7.144) in the arms of a wet nurse who has been paid to breast-feed the child. Then comes a schoolboy, with his bag of books and freshly washed and shining face, walking slowly and reluctantly to school. Having finished school, the youth now turns lover, who emits sighs like a furnace and composes pitiful or sad ballads or songs to flatter his mistress's face (as Orlando does). The lover turns soldier, uses vulgar oaths, and grows whiskers like those of a leopard. Sensitive to possible infractions of his honor, he is violent and quick in quarrels and ever ready to seek out "the bubble reputation" (2.7.152), which has nothing solid about it, even in front of a cannon. After leaving the military, the soldier becomes a judge with a fat belly caused by eating too many chickens offered to him as bribes by criminals hoping to get lenient treatment. He looks stern and wears a dignified beard; his head is full of commonplaces of moral wisdom and trite sayings in proof of his opinions. Then he declines into a ridiculous emaciated old man in slippers; he wears glasses and carries a purse of money on the side. His breeches that he has worn since his youth and preserved carefully are too big for his shrunken body. His loud masculine voice of the past has turned to that of a child, and he wheezes as he breathes. The last stage of all "[i]s second" childhood (2.7.165) and senility. He has lost his teeth, his sight, his sense of taste, everything. Jaques cannot imagine much joy or celebration in human life.

This view, in keeping with the speaker's humor, is melancholic. It should not be taken for Shakespeare's, and it is a reflection on the speaker, not the world. Jaques ignores, for example, the joys of being in love and the pleasures of a good meal.

3.2.406–424. "Yes, one, . . . spot of love in't." Meeting Orlando in the forest of Arden, Rosalind/Ganymede assures him that she/he can cure his malady of love, as "his" uncle has taught "him." Orlando is to imagine that Ganymede is his mistress and to see Ganymede every day as if wooing Rosalind. At that time, pretending to be a fickle and unpredictable young woman, Ganymede will act the reverse of Orlando's stereotype of his beautiful Rosalind. Ganymede will show the variable moods of a woman: sad, happy, capricious, proud, constant only in her inconstancy. She will love him one moment and hate him another. She will amuse and please him and promise to behave properly. She will weep because he is a mere mortal, and soon after she will spit at him. Ganymede's Rosalind will be earthly and carnal. When Orlando sees how inconsistent and erratic Rosalind is, he will give up his mad whim of love for real lunacy. He will thus be like one whom Ganymede had cured and so took an oath to withdraw completely from the world and live in a corner of a monastery. In this way Ganymede will wash Orlando's liver clean, livers being regarded as the source of the passions, including love. Of course, Ganymede is delighted with Orlando's retort: "I would not be cured, youth" (3.2.425). But even the pretence of being with Rosalind is so satisfying to Orlando that he consents to submit to Ganymede's therapy.

Rosalind's speech is paradoxical. It is, after all, better to be madly in love than to be truly mad. Moreover, Rosalind does not want to cure Orlando of his love for her, a love that she reciprocates. She does, however, want Orlando to love her as she truly is: a real woman, not a Petrarchan conceit. Hence, she must disabuse him of his naive view of women.

3.5.35–63. "And why, I pray you? . . . Fare you well." Corin wants to show to Rosalind/Ganymede and Celia/Aliena "a pageant truly play'd / Between the pale complexion of true love / And the red glow of scorn and proud disdain" (3.4.52–54) between Silvius and Phebe. Promising to "prove a busy actor in their play" (3.4.59), Rosalind/Ganymede hides with Corin and Celia/Aliena and watches the two. Phebe scorns Silvius, as Corin predicted. This attitude annoys Rosalind/Ganymede so much that she comes forward and confronts Phebe. She asks whether Phebe comes from such a good background that she has the right to insult Silvius. Ganymede claims to see no beauty in Phebe. Lacking in beauty, why is she so proud and pitiless? Suddenly, Ganymede realizes that Phebe is looking at "him" amorously. Ganymede assures her that "he" sees nothing in her to attract him. Ganymede describes Phebe as the anithesis of the ideal Renaissance beauty, with her dark eyebrows and hair and her yellow complexion.

Then Ganymede asks Silvius why he is following Phebe. Calling him a "foolish shepherd" (3.5.49), Ganymede asks why he is full of sighs and tears: Silvius is a thousand times more proper a man than Phebe is a woman; fools like Silvius give rise to ugly children all over the world; Phebe's mirror does not flatter, only Silvius does; and looking at herself through Silvius's eyes, Phebe considers herself more beautiful than her features would allow. Addressing Phebe again, Ganymede warns her, "[K]now thyself" (3.5.57), that is, don't have such an inflated opinion of your worth. Instead of scorning Silvius, Phebe should be grateful that a good man is in love with her. Ganymede tells her in a somber tone, "Sell when you can, you are not for all markets" (3.5.60). That is, get married as soon as you can; you do not have the beauty to offer yourself the world over. Beg Silvius's pardon, love him, and accept his proposal; ugliness becomes more ugly when an ugly person begins to scoff at another. Ganymede finally advises Silvius to take Phebe and bids them farewell.

Rosalind here is acting in a role similar to the one she performs for Orlando. In each case she is introducing a note of realism. Orlando thinks too highly of Rosalind. Silvius thinks too highly of Phebe and so causes Phebe to think too highly of herself. Just as Rosalind does not want Orlando to stop loving her, so she does not want Silvius to give up Phebe. But she understands that Silvius can win Phebe only if he, like Orlando, sees his beloved for who and what she is. If Silvius insists that Phebe is too good for him, Phebe will agree and reject him.

4.1.94–108. "No, faith, . . . not for love." Orlando had promised to meet Rosalind/Ganymede for a lesson in the cure of his love-sickness, but he is late. This tardiness infuriates Rosalind, but soon she gets into a holiday mood and invites him to woo her. Ganymede says that as Rosalind "I will not have you" (4.1.91–92), and Orlando responds, "Then in mine own person, I die" (4.1.93). Dying for love? No, says Rosalind, die by proxy. Trying to disabuse him of his illusions about sacrifices in love, Ganymede reminds him that in the 6,000-year-old history of the world (based on biblical calculations), no man has died in a love-cause. She builds her case: Troilus, the lover of Cressida, met an unromantic end at the hands of Achilles, who killed him "with a Grecian club" (4.1.98); even though Troilus's love, Cressida, abandoned him, he did not die because of her infidelity. Leander, another doomed classical lover, would have lived many years though Hero of Sestos had become a nun, if it had not been for a hot midsummer night. Leander didn't drown in the Hellespont because he was trying to swim to Hero. Leander just wanted to cool off in the water, got a cramp, and died. The foolish chroniclers of that age declared that his drowning was because of love. Rosalind/Ganymede concludes that "men have died from time to time, and worms have eaten them," but they never died of love (4.1.106–107). Orlando, unconvinced by Ganymede's common sense, would not have his Rosalind believe Ganymede's words, and he protests that Rosalind's frown might kill him.

Annotated Bibliography

Barber, C. L. *Shakespeare's Festive Comedy: A Study of Dramatic Form and Its Relation to Social Custom.* Princeton: Princeton UP, 1959. Analyzes the play in the social role and folk connections of Elizabethan comedy. Argues that *As You Like It* embraces both idyll and realism, and the retreat to the green world of Arden allows the characters a respite from the workaday world.

Brissenden, Alan, ed. *As You Like It.* The Oxford Shakespeare. Oxford: Oxford UP, 1993. Discusses the play's textual and performance history, its sources and themes of love, pastoral, and doubleness. Includes an appendix on the play's songs and music.

Bristol, Michael D. "Shameless in Arden: Early Modern Theatre and the Obsolescence of Popular Theatricality." In *Print, Manuscript, Performance: The Changing Relations of the Media in Early Modern England.* Ed. Arthur F. Marotti and Michael D. Bristol. Columbus: Ohio State UP, 2000. 279–306. Bristol argues that this play "experiments with a social world where the idea of mutual consent is really taken seriously. At the end of the play, an archaic fratricidal order has simply withered away, to be replaced by radically new forms of social desire" (303).

Erickson, Peter. *Patriarchal Structures in Shakespeare's Drama.* Berkeley: U of California P, 1985. An analysis of the literary representation of gender and the political implications of that representation in *As You Like It* and other plays.

Grady, Hugh. *Shakespeare's Universal Wolf: Studies in Early Modern Reification.* Oxford: Clarendon P, 1996. Examines the power relations and social structure of society in the play. Shakespeare is a product of his own historical period, and a 400-year train of contingencies has shaped those who are reading these texts now.

Knowles, Richard, ed. *As You Like It.* New Variorum Edition. New York: MLA, 1977. A comprehensive account of scholarship and criticism up to the 1970s. An annotated text of the play, this edition provides discussions of the date of composition, textual history, source material, the text of *Rosalynde* (Shakespeare's major source for the comedy), and a full bibliography.

Smallwood, Robert. *Shakespeare at Stratford: "As You Like It."* London: Thomson Learning, 2003. A critical account of the productions of the play by the Royal Shakespeare Company at Stratford-upon-Avon from 1946 to 2001. Includes cast lists and production credits.

Tomarken, Edward, ed. *"As You Like It" from 1600 to the Present: Critical Essays.* New York: Garland, 1997. A collection of articles on different aspects of the play; also, a reprint of Charles Johnson's *Love in a Forest.*

Tvordi, Jessica. "Female Alliance and the Construction of Homoeroticism in *As You Like It* and *Twelfth Night.*" In *Maids and Mistresses, Cousins and Queens: Women's Alliances in Early Modern England.* Ed. Susan Frye and Karen Robertson. New York: Oxford UP, 1999. In Shakespeare's works, women form alliances with other women. These alliances are "characterized by friendship, familial duty, socioeconomic dependence, service, the rejection of heterosexuality, and, in some cases, [by] homoerotic desire" (114). By the end of the plays, though, these bonds between women have yielded to heterosexual unions that limit female social and sexual power.

Twelfth Night

Gina Macdonald

PLOT SUMMARY

1.1. Act 1 opens with Duke Orsino and a retinue of lords and attendants (an all-male court) listening to musicians playing sweet, soulful music. The Duke is wallowing in his pose of the romantic, lovesick suitor. A piece of music is so lovely that he calls for it to be replayed ("That strain again" 1.1.4), then finds it not as sweet a second time, as if overindulgence in music, like overindulgence in eating, can cloy the senses. Orsino describes music as "the food of love" (1.1.1) because it creates in him a romantic mood and feeds his fantasies as he thinks about his love for Olivia. However, his imagery reverses the traditional pattern of the deer pursued by hounds, with the deer the woman and the hunter male. In his image, he is the deer, hunted by a destructive goddess, rather as Actaeon was pursued and killed by his own hounds as punishment for seeing Diana naked. Orsino's attendant Curio tries unsuccessfully to distract him from this melancholy moping (punning on "hart" and "heart," 1.1.16), as does Valentine, appropriately named for the saint of love. Valentine is the go-between who brings word that Olivia has vowed to mourn her dead brother for seven years (another act of excessive behavior). Orsino speculates that she will care enormously for a lover if she showers this much devotion on a brother; he feels that Cupid's golden arrow has pierced his heart and that therefore he has no choice but to love Olivia. Orsino is full of longing but seems insincere, more in love with love at this point than with a real person as he departs to languish voluptuously in his flower garden.

1.2. A shipwrecked Viola lands in Illyria, a distant, mythical place on the Adriatic coast opposite Italy, and fears for the life of her twin brother, Sebastian. The ship's captain tries to comfort her, saying that he saw her brother bound to a strong mast and riding high above the waves. The captain informs Viola about Duke Orsino, a man her father has talked about. He quotes the gossip about his unrequited courtship of Olivia, a virtuous maid in mourning, and Viola wishes she could attach herself to Olivia's service until she has a better sense of the lay of the land. However, since Olivia will not accept any new servants, Viola pays the captain to help her disguise herself as a eunuch and get into the service of the duke. The captain agrees to help. The disguise will give her the protection of being a male, rather than a weak and solitary woman. It will also explain her high-pitched voice and more feminine features, since eunuchs were castrated when young so that they could sing soprano parts in church services.

1.3. This scene introduces Sir Toby Belch, Olivia's fun-loving, drunken uncle, and Maria, Olivia's handmaiden/chambermaid. Olivia is most distressed at Sir Toby's late-night carousing, disorderly habits, and violations of her sense of propriety. Sir Toby's drinking companion, Sir Andrew Aguecheek, a tall, thin man with an income of 300 ducats a year (much of which he foolishly wastes in carousing), has been courting Olivia without success. When he enters, he and Toby joke in a silly way, engaging in puns and intentional (or unintentional) misunderstandings, until Maria can no longer stand their company. After Maria leaves, the two men continue to quibble amusingly, and Sir Toby encourages Sir Andrew to woo Olivia, because, he argues, the only competition is Duke Orsino, and Olivia will not marry above her station. The two men set off for their evening revels as they joke about dancing, food, drink, and women, and punning on multiple meanings of "caper" (a dance, a seasoning, and an adventure).

1.4. Viola, in man's attire, now supposedly the boy Cesario, has been in Count Orsino's service for an unspecified period, but Valentine remarks that the Duke has already shown Cesario favors. Indeed, Orsino enters calling for Cesario, to whom he has already revealed the secrets of his attachment to Olivia. The Duke now sends Cesario as his representative to court Olivia for him, arguing that she will pay greater heed to the pleas of youth and particularly from so womanly a young man, whose lips and neck and voice have already caught Orsino's attention. The irony, of course, is that the audience perceives Orsino already attracted to Viola's womanly appearance, but as Cesario, a man, just as very shortly they will see Olivia's growing affection for Cesario as a potential suitor. The gender confusions are part of the intrigue and humor of the story. The final lines of scene 4 reveal Viola's growing love for Orsino and the irony of her being sent to woo Olivia for him when she would have him wooing her.

1.5. Scene 5, set in Olivia's house, introduces the perceptive and quick-witted clown Feste, who cleverly converses with the equally bright Maria. Their joking about "a good hanging" (1.5.19–20) transforms a serious topic into sexual innuendo, while the pun on colors and collars (1.5.6) connects worldly deceptions, military standards, and hangman's nooses. Feste implies that Maria is attracted to Sir Toby, but Olivia enters with Malvolio before this idea can be explored. Olivia is peevish about Feste's jests, especially when he suggests that his wits are sharper than his clownish attire suggests and that she is the real fool in the household for her excessive mourning of her brother, even though she believes he has gone to heaven. She has cloistered herself like a nun, and her grief seems as much a pose as Orsino's supposed love. Olivia is displeased with Feste's criticism, but she comes to Feste's defense when Malvolio jealously denounces him. Olivia says Malvolio is obsessed with "self-love" (1.5.90) and makes mountains out of molehills.

Maria enters to announce Viola/Cesario, who is being kept from entering by a drunken Sir Toby. However, Olivia wants no more suits from Orsino and does not wish to admit Cesario. She is irritated with Malvolio, and Sir Toby is so far gone with drink that he confuses "lethargy" with "lechery" (1.5.124–125). Olivia has Feste take Sir Toby away ("the fool shall look to the madman" 1.5.137–138), but she cannot get rid of Malvolio, who describes Cesario's persistence, ill manners, and youth.

Veiled, she meets with Viola/Cesario, who begins the love-suit with exaggerated praise, but then admits that s/he cannot carry on in this vein until s/he actually sees the lady s/he has been sent to woo. Clearly, she wants to see her rival, but Olivia is taken by this unorthodox approach and finally agrees to a private meeting. Playing on Olivia's name and the association of olive branches with peace, Cesario fulfills Orsino's commission, but in doing so wins both Olivia's confession that she absolutely cannot love Orsino and, unknowingly, Olivia's love. In fact, Olivia's questions about the parentage of Cesario would suggest to Elizabethan viewers her interest in "his" acceptability as a potential marriage partner of the right social rank. When Cesario exits, Olivia comments in a soliloquy on how quickly she has fallen in love and then, on second thought, decides this sudden love is not a problem and she will not resist. She sends Malvolio after "that same peevish messenger" (1.5.300), providing her servant with a ring Cesario has supposedly left behind, but actually a gift from her to "him." Malvolio is to tell Cesario that if "he" will return tomorrow, Olivia will explain why she will not marry the Duke.

2.1. Set along a seacoast, this scene shows Viola's twin brother, Sebastian, alive, accompanied by Antonio, a sea captain wanted by Count Orsino for questionable maritime activities, possibly piracy, but one to whom Sebastian owes a major debt for having rescued him from drowning. Sebastian fears that his sister, Viola, has drowned and feels that his luck has been so bad that he doesn't want to taint Antonio with it. Antonio has many enemies in Orsino's court and, though he wishes to serve Sebastian, allows him to go to court without him because of the danger. But as soon as Sebastian leaves, Antonio follows him—out of friendship or perhaps even stronger feelings.

2.2. Malvolio catches up with Viola/Cesario and, with scornful words about Cesario's ill-treating a lady, tosses Olivia's ring at Cesario's feet. Viola, in the soliloquy that follows, is of course confused because she has left no ring with Olivia. Her understanding of female behavior makes her realize that Olivia has fallen in love with her in her disguised male persona, and she feels pity for this her rival: "Poor lady, she were better love a dream" (2.2.26). Viola continues to declaim about the frailty of women and despairs of a situation in which Orsino is in love with Olivia, Olivia is in love with Cesario/Viola, and Viola is in love with Orsino, who thinks she is a boy. She concludes that only time can untangle this mess, for it is too hard for her to unravel.

2.3. Sir Toby and Sir Andrew are up after midnight, drinking and calling for more wine from "Marian," that is, Maria (2.3.14) and for a love song from Feste. Amid the singing, drinking, and nonsensical ravings, they manage to awaken Malvolio, and he soundly berates them for disturbing the household. He calls them "mad" and witless, with "no respect of place, persons, nor time" (2.3.86, 91–92), while they mock him with song. Significantly, Sir Toby calls attention to the reality of the situation: Sir Toby is the brother of the Lady Olivia; Malvolio is merely a steward, a servant in the household. In a famous line, Sir Toby asks Malvolio, "Dost thou think because thou art virtuous, there shall be no more cakes and ale?" (2.3.114–116). That is, one person's disapproval cannot prohibit food and drink and celebrations for the rest of the world. Malvolio's puritanical outburst makes the whole group resolve to get revenge because he is extremely puffed up with his self-importance and condemns those whose values differ from his own.

While the men mock him, Maria comes up with a clever plan that will make Malvolio look incredibly foolish to Olivia. Maria, whose handwriting is much like that of her mistress, determines to write love letters to Malvolio as if they were from Olivia and thereby to encourage him to behave foolishly. Since it is already so late, Sir Toby invites Sir Andrew to stay up drinking for the rest of the night.

2.4. Orsino again calls for music, this time from the jester Feste. (Olivia's father, we learn, took great delight in Feste's humor and song.) As music plays, Orsino and Cesario speak of the imperfections of love. Cesario pretends to be in love with a woman of Orsino's "complexion," and Orsino encourages him to look for someone younger. Orsino compares women to roses, whose beauty fades quickly, while Viola/Cesario, not surprisingly, is slightly disapproving of this view. The dialogue is ironic on several levels, for the audience understands that Orsino is speaking to a woman disguised as a boy, a part actually played on the Elizabethan stage by a boy, a fact that further complicates the gender games in the play. When Cesario describes the woman he loves, it is really Viola describing the man she loves, Orsino, but of course he is blind to that fact. Feste sings a song about a man "killed" by the cruelty of a beautiful woman but is soon dismissed by Orsino, whose fickleness and changeable moods Feste criticizes.

In this odd mood, Orsino once again sends Cesario to court Olivia for him, with a jewel to prove his love. Before she goes, Viola as Cesario tries to convince Orsino that his love might not be returned; Orsino replies that women are inconstant and incapable of the depth of feeling men experience when in love. Viola, who is deeply in love with Orsino, tries to persuade him that women too can be "as true of heart" as men may be (2.4.106). Her evidence is a story she makes up about a sister who loved constantly, though she never told her love, and pined away "like Patience on a monument, / Smiling at grief" (2.4.114–115). Her speech, peppered with phrases like "were I a woman" (2.4.108), calls the audience's attention to the reality of the gender disguises and her situation and provides hints that later Orsino will look back on and understand. However, at this point he is blind to what she really is.

2.5. The subplot with Maria, Sir Toby, and Malvolio continues, with a love letter to bait Malvolio written and ready to be put in use. Fabian and Sir Andrew are present, too, and the plotters hide behind a tree to observe Malvolio's discovery of and response to Maria's contrived "Olivia" letter. As Malvolio approaches, he is already thinking of an alliance with Olivia and fantasizing about how it will change his life and free him to lord it over Sir Toby and correct his fun-loving behavior, a fact that irritates Sir Toby. The discovery of the anonymous letter, with its silly, contrived riddle, convinces Malvolio that his fantasy can indeed become reality, that Olivia loves him. The famous line about "Some are born great, some achieve greatness, and some have greatness thrust upon 'em" (2.5.145–146) convinces him of Olivia's desire, and he supposes that the letter's instructions to wear yellow stockings cross-gartered (with black) will be a sign between the lovers that the message has been received. In fact, the stockings are meant to make him look absurd and to sum up in their colors the humors, or bodily fluids, that shape his personality (black bile, or melancholy, and yellow bile, choler). Malvolio, in other words, falls for the plot; and Sir Andrew, Sir Toby, and Fabian marvel at Maria's ingenuity and Malvolio's overweening arrogance.

3.1. On her way to see Olivia, Viola/Cesario encounters Feste, who is as witty as ever. However, his quips and word games lead to the confession that he does not care for Viola/Cesario. Feste jokes that Jove needs to send her a beard (3.1.45), a line sometimes taken to mean he recognizes her gender, since he could mean that she needs a man wearing a beard. When Cesario responds that s/he is almost sick for a beard, she means Orsino's, not one of her own. Viola makes a final statement about the skill of professional fools and their knowledge of human psychology, perhaps Shakespeare's tribute to the actor who played the role of Feste.

Sir Toby jokes with Viola/Cesario at the entranceway, as Sir Andrew listens. Then Olivia and her gentlewoman arrive. Sir Andrew is impressed by Cesario's poetic courtly phrasing, as is Olivia, who quickly drives the others away so she and Cesario can speak in private. Here is a most embarrassing moment for Viola, for her male disguise has worked too well, and Olivia confesses her love. She apologizes for the ruse of the ring in 2.2 but fears he has laughed at her about it. She tells Cesario that Orsino has no hope with her and that the ring she sent after Cesario indicates where her affections truly lie, for only a thin veil hides her true feelings for him. Viola, stunned at the suddenness of this "love," speaks her thoughts directly: "I pity you" (3.1.123). Olivia argues that pity is "a degree in love," but Cesario replies, "No, . . . very oft we pity enemies" (3.1.124–125). Olivia recognizes that her proffer of love has been wasted on this youth, and in effect says that Cesario is probably still too young to appreciate a woman. But his future wife, whoever she may be, will reap the benefit of "a proper man" when he matures (3.1.133).

Though she sends him on his way, she cannot help but call him back, hoping for a change of heart. Olivia feels scorned and yet retains some hope that time will bring him to love her. In an aside to the audience she admits she finds love even in Cesario's contempt and then swears to Cesario by all she values that she loves him so much that neither wit nor reason can hide her passion, concluding "Love sought is good, but given unsought is better" (3.1.156). Viola tries to explain that s/he is not what s/he seems to be and swears, accurately, that no woman has ever been mistress of her heart. Olivia no longer indulges in grief but wholeheartedly turns to love and its pursuit, hoping for another chance to move Cesario to love and entreating him to return soon.

3.2. Sir Andrew has finally realized that Olivia is more interested in Cesario than in him. His companions, Sir Toby and Fabian, assert that, since Olivia knew of his presence, she was only pretending to love Cesario in order to make Sir Andrew jealous. Sir Toby encourages Sir Andrew to write a letter challenging Cesario to a duel in order to impress Olivia with his prowess and thereby win her affection, though Sir Toby tells Fabian that he expects such a letter will be full of lies and foolishness. He tells Fabian to incite Cesario to battle. Sir Toby thinks that neither is man enough to fight but that a forced confrontation should be amusing. Sir Toby "psychoanalyzes" Sir Andrew in terms of the humors as lacking blood, hence his paleness and his cowardice.

Maria comes in to say that the plot against Malvolio is working better than they had hoped. The steward has obeyed every instruction in her letter: the peculiar dress and the inordinate smiling. His unaccustomed smiles create more wrinkles on his face than are found on a newly published map of the world crisscrossed with lines and are bound to irritate Olivia so much that Maria is convinced that Olivia will strike him.

3.3. Antonio explains that his fear for Sebastian's safety in so dangerous and unfamiliar a territory has induced him to follow his friend. Sebastian wants to stroll through the town and see the sights, but Antonio warns that doing so could be dangerous because he (Antonio) once fought Orsino at sea and will pay dearly if captured. He has gotten them a room at an inn called the Elephant and will scout out some food while Sebastian explores the neighborhood. Antonio leaves his purse (the Elizabethan equivalent of a wallet) with Sebastian, who is without money, in case he sees some item he might wish to purchase. They then separate.

3.4. This long, complex scene brings together the different players in the various plots and subplots. It begins with the Malvolio subplot. Olivia is in the midst of making plans to entertain Cesario. She has sent for him and thinks, cynically, that Cesario might be impressed by her wealth, if not by her. Maria interrupts her planning with word about Malvolio's strange behavior, saying that he acts as if he were possessed by demons, warning Olivia to be careful around him and planting the idea that he may be insane. Olivia muses that love has perhaps made her as mad as Malvolio if extreme sadness is as mad as extreme merriment.

When Malvolio enters, his transformed demeanor, his beaming smile, his odd dress, and his insinuations about her love for him disturb Olivia. She hates cross-gartered stockings, as Maria knew when she hatched the plot. Malvolio calls attention to this part of his attire, quotes lines from the anonymous letter, thinking she will recognize them, and acts in far too bold and insinuating a fashion for a servant. Olivia is baffled but thinks this odd behavior is a passing eccentricity, a "midsummer madness" (3.4.56). When a servant brings word that Cesario has arrived, she puts Maria in charge of handling Malvolio and expresses concern for him, saying she would give up half her dowry to keep him from harm.

Malvolio, of course, interprets her concern as confirmation of the letter and proof of her love. As a consequence, when Sir Toby, Maria, and Fabian goad him and tease him about being possessed by devils or engaged in witchcraft, he rudely asserts that he does not care what they think; they are too far beneath him in importance. Fabian remarks that if Malvolio's transformation were presented on the stage, no one would believe it. This remark is Shakespeare's way of calling attention to the unreality of the stage but also to his skill in making his characters ring true despite the artificiality of the production. Fabian suggests that they try to make Malvolio truly mad, and Sir Toby contrives the idea of locking him in a dark room and treating him as if he were mad for their personal pleasure and for his reformation of character.

When Sir Andrew arrives, the merry crew of schemers is ready for another game or, as Fabian says, "More matter for a May morning" (3.4.142). Sir Toby does a comic reading of Sir Andrew's short, contradictory, back-pedaling, nonsensical letter challenging Cesario. They send Sir Andrew to the orchard to await Cesario's arrival, while Sir Toby, who has no intention of delivering the letter, because it would not frighten anyone, moves to deliver the challenge in person, hoping Sir Andrew and Cesario will be so frightened of each other that some amusing by-play will occur. Then Olivia and Cesario appear, with Olivia apologizing for speaking her heart and offering Cesario a jeweled portrait of her. Cesario still seems to plead Orsino's case, but Olivia says that all her love and honor now belong to Cesario.

After Olivia leaves, Sir Toby delivers Sir Andrew's challenge to Cesario orally and exaggerates Sir Andrew's fighting skills enough to make Cesario/Viola ready to return quickly to Orsino's house, preferably with a guard to protect him/her on the way. Sir Toby sends Fabian along with Cesario/Viola, and Fabian continues to describe Sir Andrew's ferocity and anger. In like manner, Sir Toby confronts Sir Andrew with a frightening description of Cesario's martial skills and reputation. Sir Andrew is ready to give Cesario his horse and recant his challenge when Fabian and Cesario arrive. A comic scene ensues in which the reluctant fighters try to flee their opponents while they are being pushed to attack by their seconds.

Cesario/Viola and Sir Andrew have just drawn swords, and Cesario/Viola is ready to confess the truth about her sex, when Antonio, the sea captain, comes to her rescue, thinking she is Sebastian, who has been strolling about town. (We are meant to accept the comic premise that the twins are identical despite their gender difference, and also identically garbed.) However, several of Orsino's officers arrest him. In an aside, he tells Cesario/Viola that his arrest results from trying to find him (that is, Sebastian), and Antonio unhappily asks for his money back. Antonio expresses grief that he will no longer be in a position to help his friend. Cesario/Viola, however, not knowing who he is, shocks Antonio by saying she knows nothing about any money. Antonio thinks "Sebastian" is being ungrateful, a false friend, returning ill for good. His words of disappointment, however, mention the shipwreck, the rescue, and the name Sebastian, and therefore make Viola finally realize that he has mistaken her for her brother and that Sebastian must be alive. Now that there is no more danger for him, Sir Andrew is eager to continue the fight with Cesario, though Sir Toby still thinks the duel will come to nothing because Sir Andrew is an unskilled fighter and a coward.

4.1. Feste mistakes Sebastian for Cesario and is miffed that Sebastian refuses to acknowledge their acquaintance; speaks in an aloof, stiff, and distant manner; engages in none of the word games Viola/Cesario usually enjoys; and, adding insult to injury, tosses money to get Feste to leave him alone. Sir Andrew accosts Sebastian, striking him because he thinks he is the weakling Cesario, but when Sir Toby tries to keep Sebastian from fighting back, Sebastian directs his attack at Toby. Luckily, before anyone is hurt, Olivia stops the fighting, chides her uncle, and asks Sebastian, whom she mistakes for Cesario, to "be rul'd by" her (4.1.64). Sebastian, struck by her beauty (another case of love at first sight) and thinking himself caught up in some dream, agrees to do so.

4.2. Maria brings Feste, disguised as Sir Topas, the curate, to bait and tease Malvolio. For modern readers the scene is sad and pathetic, though for Elizabethans who enjoyed bearbaiting and other such cruel sports it would have been comic. Malvolio insists on his sanity, while Feste insists on his madness. Malvolio's most significant lines herein describe his plight, locked away when he is "no more mad than you are" (4.2.47–48). He asks to have his sanity tested through questions, but Feste asks such absurd ones that no sane person could answer them. Feste also lies, telling Malvolio that the dark room is full of light provided by bay windows and creating confusing contradictions, saying windows are as transparent as barricades (which are solid) and as bright as ebony, which is black (4.2.36–38).

Sir Toby asks Feste to end the tormenting of Malvolio because "I am now so far in offense with my niece that I cannot pursue with any safety this sport t' the up-shot" (4.2.69–71). Feste, however, has not forgiven Malvolio for trying to get Olivia to dismiss him and for calling him "a barren rascal" (1.5.83–84). Feste drops his disguise to torment Malvolio even more, then fakes a conversation between himself and his other persona, Sir Topas. Malvolio begs for paper and ink so he can send a message to Olivia, and Feste exits singing a song about the character Vice, who raged angrily on the stage in medieval morality plays. During this scene Malvolio is heard but not seen; in some versions he speaks from under the stage and in others from behind the stage. This scene shows a darker side of Feste and a more human side of the tormented Malvolio.

4.3. Sebastian debates whether he or Olivia is mad. She has given him a pearl (part of her plan to use her riches to turn young Cesario's head) and treats him so like an acquaintance that he doesn't know what to think. He also puzzles over what has happened to Antonio, who he knows was looking for him. Sebastian concludes that Olivia could not command her servants and run her household so smoothly if she were mad. Olivia makes the most of his pliability and rushes him to a parson, who marries them. She promises a true wedding celebration appropriate to her social position later.

5.1. Act 5 begins with Fabian's begging Feste for a glimpse of Malvolio's letter to Olivia. They are interrupted by Duke Orsino, his attendants, and Cesario/Viola, all coming to see Olivia. After a bit of clowning between the Duke and Feste that earns the jester some money, Cesario/Viola points out Antonio, who is brought before the Duke by his officers, and tells Orsino that Antonio is the man who rescued her from Sir Andrew. Orsino remembers him as the captain of a poor ship with which he accomplished great feats against Orsino's forces. One of Orsino's nephews lost a leg in that sea battle. Antonio says he was never a thief or a pirate, though he did end up in battle with Orsino. He claims to have saved the ungrateful boy at Orsino's side (Cesario/Viola) from drowning and to have faced danger for his sake ever since, only to deny Antonio his own purse when he most needed it. He also claims to have been in town only a day, though he has been at his friend's side for three months, a statement which makes Orsino dismiss the entire story as a lie or "madness" (5.1.98) because Viola/Cesario has been in his service all that time.

Olivia and her attendants now enter, and the conversation which ensues is at cross-purposes. Olivia thinks her new husband is playing her false, not following her instructions to stay inside, pretending not to love her, and speaking perversely about his obligations to the Duke. Orsino is angry that Olivia has rejected his love and angrier still that Cesario has played him false and courted Olivia. He threatens to sacrifice the "lamb" he loves (Cesario) to spite Olivia ("a raven's heart within a dove" 5.1.130–131). To his embarrassment and to Olivia's consternation, Viola, still disguised as Cesario, declares her love for Orsino. However, when Olivia claims to have already married Cesario, and brings forth the priest to confirm the marriage, Orsino is enraged at the supposed dissembling and betrayal.

Before violence can erupt, Sir Toby and Sir Andrew charge in, complaining loudly of the damage Cesario did to them in battle. Viola is shocked and confused, but at that moment Sebastian joins the group and all the confusions suddenly become clear. He is apologizing for hurting Olivia's uncle when he realizes that everyone is gaping at him. The Duke gives voice to what all see: "One face, one voice, one habit, and two persons" (5.1.216). Sebastian is overjoyed to see Antonio again and explains how distressed he has been at having missed his friend. Antonio does not know which of the two people he sees is Sebastian. Sebastian is confused, too, because he never had a brother. The twins exchange family information to confirm their kinship, as if it were necessary, but Viola promises to confirm her identity by taking them to the captain who has her clothing and possessions and by changing into attire that will reveal her true feminine identity. (There seems to be some suggestion that Malvolio has had the captain locked up. How this could be possible is unclear.)

Sebastian realizes that Olivia thought she was marrying Viola, and the Duke is delighted that the boy he has grown to love is instead a woman whom he can marry. He feels confidant in her affection because she, in her disguise, had often said that she would never love a woman as much as she loved him. In the midst of such revelations, Fabian adds the news that Sir Toby has married Maria for her clever plot against Malvolio, and Feste finally delivers Malvolio's letter to Olivia. All agree that it does not sound like the ravings of a madman.

Malvolio's story reveals the prank played on him, a prank Fabian confirms. Olivia feels he has been "most notoriously abus'd" (5.1.379), but Malvolio, after Feste's description of their trick on him for his pomposity, can think only of revenge. Orsino looks forward happily to marrying Viola, while Feste tempers the optimism of the ending with a song about wind and rain, the pangs of maturation, and the players' wish to please their audience.

PUBLICATION HISTORY

The play seems to have been written sometime between 1599 and early 1602, with "about 1600" frequently cited as the date. Francis Meres, who listed many of Shakespeare's plays in *Palladis Tamia* (1598), did not mention it. The earliest reference to the play appears in a February 2, 1602, entry of the *Diary* of John Manningham, a Middle Temple law student (published by John Payne Collier in 1831):

> At our feast wee had a play called "Twelue Night, or What you Will," much like the Commedy of Errors or Menechmi in Plautus, but most like and neere to that in Italian called Inganni. A good practise in it to make the Steward beleeue his Lady widdowe was in love with him, by counterfeyting a letter as from his Lady in generall termes, telling him what shee liked best in him, and prescribing his gesture in smiling, his apparail, & c., and then when he came to practise making him beleeue they tooke him to be mad.

However, this is not likely to have been the play's premier performance.

Allusions in the play seem to confirm 1600 as the date of composition, particularly the following: (1) Fabian's joke about "a pension of thousands to be paid from the Sophy" (2.5.180–181), a reference to Sir Anthony Shirley's reception by the Shah of Persia (the Sophy) in 1599–1600; (2) Maria's comparison of Malvolio's smiling face to "the new map, with the augmentation of the Indies"(3.2.79–80), which refers to a 1600 map that showed America (the Indies) as larger than it had appeared in earlier projections; and (3) Viola's description of Feste as "wise enough to play the fool" (3.1.60), echoing comedic actor Robert Armin's poem "True it is, he plays the fool indeed" of 1600–1601 (see *Twelfth Night, Or, What You Will*, New Variorum Edition, ed. Horace Howard Furness [Philadelphia; J. B. Lippincott, 1901], vi–xi for discussion of dating). Some argue for 1602, not long after *Hamlet* was completed, but most agree that *Twelfth Night* was written about the same time as *As You Like It* and *Much Ado about Nothing*, and that it has similar thematic concerns.

In *The First Night of "Twelfth Night"* (New York: Macmillan, 1954), Leslie Hotson argued that the first court performance actually occurred on Twelfth Night, Janu-

ary 6, 1601, when Queen Elizabeth entertained Don Virginio Orsino, Duke of Brac-
ciano. However, since the role of Orsino would mock rather than entertain such a
visitor, most critics do not share Hotson's view. We do know that Shakespeare's
company acted a play at court on Twelfth Night, January 6, the same day as Don
Orsino's visit, and his report home to his Duchess described seeing a comedy that
contained music and dance. John Dover Wilson, in his "New Shakespeare" edition
of the play (Cambridge: Cambridge UP, 1964), found the number of legal jests indicative of an Inns of Court production (95). Likewise, G.P.V. Akrigg, in a brief
Shakespeare Quarterly article "*Twelfth Night* at the Middle Temple" (9.3 [Summer
1958]: 422–424), argues that John Manningham's diary reports a performance of the
play at the Middle Temple in February (Candlemas), 1602. He demonstrates the
precision with which the internal descriptions correspond to the Middle Temple
Hall and the many legal references that suggest that the play was first performed in
the Middle Temple, attended by justices and barristers/lawyers. Akrigg takes Malvolio's comments about ignorance and trials (4.2) to be double-edged, good-natured,
Twelfth Night humor "tailor-made" for representatives of the courts (424).

The play was one of sixteen registered by Blount and Jaggard on November 8,
1623, before publication in that year of the First Folio edition. *Twelfth Night* was
first published in the 1623 Folio, in, says Hardin Craig, a good text that followed a
theater promptbook or possibly a transcript of a promptbook, as internal references confirm. The role of eunuch, for example, implies an ability to sing, but
when Orsino asks for a song, Cesario sends for Feste, as if the boy playing Viola
was not adequate to the singing Shakespeare had intended for the role. Other signs
of emendation after performance are the confusion of Orsino's rank (the duke at
times is a count), the dropping of a song in an early version and its replacement
with Viola's more emotionally satisfying story of an imaginary sister, and the substitution of Fabian for Feste as accomplice in the Malvolio scheme to turn Feste
into more of an ironic commentator. This Folio edition contains the only surviving version of *Twelfth Night*, the thirteenth play in the Comedy section. All other
copies of the text derive from this source.

Apart from the difficulties just noted, the Folio text is unusually clean, with few
problems for an editor. The Folio version was already divided into acts and scenes—
although according to the Riverside edition (Boston: Houghton Mifflin, 1997), the
fact that the stage is cleared at 3.4.272 suggests that "a new scene probably should
have been marked at that point" (474). The anti-profanity act of 1606 might be responsible for the mildness of the swearing in the text; possibly the bookkeeper toned
down the language (like that of Sir Toby) to meet the requirements of the law. Much
ado has been made about a typesetting error in which Antonio's name was recorded
as Antonia. Robert K. Turner Jr.'s *Shakespeare Quarterly* article, "The Text of *Twelfth
Night*" (26.2 [Spring 1975]: 128–138) provides a very thorough exploration of textual
concerns and concludes that the First Folio text is "two steps away from authorial
papers and that the promptbook was not in the line of transmission" (138).

SOURCES FOR THE PLAY

Twelfth Night is based on a combination of sources. The Olivia-Orsino, Viola-
Sebastian plot derives from the story of Apolonius and Silla in Barnabe Riche's

Farewell to Militarie Profession (1581), an adaptation of Belleforest's French version (1571) of a Bandello novella (1554), based on the Sienese comedy *Gl'Ingannati* ("The Deceived," 1531). *Gl'Ingannati* has in its cast the characters Fabio and Malvolti, and a pair of separated twins. It makes references to Epiphany, or Twelfth Night, and ends with a young woman's marrying the lord for whom she has been wooing the young lady her brother eventually marries. Like Shakespeare's play, Riche's adaptation explores the multifaceted nature of love, but Riche's theme is a negative one, with the man a hunter and the lovers foolish and interchangeable (like Shakespeare's immature young lovers in *A Midsummer Night's Dream*). Riche's sea captain, for example, his marriage proposal rejected, threatens to take Silla (Viola) by force and to keep her captive for his pleasure, and the Viola and Olivia characters are very much alike. John Manningham recognized the Italian source when he saw the 1602 production and recorded the connection in his diary; more modern critics have noted the parallels between Olivia's phrasing and that of Riche's lady. The heroine, Silla, daughter of the Governor of Cyprus and disguised as the page Cesare, perhaps provided Shakespeare with the idea of Viola's disguise as Cesario. Shakespeare omitted from Riche's story the heroine's previous love for the Duke, her pre-shipwreck adventures, and her imprisonment for allegedly impregnating the Duke's beloved (an act committed by her twin brother). Riche's Viola character strips in front of the Olivia figure to prove her true gender, an action Shakespeare omits.

Charles Prouty in his edition of the play (New York: Penguin, 1978) also attributes bits and pieces of the play to Sir Philip Sidney's *Arcadia*, the play *Sir Clyomon and Clamydes*, and Emanuel Forde's *Parismus*, which includes an Olivia and a Violetta as well as a shipwreck. These sources deal in various ways with twins and with a page (a young maiden in disguise) wooing on behalf of the master (Prouty, p.15). Forde's description of the tender devotion Violetta feels for Pollipus clearly affected Shakespeare's perception of the Viola-Orsino relationship. Some critics suggest a bit of self-borrowing, for Shakespeare had already employed the gender disguise in *The Two Gentlemen of Verona*, wherein a disguised Julia acts on behalf of her false lover Proteus. The subplot and its characters appear to be Shakespeare's creation.

As Peter Phialas points out in his chapter on *Twelfth Night* in *Shakespeare's Romantic Comedy: The Development of Their Form and Meaning* ([Chapel Hill: U of North Carolina P, 1966], 256–305), the play incorporates the themes and features of earlier Shakespearean works and as such is perhaps a lesson in recreating texts to produce new meanings from old materials. Shakespeare had used the confusion of twins in *The Comedy of Errors* and the theme of a disguised lady courting another woman for the man she loves in *The Two Gentlemen of Verona* (where the disguised Julia was called Sebastian). The Antonio of this play is like Bassanio's close friend of the same name in *The Merchant of Venice*. Like *Much Ado about Nothing* and *As You Like It*, this play includes not only a disdainful lover but also the theme of education in the ways of love. In *As You Like It* Phebe anticipates Olivia's fruitless love for a man who proves to be a woman. Feste is reminiscent of Touchstone; Rosalind's balanced temperament and levelheaded approach to love is like that of Viola. In other words, Phialas's observations confirm Shakespeare's self-borrowing, using past successes in new ways, as a feature of this play.

STRUCTURE AND PLOTTING

Act 1 introduces the two significant households in the play: that of the nobleman, Orsino, Duke of Illyria, and that of the Lady Olivia, a rich countess, with Viola caught in the middle, moving back and forth between the two houses in the guise of Cesario. As Mark Rose points out in *Shakespearean Design* (Cambridge, MA: Harvard UP, 1972), by having Viola introduced in 1.2, in between the Duke in scene 1 and Olivia's household in scene 3, Shakespeare provides a sense of balance between the two. Viola's good sense counters the overdone sensibilities of Orsino and Olivia and is a "mean between extremes" (74). In terms of the humors, Viola is the balanced personality between Orsino's excessive melancholy and Sir Toby's excessive sanguineness. In terms of love, she is the balance between Orsino's luxuriating in unrequited love and Olivia's excessive grieving. In terms of action, she is energy and action set between the indolence of Orsino and the passivity of Olivia. Sir Toby's lines at the beginning of 1.3, "What a plague means my niece to take the death of her brother thus? I am sure care's an enemy to life" (ll. 1–3), express an attitude toward life in contrast to Orsino's emotionalism and Viola's practicality. The three scenes create a balanced triptych in still another way, with Orsino and Sir Toby both self-indulgent figures in contrast to the more cautious and controlled Viola. The remaining scenes in this act continue the character development, particularly of Olivia's household.

Act 2 introduces the remaining characters and sets up the complicated interactions of the households, moving from Sebastian to Viola—the twins coping with their situations—to the activities of the courts of Orsino and Olivia. Likewise, Olivia's household is coping with Olivia's mourning and Malvolio's hectoring and lecturing through strategies to shift Olivia's interest to marriage and to expose Malvolio to the ridicule he deserves.

In act 3, as Feste sings in both households, Viola/Cesario moves between Olivia, who loves her as a man, and Orsino, whom she loves behind her male disguise. The act explores the confusions and foolishness of love as it moves from the Orsino-Viola/Cesario-Olivia triangle to the ambitious but absurd wooing of Olivia by Sir Andrew and Malvolio. The subplot mixes male aggression with courtship when Sir Toby spurs Sir Andrew to battle Cesario for Olivia's favors.

Acts 4 and 5 are very short. The play is winding down, and the action is moving toward the final revelations of true identities and an explanation of the confusions that drive the plot. Sebastian and Olivia frame act 4, meeting in scene 1 and marrying in scene 3, a confirmation of the wonder and madness of love. In between is another kind of madness, the madness of hate: Feste, the very antithesis of Malvolio's puritanical abhorrence of merriment, torments the imprisoned Malvolio and tries to drive Malvolio mad. Act 5 moves forward rapidly with disturbing revelations of Orsino's and Viola's attraction to each other, Olivia's marriage, and Antonio's disillusionment followed by the entrance of Sebastian, who makes all right. He exposes the cowardice and bluster of the would-be courtier, Sir Andrew, confirms his fidelity to Olivia, restores Antonio's faith in his friendship, and explains Viola to Orsino. The order of these events is suspenseful, though the audience understands what is going on long before the characters on the stage do. Once the love concerns of the main characters have been taken care of, the scene briefly pulls together the remaining threads: Sir Toby and Maria's marriage and the trick on Malvolio. The optimism of Orsino is balanced between Malvolio's mean-spirited and dangerous promise of revenge and Feste's gentle reminder that life is not always fun and sunshine, but that pain and rain are daily realities.

For a more detailed consideration of the scene-to-scene dynamics of this play, see Jean Howard's *Shakespeare's Art of Orchestration* (Urbana: U of Illinois P, 1989).

MAIN CHARACTERS

Viola

Despite eighteenth-century Samuel Johnson's objection to Viola as an "excellent schemer" (*Johnson on Shakespeare*, The Yale Edition of the Works of Samuel Johnson, vol. 7, ed. Arthur Sherbo [New Haven: Yale UP, 1968], 312), she is one of *Twelfth Night*'s happiest achievements, a female character in the best tradition of Shakespeare's heroines. William Hazlitt (*Characters of Shakespear's Plays* [London: Printed by C. H. Reynell for R. Hunter and C. and J. Ollier, 1817], 255) found Viola responsible for the charm of the play. Unlike Helena and Hermia in *A Midsummer Night's Dream*, she has the balance of virtues so dear to the Renaissance ideal of perfection, a balance that is played off against the extremes delineated in the other characters. Amid such extremes Viola indeed proves the embodiment of the sensible and the moderate. Her speech is simple and direct, not mannered or affected. Her love for Orsino is real: she is ready to sacrifice herself for him. Such self-sacrifice is a traditional test of real love: the selfless lover puts the beloved first, while the self-indulgent one simply loves the emotions evoked by love. Viola manages her difficult situation with wit and grace, and she is attractive as a character in a way that we can appreciate only by contrasting her with the much less sympathetic Olivia.

Like Olivia, Viola seems at first to have lost a brother to death, but instead of indulging herself in ostentatious mourning, she takes action to find her bearings and to place herself in a position where she can help herself as well as her brother if indeed he has not died at sea. Viola's true, self-sacrificing love is paralleled by the true friendship shown by Antonio for Sebastian and later by the real love Sebastian has for Olivia—a sudden emotion the reality of which we must accept on faith. Furthermore, she seems to have a positive effect on others, transforming Orsino's artificial poetic phrasing to more direct discourse and Olivia's self-righteous shows of mourning to more honest speech.

Orsino

The first extremist we meet is Orsino, a self-indulgent and excessive romantic who is more in love with love than with Olivia, the supposed object of his affections. His speeches in 1.1 should be read with close attention to his metaphors, which are a sign of his exaggerated feelings. Orsino is a parody of the Petrarchan lover, and his posing, heightened by the fact that he takes himself so seriously, becomes hilarious in a good production of the play. His romantic posturing is clearly inappropriate for his position, and thus obviously meant as comic: Orsino is a duke, the ruler of Illyria, a mature man with past naval experience.

Olivia

Olivia, a noblewoman, also takes herself too seriously, as is obvious from her absurd resolve to mourn her dead brother for seven years; she refuses to see

Orsino and, "like a cloistress," or nun (1.1.27), shuts herself off from life and love. This indulgence of grief would have been seen as extreme in the Renaissance, just as it would be today. Olivia's failing, like Orsino's, is a too-ready enjoyment of the role or part she is expected to play, an exaggeration of its more emotional features. However, once she sets her sights on Cesario, she is transformed into an active, honest person, forthright about her emotions, willing to use her money and her power to aid her cause, and quick to take advantage of Sebastian's confusion to get what she wants: marriage to the man she thinks won her heart at first sight.

Malvolio

The most fanatical extremist in the play is Malvolio (*volio* = wish; *mal* = bad/evil), whose "humor" or temperament is puritanical and negative. Malvolio is humorless, overly sensitive—Olivia tells him that he takes "bird-bolts" (small, blunt arrows, that is, harmless activities) for "cannon-bullets" (1.5.93)—and ambitious; his failing is self-love of a kind far more advanced than Orsino's or Olivia's. A "humor" character in the Renaissance was a figure so dominated by a single passion or quirk of temperament that it motivated all his speech and behavior. In *A Midsummer Night's Dream* Bottom's humor, for example, is braggadocio, while in *The Taming of the Shrew* Petruchio's is cantankerousness. The word "humor" in this context pertains to an old physiologically based theory about the effects of bodily fluids on personality; it does not simply mean humor as in "funny." Shakespeare's characters can be funny if their humor is absurd and thus comic, or they can be tragic if their humor is violent or treacherous. Malvolio has an excess of both black bile and yellow bile, a fact that is conveyed visually in the costume Maria and Sir Toby persuade him to wear when he courts Olivia: black and yellow cross-garters. Critical discussion centers on the degree to which he is intended to be a stereotype of Puritanism, which originated during the reign of Elizabeth I in opposition to the established church of that time. Some critics debate whether Malvolio is supposed to be nastily revengeful at the end, or just pitiable.

Sir Toby Belch and Maria

Set against the extremes of self-love is another set of comic characters whose failings are quite the opposite: they take nothing seriously, not even themselves. Sir Toby Belch is a fun-loving prankster, a riotous figure who enjoys ale and food and jokes. His surname "belch" seems appropriate for his large appetites. He is drunk throughout most of the play, yet his language is rich in phrases that suggest he is more than simply a fool. He tosses out Latin tags like "deliculo surgere" (to get up at dawn, 2.3.2–3), yet he also alludes to elements of popular culture of the time, singing songs familiar to the Elizabethan audience, and calling Maria "Penthesilea," Queen of the Amazons (2.3.177)—a name ironic because of her diminutive size but praising the force of her wit. In fact, he turns out to be more Maria's sidekick in witty pranks than she is his. Glosses of the text often call Maria a witty servant, but doing so ignores the conventions of the time, whereby the woman who helps manage a household was not a servant in our sense of the word but a lady of chambers, usually from a good family.

Sir Andrew Aguecheek

Sir Toby and Maria are assisted in their schemes, often unknowingly, by Sir Andrew Aguecheek—a "carpet" knight of the type depicted in the ancient comic tradition of the cowardly soldier who brags about his ferocity in battle but runs away when faced with a real potential for violence. Viola/Cesario seems enough of a weakling for him to overcome, but Sebastian routs him. Sir Andrew is the opposite extreme of Malvolio in that, rather than being too censorious, he is too ready to accept any proposal that promises him a good living and a pot of ale. He has a thin, pale face and is a bit of a fool, misconstruing Sir Toby's statements and absurdly believing he has some hope of winning Olivia's affection.

Feste

A very significant minor character is Feste the clown, who, like Viola/Cesario, moves freely between the two households, Orsino's and Olivia's, and interacts with all characters "both high and low" (2.3.41). He is a paid servant who is much more important than he seems to be, despite his angling for coins. Feste worked for Olivia's father and since his death has been employed as Olivia's jester. Whereas Olivia and others see him as no more than an aging and slightly disrespectful fool, paid to entertain them with acrobatics, tumbling tricks, and clever jokes, Viola sees the depth of wisdom and understanding that lies behind his foolery, just as he, to some degree, recognizes that she is different from what she pretends to be. In fact, throughout the play Feste sees through others.

Feste first appears in 1.5 and from the start he serves as far more than comic relief. In Robert Armin, who first played this part, Shakespeare had a versatile comedic actor who could bring a depth of understanding to the role normally impossible in traditional "fools." "Better a witty fool than a foolish wit" (1.5.36), he says. Because of the supposed timing of the play, Twelfth Night, a period of festivity and revelry, the role of Feste (whose name suggests "feast" and "festival") is central to Shakespeare's purposes. Feste's genuine wit and understanding contrast with the absurd or simply foolish wit of others. Where Sir Andrew is irredeemably foolish, this licensed fool is no fool at all. His role permits him to speak the truth to dukes and countesses when others may not. To some degree Feste is a projection of Shakespeare himself, entertaining and, behind seeming foolishness, revealing truths with wit and wisdom, the authorial voice at work. (Some critics note that Feste's allusion to Cressida and Troilus at 3.1.51–55 fits with Shakespeare's work habits; he may have been toying with the two in this play as he thinks through how he will use them in a forthcoming work, *Troilus and Cressida*.) Viola says that Feste is "wise enough to play the fool" (3.1.60), a task requiring wit, close observation, and an understanding of human psychology: "He must observe their mood on whom he jests, / The quality of the persons, and the time." His job is "[a]s full of labor as a wise man's art" (3.1.62–63, 65). He links the two key households and the story lines. Feste is a performer, a close observer of human behavior, and a skilled rhetorician and storyteller. He is at once part of the action of the play and to some degree removed from it, observing the actors as they move across the stage. He is detached and self-contained, except in his deep-seated hatred of Malvolio, who embodies perhaps Shakespeare's attitude toward people who are hypocritical and arrogant spoilers of fun. Feste masquerades as Sir Topas the Curate to torment the discredited and imprisoned Malvolio, treating him as a witless lunatic.

Feste's songs carry some of the important themes of the play: the nature of love, the transience of youth, the ups and downs of life and love, the inevitability of death. His statement that "A sentence is but a chev'ril glove to a good wit" (3.1.11–12) captures the way Feste turns phrases inside out like a soft leather glove to make others see themselves and their behavior in new ways and from other perspectives. Feste has the last word, a song that undercuts the optimism of the multiple marriages by reminding the audience that "the rain it raineth every day" (5.1.392) and bringing them back to the reality of their own lives with his closing promise that the actors will "strive to please you every day" (5.1.408). Thus, he mediates between the stage illusions and the everyday realities to which the audience will return when they leave the theater.

In "A Star Is Born: Feste on the Modern Stage," *Shakespeare Quarterly* (39.1 [Spring 1988]: 61–78), Karen Greif warns,

> Too-sad Festes can turn maudlin, thereby blunting the comedy. Hack Festes make bad entertainers. Fools whose thoughts have soured or whose failings are too obvious cannot make convincing ironists, and dreary ones are worse. Gimmicky productions trivialize the fool's wisdom. Criticism-conscious productions puff him up unduly. Lastly, monotone productions that take their cue entirely from Feste's saddest utterances, or farcical versions, weighed down with a malcontent clown, too often blast the comedy's delicate harmonies. (77)

Clearly, she sees Feste as a significant character in any production, for she goes on to say, "Feste may . . . usher us out of the sheltered world of romantic comedy, but he must not be exiled from its precincts," for a Feste lacking "sympathy for love and the good life," no matter how sharp his understanding of "caprices," will be unable to awaken the audience to the "fuller vision of early life" that Shakespeare celebrates in *Twelfth Night* (77). As Greif reminds us, some fifty years earlier Sir Arthur Quiller-Couch, in his "Introduction" to *Twelfth Night* in the Cambridge University Press edition of *The New Shakespeare* (1949), asserted that modern readers and producers must recognize "Feste, Master of the Revels, to be the mastermind and controller of *Twelfth Night*, its comic spirit and president" (xxvi).

Curio, Valentine, and Antonio

The minor characters are basically functional. Curio and Valentine attend on Orsino. Valentine tries unsuccessfully to gain admission to Olivia to carry his master's words of love, and Curio accompanies Orsino to Olivia's household in the last act. The sea captain who rescues Viola from drowning and helps her disguise herself reappears at the end of the play so Viola can reclaim her clothing and possessions. Antonio, however, has more importance because of his friendship for Sebastian as revealed at the beginning and end of the play. A number of modern critics argue that Antonio's response to Sebastian is homoerotic, that Shakespeare is toying with another facet of love. Others argue that within the context of Renaissance ideas of copia, or fullness, he stands for true friendship, which is giving and loyal, not self-seeking. Shakespeare sets his true, self-sacrificing friendship in contrast to the play's images of false friendship in Malvolio and Sir Andrew (and perhaps even Sir Toby, who manages to make money off of his friends).

Sebastian

Sebastian seems more developed than he actually is because he is the masculine version of his sister, and the little we see of him suggests that they share an impulsive generosity and a willingness to accept what fate throws at them. Confused by Olivia's reaction to him and worried about his friend Antonio, he nonetheless proves equal to the situation, ready to fight or love as occasion demands.

DEVICES AND TECHNIQUES

Despite *Twelfth Night*'s focus on the extremes of love, the true value of the play rests in its comedy. The humor comes from the contrasting theories of love held by contrasting characters, and the resulting collisions and mix-ups. We can analyze the general conception of the characters but not the specific qualities that make them funny line after line. Try to picture the characters as you go over their jokes: what should Toby Belch look like? Andrew Aguecheek? How should they move? Talk? Comedy comes in part from the dramatic irony inherent in the audience's knowing more than do the characters on the stage. For example, when Olivia falls in love with Cesario, we know but she does not that the countess loves a woman.

Shakespeare here is using comic strategies that worked for him throughout his career. These include the comedy that is inevitable because of misunderstandings caused by disguises and the absurd situations in which such disguises may place one. The exaggerated behavior of Malvolio and Sir Andrew is meant to amuse, as is the image of a cowardly courtier and a battle of the sexes, in which both opponents (Sir Andrew and Cesario) look like men but behave (from an Elizabethan view) like women. The incongruity of the naturally clumsy Sir Andrew's attempts to imitate courtly grace and dancing, his absurd nonsequiturs, and his pretense at bravery when he is clearly cowardly make for both visual and verbal comedy.

Exaggerated Petrarchan language is always good for a laugh in Shakespeare's works, as are the standard quibbling over meanings of words, bawdy puns, and misunderstandings (Sir Andrew seems to misunderstand everything!). Characters use each other as the butt of their wit, make allusions that exaggerate reality, and engage in fake and often nonsensical erudition (like that of Feste as Sir Topas testing Malvolio for madness through paradoxes and absurdities). Comic descriptions (like those of Sir Andrew fearful of Cesario, and vice versa) and incongruities (Malvolio's shockingly bright stockings) add to the fun.

The imagery throughout the play is significant, revealing character and mood. Orsino's language alternates between exaggerated traditional romantic images and more cynical interpretations of such imagery. In the first scene, when he is asked whether he will hunt "the hart" (deer), he replies that he does indeed hunt Olivia's "heart" (1.1.16, 20). Yet he also sees himself transformed into a stag, as Actaeon is in Ovid's *Metamorphoses*, one who will suffer pain because of his glimpse of beauty: "O, when mine eyes did see Olivia first, / . . . That instant was I turn'd into a hart, / And my desires, like fell and cruel hounds, / E'er since pursue me" (1.1.18–22).

He repeatedly compares love to the vast and hungry sea (for example, 1.1.11), but then concentrates his discussion about the traditional image of a rose on the rose's negative qualities: the fragility of the flower speaks of the fragility of women "whose fair flow'r / Being once display'd, doth fall that very hour" (2.4.38–39). Yet the image of perishable beauty fits with the play's recurring autumnal motif and associations of love and death. It has often been pointed out that real danger often lurks behind the light foolery of Shakespearean comedy; the threat to Antonio's life is the major example here, along with the potential harm to Viola—an unprotected young woman in Illyria.

Feste compares Orsino's mind to an opal (2.4.75), a jewel of magical properties and ever-changing colors. The imagistic focus is on changeability and instability, for Feste has perceived the inconstant nature of Orsino's course. He is more in love with love than with an individual. Olivia and Sebastian connect salt-water and the sea with tears (for example, 2.1.30–32), a natural image for Sebastian, who is grieving over his sister's supposed drowning. Viola compares women's hearts to sealing wax, upon which is pressed an image of the man who rules theirs; in her guise as the cynical Cesario she suggests how easily the "proper false" can leave a lasting impression on their hearts (2.2.29–30).

Some metaphors of "contagion"—such as "contagious breath" (2.3.55, 54) alluding to disease and plague—echo, say historians, the Elizabethan worry about the plague, an outbreak of which had closed down theaters about ten years before Shakespeare wrote this play. Even love at first sight is tied to disease, as when Orsino says that Olivia "purg'd the air of pestilence" (1.1.19). Similarly, Olivia describes her sudden infatuation with Cesario as catching a fatal disease: "Even so quickly may one catch the plague?" (1.5.295). When Sir Toby and Sir Andrew apparently misuse the word "contagious" in 2.3.54–55, they are speaking of Feste's singing. Since music and love are so intimately connected in *Twelfth Night* from the very first line onward, Sir Toby and Sir Andrew can be seen as again alluding to love as a plague.

Olivia, in dealing with Viola/Cesario, draws on the traditional images of courtly love that define the courtship process as a religion having a "text" (1.5.220, 223, 232), a "doctrine" (1.5.222), and departures from it "heresy" (1.5.228). Metaphors of madness recur; obviously there are the mad delusions of lovers and the supposed madness of Malvolio. Olivia comments about Malvolio, "I am as mad as he, / If sad and merry madness equal be" (3.4.14–15), and later she concludes that his behavior is "midsummer madness" (3.4.56). Malvolio, in turn, accused of madness, finds madness in all others. The officers find Antonio's statements about Sebastian's betrayal madness, and Orsino calls Antonio mad for insisting that Cesario had spent the three preceding months with Antonio, not Orsino.

Related to the images of madness are those pertaining to the devil. Malvolio's persecutors joke about "all the devils of hell" being contained within him and "Legion" or the devil possessing him (3.4.85–86). Later "Sir Topas" claims that a "hyperbolical fiend" inhabits the steward (4.2.25). Feste's song at the end of 4.2 connects Malvolio's madness with the devil and Malvolio with the old-fashioned stage figure Vice. Likewise, Olivia, distressed at Cesario's failure to respond to her advances, whispers, "A fiend like thee might bear my soul to hell" (3.4.217).

As is typical of most Shakespearean plays, the aristocrats speak in poetic diction and the less refined characters speak in prose. In this play, however, Shakespeare sometimes changes that pattern by having Sebastian and Antonio, for example, speak in prose in 2.1 but then having Antonio revert to verse as soon as Sebastian leaves. This break in pattern certainly suggests the degree to which Sebastian is shaken by his experiences and by his grief at the supposed loss of his sister, for later he returns to the use of blank verse. Antonio's use of verse may suggest that though he is a ship's captain, he is well-born. Olivia speaks in verse and, when deeply emotional, in couplets to Cesario, who usually replies in clipped, plain diction, sometimes even creating a cool distance by choosing the formal and impersonal phrasing of a servant speaking to someone who ranks above her. As the clown, Feste continually engages in wordplay, makes witty jests, mocks obliquely, and improvises new roles for himself with great delight.

Finally, as usual, Shakespeare relies on foils, or characters and situations that explore the same theme in different ways, to carry his themes: real fools, such as Sir Andrew or Malvolio, played off against seeming fools like Feste and Fabian, who are really wise; Olivia's and Orsino's grief as a pose set against the genuine grief of Sebastian and Viola; multiple cases of love at first sight and different types, qualities, and levels of love, fake courtiers and genuine courtiers, cowardly soldiers and brave soldiers, false friends and true friends, and so on. Sometimes modern critics use the verb "mirror" or the noun "mirror-images" to express a similar idea of correspondences between characters. For example, Malvolio and Feste are mirror images of each other, and very different types of fools. The section that follows will explore this strategy at length.

THEMES AND MEANINGS

The themes of *Twelfth Night* are many. The play clearly is about love and friendship. It is full of revelry, music, and games of love. It opposes merrymakers against spoilers of fun. It explores the deceptive nature of appearances and the madness of love compared with mad, in the sense of angry, personalities. It is also about the transience of youth and happiness, and the need to seize the day before the rain and the wind, aging, and grim mortality affect us all for the worse.

The theme of love dominates the play, from the first line, which describes music as the "food of love," through statements about love's torments, jealousy, barren love, concealed love, the causes of love, and even a debate over who loves more deeply, men or women (2.4.93–121). Duke Orsino languishes in his fantasy infatuation with Olivia in the very first scene, and his self-indulgent playing at love, with music and poetry to heighten his senses, seems inappropriate in a man of his position. What is acceptable in a teenaged Romeo (and he shares with the young Romeo a romantic disposition) seems immature in an adult who wields power and authority, especially when his fancies prove changeable. He does not even go himself to the lady who supposedly causes him such pangs of love; instead, he sends representatives to do his wooing for him (his servant Valentine acts as Orsino's valentine to Olivia). His exchanges with Viola/Cesario on the nature of love reflect the conventions and imagery of the time and hence reveal a lack of experience with genuine love. His attitude reflects the medieval courtly tradition and the Petrarchan conventions of poetry, whereby the lover praises his beloved in conventional, exaggerated terms like those Shakespeare mocked in Sonnet 130. It should be clear to the audience that Orsino's romantic pose is just that, a pose.

His sudden and growing affection for and dependence on Cesario present interesting complications. He has noticed the softness of her skin, the fullness of her lip, the smooth and elegant neck without the protrusions of an Adam's apple—all clues that she is not what she seems—but from his point of view, any sexual attraction he might be feeling is for a boy, not a woman. This complication is reinforced by Elizabethan staging, since all female roles were played by young men whose voices had not yet changed, so what he sees on stage really is a boy, even though the audience is meant to imagine that the boy actor is a woman disguised as a castrated male. In other words, there is the hint of a homosexual attraction between Orsino and Cesario, but it is undercut by our knowledge of the dramatic reality: he is attracted to a woman; he just does not know it at first.

Olivia's behavior, too, exposes the complications of love. Her mourning for her dead brother has come to dominate her life but is as much of a pose as is Orsino's pretense of love for her. Even the clown, Feste, can see that she has wallowed in emotion too long. Then, another conventional event occurs: love at first sight. Orsino has said that his first glimpse of Olivia was so wondrous that he thought that she "purg'd the air of pestilence" (1.1.19). Viola also experiences love at first sight, realizing that she wants to be Orsino's wife, now that she has met him, but has put herself in a difficult situation for courtship. Then Olivia, upon first sight of Viola/Cesario, falls deeply in love with "him": "Methinks I feel this youth's perfections / With an invisible and subtle stealth / To creep in at mine eyes" (1.5. 296–298). Thus, she invents an excuse (the ring) to bring him back for another visit. Her situation, like Orsino's, is hopeless and unrequited, since Olivia has, without knowing it, fallen in love with a woman. Yet, it is the delicacy of Viola/Cesario's appearance, the cadences of her speech, and the gentle strength of her manner that win Olivia's heart, so that one wonders how well she will fare with Viola's twin, Sebastian, who is meant to seem far more masculine than does Viola in disguise.

Another case of love of first sight, but governed by practical matters of position and rank, is Sebastian's for Olivia, his social equal, and Olivia's sudden transfer of love from Viola/Cesario to her/his twin brother. This shift of love from one object of affection to a very similar one solves the problem of a man in love with a man and a woman in love with a woman. But it also comments on the changeability of love, its arbitrary nature. The sudden shifts whereby Olivia moves from love of Cesario to love of Sebastian and Orsino moves from wanting to kill Cesario to wanting to marry Viola matches the suddenness with which the lovers fell in love in the first place. This interchangeability of love objects recalls *A Midsummer Night's Dream*, where Lysander and Demetrius cannot make up their minds which woman to woo. There Shakespeare offered the excuse of a magic plant. Here one sees love's fickleness without alloy.

Another love match is Sir Toby and Maria. She may be small, but she is mighty in her cleverness, her witty retorts, and her even wittier pranks; Toby, despite her chiding, comes to appreciate her as a kindred spirit. Fabian reports in act 5 that Sir Toby has married Maria in recompense for her writing of the letter that damned Malvolio.

During the progress of the play other forms of love add to the humor: variations of inappropriate love. First is the supposed love of Sir Andrew Aguecheek, who is driven, at Toby's encouragement, to court Olivia in the hopes of the social status and rich dowry she will bring with her. In their drunken state, Sir Toby encourages Sir Andrew at one point to woo Maria (or at least to "accost" her, 1.3.49), but most of the time Sir Andrew aims his sights hopelessly at Olivia. Sir Andrew is a caricature of the traditional courtly lover. Sir Toby claims that Sir Andrew plays the "viol-de-gamboys," speaks several languages "without book" (1.3.26–27) and should pride himself on dancing and fencing, yet Sir Andrew proves incompetent at all of these courtly skills.

Then there is the overweening Malvolio, whose name in Italian means "wishes ill." Olivia rightly identifies Malvolio's pretensions, arrogance, and self-importance as self-love (1.5.90). Malvolio is only a steward in Olivia's household, but his dreams of self-aggrandizement inspire him to look above his proper rank and status for a rich and powerful lover, marriage to whom will raise him above his present rank and place him in the superior position he thinks he deserves. Thus, he is already plotting to gain Olivia's hand in marriage even before Maria and the others set out the bait that will call Olivia's attention to Malvolio's true self and gain him his deserved comeuppance. To Elizabethans, for whom the social hierarchies were an engrained rule of life, Malvolio would be seen as breaking the social class rules, his revolutionary behavior absurdly self-promotional. Whereas it was acceptable for a man to marry beneath his station and thereby elevate his wife, for a woman to marry below her rank would demean her. Hence, Sir Toby can marry Maria without upsetting the social order, whereas Olivia's marrying Malvolio would. Similarly, Orsino can wed Viola at the end of the play, and Sebastian is of sufficiently good parentage that Olivia can unite herself with him. Olivia could not stoop to Malvolio's level, and it is absurd for him to fantasize that she could.

Finally, but most importantly, there is Viola's love, a mature, adult emotion. Placed in unusual circumstances and forced to play a man's part, which she does with flair, she nonetheless is one of the frail creatures she defends. Like others of her sex, she is perforce passive, waiting for all to fall out as it should, but she uses her opportunities as best she may to educate Orsino about true love, to curb his cynicism, and to make him understand that women can love with all the depth of feeling of men and yet, unlike men, be unable to act on those feelings. She tries to prepare him gently for Olivia's rejection.

Marriage is the final result of the discovery of love and the progress toward understanding between the sexes. The marriages of Orsino to Viola, Sebastian to Olivia, and even Sir Toby to Maria bring order and harmony to the topsy-turvy, chaotic, upside-down world of the play.

Another theme in this play, closely tied to that of love, is friendship. Antonio and Sebastian's friendship is true. Antonio has saved Sebastian's life at sea, and this act has bound them to each other. Antonio would like to stick by Sebastian's side and be his guide and protector, but circumstances at first prevent him. At the end of the play, Sebastian has a chance to return Antonio's kindness. This is a friendship of equals, of male camaraderie. It is self-sacrificing. True friends are loyal to each other. Ironically, when Antonio reveals himself to his enemies to come to his friend's rescue from Sir Andrew's attack, the supposed Sebastian, really Viola, has no idea who he is and seems to spurn Antonio's sacrifice, not recognizing it for what it is. Yet Antonio has thereby proven the strength of his friendship, at great cost to himself. The friendship that grows between Orsino and Cesario is a misleading friendship, but suggests that, if not for gender getting in the way, men and women could be friends, not just lovers.

Twelfth Night contrasts fun-loving rogues with people who condemn and spoil the joy of others. The churlish Malvolio is associated with dark extremes. Wearing somber colors, chiding merrymakers, and priding himself on his superiority, he threatens the existing hierarchies by considering himself the equal or superior of his betters. Where the audience laughs with Feste and Maria, viewers/readers laugh at Malvolio when he brings his punishment and suffering on himself. Some critics have found his treatment in the play overly harsh, but he is an appropriate object of satire and of ridicule on the stage because his attitudes are precisely those that would, with time, lead to the closing of the theaters. It is ironic that it is his pretense at smiling that damns him, for a smile is so at odds with his personality that it is clear he is not himself.

In Shakespearean comedies the real world always threatens to break through, and real dangers are always near. Sebastian and Viola could have drowned at sea or been shattered against the rocks near the shore. The sea captains who rescued them could have taken advantage of their condition and held them hostage, or worse. Antonio could have been killed by his enemies. Viola could have been thrust through by Sir Andrew. Time and again danger threatens. There is even the real possibility that Orsino might kill Cesario near the play's end. While Shakespeare helps his audiences lose themselves in a fascinating story that entertains, delights, and teaches, he also warns that playgoers eventually have to go home, out into the rainy night, and face the literal and metaphorical darkness and its hidden dangers.

As always in Shakespearean plays, there is the underlying theme of the deceptive nature of appearances, the illusions that distort and hide reality. The disguises are a visual expression of this theme: Viola is a boy pretending to be a woman pretending to be a man; Malvolio is a killjoy pretending, thanks to the plotters, to be a fashion-plate and a jolly wooer; Feste is a wise man behind his jester's costume. Ironically, Malvolio's amorous overtures to Olivia take the form of references to bawdy songs about the sexual escapades of ladies who "Please one and please all" (3.4.23) or about joining one's sweetheart in bed (3.4.31)—statements out of keeping with his normally somber and condemning manner but revealing his hypocrisy. The behavior of Orsino and Olivia also confirms the contrast between who they are and who they seem to be, for Olivia immediately drops her long-standing pose of grief when she falls in love with Cesario; Orsino's romantic pose clearly hides a man of action who we know took part in battles at sea, who commands his officers, and who imprisons his enemies; in contrast, Sir Andrew pretends to be an accomplished fencer and fierce fighter when in fact he is a coward. Critics note the saturnalian license associated with the last day of the Christmas holiday, and, consequently, see the themes of the world turned topsy-turvy or upside-down as inevitable in this play.

CRITICAL CONTROVERSIES

Twelfth Night has provoked much critical debate about the nature of the comedy and of the characters, the production issues that affect credibility and theme, and the gender issues emphasized by modern productions.

One critical concern is the nature of the comedy in this play, with some seeing in the humor characters ties to the comedies of Ben Jonson, a fellow playwright in whose plays Shakespeare had acted, but with most seeing Shakespeare as reacting against Jonson's stiffer kind of comedy, with its satiric types dominated by humors. Famous nineteenth-century critic William Hazlitt, in *The Characters of Shakespear's Plays* (1817), found Malvolio more than a simple type and described him as a sympathetic figure, foolishly smiling in his yellow, cross-gartered stockings and suffering genuine anguish when cruelly locked up as part of a vengeful joke.

Taking a lighter view of the play (in "The Saturnalian Pattern in Shakespeare's

Comedy," *Sewanee Review* 59 [October 1951]: 593–611), C. L. Barber originated the term "festive comedy" to describe this type of play, because its feelings of celebration and good fun grew out of traditional Christian festivals (particularly the Twelfth Night referred to in the title). Elias Schwartz (in "*Twelfth Night* and the Meaning of Shakespearean Comedy," *College English* 28.7 [April 1967]: 508–519) again explores the play as festive comedy, whose merriment focuses on the joys of life rather than its limitations and whose characters, unlike satiric figures, win our understanding and acceptance because they are complex and hence like ourselves, even sometimes foolish. Thus, despite the weaknesses of Orsino, Olivia, and Sir Toby, they never take themselves so seriously that we the audience reject them.

Likewise, John Hollander argues that Shakespeare, disturbed by Jonson's rigid cardboard figures, aimed for more humanized characters who, rather than being static emblems, are full of kinetic energy representative of genuine human experience. According to Hollander, the festive-theatrical masquerade in the play ultimately exposes the true desires behind the conventional social guises. Helene Moglen (in "Disguise and Development: The Self and Society in *Twelfth Night*," *Literature and Psychology* 23 [1973]: 13–20) explores Freudian psychological hypotheses at work, providing a new twist to the idea of satirized humor types versus humanized comedic individuals; she finds an intriguing mix of real world absurdities and fragmented dreams and symbols. She calls Sir Toby the "Lord of Misrule" who "burlesques majesty by promoting license" (18) in keeping with the pre-Lent carnival spirit. Journal articles on revelry, charades, Sir Toby's drunken Christmas songs, and Elizabethan Twelfth Night rituals highlight the ongoing assertion that the festive characteristics of the play set it apart from satire per se.

Yet the masqueraders, imposters, self-deceivers, and counterfeiters who beguile others and themselves pull other critics back to humor theories and the concept of the comedy as "dark." Typical titles include Joan Hartwig's "Feste's Whirligig and the Comic Providence of *Twelfth Night*" (in *English Literary History* 40 [1973]: 501–513), Joseph Summers' "The Masks of *Twelfth Night*" (in *The University of Kansas Review* 22 [1955]: 25–32), and Robert Wilcher's "The Art of the Comic Duologue in Three Plays by Shakespeare" (in *Shakespeare Survey* 35 [1982]: 87–97).

How to stage this play has always been a matter of controversy. Should the same actor play both Viola and Sebastian, or should they be different actors? Should the same actor play the two roles until the very end and then a new Sebastian enter in act 5? Does it matter that sister and brother do not look alike when together? Is Feste meant to be simply a go-between connecting the two households or central to the production, a character who informs the audience of realities portrayed on stage? Is the play lighthearted in the tradition of Shakespeare's earlier comedies, or is it a darker, more problematic work like *Measure for Measure*? Should it be played for laughs, or for its darker warnings? Should the play follow the Shakespearean practice with a young man playing the role of Viola, or should a woman play that woman's part? Should the acting style suggest that Orsino is falling in love with Viola when he thinks she is a man, Cesario, or should there be sympathy of understanding but not physical attraction? If there is a physical attraction, how would it best be handled? Should Orsino, Olivia, and Malvolio be played as comic extremes, with, for instance, Orsino lolling in a lavish oriental pleasure palace or Malvolio played as the stereotypical killjoy? Or should they be more modulated, moderate in tone and manner? What is the physical and thematic place of Antonio in the final scene: when should he be pardoned, where should he stand, and what attitude should he adopt? Acting styles and thematic interests change from generation to generation and affect interpretations, with, for example, postwar productions often focusing on the darker implications of the play and productions of the late twentieth and early twenty-first centuries intrigued by gender roles and taking as vital central themes the cross-dressing and gender confusions that were standard Renaissance comic devices.

Many modern critics explore the gender questions inherent in Renaissance stage practices in which a young male actor plays a young woman, in this case one who is disguised as a young man. The complications of this youth's falling in love with the nobleman s/he serves and having the woman s/he courts fall in love with her in disguise confuses gender and raises the question of Shakespeare's comic and thematic intent: how overtly should same-sex attractions be played? In other words, critics examine the heterosexual versus the homoerotic implications of the play before the final restoration of gender order through marriage. They often judge productions in the light of how effectively they call attention to such implications, which may or may not have loomed large for a contemporary Elizabethan audience. Donald Lyons, for example (in "Review of *Twelfth Night*," *Commentary* 103 [February 1997]: 59–60), praises the Trevor Nunn 1996 film production for demonstrating the boundaries of decorum in its teasing suggestions of homosexuality that capture the awkwardness of misplaced affections but do not overstep Renaissance proprieties. In contrast, Laurie Osborne finds Nunn too conservative and his production flawed, because it fails to provide modern gender perspectives on gay and lesbian relationships that fit with the ambiguous sexuality at the heart of the play. Phyllis Rackin (in "Androgyny, Mimesis and the Marriage of the Boy Heroine on the English Stage," *PMLA* 102 [1987]: 31–35) relates Shakespearean cross-dressers/transvestites to the Renaissance divine androgyne, a representation of gender reunion and harmony. However, Christina Malcolmson (in " 'What You Will': Social Mobility and Gender in *Twelfth Night*," in *The Matter of Difference: A Materialist-Feminist Criticism of Shakespeare*, edited by Valerie Wayne [Ithaca: Cornell UP, 1991], 29–57) argues that when Viola targets Orsino as the most eligible bachelor around even before she sees him, she is acting out the standard Elizabethan pattern of upward mobility. Likewise, Marjorie Garber's *Vested Interests: Cross-Dressing and Cultural Anxiety* (New York: Routledge, 1992) finds class mobility and resistance—not sexual mobility or an imposed modern obsession with transvestite concerns—as crucial to our understanding of *Twelfth Night*. Jonathan Crewe ("In the Field of Dreams: Transvestism in *Twelfth Night* and *The Crying Game*," *Representations* 50 [Spring 1995]: 101–121) asserts that "the festive/utopian vistas" of both texts "imply the undoing of the enforced marriage plot" (102), and, as a result, Viola/Cesario serves the paradoxical function of acting as "a highly improper, gender-ambiguous object of desire" and directing desire "to its appropriate objects" (103). While Crewe rejects "an exclusively homosexual construction" of Viola/Cesario's appeal to Orsino as "historically suspect," he explores the function of "same-sex desire" as a transitional phase in the otherwise heterosexual marriage plot (108) and the crisscrossing of the "proper axis of desire" with "improper" desires to provide multiple new "selves," like Olivia's "picture" of herself (110). Crewe also finds Shakespeare playing interesting variations on Orsino as the narcissistic Petrarchan suitor.

These differences in interpretation have led to controversy over the final marriages and the question of whether the marriages that end Shakespearean comedy always embody harmony. Were eighteenth-century productions right to have stage business suggest multiple marriages and a final dance of couples to validate heterosexual love? Gender study approaches have also led to an exploration of Antonio's role in the play. Janet Adelman (in "Male Bonding in Shakespeare's Comedies" from Peter Erickson and Coppélia Kahn's edition of *Shakespeare's "Rough Magic": Renaissance Essays in Honor of C. L. Barber* [Newark: U of Delaware P, 1985], 73–103) finds Antonio crucial to the final scene, a silent "image of loss" as he sees his dearest friend commit himself to a woman (88). In contrast, Joseph Pequigney (in "The Two Antonios and Same-Sex Love in *Twelfth Night* and *The Merchant of Venice*," *English Literary Renaissance* 22 [1992]: 201–221) asserts that when Sebastian takes a wife, he remains Antonio's friend, as having them exit as a trio, arm-in-arm, visually confirms (206). In turn, Laurie E. Osborne ("Antonio's Pardon," *Shakespeare Quarterly* 45 [Spring 1994]: 108–114) surveys Folger Library promptbooks and finds mixed views of Antonio's place in the final scene. The nineteenth-century efforts to include him in the comic closure anticipate the modern critical debate about the nature of Antonio's love for his friend, says Osborne, who concludes that attempts to pardon or explain Antonio result not from Shakespeare's text but because of our own evolving "perceptions of homosexuality" (114).

PRODUCTION HISTORY

As noted earlier, the first recorded performance of *Twelfth Night* took place in the Middle Temple on February 2, 1602. The next documented production did not occur until 1618, when the play was staged before James I on Easter Monday. The *Office Book of Henry Herbert* records the King's Servants' performing the play at court on Candlemas (February 2) 1623. Leonard Digges, author of one of the commendatory poems in the 1623 First Folio edition of Shakespeare, mentioned another production presented in 1640. In 1661, William D'Avenant's version appeared at the Duke's Theatre, starring the famous actor Thomas Betterton as Sir Toby. Samuel Pepys saw this play three times, on September 11, 1661; January 6, 1663; and January 20, 1669—yet he dismissed it as "but a silly play" (January 6, 1663). Though initially popular, *Twelfth Night* lost its following in the late seventeenth century, and this attitude continued into the mid-eighteenth century. In 1703 William Burnaby recreated Shakespeare's play as *Love Betray'd; or, The Agreeable Disappointment* and produced it at Lincoln's Inn Fields. Shakespeare's play appeared at Drury Lane in 1741, starring Charles Macklin as Malvolio and Hannah Pritchard as Viola. Frederick Reynolds's operatic version, with music by Henry Bishop, came out in 1820.

In the nineteenth century the play began to appear more frequently and with more of a following than in the preceding century. Successful nineteenth-century productions added songs and funny scenes lifted from other Shakespearean works (like the betrothal masque from *The Tempest*) without regard to their appropriateness or relevance to theme. John Philip Kemble's 1810 acting edition of *Twelfth Night* cut the play drastically and realigned the scene order to make the play more neatly fit classical standards. He reduced the roles of both Feste and Malvolio, omitting the prison scene, for example. This edition became the directors' guide for productions. In 1804 New York saw its first performance of the play, and 1865 witnessed the first known production of the play with the same actress playing both Sebastian and Viola. (Jean Anouille followed this precedent when he adapted the play for French audiences.) Most Victorian productions involved elaborate outdoor backdrops that forced the action to take place in one setting. They also ignored the dark elements of the play and opted instead for humor and comic set pieces. The goal was to see the pleasure in the play but not the disturbing philosophical questions or the possible implications of male-male and female-female relationships in the play. From the early nineteenth century on, as the acting pace for playing Shakespearean roles has slowed down, the play has undergone radical cutting, partly due to time constraints. Act 2 normally undergoes the most cuts because of its length. Feste's role in the scene and Orsino's discourse on why men's love wavers were standard cuts, with Feste's role interpreted as minimally as possible.

In the twentieth century various famous productions focused on the near tragic and bittersweet qualities of the play and the psychological insights Shakespeare provided. In 1901 Herbert Beerbohm Tree transformed playgoers' vision of *Twelfth Night* with his sumptuous staging, extravagant sets, lavish costumes, and festival foolery, in which even Malvolio clowned around and Feste summed up the merry spirit of the play. In 1912 Harley Granville-Barker directed what has been repeatedly identified as a brilliant rethinking and staging of the play. This production was the first since the Renaissance to include almost all of the text, and in the original sequence. It emphasized the bittersweet undertones of the play, restored the songs and lines of Feste, and made Feste the older, wiser spokesman for the melancholy cynicism behind the confusions and courtship of the other characters. In the production, Feste is left alone on the stage at the end, the spotlight on him, his words addressed directly to the audience.

Tyrone Guthrie in 1933 went a step further in experimenting with the comedy. His goal was to break with the stodginess of earlier productions, to create a faster moving, more hilarious comedic experience. He imitated the Elizabethan stage with an architectural setting instead of scenic backdrops and made Feste a melancholy, white-haired old man. In 1957 Guthrie restaged the play for the Stratford Festival Theatre in Ontario, and, despite its inventive comic business, his version of the play demonstrated more fully than before the nearness of tears to laughter, and the darkness that dispels the sunshine. Peter Hall's productions followed Guthrie's lead, with Feste one of the humor characters. Karen Greif's article on the stage history of Feste ("A Star Is Born: Feste on the Modern Stage"), mentioned above, provides a valuable study of the Tree, Guthrie, Benthall, and Hall productions. Greif finds the degree of alienation, world-weariness, and awareness of role-playing in the characters directly related to the cultural milieu of the production's intended audience, so that trends in the theater correspond to fads in criticism and to topics in vogue and the social values of the day. Finding depictions of Feste as touchstones to the sensibilities of the time, she points out the vogue for world-weary Festes, for example, extending to productions in Paris (1961) and Stockholm (1975), and the contrast in goals between productions in which Feste seems to orchestrate the story and ones in which he is self-effacing.

A 1975 American Shakespeare Theatre production had an aquariumlike setting and presented Malvolio strapped down under a spotlight. According to *New York Times* reviewer D.J.R. Bruckner, K. G. Wilson's 1995 production at Prospect Park took full advantage of sex and low humor to win its Brooklyn audience. New York regularly produces *Twelfth Night* as part of its Shakespeare in the Park series, with varying degrees of success. Trevor Nunn's 1996 film version of the play created a good bit of critical controversy, particularly between those critics who find homosexuality affirmed in the play and those who do not. Nunn's film is an all-British costume drama set amid the wild, dramatic landscape of Cornwall rather than a more romantic, lyrical countryside, presumably the "Illyria" of Shakespeare's setting. The time period is late Victorian, when women were considered frail, delicate creatures whom males were to protect from harsh realities. The film opens with Viola and Sebastian dressed as veiled harem girls entertaining the other guests on-board ship with musical numbers. The joke is that Sebastian's voice is distinctively masculine, yet the two performers are so heavily made up and veiled that it is impossible to distinguish which is which. When Viola removes her veil revealing a moustache, she at first seems to be the female impersonator, but then Sebastian tears it off; next, when Viola removes Sebastian's veil and seems to prepare to rip off his genuine moustache, the ship founders. Incredibly, as the ship is sinking, Sebastian changes into his naval officer's uniform, while Viola removes her wig to show her genuine blonde hair. From then on, the film effectively keeps the viewer's eyes on Viola and Orsino throughout the production.

Critics Marla Magro and Mark Douglas (in "Reflections on Sex, Shakespeare and Nostalgia in Trevor Nunn's *Twelfth Night*," from *Retrovisions: Reinventing the Past in Film and Fiction* [London: Pluto P, 2001], 41–58) assert that Nunn's film uses "moments of gender and sexual ambiguity involving misrecognition and misrepresentation," such as Antonio's affection for Sebastian, Orsino's attraction to Cesario, and Olivia's love for Cesario, to "reaffirm established, normative heterosexuality," while Magro and Douglas would prefer instead that the film assert "the existence and positive cultural value of diverse and multiple sexualities." The film includes scenes in which Viola/Cesario washes Orsino's back while he is bathing, rides and jumps a horse with vigor, and later plays billiards with Orsino in a room reserved for gentlemen.

Nicholas Hytner's 1998 production of the play, starring Helen Hunt, has been particularly controversial and produced a number of reviews because of its unique sets (like something out of *The Arabian Nights*) and gender games. Aired on PBS, the opening set, rosy and speckled with peacocks, stretches far back into fantastic topography, "a delicious dreamworld," says *Time* reviewer Richard Corliss, with a carpet flanked by "two small pools, suitable for bathing and wallowing, where villains can be dunked and lovers share a kiss" ("Humming the Sets," *Time*, 31 August 1998, 72). Orsino is bare-chested and long-haired, while Sir Toby and Sir Andrew eat Chinese takeout, and Malvolio wears shorts.

Sam Mendes's 2002 New York production of *Twelfth Night* is minimalist, with no scenery; only candles hanging high and low over the actors and, upstage, a great empty picture frame. The music is haunting, the mood conveys an autumnal Chekhovian melancholy; Mendes had produced *Uncle Vanya* with the same actors he used in this Shakespeare play. Malvolio appears as a depressed intellectual who gains the audience's sympathy, and both Viola and Olivia seem to find a homosexual union as acceptable as a heterosexual one.

Tim Supple's television adaptation of the play (2002/2003) depicts a contemporary, multicultural London dreamscape, with the lead roles filled by an interna-

Kyra Sedgwick as Countess Olivia and Rick Stear as Sebastian in a scene from Lincoln Center Theater's 1998 production of *Twelfth Night*, directed by Nicholas Hytner. Courtesy of Photofest.

tional mix. Viola is played by Parminder Nagra of *Bend It Like Beckham* fame. Chiwetel Ejiofor, star of a London production of *Midnight's Children*, is Orsino, and Malvolio is acted by Michael Maloney of the Royal Shakespeare Company. The production captures both the dark, dangerous side of the play and its sensual, soulful tone. The video is distributed by 4 Ventures Ltd. (UK), Channel 4 Television Corporation, and Projection Productions.

EXPLICATION OF KEY PASSAGES

1.1.1–15. "If music be the food of love . . . high fantastical." Orsino's opening speech reveals the romantic excesses in which he (whose name, ironically, means "bear") is knowingly indulging. A supposedly love-sick Orsino draws an analogy between food and music. He extends the proverb that music makes love grow just as food makes the body grow to argue that just as overindulging in eating will make one lose one's appetite, so overindulging in music might kill his desire for love. The relevant idea is best expressed in *A Midsummer Night's Dream*: "a surfeit of the sweetest things / The deepest loathing to the stomach brings" (2.2.137–138). The music Orsino is listening to pleases him at first, particularly one melancholy chord comparable to the "sweet sound" of a gentle breeze blowing over a field of violets and carrying that perfume on the air (1.1.5). This correspondence between sound and scent is technically synesthesia, the blurring together of different senses; thematically it reveals Orsino's fine-tuned sensibilities as an aesthete and possibly as a narcissistic lover of sensation, in love with being in love. But he is fickle, as such characters conventionally are, and the music begins to displease him. He calls on the musicians to stop playing and muses on how changeable love is, stealing away the value of things, like the changeable sea, which transforms itself as it moves from high swells to the calm of low tide. His image of love as "quick and fresh" fits with the image of food, for love, like the sea, hungrily takes in more than it can swallow (1.1.9). Basically, he finds love insatiable, variable, and so imaginative ("So full of shapes is fancy") that nothing can keep up with its fantastic needs and wishes (1.1.14–15).

1.2.47–60. **"There is a fair . . . to my wit."** Viola shares her plan with the captain who has rescued her, paying him to keep her secret and assist her in her disguise. Having ascertained that Orsino is the most eligible bachelor around, of good family and good report, she will dress as a eunuch (to explain her high-pitched voice and other feminine features) and, offering her services as a musician, will communicate with Orsino through her songs. Clearly, she is not quite sure what she will do, but before she even sees him, she plans how to gain some influence over him, a reasonable strategy since, as the audience has just heard, music is the food of love. In the first lines of scene 4 Valentine already recognizes how strong that influence is, telling Viola that the Duke has favored her so much that she is already well accepted and likely to get a promotion, and in the last lines Viola herself confides to the audience that courting Olivia for Orsino will be difficult for her since she is already determined to be his wife.

2.2.18–42. **"I left no ring . . . for me t'untie."** Viola responds to Olivia's courtship ploys with puzzlement, particularly at Olivia's sending Malvolio after her with a ring that Malvolio, echoing his mistress, says s/he peevishly threw at Olivia. Viola tries to figure out what this action means, for she knows she left no ring with Olivia. She hits on the truth immediately. Heaven forbid my male appearance has taken her fancy, she exclaims, and then she declares that Olivia "loves me, sure" (2.2.22). The audience should understand that something unusual is going on here, because Viola/Cesario is not a male puzzling over the advances of a rich woman in an important position and fearing his master's reaction. Instead, Viola/Cesario, attuned to female patterns of thought and behavior, reviews behavior that confirms her fears: Olivia's careful perusal of Cesario and difficulty speaking, as if excited. Viola correctly concludes that Olivia's sudden love has made her seek some immediate means to bring Cesario back again, and the ring and its rude delivery are her instruments. Orsino sent Olivia no ring, so Viola/Cesario must be the object of this ruse, Viola reasons.

The result of her discovery is pity, for she calls Olivia "Poor lady" (2.2.26), in the sense of pitiable, and tells the audience that Olivia might as well be in love with a dream. Viola thus realizes how easily her disguise has given the devil scope to do his work and how susceptible women are to handsome and presentable philanderers. Her conclusion is that the frailty or weakness of women (or of their situations in life) is to blame; that is, women are what they are and must be what they must be. Thus, where Olivia accepts her fate, Viola accepts her gender role. In the final lines of this soliloquy, Viola contemplates how this confusion will end, since she assumes that Orsino loves Olivia as she (Viola) loves him and as Olivia loves her, thinking she is Cesario. But she has no answers as to how this situation will work out. As a man, she has no chance to win Orsino's love; as a woman in love herself, her sympathies are with Olivia and the futility of her love. She concludes that only time can untangle this situation because it is too complicated a knot for her to untie by herself.

This willingness to let time solve problems allows *Twelfth Night* to be comedic. When characters insist on haste, as when Romeo rushes back to Verona from Padua and kills himself before Juliet can awake, or when Macbeth refuses to let chance make him king as the weird sisters promised and instead kills Duncan, tragedy ensues. Comedy is often viewed as allowing characters to transcend human limitations, whereas tragedies are about their inability to do so. Perhaps another way of describing the difference between the two genres is to say that in tragedies characters try to over-reach their limits and so are defeated, whereas in comedy they recognize and accept those limits and so succeed.

2.5.82–179. "What employment have we here? . . . thou wilt have me." Malvolio finds the letter Maria has written and placed in his path and begins to read it aloud, puzzling out its meanings as he goes, while Sir Toby, Sir Andrew, Maria, and Fabian watch from their hiding places and comment on his responses. The humor comes from his arrogance and the ease of the deception, but also from the obscenities embedded in the lines and the audience's participation in the plot to embarrass him. Malvolio considers his finding the anonymous letter a matter of luck, and he immediately leaps to the conclusion that Maria intended, that the letter is from Olivia. Maria had prepared him for this by telling him, as he remembers, that Olivia fancied him (2.5.23–24), and he has convinced himself that Olivia has hinted to him of her affection, suggesting that if she ever fell in love, it would be with someone of his type (though she probably really meant someone of his seriousness). He takes the respect with which she treats him as further confirmation of her affection. For Elizabethans, he is out of line in his ambitions, since, as house steward, he is too far beneath Olivia in rank ever to be considered a possible suitor, as he should know. Yet he recalls a situation in which a lady of property married a servant and takes that union for a precedent he might follow (2.5.39–40).

In fact, even before he finds the letter, he begins to imagine what he would do if he married Olivia. After three months of marriage, dressed in a fashionable velvet robe and leaving Olivia in bed sleeping, he would call his servants, he daydreams in lines 44–80, and then would summon Sir Toby to make Toby understand his place. Malvolio, who is now lord of Olivia's estate—in his imagination—extends his ring to be kissed and insists that Toby give up drink and his friendship with Sir Andrew ("a foolish knight," 2.5.78).

Upon finding the forged letter Malvolio expresses his recognition of Olivia's handwriting in bawdy terms. He cites "her very c's, her u's, and her t's," (2.5.87, with "and" pronounced as "n"), adding, "and thus makes she her great P's" (2.5.87–88), in the sense of urinate, a joke Sir Andrew, dense as usual, does not understand (2.5.89), though his very questioning of those particular letters calls the audience's attention to the bawdy innuendo. Malvolio claims to recognize Olivia's style and wax seal impression of Lucretia, a noble Roman matron who killed herself to save her honor (the subject of one of Shakespeare's long narrative poems). The silly, cryptic verses enclosed admit loving but call for secrecy, suggest power over the loved one, and provide letters (M.O.A.I.) to identify the secret object of adoration (2.5.96–99, 104–107). These letters probably stand for the four elements to which Malvolio so often refers: Mare (sea), Orbis (earth), Aer (air), and Ignis (fire). Malvolio figures out right away that Olivia is superior and therefore fits the lines, though he finds the letters puzzling, finally seeking satisfaction in the fact that they all are letters from his name.

The encouragement not to fear greatness and the suggestion that some have greatness thrust upon them when Fate helps them to rise combine to convince Malvolio that he should follow the letter's advice: to be proud and pushy, to argue with "a kinsman" (2.5.150), whom he takes to be Sir Toby, to be surly and unfriendly with servants, to talk about lofty matters, to wear yellow stockings cross-gartered, and thereby to embrace his fate. Malvolio takes these admonitions to be the advice of Olivia and resolves to better himself in this way, because the letter warns at its close that if he does not take a chance on love and advancement, he will remain a steward and a servant forever. The signature emphasizes the lady's willingness to make him her lord. Malvolio resolves to follow these instructions precisely, convincing himself that Olivia praised his yellow stockings and his cross-gartering (black lacing that runs from thigh to ankle, a fashion extreme worthy of laughter). The postscript adds one more instruction: Malvolio has a lovely smile and is therefore asked to go about his duties smiling hugely as proof of his love and to smile all the more in Olivia's presence. Maria knows that smiles are an insult to Olivia's pose of grief, that yellow is a color she detests, and cross-gartering a fashion she loathes, so Maria expects that Malvolio's resolve to be true to the letter is bound to result in Olivia's fury. Sir Toby is so taken with the cleverness of the letter that he promises to marry Maria as a reward. The humor that follows derives from the audience's anticipating Malvolio's behavior and Olivia's response and finding those anticipations played out most hilariously.

4.3.1–21. "This is the air, . . . the lady comes." Sebastian's soliloquy responds directly to Olivia's behavior. She has mistaken him for Cesario in 4.1 and has aggressively taken advantage of his hesitation (and bewilderment). Sebastian, believing his twin is dead, does not know what to think. He has to convince himself that he is still in the real world, breathing air, enjoying the sunshine, because this stranger greeted him like a lover, gave him a pearl that he can see and feel so he knows it is real, and has left him doubting his own sanity. He would like to get his friend Antonio's advice in this matter, but he did not find him at the Elephant Inn, though Antonio had been there, paid for a room, and told the innkeeper that he was going in search of Sebastian. Sebastian thinks that Antonio's input would be worth its weight in gold. As it is, however, Sebastian is on his own. Common sense tells him to be distrustful, and even though he believes what is going on is due to some accident, not madness, yet these experiences are so out of the ordinary that he does not quite trust his eyes or even his own logic.

Maybe he is mad, or maybe Olivia is. Yet, he reasons, if she were truly mad, she would not be able to run her household, command her servants, or manage her business matters so competently, confidently, and smoothly as he sees she does. The only reasonable conclusion, then, is that something is going on that he does not fully understand. Having reasoned his way to this conclusion, Sebastian is prepared to act on instinct when Olivia returns, and he agrees to follow her to a priest and marriage. This done, viewers can anticipate the ending: Orsino's anger, Viola's unveiling, and a restoration of balance and order through other marriages. Like Olivia in 2.2.41, he is willing to let events unfold as they will. He does not seek to impose his will upon them, and the result is favorable.

5.1. 389–408. "When that I was . . . every day." Feste's song ends the play. Music opened this production, and music closes it. The repeated jokes about "dryness" throughout the play in contrast to Olivia's tears and Sir Toby's drinking are replaced at the end with the wet, rainy world of Feste's song: "For the rain it raineth every day" (5.1.392ff). Feste, who has moved between both households, commenting ironically on both, in modern productions is left alone on the stage to sing the final words directly to the audience. One of his earlier songs had warned that youth does not endure (2.3.52). The song in act 5 confirms that idea. It moves forward chronologically from childhood to old age, a quick summation of the ages of man, and emphasizes the changes in perception undergone through maturation: The tiny boy, foolishly playing, his childish folly little regarded; the mature adult male being turned away from homes as a rogue or a possible thief, and needing himself to guard against knavery; the married man, whose boasts do not feed or clothe his family or sweeten his marriage; and later, the drunkard sleeping with drunks, for youth and beginnings came a long while ago. In each case, too, the reference could be to the fool's maturation from childish tricks and toys that amuse to cynicism that threatens respectable society, so the fool is shut out at the gate, to finally the swaggering, dissembling, and drunkenness of the aging fool. Yet throughout a lifetime the wind and rain persist, reminders of the unchanging harshness of reality. They keep the child indoors, the youth drenched, and, after revels, they must be faced again. Still, Feste is "for all waters" (4.2.63) and thus for all humors.

This is a melancholy song, bittersweet, a song of transition that awakens the audience from the dream or illusion of the play, in which, despite the potential for disaster, violence, and death, all ends happily in marriages and social order. Now that the play is done, the audience must face the wind and the rain on their own. However, the promise of the playwright, and of the actors, is that there will be other plays to entertain and to help the audience escape from daily toil, and the writer's and players' goal will be to amuse and please when the audience returns for another show.

Annotated Bibliography

Booth, Stephen. *Precious Nonsense: The Gettysburg Address, Ben Jonson's Epitaphs on his Children, and "Twelfth Night."* Berkeley: U of California P, 1998. The last chapter of this book, a close reading of the texts listed in the title, focuses on the role and value of nonsense in the play: the opposition of significant and insignificant imagery, of propriety and impropriety, of closure and lack of closure. Booth analyzes the syntax of a number of speeches, criticizes the treatment of Malvolio, and questions the neatness of the ending.

Box, Terry. "Shakespeare's *Twelfth Night*: 'The Miller's Tale' Revisited." *CLA Journal* 37 (September 1993): 42–55. Shakespeare incorporates into his play satirical elements analogous to those Chaucer used in "The Miller's Tale." Both authors satirized conventions of courtly love; both used numbers, sex-role reversal, and details of character development to satirize romantic love.

Cahill, Edward. "The Problem of Malvolio." *College Literature* 23 (June 1996): 62–82. The Malvolio subplot involves comic errors, disguise, and performance; its comic force drives the subplot and the main story. Cahill uses modern identity theory to explore the flaws in Malvolio's character.

Edgecombe, Rodney. "Shakespeare's *Twelfth Night*." *Explicator* 55 (Summer 1997): 200–202. Shakespeare purposely selected the colors of his players' costumes to accord with the natures of the characters who wore them and to capture visually the clash between gallantry and Puritanism. To Elizabethan audiences the waspish colors yellow and black suggested usurpation and sexual aggression.

Gras, Henk K. "Direct Evidence and Audience Response to *Twelfth Night*: The Case of John Manningham." *Shakespeare Studies* 21 (1993): 109–155. Gras examines Manningham's diary account of Elizabethan audience responses to the play, its humor and its wit.

Hollander, John. "*Twelfth Night* and the Morality of Indulgence." In *Modern Shakespearean Criticism*. Ed. Alvin B. Kernan. New York: Harcourt, Brace & World, 1970. 228–241. Shakespeare, who acted in Ben Jonson's play *Every Man in His Humour* in 1598, wrote *Twelfth Night* to counter Jonson's more didactic and emblematic comedy. Shakespeare aimed for moral comedy in which he represented human experience through "fully dramatized metaphor rather than a static emblematic correspondence" (241). The result is a moral vision "as intense as that of the problem comedies" (241).

Osborne, Laurie E. "Antonio's Pardon." *Shakespeare Quarterly* 45 (Spring 1994): 108–114. Osborne analyzes the theatrical interpretation of Antonio's pardon at the end of the play and his homoerotic love for Sebastian. He discusses three performance editions at the Theatres Royal, Drury Lane, and Covent Garden in 1808; revision by J. P. Kemble and publication and performance at the Theatres Royal in 1815; and performance by Madame Helena Modjeska in 1883.

———. "Cutting up Characters: The Erotic Politics of Trevor Nunn's *Twelfth Night*." In *Spectacular Shakespeare: Critical Theory and Popular Cinema*. Ed. Courtney Lehmann and Lisa S. Starks. Madison, NJ: Fairleigh Dickinson UP, 2002. 89–109. Trevor Nunn's film adaptation of the play combines stage conventions and theatrical traditions of this play with heavy-handed modern film editing strategies (like crosscutting) to keep the focus on character continuity, with Viola and Orsino his central cinematic figures. Nunn complicates Viola's character, using her to explore both romantic and twentieth-century gender ideologies as he makes her plausible to modern viewers. The result of providing a complex weave of gender identity is an interesting but flawed production.

Troilus and Cressida

Charles R. Trainor

PLOT SUMMARY

The Prologue. An actor dressed in armor enters and announces to the audience that the play starts in the middle of the Trojan War after the city of Troy has been under siege for several years.

1.1. As the action begins, we meet Troilus, the youngest son of Priam, King of Troy. Troilus is so lovesick over Cressida that he feels unable to take up arms. Troilus asks Cressida's uncle, Pandarus, to arrange a meeting, although the go-between complains that he has received little thanks for his efforts to date. Troilus comments to himself that Pandarus is difficult to deal with but concedes that "I cannot come to Cressid" except through him (1.1.95). Aeneas then arrives with the news that Menelaus has wounded Paris, and Troilus leaves to join his fellow Trojans in the fight.

1.2. Cressida's servant informs her that on the preceding day, the Greek warrior Ajax got the better of Hector, who is now battling fiercely in an attempt to redeem himself. Pandarus then enters, and he and Cressida comment on the Trojan lords as they watch them return from the field. Pandarus has kind words for each but insists that none can compare to Troilus, and he promises to bring his niece a love token from the young man. After he exits, Cressida admits in soliloquy that she returns Troilus's affection but is coyly pretending otherwise since "Men prize the thing ungain'd more than it is" (1.2.289).

1.3. In the Greek camp, Agamemnon asks his commanders why they seem depressed. It is true that their long siege of Troy has so far proven fruitless, but he argues that they should not despair. After all, only adversity brings out true greatness. The elderly Nestor concurs with the King, but Ulysses asserts that their army has a serious problem. Rather than being unified, it has disintegrated into factions, and this is in large part the fault of Achilles. Grown "dainty of his worth" (1.3.145), he petulantly refuses to take orders and lounges in his tent with his lover, Patroclus, who clownishly mocks the efforts of the rest. Achilles' insubordinate ways have been spreading to the other soldiers, and as a result the Greek forces are paralyzed.

As the commanders begin to discuss the issue, Aeneas arrives from Troy to announce that Hector has issued a challenge to single combat. Ulysses suspects that this is meant for Achilles, the only Greek warrior who could hold his own against Hector. However, Ulysses thinks it would be unwise to allow Achilles to be their champion. If he won, he would become even more insolent, and if he were to be defeated, the loss would demoralize their whole side. Consequently, Ulysses proposes that Ajax should meet Hector. If he fails, the Greeks can allege that Achilles would have won, and by selecting the oafish Ajax, they will aggravate Achilles. Ulysses hopes that this snub will wound the man's pride enough to bring him back to the field.

2.1. Ajax orders Thersites to bring him news of Hector's challenge, but the malcontent Thersites responds with insults. These lead Ajax to beat him, and when Achilles and Patroclus enter, Thersites curses them as well. Achilles informs Ajax about the single combat and tells him that their champion will be chosen by lottery.

2.2. In the king's palace in Troy, Priam and four of his sons discuss whether they should go on with the war or simply give Helen back to the Greeks. Hector argues that "she is not worth what she doth cost" (2.2.51), and his brother Helenus agrees. Their sister Cassandra suddenly appears and warns that if they do not return Helen, Troy will be destroyed. Troilus, though, dismisses her as mad and declares that they must continue the war at any cost, a position that Paris endorses. In response, Hector says that the reasons offered by Troilus and Paris reveal that the young are unfit to make important decisions: they are ruled by emotion, not reason. Troilus, however, asserts that in waging war for Helen, they are not fighting merely for her but for their honor, and Hector finally gives in.

2.3. In soliloquy, Thersites jeers at Ajax and Achilles, and after Patroclus comes on stage, Thersites mocks him, too. Achilles then enters but quits the scene when the Greek leaders draw near. Agamemnon requests his presence, but Patroclus lies and says that Achilles is sick. When Ulysses nevertheless goes into his tent to speak with him, he remains uncooperative, leading Agamemnon to propose that Ajax appeal to him. Ulysses, though, opposes the idea, and after complimenting Ajax, the leaders nominate him as their champion and leave Achilles to sulk in seclusion.

3.1. In Priam's palace, Pandarus requests that Paris and Helen make excuses for Troilus's absence if the king calls for him at supper that evening. The couple is curious as to where Troilus will be, but Pandarus will not say. They both infer, however, that he will be with Cressida and proceed to make sexual jokes about love. Pandarus contributes by singing an off-color song on the subject, but after the sound of a retreat is heard, they leave to meet the soldiers.

3.2. On his arrival home, Pandarus finds Troilus awaiting him. The young prince begs him to set up a meeting with Cressida, and Pandarus agrees to bring her to him, a piece of news that leaves Troilus overjoyed. When the uncle does indeed return shortly with his niece, the two young people confess their feelings for each other and swear to be eternally true. Troilus goes as far as to declare that future lovers will pronounce themselves "as true as Troilus" (3.2.181), and Cressida replies that should she ever betray him, she hopes that fickle lovers will henceforth be termed "[a]s false as Cressid" (3.2.196). Pandarus then takes the happy couple off to consummate their relationship.

3.3. In the Greek camp, Cressida's father, Calchas, a Trojan priest who has defected, beseeches Agamemnon to trade a captured soldier for his daughter. The King orders it to be done and puts Diomedes in charge of the matter. At Ulysses' urging, the Greek leaders then parade by Achilles, contemptuously slighting his greetings. When the confused Achilles seeks to know the reason for these snubs, Ulysses explains that a man cannot rest upon his laurels. It is now Ajax and not Achilles who is viewed with approval, since past achievements are quickly forgotten and "the present eye praises the present object" (3.3.181). Ulysses adds that he knows Achilles is secretly in love with Hector's sister Polyxena and cautions that the Greek would do well to give her up and return to battle. When Ulysses leaves, Patroclus urges his companion to follow that recommendation, and Achilles says that he will. Thersites then enters and imitates Ajax's pridefully strutting about, after which Achilles exits with Patroclus.

4.1. When Diomedes arrives in Troy to arrange the trade for Cressida, he is warmly welcomed. Aeneas and Paris agree, however, that this turn of events will be hard on Troilus, and Aeneas leaves to explain the situation to the young man. Paris asks Diomedes whether he thinks Paris or Menelaus is worthier of Helen, and Diomedes caustically responds that since the two are deluded enough to fight over "contaminated carrion" (4.1.72), they merit her alike.

4.2. With the coming of dawn, Troilus is about to leave Cressida, who begs him to tarry a little. After Pandarus enters and makes lewd jokes about the lovers' night together, Aeneas arrives and tells Troilus that Cressida is to join her father with the Greeks. As the youth accompanies Aeneas to the palace, Pandarus informs the grief-stricken Cressida of what has been decided.

4.3. The disconsolate Troilus agrees to tell his love that she must accompany Diomedes to the enemy camp.

4.4. Pandarus is unable to comfort Cressida in her misery, and on Troilus's return the pair swear to be eternally true. He tells her that he will bribe the Greek sentries and visit her often, and when Diomedes enters, the young man threatens to kill him if he lets anything happen to Cressida. Diomedes responds that he will not take orders from Troilus and will treat her as he judges fit.

4.5. When Diomedes and Cressida reach the Greeks, the leaders welcome her courteously, and after Agamemnon kisses her, Ulysses urges everyone else to do so as well. In a passage full of rhyme and wordplay, she uncomplainingly bestows a round of kisses, causing Ulysses to brand her one of the "sluttish spoils of opportunity / And daughters of the game" (4.5.62–63).

The Trojans enter for the single combat, but Aeneas notes that Hector is likely to fight only halfheartedly since he and Ajax are cousins. Soon after the fight begins, Hector does indeed call it to a halt on the grounds that Ajax is his father's sister's son, and the two relatives embrace. Ajax then invites "My famous cousin to our Grecian tents" (4.5.151), and Hector and the enemy leaders warmly praise each other. When he faces Achilles, however, the pair exchange harsh words and pledge to meet the next day in battle. As Hector goes off to feast with the Greeks, Troilus queries Ulysses on where he may find Cressida's father. Ulysses agrees to guide the prince to him although he adds that Diomedes has already been openly admiring the young woman.

5.1. Achilles receives a letter from Hecuba, the mother of the Trojan princess with whom he is involved. In it, she and her daughter plead with him to keep his promise not to fight, and he informs Patroclus that he will honor the request. After the two men leave, Thersites rails against the Greeks and then watches Diomedes head off to visit Cressida, followed first by Ulysses and Troilus and then by Thersites himself.

5.2. At her father's tent, Cressida greets Diomedes as Troilus and Ulysses eavesdrop from one spot and Thersites from another. Diomedes flirts with her, and she reacts coquettishly by alternately putting him off and leading him on. She offers him the love token that Troilus just gave her but immediately retracts it, only to present it to him once again. He says that he will wear it on his helmet, and she promises to sleep with him that night. After they exit, Troilus is wrenched with despair over her betrayal. At first, he even tries to deny the reality of what he has seen but then vows to seek out Diomedes and kill him in combat.

5.3. As morning approaches, Hector prepares for the day's fighting despite strong opposition from his wife, Andromache, and his sister Cassandra. Andromache has had terrifying dreams about his death, but he ignores both women's fears. Troilus then enters and announces his intention to join the battle despite the fact that Hector thinks him too young. Troilus in turn criticizes Hector for showing mercy to his enemies, at which point King Priam enters to beseech Hector to stay home. The warrior, though, is unswayed and leaves as Pandarus arrives with a letter from Cressida. Troilus reads it only to reject it as "Words, words, mere words" (5.3.108), after which he goes off to face the Greeks.

5.4. In the midst of the fighting, Thersites rages against anyone and everyone and watches as Troilus and Diomedes, locked in combat, pass through. Next Hector comes on the stage and is about to engage Thersites, who begs off on the grounds that he himself is not a man of honor.

5.5. Diomedes is arranging to present Troilus's captured horse to Cressida when Agamemnon arrives and tells him to rejoin the battle. Hector has killed Patroclus, and the fighting is going badly for their side. At Nestor's bidding, Patroclus's body is taken to Achilles, who at long last takes up arms in pursuit of revenge.

5.6. Like one possessed, Troilus fights with both Ajax and Diomedes simultaneously. Achilles begins to battle Hector, but the Greek tires quickly and exits, at which point Troilus returns and declares his resolve to rescue Aeneas, whom Ajax has taken prisoner.

5.7. Achilles orders his men to help him search for Hector and to "Empale him with your weapons round about" (5.7.5). After they leave, Thersites watches Paris and Menelaus fight but flees when the illegitimate son of Priam (Margaleron) challenges him to combat.

5.8. As the day approaches its end, Achilles and his men come upon the resting Hector, who has laid down his sword. The Greek commands his soldiers to kill the unarmed Trojan, whose body they then tie to his horse's tail so that he may drag it after him.

5.9. The Greek leaders hear that Achilles has slain Hector, and Agamemnon now believes that "Great Troy is ours, and our sharp wars are ended" (5.9.10).

5.10. As Aeneas leads the Trojans back to their city, Troilus vows revenge against Achilles and curses Pandarus, who remains alone onstage to speak the epilogue. In it, the go-between complains about his ill treatment after all his efforts, and he promises to bequeath his diseases to the audience.

PUBLICATION HISTORY

We know that *Troilus and Cressida* was written by 1603. On February 7 of that year, James Roberts entered it in the Register of the Company of Stationers, that is, of publishers and booksellers, although in the past a few scholars tried to argue that the play was written as far back as the late 1590s. For example, Arthur Acheson assigned it to 1598–1599 because he believed the work to be directed against George Chapman's idolatry of Homer as demonstrated in his 1598 translation of the *Iliad* (*Shakespeare and the Rival Poets* [New York: John Lane, 1903], 175). Similarly, Leslie Hotson (in *Shakespeare's Sonnets Dated* [New York: Oxford UP, 1949], 37–43) placed the drama before 1598 based on his theory that it was actually the *Love's Labours Won* referred to by Francis Meres in that year. However, the preponderance of evidence, along with the poetic maturity of scenes like those of the Greek and Trojan councils, makes it likely that the play dates from around 1602. The Prologue itself may offer additional proof in its mention of "a prologue armed" (l. 23), a possible allusion to the armed Prologue in Ben Jonson's *Poetaster* (1601). In fact, the figure of Ajax in the play may be a satirical jab at Jonson himself.

Another figure whom Shakespeare may be parodying in the drama is the Earl of Essex, whose failed rebellion had occurred in 1601. Shakespeare's source, Chapman's translation of the *Iliad*, is dedicated to the earl, whom it explicitly compares to Achilles, and critics like John Dover Wilson see parallels between the Greek warrior and Essex in *Troilus and Cressida* as well (*The Essential Shakespeare* [Cambridge: Cambridge UP, 1932], 101–102). Just as Achilles has withdrawn to his tent and refuses to return to action, Essex left court after a rebuke from the Queen and retired to his estate at Wanstead. Moreover, just as Ulysses warns Achilles of the need to come back to the fold, Essex remained in self-imposed exile for so long that his friends gave him similar advice. However, most critics argue against there being a sustained political allegory in the play. As Oscar Campbell points out, Essex's withdrawal was over by the end of 1600, in other words, probably before the drama was even written (219–223). In fact, the work was likely composed not while Essex was sulking in seclusion but a short time after he was executed for his failed rebellion.

Nonetheless, while Achilles may not be Essex, the play does have a topical connection. While it takes place during the dying years of Troy, its overall mood reflects that of the dying years of Elizabeth's England. Economic and social changes, Essex's revolt, and the queen's declining health gave rise to a sense of threatening instability, of anxious helplessness, that may lie behind the air of disorder and disillusionment that marks the work. In fact, much as *Troilus and Cressida* shows how insubordination compromises the body politic, the England of Elizabeth's last years was itself racked with factions and feuds. Consequently, if there seems a palpable urgency to Ulysses' plea that order be reestablished before chaos descends, Shakespeare may well have had the contemporary situation in mind.

It was indeed shortly before Elizabeth's death in 1603 that James Roberts recorded *Troilus and Cressida* in the Stationers' Register. He then had the right to print the play once he had gotten permission from Shakespeare's acting company. However, either the entry was simply a holding one—in other words, an entry made simply to prevent piracy—or else permission was never granted since the work remained unpublished. On January 28, 1608, the drama was again recorded in the Stationers' Register, this time by Richard Bonian and Henry Walley, who subsequently did print the play in quarto—that is, in a single-play edition. It appeared in 1609 with the title *The Historie of Troylus and Cresseida. As it was acted by the Kings Majesties servants at the Globe.* Strangely, however, during the course of the printing, the title page was altered to read *The Famous Historie of Troylus and Cresseid. Excellently expressing the beginning of their loves, with the conceited wooing of Pandarus Prince of Licia*. Along with this change the printer added a prefatory epistle, but these were the only changes. Moreover, they were probably made before any copies of the quarto had been circulated, so the two different versions of the quarto should be regarded as simply variant states of the same issue.

Finally in 1623, John Heminge and Henry Condell included *Troilus and Cressida* in their anthology of Shakespeare's plays, the First Folio, but once again the circumstances were peculiar. Isaac Jaggard, the printer, had intended to place it after *Romeo and Juliet* and had even set three pages in type when, presumably because of copyright problems, he had to stop the press. Then, at the last moment the play was reinserted between the histories and tragedies but without page numbers and too late to be listed in the table of contents.

The Folio presents essentially the same text as the quarto with the addition of the prologue, a number of stage directions, and about forty-five new lines. The quarto was likely based on a transcript of Shakespeare's original draft, while the Folio may have been printed directly from the quarto collated with another manuscript. Each text has its champions, but in recent years the quarto has generally been accepted as the more authoritative version of the drama.

SOURCES FOR THE PLAY

For the military scenes, Shakespeare's major source was Homer's *Iliad*, primarily the seven books of George Chapman's 1598 translation. There Shakespeare found the story of Achilles, Ajax, and Hector as well as the basic personality of Thersites. For other aspects of the war scenes, such as Hector's visit to the Greek camp and his stripping an enemy of his armor, he was indebted to William Caxton's translation of Raoul Lefevre's *Recueil des Histoires de Troyes* (1475), newly edited in 1596, and John Lydgate's moralistic *Troy Book* (ca. 1412–1420).

For the love story, Shakespeare's use of sources is somewhat complex. He relied principally on Chaucer's narrative poem *Troilus and Criseyde* (ca. 1385–1386), which he followed in incident and outline, but since the tale of the young couple's ill-fated romance was highly popular throughout the sixteenth century, Shakespeare could readily have found material in other places as well. In fact, satirists and balladeers had retold the story so frequently that many of the characters had been reduced to caricatures in the public imagination. For example, Pandarus had become notorious as a go-between and procurer to the point that the word "pander" had turned into the occupational noun it remains. Similarly, Cressida's moral laxity was so well known that the phrase "a woman of Cressid's kind" was synonymous with a prostitute. Thus, in *Henry V* Pistol refers to Doll Tearsheet as "the lazar kite of Cressid's kind" (2.1.76), that is, the leprous whore like Cressida. As for why he would call her leprous, *The Testament of Cresseid* (1593), by the Scottish poet Robert Henryson, is most likely responsible. In early Chaucer anthologies, Henryson's piece was printed as an appendix to *Troilus and Criseyde*, and it presents its dying heroine as suffering from leprosy. In fact, she has been cast off by Diomedes, reduced to beggary, and is so altered that Troilus fails to recognize her when he offers her alms.

Given their contemporary degradation, it is not surprising that Shakespeare's characters are less sympathetic than Chaucer's; Shakespeare may follow his predecessor in substance but not in spirit. However, E. Talbot Donaldson points out that it would be wrong to view the playwright as simply "a victim of literary determinism" (77). After all, the man whose source for *King Lear* was a tale with a happy ending can hardly be considered a slave to received tradition. Indeed, even with the public debasement of the legend, Shakespeare goes out of his way to darken the story. As Heather James notes, he unerringly "selects the least reputable versions of characters and events and heightens their unsavory aspects" (93). Shakespeare, as usual, is in command of his materials and elects to present the tale as he does.

STRUCTURE AND PLOTTING

In terms of plotting, *Troilus and Cressida* presents difficulties. At the start the play seems structurally balanced: a scene between Troilus and Pandarus is followed by a scene between Cressida and Pandarus; the Greek council debates what to do about Achilles, and the Trojan council debates what to do about Helen. However, by act 5 the symmetry has completely collapsed. In fact, the work ends with a notably inconclusive conclusion in which the faithless heroine is unpunished, her anguished lover is unavenged, and a disreputable pimp gets the last word. So disjointed seems this fifth act that when John Dryden adapted the work for the Restoration stage, he simply wrote a new one. To complicate matters further, the plot repeatedly rouses audience expectations only to frustrate them. For example, Hector's much-touted single combat with Ajax quickly concludes in a draw, and his initial fight with his archrival Achilles ends abruptly when the latter grows tired and leaves. Moreover, when the two great warriors do reengage, instead of a climactic confrontation, we get Achilles ordering his minions to ambush his unarmed adversary.

However, as the very consistency of this deflation suggests, there is a structure to the play, although a deliberately unsatisfying one. Much as Thersites uses invective to undercut the characters, Shakespeare uses anticlimax to undercut events. Indeed, Joyce Carol Oates argues that the plot itself functions as a tool of irony. By continually puncturing the anticipated glories of love and war, the play intentionally highlights the discrepancy between humans as they ought to be and humans as they are. For instance, Achilles may present himself as the supreme soldier, but we ultimately see him behave not like a hero but like a thug. Cressida may pledge her eternal devotion to Troilus, but we ultimately see her affections change as quickly as her surroundings.

In fact, Troilus's reaction on observing Cressida's betrayal could serve as a metaphor for this very disjunction between what people profess and what they do. When she proves unfaithful, his vision of her breaks in two as he cannot reconcile what he sees with what he believes: "If there be rule in unity itself, / This is not she. . . . / This is, and is not, Cressid!" (5.2.141–146). With that hopeless dualism, the indivisible is split asunder, as "a thing inseparate / Divides more wider than the sky and earth" (5.2.148–149). Hence, all he can do is rage like another Thersites and join in the jumble that ends the play. Viewed from this perspective, the plot's descent from coherence into confusion simply mirrors the overall breakdown in unity that the drama records. If Ulysses' speech on the Chain of Being (1.3.75–137) predicts that anarchy will follow when order fragments, it is just that disintegration of symmetry that the play records as the structure collapses into apparent chaos.

MAIN CHARACTERS

Troilus

Troilus and Cressida includes a panoply of fascinating characters who have been the subject of much critical debate. Troilus is undeniably a brave youth, as his simultaneously fighting Diomedes and Ajax shows. Ulysses calls him, "a true knight, / . . . His heart and hand both open and both free, / . . . Manly as Hector, but more dangerous" (4.5.96–104), and once he takes the field he does indeed prove as determined and "manly as Hector." However, in his role as a romantic, Troilus often seems more princeling than prince, more boy than man. He is presented from the start as being in love with love and seems as overwhelmed by his feelings as the adolescent Romeo. Indeed, the experience Troilus aspires to is so all-encompassing and absolute that even he seems to suspect that it may be unattainable. As he tells Cressida, "This is the monstruosity in love, lady, that the will is infinite and the execution confin'd, that the desire is boundless and the act a slave to limit" (3.2.81–83). Similarly, on parting from her for the last time, he appears half-aware that the eternal and unwavering bond that he seeks may not lie within the realm of possibility. In a sense, he is like another Jay Gatsby; he asks too much. In his innocent idealism, he tries to capture a perfect love in an imperfect world, and the attempt leads him to his doom.

Moreover, if Troilus is unrealistic, that may not be his only flaw. In a play in which intellect is prized, he repeatedly shows himself to be the slave of passion. For example, when Troilus argues for continuing the war, Hector notes with disapproval that his brother has allowed his feelings to overcome his rationality and asks him pointedly, "[I]s your blood / So madly hot that no discourse of reason, / Nor fear of bad success in a bad cause, / Can qualify [moderate] the same?" (2.2.115–118). All too often Troilus is indeed ruled by emotion. He absents himself from his military duties at the start of the play because he is overcome with love, and when he finally joins the battle at the end, it is out of a desire for "venom'd vengeance" (5.3.47). In fact, that desire is so intense that he actually condemns Hector for showing mercy toward fallen enemies.

Even the quality of his celebrated love is open to question. Certainly he insists on its purity and sincerity, as when he assures Cressida, "I am as true as truth's simplicity, / And simpler than the infancy of truth" (3.2.168–170). His rhetoric in such passages, though, is so narcissistic and extreme that one wonders how seriously to take the youth. Moreover, in anticipating his night with Cressida, Troilus sounds on occasion more like the sensualist than the ideal lover, worrying whether she will prove so ravishing a morsel that she will dull his palate for future delectations.

Cressida

Cressida's personality is as problematic as is that of Troilus. Nestor calls her "[a] woman of quick sense" (4.5.54), and in her first appearance she is indeed lively and self-possessed, easily besting her uncle in wit. It is perhaps for this reason that George Bernard Shaw admired her greatly and declared Cressida to be the first real woman in Shakespeare's plays (*Shaw on Shakespeare*, Edwin Wilson, ed. [London: Cassell, 1961], 186). In Elizabethan times, however, Cressida was famous not for her clever mind but for her sexual looseness, and she in fact demonstrates a ready skill in the game of love. She admits that she has been toying with Troilus in order to prolong his wooing (1.2.286–295), and later she deliberately teases Diomedes to whet his amorous appetite. Moreover, the fact that she switches so effortlessly from exchanging love tokens with Troilus to dispensing kisses to a receiving line of Greeks lends support to Ulysses' contention that she is a knowing and shallow seducer of men.

Nonetheless, when she tells Troilus that she loves him, she sounds almost wistfully sincere, and on hearing the news that she must leave Troy, she actually appears more heartbroken than he. Given such facts, recent scholars like Richard Hillman have argued that she is no calculating sophisticate but simply a lone and helpless female cast adrift in a predatory world, an innocent who never means to deceive or betray. Certainly, Cressida does appear to recognize her precarious situation and the need to protect herself. Thus, she tells her uncle that she lies "Upon my back, to defend my belly, upon my wit, to defend my wiles, upon my secrecy, to defend mine honesty, my mask, to defend my beauty, and you, to defend all these" (1.2.260–263). But of course Pandarus does not defend her. Rather, he virtually serves her up on a platter to Troilus, much as her father seems willing to offer her to Diomedes. Consequently, if Cressida is sometimes coy, she may simply be employing a defensive strategy that allows her to fend off her male pursuers at least for a time.

Ulysses

Ulysses' personality has proven controversial as well. Traditionally, this legendary hero has been portrayed as the craftiest of the Greeks, and Shakespeare does indeed depict him as a shrewd man who, unlike Troilus, understands the world only too well. It is he who correctly diagnoses the problem within the Greek army and who proposes the scheme to manipulate Achilles and Ajax. In addition, with his praise of Troilus and courtesy toward Hector, he appears to demonstrate a level of decency rarely seen in the treacherous world of this play.

There may, however, also be a less positive side to Ulysses, who is sometimes more eloquent than effective. For instance, he may cleverly play Achilles and Ajax against each other, but his plan ultimately "is not prov'd worth a blackberry" (5.4.11–12), as Thersites observes. Moreover, if he shows intelligence, it is often less true wisdom than the political cunning of an operative for the state. Particularly chilling in this regard is his warning to Achilles that he has secret knowledge of that man's romance with an enemy princess: "All the commerce that you have had with Troy / As perfectly is ours as yours, my lord" (3.3.205–206). Critics like Harold Bloom sense an allusion here to Elizabeth's network of informants, turning Ulysses into a dreaded spymaster like Francis Walsingham (340). Furthermore, there may be a certain maliciousness to the man. For example, his quick condemnation of Cressida as nothing but a whore could be taken as an illustration less of keen insight than of harsh judgment, especially given the fact that he himself was the one who initiated the round of kissing. Similarly, out of alleged indignation he may inform Agamemnon and Nestor of how Achilles and Patroclus mock them, but he repeats their insults in such loving detail that it borders on the cruel.

Hector

However, if the personalities of some characters have sparked debate, others are more straightforward. For instance, Hector is widely regarded as closer to a hero than anyone else in this antiheroic play. Indeed, when he issues his challenge to single combat in the name of his lady love, he seems a figure of medieval romance, a knight "sans peur et sans reproche" (as was said of the chivalric Bayard—without fear and without reproach). Almost alone among the characters he is consistently portrayed as honest, honorable, and kind. The mercy shown by this great soldier is remarked upon repeatedly; and while Troilus, Paris, and Achilles may absent themselves from battle to pursue their own agendas, Hector never shirks his duty, not even when his father, wife, and sister all beg him to do so. Still, admirable as he is, no one in the cynical world of this play is depicted as ideal. Thus, after making a clear-sighted and convincing plea for Troy to return Helen and to end the war, he cavalierly reverses himself and almost offhandedly embraces her cause. Moreover, he meets his demise when he pursues a fleeing enemy out of a whimsical desire for his gaudy armor—an action unworthy of such a worthy man.

Thersites

If *Troilus and Cressida* features an array of flawed characters, however, few are more defective than Thersites. This bitter misanthrope is malice incarnate, a figure so repellant that others physically attack him. In many ways, he is less a participant in the action than an observer, as he comments like an endlessly cynical chorus on the "wars and lechery" (5.2.195) that surround him. Furthermore, his "spiteful execrations" (2.3.7) are not intended to improve others; they are simply an end in themselves. Thersites gleefully points out the world's scurrility as if to justify his own. Indeed, if he recognizes the baseness of his fellow Greeks, it is because he himself is so base.

"[L]ost in the labyrinth" of his own lacerating rage (2.3.1–2), his universal hatred has warped his perception and left Thersites as deformed in soul as in body. He himself admits as much: "I am bastard begot, bastard instructed, bastard in mind, bastard in valor, in every thing illegitimate" (5.7.16–18). If he despises, he is despicable; if he scorns, he is scorned. Nevertheless, the reality around him is so vile that one cannot help but partly agree with him as he strips the strutting heroes of their self-proclaimed grandeur to reveal the rottenness within.

DEVICES AND TECHNIQUES

Troilus and Cressida is filled to an unusual degree with abstract thought and philosophical reasoning. G. Wilson Knight (in *The Wheel of Fire: Essays in Interpretation of Shakespeare's Sombre Tragedies* [London: Oxford UP, 1930], 60–61) notes a clear sign of the play's intellectuality: the characters repeatedly criticize each other's stupidity. For instance, the blockheaded Ajax is continually satirized, and Ulysses assails men like Achilles and Patroclus because they "[f]orestall prescience, and esteem no act / But that of hand. The still and mental parts, / That do contrive how many hands shall strike / . . . Why, this hath not a finger's dignity" (1.3.199–204).

With its cerebral tone, however, the work's language can be challenging. It is re-plete with such Latinate forms as "protractive" and "persistive" (1.3.20–21), and, as in *Julius Caesar*, the drama contains a substantial amount of formal disputation, most notably in the scenes of debate in the Greek and Trojan councils. Moreover, as Caroline Spurgeon has demonstrated in *Shakespeare's Imagery and What It Tells Us* (Cambridge: Cambridge UP, 1935), it is rich with patterns of imagery. For ex-ample, it is no accident that the play concludes with the word "diseases" because through repeated allusions to illness it stresses the corruption infecting the worlds of both love and war. Thus, the doting Troilus's heart is an "open ulcer" (1.1.53) and his pulse "feverous" (3.2.36); his love-inflicted wounds require "oil and balm" (1.1.61). Moreover, the man who brings the young couple together is himself a ver-itable compendium of diseases, with Pandarus complaining that "a whoreson ras-cally tisick [cough] so troubles me . . . and I have a rheum in mine eyes too, and such an ache in my bones" (5.3.101–105).

If lovers like Troilus and Paris suffer from "distemper'd blood" (2.2.169), so too do the soldiers, who are also linked with images of sickness. For instance, Achilles' behavior needs "physic" (1.3.377), and Thersites delights in the idea of Agamemnon covered with running boils and Ajax turning into "the loathsomest scab in Greece" (2.1.28–29). In fact, if he had his way, their entire cause and army would be stricken with the "Neapolitan bone-ache" (syphilis) and the "dry suppeago" (that is, ser-pigo, a skin disease, 2.3.18–19, 74).

Such allusions give the play a sense of physical blight, and a second pattern of imagery also links the characters to physicality. While their words may speak of the spiritual and pure, their deeds are often mired in bodily appetite, a fact that Shake-speare stresses through frequent references to food. Thus, Troilus looks forward to meeting his love with all the gusto of a discriminating gourmet:

> I am giddy; expectation whirls me round;
> Th' imaginary relish is so sweet
> That it enchants my sense; what will it be,
> When that the wat'ry palates taste indeed
> Love's thrice-repured nectar? (3.2.18–22)

He repeatedly refers to Cressida as if she were a luscious meal, as "food for for-tune's tooth" (4.5.293). When she betrays him, he reels with disgust on finding that the "scraps, the bits and greasy relics / Of her o'ereaten faith, are given to Diomed" (5.2.159–160). Similarly, food imagery is linked with Cressida's love for Troilus. For example, Pandarus urges his niece to sleep with the youth because he has all the "spice and salt that season a man" (1.2.255), and later when the go-between begs her to control her sorrow on parting from Troilus, she responds, "How can I moder-ate it? / If I could . . . brew it to a weak and colder palate, / The like allayment could I give my grief" (4.4.5–8).

However, if love is a physical appetite, one can also have a taste for war, and the play applies the same food imagery to the military realm. Thus, Ajax threat-ens to "knead" the haughty Achilles and make him "eat swords" (2.3.221, 217), while Ulysses says that that proud warrior "bastes his arrogance with his own seam [lard]" (2.3.185). Moreover, Ulysses concludes his great speech on order with a warning on the very subject of appetite. Branding it the "universal wolf," he states that if "seconded with will and power," appetite "[m]ust make perforce an universal prey / And last eat up himself" (1.3.121–124). In other words, if unleashed and empowered, a devouring hunger is the ultimate annihilator, consuming all within its reach and bringing a return to primal chaos. It is through his use of food imagery that Shakespeare embeds this notion of the dangers of appetite throughout the entire play.

THEMES AND MEANINGS

Troilus and Cressida presents a world in which both war and romance are reduced to sordidness and stupidity. People may strive for the glory of battle and the heaven of love, but chivalry and affection are ultimately trumped by treachery and lust. To make matters worse, even their suffering seems futile, as it does not purify its victims but simply leaves them disillusioned or dead.

With all virtue under attack, it is not surprising that the characters repeatedly turn their attention to the concept of value. Frank Kermode notes that they focus in particular on two opposing viewpoints, namely, the idea that the worth of an object is intrinsic and the idea that its worth is simply the price we choose to assign it (129). When the Trojans debate the return of Helen, this opposition comes out clearly in the interchange between Troilus and Hector:

> *Troilus*: What's aught but as 'tis valued?
>
> *Hector*: But value dwells not in particular will;
> It holds his estimate and dignity
> As well wherein 'tis precious of itself
> As in the prizer. (2.2.52–56)

Ulysses raises this same question of the source of value when he advises Achilles that the determinant of merit is not inner but outer, that no matter how deserving you may be, you can gauge your superiority only by its reflection in the eyes of those around you:

> [N]o man is the lord of anything,
> Though in and of him there be much consisting,
> Till he communicate his parts to others;
> Nor doth he of himself know them for aught,
> Till he behold them formed in th' applause
> Where th' are extended; who, like an arch reverb'rate
> The voice again, or, like a gate of steel,
> Fronting the sun, receives and renders back
> His figure and his heat. (3.3.115–123)

Such allusions to worth fill the play, with the value of individuals reduced at times almost to a commercial matter. For example, on meeting Hector, Achilles examines and re-examines him, as if to set a price: "I will the second time, / As I would buy thee, view thee limb by limb" (4.5.237–238). Similarly, Troilus refers to both Cressida and Helen as pearls and their lovers as merchants (1.1.100–104, 2.2.81–83). Indeed, Hector feels that the Trojans have paid too much for Helen, who "is not worth what she doth cost" (2.2.51–52), an opinion that Diomedes would extend to his side as well (4.1.69–75).

If value is reassessed as changes occur and events unfold, time itself emerges as a major theme in the drama. According to Ulysses, "beauty, wit, / High birth, vigor of bone, desert in service, / Love, friendship, charity, are subjects all / To envious and calumniating Time" (3.3.171–174), and in *Troilus and Cressida* its ceaseless flow is in fact the great destroyer. Thus, about the armed conflict between their nations, Hector tells Ulysses, "the end crowns all, / And that old common arbitrator, Time, / Will one day end it" (4.5.224–226), and the approaching doom of Troy and of Hector himself does in fact hang over the entire play. Moreover, time the leveler is powerful not only in the world of war but also in the world of love, as Troilus's example tragically proves. The young man yearns for an unending experience, declaring that he loves with an "eternal" and "fix'd" soul (5.2.166). In effect, he envisions love as timeless, and when it does not stand the test of time, he is left raging at this impermanent world of flux.

However, if the work concludes in betrayal and defeat, not all the blame can be laid at time's doorstep. The characters themselves act in ways that precipitate their problems. In a play that decries irrationality, Troilus foolishly lavishes love on an unworthy woman, much as the Greeks and Trojans foolishly wage war over one. As for why they make such grave errors, the debate in the Trojan council provides the key. When Paris and Troilus argue for continuing the fight, Hector reprimands his brothers:

> The reasons you allege do more conduce
> To the hot passion of distemp'red blood
> Than to make up a free determination
> 'Twixt right and wrong; for pleasure and revenge
> Have ears more deaf than adders to the voice
> Of any true decision. (2.2.168–173)

Hector is correct. Consistently, and to their detriment, characters are not guided by morality or reason but by their feelings. For example, while Hector may dutifully fight for his country even in a war with which he disagrees, Paris and Troilus absent themselves to wallow in their love. Similarly, Achilles chooses to lounge self-indulgently in his tent rather than fulfill his obligations to the group. In fact, when Troilus and Achilles finally do take to the field, it is only to avenge the loss of their loves. It is as if the Trojan War is not being waged out of any rational commitment to the common good but has degenerated into a series of private quarrels based on anger and pride.

It is significant in this regard that Hector argues against the conflict because he subscribes to a higher law, a standard transcending individual desire. He believes in a law "[o]f nature and of nations" (2.2.185) that opposes fighting to retain another man's wife. Indeed, it is no accident that the play also contains Ulysses' speech on the hierarchy governing the universe with its divinely established rules and roles (1.3.75–137). Furthermore, he warns the Greek council,

> Take but degree away, untune that string,
> And hark what discord follows. Each thing meets
> In mere oppugnancy: the bounded waters

Should lift their bosoms higher than the shores
And make a sop of all this solid globe. (1.3.109–113)

Troilus and Cressida shows exactly that—the triumph of anarchy over order, as people ignore the general welfare to pursue their personal pleasure. The result is not community but chaos and a world in which "the bonds of heaven are slipp'd, dissolv'd, and loos'd" (5.2.156).

CRITICAL CONTROVERSIES

Troilus and Cressida may be Shakespeare's most unsettling play. It depicts celebrated heroes unheroically and a celebrated romance unromantically. Indeed, while it presents a legendary love and a legendary war, it presents the underside of that love and that war. We see a young man seeking a transcendent bond, but we also see a jaded procurer whose only aim is to bring the couple to bed. We see a passionate advocate who envisions the Trojan War as a matter of honor and renown, but we also see a hardened cynic who declares that "all the argument is a whore and a cuckold" (2.3.72–73).

The result of such destabilizing shifts is a discordant drama whose very nature is difficult to fix. For example, the title page of the 1609 quarto describes the play with the neutral word "history"—a designation that had no more specific meaning in those days than "story." However, the attached epistle then proceeds to label the work "comical," even comparing it to "the best comedy in Terence or Plautus." To add to the confusion, the Folio editors regarded it as neither a history nor a comedy but *The Tragedie of Troylus and Cressida*. In fact, they initially planned to position it immediately after *Romeo and Juliet*, although because of copyright difficulties they ultimately inserted it between *Henry VIII* and *Coriolanus* instead, that is, between the histories and the tragedies.

Faced with the enigmatic nature of the play, some twentieth-century scholars went so far as to invent new categories in which to place it. For instance, in 1931 W. W. Lawrence grouped it with *All's Well That Ends Well* and *Measure for Measure* as a problem comedy, a type of drama that lacks a tragic ending but incorporates a "preoccupation with the darker sides of life, serious and searching analysis of character and conduct, and drastic realism" (*Shakespeare's Problem Comedies* [New York: Frederick Ungar Publishing, 1960], 231). Oscar Campbell made yet another attempt at classification two years later; he argued that the work is not a problem comedy but rather a comical satire, a genre developed by Ben Jonson and John Marston between 1599 and 1602 and popularized by Jonson's *Every Man out of His Humour* (1599). Such a play features a collection of rogues and fools brought together in a loose plot that gains its unity from the presence of a sharp-tongued commentator like Thersites.

To this day there is no consensus on how to categorize this drama, which is unlike any other in the Shakespearean canon. His works regularly show love as eternal, but here it ends abruptly, and Ulysses asserts that it is always cut down by time. His works regularly show the need for forgiveness, but here Troilus faults Hector for demonstrating the "vice of mercy" (5.3.37). His works regularly show a humanity and generosity of spirit; here the play concludes not with Puck's wishing all a good night but with a pimp's wishing his diseases on the audience.

So pervasive is the play's cynicism that one is even left in doubt about what to take seriously. A case in point is Ulysses' majestic sermon on order. The picture that it paints of a hierarchical universe filled with corresponding harmonies is validated in works like *King Lear* and *Macbeth*, where chaos in the state creates chaos in nature. However, within *Troilus and Cressida* itself, it is not clear how fully we are meant to accept Ulysses' demand that we respect and bow to established authority. After all, the crafty Ulysses is himself part of the power structure and an operative for the state, and the worth of a ruler like Agamemnon is open to question. Aeneas, expecting "most imperial looks" (1.3.224) in the Greek leader, pointedly fails to recognize the ineffectual king, who generally seems more prolix than productive.

This interpretive uncertainty is not limited to the characters' speeches but extends to their personalities, where it is aggravated by inconsistencies of behavior. For example, Hector gives a long and well-reasoned condemnation of the war, only to conclude by suddenly reversing himself. Similarly, Troilus begins the play by condemning the Greek and Trojan soldiers as

> Fools on both sides! Helen must needs be fair,
> When with your blood you daily paint her thus.
> I cannot fight upon this argument;
> It is too starv'd a subject for my sword. (1.1.90–93)

One act later, however, we find him forcefully arguing for the validity of Helen's cause and the necessity of continuing the war at any cost. Indeed, Troilus's conduct throughout the play seems marked by contradictions. For instance, he professes to be hopelessly in love with Cressida during the first two acts, but after their night together in act 3 he appears almost eager to be gone. Moreover, on hearing that she is to be handed over to the Greeks, he is surprisingly self-possessed—"Is it so concluded?" (4.2.66)—and he acquiesces to her departure virtually without a fight. Given that he vehemently insisted on the need to keep Helen and not return her to the Greeks, his instant willingness to surrender Cressida is puzzling at best.

Such inconsistencies have led to widely divergent interpretations of the work's major characters. Is Troilus a tragic idealist betrayed by a heartless woman, or is he a self-centered sensualist who is glad to be rid of Cressida after fulfilling his lust? Is Cressida a knowing sophisticate who enjoys the games that she plays, or is she a defenseless innocent who is used and abused by the men who control her? Is Ulysses the author's spokesman and wisest of counselors, or is he a sinister manipulator whose words are empty and schemes unsuccessful? The characters' erratic actions that occasion such antithetical opinions may, however, be there for a reason. The play after all focuses on inconstancy as embodied in Cressida's betrayal and Achilles' rebelliousness, and it is possible that the characters' capricious conduct is meant to reinforce this idea. If Polonius advises, "This above all: to thine own self be true" (*Hamlet*, 1.3.78), then the ultimate form of betrayal is the very infidelity to one's stated beliefs that surfaces repeatedly in *Troilus and Cressida*.

Still, whatever the cause of the play's jarring shifts in tone and characterization, the result is a fundamental ambiguity, a pervasive ambivalence in which arguments are made only to be mocked, much as Achilles and Patroclus mock the Greek generals and Thersites ridicules all. The latter's assertion that opinion may be worn "on both sides, like a leather jerkin" (3.3.264–265) could easily apply to the work as a whole, a fact that has made *Troilus and Cressida* among the most critically disputed of Shakespeare's dramas.

PRODUCTION HISTORY

Many aspects of *Troilus and Cressida* invite controversy, even the date of its initial production. The 1603 entry in the Stationers' Register states that the play was "acted by my Lord Chamberlain's Men," apparently documenting its performance by Shakespeare's company at the Globe Theatre, probably during the winter of 1602–1603. Similarly, the original title page of the 1609 quarto states that the play was acted at the Globe by the King's Men, the "King's Men" being the new name for the Lord Chamberlain's Men. Oddly, however, the second issue of the quarto not only omits any reference to a production but also includes a preface asserting, "[Y]ou have heere a new play, never stal'd with the Stage, never clapper-claw'd with the palmes of the vulgar [or] sullied, with the smoaky breath of the multitude." In other words, it alleges that the drama had never been publicly performed.

As Daniel Seltzer points out in his introduction to the work in *The Complete Signet Classic Shakespeare* (New York: Harcourt Brace Jovanovich, 1972), this apparent contradiction has fueled numerous hypotheses. Perhaps the play was in rehearsal but proved too difficult and was withdrawn without being acted. Perhaps it was acted but not for the "vulgar" at the public theater. Perhaps it was staged instead for a private audience at the Inns of Court, where young men studied law and would appreciate the work's intellectual appeal. Perhaps it actually was produced at the Globe but failed and in that sense was "never clapper-claw'd" by "the multitude" (1000). It must be borne in mind, however, that such theories arise only because of the revised 1609 title page and added preface, and it may be a mistake to take these too seriously. The epistle's statement that this is "a new play" is clearly untrue, and the preface as a whole sounds like a marketing ploy aimed at convincing elitist readers that only they can savor such sophisticated fare. The evidence of the 1603 entry in the Stationers' Register and the first 1609 title page still stands, and both state unequivocally that Shakespeare's company had acted the drama. In the final analysis, any other suggestions are purely conjectural.

Whatever its original production history, *Troilus and Cressida* did not reappear on the London stage until 1679 and then not in its original form. Rather, it was performed in an adaptation by John Dryden, who presents Cressida as a completely faithful woman. In his rendering she merely pretends to love Diomedes as part of a scheme to escape, and when Troilus tragically misinterprets her actions, she kills herself. This version of the play, which Dryden fittingly subtitled *The Truth Found Too Late*, held the boards until 1734, after which *Troilus and Cressida* remained unstaged until 1898. In that year the Munich Literary Society mounted a production that significantly cut the text in order to insert scenes of Elizabethan theatrical life. This was followed by a single performance of the play in 1899 in Berlin and by subsequent stagings in Budapest (1900) and Vienna (1902). In 1904 Berliners again had the opportunity to see the work when it was produced at the Deutsches Theater.

It was not until 1907, however, that *Troilus and Cressida* was again presented to an English audience. This costume reading at the Great Queen Street Theatre was followed five years later by a production directed by William Poel for the Elizabethan

Stage Society. With a cast that included Edith Evans as Cressida and Hermione Gingold as Cassandra, it proved successful enough to be revived at Stratford-upon-Avon the next year. From that point on, performances of *Troilus and Cressida*, while never numerous, began to appear with some regularity in England. For example, it made its first appearance at the Old Vic in 1923, was acted at Stratford-upon-Avon in 1936 and at the Westminster Theatre in 1938. In the United States the first recorded production took place at Yale University in 1916, and by the end of 1941 there had been six more appearances of the work around the country. Germany, though, continued to lead the way with four stagings of the drama in 1925 alone.

World War II marked a turning point in *Troilus and Cressida*'s fortunes. With the cynicism that followed that war, the play's bitter satire on the glories of love and war resonated with audiences as never before, and since 1945 it has been acted repeatedly at the major Shakespearean venues, often with notable directors involved. To name only a few, Tyrone Guthrie staged it at the Old Vic (London) in 1956 in a production that was then taken to the Winter Garden in New York. Peter Hall and John Barton directed it at Stratford-upon-Avon in 1960, and Joseph Papp did the honors at the New York Shakespeare Festival in 1965. John Barton mounted it twice more for the Royal Shakespeare Company: in a 1968 production featuring an Achilles in drag and then again in 1976. Alvin Epstein directed the drama in 1976 at Yale Repertory, and Howard Davies did so in 1985 at Stratford-upon-Avon, which was also the scene of Sam Mendes's 1990 revival.

Troilus and Cressida has now earned a place of respect in the Shakespearean repertory. Indeed, in 1999 alone it appeared in five separate productions in England and the United States, including Trevor Nunn's lavish staging at the Royal National Theatre. Nonetheless, there has never been a motion picture of the work, although the British Broadcasting Corporation (BBC) has televised it three times. In 1954 the BBC aired an ambitious version that drew a negative reaction from critics and viewers alike. In 1966 the network televised the drama again, this time as acted by the National Youth Theatre, and in 1981 the BBC mounted a new production as part of its series "The Shakespeare Plays." Directed by Jonathan Miller, this capable interpretation featured a solid group of actors, received generally positive reviews, and is available on videocassette and DVD.

EXPLICATION OF KEY PASSAGES

1.3.75–137. "Troy, yet upon his bases . . . not in her strength." Ulysses' impassioned address on the natural and social hierarchy is among the most famous political speeches in Shakespeare, in part because it offers a concise statement of Elizabethan cosmology. Indeed, while some critics have sought to find specific sources for it, the ideas that it expresses are essentially the standard beliefs of the day. Thus, it was commonly accepted that God had imposed a universal order on his creation, a structure in which every aspect had its divinely appointed role. As the Church of England's 1547 homily "An Exhortation to Obedience" puts it: "In the earth God hath assigned kings princes with other governors under them, all in good and necessary order. The water above is kept and raineth down in due time and season. The sun moon stars rainbow thunder lightning clouds and all birds of the air do keep their order" (quoted by E.M.W. Tillyard in *The Elizabethan World Picture* [New York: Macmillan, 1944], 82). In fact, Shakespeare illustrates this idea

Joseph Fiennes as Troilus and Victoria Hamilton as Cressida in the Royal Shakespeare Company's 1996 production of *Troilus and Cressida*. Courtesy of Photofest.

of corresponding harmonies time and again in his works. For example, in *Macbeth* the murder of King Duncan leads to the disruption of nature as does the fighting of the King and Queen of the fairies in *A Midsummer Night's Dream*. However, it is in this speech by Ulysses that the playwright gives these ideas their fullest and most explicit treatment.

Ulysses begins by stating his premise: in the Greek army "the specialty of rule" (1.3.78)—that is, the prerogatives of supreme authority—has been neglected, with predictably bad results. To illustrate the problem, he compares society to a colony of bees, a familiar Elizabethan analogy that also appears in *Henry V* (1.2.187–204). Ulysses asks, if individual soldiers do not serve the general as bees do the hive, then "[w]hat honey is expected?" (1.3.83). His underlying thesis is that organized societies flourish only if all members respect the hierarchy and pursue, not their private pleasures, but the general welfare. Whatever their rank, they must fulfill their obligations to the whole, and if this structure is preserved and order maintained, the community will thrive. Indeed, in Ulysses' opinion, authority should make itself visible to all, or else the lowest might seem as worthy as the highest.

He then expands his argument for hierarchy to the entire universe, invoking the cosmic parallels that knit creation together. Declaring that the heavens themselves observe degree, he notes that the sun keeps the planets in alignment, without which they would wander into astrological positions that would wreak havoc on Earth. All is well as long as the sun rules as intended, but everything would go awry in the sea, in the air, and on the land if the planets proved unruly and spun out of control. Disorder in the celestial realm would lead to plagues, storms, earthquakes, and other natural disasters throughout the world. In essence, Ulysses is arguing that when authority is not maintained, anarchy results and the universe reverts to original chaos.

Given that all communities, schools, and commerce rest upon hierarchy, respect for it must be observed not only on the heavenly but also on the human plane. Alluding to the Elizabethan concept of creation as a great stringed instrument producing divine harmony, Ulysses says, "Take but degree away, untune that string, / And hark what discord follows" (1.3.109–110). The oceans would overwhelm the shores, sons would kill fathers, and might would make right, as brute strength triumphed and justice and morality disappeared. In their place, power, desire, and appetite would succeed each other as the dominant force and would ultimately consume all that exists. Thus, when degree is not respected, societies founder and humans become bestial and destroy themselves.

Ulysses' view of the consequences of hierarchy's collapse may sound unreasonably apocalyptic, but it was in fact a commonplace of the period with parallels in the works of other authors. For example, in his 1531 treatise *The Gouernour* (New York: E. P. Dutton, 1937), Thomas Elyot declares: "Take away ordre from all thynges what shulde than remayne? Certes nothynge finally, except some man wolde imagine eftsones *Chaos*. . . . Also where there is any lacke of ordre nedes must be perpetuall conflicte: and in thynges subjecte to Nature nothynge of hym selfe onely may be norisshed; but whan he hath distroyed that where with he dothe participate by the ordre of his creation, he hym selfe of necessite muste than perisshe; wherof ensuethe uniuersall dissolution" (3).

Having established the philosophical framework, Ulysses then brings his argument home with its application to the Greeks' situation. In all organizations there are those whose lot is to rule, and in the Greek army that individual is Agamemnon. Nonetheless, "the general's disdain'd / By him one step below" (129–130)—an obvious reference to Achilles' refusal to obey his superior's commands. Most Elizabethans would have shared Ulysses' view of this disobedience as a very grave infraction. In fact, one need only consider the conduct of another Shakespearean soldier to appreciate how wrongly Achilles is behaving. Unlike his Greek counterpart, Talbot in *1 Henry VI* shows the proper deference to his ruler:

> In sign whereof, this arm, that hath reclaim'd
> To your obedience fifty fortresses,

Twelve cities, and seven walled towns of strength,
Besides five hundred prisoners of esteem,
Lets fall his sword before your Highness' feet,
And with submissive loyalty of heart
Ascribes the glory of his conquest got
First to my God and next unto Your Grace. (3.4.5–12)

Achilles by contrast mocks those above him, and as a consequence, as Ulysses concludes, disrespect for authority has infected the entire army. Soldier after soldier imitates the insubordination that he sees before him, with the result that it is not the strength of the enemy but this spreading anarchy that keeps Troy standing.

2.2.163–193. "Paris and Troilus . . . joint and several dignities." Hector, too, stresses the need for order in his words to the Trojan council in act 2. That body is debating whether to go on with the war over Helen or to return her to the Greeks, and Troilus and Paris have spoken in favor of continuing to fight. Hector begins by saying that his brothers have argued eloquently but superficially, as is typical of youth. In an anachronistic reference to the *Nicomachean Ethics* (1.3), he adds that Aristotle himself considered young men unfit to discuss moral philosophy since, as Troilus and Paris have shown, they are ruled not by logic but by "the hot passion of distemper'd blood" (2.2.169). Indeed, says Hector, emotions are not to be trusted since they are "more deaf than adders to the voice" of reason (2.2.172), a reference to a popular misconception that dates back at least as far as Psalms 58:4–5. According to this belief, adders could make themselves deaf at will by putting their tails in one ear while laying the other against the ground.

Echoing Ulysses' views on a structured and regulated universe, Hector then asserts that a basic law of nature joins husband and wife. In fact, rather than permit one spouse's extramarital lust to violate the union, every nation has civil rules that reinforce nature's and prevent such a breach. It might be added that in raising this notion of parallel systems of law supporting each other, Hector is simply expressing an accepted view of the period. For example, in his 1593 work *Of the Laws of Ecclesiastical Polity* (New York: E. P. Dutton, 1907), Richard Hooker argues that the part of God's original plan "which ordereth natural agents we call usually Nature's law; . . . the law of Reason, that which bindeth creatures reasonable in this world, and with which by reason they may most plainly perceive themselves bound; . . . Human law, that which out of the law either of reason or of God men probably gathering to be expedient, they make it a law" (1.154–155).

Given such an ethical imperative, Hector contends that it is their obligation to return Helen to her husband in accordance with "these moral laws / Of nature and of nations" (184–185). Strangely, however, after forcefully explaining the necessity of surrendering the Spartan king's wife, he concludes by abruptly reversing himself and yielding to Paris and Troilus's position. Almost as if all that preceded were no more than an academic exercise, he agrees that they should keep Helen and continue the war since their honor and dignity are now engaged.

3.3.145–190. "Time hath, my lord, . . . great Mars to faction." Time is an important subject in *Troilus and Cressida*. The play features a walking exemplar of the concept in the aged Nestor, a "good old chronicle / That hast so long walk'd hand in hand with Time" (4.5.202–203), and hanging over the entire work is the impending ruin of Troy by this unstoppable force. Indeed, the drama includes repeated allusions to time's destructive power, with Troilus's own tragedy resulting from his mistaken belief that love transcends its grasp. It is, though, in Ulysses' speech to Achilles that this critical theme receives its most extensive statement.

He begins by asserting that uncaring time has on its back a "wallet" (3.3.145), that is, a large bag, an image that also appears in earlier works like Edmund Spenser's *The Faerie Queene* (1590–1596). However, whereas the wallet in most other sources stores faults, in this instance it contains a person's "good deeds" (3.3.148). Moreover, once deposited there, they are quickly forgotten and consigned to oblivion. Consequently, the only way to maintain your reputation is to be sure that your actions keep pace with time, since victories, once won, become like unused armor rusting on a wall. There are a thousand people waiting to replace yesterday's hero; and if you wander off the path of accomplishment for a moment, they will rush by you and leave you in their dust, much like a brave horse that falls in battle only to be trampled by lesser ones advancing from the rear.

Indeed, even if the present achievements of others are inferior to yours in the past, their deeds will receive more attention since time is like the host of a party who extends a tepid good-bye to those leaving while rushing to greet new arrivals with open arms. The flux of events lays all low. "[B]eauty, wit, / High birth, vigor of bone, desert in service, / Love, friendship, charity" (3.3.171–173)—nothing stands the test of time. Rather, it is human nature to love the new, no matter how derivative. We live in the present and so praise most highly that which is currently before our eyes. Therefore, Ulysses tells Achilles, you must not be surprised if the Greeks now worship Ajax instead of you; he is visible while you retire from view. You were previously acclaimed and might be so again if you did not stay hidden in your tent, a point that Ulysses then reinforces with a possible allusion to Book V of the *Iliad*. As he reminds Achilles, you once performed deeds so glorious that they led the very gods to join the battle and drove even "great Mars" to take sides (l. 190).

Annotated Bibliography

Bloom, Harold. *Shakespeare: The Invention of the Human.* New York: Riverhead Books, 1998. A comprehensive interpretation with a chapter devoted to each play. Bloom argues that Shakespeare created the representation of cognition, personality, and character as we know it today.

Campbell, Oscar James. *Comicall Satyre and Shakespeare's "Troilus and Cressida."* San Marino, CA: Henry E. Huntington Library and Art Gallery, 1959. A major study that attempts to categorize the play as a comical satire like Ben Jonson's *Every Man out of His Humour.*

Charnes, Linda. *Notorious Identity: Materializing the Subject in Shakespeare.* Cambridge, MA: Harvard UP, 1993. An investigation of Shakespeare's depiction of the culturally authorized figures of Richard III, Troilus and Cressida, and Antony and Cleopatra.

Donaldson, E. Talbot. *The Swan at the Well: Shakespeare Reading Chaucer.* New Haven: Yale UP, 1985. An analysis of Shakespeare's debt to Chaucer in the character of Falstaff and in the plays *A Midsummer Night's Dream*, *Two Noble Kinsmen*, *Troilus and Cressida*, and *Romeo and Juliet.*

Godshalk, W. L. "The Texts of *Troilus and Cressida*." *Early Modern Literary Studies* 1.2 (1995): 1–54. A review of the textual history of the work that offers several hypotheses about the Folio, its differences from the quarto, and the stage directions in the two texts.

Hillman, Richard. *William Shakespeare: The Problem Plays.* New York: Twayne, 1993. An examination of *Troilus and Cressida, All's Well That Ends Well,* and *Measure for Measure* that applies intertextual and metadramatic criticism to the problem plays, a genre which it views as problematic in itself.

James, Heather. *Shakespeare's Troy: Drama, Politics, and the Translation of Empire.* Cambridge: Cambridge UP, 1997. A study of Shakespeare's political use of the Troy legend in *Timon of Athens, Troilus and Cressida, Antony and Cleopatra, Cymbeline,* and *The Tempest.*

Kermode, Frank. *Shakespeare's Language.* New York: Farrar, Straus, Giroux, 2000. An analysis of the language in the plays that discusses *Troilus and Cressida*'s concentration on questions of opinion, truth, and value.

McCandless, David. *Gender and Performance in Shakespeare's Problem Comedies.* Bloomington: Indiana UP, 1997. An exploration of sexual difference in *All's Well That Ends Well, Measure for Measure,* and *Troilus and Cressida* using feminist-oriented performance criticism.

Oates, Joyce Carol. "The Tragedy of Existence: Shakespeare's *Troilus and Cressida.*" In *The Edge of Impossibility: Tragic Forms in Literature.* New York: Vanguard, 1972. 9–36. An essay that interprets the play as an almost modern and existential drama.

All's Well That Ends Well

Regina M. Buccola

PLOT SUMMARY

1.1. The play begins in the French palace of Rossillion, which is steeped in sadness. The Countess is mourning both the death of her husband, the Count of Rossillion, and the loss of her son, Bertram, who is preparing to leave for Paris to live with his new guardian, the King of France. Helen, daughter of the celebrated court physician at Rossillion, Gerard de Narbonne, became the ward of the Countess upon her father's death six months earlier. Having grown up at the palace where her father served, Helen has fallen in love with the companion of her childhood, Bertram. As Bertram leaves, Helen speaks of her love for him in an eloquent soliloquy, lamenting the class distinctions that she fears will make it impossible for him, a noble, to love her, the daughter of a court physician: "'Twere all one / That I should love a bright particular star / And think to wed it, he is so above me" (1.1.85–87).

Helen is interrupted in her reverie by Parolles, Bertram's lewd, cowardly friend, who draws her into a lengthy meditation on virginity and a consideration of Helen's daring query, "How might one do, sir, to lose it to her own liking?" (1.1.150–151). When Parolles departs, Helen determines to use whatever means are necessary to secure Bertram's love: "Our remedies oft in ourselves do lie, / Which we ascribe to heaven. . . . Who ever strove / To show her merit, that did miss her love?" (1.1.216–217, 226–227).

1.2. The King of France, weakened by a long illness that none of his physicians can cure, welcomes Bertram to Paris, and reminisces about the kindness and virtue of the deceased Count of Rossillion. With his courtiers the King discusses an ongoing war in Italy, ultimately deciding not to commit French troops formally, but authorizing them to enlist independently as paid soldiers if they wish. The scene concludes with the King's self-interested sorrow at the death of Gerard de Narbonne, noting, "He was much fam'd. . . . If he were living, I would try him yet" (1.2.71, 72).

1.3. Rinaldo, the Countess's steward and most trusted servant, overhears Helen agonizing over her love for Bertram and tells the Countess what he has heard. Sympathetic to her young ward, the Countess coaxes from Helen a confession of love and is ultimately persuaded to support Helen's plan to win Bertram by curing the King of his long illness. The Countess is not without her doubts, however. She asks Helen, "How shall they credit / A poor unlearned virgin, when the schools, / Embowell'd of their doctrine, have left off / The danger to itself?" (1.3.239–242). Invoking the mysticism that will surround Helen's cure of the King and long quest for Bertram's hand and heart, Helen enigmatically replies, "There's something in't / More than my father's skill" (1.3.242–243).

2.1. The King confers his blessing on a group of French lords who have decided to join the Italian wars. Foreshadowing the way that he will deal with Bertram and Helen, the King cautions his young soldiers, "see that you come / Not to woo honor, but to wed it" (2.1.14–15). At the King's behest, Bertram is left behind; he frets, "I am commanded here, and kept a coil with / 'Too young' and 'the next year' and ''tis too early'" (2.1.27–28).

The King's trusted servant, Lafeu, enters to announce the arrival of "Doctor She," bearing "a medicine / That's able to breathe life into a stone" (2.1.79, 72–73). His interest piqued, the King agrees to see her. Helen convinces the King to try her ministrations for forty-eight hours; at the end of that time, if she has not succeeded in curing him, she proposes that she be punished with a shameful death. In return, the King agrees to her condition if she does succeed: "Then shalt thou give me with thy kingly hand / What husband in thy power I will command" (2.1.193–194).

2.2–3. The King dances into the court with Helen, cured of his ailment, and calls his lords before him in fulfillment of his promise to allow her to choose a husband from among them. When she chooses Bertram, he reacts in horror. Shamed, Helen begs the King not to force the issue, but he insists. Meanwhile, Lafeu sizes up Parolles, perceiving him for the bombastic fool that he is. Taking his cues, for the moment, from Parolles, Bertram determines upon the duplicitous course of sending Helen home to Rossillion and running away from her to the Italian wars.

2.4. Bertram sends Parolles to do his dirty work for him, giving Helen the news that she must return to Rossillion at once, leaving her marriage unconsummated. She complies: "In every thing I wait upon his will" (2.4.54).

2.5. Lafeu tries to open Bertram's eyes to the low character of Parolles: "there can be no kernel in this light nut; the soul of this man is his clothes" (2.5.43–44). Unmindful of this advice, Bertram prepares to depart for Italy with Parolles. Helen comes to take her leave of him, pathetically begging at least a kiss of her husband: "Strangers and foes do sunder, and not kiss" (2.5.86). There is no stage direction to indicate Bertram's response to this request.

3.1–2. The Countess learns in a letter from her son regarding Helen that he has "wedded her, not bedded her" (3.2.21). Helen arrives bearing a letter of her own from Bertram, which vows that she can call him husband, "'When thou canst get the ring upon my finger, which never shall come off, and show me a child begotten of thy body that I am father to'" (3.2.57–59). Convinced that she has driven Bertram to endanger himself by entering the war, Helen decides, "I will be gone. / My being here it is that holds [him] hence" (3.2.122–123).

3.3. Bertram greatly impresses the Duke of Florence with his prowess on the battlefield.

3.4. Back at Rossillion, the Countess and Rinaldo discover Helen's flight.

3.5. Helen arrives in Florence, under the guise of making a religious pilgrimage. The Widow who runs the lodge for religious pilgrims introduces Helen to her daughter, Diana, noting Bertram's attentions to her.

3.6. Picking up where Lafeu left off, the Lords Dumaine attempt to convince Bertram of Parolles's unscrupulousness.

3.7. Helen admits that she is Bertram's wife and persuades the Widow and Diana to collaborate with her in tricking Bertram into sleeping with her and giving her his ring in exchange for a handsome dowry with which to marry Diana respectably. Continuing the play's riddling advancement of the plot, Helen declares this plan "Is wicked meaning in a lawful deed, / And lawful meaning in a [wicked] act, / Where both not sin, and yet a sinful fact" (3.7.45–47).

4.1. The Lords Dumaine trick Parolles into believing that they are members of a hostile army, and they take him hostage.

4.2. Diana arranges an assignation with Bertram, persuading him to give her his family ring, pointing out that, "Mine honor's such a ring, / . . . Which were the greatest obloquy i' th' world / In me to lose" (4.2.45, 48–49). She establishes the conditions for the momentous event that goes unstaged, Bertram's midnight rendezvous with Helen—whom he believes to be Diana—in total darkness. In soliloquy, Diana reveals that Bertram has vowed to marry her, once Helen dies.

4.3. The French lords interrogate the blindfolded Parolles in front of Bertram, proving him a disloyal coward.

4.4. Helen reports to the Widow and Diana of her success in the meeting with Bertram. Meanwhile, she has given out a story of her death in Florence, which has, in turn, made its way back to the court at Rossillion, hoping that the news will bring Bertram home from Italy.

4.5. Lafeu tells the Countess that both Bertram and the King are on their way to Rossillion, and that he has offered his own daughter's hand in marriage to Bertram, presumed to be a widower. Consumed with grief over Helen's reported death, the Countess agrees.

5.1. Helen, Diana, and the Widow have a difficult time trailing the King of France, but eventually overtake him upon his arrival at Rossillion.

5.2. Lafeu makes amends with the cast-off Parolles, considerably reduced in fortune and bravado.

5.3. The King and the Countess welcome a seemingly chastened Bertram back to Rossillion, forgiving him both for his defiance and for his ill treatment of Helen. The King then informs Bertram that he has already disposed of him in marriage once again, to Lafeu's daughter, Maudlin.

Bertram accepts this second marital choice, claiming, "At first / I stuck my choice upon her" (5.3.44–45). Asked to send a token of his esteem to Maudlin, Bertram produces a ring that Helen gave him during their night together in Florence. It turns out to be the King's own ring; Bertram's possession of it excites the King and Countess's suspicions that he had a hand in Helen's death. In horror, Lafeu withdraws his offer of his daughter's hand in marriage, just as a gentleman arrives with a letter announcing Diana's complaint against Bertram: he promised to marry her upon the death of his wife, and then fled the country when her death was announced. Using Bertram's ring as evidence against him, Diana brings the play to its riddling conclusion: "He knows himself my bed he hath defil'd, / And at that time he got his wife with child. / Dead though she be, she feels her young one kick. / So there's my riddle: one that's dead is quick" (5.3.300–303). This is Helen's cue to enter and present herself to Bertram in compliance with the conditions of his earlier letter about acquiring his ring and a child of his body. The play ends with a bittersweet reunion of husband and wife, bound together a second time under the eyes of the King and Countess.

Epilogue. The King comes to the edge of the stage to announce that with the end of the play he is again a common beggar (as actors were regarded if they lacked a patron). So he has come to beg the audience's applause. In exchange for the spectators' hands (applause), the actors will give their hearts (love) in a symbolic marriage.

PUBLICATION HISTORY

The textual history of *All's Well That Ends Well* is very straightforward, which has, paradoxically, produced a wide array of textual problems. There is no known reference to *All's Well* in Shakespeare's lifetime, nor any record that it was ever printed until its inclusion among the comedies in the First Folio (1623). This leaves scholars curious about the play's date of composition and early production history.

Since there are no surviving manuscript copies of any of Shakespeare's plays, scholars in the late nineteenth and early twentieth centuries developed an array of text-based analytical tools designed to help confirm Shakespeare's authorship and to develop a reliable chronology for the plays. While a case has been made for *All's Well* as an early play, today most scholars concur that the trio of "problem plays" (see "Critical Controversies," below) dates from the early seventeenth century. Both *All's Well* and *Measure for Measure*, the latter typically dated to 1603–1604, employ the plot device of a bed trick. There is no definitive way to determine the order of composition of these two plays, but a variety of similarities in their respective themes and tones suggest that they were composed in close proximity to one another. The general consensus runs to a date of approximately 1604–1605 for *All's Well*.

Part of the rationale for dating the play to the 1590s, the early part of Shakespeare's dramatic career, was the tantalizing possibility that *All's Well* might, in fact, be *Love's Labor's Won*, the sequel to *Love's Labor's Lost* attributed to Shakespeare in Francis Meres's *Palladis Tamia* in 1598. Such a connection would have resolved two problems with respect to the Shakespearean canon: the date of *All's Well* and the unaccountable loss of at least one of his plays. Scholars eager to find *Love's Labor's Won* in *All's Well* pointed to the relatively high incidence of rhymed verse that it contains—a feature deemed more prominent in Shakespeare's early, romantic comedies. However, as David Bevington has argued, Shakespeare does, in fact, employ rhymed verse in an anachronistic fashion in the romances—late plays that share with *All's Well* a reliance on an almost mystical resolution of nearly tragic life events (Introduction, *All's Well That Ends Well*, in *The Complete Works of Shakespeare*, 4th ed. [New York: Addison Wesley Longman, 1997], 362).

In addition, *All's Well* shares many features with Shakespeare's late tragedies, particularly *Hamlet*. Both plays open with fathers recently deceased, both contrast being and seeming (Helen declares, "I do affect a sorrow indeed, but I have it too" [1.1.54], while Hamlet protests of his grief, "Seems, madam? Nay, it is, I know not 'seems'" [1.2.76]), both feature heroes with problematic attitudes toward adult sexual relationships, and both feature officious fools in significant relationships with the hero (Polonius in *Hamlet* and Parolles in *All's Well* (see Susan Snyder, Introduction, *All's Well That Ends Well*, The Oxford Shakespeare [New York: Oxford University Press, 1993], 19–21). However, these connections are not entirely incompatible with an early date of composition, as it is possible that the play was written in the 1590s and revised in the early seventeenth century.

Indeed, as those who have performed extensive textual analysis of the First Folio have demonstrated, the text as we have it offers some evidence for possible authorial revision at a later time. However, such revisions could have been made within a matter of days after the original composition, rather than years later. It seems quite likely that the compositors who set the type for the First Folio were, in fact, working from authorial manuscripts, or, foul papers. Susan Snyder lists the following central features that mark this first surviving text of *All's Well* as derived from foul papers: speech prefixes that vary from scene to scene, or even within a single scene; vague or duplicated entry directions, or entries provided for characters who do nothing in the scene in question; and extraneous information in stage directions that seem to have been notes toward dialogue, rather than plans for stage action (ibid., 53). Curiously, however, there are also several calls in stage directions for musical instruments, including cornets, which were rare on the stage prior to 1609. This feature has produced the theory that the First Folio was typeset from a script that at some point had been annotated for performance, quite possibly after Shakespeare's retirement (ibid., 54).

The many confusions with respect to speech prefixes throughout the First Folio *All's Well* suggest a text set from an authorial manuscript with numerous additions in the margin. Such marginalia often prove confusing for a compositor and lead to speeches that appear out of sequence or are assigned to the wrong character. One of the most interesting disparities in the text concerns the names of the heroine and her partner in the bed trick. In the opening scene, Helen is referred to as "Helena" in dialogue, and this name is used with reference to her on three other occasions within the first two acts of the play, all stage directions. Given the relative paucity of these references, most modern editors refer to her throughout as "Helen." The First Folio also contains a cryptic reference to a mysterious character named "Violenta" in act 3, scene 5, in the company of the Widow and Mariana. Both of them have lines, while Violenta does not, leading to speculation that this was originally intended as the name of the Widow's daughter. If so, the shift to Diana is significant, suggesting as it does the contrast between Helen, classically associated with the sensuous Venus, and Diana, paragon of chaste virtue (ibid., 56–57, and G. K. Hunter, Introduction, *All's Well That Ends Well*, The Arden Edition of the Works of William Shakespeare, 5th ed. [London: Methuen, 1986], xii).

There is less editorial agreement regarding how to handle a trio of paired characters, referred to variously as "gentlemen," "messengers," and "French lords," with a corresponding array of speech prefix abbreviations for each label. This essay follows the conclusion of Oxford Shakespeare editor Susan Snyder that "at some point as the writing proceeded, Shakespeare reviewed the text with an eye to dramatic economy and found that these pairs of lesser characters could be amalgamated with the French lords" (Snyder, p. 61). Editors and directors have variously addressed the mishmash of character designations with which the First Folio leaves us, with conflation being the simplest for theatrical purposes (Hunter, pp. xvi–xvii).

There are two places where the text is seemingly hopelessly corrupt (that is, it has been changed too much from the original text by persons other than Shakespeare). The first of these is a clearly misplaced line in act 1, scene 1, Lafeu's query, "How understand we that?" which has been variously placed at line 55, line 59, and line 61. The question seems abrupt for the context, a discussion of grief in parting, whether it be for a journey in life, or out of it. In consequence, many directors choose to cut it out entirely, lacking a clear sense of its proper placement. The second instance is a corrupt line delivered by Diana in the midst of the bed trick negotiation with Bertram, which reads in the First Folio, "I see that men make rope's in such a scarre" (4.2.38). Nicholas Rowe, in his edition of the play (*The Works of Mr. William Shakespear* [London: Printed for Jacob Tonson, 1709], 2.793), changed the curious words to "make Hopes in such Affairs," and John Payne Collier in 1853 proposed "make hopes in such a suit" (*Notes and Emendations to the Texts of Shakespeare's Plays* [New York: Redfield, 1853], 186).

SOURCES FOR THE PLAY

The central plot elements of *All's Well That Ends Well* would have been well known to Shakespeare and his audience from oral tradition, which had, in turn, been immortalized in print in Giovanni Boccaccio's *Decameron* and its English translation, William Painter's *Palace of Pleasure*, Novel 38. Although Ben Jonson famously ascribed to Shakespeare "small Latin, and less Greek" (Ben Jonson, "To the Memory of My Beloved, the Author, Mr. William Shakespeare, and What He Hath Left Us," *The Longman Anthology of British Literature*, vol. 1, 2nd ed., David Damrosch, ed. [New York: Longman, 2003], 1634), Howard C. Cole has persuasively argued that the Bard might also have known a medieval Italian play that relates the same basic story, Bernardo Accolti's *Virginia* (1494), as well as an anonymous French romance, *Le Livre du Très Chevalereux Comte d'Artois* (4–5, 8). Since one of the differences between Painter's somewhat sanitized versions of racy continental tales and Shakespeare's play is the seamy sexuality that pervades many aspects of the plot, it is indeed possible that Shakespeare knew the unexpurgated Italian or French version of this tale in some capacity. Finally, Susan Snyder follows G. K. Hunter in arguing that Shakespeare might also have been drawing on Erasmus's colloquy "Proci et puellae," a text with which he would have been familiar from grammar school. This dialogue between a young woman and her suitor contains many passages of sexual/marital negotiation that resonate with Helen and Bertram's situation.

W. W. Lawrence was the first to trace the main character traits and plot points in *All's Well* to their roots in popular lore. In Helen, he sees an echo of the Clever Wench popularized in such medieval tales as the story of Patient Griselda, one of the tales told in Chaucer's *Canterbury Tales* (*Shakespeare's Problem Comedies*, 2nd ed. [New York: Frederick Ungar Publishing, 1931], 47–50). As Geoffrey Bullough observes, Shakespeare had already employed this sort of character himself by the time he wrote *All's Well*, in the person of Hero in *Much Ado about Nothing* (376). Helen needs to be clever in order to meet the demands of the first plot strand Lawrence identifies in the play, the Healing of the King. The cleverness that she manifests here is directly related to her ability to satisfy the requirements imposed by the second plot outline that, in Lawrence's view, Shakespeare derived from popular tradition, the Fulfillment of the Tasks (55–60). The tasks in question are those imposed upon her by Bertram before he will agree to accept his role as her husband.

The closest analogue to the *All's Well* story is the tale of Giletta of Narbon, the ninth story told on the third day in Boccaccio's *Decameron*, a day devoted to tales of fickle Fortune, and the acquisition or restoration of something badly desired. In Painter's English version, Giletta is the wealthy daughter of Gerardo of Narbona, physician to the Count of Rossiglione. The Count's death precedes, rather than follows, that of Giletta's father in this account, somewhat mitigating the wondrousness of his skills, while by virtue of her wealth she is not as distant from the Count's son as Shakespeare represents Helen to be from Bertram. The Count's son, Beltramo, departs for Paris to enter the custody of the King. Shortly thereafter, Gerardo dies, and the grief-stricken and lovesick Giletta follows Beltramo to Paris.

Once there, she determines to use healing arts learned from her father to cure the King. She strikes the same husband-for-a-cure deal with the monarch that Helen arranges in Shakespeare's play, but Giletta allows herself eight days to effect this cure (Bullough, 391), whereas Helen must accomplish the feat in two days. Although Beltramo acquiesces to the King's demand that he marry Giletta once she has succeeded in curing him, he promptly sends her back to Rossiglione and departs for the Tuscan wars. Painter's prose version of the tale lingers over Giletta's time in Rossiglione, showing the facility with which she fills in for the absent Count, winning the love of his subjects.

It takes quite some time for Giletta to realize that Beltramo will not return to Rossiglione as long as she is there. Once he stipulates that he will not live with her as a husband until she presents him with their child and his ring, she leaves and, like Helen, meets up with Beltramo in Florence. She stays in the home of a widow who lives next-door to a young woman with whom Beltramo is in love. Giletta convinces both of them to help her trick Beltramo into sleeping with her—a deception which they practice repeatedly until she is certain that she is pregnant. In Shakespeare's greatly compressed account of these events, the Widow is also the mother of the young woman, whom he names Diana, and Helen performs the bed trick only once.

Giletta does not confront Beltramo until she has given birth to twin sons, who resemble him to such a degree that he is forced to acknowledge them. She also presents him with his ring, and he accepts her as his wife. Although Shakespeare heightens the tension by truncating many aspects of the plot, he adds a large number of characters, including three significant ones: the Countess, Lafeu, and Parolles (Bullough, p. 381). Both Lafeu and Parolles have many ancestors on the stage, as the types of the wise servant and braggart soldier, respectively. As Geoffrey Bullough notes, Shakespeare also adds the scene in which Helen selects her husband from among a group of courtiers, and the second ring, which serves as the King's clue that Helen is trying to communicate something of urgency to him. Finally, Helen presents Bertram with a child still in the womb, rather than with live twins. This alteration might well have been made to save the trouble of representing twin infants on the stage (Bullough, pp. 380, 381).

STRUCTURE AND PLOTTING

The play closely follows the story of Giletta of Narbon in its primary outlines, and its main structure likewise follows that of Boccaccio's narrative, producing a plot familiar to modern readers as a fairy tale. Like most such tales, the play has a happy ending, featuring the restoration of one thought lost or dead, the reunion of a separated couple, and the promise of a future reward for Diana, who has served the heroine truly. *All's Well* is, therefore, regarded on the most basic level as a comedy, since it ends with renewal rather than the death that marks tragedies of love, such as *Othello*. However, its genre has produced a great deal of critical controversy, with many critics convinced it occupies a comic sub-genre, such as tragi-comedy (see "Critical Controversies," below). Drawing upon the "wicked angel" role played by one of Shakespeare's additions to the source tale, the character Parolles, M. C. Bradbrook suggests that *All's Well* also has some affinity with the morality play tradition, in which a hero must overcome the temptations of a personified vice, or group of vices ("Virtue Is the True Nobility," *Review of English Studies* n.s. 1.4 [October 1950]: 289–301, reprinted in Bradbrook, *Shakespeare and Elizabethan Poetry: A Study of His Earlier Work in Relation to the Poetry of the Time* [London: Chatto and Windus, 1951], 162–170).

As he does in most of his plays, Shakespeare develops a series of interlocking, parallel plots in *All's Well*, some of which are unique to his play, having no known basis in the sources that he is conjectured to have used. The symmetry between these plots is perhaps nowhere more apparent than in the first two acts, which oscillate between the household at Rossillion and the French court. Ultimately, these two plot lines and the characters associated with them will converge, but first there is another location and plot strand added in the form of the play's complication—Bertram's flight to the Florentine wars to escape from his new bride. The third act begins with a pair of alternations between Florence and Rossillion before focusing exclusively on the Florentine location of both the hero and heroine for the duration of act 3 and all but the final scene of act 4. Act 5 begins with the progress of Helen toward Rossillion, and the remaining scenes bring the action full circle to the place where the story began.

The play features paired characters and story lines to complement its paired settings. Bertram and Helen have each lost a father; the King and the Countess are each given the charge of a fatherless child; Bertram, who must learn to see beyond the surface, is dogged by the superficial Parolles; and Helen, who must impugn a virgin's honor to redeem her own, is paired with the chaste Diana. Frequently likened to war both in the play and in early modern commonplaces, love is figured as a pitched battle here, in which strategic siege is necessary for complete conquest (G. Wilson Knight, "The Third Eye," in *The Sovereign Flower*, 2nd ed. [London: Methuen, 1966], 110–111). The metaphorical war that Helen imagines herself waging in her act 1 meditation on virginity with Parolles (1.1.105–198) is literalized in the play as the Florentine battlefield, which her husband prefers to her bed (see "Themes and Meanings," below). The cowardly deceit and betrayal that Bertram so disdains in the act 4 unmasking of Parolles (4.3) will become his own downfall in his dealings with Diana. Consumed with the mark against his honor that marriage to a poor physician's daughter would constitute, Bertram must undergo public excoriation of his conduct and character that is commensurate with the class disparagement he so feared.

In addition to the way in which Parolles's poor conduct and its public revelation mirrors Bertram's story, the clown Lavatch's courtship and subsequent disenchantment with the Countess's "woman," Isbel, refracts the main story line through biting satire. When Lavatch says, "I have no mind to Isbel since I was at court" while the Countess reads Bertram's letter declaring with respect to Helen, "I have wedded her, not bedded her" (3.2.12, 21), it is clear that their crass disregard for their wives is of a piece despite the vast gulf that separates them socially. Bertram is the principal student set to learn the play's central lesson: "Where great additions swell's, and virtue none, / It is a dropsied honor. . . . That is honor's scorn, / Which challenges itself as honor's born / And is not like the sire" (2.3.127–128, 133–135).

MAIN CHARACTERS

Helen and Bertram

The critical controversies associated with *All's Well* are closely aligned to the perception of the play's major characters (see "Critical Controversies," below). Perhaps nowhere is the difference of opinion more stark than in the response of critics and theatergoers over the years to the two main characters: Helen and Bertram. Helen has been seen as everything from a semidivine representative of heaven on earth to a manipulative, scheming social climber with powerful tendencies toward nymphomania. Bertram has been positioned on a spectrum ranging from a crude and perhaps even misogynistic boor to a much-maligned victim of feminine wiles. Lawrence finds Shakespeare's innovations with respect to Bertram's character utterly condemnatory: "Shakespeare goes farther than Boccaccio: he makes the rejection of Helen depend . . . upon Bertram's own vanity, intolerance of control, and inability to see the finer qualities of Helen. He turns Bertram, in short, into a thoroughly disagreeable, peevish, and vicious person" (61).

Casting Bertram in this negative light has necessary implications for one's assessment of Helen, since she falls so intensely in love with him that she is willing to risk her reputation—indeed, her very life—to secure him for her husband. Susan Snyder observes that "The mysterious Helen in *All's Well* is highly unusual among Shakespeare's comic heroines in that she not only loves before she is loved but actively, overtly, chases the man she wants" ("*All's Well That Ends Well* and Shakespeare's Helens: Text and Subtext, Subject and Object," *English Literary Renaissance* 18.1 [Winter 1988]: 70). Snyder goes on to note that the only other Shakespearean heroine who fits this description is a second Helen: Helena of *A Midsummer Night's Dream*. She concludes, "The repetition of name and situation is striking, especially since as far as we know Shakespeare chose the names in both cases. He seems to have invented the *Midsummer* lovers and their story; and for *All's Well*, he deliberately rejected the name supplied by his source, Giletta, and substituted that of Helena or Helen" (70). As Lavatch notes, this name was evocative of adultery, deception, and danger by virtue of its association with the story of Helen of Troy (1.3.70–89). Helen's character is marked by a degree of opacity that defies glib classification. She is a paradox, every bit as enigmatic as the riddles used to re-introduce her into the household at Rossillion after her faked death.

The Countess, the King, and Lafeu

In this play of sharp contrasts, Helen and Bertram are almost universally perceived in opposition to one another, and the characters of their generation in the play are, in turn, typically seen in contrast to their elders, chief among them the Countess, the King, and Lafeu. This trio of elders—the repository of wisdom and temperance in a play rife with headstrong passions and contests of will—offers unreserved approval of Helen, an authorial choice often perceived as a way of tacitly mitigating the potential sordidness of her unabashed pursuit of Bertram and the devious means she employs to bed him. Likewise, the King's critical remonstrance of Bertram's bad behavior directs the audience to sympathize with Helen's claim upon him, rather than with his churlish rejection of her. As soon as the King meets Bertram, he recalls the recently deceased Count of Rossillion in a manner that anticipates the disregard for class rank that the King will demonstrate in betrothing Bertram to Helen and the wide rift between the conduct of the older generation and the manner in which young courtiers like Bertram and Parolles comport themselves. Of Bertram's father, the King says:

> his honor,
> Clock to itself, knew the true minute when
> Exception bid him speak, and at this time
> His tongue obey'd his hand. Who were below him
> He us'd as creatures of another place,
> And bow'd his eminent top to their low ranks,
> Making them proud of his humility,
> In their poor praise he humbled. Such a man
> Might be a copy to these younger times;
> Which followed well, would demonstrate them now
> But goers-backward. (1.2.38–48)

Although the King clearly hopes that Bertram is cut from the same cloth as his father, the son proves himself to be a "goer-backward" until hard lessons turn him round about.

Parolles

The King's aging lord, Lafeu, is an important crossover character in the parallel plots centered on Rossillion and Paris, linking the contrast delineated in the moral fiber of Helen and Bertram, as well as the mirroring of Bertram and his profligate companion, Parolles. Parolles is at one and the same time a theatrical type and an inspired Shakespearean creation. As an example of the miles gloriosus, or self-aggrandizing fool, of the Italian commedia dell'arte tradition, Parolles has many theatrical precedents (for a different view of Parolles, see Hunter, pp. xlvii–xlviii). By Shakespeare's day, the braggart soldier of Plautus and Terence was a stage convention. However, as an addition to the basic source story about Giletta of Narbon from Boccaccio, Parolles is an innovation. Lafeu immediately recognizes Parolles for what he is, and it is an index of how much Bertram lacks of maturity and powers of discernment that he fails to do so. Parolles's very name—French for "words"—reveals him as a man of voluble speech unsupported by action. In this, he forms a sharp contrast to Helen, who twice wins Bertram as her spouse by her actions (Frederick Boas, "The Problem-Plays," in *Shakspere and His Predecessors* [New York: Charles Scribner's Sons, 1902], 355). It is telling that the military action that most excites Parolles is the recovery of his regiment's drum, a matter rather of pride than import and an object that, like himself, makes a good deal of noise.

However, Parolles is not merely amusing; he is drawn with sufficient care to elicit some degree of audience sympathy. As A. P. Rossiter notes, when the Lords Dumaine expose him for a coward and a knave, he does not try to lie his way out of the situation, as perhaps the most famous of Shakespeare's braggart soldiers, Falstaff, repeatedly does in the *Henry IV* plays. Instead, Parolles acknowledges the fact that he has been caught in a shameful act, a stage moment embarrassing not only for him but also, Rossiter suggests, for the audience ("*All's Well That Ends Well*," in *Angel with Horns and Other Lectures on Shakespeare*, Graham Storey, ed. [New York: Theatre Arts Books, 1961], 93–95). Even in his moment of defeat, however, Parolles continues to shadow Bertram. As Vivian Thomas observes of this scene of degradation, "Being the last to discover Parolles, Bertram is also the most cruel in his condemnation and the least forgiving. Thus Parolles in a number of ways acts as a mirror in which we see Bertram" (*The Moral Universe of Shakespeare's Problem Plays* [London: Croom Helm, 1987], 66). Both Bertram and Parolles are cast in the mold of a standard narrative figure, that is, the deceiver deceived.

Lavatch

Parolles is paired with a second clown figure in the play, the Countess's scurrilous servant, Lavatch. Although Lavatch's ribald humor greatly eases the dramatic tension at several key junctures in the plot, he provides far more than comic relief. His first appearance before the Countess punctuates the steward Rinaldo's revelation of Helen's feelings for Bertram. The nature of Lavatch's errand to the Countess is to secure her blessing to marry a fellow servant, Isbel. This anticipates the much thornier blessing that Helen hopes to secure: the Countess's good will toward her as a potential daughter-in-law, and toward her proposed venture to Paris to cure the King. However, it also anticipates the sexual stipulations that will circumscribe Helen's marital relationship. When asked why he wishes to marry Isbel, Lavatch responds, with crude candor, "My poor body, madam, requires it. I am driven on by the flesh, and he must needs go that the devil drives" (1.3.28–30).

In a scene that fills the time between Helen's attempt to cure the King and her triumphant appearance in the French court after she has succeeded, Lavatch plays the courtier before the Countess. Demonstrating his full awareness of the superficiality of interactions at court, Lavatch saucily observes, "He that cannot make a leg, put off 's cap, kiss his hand, and say nothing, has neither leg, hands, lip, nor cap; and indeed such a fellow, to say precisely, were not for the court" (2.2.9–13). In the very next scene, Bertram will prove himself an inept courtier by these superficial standards in his coarse refusal to submit to being Helen's spousal reward for services rendered to the King.

DEVICES AND TECHNIQUES

All's Well contains a rich mix of prose, blank verse, and patterned, rhymed verse that identifies it as a work completed at the zenith of Shakespeare's creative powers. Perhaps nowhere is the commingling of these styles clearer than in act 1, scene 1, when Helen delivers two verse soliloquies (1.1.79–98 and 216–229) punctuated by a lengthy prose dialogue with Parolles (1.1.106–215; see "Explication of Key Passages," below). Helen's verse exchange with the King in act 2, scene 1 is also noteworthy for its mystical language and incantatory rhyming couplets as well as the frequent incidence of shared lines between Helen and the King, foreshadowing structurally the accord they are on the verge of forging. The riddling rhymed couplets delivered by Diana in the play's denouement give way to an extended run of rhymed couplets (5.3.313–334 and Epilogue) that sound a note of finality in a play whose ending has struck many as quite ambiguous.

Like many of Shakespeare's other clowns, Parolles and Lavatch speak primarily in prose. Parolles is the inspiration for one of the most outrageous comic devices employed in the play, the fabricated language of his alleged enemies in act 4, scene 1. The Lords Dumaine mastermind the exposure of Parolles as a fraud, and they achieve their end by convincing a blindfolded Parolles that they are an enemy army by babbling in nonsense language that one of their number then "translates" into threats and interrogation of Parolles. Amusing on the page, this scene almost never fails to leave theater audiences helpless with laughter when staged.

As in many other Shakespeare plays, several important plot points are communicated via letters that are read aloud. Bertram writes to his mother of his marriage to Helen, promising "to make the 'not' eternal" in a crude pun predicated on his refusal to "tie the knot" by consummating the union (3.2.21–22). Helen, likewise, has a letter from Bertram establishing the conditions whereby he will accept his role as her husband. She reads parts of this letter aloud in act 3, scene 2 and in the play's final scene, when she demonstrates that she has succeeded in getting his family ring and getting herself with child by him. These letters are in prose; the letter that Helen leaves for the Countess announcing her intention to travel as a religious pilgrim so that Bertram will not remain in the danger of his self-imposed military exile from Rossillion is a sonnet (3.4.4–17), a poetic form associated with love. Having long conceived of Bertram as an object of religious devotion, Helen now imagines a religious pilgrimage as a means of salvation for him, fearing that he will be killed in battle while trying to avoid marriage to her: "Bless him at home in peace, whilst I from far / His name with zealous fervor sanctify" (3.4.10–11).

In a movement that has been variously interpreted by critics as providential and strategic on Helen's part, she does not complete a pilgrimage, in fact, but tracks Bertram to Florence. It is here that the plot device over which the most ink has been spilled is set: Helen's bed trick consummation of her marriage to Bertram. By far the best survey of the bed trick as an early modern theatrical device is provided by Marliss Desens. Of the numerous extant early modern plays that employ this plot device, Shakespeare is responsible for at least two: *Measure for Measure* and *All's Well*.

Richard Wilson notes the central contrast between the bed trick as played in *Measure for Measure* and that in *All's Well*: the fact that in the former play the deception is orchestrated by a man, and the center of political power, whereas in *All's Well* Helen masterminds the ploy ("Observations on English Bodies: Licensing Maternity in Shakespeare's Late Plays," in *Enclosure Acts: Sexuality, Property, and Culture in Early Modern England*, Richard Burt and John Michael Archer, eds. [Ithaca: Cornell UP, 1994], 129). Linking the theme of divinity with the device of the bed trick, Peggy Muñoz Simonds asserts that the bed trick "is a device in the cultural tradition of Western civilization to provide for the conception of a divine child who *must be born* into the world of man" ("Overlooked Sources of the Bed Trick," *Shakespeare Quarterly* 34.4 [Winter 1983]: 433). Like Wilson, A. P. Rossiter compares the bed tricks in *All's Well* and *Measure for Measure*, noting that "the two plays are certainly alike in making a tortuous trial-scene of the penultimate *exposé* by the conniving females. The exposure of the iniquity and meanness of both men is not tragic, yet it jars discordantly with the comedy ending in marriage: in both cases not to the women of their choice" (125). Bizarre though it may seem to us, the bed trick was considered in Shakespeare's time a satisfactory resolution to relationship conflicts of various kinds in a number of comedies. It is left to modern readers, directors, and theatergoers to determine whether the trick is a feminine connivance or not.

THEMES AND MEANINGS

Many of the themes central to *All's Well That Ends Well* can be traced to its proverbial title. As Susan Snyder notes, the chief meaning of the proverb seems to be that, as long as efforts yield success in the long run, any pain endured will be worthwhile; however, "the proverb can also carry a message more Machiavellian, that the desirable end justifies the questionable means used to achieve it" (Introduction, *All's Well That Ends Well*, 49). The title has implications for Helen's mysterious and potentially inappropriate cure of the King, the deal that she strikes with the King for Bertram's hand in marriage, and the subterfuge in which she implicates Diana in fulfilling Bertram's condition that she somehow consummate a marriage that he shuns. All of these plot points relate to the themes of ambition and honor, manifest in Helen's quest to win Bertram and to prove herself her father's daughter in curing the King, as well as to Bertram's initial refusal as a noble to consent to marry the daughter of one of his former household servants, and his desire to earn commendation as an officer in the Florentine wars.

A virtual doppelganger to Bertram, Parolles represents two important lessons that Bertram must learn over the course of the play: appearances can be deceptive, and honor is earned rather than inherited. Susan Snyder points out that Parolles can reflect on Helen, too, as a rival for Bertram's attention: "posing this fraudulent figure in structural parallel to the heroine, as another middle-class character aspiring to intimacy with the noble Bertram may also open the way to interpretation of Helen as another kind of unscrupulous social climber" (Introduction, *All's Well That Ends Well*, 3). The pitched battle between Helen and Parolles for sway over Bertram occasions one of the play's main metaphors, that of love as war (see "Structure and Plotting," above).

The older characters in the play—the Countess, the King, and Lafeu—look with hope to Bertram to fulfill his father's honorable legacy, but ultimately they anoint Helen the successor to their generation's heritage. Their profound admiration of Helen often casts her in terms of an agent of heaven, pointing to another of the play's central themes, divinity. Like many of Shakespeare's late "romance" plays, such as *Cymbeline*, *All's Well* frequently invokes the power of heaven. In her mystical cure of the King, her sly "salvation" of Bertram from the sin of adulterous lechery, and her act 5 "resurrection" of her allegedly dead self, Helen emerges as the play's divine agent, a dea ex machina (Knight, pp. 144–145). After hearing her overture respecting the cure she wishes to attempt, the King avers, "Methinks in thee some blessed spirit doth speak," (2.1.174), while Lafeu greets her success in curing the King with the declaration, "A showing of a heavenly effect in an earthly actor" (2.3.23–24).

Even here Shakespeare complicates the perception of Helen, however, as she frequently characterizes her love for Bertram as idolatrous, uses a religious pilgrimage as an excuse to see him, and asks the rector of Saint Jaques le Grand to collude in the stories of her death (4.3.57–59). Mourning Bertram's parting in act 1, Helen announces, "my idolatrous fancy / Must sanctify his reliques" (1.1.97–98). In keeping with the play's theme of the deceptive nature of appearances, Helen, like Bertram, must learn to see beyond the surface. Helen's early devotion to Bertram has much of blindness in it, but she will see him and all men in a different light after the bed trick: "But O, strange men, / That can such sweet use make of what they hate, / . . . so lust doth play / With what it loathes for that which is away" (4.4.21–22, 24–25). Lust is a superficial attraction; love requires a depth of understanding that goes beyond physical passion. Like Bertram, Helen must learn difficult lessons about life and love before she can finally approach him, soberly, as a marital partner in the final act. The play's enduring fascination stems largely from the variety of possible perspectives on Helen and the plot of which she is the prime mover.

CRITICAL CONTROVERSIES

One of the best surveys of the critical debate over *All's Well* up to the mid-twentieth century is provided by Joseph G. Price in the aptly named *The Unfortunate Comedy: A Study of "All's Well That Ends Well" and Its Critics*. Price begins by observing that the critical history of the play parallels, to a large extent, its theatrical history (see "Production History," below):

> Both demonstrate the comic delight of the eighteenth century, the ethical norms and sentimental inclinations of the late eighteenth and early nineteenth centuries, the concern for the heroine and melodrama throughout much of the nineteenth century. Near the end of the century, both record the increasingly realistic reaction against this melodramatic approach. In the twentieth century, the studied theatrical experiments of the directors are matched in the critical history by extensive conjecture upon the "inherent failure" of *All's Well*. (75)

By the point at which Price's study terminated, in the mid-1960s, a critical revaluation of the play had begun, which continued into the latter part of the century. The proliferation of stage productions of the play beginning in the 1950s facilitated new critical approaches. The class and gender issues so prominent in the play came in for scrutiny as feminist and new historicist criticism of Shakespeare rose to the forefront in the 1980s and 1990s. Making an asset of what had previously been seen as a liability, many recent critics and directors have found the play's complexity a fruitful ground for exploration, rather than an obstacle to understanding.

In the eighteenth century, critical commentary on *All's Well* focused, as stage productions did, on Parolles, typically perceived as vying with Falstaff for the title of greatest comic creation in the Shakespeare canon. The praise ended there, however, as eighteenth-century critics found fault with virtually everything else, including the plot, the hero, and the heroine (Price, pp. 76–78). Throughout the critical history of this play, the central problem with Helen has been how to interpret the ambition in her love. Is she a gold-digging nymphomaniac who secures a husband beyond her station by bartering for the King's life? Or is she an agent of heaven, divinely inspired to cure both the King and her wayward husband? In addition to her enterprising means of attaining a noble husband and greater social stature for herself, the bed trick ploy by which she wins Bertram a second time has also come under scrutiny repeatedly in analyses of her character (see "Devices and Techniques," above).

What the criticism of the eighteenth and early nineteenth centuries initially held in common was the consistent valuation of the play as a comedy. By the mid-nineteenth century, this view had begun to shift, with increasing attention paid to the play's tragic elements, along with a return to critical treatment of the machinations of its heroine. The harsh, public shaming of both Bertram and Parolles enabled a plausible reading of the play in the light of moral didacticism. Whatever lesson the play had to offer, however, rapidly came to be seen as too bitter a pill to swallow, and the play's stock with critics began to plummet (Price, pp. 86–87).

There were exceptions to this negative view, of course, chief among them being the opinion of George Bernard Shaw, who regarded the play as too sophisticated, in fact, for the audiences and readers who disdained it. Shaw's judgment as a dramatist could not tip the balance of early-twentieth-century criticism, however, which consistently identified three basic ways in which the play failed: "inconsistency in the character of Helen, the demands upon the audience, and the ineptness of Shakespeare's dramatic powers at the time of composition" (Price, pp. 95, 99). The last of these reasons hinges on an early date for the play, an issue that has, in its turn, been the subject of critical controversy.

The central critical controversy concerning *All's Well* is the longstanding debate over the play's genre. Grouped with the comedies in the First Folio, *All's Well* nevertheless has many affinities with the tragedies, such as *Hamlet*, thought to have been composed in the same period of Shakespeare's career, as well as the late plays critically regarded as generic hybrids and labeled "romances," such as *Pericles*. The uncertainty and ambiguity that riddle this play as well as *Measure for Measure* and *Troilus and Cressida* led Frederick Boas to group them, along with *Hamlet*, under the rubric "problem plays." For Boas, throughout all of these plays "we move along dim untrodden paths, and at the close our feeling is neither of simple joy nor pain; we are excited, fascinated, perplexed, for the issues raised preclude a satisfactory outcome" ("The Problem-Plays," in *Shakspere and His Predecessors*, 345). Ironically, the term "problem play" has itself become problematic since its coinage.

W. W. Lawrence, for one, attacked the notion of problem comedies, defending *All's Well* specifically on the grounds of Shakespeare's reliance on a source that would have been well known to his audience and with which, therefore, he was not free to take creative liberties (68–69). G. K. Hunter maintained that the attributes of *All's Well* situate it most logically with the late plays typically identified as romances (Hunter, pp. l–lvi). R. A. Foakes found that the play's intractable realism, which he located in the sardonic humor that radiates from Parolles and Lavatch, stymied what might otherwise "have been a straightforward romantic comedy" ("Shakespeare and Satirical Comedy," *Shakespeare—The Dark Comedies to the Last Plays: From Satire to Celebration* [Charlottesville: UP of Virginia, 1971], 17). By far the harshest condemnations of the play, however, were issued by its early-twentieth-century editors. Sir Arthur Quiller-Couch and John Dover Wilson roundly criticized *All's Well* in their introduction to the New Cambridge Edition (1929), basing their critique largely on extra-textual speculation about character and motive. This trend continued well into the twentieth century. As recently as 1980, Richard Levin could argue that "Helen's success depends on guile," building the case largely on extra-textual evidence, such as the notion that her lament over her love for Bertram was staged for Rinaldo's benefit, and that she had suborned the Lords Dumaine to help her catch Bertram in acts of lechery and deception (*"All's Well That Ends Well*, and 'All seems well,' " *Shakespeare Studies* 13 [1980]: 131, 133, 138).

In the second half of the twentieth century, *All's Well*'s stock began, finally, to rise again. The early-twentieth-century focus on authorial intention and psychobiography became passé with new critical paradigms grounded in the text itself and its historical context beyond the life narrative of its author. One of the approaches taken by twentieth-century critics eager to defend the play has been to focus on the play's themes, such as chastity, honor, friendship, virtue, ambition, and the cycle of life from youth to procreation to old age. Long censured, Bertram finally became the object of critical defense in the last half of the twentieth century, an enterprise that often had as its corollary an assault on Helen as a cold-eyed, social-climbing harpy (Price, pp. 119–120, 123–124). Without condoning this assessment, Marilyn Williamson found that Helen's sexual excess is what renders the play problematic for so many critics, since she "exceeds most audiences' sense of limits on women's assertiveness" (*The Patriarchy of Shakespeare's Comedies* [Detroit: Wayne State UP, 1986], 61).

In the last two decades of the twentieth century, feminist criticism, in particular, began to reassess Helen along with the riddle-weaving Diana. Attacking those who see Helen as manipulative on the grounds that they are viewing her through restrictive notions of gender roles, David McCandless asserts that "Helena's essential provocation lies in her capacity for forcing masculine and feminine modes of desire to collide" ("Helena's Bed-trick: Gender and Performance in *All's Well That Ends Well*," *Shakespeare Quarterly* 45.4 [Winter 1994]: 455). Marliss Desens holds a similar view of Helen, arguing that she fits neither the stereotype of the "manipulative vixen" nor the "idealistic wife willing to sacrifice all to redeem her husband. . . . [S]he is only a person fighting for a place in a society that severely limits the options available to a woman" (67). Emphasizing the extent to which Helen violates both class and gender norms in her pursuit of Bertram, Dolora Cunningham sets her off against her peers in the Shakespearean canon as well, noting that she "is the only heroine who does not at any time dress herself up as a man in order to get a hearing in the world of affairs" ("Conflicting Images of the Comic Heroine," in *"Bad" Shakespeare: Revaluations of the Shakespeare Canon*, Maurice Charney, ed. [Madison, NJ: Fairleigh Dickinson UP, 1988], 123). As postmodern criticism and dramatic practice continue to evolve into post-post-modernity, undoubtedly new perspectives on this play and its complicated central characters will emerge.

PRODUCTION HISTORY

Perhaps because *All's Well That Ends Well* is so difficult to pin down in terms of genre and overall tone (see "Critical Controversies," above), it has not been popular with directors over the centuries. As the issues of class and gender so central to the play became of significant social concern in the twentieth century, however, the play began to appear on stage more frequently. In fact, there were more than twice as many major productions of *All's Well* after 1900 than there had been in the preceding three centuries.

The lack of information about when Shakespeare wrote the play is closely intertwined with a concomitant lack of knowledge about its early stage history. The first formal record of a production of the play occurs in 1741, when it appeared at Goodman's Fields. Henry Giffard mounted the play with the relatively unknown Joseph Peterson cast as Parolles. The role proved so popular for Peterson that he took the show on the road, playing Parolles throughout Britain (Price, pp. 5–6). After over a century of neglect, *All's Well* was revived again the very next year in a production that posed a serious challenge to the superstitions associated with "the Scottish play" (*Macbeth*): one night the actress playing Helen fainted on the stage, and the actor cast in the role of the ailing King of France took method acting to the extreme by dying during the run (Styan, p. 2).

In the eighteenth century, when theater audiences' tastes ran to the broadly comic, directors took Giffard's lead and trained their attention on Parolles. The renowned eighteenth-century actor and director David Garrick drastically cut the play to make Parolles and not Helen the central character. Garrick's Parolles, Harry Woodward, portrayed the bombastic "soldier" in the Harlequin style to wild enthusiasm from the audience. John Bannister took this trend to its extreme in 1785, stripping the play of all but its most Parolles-focused moments in a production at London's Haymarket Theatre (Price, pp. 11–14, 20).

Director John Kemble restored Helen to a central position in his 1794 version of *All's Well* at Covent Garden, which shifted the play's register from the comic to the romantic. The clowns Parolles and Lavatch fared badly in this script, in order to give precedence to Helen's passion for Bertram. Both the 1794 production and an 1811 revival of Kemble's script by his younger brother, Charles, were poorly received, despite Kemble's assiduous attempts to sanitize the script by bowdlerizing Bertram's letter to require only the production of his ring, and not a child (Price, pp. 23–24, and Styan, p. 3). By the time *All's Well* returned to the stage at Covent Garden in 1832 it had been transformed yet again, this time into an opera. The play enjoyed one final staging in 1852 at Sadler's Wells, but Victorian audiences were scandalized by the more prurient aspects of the plot. The play was effectively banished from the stage until an irregular group of productions between 1916 and 1935, mostly for the Stratford-upon-Avon theater festivals (Price, pp. 43–61).

The first breakthrough in the theatrical treatment of *All's Well* came in the 1950s. Director Tyrone Guthrie opened and closed this remarkable decade of renewed interest in the play with productions for the 1953 festival at Stratford, Ontario, and the 1959 season at Stratford-upon-Avon. Both of Guthrie's productions emphasized refinement, with elegant set pieces and formal costumes. In a subtle bit of stage business, Guthrie replaced the romping Elizabethan coranto with which Helen and the King enter in act 2 (2.3.40) with a graceful waltz, heightening the sense that Helen can, in fact, meet her noble husband on equal terms (Styan, p. 26).

Guthrie and the other directors who tackled *All's Well* in the 1950s were creating a work for a post–World War II theatergoing audience, eager for happy endings. For his 1953 production at the Old Vic in London, director Michael Benthall emphasized the fairy tale elements of the play. Claire Bloom played Helen with wide-eyed innocence, and the entire cast wore costumes emblazoned with symbolic representations of their social status and the nature of their characters.

With the sexual revolution of the 1960s, audiences were finally ready for the full complexity of Shakespeare's frank exploration of sexual relations. When Joseph Papp, celebrated producer of the New York Shakespeare Festival, directed a dark version of *All's Well* for Central Park's open-air theater in 1966, he emphasized the play's seamy side. The following year, John Barton, who considered Helen's sexuality central to the plot, directed *All's Well* for England's Royal Shakespeare Company. Barton instructed his Helen, Estelle Kohler, to flirt knowingly with Parolles, with her potential husbands in the French court, and even with the King. He staged the private scene in which Helen persuades the King to attempt her cure in his bedroom. Kohler sat by the King's bedside as she defended her healing arts, and she sealed her cure/husband deal with the King by giving him a kiss.

British director Jonathan Miller returned to the Elizabethan period for the design of his 1975 production at the Greenwich Theater. Taking seriously Lafeu's claim that Parolles is a bad influence on a naive Bertram (4.5.1–3), Miller broke with a long stage tradition in which Parolles was considerably older than Bertram to cast actors of approximately the same age and physical characteristics in the two parts (Styan, p. 31). Miller effectively made the two characters carbon copies of one another, dressing them in identical costumes, investing the scenes in which it is revealed that Parolles has attempted to woo Bertram's love, Diana, for himself with a sinister aspect (4.3.201–220).

By the 1980s, the general theatrical trend was toward gritty realism and direct confrontation with pressing social issues. In 1980 Trevor Nunn, who has directed both stage and film versions of Shakespeare's plays (*Twelfth Night*), trained the spotlight on the class differences separating Helen and Bertram. In addition, the King of France was confined to a wheelchair, a bit of stage business employed in many late-twentieth-century productions of the play, which renders his restoration to caper-cutting with Helen the more dramatic. Renowned actress Peggy Ashcroft took the role of the Countess, her last appearance with the Royal Shakespeare Company in a long and illustrious career.

Jonathan Miller produced *All's Well* for the British Broadcasting Company in 1981; in this video version of the play, director Elijah Moshinsky reprised Barton's coy bedroom staging of the cure negotiation between Helen and the King. Barry Kyle closed out the 1980s with a 1989 production for the Royal Shakespeare Company, which conceived of the play as a journey from youth to maturity, and emphasized the semi-sibling status of Helen and Bertram, offering some degree of rationale besides class consciousness for his repulsion at the idea that he should marry her.

Sir Peter Hall, founder of the current incarnation of the Royal Shakespeare Company at Stratford-upon-Avon, came out of retirement in 1992 to direct *All's Well* in the intimate setting of the Swan Theatre. Meanwhile, on the other side of the globe, Henry Woronicz raised the bar considerably in the twentieth-century explorations of the class disparity between Helen and Bertram by casting Luck Hari, a native of Calcutta, India, as the heroine in a production for the Oregon Shakespeare Festival (Alan C. Dessen, "Taming the Script: *Henry VI*, *Shrew*, and *All's Well* in Ashland and Stratford," *Shakespeare Bulletin* 11.2 [Spring 1993]: 36–37). Cross-racial casting

Judi Dench as the Countess of Rossillion and Claudie Blakley as Helena in the Royal Shakespeare Company's production *All's Well That Ends Well* at the Swan Theatre. © Robbie Jack/Corbis.

was used in several twentieth-century productions, adding force to Helen's sense that Bertram is unattainable in a society in which class distinctions alone are less prohibitive to romance than they were in earlier ages.

Mary Beth Rose has argued that *All's Well* is the Shakespearean comedy that comes closest to depicting female characters who also happen to be mothers as powerful protagonists ("Where are the Mothers in Shakespeare? Options for Gender Representation in the English Renaissance," *Shakespeare Quarterly* 42.3 [Fall 1991]: 291–314). The Royal Shakespeare Company mounted a production of *All's Well* once again, in both Stratford-upon-Avon and London, in the 2003–2004 season. Under the direction of Gregory Doran, Academy Award-winner Dame Judi Dench made her first appearance with the RSC in over a decade when she played the Countess of Rossillion, thus continuing the by-now established tradition of reserving this role as a plum for a revered actress.

EXPLICATION OF KEY PASSAGES

1.1.79–229. "O, were that all! . . . will not leave me." The last half of the opening scene of *All's Well That Ends Well* includes Helen's infamous exchange with Parolles on the subject of virginity, bracketed by two significant soliloquies that reveal her love for Bertram and her ambitions with respect to it. Ambition is the governing theme throughout the passage, as Helen shifts from semi-despairing surrender to the impossibility of her love, to an aggressive conversation with a man about how women may alternately "barricado it [virginity] against him [man]" (1.1.113) and "lose it [virginity] to her own liking" (1.1.150–151), to, finally, a firm resolve to pursue Bertram irrespective of the consequences: "my intents are fix'd, and will not leave me" (1.1.229). A second significant theme for the play as a whole, the deceptiveness of external appearances, is also introduced in this passage (see "Themes and Meanings," above).

In the soliloquy that opens this passage, Helen details her intense love for Bertram, which has replaced her devotion to her recently deceased father. The nature of her attraction to Bertram is revealed in the brief blazon that she delivers of her love, focused entirely on his physical attributes:

> 'Twas pretty, though a plague,
> To see him every hour, to sit and draw
> His arched brows, his hawking eye, his curls,
> In our heart's table—heart too capable
> Of every line and trick of his sweet favor. (1.1.92–96)

Paradoxically, though blinded by her physical attraction to Bertram, Helen is capable of seeing beyond the surface of his boon companion, Parolles, whom she characterizes as "a great way fool, soly [solely] a coward" (1.1.101). This ability to see through external appearances allies Helen with the older generation in the play, particularly Lafeu, who also looks through Parolles as through a pane of glass: "Thy casement I need not open, for I look through thee" (2.3.214–215). However, rather than following her own instincts with respect to Parolles, she follows Bertram's lead in this as she will in so many other things throughout the play and avers, "I love him [Parolles] for his [Bertram's] sake" (1.1.99).

What ensues is a ribald exchange with Parolles about virginity and its vulnerability in the face of male sexual assaults, ranging from persuasive seduction to coercive rape. Given the sexual stipulation that Bertram will ultimately attach to his marital contract with Helen and the machinations to which she will resort in order to meet it, this exchange serves a crucial function in the advancement of the plot. However, many directors since the eighteenth century have elected either to curtail this conversation or to delete it entirely out of a fear that it makes the heroine seem too sexually aggressive. Helen's ambition with respect to sex, specifically, comes through clearly in this scene, as she deplores the fact that men are given the offensive position in sexual struggles, leaving her to ask, "Is there no military policy how virgins might blow up men?" (1.1.121–122). Evoking the battlefield for which Bertram will eschew his own marriage bed, Helen likewise unwittingly foreshadows with this question the strategic siege she will be required to lay to Bertram in order to lose her virginity "to her own liking."

Although she concludes her conversation with Parolles with a cryptic reference to her lowly status with respect to Bertram, mourning the "baser stars" that govern her fortunes (1.1.183), her final soliloquy shifts rapidly from a perception of fortune as a preordained course in life to a notion of fortune as a course subject to human intervention. Reasoning that "The fated sky / Gives us free scope, only doth backward pull / Our slow designs when we ourselves are dull" (1.1.217–219), Helen resolves to follow Bertram to Paris.

2.3.66–183. "I am a simple maid . . . else, does err." Although Helen proposes the husband-for-a-cure deal to the King, in the event she becomes prophetically nervous at the possible outcome: "The blushes in my cheeks thus whisper me, / 'We blush that thou shouldst choose'" (2.3.69–70). Heightening the tension in this scene is Lafeu's running commentary on it. Shakespeare groups Lafeu, Bertram, and Parolles together, creating two basic staging possibilities. Either Lafeu cannot hear Helen politely turning aside the lords' preferred favors, so he assumes that they have all rejected her—"These boys are boys of ice, they'll none have her" (2.3.93–94)—or the French lords deliver their lines of seeming accord to Helen in a tone that makes it clear that Lafeu is interpreting their attitude correctly. Either staging works on two levels: Lafeu's fears foreshadow Bertram's flat rejection of Helen, while the other lords' responses to her either establish Bertram as the odd man out in his negative assessment of her or create some degree of sympathy for Bertram by making his sentiments the general consensus of the young nobility.

Helen's trepidation at publicly naming her spousal choice underscores the central theme in this scene, honor (see "Themes and Meanings," above). Helen fears being maligned with "A strumpet's boldness, a divulged shame" (2.1.171), public shaming being the inverse of honor, as Parolles finds at the taunting hands of the Lords Dumaine (4.3). Aghast at the social gulf that separates them, Bertram bases his refusal of Helen's hand on the status he feels that he will lose as a consequence of such a match: "A poor physician's daughter my wife! Disdain / Rather corrupt me ever!" (2.3.115–116). The trump card in this battle of reputations, however, is held by the King: "My honor's at the stake, which to defeat, / I must produce my power" (2.3.149–150). The royal honor supersedes all others, as Bertram learns to his cost.

However, the King's justification of his face-saving power play is built on the commonplace that virtue is the true nobility. Paradoxically, the King urges Bertram to ignore Helen's station in life even as he uses his own social position to bend Bertram to his will. The King asserts that "The property by what it is should go, / Not by the title. . . . Honors thrive, / When rather from our acts we them derive / Than our foregoers" (2.3.130–131, 135–137). This platitude is spoken by a monarch who holds his crown and the honor attendant upon it through lineal descent.

Bertram provides the acquiescence that the King clearly requires:

> Pardon, my gracious lord, for I submit
> My fancy to your eyes. When I consider
> What great creation and what dole of honor
> Flies where you bid it, I find that she, which late
> Was in my nobler thoughts most base, is now
> The praised of the King, who, so ennobled,
> Is as 'twere born so. (2.3.166–173)

This passage begins with the same focus on the superficial evinced by Helen in her act 1 declarations of love for Bertram. In Bertram's case, however, it is not even his own eyes that are subject to the dictates of fancy, but, rather, his fancy is dazzled by proxy, through the eyes of the King: "I shall beseech your Highness, / In such a business, give me leave to use / The help of mine own eyes" (2.3.106–108).

In a series of backhanded concessions to both the King and Helen, Bertram underlines the class disparity between himself and his bride, noting her as one "in my nobler thoughts most base." However, he acknowledges the King's unique ability to bestow honor and to create nobility where he finds that virtue warrants it. As the

King puts it, "I can create the rest. Virtue and she / Is her own dower; honor and wealth from me" (2.3.143–144). All of the monarchical blessings in the world, however, cannot create native nobility, a birthright perceived by centuries-old aristocracy like Bertram and, paradoxically, by the King himself as God-given, irrevocable, and not to be challenged.

5.3.309–334. "O my good lord, . . . more welcome is the sweet." Although Helen's public selection of a husband from among the bachelors of the French court has something of a Cinderella quality to it, it is to the play's riddling final scene that most critics look when making a case for the fairy tale aspects of *All's Well* (see "Structure and Plotting," above). Here, the theme of honor shares the stage with enigmatic rhyming couplets and the miraculous restoration of one believed to be dead, like Hero in *Much Ado about Nothing* and Hermione in *The Winter's Tale*. In a final bit of irony, Parolles returns to the court just in time to give evidence against Bertram, turning Bertram's participation in Parolles's public shaming (4.3) back upon him.

Upon her dramatic entry into the scene, seemingly from the grave, Helen reminds Bertram of her charge by producing and reading to him the letter containing his original conditions. While the title of the play asks the audience to believe that a positive resolution absolves all prior faults, the final moments of the play are heavily weighed with hypothetical statements that somewhat belie this cheerful outlook. When Helen asks Bertram, "Will you be mine now you are doubly won?" (5.3.314), he replies not to her, but to the King, "If she, my liege, can make me know this clearly, / I'll love her dearly, ever, ever dearly" (5.3.315–316). Having been presented with his ring and her pregnant body, it is unclear what further Helen will have to do in order to satisfy this new condition, and make Bertram know it "clearly." Before the King has time to respond, Helen intercedes with a hypothetical retort of her own, addressed directly to Bertram: "If it appear not plain and prove untrue, / Deadly divorce step between me and you!" (5.3.317–318). Unconventional from beginning to end, Helen proposes a divorce—unattainable under all but the most extraordinary of circumstances in early modern England—to the husband to whom she was compelled to propose marriage in the first place. She may mean, though, that she wishes she will die or be killed if she is lying. Bringing all full circle in a manner that leaves one wondering if he has learned anything from experience, the King delivers his own hypothetical proposition to Diana: "If thou beest yet a fresh uncropped flower, / Choose thou thy husband, and I'll pay thy dower" (5.3.327–328). This offer threatens to launch a second version of *All's Well*, with Diana as the beleaguered heroine.

In a final reprise of the play's title, hitherto spoken only by Helen (4.4.35 and 5.1.25), the King concludes much less optimistically, "All yet seems well; and if it end so meet, / The bitter past, more welcome is the sweet" (5.3.333–334). Not only does this, the play's concluding couplet, modify "all's well" to focus on external appearances—what seems to be the case—it also introduces another hypothetical statement: "if it end so meet." Ultimately, the epilogue delivers the final hypothetical proposition of the play: "All is well ended if this suit be won" (Epilogue 2), the suit in question being a request for applause. The audience must decide if all ends well, a decision on which theatergoers have been leaving the playhouse divided for four centuries and will likely continue to do for centuries to come.

Annotated Bibliography

Bullough, Geoffrey, ed. *"All's Well That Ends Well."* In *Narrative and Dramatic Sources of Shakespeare.* Vol. II: *The Comedies, 1597–1603.* New York: Columbia UP, 1958. 375–396. Discusses the stories on which Shakespeare based the plot of *All's Well,* including Boccaccio's *Decameron* and its English translation, William Painter's *Palace of Pleasure.*

Cole, Howard C. *The All's Well Story from Boccaccio to Shakespeare.* Chicago: U of Illinois P, 1981. Expands the field of sources available to Shakespeare to include Accolti's play *Virginia* and *Le Livre du Très Chevalereux Comte d'Artois et de sa Femme.*

Desens, Marliss C. *The Bed-Trick in English Renaissance Drama: Explorations in Gender, Sexuality, and Power.* Newark: U of Delaware P, 1994. Traces the English stage history of the bed trick as a plot device.

Free, Mary. *"All's Well That Ends Well* as Noncomic Comedy." In *Acting Funny: Comic Theory and Practice in Shakespeare's Plays.* Ed. Frances Teague. Rutherford, NJ: Fairleigh Dickinson UP, 1994. 40–51. Traces Shakespeare's use, from his own previous plays, of plot devices and characters in *All's Well.*

Frye, Northrop. *The Myth of Deliverance: Reflections on Shakespeare's Problem Comedies.* Toronto: U of Toronto P, 1983. Dismisses the notion that *All's Well* is a problem play, maintaining that it is simply a romantic comedy.

Jardine, Lisa. "Cultural Confusion and Shakespeare's Learned Heroines: 'These Are Old Paradoxes.'" *Shakespeare Quarterly* 38.1 (Spring 1987): 1–18. Analysis of the dark aspects of Helen's character.

Lawrence, William Witherle. *Shakespeare's Problem Comedies.* 2nd ed. New York: Frederick Ungar, 1931. Finds that Shakespeare's plot is based on two classic motifs, the Healing of the King and the Fulfillment of the Tasks.

Price, Joseph G. *The Unfortunate Comedy: A Study of "All's Well That Ends Well" and Its Critics.* Toronto: U of Toronto P, 1968. Establishes a historical framework for both literary and dramatic criticism of *All's Well.*

Styan, J. L. *All's Well That Ends Well.* Shakespeare in Performance Series. Ed. J. R. Mulryne. Manchester, Eng.: Manchester UP, 1984. Overview of British and American stage productions of *All's Well* with an act-by-act analysis of significant directorial choices.

Thomas, Vivian. *The Moral Universe of Shakespeare's Problem Plays.* London: Croom Helm, 1987. Meditation on the problem comedies, with emphasis on the themes of honor and virtue in *All's Well.*

Measure for Measure

Nicholas Birns

PLOT SUMMARY

1.1. The Duke of Vienna announces that he is leaving the city for a long sojourn in Poland. He appoints the young Angelo, who is known for his absolute strictness in implementing justice, to hold power in his stead. The Duke commends Angelo for his virtue. Angelo says that he is not worthy of the honor, but the Duke persists in his purpose.

1.2. After the Duke leaves, Lucio, a young ruffian, talks with two gentlemen and learns that his acquaintance Claudio is in prison for impregnating Julietta. It soon emerges that Claudio's arrest is part of a general crackdown by Angelo on prostitution and immorality. Lucio talks to Claudio and confirms the story.

1.3. The audience discovers that the Duke has not, after all, left Vienna, but is still in the city, disguised as a friar (an itinerant priest who lives among the people) named Lodowick. He reveals that he has appointed Angelo both to enforce a stricter standard of justice than his own lax rule and to test the scope of Angelo's character.

1.4. Lucio speaks to Isabella, Claudio's sister, who is on the verge of entering a convent. Lucio tells Isabella of Julietta's pregnancy and her brother's arrest. Isabella finds out that Angelo is responsible for her brother's situation. Spurred by Lucio, she resolves to appeal to Angelo.

2.1. The wise old counselor Escalus advises Angelo to soften the rigor of his rule. But Angelo persists in thinking his firm course the right one. He is determined to make Claudio an example of this firmness and vows to execute him the next morning. Several people of the lower class come before Angelo. These include Elbow, who complains that Froth has had an affair with Elbow's wife. Froth counters by denigrating the lady's low standard of virtue. Angelo decides the matter is too complex for him and so leaves Escalus to deal with it.

2.2. Isabella eloquently appeals to Angelo for leniency for her brother. Angelo rigidly refuses to consider her request. But inwardly he lusts for Isabella and is anguished by this human weakness.

2.3. The Duke meets Julietta and finds that she and Claudio truly love each other and have a strong, mutual commitment.

2.4. Angelo postpones Claudio's execution, hoping to lure Isabella with this mercy. He presses his suit with Isabella, who rejects him. Isabella vows to complain about Angelo's advances, but Angelo tries to persuade her that his reputation for virtue will prevent anyone from taking her seriously.

3.1. The Duke, pretending to take confession from Claudio, talks of the virtues of death. Claudio begins to feel consoled for his presumably upcoming loss of life. Isabella finds Claudio and tells her brother of his reprieve. When she lets him know that it will be permanent if she gives way to Angelo's lusts, Claudio pleads with her to do so. Isabella will not compromise her virtue, though, even if her refusal means that her brother dies. The Duke advises Isabella that Angelo is only pretending to seduce her in order to illustrate Isabella's virtue; therefore there is no way out for Claudio. The Duke advises Isabella that Angelo is secretly betrothed to Mariana, the sister of the late sailor Frederick. Angelo has abandoned Mariana because her dowry is small. The Duke persuades Isabella to trick Angelo by promising to have sex with him and then having Mariana take her place with Angelo; by the substitution of one woman for another, Angelo will be trapped.

3.2. The Duke in disguise attempts to bring peace to the men of the lower orders. In the process, he lures Lucio into making several remarks disrespectful of the Duke, although Lucio makes clear he prefers the Duke's easygoing ways to Angelo's rigor and austerity. Escalus, again dealing with the actual mechanics of administration Angelo eschews, meets the Duke (whom he does not recognize), and advises him, as a friar, to prepare Claudio spiritually for death.

4.1. Mariana, at her home in "the moated grange" (3.1.264) laments her loss of the absent Angelo. The Duke and Isabella arrive, and Isabella (offstage, in a moment of what would today be called girl talk) coaches Mariana in her role in the plot against Angelo.

4.2. The Provost hires a clown to assist Abhorson, the executioner, in executing both Claudio and a common criminal, Barnardine. Angelo orders Claudio to be beheaded in the morning, Barnardine in the afternoon. The Duke, using his moral authority as a friar, persuades the Provost to substitute Barnardine's head for Claudio's. This gives Claudio a slight reprieve. But Barnardine refuses to die, seemingly paralyzing Abhorson and the rest of the executioner's staff. Since a head must be found, the Provost uses the head of Ragozine, a dead pirate, who, as a substitute for a substitute, is offered to Angelo in place of the head of the still-living Claudio.

4.3. The Duke as friar lies to Isabella, telling her Claudio has been killed. Lucio attempts to comfort Isabella. The friar says that the Duke returns tomorrow and urges Isabella to inform the returned potentate of Angelo's actions.

4.4. Angelo and Escalus discuss the strange letters the Duke has sent from his feigned sojourn abroad. These letters command the worthies of the city to meet him at the gates.

4.5. The Duke gives Friar Peter more letters to deliver.

4.6. Isabella escorts Mariana to the city gates and her imminent confrontation with Angelo (4.6).

5.1. The Duke officially returns. He is welcomed by Angelo and Escalus. Isabella petitions the Duke to redress what she thinks is the death of her brother. Isabella informs the Duke of the hypocrisy revealed by Angelo's overture toward her and brings out the wronged Mariana as proof of Angelo's dishonesty. Angelo tries to foist off the accusations as lies fostered by Friar Lodowick, little knowing that the friar and the Duke are the same person. Lucio heartily joins in the denunciation of the friar. The Duke, who goes off and returns disguised as the friar, is arrested and denounced by Angelo and Escalus. Lucio, fired with zeal at what he thinks is his apprehension of the criminal, pulls off the friar's disguise—only to reveal the Duke. Mortified, Lucio realizes he is in deep trouble. Angelo also realizes that he has been caught and that the Duke has witnessed all his hypocrisies. Angelo begs for mercy; the Duke compels him to acknowledge his marriage to Mariana. Still pretending to Isabella that Claudio is dead, the Duke declares that he is about to kill Angelo as requital for Claudio's murder. Mariana pleads for Angelo's life. The Provost brings out the still-living Barnardine, followed by Claudio. Lucio is punished by being forced to marry one of the many prostitutes with whom he has consorted. To complete the tableau, the Duke extends his hand in marriage to Isabella.

PUBLICATION HISTORY

It is generally agreed that *Measure for Measure* had its premiere in the banquet room at the royal court in Whitehall (London) on St. Stephen's Day (December 26) 1604, as is recorded in the Revels Account. The play might have been written and conceivably performed earlier, though London's theaters were closed because of the plague from May 1603 to April 1604, leaving only a small window for an earlier production. Scholars are sure that it cannot have been written before 1603. This dating is important for a historically based understanding of the play, as its premiere is placed securely in the reign of the new king, James I, providing a horizon against which Shakespeare's portrait of governance in the persons of the Duke and Angelo would have been understood. Of course, whether the new King is intended to be represented by the Duke or by Angelo can, at the interpreter's preference, be used to indicate whether the play is seen as pro- or anti-monarchical. Most of those who have chosen to read the play historically have chosen the former option. Shared themes and motifs with chronologically proximate plays also testify to the play's date. Angelo's certainty, for instance, has many inverse resemblances to Hamlet's doubt. The Duke's presence while others think he is absent is reminiscent, on a less spectral level, of the ghost of Hamlet's father.

The text of the play, transcribed by Ralph Crane, comes from the First Folio (1623), collected by John Heminge and Henry Condell. As is true for about half of Shakespeare's plays, there is no earlier Quarto version. There are few stage directions in the text. Scholars therefore presume that the Folio text was taken from a promptbook used by actors of Shakespeare's company, who knew the play sufficiently well not to need stage directions. An alternate theory is that Crane's text is derived from Shakespeare's foul papers, or original manuscript. This paucity of stage directions has given directors an unusual degree of freedom in producing the play while yet remaining faithful to the text. Some have thought that Crane slightly bowdlerized the text, amending certain sentences to avoid sexually explicit implications. Yet none of the passages said to have been altered by Crane are nearly as explicit in this respect as Pompey's "Groping for trouts in a peculiar river" (1.2.90) to describe Claudio's getting Julietta pregnant. It is this very scene that is the focus of what textual speculation there is about the play. The fact that Claudio's arrest is explained twice has led some scholars to suppose that 1.2 must have been emended by another hand, perhaps Thomas Middleton. The argument, though, could well be made that the double explanation is needed not by the audience but by different sets of characters within the play.

The ballad "Take, O take, those lips away" (4.1.1–6), sung by Mariana's page to console her, is also found in a later work by John Fletcher. This fact has led some scholars to think that Fletcher first wrote it and that it was later interpolated into Shakespeare's text. But it is at least as likely that Fletcher was here appropriating a song from the earlier Shakespeare play. The song's publication in a 1640 edition of Shakespeare's poems indicates that it might have originated as an independent composition by Shakespeare and was then inserted into *Measure for Measure*. Whether the song was interpolated by Shakespeare himself or by later redactors we do not know.

The original printer did not correct typographical errors in all copies, so very few copies of the 1623 text are alike. Editors therefore have had to decide about spelling and punctuation. Nonetheless, there have been few major textual controversies in *Measure for Measure* scholarship.

SOURCES FOR THE PLAY

Shakespeare's immediate source for the plot of *Measure for Measure* was George Whetstone's two-part, ten-act tragicomedy *The Right Excellent and Famous Historye of Promos and Cassandra: Divided into Commercial Discourses* (1578). In this version, Promos is the character later called Angelo by Shakespeare, and Cassandra occupies the role eventually to be that of Isabella. The story is also to be found in a prose narrative, *Heeptameron* [*sic*] *of Civil Discourses*, published by Whetstone in 1582. Whetstone was a quasi-aristocratic writer of Puritan sympathies who wrote prose fiction, conduct books, and accounts of military action as well as plays. He died relatively young after a duel in the Low Countries. Whetstone, in turn, had borrowed from an earlier source, the Italian author Cinthio's (Giovanni Battista Giraldo) collection of stories called *The Hecatommithi* (100 stories), written in 1565. (This work also provided the source for *Othello*.) Cinthio wrote a play, *Epitia*, on the same subject, which was published after his death in 1583. In Cinthio's story, the Isabella character is named Epitia, the Angelo character Juriste. Shakespeare's Duke is Cinthio's Maximian (recalling the late-third century A.D. Roman emperor). The Claudio character is named Vico, perhaps transposed by Shakespeare to the Duke's assumed name as friar, Lodowick, which is the English version of Ludovico. The Duke's city is Iulio (Innsbruck), not Vienna. Innsbruck, now famous as a mountain resort, was a lesser city more suited to the merely ducal status of Shakespeare's ruler. Perhaps Shakespeare changed the setting to Vienna because the London theatergoer would not have heard of the smaller city. Scholars generally agree that Shakespeare, whether through reading the original in Italian or through some other access, knew of Cinthio's account as well as Whetstone's English rendering of it.

Some critics have postulated that Cinthio derived his story from *Philanira*, a 1556 Latin drama by Claude Rouillet that was translated into French in 1563. This source may also have been used directly by Whetstone. A similar story is found in the works of François de Belleforest, a major source for *Hamlet*. A possible nonfiction source is a letter that Joseph Macarius, a Hungarian, wrote from Vienna about an incident in Milan where an administrator had forced a man to act honorably much as the Duke does in the cases of Angelo and Mariana, Lucio and Kate Keepdown. This letter not only displays the drama's core anecdote but also occupies the geographical settings used in Shakespeare's play. Another possible source is two stories told consecutively by Andreas Hondorff, a German writing in Latin, in his 1575 book *Theatrum Historicum* and perhaps also in the same writer's earlier work, *Promtuarium Exemplor* (1572).

Some critics have seen Mariana's forwardness in securing marriage from Angelo as indebted to the interaction of Judah and his former daughter-in-law Tamar in Genesis 38. Though far-fetched (especially as Tamar's trick involved disguising herself, not substituting someone else Judah already knew), this thought cannot be entirely dismissed in such a biblically conscious play. Nor for that matter can Laban's substitution of Leah for his other daughter, Rachel, as a bride for Jacob some chapters earlier in Genesis. The Duke's praise of death has also been cited for its reminiscence of Socrates' commendation of death in Plato's dialogue *Phaedo*. Cognate possible sources are also available in Plotinus and later Neoplatonic thinkers. The Duke's disguising himself as a commoner was a standard motif in Elizabethan and Jacobean drama (for example, John Marston's *The Malcontent* and *The Fawn*, Thomas Middleton's *The Phoenix*). But the way Shakespeare mixes this plot element with the idea of the Duke as stage manager of the action, making him the surrogate of the author, hearkens back to earlier sources. The entire notion of the ruler in disguise as a common man and mingling with his people, as a kind of enactment of the art of storytelling itself, is seen most prominently in the Arabic short story collection *The Thousand and One Nights* (*Alf Laylah Wa Laylah*). This work, though, would have had to reach Shakespeare through intermediaries since it was in his time not available in Western languages. A previous play in the Shakespeare canon, *Henry V*, also had the King passing incognito among his troops, giving them "a little touch of Harry in the night" (Chorus to act 4, l. 47).

The basic incidents and course of the plot are to be found in the sources mentioned above. But Shakespeare enlarged and re-imagined them, giving his play an endogenous rationale and pulse. The sources cannot really yield much insight into the meaning of the play. In terms of imaginative kinship, there is far more resemblance between this play and the others Shakespeare wrote during this period than between *Measure for Measure* and any of its ascribed sources. Walter Pater underscores this fact when he reminds us of the difference between the effect of a title such as *Promos and Cassandra*, which implies that the drama is about a determinate relationship between two individuals, and *Measure for Measure*. The latter title suggests an entire tableau involving moral and conceptual issues as much as it does discrete relationships. Pater also points out that "Shakespeare, in *Measure for Measure* has refashioned, after a nobler pattern, materials already at hand, so that the relics of other men's poetry are imported into his perfect work" (504). Shakespeare has transmuted his source material into something thoroughly his own. That this happens so powerfully in *Measure for Measure* may well be the reason that, despite its mixed general reception, the play has seemed to be a special favorite of the major Shakespeare scholars of the past hundred years.

STRUCTURE AND PLOTTING

The disguise of the Duke is more than the precondition for the story of the play; it is the linchpin of its structure. The Duke in dramatizing himself, in casting himself in the role of friar, initiates the play's action. In most respects, the play unfolds as he has presumably intended. Angelo, given scope to implement his own harsh justice, proves both intolerably severe and hypocritical. But the Duke must innovate in mid-course because of Claudio's plight and Isabella's desperate attempts to save her brother. Success results not through the machinations of the Duke but through the providential appearances of two utterly disparate creatures: the abandoned Mariana and the adamant, unfazed criminal Barnardine.

Claudio and Isabella also stage-manage to a degree. Claudio casts Isabella in the role of subservient follower by asking her to sacrifice her moral virtue, what Walter Pater calls her "cloistral whiteness," in order to sway Angelo to relent (502). By casting his sister as an adjunct in the drama of his own salvation, Claudio reveals that he is as adept at the dark side of stage-managing as is the Duke himself. And Isabella is not exempt, either. Though her deployment of Mariana to trick Angelo has benevolent results—Claudio is saved and Mariana recovers Angelo as husband—she certainly employs trickery and sexual opportunism not totally in keeping with her presumed chastity and constancy as a young novice.

Mariana's discovery, and her enrollment in the plot to counter Angelo's tyranny, is a turning point. Once she is enlisted to help Isabella, the forces of good have regrouped, and the audience recognizes that these forces will prevail. In this way and in the general idea of the cunning of reason, or the whirligig of time, triumphing over tragedy and ill intentions, the play has structural affinities to the late romances.

Yet the bed trick by which Mariana is substituted for Isabella does not have any of the magic or mystery of the late plays. It is a piece of expedient sexual connivance that unmasks Angelo's hypocrisy by means that are themselves underhanded. The bed trick seems out of place with the high thinking of the play, especially since most of that high thinking is dealt out by the trick's two formulators, the Duke and Isabella. Yet the denouement of the play simply could not transpire without it. The bed trick is disorienting. There is a disparity of scale and posture between its raunchy salaciousness and the play's serious moral and political philosophy. This incongruity may well be a function of adapting an anecdote in a Renaissance tale to a full-scale, five-act Elizabethan drama.

MAIN CHARACTERS

The Duke

Do we like the Duke? He is definitely the play's protagonist. But is he its hero? The Duke pretends to leave the city and disguises himself as a friar in order to test Angelo and to find out how the city will work without him. The role of the Duke, as dramaturge, or shaper of the play, has led some readers to make him into a kind of demiurge, or semi-deity. Criticism has run the gamut from seeing the Duke as an incarnation of God Himself to a more cautious conclusion that he represents pure Christian principles. There is also a substantial body of opinion that the Duke represents Shakespeare, as playwright, in the way he deliberately steps away from his supreme status, then wields it subtly behind the scenes when no one is looking. The Duke, at the end of act 3, says that the ideal ruler "Should be as holy as severe; / . . . / More nor less to others paying / Than by self-offenses weighing" (3.2.262, 265–266); whenever the Duke is particularly sententious, he speaks in tetrameter. Unlike the rigid Angelo, the Duke is open to self-criticism. But this self-criticism can also be a form of self-buffering. All the insight available cannot weaken his inherent sense of mastery. The Duke, in this respect, resembles Prospero in *The Tempest*, as has often been said. This resemblance, though, lies not just in their benign traits but also in what the twentieth-century British novelist Anthony Powell calls "certain rather disagreeable aspects" (*Journals 1990–92* [London: Heinemann, 1997], 85).

Angelo

Angelo, when first chosen by the Duke, has a moment of self-doubt. "Now, good my lord," he says to his superior who has suddenly bestowed this boon on him, "Let there be some more test made of my mettle / before so noble and so great a figure / Be stamp'd upon it" (1.1.47–50). Whether or not this request is sincere, whether he is only feigning humility, is less important than that this admission of vulnerability does, even before he has been fully presented to us, somewhat humanize the character. Indeed, his protest that he cannot live up to the Duke's glowing characterization of him may be, in the end, what justifies his pardon, occasions the mercy shown to him in spite of his many misdeeds and dishonesties. When Isabella says to Angelo, "O, it is excellent / To have a giant's strength; but it is tyrannous / To use it like a giant" (2.2.106–109), she is making a double critique of his rule. She is criticizing his harshness and his lack of leniency as a personal attribute. But she is also implying that Angelo is a bad politician, that he does not have the knack of keeping his strength in reserve, the way the truly successful leader does. In throwing his weight around, Angelo is making the banal gesture of actually using the fullest potential, what Claudio calls the "unscour'd armor" (1.2.167), of the power he possesses.

Angelo cannot be taken seriously, especially by the common people. They treat him as a sort of robot, someone so inhuman that his "blood / Is very snow-broth" (1.4.57–58). Far from inspiring fear among the multitude, Angelo's overdone severity marks him out as a target of jest and abuse. Angelo shows a similar inflexibility in his personal life. His betrayal of Mariana may be inconsistent with both his political profile and his political skills: why leave your enemies such an opening to exploit? But their common trademark is rigidity. Once Angelo has decided to do something, he never revises his opinion, and so he is an obvious foil for the far more morally flexible Duke. There is an element of Malvolio (*Twelfth Night*) in Angelo. Both characters are ambitious arrivistes trying to step into higher social levels, though Angelo is of a far higher background and has in any event been chosen for the role, not had it thrust upon him. But both are brought down by their inflexibility, which seems to be a side effect of their social insecurity. Like so many who claim to be the embodiment of morality or authority, Angelo places more of his energy in premise than execution (despite Angelo's yen for executions in the other sense of the word). Angelo yearns to exercise authority. But when the details of legal disputes among the rank and file become tedious, he leaves the actual administration to Escalus, who manages to do the job diligently, responsibly, and inconspicuously.

Isabella

Isabella may well be Shakespeare's most vexatious heroine. Unlike the character who in many ways parallels her, Helena in *All's Well That Ends Well*, she is less a totally good person caught in a bad situation than a person whose morality seems to shift with the wind. At one point she is the virtuous sister, ready to plead for her brother's life. At the next she is unwilling even to consider seducing Angelo to save Claudio. Her choice to preserve her own virtue even at the expense of Claudio's life is morally understandable from several perspectives. But it is out of kilter with her earlier dramatic devotion to her brother's cause. Similarly, Isabella, on the verge of entering a convent at the beginning of the play, is most unlike a nun at its end. She has used sex to bring down an opponent (albeit substituting Mariana's body for her own). In addition, she is perhaps to be married to the Duke, to become the final thread in the unification of marital economy that occurs at the end of the play, with the proclaimed marriages of Angelo, Claudio, and even Lucio (to Kate Keepdown). Is the Duke, as Mario DiGangi puts it, working "underhandedly to transform her virginal body into a womanly one?" (in Wheeler, p. 185). Is his will running rampant over Isabella's previously much-discussed chastity? The fact that the Duke's proposal is left hanging at the end (a hint taken full advantage of by several recent productions of the play) does, however, give Isabella some independence.

Mariana

Mariana is at first an object of pathos. She is the lonely, abandoned woman, transformed by her fiancé's abandonment of her from society's most desirable prize to its most expendable and superfluous element. But Mariana's "brawling discontent" (4.1.9), so splendidly captured by Alfred, Lord Tennyson, in his nineteenth-century poem on the subject, is only one element of her character. On another level, Mariana is more than up to the task. Her forthright "Fear me not" (4.1.69) is spoken in the tones of a trusty foot-soldier eager to show that she can perform her mission. Mariana's residence in the moated grange also should not be read to signify that she is living in a sort of almshouse. The moated grange was most likely an estate of reasonable substance left to Mariana by her seafaring brother, Frederick, apparently a prominent member of the community, even if Mariana's dowry was insufficient for the money-hungry Angelo.

Lucio

Lucio is at home in both the "high" and "low" worlds of the play. Unlike Angelo, whose punitive regime is, at least in theory, a way to honor the Duke's intention, not subvert it, Lucio overtly insults the Duke, even to his face. However, as Lucio does not know that the friar in front of whom he insults the Duke is in fact the Duke, the element of intention is missing. That the Duke should fume at Lucio and should find him a particular object of punishment when he comes back into power is understandable. But to sentence Lucio to death seems severe. Lucio is ultimately pardoned, though forced to marry Kate Keepdown, whose child by him is already more than a year old. Although the Duke must be seen as the principal self-representation of the playwright in the play, Lucio, with his trickery, his ability to bridge worlds, and his savage wit, resembles that character. This similarity between Lucio and the Duke is seen when Lucio, described in the list of characters as a "fantastic," describes the Duke as "fantastical" (3.2.92).

Barnardine

A character whom critics such as Harold Bloom have found to be particularly appealing is Barnardine, a Bohemian (Czech) brought up in Vienna. He has been imprisoned for nine years. Though he has confessed to a crime he has obviously committed, his friends (not his own efforts) have so far won him a reprieve; Angelo's new severity, however, has annulled these efforts. (It is intriguing, in general, how much information this play provides by way of background about even minor characters, while still clothing many large themes and motives in a cloak of mystery.) Barnardine, when scheduled to be executed by the Provost, simply will have none of it. The most winning feature of this stance is that it is not premised on conscience, or appeals to the better angels of our nature, but on sheer force and desire. He will not allow himself to die. Unlike so many others in the play, Barnardine is not a rhetorician. He states what he means, and no more than that. His caretakers have concerns for the state of Barnardine's soul. But Barnardine has none. The Provost and Elbow, used to the world of persuasion in which they are immersed, have no rejoinder, so Barnardine lives. The case of Barnardine has been used by the contemporary legal scholar Robert Batey to demonstrate the "fallacies of trying to hold too tight a rein on the human propensity towards crime" (*Oklahoma City Law Review* 26.1 (2001): 278). This is indeed Angelo's problem. But this may not be Barnardine's moral. He may represent sheer life itself, without rationale.

The release of Barnardine in favor of the execution of someone else inevitably brings to mind the release of the similarly named Barabbas in the Gospels, and the consequent crucifixion of Jesus. Like Barabbas, Barnardine is released. But the person who is executed is not the unjustly punished (though, unlike Jesus, not unjustly accused) Claudio, but someone else, someone already dead. The corpse of the pirate Ragozine must be beheaded to provide Angelo with a substitute for Claudio. The name "Ragozine" is reminiscent of "argosy," that is, ships that brought all manner of goods to the harbors of cities. Though in this play we are inland in Vienna, the mercantile analogy still applies. Ragozine is like the burden of an argosy, a product to be traded to others—though in this case the product is a human body, not spices or fabric. Also, the pirate's razing of the commandment against stealing (1.2.7–11) alludes to two of the key consonants in the name Ragozine, which is so unusual that it cries out for this sort of interpretation, especially given the fairly obvious Barnardine-Barabbas parallel just elucidated and the similarity between the endings of the names Barnardine and Ragozine. Ragozine is the key to the play: without Ragozine's availability to be substituted, Claudio would be dead. But there really is no Ragozine; when his name is mentioned, he is already dead. As Jane Malmo puts it, "The dismembered remains of Ragozine stay un-remembered, un-mourned" (144). Characters in *Measure for Measure* are inward personalities, but they are also tokens to be moved around on the stage. In this ensemble play, drama may well prevail over individuated personality.

DEVICES AND TECHNIQUES

Whether or not the Duke is the hero of the play, he is certainly, in rhetorical terms, its frame. His voice begins and ends the play. In both cases, what he says, or means, is rather opaque. When he addresses Escalus, "Of government the properties to unfold / Would seem in me t' affect speech and discourse" (1.1.3–4), the Duke is saying that his political office confers on him rhetorical skills or, more aptly, responsibilities. The Duke then seems to say that Escalus by his "science" (1.1.5), that is, his learning in statecraft, knows as much about ruling Vienna as he, the Duke, does by rank. Yet the Duke does not grant rule to the seasoned Escalus but to the untried, if ardent, Angelo. From being the personification of power to its rhetorical fount, the Duke, once he appoints Angelo in his stead, becomes the opponent of power. By laying aside his responsibilities and lending them to Angelo, he in effect becomes the opponent of his former self. And he seems more comfortable in this position, especially when he impersonates a friar, mingling with the poor and the outcast, proceeding, in Lucio's words, to "usurp the beggary he was never born to" (3.2.93–94). All the while, though, he still actually holds the reins of power. Indeed, his power is heightened, not diminished, by his nominal abdication, as he becomes a kind of hidden sword of Damocles over Angelo and the entire substitute regime.

The paradox that the Duke wields more power as friar, by being who he is not, extends throughout the play. Angelo is constrained, not enabled, by his literal possession of power. His moral hypocrisy is a liability in a way it might not be otherwise—and not just because he has affected such moral stringency. His predicament arises from the way he has insisted on making his power as literal as possible by exercising to the minutest extent the letter, not the spirit, of his sway. Isabella, in contrast, seems to cloister herself off from the world by becoming a nun. But this gesture of renunciation, by endowing her with a reservoir of virtue, actually gives her a more capacious staging ground within the world. Mariana's abandonment in the moated grange eventually helps her achieve her goal of being acknowledged by Angelo as his wife.

This is the play's central device: that nothing is as it seems. Everything can be substituted for anything else. Yet all is not totally anarchic. The Duke, both engineer and chief mover within the play, makes sure of that. The Duke provides measure not only in terms of retribution (the manifest meaning of the title) but also in the sense of proportion. Unlike Angelo, he does not overdo his power. Shakespeare's language in the play also takes advantage of the benefits of this sort of measure. He lets a little say a lot, as with the image of the torches in the Duke's major speech in act 1 (1.1.26–47) and that of man's "glassy essence" in Isabella's speech in act 2 (2.2.120). The language is also capable of expressing humor, as in Mariana's aside to the Duke when he intrudes upon her singing, "I . . . well could wish / You had not found me here so musical" (4.1.10–11), which is a witty way of saying that she feels somewhat embarrassed that the Duke has caught her in such an overt display of emotion.

THEMES AND MEANINGS

The historical setting of the play is imprecise. Vienna had been the seat of the Hapsburg family, the ruling dynasty of the Holy Roman Empire, for centuries, and yet the Duke is only the ruler of a city-state, not the head of an empire. The nomenclature and the entire atmosphere are Italian, not Austrian, even though Central European countries like Bohemia (native clime of Barnardine) and Poland are named in the text (and for that matter, "Russia, / When nights are longest there," is mentioned at 2.1.134–135). Comparable references to Italian cities are lacking. The play also assumes Roman Catholic religious institutions as basic features of the society depicted therein. In general, we are in the Renaissance era, where statecraft is an art, and princes can be either beneficent or malevolent. In this milieu, a complex urban society leads to the possibility of endless machinations, combinations, plots, and counterplots. Nonetheless, in many other ways the setting of the play is demonstrably Shakespeare's own time and place, early Jacobean London; the drama pulses with the exuberance, complexity, and roughness of a great city chronicled by a curious and responsive inhabitant.

The title of the play has two different reverberations for the reader. If modern audiences are ignorant of the New Testament source of the title (as the original Elizabethan theatergoers most likely would not have been) they might see it as denoting a kind of tit-for-tat, as every move Angelo makes is countered by the Duke behind his surreptitious cloak. Those aware of the Bible reference will expect the issues of mercy and justice that are indeed in the play, though surely in a far less straightforward way than the audience may anticipate.

That *Measure for Measure* lies between tragedy and comedy is not to say that it is only half-tragic or half-comic, but rather that strongly comic and strongly tragic elements uneasily coexist. Much of *Measure for Measure*, from individual lines to extended comic scenes or patterns, is downright funny. For instance, the fact that Angelo boasts of his zeal for justice and then backs off and lets Escalus actually handle the situation when the Elbow-Froth confrontation becomes a bit too involved for his liking is hilarious, and it aptly functions as an early notice of Angelo's hypocrisy. Similarly, the Duke's rapid changes from friar to Duke and back again surely provoke merriment in the audience even as it is aware that the Duke's transformations are leading to the play's denouement. Mariana and Isabella's going off-stage to discuss the Angelo marriage issue, as if these issues could not be discussed in front of men or that they would offend the virtue of the presumed friar, is also witty in its use of stage movement to indicate the idiosyncrasy of characters.

Yet tragedy looms large also. The fact that nobody dies in the play (even the severed head offered up in place of Claudio is that of the already-dead Ragozine) does not cloud the fact that much of the play is devoted to death in the abstract, and death is the threatened fate of, at different times, Claudio, Angelo, Barnardine, and Lucio. A play in which death is such a persistent motif cannot be wrapped up in a comic, redemptive ending, even if the final nuptials of the major characters were more reassuring than they are. Only the Duke's intervention at the end prevents disaster from occurring, and his actions are so late and so extrinsic to the previous course of the action that any sense of full comic restoration or harmony is forestalled.

One of the paradoxes of the play is that, as discussed in most critical analyses, it is a play about the Duke, Isabella, and Angelo. These characters are those most discussed in the criticism. Their roles are given to the most prominent actors and actresses when the play is produced. Yet what might be termed the "downstairs" characters—Pompey, Elbow, Mistress Overdone, the Provost—have a considerable amount of stage time. The other so-called problem plays, *All's Well That Ends Well* and *Troilus and Cressida*, do not give nearly this amount of presence to the lower-class characters. Their prominence in *Measure for Measure* gives substance to the way the Duke, as friar, disappears into the underworld. Their presence illustrates the inverted quality of the entire milieu.

They also serve as objects for Angelo's righteous indignation. In fact, it is as potential victims of Angelo that the audience comes to empathize with the "downstairs" characters rather than just be amused by them and see them as objects of mockery. Abhorson and Elbow as, respectively, chief and deputy contrast or parody the relationship between the Duke and Angelo. Elbow is certainly less corrupt than his "upstairs" counterpart, thus forestalling any condescension on the part of the audience. The audience might be similarly tempted to scorn Pompey, who bears the name of a famous ancient Roman general, and one of the Nine Worthies. But this Pompey, a bawdy wastrel and procurer, does not live up to his name. Both Escalus and Lucio taunt Pompey about this incongruity. However, such mockery anticipates, and thereby precludes, a negative response from the audience. So Pompey is insulated from our excessive scorn.

The fact that Mistress Overdone's name refers to her being "done" sexually too many times (Kate Keepdown's name has a similar erotic provenance) and the eminent rancidity of her profession and life are forgotten because, whatever her sins, they are venial next to the cruel repression launched by Angelo. Better to be dissolute than hypocritical, and better to profit from human frailty than interfere with and control other people's lives. Even more than the individual case of Claudio, the collective danger faced by the bawds and wenches makes us frightened of Angelo's self-styled campaign for justice. We identify with the lower-class characters because they are we. They are not just comic relief; taken together they embody positive values that they lack as individuals, and that even the "good" aristocratic characters such as the Duke, Isabella, and Mariana cannot personify.

For whatever reason, Shakespeare has the lower-class characters make most of the references to the precise passage of time. It is mentioned that Froth's father died on All Hallows' Eve (October 31). Similarly, Mistress Overdone says of the child of Kate Keepdown, whom Lucio has fathered, that it will be a year and a quarter old, "come Philip and Jacob" (3.2.201–202). The feast day of St. Philip and St. James (James and Jacob are versions of the same name, and the Latin version of James is Jacobus) is May 1; it is from this feast-day that the modern idea of May Day is derived, though the saints' day itself is said to be derived from pagan spring festivals. If the child was a year and a quarter old on May 1, it must have been born around the beginning of the previous February. This curious precision (just what does it matter when Lucio's child was born?) is absent in the recollections of the Duke and Isabella. It testifies that, in the world of this play, it is the salt of the earth like Mistress Overdone and Froth who are the monitors of time, who keep things straight, who maintain the collective memory.

A character who is certainly not lower-class, but who is not one of the inner ruling circle either, is the Provost. The argument could be made that it is the Provost, rather than the Duke, and certainly rather than Angelo, who is the most responsible and compassionate wielder of power in the play. The Provost's inconspicuously snide comments on Angelo's "good correction" (2.2.10) sum up Angelo's limitations with powerful concision. Though enjoined to execute Claudio, and willing to carry out this duty as commanded, he earnestly hopes for "some pardon or reprieve / For the most gentle Claudio" (4.2.71–72) and says to Claudio himself, "by eight to-morrow / Thou must be made immortal" (4.2.64–65). The Provost is concerned for both the stable exercise of his own authority and the moral welfare of those upon whom his authority is exercised. Even the far cruder Abhorson, the executioner, is no sadist. The man is better than the job.

Mistress Overdone, Elbow, Forth, Pompey, the Provost, Abhorson, and Kate Keepdown have little in common besides not being involved in the strange love pentangle of the Duke, Angelo, Claudio, Isabella, and Mariana, all of whom end the play in love with one of the others, except for Isabella and Claudio, who are siblings. But these lower-class characters, together with the Provost, are necessary because their collective humanity reminds us of the world of humanity that Angelo ignores through his excessive severity.

One is tempted in this play to judge, to condemn Angelo, for example, or to find Lucio annoying and impertinent. Shakespeare invites his audience to take sides, only to trap us at 5.1.411 with the reminder of the source of the play's title. In the words of the Geneva Bible, Matthew 7.1–2 reads: "Judge not, that ye be not judged. For with what judgement ye judge, ye shall be judged, and with what measure ye mette [mete], it shall be measured to you againe." To condemn Angelo is to become like Angelo. Shakespeare's humanity is evident in this play, as it is throughout his works, as he advocates understanding and forgiveness.

CRITICAL CONTROVERSIES

Debate about *Measure for Measure* has long been conducted within the parameters of the idea of "the problem play." The problem play, as a Shakespearean category, is said to include *All's Well That Ends Well* and *Troilus and Cressida* along with this play. The term was first used in 1902 by Frederick S. Boas (*Shakespeare and His Predecessors* [New York: Charles Scribner's Sons, 1902]), was amplified in the 1930s by W. W. Lawrence (*Shakespeare's Problem Comedies* [New York: Macmillan, 1931]), and has become standard critical usage for these plays, which seem to be neither tragedy nor comedy. Thus, in terms of genre, they are a problem; they do not fit easily into any preconceived classification or category. But there is another sense in which these three are "problem plays." They raise moral or psychological issues that are not easily resolved.

In terms of the problematic aspects of the play itself, foremost is its relationship to Christianity and to the New Testament. Shakespeare, rarely one to use the Bible as a source for his titles, refers here to one of the most famous passages from the Gospels, Christ's Sermon on the Mount as recorded in the Gospel according to St. Matthew (7.1–2). In judging others with severity, Angelo has called down the same severity upon himself. Jesus's ethic of mercy (Jesus would prefer people not to judge each other at all) supersedes the Old Testament idea of *lex talionis*, or the law of exact compensation, eye for eye, tooth for tooth (explicitly denounced, or superseded, by Jesus in the Sermon on the Mount, Matthew 5.38). Mercy and grace re-place the old dispensation.

The play makes overt references to the Old as well as the New Testament. The Ten Commandments (Exodus 20) are mentioned at 1.2.7–11, with Lucio's joke about one commandment being "razed," that is, erased, by the pirate ("Thou shall not steal"). But as far as the main theme of the play is concerned that erased com-mandment could better be viewed as "Thou shalt not commit adultery." The Ten Commandments are not mocked by the play, even though the negatively portrayed Angelo enforces them strictly, arguably too strictly. Similarly confusing is the Duke's interpretation of the Sermon on the Mount, which in his gloss initially seems to offer little mercy. Rather, it appears to be as retributive as any interpretation of the Old Testament law. Pretending that Claudio has died, he insists that Angelo must die too. He is not only being punitive, but deceptive, and, indeed, sadistic, given the emotions of Isabella and Mariana—both of whom fear the loss of someone dear to them. Clifford Leech puts it well when he says that the play possesses a "Chri-stian coloring" that comes from Shakespeare's "unconscious inheritance," but straightforward Christian doctrine does not "determine the play's characteristic ef-fect" (111). However, even though their application is inexact, surely the ideals of justice and mercy are paramount here. The play endorses mercy. But is this mercy exemplified by the Duke?

The role of the Duke is the most obvious barometer to measure how people cal-ibrate the play. "Mystification is his ruling passion," says Leech (114). Broadly speak-ing, modernism, as the cultural currents prevailing from 1900 until roughly 1970 are most often characterized, seemed to endorse the Duke. Modernism often em-phasized abstraction and fragmentation. Thus the play, with ample provisions of both qualities, was valued in the twentieth century as it had not been in the nine-teenth. But modernism, equally, had a conservative side. Many modernist critics (especially modernist Shakespeareans such as G. Wilson Knight) prized hierarchy and ceremony, although more in a mythic than literal way. The Duke, at once desta-bilizing and authoritative, perfectly fitted these often competing priorities. Unsur-prisingly, the Duke has been less favored by postmodernism, with its almost automatic mistrust of constituted authority. Most of the criticism since about 1970 has stripped the benign veneer from the conduct of the Duke and focused on its manipulative and even depraved aspects. It is possible, though, that the pendulum has swung too far and that the Duke is now too routinely vilified, when, though a flawed man and not ideal (as no one in the play is), he is not in fact a villain. Few, for instance, would deny that when it is demonstrated to the city at large that Lodowick, the friar, is in fact Vincentio, the Duke, this disclosure comes across as a moment of startling revelation that has an unexpected hint of plenary grace.

Basically, then, modernist critics trusted the Duke; postmodernist ones distrust him. For this postmodernist view, see, for example, Jane Beverly Malmo, cited in the annotated bibliography below. See also Michael Long, *The Unnatural Scene: A Study in Shakespearean Tragedy* (London: Methuen, 1976), who argues that the Duke "feels himself licensed to lie, manipulate and bamboozle, responsive only to the neat execution of his own designs" (87). Harriett Hawkins, *Measure for Mea-sure* (cited in the annotated bibliography) also regards the Duke's actions as arbi-trary. Despite the Duke's problematic aspects, though, it is most likely that it is not he, but Isabella, who is the character most responsible for audiences' frequent unease with the play. Isabella seems to be at first our "rooting interest"—the virtuous maid, selflessly trying to save her brother's life, only to have to dodge the unwanted embraces of the vile Angelo. But Isabella reveals herself to be someone of more practical motive, not only willing to let Claudio die to save her virtue but, in her cooperation with the Duke in staging the Mariana substitution, just as much a schemer and puppet-master as the Duke himself. Not only is Isabella not the fresh and winsome lass like those nineteenth-century portrayals of Imogen in *Cymbeline*, Perdita in *The Winter's Tale*, and Miranda in *The Tempest*, but she is more morally ambiguous than either of the female leads in the two other "problem plays." The entire argument of *All's Well That Ends Well* is based on how virtuous Helena is and thus how truly disgraceful is the behavior of the recalcitrant and ungentlemanly Bertram, and the entire argument of *Troilus and Cressida* rests on the perfidy of Cressida, how she has betrayed not only Troilus but also her own earlier self. But Isabella neither confirms nor betrays her virtue in the audience's eyes; she is caught in the middle of the skein of human motive. Though not bad, neither is Isabella spectacularly virtuous. She is good in an ordinary kind of way, and thus the audience cannot flatter itself by seeing her as its vicarious advocate onstage, or as kind of a refined, demure sex object.

There is constant talk about how rancid and cynical the play is. This probably constitutes an overreaction to Shakespeare's success in creating, in Isabella, an ordinary woman, as compromised by the inadequacies of humanity as the gamut of male characters stretching from the Duke to Lucio. The complexity with which Shakespeare endows Isabella's character gives the play what later centuries would term a novelistic quality.

PRODUCTION HISTORY

After its premier, *Measure for Measure* was apparently never acted again in Shakespeare's lifetime or in the years immediately after he died. The theaters were closed by the Puritan Parliament in 1642, so *Measure for Measure* was not restaged until 1662, in a highly redacted version by the epic poet, and Poet Laureate, Sir William Davenant, with its title altered to *The Law against Lovers*. As the title indicates, Davenant rendered the conflicts in the play in a far more straightforward manner. Another modernization (by the lights of that era), by Charles Gildon, with the original title restored but with the subtitle *Beauty the Best Advocate*, was played at the same theater, Lincoln's Inn, as was Davenant's version. Gildon's adaptation, incongruously, interspersed music from Henry Purcell's opera *Dido and Aeneas* (to which Angelo listens in an unsuccessful attempt to soothe his lust for Isabella) with the remnants of Shakespeare's drama, constructing a multimedia spectacle. Both adaptations, as is indicated by their titles, centered their action on Isabella's pleas to Angelo for mercy in the case of Claudio.

The first "restored" Shakespearean version was acted in 1720. The play became a recurrent if never popular staple of Shakespearean production. Angelo was often seen as a representation of the Whig and often corrupt prime ministers of the day. The play became more popular when Isabella was portrayed by the renowned actress Sarah Kemble Siddons (beginning in the 1770s). A 1794 production in which Siddons participated is fascinating because her brother J. M. Kemble performed in the play. But Kemble did not play Claudio, Isabella's brother. He played the Duke, her eventual husband. This casting raises what for a modern audience would be disturbing issues of incest and interchangeability, but ones that did not seem to disturb contemporary audiences.

During this period, the play was not held in high critical esteem, and this surely had an impact on the frequency with which it was staged. The dislike of and discomfort with the play felt by writers as different in provenance and viewpoint as John Dryden, Charlotte Lennox, and Samuel Taylor Coleridge coincided with its perceived lack of visceral appeal to an audience to ensure that it occupied a distinctly secondary place in the repertoire. Perhaps not coincidentally, as twentieth-century critics began to revalue the play, the theater began to pay more attention to it.

The role of Isabella, though played by such prominent actresses as Helena Modjeska, was nonetheless not the tour de force vehicle of, say, Imogen in *Cymbeline*, Portia in *The Merchant of Venice*, or Rosalind in *As You Like It*. The fact that Modjeska's portrayal in 1881 was more sexually forthright than the typical nineteenth-century Shakespeare stage heroine—demure and chaste, though spunky—reveals the inherently different nature of the role. Isabella is not this sort of proactive, devil-may-care, vivacious yet comely heroine. She tries to save Claudio, but she cannot—at least not without compromising her virtue. As her virtue makes her who she is, to compromise it would be to compromise herself in her own eyes as well as in the eyes of the audience. To maintain her character and maintain her altruism become competing priorities for Isabella in a way they are not for Imogen. Most likely, the ideal Isabella would be a kind of actress not customarily cast in the other Shakespearean comedic female roles. Perhaps someone more of a "character actor" mainly assigned subordinate roles in other plays would make the ideal lead in this one.

As the play became more frequently staged, productions of it were nonetheless troubled by a kind of unstated pressure to clothe the Duke in as much majesty as possible. This approach yielded an impression that the director saw his own authority, and that of the play, as bound up with the Duke's own stage managing within the drama. This was, from all accounts, true of Peter Brook's memorable production at Stratford, England, in 1950, with John Gielgud as Angelo, Barbara Jefford as Isabella, and Harry Andrews as the Duke. With a simple but flexible set built around stone megaliths and arched entryways with skulls and bones emblazoned on screens in the background, Brook's production emphasized the actors rather than the scene, and the general over the specific. Brook also highlighted the separateness of the upper-class world of the Duke, Isabella, Angelo, and Mariana from the lower-class world of Pompey, Elbow, and Mistress Overdone, staging the play as if these strands were on two separate levels of reality. Though innovative in theatrical terms, later taste would find Brook's view of the play too close to the Christian idealization of the Duke to escape postmodern critique.

Directors have faced the dilemma of what to do with the play's Viennese setting. The options are to play it down, acting as if it was Shakespeare's London or resituate it in some other setting, or to play it up, clothing Shakespeare's Vienna in the much later associations a contemporary audience would have of the Austrian capital: of the late Hapsburg dynasty, fin-de-siècle decadence, and Freudian psychoanalysis. Directors such as John Barton, in his 1970 production for the Royal Shakespeare Company at Stratford-upon-Avon, and Trevor Nunn in his 1991 production for the same troupe, have made the latter choice. It must be stressed, given the thin aspect of the play's setting, and the differences between Renaissance Vienna and its modern counterpart, that this latter approach is as interpretive a move as any more radical redeployment.

Similarly, productions of the play that give a feminist emphasis to the portrayal of Isabella have had to cope with new insights in feminist thought. When Estelle Kohler, playing Isabella in Barton's production, openly turned away from the Duke's closing marriage proposal, it was viewed as a clear sign of feminist assertiveness. Later productions, though, equally feminist in intention, placed the stress more on how Mariana, in her abandonment, and Isabella, in her attempted manipulation by both Angelo and Claudio, persevere amid difficult circumstances.

Five widely seen productions from 1976 to 2001 made significant strides in addressing the complexities of the play. The 1976 Public Theater production, innovative in casting and staging, featured Sam Waterston in what might be seen as the last gasp of the "benevolent Duke" tradition. Waterston's patrician, assured, gracious portrayal of the Duke was interestingly juxtaposed to Meryl Streep's spirited and complex Isabella. Far more than Kohler's earlier rendition of the role, Streep's extraordinary psychological range as an actress heralded the more varied treatment of Isabella possible in the wake of feminism and the greater tonality available for women's roles onstage that finally matched the inherent complexity of Shakespeare's character.

The 1978 Desmond Davis-directed production by the British Broadcasting Company and Time-Life (shown in 1979 on television in the United States) cast Kenneth Colley as the Duke, Tim Pigott-Smith as Angelo, and Kate Nelligan as Isabella—and was much criticized for simplifying the play. But it did, competently and winningly, give the beginning viewer the basics of the work, and it more than adequately brought home its interest in what might be called the cunning of reason. Pigott-Smith's Angelo, in his maniacal sadism, anticipated the same actor's portrayal of Ronald Merrick in the later BBC miniseries *The Jewel in the Crown*. As with many of the televised plays in this series, whose general producer was Cedric Messina, a lukewarm critical response has made this version less admired and influential than it should rightly be. The sets, with their depiction of a dark world where the characters descended through arches, carrying torches as if to bring a smidgen of light into a degraded world, suffuse the entire production with the spirit of the line, "Heaven doth with ourselves as we with torches do, / Not light them for themselves" (1.1.32–33).

A second BBC television adaptation in 1994, directed by David Thacker (Tom Wilkinson as the Duke) was more acclaimed and presented a darker view of the major characters. It also presented the scene more realistically, making issues such as the plausibility of the Duke's disguise and, for that matter, of Mariana's continued pining over Angelo, more debatable than did Davis's more stylized production. Thacker, though, introduces a note of anachronism and metadrama by having the Duke's return in 5.1 covered by a television news team. David McCandless's 1995 production in Berkeley, California, took Angelo's behavior toward Claudio clearly as an expression of homoerotic sadism.

Studying cast lists and seeing productions of the play reveal, more than would a private reading of the play, that Angelo and Isabella are the lead male and female roles in dramatic terms. Thus, the fact that they do not end up together is dramat-

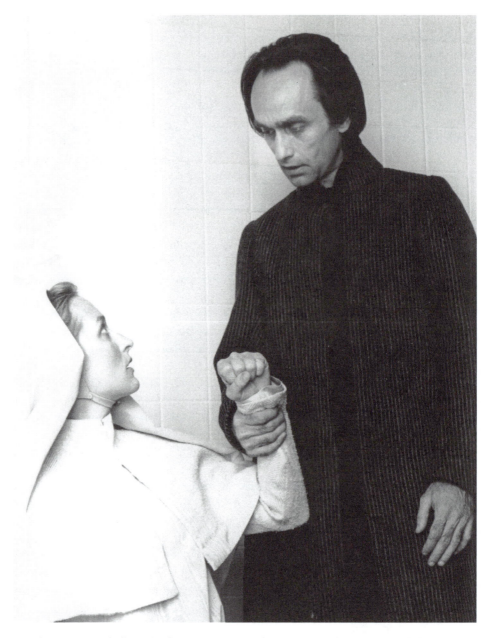

Meryl Streep as Isabella and John Cazale as Angelo in the Joseph Papp Public Theater/New York Shakespeare Festival 1976 production of *Measure for Measure*. Courtesy of Photofest.

ically important. We see thereby a standard marriage-plot template against which Shakespeare, on the authorial level, and the Duke, on the level of action, swerve by introducing Mariana into the weave. When the director recognizes this feature of the play, and tries to make it more of an ensemble piece and less of a star vehicle, its complexity can be fully rendered on the stage. Mary Zimmerman's 2001 production, staged in Chicago and New York, placed as much emphasis on Daniel Pino's performance of Claudio and Felicity Jones's of Mariana as the traditional lead actors (Billy Crudup as Angelo, Sanaa Latham as Isabella, and Joe Morton as the

Duke). It also managed to balance a sense of the Duke's manipulations as beneficent with a genuine sense of the impure motives of everyone in Shakespeare's Vienna. Far from following a consensus about the play reached by previous productions, Zimmerman's version offers a new approach, indicating that theatrical interpretations of the play will not remain static. *Measure for Measure* will continue to perplex and fascinate audiences in the twenty-first century.

EXPLICATION OF KEY PASSAGES

1.1.26–47. "Angelo: / There is . . . thy commission." The Duke explains why he has chosen Angelo to lead Vienna in his absence. Angelo's life history reveals itself to the outer world as plainly as to Angelo himself. Already, there is a double sense here. Angelo's character is "not thine own so proper" (1.1.30) in the sense that other people notice it, take its measure. But the Duke, on a less immediate level, also stresses that this lack of proper ownership of self shows how implicated we all are in each other, a point that Angelo neglects to his own peril, and of which the Duke does not hesitate to remind him later. The extended torch simile is one of the most eloquent in the play. It demonstrates how a person can be a light for others, a flare to show the way. Personal integrity—what Walter Pater, in speaking of the play, calls "that which the person, in his inmost nature, really is"—is too valuable to be kept for oneself (Pater, p. 505). Properly distributed on behalf of others, it can illuminate their lives for them. Comparing the selves of persons to the light on torches emphasizes both the utility and luminescence of the self.

There is an underside, though, to the Duke's phrasing that will not prove so flattering to Angelo. If we cannot exist wholly unto ourselves, if we are only truly visible when we gain the approval of other people, our own judgment cannot be sufficient. If our souls are ultimately lit by our creator, the wisdom even of the most just person is not unlimited. Angelo, who is not as just as he thinks he is, even if far more perfect would not be able to live up to his own view of himself. On the most literal level, what the Duke is saying when he speaks of nature lending her "excellence" (1.1.37) to persons and becoming a kind of "creditor" (1.1.39) is that the Duke has noticed Angelo's good qualities. But a deeper reading indicates a more general application: we all notice each other's qualities, both good and bad.

The phrase "Mortality and mercy in Vienna" (1.1.44) has a portentous, emblematic quality to it, as if it could be extracted from its immediate context. The emphasis given the line by the Duke indicates the broad coverage of the responsibilities accorded Angelo. It also emphasizes that need for balance, for measure, that Angelo will fail to recognize when he assumes power.

2.2.110–123. "Could great men thunder . . . laugh mortal." Isabella excoriates Angelo for prescribing death as retribution for Claudio's sexual offense. But she also makes a more general statement about power. Jove (Jupiter), the most powerful god of the classical pantheon, only hit people with a thunderbolt when he really needed to do so. It is wrong for someone like Angelo to use his power to its full theoretical extent. Power is there as a horizon, an emblem, not always to be used—if it were constantly exercised, we would have "[n]othing but thunder" (2.2.114). There would exist a regime of permanent fear, permanent punishment. Nature itself has more wisdom than have humans, since a bolt of thunder is more likely to split the powerful oak than the myrtle, an inconspicuous creeping plant. But people think more of themselves than nature does, and they thereby diminish themselves. Human authority, in its overweening posturing, makes us fools and causes the angels to weep, though if they had spleens (regarded as the seat of laughter) they would laugh at our efforts to seem powerful.

Isabella's lines have become famous for their delineation of what human existence constitutes and what it does not. The American philosopher Richard Rorty, for instance, took what Isabella calls people's "glassy essence" line (2.2.120) in his book *Philosophy and the Mirror of Nature* (Princeton, NJ: Princeton UP, 1979) to epitomize the idea of innate or inherent qualities in human nature. Interestingly, Isabella herself undermines this conception. Her imagery of the "angry ape" casts man as a simian mimic who only imitates what he is supposed to be, who is nothing but his own imitation. Furthermore, human identity itself seems to be but one of the items in a bag of tricks that are played out with no permanent sanction or effect. Isabella's anger at Angelo's arbitrariness turns into a scathing denunciation of all human pretension.

3.1.5–41. "Be absolute for death: . . . odds all even." The Duke (as Friar Lodowick) urges Claudio to accept his imminent death. Once Claudio accepts death, it will not faze him, and if by chance he continues to live, his having opted for death will make life sweeter and give him a kind of pleasing detachment from the excessive investments most people make in their own existence. Life, or living people (it is hard to work out how much the figure of "life" is explicitly allegorical here), are afflicted with many disadvantages. They are at the beck and call of nearly everything, of every stray whim, demand, or circumstances that comes along. And everything in life dances to death's tune. Death is always calling the shots, so why not acknowledge this publicly, face up to it, and be done with it? We love sleep, and see it as a respite from life's torments. But death is only an extended sleep. So, the argument continues, what is so bad about death? In death, we no longer want what we do not have. And we no longer suffer from the defects of possessing what we do have. For instance, even the rich are in fact poor, as they cannot take their money with them after death, and wealth becomes a burden that is as oppressive as it is beneficial. Those with many friends cannot truly be satisfied, because even dissident parts of their own body rebel in festering illness. When we are young, we are weak and inhibited. When we are old and have what we need in life, we no longer have the strength to enjoy it. Nothing in life is real. It is all an insubstantial daydream. So it is not really "life" as we conceive it. Yet we still fear death. The closing line about death, that it "makes these odds all even" (3.1.41) is ambiguous. There is a sense of salutary straightening-out. The rough edges of life will be smoothed out by the consoling regularity of death. Yet the "thousand deaths" of life (3.1.40), in their variety and plurality, may be preferable to the simplifying tread of death. The Duke thus leaves an opening of doubt amid what Richard Wheeler calls his "nihilistic dignity" (26) that will be capitalized on by Claudio in the play's next pivotal passage.

3.1.117–131. "Ay, but to die, . . . we fear of death." In a speech that has several echoes in Shakespeare's other plays, most notably *Hamlet* (3.1.55–87), Claudio voices the basic human uncertainty about death. What is death? Do we exist after it? If so, where will we exist? And in what form? Do we simply decay, as a physical body, and become mixed with the earth? Or do we suffer in "fiery floods" and "thick-ribbed ice" (3.1.121, 122), both images of hell? As a condemned criminal, Claudio has every reason to believe he will be confined to the lowest portion of the physical map Christianity had devised to illustrate its metaphysical ideas of life after death. The image of being blown about by "viewless winds" (3.1.123) not only sets up a long poetic tradition (to eventuate in as unlikely a successor as the "viewless wings of poesy" in John Keats's "Ode to a Nightingale") but also connects us again to *Hamlet*, this time with the image of the ghost of Hamlet's father (1.5.10–20).

If one's fate in death were a certainty, there would be some consolation, no matter how bad that certainty. But Claudio feels no certainty at all. The apprehension, the doubt, about what is to come makes even the most intolerable aspects of life, all its suffering, whether inevitable or optional, preferable. Compared with death, indeed, Claudio finds his imprisonment and humiliation "paradise" (3.1.130). When contrasted to the factitiousness of the Duke's previous speech on death, Claudio's words are persuasive. What, after all, does the Duke know of death, other than the religious understanding his false identity as a friar imputes to him in the eyes of others? Claudio's sentiments seem far more personal. They ring more true than the Duke's vaporous generalities.

5.1.400–416. "For this new-married man . . . Away with him!" The Duke asks Isabella to pardon Angelo for Mariana's sake. This is somewhat paradoxical as Mariana had only become known to Isabella through the Duke's machinations. Angelo's "salt imagination" (5.1.401) means "lecherous intentions." In the middle of line 403 the Duke abruptly switches course and says that despite Isabella's pardon Angelo must be sentenced to death—because he had intended this fate for Claudio. Angelo had not only made uncouth sexual demands on Isabella but had not even granted the boon for which Isabella had pleaded: Claudio's pardon. So he was deceptive on two counts. Using highly contradictory language, the Duke says that the "mercy" of the law—not, here, a sense of equity, but the law's full power, its punitive vigor—demands that Angelo be given the punishment he had designed for Isabella's brother. Lines 410–411, which give the play its title, imply a fabric of compensation, of equally apportioned fate. They also may well refer to the Duke's scheming and the way that it has, slowly but surely, brought justice about, or remedied the false justice intended by Angelo. But is Angelo to be the victim of injustice in turn? The concluding "Away with him!" is peremptory. We understand why Mariana is so appalled, not only by the content of the Duke's statement but also by its manner. Is the Duke redeemer, manipulator, or a close-twinned mixture of the two? The crux of this dilemma is contained within this culminating, though hardly decisive, passage.

Of course, the Duke will in fact balance "Mortality and mercy in Venice" (1.1.44). Angelo will not die, and the play will end with various marriages, happy or unhappy as the case may be.

Annotated Bibliography

Barnaby, Andrew, and Joan Wry. "Authorized Versions: *Measure for Measure* and the Politics of Biblical Translation." *Renaissance Quarterly* 51 (Winter 1998): 1225–1254. Analyzes the play's overt relation to the Gospel and covert registering of several Old Testament passages with King James I's project of translating the Bible into English, which resulted in the Authorized (King James) Version. Does not simplistically see the Duke as James and the Duke's quotation of Gospel passages as allegorizing James's translation project, but nimbly takes account of possible reverberations of the translation project in the play. In general, represents an innovative use of the play's relation to biblical materials.

Battenhouse, Roy. "*Measure for Measure* and the Christian Doctrine of the Atonement." *PMLA* 61 (1946): 1029–1059. An older yet still frequently cited article that enunciates most fervently the proposition that the play is an emblematic display of Christian attitudes. The Duke is seen as not only a pattern of virtue but also a surrogate for God himself. Influenced many subsequent critics and certainly has emphases in parallel with Peter Brook's 1950 production even if there was no direct linkage (and even though Brook's manifest intentions seem far more "modernist").

Bloom, Harold. *Shakespeare and the Invention of the Human.* New York: Riverside, 1998. 358–380. Bloom is the critic who has paid the most thorough attention to Barnardine, seeing in his refusal to die a manifestation of the exuberance of character that is apparent in a larger compass in such major Shakespeare characters as Hamlet and Falstaff. *Measure for Measure* has always been one of this critic's favorites, and this enthusiasm is well conveyed to the reader.

Friedman, Michael D. *The World Must Be Peopled: Shakespeare's Comedies of Forgiveness.* Madison, NJ: Fairleigh Dickinson UP, 2002. In a way, the opposite perspective from the Shell book cited below; a fresh, affirmative reading of the play that, unlike the mid-twentieth-century consensus, does not rely on overly romantic notions of authority and Providence.

Gless, Darryl. *"Measure for Measure," the Law, and the Convent.* Princeton: Princeton UP, 1979. Argument for the Duke as representing a providential order of grace. Gless gives a Christian reading, and a reading of Christianity, without being simplistic or forcing the data of the play into rigid paradigms.

Hawkins, Harriett. *Measure for Measure.* Boston: Twayne (G. K. Hall), 1988. This introductory book focuses on certain themes and aspects of the play to the exclusion of others; unlike most books in this series, it is not comprehensive, but still is of substantial use to a beginning reader of the play.

Leech, Clifford. "The Meaning of *Measure for Measure*." In *Shakespeare: The Comedies.* Ed. Kenneth Muir. Englewood Cliffs, NJ: Prentice-Hall, 1965. 109–118. This essay by a Canadian scholar, even though written in 1950, is still the most succinct and lucid discussion of the basic issues at stake in the analysis of the play. Especially astute on warning the reader away from certain simplistic interpretations.

Malmo, Jane Beverly. "Beheading the Dead: Rites of Habeas Corpus in Shakespeare's *Measure for Measure*." *New Formations: A Journal of Culture/Theory/Politics* 35 (Autumn 1998): 135–144. Malmo, a former defense attorney who later taught at the John Jay College of Criminal Justice, argues that the Duke is a sponsor of an arbitrary justice system that institutionalizes violence. One of the few analyses to pay due attention to Ragozine and how the superfluous beheading of his already dead corpse is a metaphor for how so-called civilization is premised on the victimization of the outcast and the rejected. "Stripped of his name and his identity, Ragozine is murdered symbolically when his death is given over to another man" (144).

Marx, Steven. *Shakespeare and the Bible.* New York: Oxford UP, 2000. Definitive treatment of issues of biblical interpretation as they relate to the New Testament echoes of the play. Written in an engaging and accessible style. Does not just trace sources and citations but gets to the heart of the questions of meaning that these Shakespearean-biblical connections pose.

Pater, Walter. "*Measure for Measure*." In *Appreciations, with an Essay on Style* [1893]. Republished in *Walter Pater: Three Major Texts,* edited with an introduction by William E. Buckler. New York: New York UP, 1986. 497–505. In this essay, originally written in 1874, the author, a renowned aesthete, gives the first fully grounded modern critical response to the play. Pater speaks of the "finer justice" that the dramatic design manifests by the finale. Pater also pays more attention to Claudio than do most subsequent commentators. Aside from a short paragraph from Ralph Waldo Emerson, Pater's is the first serious consideration of *Measure for Measure.*

Phillips, Stephen J. "'Adapted for Television': David Thacker's *Measure for Measure*." *Forum for Modern Language Studies* 35 (January 1999): 23–33. This discussion of the directorial choices involved in the television version now available as a videocassette in many libraries is also relevant to the question of adapting and, for that matter, staging the play in general.

Shell, Marc. *The End of Kinship: "Measure for Measure," Incest, and the Ideal of Universal Sibling-hood.* Baltimore: Johns Hopkins UP, 1988. Shell uses insights from psychology, anthropology, and religious studies to discuss not only the Claudio-Isabella relationship but also all of the parallels and substitutions in the play in terms of the different but interlocking relationships of envy, emulation, and empathy. Complicated but essential to any contemporary understanding of the play.

Shuger, Deborah Kuller. *Political Theologies in Shakespeare's England: The Sacred and the State in "Measure for Measure."* New York: Palgrave, 2001. In this excellent and innovative treatment, Shuger uses political theology—the theory of how God wants the world to be run and how the way the world is run accords with the idea of God—as a prism to generate a thorough and complex rereading of the play. Shuger sees the Duke and the social order he incarnates positively as leading to a penitential theology of reconciliation and concord. Heavily contextual; hence the Gless book, which maintains a similar position, is more accessible for the beginner.

Westlund, Joseph. *Shakespeare's Reparative Comedies: A Psychoanalytic View of the Middle Plays.* Chicago: U of Chicago P, 1984. Proceeding from the "object-relations" theories of Melanie Klein and D. W. Winnicott rather than the traditional instinctual emphases of Freud (or rather reductive Freudianism), Westlund arrives at a mature, cautiously optimistic reading of the moral reparation achieved by the major characters—and the text itself—at the end of the play.

Wheeler, Richard P., ed. *Critical Essays on Shakespeare's "Measure for Measure."* New York: G. K. Hall, 1999. This collection is substantial and includes several essays with varied viewpoints and themes, reflecting the contextual and historical emphases of recent criticism. Includes Mario DiGangi on female sexuality, Leah Marcus on London, and Harry Berger Jr. on disguise. Though Wheeler's collection lacks a basic overview essay like the one by Clifford Leech mentioned above, this anthology will situate the reader in debates about the play as they occurred in the 1990s.